Andrew C. Brunson

Psalm 118 in the Gospel of John

An Intertextual Study on the
New Exodus Pattern
in the Theology of John

Mohr Siebeck

ANDREW C. BRUNSON, born 1968; 1988 BA; 1991 MA; 1992 M. Div.; 2001 Ph.D. University of Aberdeen; since 1993 Minister in Turkey.

ISBN 3-16-147990-4
ISSN 0340-9570 (Wissenschaftliche Untersuchungen zum Neuen Testament 2. Reihe)

Die Deutsche Bibliothek lists this publication in the Deutsche Nationalbibliographie; detailed bibliographic data is available in the Internet at http://dnb.ddb.de.

The book was printed by Druck Partner Rübelmann GmbH in Hemsbach on non-aging paper and bound by Buchbinderei Schaumann in Darmstadt.

Wissenschaftliche Untersuchungen
zum Neuen Testament · 2. Reihe

Edited by
Jörg Frey, Martin Hengel, Otfried Hofius

158

Preface

This book is a slightly revised version of a doctoral thesis completed under the supervision of Prof. I. Howard Marshall and submitted to the University of Aberdeen in the fall of 2001.

In thinking about a thesis topic I very much wanted to work in an area that would focus on the work and person of Jesus. This is precisely where I ended up, although when I first started exploring Ps 118 it did not seem the most obvious route to the desired destination. I am grateful to have had this opportunity, and would like to acknowledge and thank those who have made it possible.

Doctor Brian Rosner first sparked my interest in the study of the OT in the NT. His expertise in this area is matched by few, and I benefited greatly from his supervision during the first year of my studies. I am especially grateful to Prof. Howard Marshall, who upon Dr. Rosner's return to Australia graciously agreed to supervise my work even though he had recently retired. His example of careful, precise, and thorough scholarship set a high standard to emulate, his suggestions significantly improved this work, and the encouragement he offered did indeed encourage. I count it the highest privilege to have worked under Prof. Marshall.

I also extend my thanks to several others who provided valuable assistance. At Aberdeen Prof. Paul Ellingworth gave some helpful advice at the beginning stages of my research. I am grateful to Prof. Bill Kuykendall of Erskine Theological Seminary for reading portions of my work and making available to me his expertise in OT studies. My postgraduate colleagues Drake Williams and David Matthewson helped introduce me to this field of study. Although our time in residence at Aberdeen was limited, friendships developed with some exceptional people. Among these we owe special thanks to Paul and Meg Wraight, whose kindness eased our way and made Aberdeen a much warmer place.

This study would not have been possible without the support of World Witness, the Board of Foreign Missions of the Associate Reformed Presbyterian Church. In addition to meeting the financial costs, they allowed for some extended periods of research and also released me from some of my ministry responsibilities while on the field in Turkey. I express my deep appreciation to the Board, and am particularly grateful to John Mariner, the Executive Director of World Witness, who enthusiastically supported this project from beginning to end.

Acknowledgements would be incomplete without mentioning my family. My wife, Norine, has supported me with constant encouragement and love, and has shown great patience with this great distraction of mine. Although she would deny it, this book is as much hers as mine. Two children, Jacqueline and Blaise St. John, have joined our oldest son Jordan in the course of this study. Each has been a source of joy, and the older two especially will be glad to know that their daddy has finished his "big book," as they know it.

I am grateful to Prof. Dr. Jörg Frey, who read and accepted my thesis for publication in the WUNT 2 series, and to the staff at Mohr Siebeck for their assistance. As this book was submitted in camera-ready copy I am completely responsible for any errors that remain – I am quite sure that some have escaped my notice.

Finally, as a result of this study I have gained a much deeper appreciation for the redeeming work of Jesus and the revelation of the Father in the Son, but this is the high point of a process that started many years ago. I would be remiss not to mention the three men who have most influenced me along the way. My father, Ron Brunson, inculcated in me a deep respect and appreciation for the Scriptures from childhood: He laid a good foundation. Peter Mehegan with the eye of faith saw in me what was not there to see, and introduced me to the renewing work of the Holy Spirit at just the right time. Lyle Dorsett, master builder and discipler of men, shaped me by word and example: He was and remains my mentor. I am deeply indebted to these men, and it is to them that I dedicate this thesis.

Table of Contents

Abbreviations

Bibliographic entries for all materials in the footnotes are normally cited by author, title and page number. A second citation will include author, shorter title and page number. Commentaries on John are cited by author's name only. Other commentaries are normally cited by author's name only, except where this may cause confusion, in which case a short title is used. Standard reference works are cited either by author or abbreviated title. Abbreviations for primary sources, periodicals, reference works, and serials follow *The* SBL *Handbook of Style: For Ancient Near Eastern, Biblical, and Early Christian Studies* (edited by P. H. Alexander et al; Peabody, Mass.: Hendrickson, 1999). For biblical books, intertestamental literature, and rabbinic literature, a period has been used to separate chapter and verse. Normally parentheses within a quotation are original to the quote, and brackets indicate my additions.

Chapter 1

Introduction

I. Introductory Remarks

The use of Scripture within Scripture, and particularly of the OT in the NT, continues to generate interest for scholars.[1] It is also an area that continues to repay study, especially with the recent emphasis on literary approaches.[2] This work is intended to contribute to the field of study by examining the presence and function of Ps 118 in the Gospel of John. Several observations justify the focus on Ps 118: the NT uses the psalm in high profile and significant contexts; the quantity and distribution of use signals its importance; and last, there has been no comprehensive study of the psalm's function either in the NT or in John.

It is not unusual for scholars to note the use of Ps 118 in the NT as significant. K. Snodgrass, for example, claims that Ps 118.22–26 stands out as one of the several OT texts that "provided the framework for Jesus' understanding of his ministry."[3] This high praise is echoed by others like C. H. Dodd, who considers it one of the primary sources of testimonies for the

---

[1] See for example the articles and bibliographies in D. A. Carson and H. G. M. Williamson, *It is Written: Scripture Citing Scripture: Essays in Honour of Barnabas Lindars*; C. A. Evans and W. R. Stegner, *The Gospels and the Scriptures of Israel*; C. A. Evans and J. A. Sanders, *Paul and the Scriptures of Israel*; C. M. Tuckett, *The Scriptures in the Gospels*.

[2] Especially in view is intertextuality and the mediation of Scripture through Jewish writings. For the latter see for example the approach of B. Rosner, *Paul, Scripture and Ethics: A Study of 1 Corinthians 5–7*; T. Moritz, *A Profound Mystery: The Use of the Old Testament in Ephesians*; H. H. D. Williams, *The Wisdom of the Wise: The Presence and Function of Scripture within 1 Cor. 1:18–3:23*. For the former see R. Ciampa, "What Does the Scripture Say? An Analysis of the Presence and Function of Scripture in Galatians 1–2"; S. Moyise, *The Old Testament in the Book of Revelation*; R. Hays, *Echoes of Scripture in the Letters of Paul*; J. Fekkes, *Isaiah and Prophetic Traditions in the Book of Revelation*; D. L. Matthewson, "The Meaning and Function of the Old Testament in Revelation 21.1–22.5."

[3] Snodgrass, "The Use of the Old Testament in the New," 40. Alongside the psalm he lists Isa 61.1–3 and Dan 7.13–14. Cf. idem, *The Parable of the Wicked Tenants: An Inquiry into Parable Interpretation*, 112. Jeremias similarly claims that Jesus "was very much concerned with Ps.118," interpreted it messianically, saw in it a prophecy of his

early church,[4] and B. Lindars, who calls it "the great Resurrection Psalm"[5] and argues that it played a primary role in the church's apologetic.[6] Such claims, if true, would suggest that Ps 118 should rank among the most important OT passages quoted in the NT. Among its occurrences in the NT it is linked with the Son of Man in the passion predictions, voiced in Jesus' lament over Jerusalem, quoted in the Entrance to Jerusalem Narratives, and is key to understanding the parable of the Wicked Tenants.

The quantity of usage of Ps 118 leaves no doubt that the psalm was popular in early Christianity. The tables of quotation in UBS[3] and NA[27] show that Ps 118 is the most frequently quoted psalm in the NT,[7] and may be the most quoted OT chapter.[8] According to NA[27], Ps 118 is quoted 11 times,[9] with a further 13 allusions.[10] That in the eyes of these authorities

---

own death and exaltation, and "found in Ps 118 how God would guide his Messiah through suffering to glory" (*The Eucharistic Words of Jesus*, 259). Jeremias also argues that the psalm significantly influences the interpretation of the Last Supper (ibid., 260–261).

[4] Dodd, *According to the Scriptures: The Sub-Structure of New Testament Theology*, 108. Dodd classifies according to kerygmatic themes 15 or so different passages from the OT which he believes functioned crucially in the early church's understanding and proclamation of Jesus' life, death, resurrection, and exaltation: 1) Apocalyptic-eschatological; 2) Scriptures of the New Israel; 3) The Servant of the Lord and the Righteous Sufferer (ibid., 61–103). These three groupings, in corresponding order, were used to formulate the church's understanding of its 1) place in God's eschatological plan; 2) identity; 3) and Christological formulations with respect to Jesus. Dodd includes Ps 118 in the first and third category, writing that "the importance of this psalm as a source of testimonia is manifest" (ibid., 100).

[5] Lindars, *New Testament Apologetic*, 185–186.

[6] Lindars argues that Ps 118 played an important part in what he categorizes as the Resurrection Apologetic (*Apologetic*, 171–172), Passion Apologetic (ibid., 113, 170–171), and Apologetic of Response (ibid., 173, 255–257).

[7] Many mention in passing that Ps 110 is the most quoted psalm. In both the UBS[3] and NA[27] tables of quotation, however, it is listed as quoted less than Ps 118 (although both list Ps 110 as having more allusions than Ps 118). According to NA[27], Ps 118 is quoted or alluded to 24 times, and Ps 110 a total of 26. The point of the comparison is not to say that one is more important than the other, but to show that, if the number of alleged citations is considered an important factor, then Ps 118 is perhaps more significant than sometimes thought. The term "citation" is used in this study to refer to the act of evoking a prior text, whether this be through quotation, allusion or echo. That is, it is not used as a technical term for "quotation."

[8] According to UBS[3], Ps 118 is the most quoted OT chapter in the NT, a distinction shared only with Exod 20. Deuteronomy 5 and Ps 110 run a close second.

[9] Ps 118.6 in Heb 13.6; Ps 118.22 in Luke 20.17 and 1 Pet 2.7; Ps 118.22–23 in Matt 21.42 and Mark 12.10; Ps 118.25–26 in Matt 21.9, Mark 11.9, and John 12.13; Ps 118.26 in Matt 23.39, Luke 13.35 and 19.38.

[10] Ps 118.6 in Rom 8.31; Ps 118.15–16 in Luke 1.51; Ps 118.16 in Acts 5.31; Ps 118.17–18 in 2 Cor 6.9; Ps 118.19–20 in Rev 22.14; Ps 118.20 in John 10.9; Ps 118.22 in Mark 8.31, Acts 4.11, and 1 Pet 2.4; Ps 118.24 in Rev 19.7; Ps 118.25 in Matt 21.15;

Ps 118 occurs relatively often compared to other OT passages constitutes a *prima facie* case for investigation.[11] Other possible allusions to Ps 118 may occur in John 8.56 (Ps 118.24);[12] John 10.24 (Ps 118.10–12);[13] John 11.41–42 (Ps 118.5, 21, 28c [LXX]);[14] Luke 9.22 and 17.25 (Ps 118.22);[15] Eph 2.20 and Rom 9.32–33 (Ps 118.22);[16] 1 Pet 2.9 (Ps 118.23);[17] Acts

---

Ps 118.26 in Matt 11.3 and Luke 7.19. UBS[3] differs from NA[27] in several places. It lists 12 quotations, including Acts 4.11 (quoting Ps 118.22) which NA[27] regards as an allusion. As for allusions, only four are listed, all of which are included in the NA[27] list. The total for the UBS[3] tables is 16, compared to NA[27] which lists 24. It is true that the list of separate occurrences is rather reduced if one bears in mind the existence of Synoptic parallels. However, even if dependent on a prior source that included a quotation or allusion, the later gospel writer is responsible for the quotation and its function if, when he incorporates it into his text, he is conscious of having done so. It will be argued below that each of the Synoptic evangelists demonstrates independent knowledge of Ps 118, with the result that the parallel uses of the psalm can legitimately be considered intentional and therefore each counted in its own right.

[11] It is evident, even from the differences between the NA[27] and UBS[3] lists, that a number of the proposed allusions are questioned in varying degrees. We do not assume, therefore, that inclusion in the UBS[3] or NA[27] tables obviates the need for each citation to be examined critically, and it is possible that careful scrutiny would cast doubt on some. The scope of this study precludes examining those that occur outside the Gospels. For an extensive list of possible parallels to Ps 118 see further W. Dittmar, *Vetus Testamentum in Novo: Die alttestamentlichen Parallelen des Neuen Testaments im Wortlaut der Urtexte und der Septuaginta*, 338–339.

[12] See ch. 8 of the present study. This allusion has not previously been suggested.

[13] See A. T. Hanson, *The Living Utterances of God: The New Testament Exegesis of the Old,* 127; Dodd, *According to the Scriptures*, 99; Lindars, *Apologetic*, 171. Although they point to Ps 118.10, it is likely that the wider Ps 118.10–12 underlies the passage. See ch. 10 of this study.

[14] See Hanson, *Living Utterances*, 127; idem, "The Old Testament Background to the Raising of Lazarus"; M. Wilcox, "The 'Prayer' of Jesus in John XI.41b–42." See further ch. 10 of this study.

[15] See ch. 3 of the present study. Cf. J. R. Wagner, "Ps 118 in Luke-Acts: Tracing a Narrative Thread," 162, 164. Note that Wagner's list of allusions to and echoes of Ps 118 in Luke-Acts would add a considerable number to the list above (see esp. ibid., 176–178).

[16] Snodgrass (*Wicked Tenants*, 109–110) argues that the Isaiah stone texts were joined to Ps 118.22 by the church and applied theologically in a variety of ways, including in these two references. Although Ps 118 is not explicitly quoted or directly alluded to, he claims it provides a contextual background for the passages. In support of Eph 2.20 alluding to Ps 118.22 see Briggs, 2.407; Bratcher and Reyburn, *A Translator's Handbook on the Book of Psalms*, 993; VanGemeren, 735; J. P. Peters, *The Psalms as Liturgies*, 428; Delitzsch, 214; Allen, 125. Dittmar (*Vetus Testamentum*, 339) notes the parallel. E. E. Ellis suggests that Eph. 2.20 "simply takes the Christian reference [Ps 118.22] for granted" ("Midrash, Targum and New Testament Quotations," 68).

[17] See J. R. Michaels, 111–112.

2.33 (Ps 118.16);[18] and Matt 26.30 and Mark 14.26 (Ps 118).[19] If these can be sustained,[20] it is possible that the NT uses Ps 118 as many as 35 times.[21]

It is not only the suggested number of citations that argues for significance, as the breadth of material taken from the psalm indicates that the NT writers found it a particularly rich source. As many as 18 different verses from Ps 118 may be used in the NT.[22] Furthermore, the distribution of quotation and allusion across different NT corpora[23] attests that its importance was widely recognized. Five verses are quoted in at least two different corpora which do not *prima facie* depend one on the other, and one of these occurs in four corpora.[24] Of interest is Ps 118.26, which is quoted in each of the Gospels. How widespread was its use? Psalm 118 may be cited in Matthew, Mark, Luke-Acts, John, the Pauline corpus (Rom, 2 Cor, Eph), Hebrews, 1 Peter, and Revelation. The only corpora where an allusion has not been suggested are James and Jude.

---

[18] See Wagner, "Ps 118," 172–173. Dodd (*According to the Scriptures*, 99) claims there is a "clear echo," and Lindars (*Apologetic*, 171) that the psalm has a "literary influence." See further ch. 3 of the present study.

[19] Although there is no citation of any particular verse of Ps 118, the hymn mentioned in these two passages refers to the Hallel (Pss 113–118), which was sung at Passover. See further ch. 3 of the present study.

[20] At this point there is no attempt to distinguish between allusion and echo. Although a number of the proposed allusions not included in the UBS[3] and NA[27] lists are suggested by one or more scholars, by gathering them here we are not endorsing them as valid. They are offered as possible examples of the use of Ps 118 in the NT. This study will argue on a case by case basis for each of the proposed allusions found in the Gospels. The remaining are simply listed as material to be investigated, with no reference to the plausibility of the suggestion.

[21] To compare this again with Ps 110, in the most comprehensive study of this psalm in the NT, D. Hay (*Glory at the Right Hand: Psalm 110 in Early Christianity*, 15) claims 33 quotations and allusions, several more than the 26 listed by NA[27].

[22] That is, Ps 118.5, 6, 10–12, 15–26, 28c.

[23] The Synoptic Gospels will be counted as one corpus since independence cannot be assumed. Although Luke and Acts will be considered as one body of work, citations in Acts which have no parallel passage in Matthew and Mark will be considered *prima facie* independent from the Synoptics, as is John. Cf. Dodd, *According to the Scriptures*, 28–31.

[24] The five verses are 1) Ps 118.6 in Rom and Heb; 2) Ps 118.22 in Matt-Mark-Luke, Acts, Rom-Eph, and 1 Pet; 3) Ps 118.23 in Matt-Mark, and 1 Pet; 4) Ps 118.25 in Matt-Mark, and John; 5) 118.26 in Matt-Mark-Luke and John. Psalm 118.22 occurs in four corpora.

Table 1: Possible Extent of the NT Use of Ps 118

	Ps 118	5	6	10–12	15	16	17–18	19	20	21	22	23	24	25	26	(28c)
Matt 11.3															X	
21.9														X	X	
21.15														X		
21.42											X	X				
23.39															X	
26.30	X															
Mk 8.31											X					
11.9–10														X	X	
12.10–11											X	X				
14.26	X															
Luke 1.51					X	X										
7.19															X	
9.22											X					
13.35															X	
17.25											X					
19.38															X	
20.17											X					
Acts 2.33					X											
4.11											X					
5.31					X											
John 8.56													X			
10.9									X							
10.24–25				X												
11.41–42		X							X							X
12.13														X	X	
Rom 8.31			X													
9.32–33											X					
2 Cor 6.9							X									
Eph 2.20											X					
Heb 13.6			X													
1 Pet 2.4											X					
2.7											X					
2.9													X			
Rev 19.7													X			
22.14								X	X							

Considering the apparent importance of Ps 118 in the NT, it is surprising that no full-length study has been devoted to exploring its presence and function there. Numerous articles address Ps 118 to some degree, and there is no lack of monographs that at some point refer to it, but the majority of the latter do so briefly, and often cursorily. Even those who have recognized the psalm's significant role have not given it full treatments.[25] Studies that include significant work on Ps 118 tend to fall into one of several categories: 1) tracing the stone *testimonia* through the NT;[26] 2) dealing with a citation from Ps 118 which is included in the larger event on which the primary focus lies;[27] 3) investigating the citation of a specific verse from Ps 118 and its parallels;[28] 4) examining a single citation of the psalm;[29] 5) and treatments in commentaries. Although some psalms have received attention in full-length studies,[30] there has been no comprehensive or systematic analysis of early Christian interpretations of Ps 118.

Furthermore, what studies there are suffer from incompleteness. First, none has examined the function of Ps 118 either in the NT as a whole, in the Gospels where it is most quoted, or even in a single book or one writer's body of work.[31] As a result, although many studies are of high quality, they generally have not investigated the possible coherence of allusions to Ps 118. Second, due consideration has not been given to the

---

[25] For example, Lindars (*Apologetic*), Dodd (*According to the Scriptures*), and Jeremias (*Eucharistic Words*).

[26] This generally includes, along with Ps 118.22, texts from Isaiah and Daniel. See for example W. C. Pender, "The Christological Interpretation of Old Testament and Rock Texts in the New Testament"; K. Snodgrass, "The Christological Stone Testimonia in the New Testament"; U. Maiburg, "Christus der Eckstein: Ps. 118,22 und Jes. 28,16 im Neuen Testament und bei den lateinischen Vätern." For a survey of the secondary literature see M. Berder's recently published thesis, *"La pierre rejetée par les bâtisseurs": Psaume 118,22–23 et son emploi dans les traditions juives et dans le Nouveau Testament*, esp. 9–15.

[27] The Entry to Jerusalem and the parable of the Wicked Tenants stand out. See for example W. Weren, " Jesus Entry Into Jerusalem: Mt 21,1–17 in the Light of the Hebrew Bible and the Septuagint"; Snodgrass, *Wicked Tenants*. Similarly, the majority of articles may look at a citation of Ps 118 while focusing on the larger passage where it was quoted. That is, Ps 118 is dealt with incidentally.

[28] In this category would fall a number of the studies on "Hosanna." See for example J. A. Fitzmyer, "Aramaic Evidence Affecting the Interpretation of Hosanna in the New Testament."

[29] For example, C. Breytenbach's study, "Das Markusevangelium, Psalm 110,1 und 118,22f.: Folgetext und Prätext," focuses on Mk 12.10f.

[30] For example, M. S. Kinzer, "All Things Under His Feet: Psalm 8 in the New Testament and in other Jewish Literature of Late Antiquity"; Hay, *Psalm 110*.

[31] A recent exception to this is Wagner's "Ps 118 in Luke-Acts," which deals with some of this study's concerns, albeit briefly.

wider OT context of the psalm as a whole. Third, there has not been an adequate investigation of the possible mediation of the psalm through the intertestamental writings and liturgical traditions of early Judaism.[32] The importance of Ps 118 in early Christian thought, the quantity and spread of citation, and the lack of a comprehensive study, suggest that further attention is warranted.

II. Method and Approach

We will make use of several methodological approaches: the literary theory of intertextuality as it has been applied recently to NT studies; the inter-testamental mediation of Scripture; and the recognition of literary context fields. These have not been applied to Ps 118 in such a blended combination before.

A. Intertextuality

1. The Theory of Intertextuality

Until recently the dominant approach to the study of the use of the OT in the NT has been diachronic, with the focus on determining which texts from the OT are cited in the NT, how they have influenced the text tra-dition, on which level of the text tradition this happened, and on the form of the text. In general it is a quest for source that dominates. Attention has been paid primarily to quotations that are "certain," often restricting analysis to those accompanied by a quotation formula, and rarely moving beyond the occasional allusion. Intertextuality,[33] which was first used as a technical term in literary criticism, has only recently been applied to

---

[32] Those studies that have paid significant attention to early Jewish interpretation have focused primarily on stone *testimonia*, and thus have not offered a full treatment of the breadth of traditions and associations linked to the psalm.

[33] There is disagreement over what exactly intertextuality refers to (see Porter's criticism in "The Use of the Old Testament in the New Testament: A Brief Comment on Method and Terminology," 84–85). E. Van Wolde has sounded a warning that while the subject repays study, many have jumped on the bandwagon, using the terminology "as a modern literary theoretical coat of veneer over the old comparative approach" ("Trendy Intertextuality?" 43). Obviously, intertextuality will not contribute much to biblical exegesis if it is primarily a source of labels. For an example of a variety of applications of the theory of intertextuality see articles in S. Draisma, *Intertextuality in Biblical Writings: Essays in honour of Bas van Iersel*; Tuckett, *The Scriptures*. Tuckett ("Introduction") comments on the diversity of understanding of intertextuality among contributors.

biblical studies, where it has significantly broadened the horizons of investigation.[34] There is growing appreciation that the NT use of the OT goes far beyond the clearer quotations and allusions, and that the meaning effects created by allusion are important for interpreting the passage in which they are embedded. Intertextuality raises questions rarely asked in the past, dealing with the relationship between texts created by alluding to or echoing a prior text, the changes of meaning and significance which the anterior text imports to the later text, and the continuity and discontinuity ("intertextual transformations") that takes place.

In order to be an effective exegetical tool the focus of intertextuality needs to be narrowed, for in its broadest sense it advances that all text is constructed of a dialogue with precursors.[35] This approach, although it has value,[36] can easily degenerate into incomprehensibility.[37] As J. Culler notes,

---

[34] Hays' *Echoes* was one of the earliest, and remains one of the most influential, studies to apply intertextuality to biblical studies. See reviews interacting with Hays, the first two positively, the latter negatively: C. A. Evans, "Listening for Echoes of Interpreted Scripture"; J. A. Sanders, "Paul and Theological History"; W. S. Green, "Doing the Text's Work for It: Richard Hays on Paul's Use of Scripture"; J. C. Beker, "Echoes and Intertextuality: On the Role of Scripture in Paul's Theology." See further Hay's response, "On the Rebound: A response to Critiques of *Echoes of Scripture in the Letters of Paul*". Other studies which have influenced my approach include Ciampa, "Galatians"; Williams, *The Wisdom of the Wise*; Matthewson, "Revelation"; Rosner, *Scripture and Ethics*; Moyise, *Revelation*.

[35] Intertextuality has advanced the theory that a text cannot be construed as isolated and unaffected by the context in which it was created, a context determined by the culture in which it takes place, and which in turn "determines everything and forms the universal, trans-subjective or collective text" (Van Wolde, "Texts in Dialogue with Texts: Intertextuality in the Ruth and Tamar Narratives," 3). In this sense, intertextuality "refers to the whole complex of relationships between texts within the general 'text of culture'" (idem, "Trendy Intertextuality?" 45). As Ciampa argues, "All language can be understood as taking place in an intertextual context – that is, that all discourse depends upon, builds upon, modifies and/or reacts to prior discourse and the prior use of words, concepts and sentences" ("Galatians," 21).

[36] Ciampa ("Galatians") and Rosner (*Scripture and Ethics*) have shown the value of a careful application of the broader concept of intertextuality to NT studies, demonstrating that even in places where there may not be a clear citation of Scripture, Paul's conceptual framework, his thought world, is formed by Scripture.

[37] If "the intertextual relationships of any work of literature are theoretically infinite" (so O. Miller, *Identity of the Literary Text*, 24–25), and "text becomes a network of traces; it is no more a unitary object which is knowable, or a completed work with a centre and an edge which is recoverable" (W. Vorster, "Intertextuality and Redaktionsgeschichte," 21), then the task of the exegete is impossible. Van Wolde correctly questions this broad approach to intertextuality, arguing that if everything has become an intertext, then intertextuality no longer functions as a distinct concept. It can only function as an effective "instrument of analysis and an explanatory model when it is defined

intertextuality can be a difficult concept to use because of "the vast and un-defined discursive space it designates. Theories of intertextuality set before us perspectives of unmasterable series, lost origins, endless horizons."[38] For a text to have a meaningful dialogue with its precursors, one must be able to determine what these were. Accordingly, the vagueness which characterizes the broader intertextual approach must yield to clearer boundaries if one is to engage in fruitful interaction with the texts. In this light it is important, first, to note that an author may signal, or a text may indicate, what prior discourse is most significant for understanding the intertextual relationship, which texts are designated as presupposed. Second, whereas in the field of literature the vast number of cultures and social contexts ensures that the range of possible intertexts is staggering, the major fields of significant prior discourse are more limited for the NT writer.[39]

The NT writer was heir to a phenomenon of intertextuality in Jewish culture that extends back into the writing of the OT itself.[40] In the same way as for the Jew, the Scriptures of Israel were the Bible of the early Christian. If for Israel "all significant speech is Scriptural or Scripturally-oriented speech,"[41] then although there may be other significant prior bo-dies of discourse with which the NT writer interacts, it is not unreasonable to expect that Scripture would prove the most significant source of symbol

---

more closely, and the repetition of the elements to which it refers is well articulated" ("Texts in Dialogue," 3–4).

[38] Culler, *The Pursuit of Signs: Semiotics, Literature, Deconstruction,* 109.

[39] As Ciampa correctly observes, "One of the distinctive characteristics of sectarian or closely knit religious groups would be that their discourse takes place within the context of a more narrowly defined, clearly recognized and fully accepted intertextual framework than other communities. The foundational documents and traditions of such a group play a significant role in establishing the particular intertextual and hermeneutical framework within which the community's discourse is to take place and within which it yields a more consistent meaning. In this context it can be affirmed that virtually all Jewish religious literature and discourse of the first century has its intertextual context firmly rooted in the Scriptures of Israel and discourse based on the interpretation of those Scriptures. That is to say that most if not all of early Judaism were communi-ties whose discourse was intertextually linked to Jewish scriptural interpretation" ("Galatians," 22–23).

[40] M. Fishbane has convincingly demonstrated that the complex intertextuality of Jewish culture extends back into, and is rooted in, the writing of Scripture: "Older traditions fostered new insights which, in turn, thickened the intertextual matrix of the culture and conditioned its imagination . . . the Hebrew Bible not only sponsored a monumental culture of textual exegesis but was itself its own first product" ("Inner Biblical Exegesis: Types and Strategies of Interpretation in Ancient Israel," 20–21, 33–34).

[41] So Fishbane, "Inner Biblical Exegesis," 34.

and language for a movement that arose in a Jewish context. The Scriptures of Israel formed the "canon," were the major symbolic field, the single great textual precursor, for the NT writers.[42] To use the language of intertextuality, the Scriptures of Israel provided their "cave of resonant signification."[43]

This study will use "intertextuality" in this stricter sense, narrowing the scope of significant prior discourse and stipulating that a pre-text be recognizable and recoverable. In this more limited sense the term is concerned with prior texts, or fragments thereof, embedded in later texts. The aim is to discern the influence of one text on another, the meaning effects generated when a later text alludes to and absorbs an earlier text, thus activating and bringing it into interaction with a new context.

2. The Recovery and Function of Allusions and Echoes

The theory of intertextuality has made several significant contributions to the study of the OT in the NT, most notably in advancing the search for echoes and allusions within an author's work which would otherwise not receive attention because they are not sufficiently explicit, and in stressing the recovery of the meaning effects created. Several observations are in order. First, as a result of paying attention to the "more finely tuned signals"[44] of subtle allusions, it is now commonly recognized that an author need not quote explicitly in order to refer to a prior text. As Hollander observes, "A single word or phrase, then, . . . may easily carry rumors of its resounding cave."[45] Consequently an intertextual relationship may be created through an echo or subtle allusion to Scripture whose significance may be disproportionate to its degree of explicitness. Second, citation brings prior and later texts into a mutually interpreting relationship: the former is transformed by the new context into which it has been introduced, at the same time changing the new context and generating new meaning.[46] That is, intertextual relationships are not

---

[42] Cf. Hays, *Echoes*, 14–16.

[43] The phrase is J. Hollander's, *The Figure of Echo: A Mode of Allusion in Milton and After*, 65.

[44] The discovery of these is what Moritz (*Ephesians*, 3) describes as the aim of intertextual study.

[45] Hollander, *The Figure of Echo*, 95.

[46] Citation of Ps 118 inevitably causes the psalm to be read through the lenses of the new context into which it has been introduced, from that point changing how the reader looks at the psalm. Such a re-reading is part of the remit of the student of intertextuality, and is made possible only by an original re-reading of the pre-text by the author who cited it. Our interest, however, lies not in reading the NT into the OT, but in discerning

static. As Moyise observes, "Alluding to a past work sets up a link or correspondence between two contexts. The reader is asked to follow the current text while being mindful of the previous context."[47] This further suggests that interpretation should not isolate the pre-text from its original context.

A third point is that communication is not limited to what is stated. An allusion or echo in the form of a single phrase or word may appear atomistic, but when read against its original literary context, and in relation to its new setting, numerous unstated parallels and "harmonics" may be overheard even though they have not been openly voiced. Consequently the task is not only to identify an allusion and its source, but to "recover the transumed material."[48] The writer may, with a short phrase, activate the memory of a larger context, bringing to mind a number of thematic parallels between the earlier and later texts. These parallels remain unstated, but resonate to one who is familiar with the literary unit alluded to.[49] Fourth, the dialogue established between two texts by means of allusion can create tension between them. Discontinuity between texts, however, can be as important as continuity for interpreting the allusion's meaning effect in the passage.[50]

3. Definitions and Criteria for Identifying Citations

a. Definitions

There is no formally recognized, universally accepted, or standard way of using the words "quotation," "allusion," and "echo." In a recent study,

---

the function and meaning effects that the writer brings to the new text through his reading of the old.

[47] Moyise, *Revelation*, 19.

[48] Hollander, *The Figure of Echo*, 115. The word "transumed" is not in *Webster's Ninth New Collegiate Dictionary*. The intended meaning appears to be "unstated correspondences." Cf. Hays, *Echoes*, 20: "Allusive echo functions to suggest to the reader that text B should be understood in light of a broad interplay with text A, encompassing aspects of A beyond those explicitly echoed. . . . [placing] the reader within a field of whispered or unstated correspondences."

[49] Cf. Hays, *Echoes*, 21–23.

[50] For example, it is the discontinuity between the use of Ps 118 in Luke 19.28–40 and the interpretation of the psalm in contemporary Judaism that is most striking, and to which Luke draws the reader's attention. The recovery of the unstated material significantly changes the meaning effects of the quotation and the points of thematic correspondence with Ps 118. See further ch. 3 of this study. For a number of relevant examples see Moyise, "Intertextuality and the Book of Revelation"; idem, *Revelation*.

Porter surveys a number of works that have attempted to define more precisely one or more of the terms, concluding that none has succeeded even with the apparently straightforward term "direct quotation."[51] It should be noted that quotation cannot be defined merely by the presence of a quotation formula,[52] and that the categorization of a citation does not determine its significance in the passage.[53] Furthermore, since it is unlikely that the ancients placed as high a premium on the classification of citations as modern scholarship does, one should hesitate to impose on the text – and assign too great a significance to – what may be somewhat artificial categories.[54] In any case, the lack of standardization reflects the great difficulty one faces in attempting to class the various uses of Scripture, and suggests that the terms should be employed flexibly.[55]

In general I agree with Hays that "quotation, allusion, and echo may be seen as points along a spectrum of intertextual reference, moving from the

---

[51] Porter, "Terminology." Many scholars do not define how they use the terms of citation, thus contributing to the confusion. Some who have done significant work in the area include C. D. Stanley, *Paul and the Language of Scripture: Citation Technique in the Pauline Epistles and Contemporary Literature*; M. Thompson, *Clothed with Christ: The Example and Teaching of Jesus in Romans 12.1–15.13* (esp. 28–36). See also Fekkes, *Isaiah*, 14–15, 280–81; J. Paulien, "Elusive Allusions: The Problematic Use of the Old Testament in Revelation." Porter especially interacts with Thompson, Stanley, Rosner (*Scripture and Ethics*), and Hays (*Echoes*), although covering a number of other scholars as well. In effect Porter shows that when the definitions used are too complicated or restrictive, this merely compounds the problem. It may not be possible to define these terms with the clarity and precision that many would like.

[52] Such an understanding is unnecessarily restrictive. Some clear quotations do not have introductory formulae. This is the case for the citation of Ps 118 in the Entrance Narratives, which UBS³ and NA²⁷ acknowledge as a quotation in spite of the lack of a quotation formula. On the other hand, some references accompanied by a quotation formula are not clear quotations. For example, see R. T. France's discussion of the quotation in Matt 2.23, which may not in fact quote the OT ("The Formula Quotations of Matthew 2 and the Problem of Communication"). For similar practice in John see further ch. 4 of this study.

[53] As Porter ("Terminology," 89) notes, passages with explicit quotations still have priority in the discussion. It would appear from this that an allusion may be thought to have less significance than a quotation, and an echo less than an allusion. This is, however, not necessarily the case, since the pre-text's significance depends on its function in the passage and the meaning effects created.

[54] Formal quotation would at best make up a small percentage of the intertestamental use of Scripture. See further C. D. Stanley, "The Social Environment of 'Free' Biblical Quotation in the New Testament." Even if not accompanied by quotation formulae, scriptural phrases and allusions to OT events and/or figures would, when recognized, have activated the "canonical memory" of someone steeped in the Scriptures.

[55] The difficulty in defining and applying precise categories does not obviate the need to attempt to do so. However, the nature of language and the lack of agreement in defining these suggests that this will be a fluid scale.

explicit to the subliminal."[56] I will use the term "quotation" to refer to passages in which there is more or less verbatim correspondence with an antecedent text, sufficiently long to be recognizable as such.[57] I will use the term "allusion" to cover all citations that do not fall under quotation, referring to the nonformal and intentional use of a recognizable prior text with some degree of verbal and perhaps thematic correspondence. This covers the term "echo" as well, since I will make no systematic and formal distinction between echo and allusion, except that the former pertains particularly to the more subtle of references.[58] The line between each of these is blurry and classification inevitably subjective, for which reason the terms are intentionally – and I would suggest necessarily – employed here in a broader sense than usually understood.[59]

The broader theory of intertextuality has argued that the presence of echo does not depend on authorial intention, thereby encouraging a reorientation toward the possible response of the audience.[60] In accord with the narrower use of the term in this study, our approach will be author oriented rather than reader centered. That is, the focus of investigation is on what the author is attempting to do, rather than what the reader may or may not have perceived, with the understanding that the former may shed light on the latter.[61]

---

[56] Hays, *Echoes*, 23.

[57] These may or may not be accompanied by a quotation formula. Note that this still leaves the question of how many words are necessary to qualify as a quotation. Cf. Porter, "Terminology," 95. Moritz is close to this in defining quotations as "passages in which several words have been taken over directly from the *Vorlage* with little or no variation" (*Ephesians*, 2).

[58] Cf. Porter, "Terminology," 95; Hays, *Echoes*, 29; Wagner, "Ps 118," 157. In defining allusion, Moritz looks for coincidence of "just one or two words or one short phrase" (*Ephesians*, 2). Again, it is unclear what number of words would divide quotation from allusion.

[59] In this my approach echoes Porter's ("Terminology," esp. 95) call for broader definitions and greater flexibility. This study does not have as its primary aim to provide, if that were possible, the coherent and comprehensive classification system which has eluded previous studies. For our purposes, what is important is to demonstrate the presence of Ps 118 in the NT passages in question, and to evaluate its possible meaning effects.

[60] For example, Hollander states, "Echo is a metaphor of, and for, alluding, and does not depend on conscious intention," (*The Figure of Echo*, 64). Similarly, Thompson, *Clothed with Christ*, 30: "'Echo' refers to cases where the influence of a tradition seems evident but where it remains unclear whether the author was conscious of the influence." Cf. Paulien, "Elusive Allusions."

[61] Author intentionality is critical to the sense in which I use the terms "echo" and "allusion" in this study. A judicious use of the broader intertextual approach (e.g., Ciampa, "Galatians") can yield valuable insights into how the language, conceptual framework and worldview of Scripture unconsciously affects the writer and underlies his

b. Tests for Allusions and Echoes

Several recent studies have proposed criteria for identifying allusions and echoes,[62] attempting to give more precision to a discipline which can easily fall prey to "parallelomania."[63] To avoid this charge intertextual study must be guided by external constraints. That is, it is necessary to demonstrate that there is a substantial parallel (similarity) between two texts, and to establish through critical investigation the likelihood or existence of a relationship.[64] This study will employ the following criteria where appropriate. First, of critical importance is showing verbal coherence between the passages, or a marker that in a relatively clear way, without verbal correspondence, points to a particular text.[65] Obviously the repetition of distinctive and unusual verbal combinations enhances the likelihood of allusion. Second, it should be established that the author could reasonably be expected to have known the text in question.[66] Third, if the author has cited the passage elsewhere this increases the possibility

---

work, and what this communicates to the reader. This study's interest, however, lies in establishing how one author (John) uses Ps 118. Accordingly, we agree with Porter that "it would appear imperative to orient one's discussion to the language of the author, rather than the supposed, reconstructed 'knowledge' of the audience" ("Terminology," 95). I recognize that the concept of author intentionality is viewed with strong revulsion in some literary circles, but I suggest that if one is to speak with any coherence about the possible meaning effects created by reference to a prior text it is necessary to examine first whether the author intended to refer to said text. Otherwise meaning is determined purely by what the reader reads into the text, which very possibily could be something that was not there to begin with.

[62] See especially Hays, *Echoes*, 29–32; Thompson, *Clothed with Christ*, 30–36; Rosner, *Scripture and Ethics,* 18–20.

[63] The famous term is S. Sandmel's ("Parallelomania," 1). He especially takes Strack-Billerbeck to task, defining the danger as one of "extravagance," which leads to seeing parallels where there are none, and exaggerating the significance of those that are found. Cf. T. L. Donaldson, "Parallels: Use, Misuse, and Limitations." On the dangers of misusing Jewish backgrounds see further S. Hafemann, *Paul, Moses and the History of Israel: The Letter/Spirit Contrast and the Argument from Scripture in 2 Corinthians 3,* 89–91.

[64] Cf. Donaldson, "Parallels," 198–204. He argues further that the precise nature of the relationship between the texts should be specified. However, this is possible only if strict and comprehensive categories are defined, a task which in the very fluid field of language may be as impossible as it is unnecessary.

[65] Such a marker could be the recollection of a person, distinctive event, or liturgical practice.

[66] Although the author's knowledge of the prior text is determinative for establishing intentional allusion/echo, if it can be demonstrated that the intended audience could also be expected to have knowledge of the text this increases the plausibility of citation. It is not unreasonable to expect that the writer would especially make use of prior texts which his audience would be able to recognize.

of recurring allusion, especially if the cited text is distinctive and well-known, and if the author has used it in a high profile way.[67] Fourth, attention should be paid to structural correspondences such as similar contexts and circumstances. Particularly relevant to this study is cultic setting, in light of the prominent role Ps 118 occupies in Jewish liturgical practice. In addition, Hays proposes several tests which, although more concerned with evaluating the interpretation of an echo than determining its presence, aid in grading the plausibility of citation. The criterion of "thematic coherence" asks how well the proposed echo fits the author's argument;[68] "historical plausibility" questions whether the author could have intended the suggested meaning effect;[69] "history of interpretation" inquires whether others have recognized the same echo;[70] and "satisfaction" queries whether the proposed reading makes sense.

The criteria suggested above cannot provide certainty in identifying allusions and echoes. This is not because they are insufficiently rigorous, but is due rather to the nature of exegesis itself, which is inexact and must be measured in degrees of probability. Although no single test can on its own prove a relationship between two texts,[71] the more of these that a

---

[67] Hays proposes a similar test which he calls "recurrence." He correctly broadens this to apply not only to specific verses or words cited more than once, but also to larger portions of Scripture which may be referred to often. Acknowledging that this test is similar to that proposed by Dodd (*According to the Scriptures*), Hays writes, "Where such evidence exists that Paul considered a passage of particular importance, proposed echoes from the same context should be given additional credence" (*Echoes*, 30).

[68] Cf. Thompson (*Clothed with Christ*, 32), who calls this "conceptual agreement." Significantly, he claims that "allusion requires some notable allusive marker or sign, but echo does not require any shared vocabulary, as long as the shared idea(s) is sufficiently distinct" (ibid., 32). I suggest that although it is not impossible to overcome the lack of verbal correspondence, it is difficult to establish allusion or echo without it.

[69] Hays (*Echoes*, 30) adds the question of whether the readers could have understood the meaning effect, while warning that one should always be aware that an author may have written things that were not readily intelligible to his readers.

[70] This is, as Hays acknowledges, the least reliable test. First, it appears that "Gentile Christian readers at a very early date lost Paul's sense of urgency about relating the gospel to God's dealing with Israel and, slightly later, began reading Paul's letters within the interpretive matrix of the New Testament canon" (Hays, *Echoes*, 31). Second, in some cases the task is to recover echoes which have been lost. As Hollander observes, "The reader of texts, in order to overhear echoes, must have some kind of access to an earlier voice, and to its cave of resonant signification, analogous to that of the author of the later text. When such access is lost in a community of reading, what may have been an allusion may fade in prominence; and yet a scholarly recovery of the context would restore the allusion, by revealing intent as well as by showing means" (*The Figure of Echo*, 65–66).

[71] Obviously there can be relative certainty with a quotation that reproduces verbatim and at length a prior text. For allusions and echoes verbal coherence is a critical but insufficient test apart from corroborating evidence.

proposed allusion satisfies, the greater the possibility that the allusion is valid.[72]

B. *Intertestamental Mediation of Scripture*

Judaism in the first century was characterized, as were its predecessors, by its love for the Scriptures. The Jews were a people of the Book, but this is not the only place where the Scriptures could be found, for Jewish intertestamental writings contain a significant amount of Scripture.[73] It was not mainly the recitation and reproduction of the Scriptures in this literature that interested them, but their interpretation. As Charlesworth observes, "The Pseudepigrapha, like all early Jewish religious writings, generally tended to be in some way exegetical."[74] This emphasis on the interpretation of Scripture is the successor of a process begun within the canon itself.[75] Fishbane argues persuasively that although the received tradition maintained its preeminence, scribal interpretation, seeking to explicate and make more comprehensible a passage of Scripture, would at times "invade" the text.[76] This was not necessarily a sign of disregard for the authority or inviolability of Scripture, but an attempt to apply it and make it understandable in changing circumstances. Later writers of Scripture also took up previous passages of Scripture, reinterpreting and reapplying them in their own contemporary context.[77]

---

[72] As Thompson notes, the value of the tests "lies in assisting the judgment of relative probability" (*Clothed with Christ*, 36).

[73] For a list of Jewish intertestamental writings see Schürer, *The History of the Jewish People in the Age of Jesus Christ (175 B.C. – 135 A.D.)*, III.1 and III.2. Cf. J. J. Scott, *Customs and Controversies: Intertestamental Jewish Backgrounds of the New Testament*, 357–363. On the extensive use of Scripture in intertestamental writings see P. S. Alexander, "Retelling the Old Testament," esp. 117; and articles in M. J. Mulder, *Mikra: Text, Translation, Reading and Interpretation of the Hebrew Bible in Ancient Judaism and Early Christianity.*

[74] J. H. Charlesworth, "The Pseudepigrapha as Biblical Exegesis," 152. Cf. idem, "Biblical Interpretation: The Crucible of the Pseudepigrapha," 67: "The Crucible of the Pseudepigrapha was Torah interpretation."

[75] In his detailed study, *Biblical Interpretation in Ancient Israel*, M. Fishbane has credibly demonstrated that the Hebrew Bible was itself a product of an ongoing process of exegesis. Cf. idem, "Inner Biblical Exegesis," 36: "Within ancient Israel, as long as the textual corpus remained open, Revelation and Tradition were thickly interwoven and interdependent, and the received Hebrew Bible is itself, therefore, the product of an interpretive tradition." For examples of this see further the articles in Carson and Williamson, *Scripture Citing Scripture*, section 2 (esp. 25–83).

[76] Fishbane, "Inner Biblical Exegesis," 20–21, 34.

[77] Fishbane, *Biblical Interpretation*, 542–543: "The whole phenomenon of inner-biblical exegesis requires the latter-day historian to appreciate the fact that the texts and

The same issues that gave rise to the phenomenon of inner-biblical exegesis – that is, the need to interpret and apply the Scriptures in changing contexts and historical situations – ensured that this would be an on-going process. For a people who wanted to put into practice God's commands, who wanted to know his plans and purposes for history and how they fit into them, it was of the utmost importance to understand the Scriptures. This meant that "for contemporary Judaism, generally, there is no Mikra [Scripture] *without* its interpretation; indeed, there is only the Mikra *through* its *legitimate* and *proper* interpretation."[78] This preoccupation with interpreting Scripture was widespread and not isolated to sectarian groups on the fringes of mainstream Judaism.[79] As a result, the intertestamental writings are keys to understanding early Jewish thought, and this in turn is crucial to understanding the NT use of the OT.

Appreciation of the importance of intertestamental Jewish writings for properly interpreting the NT is growing among scholars.[80] This has generally developed along two interconnected lines. The first is that Jewish intertestamental literature is the backdrop against which the NT use of the OT should be read. There were many interpretive traditions that both Jews and Christians would have been familiar with, and which would have affected the way they read and understood Scripture.[81] Accordingly,

---

traditions, the received *traditum* of ancient Israel, were not simply copied, studied, transmitted, or recited. They were also, and by these means, subject to redaction, elucidation, reformulation, and outright transformation. Accordingly, our received traditions are complex blends of *traditum* [received text] and *traditio* [process of transmission, scribal process] in dynamic interaction, dynamic interpenetration, and dynamic interdependence. They are, in sum, the exegetical voices of many teachers and tradents, from different circles and times, responding to real and theoretical considerations as perceived and anticipated."

[78] M. Fishbane, "Use, Authority, and Interpretation of Mikra at Qumran," 376; emphasis original.

[79] In support of this being a widespread practice see Charlesworth, "Crucible"; Fishbane, "Mikra at Qumran"; D. Dimant, "Use and Interpretation of Mikra in the Apocrypha and Pseudepigrapha"; Y. Amir, "Authority and Interpretation of Scripture in the Writings of Philo"; L H. Feldman, "Use, Authority and Exegesis of Mikra in the Writings of Josephus"; R. Kasher, "The Interpretation of Scripture in Rabbinic Literature"; C. C. Rowland, "Apocalyptic Literature."

[80] For example, in summarizing the results of the contributions to *The Scriptures in the Gospels*, Tuckett notes that "all were agreed upon the great importance of understanding the potential significance of the background in Jewish scriptures, and the subsequent interpretation of those scriptures by other contemporary writers, for interpreting the New Testament gospels and the traditions they contain" ("Introduction," xxiv).

[81] See for example W. D. Davies, "Canon and Christology in Paul," 33: "Between the Tanak and the New Testament lies a vast exegetical-interpretative activity within Judaism . . . In confronting Judaism the early church, like Jesus and Paul, faced not only both a written and an oral Torah but also ways of understanding these, that is, long-

although this study emphasizes the necessity of examining the original
literary context of an OT passage quoted in the NT, this is not the only step
in determining meaning. It is important also to ascertain whether, and if
so in what way, contemporary Jewish exegesis interpreted the passage,
since this is the thought world and context within which Christian exegesis
was born and developed.[82] The second line of research, which is a natural
development of the first and dependent on it, is that intertestamental writings mediated portions of Scripture. The NT writers used the Scriptures,
but it was an interpreted Scripture they interacted with, one with multiple
exegetical traditions.[83]

An examination of Ps 118's function in the NT thus benefits from
understanding how it was used and interpreted in the intertestamental
period, especially since the prominent use of the psalm in the early
apologetic of the church suggests there were pre-existing traditions which
facilitated such employment.[84] It is important to look not only for allusions
to the psalm, but also for echoes of the *interpreted* Ps 118. A particular
difficulty in examining the psalm from this vantage point is that few if any
allusions to the psalm have been identified in intertestamental literature.
Instead, the primary pre-existing interpretive context is its liturgical use in
the main festivals. It is in the light of this cultic context that Ps 118 was
interpreted and mediated to Jews at the time of Jesus, and therefore at
least partly against this backdrop that Ps 118 is used in the NT. The
intertestamental mediations of Ps 118 open a window which allows us to

---

standing exegetical traditions. They assumed these, and it was to these traditions of
exegesis and interpretation rather than to the Tanak itself in its textual nudity that they
related."

[82] Daube's warning is worth heeding: "When dealing with the Old Testament in
the New we ought to read it as it was read by Jews of that era. The references without
exception come from their midst, are founded on their interpretation. . . . Unless we
do, we may miss parts – from relatively minor to very major – of the New Testament
message conveyed by means of the reference" ("The Old Testament in the New: A
Jewish Perspective," 3).

[83] Rosner has effectively advanced this methodology in his study of Paul's ethical
teaching, arguing that "early Jewish moral teaching represents an intermediary stage
which stands between the Scriptures and Paul and mediates Scripture to Paul. Scripture
influenced moral teaching, which in turn influenced Paul's ethics" (*Scripture and Ethics*,
26). As Rosner further explains, "in part he [Paul] heard the moral demands of Scripture
through this Jewish 'filter' . . . He did not receive his Bible in a vacuum . . . he used a
'diffused' Bible" (ibid., 57). In a similar vein, Kinzer ("Psalm 8") concludes through an
analysis of rabbinic, pseudepigraphic, and other contemporary literature, that the NT
appropriation of Ps 8 was based on pre-existing exegetical traditions that provided the
primary impulse for its christological reading.

[84] Lindars has observed that "the Scriptures used to defend the primitive faith were
those already commonly employed in apocalyptic-eschatological speculation, which is
thus the proper Jewish background to Christianity" (*Apologetic*, 284).

see the continuity and discontinuity between the old and the new, and therefore to better understand its attraction for the NT writer.

C. Context Fields

C. H. Dodd initiated the contemporary debate on respect for context in the citation of Scripture, arguing that the NT writers, far from quoting in an atomistic way or "prooftexting," show a high regard for the original context of the OT passages they refer to. The quoted verse or phrase functions as a "pointer" to a larger section of Scripture, so that "it is the total context that is in view, and is the basis of the argument."[85] Many scholars remain unconvinced, the conventional wisdom holding that the NT writers generally chose verses which would fit their arguments, with little regard for how these functioned in the original passage. To demonstrate that the writers always quoted with respect for original context lies beyond the scope of this study. What is argued, however, is that the citation of a prior text is a signal that the later text should be read in light of the former.

There is a sense in which all OT quotations are taken out of context, for the act of citation establishes a relationship between old and new text in which each affects the reading of the other. Inevitably the old text acquires a new meaning and function within the passage to which it has been introduced. As Moyise suggests, "The relevant question becomes not 'did the author respect the OT context?' but 'in what ways do the two contexts interact?'"[86] This does not, however, minimize the significance of the original context, for the citation continues to point the reader back to the original text.[87] Ignoring the context of the prior text exposes one to the danger of losing the correspondences and (possibly) disjunctions intended by the author. In fact, that the prior text should not be considered in isolation is presupposed by the atomistic form in which quotations and allusions are often found.[88]

---

[85] Dodd, *According to the Scriptures*, 126. Studies supporting and questioning Dodd's argument have continued to appear. For representative articles on both sides of the issue see Beale, *The Right Doctrine from the Wrong Texts? Essays on the Use of the Old Testament in the New*, 137–295. One of Dodd's most widely cited critics, A. C. Sundberg ("On Testimonies"), has in turn been strongly criticized by I. H. Marshall ("An Assessment of Recent Developments"), who demonstrates that Sundberg's statistics actually bolster Dodd's claims.

[86] Moyise, *Revelation*, 19.

[87] Cf. Weren, "Jesus' Entry," 123; Hays, *Echoes*, 20.

[88] Although contemporary supporters of the theory of intertextuality have brought new vigor to the argument that the original context of quoted verses should be studied, some of the strongest reasons may come from antiquity. D. I. Brewer (*Techniques and*

This thesis will attempt to defend the suggestion that the citation of a verse or phrase from Ps 118 points beyond that single verse to its immediate surrounding context, and further to the entire psalm, which is its larger literary unit. That is, the citation, however brief, may function to draw in the entire context from which it comes, so that the receiving text should be examined in broad interaction with the entire psalm. In this sense, the argument here for the validity of larger context fields goes hand in hand with the approach characterized by intertextuality.

III. Distinctives and Plan of Study

This study has several distinctives. First, our approach differs somewhat from most studies of the OT in the NT, which often fall into one of two camps. Many start with a NT passage and trace quotations, allusions, and echoes back to their OT source.[89] As a result the NT passage is studied in reference to several different intertextual links, with the focus on how each functions individually within the new context. The other most common approach is to examine the influence of one OT book on one NT book.[90] The approach taken in this study – examining how a restricted literary unit (Ps 118) functions in several new restricted literary contexts (across the Fourth Gospel) – is seen less often, and lends itself to answering some questions that other approaches cannot ask as easily. It can reveal whether the same verse or passage is used in different ways and

---

Assumptions in Jewish Exegesis Before 70 CE), in his analysis of exegeses in rabbinic literature which he argues are likely to have originated before 70 AD, concludes that "every single" example which he examined demonstrates respect for context (ibid., 167). Whether or not such a claim can be sustained, at the very least Brewer's work demonstrates that context was often not disregarded, and that many obscure passages "cannot be understood at all without reference to the context of the text which is quoted" (ibid., 169). This would seem to be the exegetical assumption articulated in Hillel's seventh *middah*: "Meaning is learned from context." (For the seven *middoth* of Hillel and other lists of *middoth* see ibid., 226–231.) Brewer notes in contrast that the later rabbis frequently ignored the original context (for extended discussion see ibid., 165–171, 222), as did other pre-70 commentators (see ibid., 187–212). Although Brewer has been disputed, for the most part objections do not center on questioning his attention to context. See S. C. Reif, Review of D. I. Brewer; A. J. Saldarini, Review of D. I. Brewer.

[89] For example, Rosner, *Scripture and Ethics*; Ciampa, "Galatians"; Williams, *The Wisdom of the Wise*; Hafemann, *History of Israel*; Matthewson, "Revelation"; Moritz, *Ephesians*.

[90] For example, Fekkes, *Isaiah*; G. K. Beale, *The Use of Daniel in Jewish Apocalyptic Literature and in the Revelation of St. John*; M. Knowles, *Jeremiah in Matthew's Gospel: The Rejected Prophet Motif in Matthean Redaction*.

with varying meaning effects by a single (or several) writers,[91] and also affords the opportunity to investigate whether there is coherence between the various references to the pre-text in a particular NT book.

Second, although there is value in the traditional historical-critical paradigm, this will be supplemented by making use of the theory of inter-textuality, which aids in recognizing and recovering more subtle uses of Scripture. The Fourth Gospel provides an especially appropriate source in which to test this method, for John's use of Scripture is especially subtle, and contains only one clear citation of Ps 118. It will be argued that John's use of Ps 118 is more significant and extensive than has been previously recognized.

Third, an examination of Ps 118's literary context will provide an opportunity to test in John the thesis that a citation refers one to the whole context from which it was drawn. Together with this, and fourth, the history of interpretation of Ps 118 will be considered to determine whether pre-existing traditions influenced the NT use. In conclusion, this investigation will proceed diachronically (considering the meaning of the pre-text in its original context and its history of interpretation) and synchronically (considering the function and meaning of the pre-text in its new context). We will ask what the place and function of the allusion is both in its ori-ginal and new literary context, whether there is coherence of the various references to Ps 118 in the Fourth Gospel, and whether these serve a wider purpose apart from the individual citation.

The study proceeds as follows. Chapter 2 surveys the use of Ps 118 outside the NT, with special attention to its original historical context and its role in Jewish liturgy. The Synoptic use of the psalm is examined in ch. 3, with each evangelist treated separately before addressing the relationship of the Synoptics to John. In ch. 4 the broader context of John's use of Ps 118 is explored, with attention focusing on his use of the OT and a pattern of New Exodus. Chapter 5 analyzes the only clear quotation of Ps 118 in the Fourth Gospel, which appears in the Entrance Narrative. Chapter 6 argues for recognition in the Gospel of a coming-sent motif linked with the psalm, with ch. 7 proposing a subsequent re-reading of the Entrance Narrative in light of the motif's function. Chapters 8–10 attempt to establish four additional allusions to Ps 118. The final chapter summarizes the results of the study and suggests some possible implications.

---

[91] A brief survey of the Synoptic evangelists' use of Ps 118 in ch. 3 of this study provides a basis for comparison with John's use.

Chapter 2

Psalm 118 in its Jewish Setting

This chapter proposes to contribute in two main areas to the interpretation of Ps 118 in the NT. First, we will argue that Ps 118 was probably interpreted eschatologically and/or messianically in Second Temple Judaism. This in itself is not a new claim, as many NT scholars assume such an understanding of Ps 118. Jeremias, for example, declares that Ps 118.24–29 is depicted as the antiphonal choir of the *parousia* which will welcome the Messiah.[1] However, the problem with Jeremias' work, and of those who argue from the same evidence, is that the sources adduced are rabbinic.[2] There is no question that both Ps 118 and its liturgical unit the Hallel (Pss 113–118) were interpreted eschatologically in rabbinic literature, but because of their late date it is not possible to use these sources with confidence. Accordingly we will attempt to build a cumulative case which uses rabbinic material only as corroborating evidence. Some rabbinic material is based directly on, or is an expansion of, antecedent traditions, but the difficulty is determining which material reflects earlier streams of tradition.[3] Therefore the direction of our argument is from pre-rabbinic to rabbinic. In this way we hope to provide a more solid foundation for what is too often simply assumed.

Second, we will examine several different contexts which we suggest provide the interpretive horizons for Ps 118 in Second Temple Judaism. One of the difficulties in finding the hermeneutical clues for intertesta-

---

[1] Jeremias, *Eucharistic Words*, 256–261. Cf. D. Cohn-Sherbok, "A Jewish Note on ΤΟ ΠΟΤΗΡΙΟΝ ΤΗΣ ΕΥΛΟΓΙΑΣ," 708; Kraus, *Theology of the Psalms*, 193; E. Werner, "'Hosanna' in the Gospels," 114–117.

[2] On the dangers of relying heavily on rabbinic material see Sandmell, "Parallelomania"; and especially C. A. Evans, "Early Rabbinic Sources and Jesus Research."

[3] Rabbinic literature is of value and can be used, but this must be done carefully and critically. Evans' ("Early Rabbinic Sources," 53–56) criteria for establishing the relevance of particular rabbinic parallels are a good starting point. One should look for antecedent documentation, contamination by Christian sources, provenance, and coherence between the rabbinic parallel and the passage being considered.

mental interpretation of Ps 118 is that it is not quoted explicitly in the pseudepigrapha, Philo, Josephus, or other early sources.[4] However, the fact that it is quoted extensively in rabbinic literature and the NT requires asking why it received such attention. We will look first for an original setting and possible role for Ps 118 in the autumn festival during the monarchic period. Since the themes and complex of associations which characterized each of the feasts may have influenced the interpretations that Ps 118 would acquire, it is important to investigate its use in the Jewish festivals, especially Tabernacles and Passover. Finally, we will look more closely at the Hallel and its special place in the Jewish heart and imagination before examining Ps 118 in relation to its immediate literary context (Pss 113–118), its larger literary unit (Pss 107–118), and its place in the Psalter. Such a "literary" approach will suggest various ways Ps 118 could have been read. Each of these areas will provide clues for the interpretation of Ps 118 and may indicate why it played such an important role in the NT. No study has systematically examined and gathered together the different Jewish contexts in which Ps 118 was used.

I. The Original Setting of Ps 118

A. Options Proposed

Recovering the original *Sitz im Leben* of a psalm is an uncertain task at best. No doubt many of the psalms were composed for or in response to a specific historical situation, but the historical context is seldom specified in the psalm or by the surrounding literary unit. Where a biographical or historical ascription is included in the title, this is thought by the majority of scholars to be the work of later editors and not reliable historically. The range of settings proposed for Ps 118 bears witness to the difficulty of determining an original context. Psalm 118 has been identified or associated with the annual liturgy of ritual humiliation and exaltation of the Davidic

---

[4] An exception is 4QpPs[b] frag. 5, which appears to contain a quotation of or allusion to Ps 118.20. See J. M. Allegro, *Qumran Cave 4.I (4Q158–4Q186)*, 51–53 and pl. XVIII. M. Horgan (*Pesharim: Qumran Interpretations of Biblical Books*, 266) argues that the fragment is not a pesher and is later than the other fragments, but notes the possible quotation. 4QpPs[b] frag. 4 may also quote Ps 118.26, 27. In any case, because of the poor state of the fragments it is not possible to recover the context. In adddition, Ps 118.22 is quoted in *T. Sol.* 23.4 by Solomon in reference to the building of the temple. However, its date is disputed and it is unlikely that it comes from the Second Temple period (see D. C. Duling, "Testament of Solomon: A New Translation and Introduction," 940–943). For a discussion of the quotation see Berder, *"La pierre rejetée,"* 170–180.

king;[5] the annual enthronement of the king at the fall festival;[6] Hezekiah as the individual in the psalm, in the eighth century BC;[7] an annual commemoration of earlier military victories which took place at the Autumn Festival of Yahweh;[8] a king thanking God at Tabernacles for victory in battle;[9] a Davidic king leading a procession of pilgrims in a thanksgiving service after a period of anxiety;[10] a king's hymn of thanksgiving for delivery from death and for a military victory;[11] a post-exilic psalm which borrows old royal elements and becomes a thanksgiving for a private individual who has brought his celebration into the midst of the congregation after healing from sickness;[12] an originally royal thanksgiving for a military victory adapted for communal and private use in post-exilic times;[13] a post-exilic grand celebration, possibly an old psalm that has received a new interpretation after the exile;[14] the first celebration of Tabernacles in the seventh month of the first year of return from exile

---

[5] J. H. Eaton, *Kingship and the Psalms*, 129–130. Others who support this position include A. R. Johnson, *Sacral Kingship in Ancient Israel*, 125–126; and Anderson (2.797, 800), who concludes it is an annual cultic experience belonging to the Feast of Tabernacles, including the ritual humiliation of the king. Similarly, S. Mowinckel (*The Psalms in Israel's Worship*, 1.180–181) identifies it as an entrance liturgy used in the fall festival and perhaps in a dramatic presentation of the "myth about the fight of nations."

[6] J. A. Sanders, "A New Testament Hermeneutic Fabric: Ps 118 in the Entrance Narrative," 180; Zerr, 264. Note that the immediately preceding position may include an annual enthronement.

[7] Barnes (cited by McCullough, 616); McCullough, 616. H. May ("Psalm 118: The Song of the Citadel," 97, 103–106) argues that the psalm was not composed in connection with a specific event, but had its origin in one of the royal border-fortresses along the Judaean frontier during the period of Hezekiah and Jerobam.

[8] Weiser, 725.

[9] Bratcher and Reyburn, *Translator's Handbook*, 986.

[10] VanGemeren, 729.

[11] Dahood, 3.155. Wagner ("Psalm 118," 157) follows Dahood. Also in favor of a straight military victory see L. Jacquet, *Les Psaumes et le coeur de l'Homme: Etude textuelle, littéraire et doctrinale*, 3.304–305. Dahood believes this is not best understood as part of the annual liturgy in which the Davidic king was prominent. Allen (123) agrees with Dahood, suggesting it is set in the context of a processional liturgy.

[12] Gunkel, *Die Psalmen*, 504ff. Rodgerson and McKay (83) suggest that the psalm is composed of several previously separate liturgical fragments, but do not specify a date.

[13] S. B. Frost, "Psalm 118: An Exposition," 157–161. Elsewhere Frost claims that Ps 118 includes a ritual for the readmission of a worshipper to the temple after a period in which he appeared to be excluded from divine favor ("Asseveration by Thanksgiving," 380).

[14] VanGemeren, 730. This does not necessarily contradict VanGemeren's earlier acknowledgement that the psalm may be pre-exilic, since he notes it was readily adapted to other contexts.

(Ezra 3.1–4);[15] the laying of the foundation stone of the temple in the second month of the second year of return (Ezra 3.8–13);[16] the dedication of the completed temple in the twelfth month of the sixth year of Darius (Ezra 6.15ff);[17] the Passover celebrated after the dedication (Ezra 6.19–22);[18] a psalm written for Passover after the reconstruction of the temple;[19] the Tabernacles celebrated in 444 BC after the repair of the walls of Jerusalem had been completed (Neh 8);[20] a post-exilic thank offering hymn for use at the sacrifices of a pilgrim festival, recalling David and telling of his victories as a prophecy of the future triumph of Israel;[21] a liturgy for the circumcision of a notable proselyte;[22] a text of praise for the remembered salvation of exodus and return from exile;[23] a gate liturgy for entering the temple area during a festival of thanksgiving, used by an individual with his companions;[24] a psalm inspired by the appearance of Alexander the Great;[25] the celebration of a Maccabean victory against Syrian oppressors;[26] the purification and reconsecration of the temple by Judas the Maccabee in 165 BC;[27] Simon's driving the Syrians out of the Acra and celebrating the triumph;[28] a prayer for rain in Second Temple

---

[15] G. H. Ewald. Cited by May, "Ps 118," 102 n. 3.

[16] Hengstenberg. Cited by Perowne, 2.286.

[17] Delitzsch, 3.208. He does not hold this position strongly.

[18] Kirkpatrick (3.693) lists this as an option but rejects it.

[19] Kissane, 536–537.

[20] Kirkpatrick, 3.693; Baethgen, 347. Berder ("La pierre rejetée," 89, 105) suggests this is the most probable setting, adding however that a composition in stages should not be excluded. Perowne (2.287) also concludes that the most probable setting is the Tabernacles celebration of Neh 8, yet he associates this with the completion of the second temple. It is possible that Neh 1.11 alludes to Ps 118.25. It is more likely that Nehemiah echoes the well-known psalm as a paradigm for his own situation than that the psalm, which probably was used at Nehemiah's Tabernacles festival, was created especially for that festival.

[21] Peters, *Liturgies*, 426–428.

[22] W. Robinson, "Ps 118: A Liturgy for the Admission of a Proselyte," 180. He suggests it may have been a former troubler of Israel, perhaps a Syrian army leader.

[23] J. L. Mays, "Psalm 118 in the Light of Canonical Analysis," 143. Mays argues that there is no particular cultic occasion or historical event with which the psalm can be connected with any certainty.

[24] Kraus, 395–396. Cf. with other entrance liturgies in Pss 15 and 24.

[25] Buttenwieser, 659, 664–670. The date he proposes is ca. 331–332 BC

[26] Briggs, 2.404. Duhm (414) suggests that it relates to victory over Nicanor (1 Macc 7.48–49).

[27] T. K. Cheyne. Cited by Kirkpatrick, 3.694. See 1 Macc 4.36–59 and 2 Macc 10.1–8.

[28] Venema; Rosenmüller. Cited by Kirkpatrick, 3.694. See 1 Macc 13.51;14.4ff.

Tabernacles ritual;[29] and a late post-exilic psalm for public worship which developed from a personal psalm of thanksgiving for deliverance.[30]

This representative list of proposed settings raises the question whether it is possible to recover with any degree of certainty such a historical venue for Ps 118. The obvious difficulty leads to a further question, namely, whether recovering an original setting for the psalm is necessary for understanding its use in Judaism and in the NT. Although this is a complicated question, essentially the answer is No. Far from being static, psalms were taken up and reinterpreted in new contexts, acquiring new meaning in the process. This is especially true for pre-exilic psalms associated with kingship and/or used in the royal cult.[31] In support, the NT quotes most often from the Psalter, even though few of the psalms can be linked absolutely to an original setting, suggesting that it was the association of individual psalms with broader themes in the Psalter (messianism, royalty, eschatology) that excited the imagination of the NT writers.[32] Consequently, our concern is to explore what associations were linked with Ps 118 during the intertestamental period. What thoughts sprang to the Jewish mind when encountering Ps 118? A proposed original context is only the first of several significant life settings from which Ps 118 gathers its associative meanings in Judaism.

B. The Autumn Festival

Psalm 118's use in the post-exilic festival liturgies is documented, but as with most psalms there is no explicit mention of what its liturgical

---

[29] J. Petuchowski, "'Hoshi'ah na' in Psalm 118.25: A Prayer for Rain," 270–271.

[30] Oesterley, 2.480–481.

[31] The use of Ps 118 in the various liturgical contexts of the major annual festivals is but one example. See for example J. Becker's approach in *Israel deutet seine Psalmen: Urform und Neuinterpretation in den Psalmen*; idem, *Wege der Psalmenexegese*. Becker (*Israel*, 56–57) considers Ps 118 an eschatological thanksgiving composed of different parts of pre- and post-exilic thanksgiving liturgies. Note also Frost ("Psalm 118," 157–161), who argues that Ps 118 was re-interpreted and adapted to post-exilic use.

[32] In support of his argument that the Psalter became the most important book of prophecy for early Christianity, M. Hengel ("The Old Testament in the Fourth Gospel," 382) counts verbatim citations with introductory formulas in the NT (using NA[25]) with the following results: Psalms, 55; Isaiah, 51; Deuteronomy, 45 (of which 14 are from the Decalogue and love commandments). After these three the numbers drop off, the next most cited being Exodus with 23 (10 of which come from the Decalogue). As a result, it appears that sixty percent of unambiguous citations in the NT come from Psalms, Isaiah, and Deuteronomy. It is reasonable to assume that the number of citations for Psalms would grow considerably if quotations and allusions which do not have introductory formulas were included.

function may have been in the pre-exilic temple cult, had it taken shape there. It is therefore necessary to make a distinction between the function and possible composition of Ps 118 in connection with the autumn festival, where it would most likely have featured, and its later use in the Feast of Tabernacles. In this regard it is important to note a welcome shift in Psalms research towards emphasizing a liturgical origin for the majority of psalms, especially since the cult found its apex in the autumn festival.[33] There is general agreement that the autumn festival was the most important of the three great festivals in ancient Israel, especially during the monarchy,[34] and it is also clear that although there is some complexity in determining the development of the cultic calendars and the evolution of the festivals – issues which lie beyond the scope of this study – the autumn festival came to be called Tabernacles.[35] Ps 118 is associated most closely with Tabernacles in later Judaism, and I suggest that this may well pre-date the exile. Accordingly we will look briefly at previous attempts to reconstruct the autumn festival before suggesting an original setting for Ps 118.

---

[33] E.g., Gerstenberger, "Psalms," 197; D. Howard, "Editorial Activity in the Psalter: A State-of-the-Field Survey," 58. Robinson ("Psalm 118," 179) claims a degree of consensus for the view.

[34] See Kraus, *Worship in Israel: A Cultic History of the Old Testament*, 62ff.; N. H. Snaith, *The Jewish New Year Festival: Its Origins and Development*, chs. 1 and 2; Eaton, *Kingship*; Weiser, "Introduction" in *Psalms*; J. Rubinstein, *The History of Sukkot in the Second Temple and Rabbinic Periods*, 30. That Tabernacles was preeminent among the pilgrimage festivals can be seen by its being called the "festival of Yahweh" (Lev 23.41; Num 29.12), or simply "the festival" (1 Kgs 8.2, 65; 12.32; Ezek 45.25; Neh 8.14; 2 Chr 5.3; 7.8) a title which the autumn festival shares (Lev 23.39; Hos 9.5; Judg 21.19). The title of "festival" without further qualification points to its position as the feast *par excellence*. It was used for the inauguration of the temple (1 Kgs 8), and its importance apparently led to Jeroboam's establishing a rival festival in its place (1 Kgs 12.32). At some point Tabernacles was expanded from a seven-day festival to include the feasts observed on the first (Rosh Hashanah) and tenth (Atonement) days of the month (Lev 23.23–24).

[35] For the purposes of this study there is no distinction made between Tabernacles and the autumn festival. The terms are used interchangeably, although the autumn festival refers exclusively to the period of the monarchy. For a detailed discussion of the issues involved see Kraus, *Worship*, 26–69; Rubenstein, *Sukkot*, 13–30; G. W. MacRae, "The Meaning and Evolution of the Feast of Tabernacles." For the cultic calendars see Exod 23.10–19; 34.18–26; Deut 16.1–17; Lev 23.4–44; Num 28 and 29.

1. Reconstruction of the Festival

Mowinckel's reconstruction of the autumn festival has proved both en-during and controversial.[36] He argues that many of the psalms, including Ps 118, can be understood only in the framework of an Israelite fall festival, at the beginning of the New Year,[37] central to which is a ce-lebration and dramatic enactment of Yahweh's enthronement as the universal King.[38] The New Year basis of the festival falters on several points, not least of which is the questionable reliance on Near Eastern parallels,[39] and the lack of OT evidence for a New Year's festival as such in ancient Israel.[40]   Criticism has also centered on Mowinckel's "enthronement of Yahweh," for which he depended most heavily on the enthronement psalms (Pss 47; 93; 95–99) and the phrase "*Yahweh malakh*," which he takes to mean "Yahweh has become King."[41]   It is

---

[36] Mowinckel, *Psalmenstudien*; idem, *Israel's Worship*.

[37] Tabernacles is said to be in the first month or alternatively in the seventh.   It appears that the turn of the year was transferred from autumn to spring under the influence of the Babylonian calendar.   Kraus (*Worship*, 45) suggests this took place by the end of the eighth century BC, although the date is not certain.

[38] Cf. P. Volz, *Das Neujahrsfest Yahwes*; H. Schmidt, *Die Thronfahrt Jahwes am Fest der Jahreswende im alten Israel*. Gunkel (*Einleitung in die Psalmen*, 105) also accepts the basic premise, but disputes the importance of the enthronement festival in the worship of Israel and suggests that Mowinckel associated too many psalms with it.

[39] For criticism of Mowinckel's reconstructed festival see C. R. North, "The Religious Aspects of Hebrew Kingship," 35; L. I. Pap, *Das israelitische Neujahrsfest*. See also the discussion by H. H. Rowley, *Worship in Ancient Israel: Its Forms and Meaning*, 184–203.   Although Rowley supports a New Year festival, he correctly questions the comparisons with the Babylonian New Year festival.   We suggest that reconstructing an Israelite festival on the basis of the *Akitu* festival is hazardous at best: It assumes uniformity of cultures in the Near East, and that Israel would have shared all the features of the Babylonian one.   Included in the Babylonian ritual was a representation of the death and resurrection of the god and of the creation myth, a dramatization of the god's fight with his enemies in ritual combat, a sacred marriage in which the god was represented by the king and by which the springs of fertility for the nation were believed to be released (cf. Rowley, *Worship*, 185–186).   The myth-and-ritual group, led by S. H. Hooke (see articles in the works he edited: *Myth and Ritual*; *Myth, Ritual, and Kingship: Essays on the Theory and Practice of Kingship in the Ancient Near East and in Israel*; and *The Labyrinth: Further Studies in the Relation Between Myth and Ritual in the Ancient World*), advanced arguments for a wide use of parallels, going well beyond Mowinckel.   To read this kind of ritual into the OT goes well beyond the evidence.

[40] Cf. R. de Vaux, *Ancient Israel: Its Life and Institutions*, 501–502.   For the evidence in favor of a New Year festival see Snaith (*Jewish Near Year Festival*), although he criticizes Mowinckel's reconstruction.

[41] See Mowinckel, *Israel's Worship*, 1.107–192.   A variety of translations have been suggested, including "Yahweh is King" (Johnson, *Sacral Kingship*, 77 n. 1), and "Yahweh rules as King" (D. Michel, "Studien zu den sogennanten Thronbesteigungspsalmen").

common to read, in a variety of recensions, that Mowinckel is suggesting that the king represented Yahweh and was enthroned in his place. Lurking in the background are whispers of a fertility rite, possibly a dying and rising god, and other Near Eastern parallels. However, it may be that Mowinckel has been misunderstood and unjustly associated with the radical views of the myth-and-ritual school of thought.[42] The attention focused on the enthronement of Yahweh, which takes place on only one day of the festival, has obscured both Mowinckel's broader festival reconstruction and its emphasis on acknowledging and celebrating Yahweh's kingship.[43] According to Mowinckel, the enthronement psalms show Yahweh as coming, making himself known, revealing himself and his salvation, and renewing the covenant and the life of nature. The festival is therefore a celebration of the epiphany of Yahweh, the day of his cultic coming and revelation as King.[44]

While correctly questioning the New Year basis of the festival, a number of scholars have built upon Mowinckel's legacy and supported some of his festival emphases. Gerstenberger has accentuated the idea that creation was dramatically reenacted, since one of the main concerns of the Israelite farming communities had to be rain and the fertility of their fields.[45] Weiser has proposed a Covenant Renewal Festival that recalls the election of Israel at Sinai, and argues that the cultic traditions associated

---

For a survey and discussion see Eaton, *Psalms of the Way and the Kingdom: A Conference with the Commentators*, 116–118. De Vaux (*Ancient Israel*, 505) argues that the so-called enthronement psalms are not for enthronement but deal with the kingship of Yahweh, a position that would support an emphasis on Yahweh's kingship at a major festival. Unfortunately he thinks they cannot be pre-exilic because of their close connections with Second Isaiah, failing to consider that Isaiah could be dependent on Psalms.

[42] N. K. Gottwald (*The Hebrew Bible: A Socio-Literary Introduction*, 534) has also recognized the linking of Mowinckel with ideas he did not propound. See Mowinckel, *Israel's Worship*, 1.58–59. On the myth-and-ritual school see this study's bibliography under S. H. Hooke.

[43] In Mowinckel's reconstruction the festival included dramatizations of Yahweh's enthronement and kingship based on his victory over the powers of chaos and the primeval ocean; the creation; a repetition and re-experience of these 'facts of salvation'; the renewal of the historical salvation (i.e., the election and deliverance from Egypt) and the covenant; the personal presence of Yahweh symbolized by the ark; a repeated consecration of the temple; and the renewal of the covenant with David and the royal house (Mowinckel, *Israel's Worship*, 1.129–130).

[44] Mowinckel, *Israel's Worship*, 1.118–119, 142.

[45] Gerstenberger, "Psalms," 213. He further writes, "The Yahweh kingship psalms are sufficient evidence for an Israelite festival which praised Yahweh's taking power over the nations" (ibid., 215).

with such a festival dominate the book of Psalms.[46] Kraus reconstructs a Royal Zion Festival, observed on the first day of Tabernacles, in which "Yahweh does not become King, but he comes as King."[47] The festival includes an ascent of the ark to the Temple Mount, and a celebration of the election of David and his dynasty and of Zion as the abode of the ark and the site of the temple. Whatever other particular emphases it may have had, it is likely that the celebration and recognition of Yahweh's kingship was central to the autumn festival.[48]

2. The Role of the King in the Cult

At the same time that the autumn festival is associated with the kingship of Yahweh, it is also linked closely with the Davidic king. It is possible that the accession of a king took place at the autumn festival, and if there was an annual re-enactment of the enthronement ceremony it would have occurred then as well.[49] J. B. Segal plausibly states that "throughout Israelite history it appears to be Tabernacles which is the royal festival *par excellence*."[50] The rise of the monarchy and the centralization of the cult in the Jerusalem temple with its royal associations ensured that the king would have a pivotal role in the nation's religious life and the cult. When coupled with the centrality of the king in ancient Israel, the large number of psalms which concern him suggest that he was present and perhaps

---

[46] Weiser, 23–45. H. Ringren (*Israelitische Religion*, 183) argues that in pre-exilic times Israel celebrated Yahweh as Creator and King at the autumn festival and renewed the covenant with him. G. von Rad (*The Problem of the Hexateuch and Other Essays*, 36f.) calls the autumn festival a Covenant Festival. For Mowinckel's covenant element see *Israel's Worship*, 1.155.

[47] Kraus, *Worship*, 214. This emphasis on Yahweh not becoming King is a mistaken reaction to Mowinckel. One should note that Mowinckel does not suggest that at any time Yahweh is not King. His emphasis on Yahweh's coming to be acclaimed as King is to highlight Israel's allegiance and submission to Yahweh as King of Israel and the universe.

[48] See Eaton (*Psalms of the Way*, 123) for a list of scholars who accept the linkage of a celebration of Yahweh's kingship with the autumn festival.

[49] Cf. Kraus, *Worship*, 222. Eaton (*Kingship*, 130), A. R. Johnson ("Hebrew Conceptions of Kingship," 235), and Mowinckel (*Israel's Worship*, 1.60, 66) argue for an enthronement ceremony repeated annually at the festival. Cf. Segal's comments: "We find an identical term for the ceremonial blowing of the trumpets at the proclamation of the king and at the opening of battle when the king went at the head of his army . . . and the same rite at the Israelite autumn festivals, on the other. The term is used still in the Mishnah to describe the blowing of trumpets on the second day of Tabernacles; *it is perhaps a reminder of the times when the king ascended his throne at that festival*" (*The Hebrew Passover: From the Earliest Times to AD 70*, 154; emphasis added).

[50] Segal, *Passover*, 154.

participated when they were used.[51] In fact there are numerous examples in the OT that depict the king as the leader in worship, offering sacrifices, associated with religious ceremonies, and performing a central role in the festivals and cult.[52] All of this suggests that the Davidic king played a significant part in the autumn festival, although attempts to reconstruct his role are complicated by the uncertainty over the exact nature and details of the royal ceremonies included in the festival.

A fairly convincing argument can be made for a dramatic presentation that included the king's participation in ritual combat.[53] Suffering at the hands of his enemies, the king calls upon Yahweh, who delivers and gives him victory. It is not implausible, although the evidence is less strong, that the ceremonies may have included a ritual humiliation/cultic suffering

---

[51] Cf. Miller, *Interpreting the Psalms*, 8; Rowley, *Worship*, 191. De Vaux observes that the king was considered a sacred person and therefore was "empowered to perform religious functions" (*Ancient Israel*, 113).

[52] The following are examples of the king as leader in acts of worship: David sets up the first altar for Yahweh in Jerusalem (2 Sam 24.25), plans the building of a temple for Yahweh (2 Sam 7.2–3), and plans in detail how the temple is to be served (1 Chr 22–29); Solomon builds the temple opposite his palace and dedicates it (1 Kgs 5–8); Jeroboam establishes the sanctuary in Bethel, provides its clergy, and arranges the festal calendar (1 Kgs 12.26–33); chief priests are nominated and dismissed by the king (2 Sam 8.17; 20.25; 1 Kgs 2.26–27; 4.2); Joash issues instructions regarding the repair of the temple and the collection of offerings (2 Kgs 12.4–16); Josiah ensures that the repairs are undertaken (2 Kgs 22.3–7) and takes the initiative in reforming the worship, reinstituting Passover, and renewing the covenant (2 Kgs 23); Ahaz offers sacrifices on an altar he ordered Uriah the Priest to build (2 Kgs 16.10–18). The king also performs priestly acts at times: Saul offers sacrifices at Gilgal (1 Sam 13.9–10); David offers sacrifices at Jerusalem (2 Sam 6.13, 17–18; 24.25); Solomon does the same at Gibeon (1 Kgs 3.4, 15), at the dedication of the temple in Jerusalem (1 Kgs 8.5, 62–64) and at the yearly three great festivals (1 Kgs 9.25). David leads the procession bringing the ark to Jerusalem, wearing the vestments of a priest, ordering sacrifices, and blessing the people (2 Sam 6.12–20); Solomon also blesses the people in the sanctuary (1 Kgs 8.14), and consecrates the middle court of the temple (1 Kgs 8.64).

[53] See especially A. R. Johnson, "The Role of the King in the Jerusalem Cultus," 71–111. He gives a prominent place to Ps 118 in his reconstruction of the king's role. In this article Johnson focuses on Yahweh replenishing society through the drama: Yahweh defeats the powers of darkness and death, which are represented by the kings of the earth who are attacking Jerusalem. Yahweh's ruler in Jerusalem, the Davidic king, engages in battle, representing Yahweh and Israel. In later writings (*Sacral Kingship*; "Conceptions," 235) Johnson invests the drama with eschatological significance as representing Yahweh's final triumph over the gods and nations of the earth and as an affirmation of his universal kingship. For a summary of Johnson's festival reconstruction and its elements see *Sacral Kingship*, 101–102, 134–136; "Conceptions," 235. Strong support for the king participating in ritual combat comes from Mowinckel (*Israel's Worship*, 1.244–245) and Rowley (*Worship*, 191).

(perhaps in the mock battle) and reconsecration of the king.[54]   The strongest support for such rituals comes from the psalms themselves (not least Ps 118), which offer numerous examples of the humiliation and restoration of a king.[55]   Accordingly, the autumn festival may have combined a celebration of Yahweh's kingship with a confirmation of the Davidic office.

3. Difficulties with Festival Reconstructions

Attempts to reconstruct the autumn – or any other – festival in ancient Israel stumble on the fact that the OT historical and legal traditions give very little information on the details of the temple cult and the historical development and liturgical particulars of the yearly festivals.   Added to this is the questionable value of Near Eastern parallels.[56]   Those who have proposed reconstructions acknowledge the problem.   For example, Johnson, Goulder, Eaton, Rowley, and Kraus acknowledge that there is not always explicit evidence to reconstruct a festival, so that attempts rest primarily on implicit evidence deduced from passages – especially the

---

[54] Whether the king underwent ritual humiliation is unresolved, and Johnson's position has been criticized. For example, W. S. McCullough accepts that there was a festival in the autumn at which Yahweh's powers were celebrated, yet he suggests Johnson has an overactive imagination: "No clearly discernible vestiges of a [ritual drama] have survived" ("Israel's Kings, Sacral and Otherwise," 147). See Johnson's scathing response, "Old Testament Exegesis, Imaginative and Unimaginative," whose title makes clear his view of McCullough's approach. M. D. Goulder (*The Psalms of the Sons of Korah*, 21) has also questioned the idea of the humiliation and reconsecration of the king as proposed by Johnson, Eaton (*Kingship*), and I. Engnell (*Studies in Divine Kingship in the Ancient Near East*), claiming there is no evidence of the humiliation of the king in northern traditions.   However, Goulder's recreation of the autumn festival at Dan (proposed in *Sons of Korah*) and a similar one at Bethel (*The Psalms of Asaph and the Pentateuch: Studies in the Psalter III*, esp. 38–176) contains many similar emphases (e.g., Yahweh as victorious over the waters and human enemies, a sham fight, creation, royal blessing, anointing, enthronement and procession, and what appears to be a reconsecration of the king).   Johnson's strongest support has come from Eaton, who argues persuasively that the portrayal of kingship in the royal psalms points to a drama of humiliation and restoration (see Eaton, *Kingship*, 111–129).

[55] Johnson ("The Role of the King," 71–111) gives a prominent place to Ps 118 in his reconstruction of the king's role.

[56] This leads Mettinger (*King and Messiah: The Civil and Sacral Legitimation of the Israelite Kings*, 306, 308), who acknowledges that a celebration of kingship and dynasty appears to be a natural and integral part of the festival, to leave the question open.   For further cautions see Gerstenberger, "Psalms," 197, 212; Kraus, *Worship*, 208–209; idem, *Theology*, 84–86; Brueggemann, "Response to James L. Mays: The Question of Context," 31.

psalms – that appear to assume such a festival.[57] In this regard it would do well to recognize that lack of imagination in historical research may distort results no less than unrestrained speculation does. Insight into the festivals is possible because of the growing willingness to accept that many of the psalms were shaped by and reflect the cult and therefore provide a window onto ancient Israel's worship practices.[58] This suggests that although the elaboration of precise details is to some degree speculative, careful research can hint at what may have taken place in a festival week, and at the least reveal major themes and emphases of the festival.

The extent of agreement in the various proposed reconstructions of the autumn festival appears to support this, for although in their details there is divergence, there is a great deal of convergence in the major themes. Kraus' Royal Zion, Weiser's Covenant Renewal, and Mowinckel's Enthronement Festival share the same emphases, including most prominently the central role of the Davidic king and the celebration of Yahweh's kingship and power in creation.[59] In conclusion, I suggest it is probable that the autumn festival included a central role for the king in the cult, and was characterized by a celebration of kingship, both that of Yahweh and his vice-regent, the Davidic king.[60] It is not implausible that the festival included an enthrone-

---

[57] For example, Kraus notes that "the most we can do is to take separate points of detail from the tradition and try to co-ordinate them" (*Worship*, 208–209). Referring specifically to Weiser and Mowinckel, he further warns of the danger of imposing on the cult "an order based on an alien principle," yet apparently is convinced that there is enough material to support his own reconstruction of a Royal Zion Festival. Similarly, at the same time that Eaton argues that the chief elements of the festival are recoverable, he acknowledges that "the order of the ceremonies and texts remains uncertain" (*Kingship*, 133).

[58] For example, Gerstenberger can say that "the seasonal pattern of feasts set the stage for most of the hymns preserved in the Old Testament Psalter" ("Psalms," 212). C. Westermann's comment summarizes well the growing consensus: "As an assured result [of research on the cultic/liturgical setting of the psalms] it has been established that much more about Israel's worship services, festival, and cultic activities can be seen in the Psalms than had been noticed earlier" (*The Psalms: Structure, Content and Message*, 28). Cf. Kraus, *Theology*, 84–85.

[59] Rubenstein similarly notes how, in spite of differences in detail, the covenant-renewal and Zion festival reconstructions are remarkably similar to the enthronement festival. For the first of these, proponents concede that their hypothetical festival evolved into an enthronement-type festival in the later monarchy; as for Kraus, his emphasis on the election of David and Zion is "all in all, an enthronement festival with a more pronounced Israelite stamp" (Rubenstein, *Sukkot*, 25).

[60] Gottwald (*Hebrew Bible*, 534) takes a similar position. Although he points out the lack of OT evidence, he says "it is almost certainly correct" to see a modified festival with an emphasis on Yahweh's kingship and with a central role for the king. In contrast see de Vaux (*Ancient Israel*, 506), who in claiming that Tabernacles, although it

ment ceremony for the king. Even though speculative, it is possible that
the king participated in a ritual battle, humiliation, and reconsecration.
Although this study will not take a position on the specific details of the
festival, the complex of Tabernacles themes is significant for possible
associations with Ps 118.[61]

C. Psalm 118's Royal Associations

Although recognizing that Ps 118 has royal style and language and that the
hymnic framework suggests a major national festival, scholars such as
Gunkel and Kraus have suggested that it is not royal. One of the main
reasons for this is the phrase "the ones who fear the Lord" (118.4), which
they take to be a reference to proselytes. However, this may simply refer
to the gathered worshippers, to all the devout of Israel.[62] Even if the term
does concern proselytes, a post-exilic date would not be required, as this
was not a late phenomenon.[63] Like Gunkel, Kraus states that Ps 118
borrows from royal language. It adopts older forms and metaphors from
royal psalms, and is a composite including a gate ritual and elements
rooted in "the ancient festival of covenant renewal."[64] The question
remains why a psalm with royal themes and elements is not considered to
be royal, especially as the criteria for making these distinctions depend
entirely on internal evidence.

Eaton has effectively questioned Gunkel's contention that there are very
few royal psalms, suggesting instead that there are good reasons to enlarge

---

developed and came to be invested with much more meaning, was from the beginning
and remained an agricultural festival, supposes to dismiss any of the associations
proposed by Eaton, Mowinckel, Kraus, Johnson, Gerstenberger, and Weiser. Cf. Rowley,
Worship, 202.

[61] Rubenstein's summary of the reconstructed festival underlines – and draws heavily
on – practices associated with Tabernacles in later literature. In addition to a
considerable amount of shared symbolism, there is a significant emphasis on Yahweh's
kingship and his advent. He concludes, "In addition, the festival gave expression to
fundamental beliefs of the Israelites: the revelation and theophany, salvation of Israel,
the exodus, renewal of the covenant, and the inviolability of Jerusalem. Rituals and
beliefs that eventually coalesced into three independent observances . . . [Rosh Hashana,
Yom Kippur and Sukkot] all took place during this festival. The original Israelite
autumnal festival, the ancient Sukkot festival, embodied this panoply of myth and ritual"
(*Sukkot*, 21).

[62] In support see May, "Ps 118," 97–98.

[63] E.g., Exod 18.10; 1 Kgs 8.41–43; 2 Kgs 5. Cf. Rodgerson and McKay, 85.

[64] See Kraus, 398–401; Gunkel, *Die Psalmen*, 509. Gunkel gives a post-exilic date
and argues against the king's being the speaker in the psalm.

the list.[65] Indeed, the trend in nineteenth century criticism, which Goulder humorously describes as "a stampede for the Maccabaean lake,"[66] has given way to a tendency among more modern scholars to judge many of the psalms as pre-exilic.[67] The willingness to accept pre-exilic dates for many psalms leads in turn to recognizing royal connections which had been largely disregarded. Eaton's claim for more royal psalms is thus plausible and deserves the support voiced by a number of scholars.[68]

---

[65] See Eaton, *Kingship*, 1–26, esp. 20–26. Eaton proposes a number of considerations favoring extensive royal interpretation. First, the headings of many psalms (73 in MT; 84 in LXX) retain a royal link. It should be noted that although the heading *of/for David* may be anachronistic or a historicizing addition by later editors, it may refer to his dynasty or the royal office, and in any case evinces a royal interpretation for these psalms. Second, modern studies of kingship have shown the important role the king took in religious affairs, and it is to be expected that his prayers and psalms (or those referring to him) would form a significant part of the worship in the royal temple. Third, of all the subjects and situations proposed for psalms of the individual, only that of the king is known for certain to exist in the Psalter. Fourth, there is a prevailing similarity between the psalms, which is in keeping with an origin within a restricted range of royal and national cultus. Fifth, there is continuity, especially in the portrayal of enemies, between psalms classified as royal by Gunkel and others which he classifies as psalms of an individual. Sixth, the problem presented by *I* and *we* alternating in a psalm makes sense in terms of a king, as he can pray both as an individual and as a national representative. Seventh, throughout the so-called psalms of the individual, motifs or expressions occur which are royal or at least can be applied appropriately to a king. Eighth, it is reasonable to regard royal items as evidence of royal psalms rather than royal motifs which are used of ordinary people. Ninth, royal elements in a psalm should not be explained away simply as later redactions, especially when a royal interpretation many times leads to a gain in cohesion for the psalm. Tenth, it is difficult to believe that very few prayers or supplications of a king were preserved in a collection rooted in a royal temple, but that numerous intercessions and petitions from other individuals were carefully treasured in the official corpus. Eleventh, the lack of majestic language in a psalm need not disqualify it for association with a king, as they were also presented as humbly approaching God in supplication, a time when exalted language would not be applied to the king but to God.

[66] Goulder, *The Prayers of David (Psalms 51–72): Studies in the Psalter, II*, 14.

[67] The shift has been so dramatic that R. Coggins (Review of M. D. Goulder, 56) can write that the claim that many psalms originate from the cult of pre-exilic Jerusalem is among the few which have established themselves as part of the modern scholarly consensus concerning the Psalter. Gottwald (*Hebrew Bible*, 26) similarly notes the trend of judging many of the psalms to be pre-exilic, and those that are post-exilic to have been probably all composed before Maccabean times.

[68] For example, P. D. Miller ("The Beginning of the Psalter," 88–89) supports Eaton's claim that many more psalms than some have thought have royal content. For Book I of the Psalter he argues in support of Eaton's suggestion that some 21 of 41 psalms have royal content, and even adds to Eaton's list. See also Engnell (*Divine Kingship*, 176), who argues that the majority of the psalms in the Psalter had originally been composed for use by the king. Clements ("Interpreting the Psalms," 114–115)

1. Evidence Internal to Ps 118

Internal evidence from Ps 118 gives no indication of a specific historical
occasion to which it was related, pointing instead to a regularly repeated
ritual/liturgy that is not restricted to any one historical occasion.[69] It is
clear that it is a processional psalm whereby the participants enter the
temple and proceed to the altar (118.19–27), and that it presupposes a
festal occasion (118.27). Although a king is not specifically mentioned,
the language of the psalm is consistent with other royal psalms. It is
obvious that the person leading the procession and speaking much of the
central part of the psalm is of high rank. Who else could be attacked by
the nations? He also has led the fight against these nations and defeated
them (118.10–13), which was one of the main roles of the king. Mowinckel
is correct in stating that "there can be no doubt that he is the leading man
of the people, the king or a corresponding figure among the people."[70]
There is good reason, then, to consider Ps 118 as royal, a position supported
by a number of commentators and scholars.[71]

It is reasonable also to suggest that Ps 118 was used in the autumn
festival. There is no reason to reject the Mishnaic traditions that link
Ps 118 closely with Tabernacles,[72] and we have argued that Tabernacles
and the autumn festival refer to the same event. The exact way in which
Ps 118 was used in the autumn festival is not clear, however, and most
suggestions depend primarily on internal evidence. The psalm centers
around thanksgiving for salvation from great distress, which when joined
to references of a fight against the nations (118.10–13) may indicate a
dramatic presentation along the lines suggested by Johnson and Eaton in

accepts that there are a number of royal psalms, but questions whether there was an
elaborate cult-drama in which the king had a central part.

[69] Johnson gives examples of songs which are specifically related to a historical
situation, characterized by concrete language and clarity of reference ("Old Testament
Exegesis," 179). See the Song of Deborah (Judg 5); David's lament over Saul and
Jonathan (2 Sam 1.17f); Pss 74; 79; 137. Weiser suggestively writes, "The absence of
any concrete allusions and the general character of the liturgy . . . point to the autumn
festival of Yahweh, as does the Jewish tradition relating the psalm to the Feast of
Tabernacles" (724–725).

[70] Mowinckel, *Israel's Worship*, 2.28.

[71] These include Eaton, *Kingship*, 129–130; Johnson, *Sacral Kingship*, 125–126;
Anderson, 2.797; Weiser, 725; McCullough, 616; Bratcher and Reyburn, *Translator's
Handbook*, 986; VanGemeren, 729; Dahood, 3.155; Allen, 123; Mowinckel, *Israel's
Worship*, 1.180–181; Frost, "Ps 118," 157–161; Sanders, "Ps 118," 180. Although
Mettinger (*King and Messiah*, 100) unnecessarily limits the number of royal psalms to
12, he includes Ps 118 in his list. Peters (*Liturgies*, 426–428) does not think it is a royal
psalm, but argues that it is written concerning David. Note that many of these are more
modern scholars, in keeping with the trend noted above.

[72] For example, *m. Sukk.* 4.5.

their festival reconstructions. Certainly the elements of such a ceremony – the king goes through a ritual humiliation and finds himself in dire distress, only for Yahweh to rescue and exalt him, after which he leads his people into the temple in a procession of thanksgiving – would not be foreign to the content and structure of Ps 118.[73] However, although it is tempting to accept this reconstruction, it is by no means certain. The psalm does have a connection with military victories, and although Dahood does not consider this to be part of the annual ritual in which the Davidic king was prominent, tying it instead to a literal battle and subsequent thanksgiving procession, this need not pose a problem to our position.[74] As previously pointed out, there is no clear connection to any specific historical occasion. Weiser has plausibly suggested that Ps 118 was used in an annual commemoration of previous military victories as part of the autumn festival.[75] It may be that Ps 118 was composed originally in celebration of a military victory and was then incorporated into the liturgy of the festival, whether on the model suggested by Weiser or one more in keeping with Eaton, Johnson and Mowinckel.[76] What is most important here is Ps 118's probable association with the Davidic king, even if the exact details of its role in the festival cannot be known with certainty.

2. Post-exilic Royal Associations of Ps 118

That Ps 118 was associated with kingship during the monarchy is most probable. However, its connection with royalty and kingship does not depend on establishing an original setting, since it is linked with these in the Second Temple period and beyond. First, there is a strong connection between the Psalter and royalty in general. This goes beyond the headings which include David's name and the tradition that sees David as an author of psalms,[77] for the OT also attributes the temple's music, guilds of musicians

---

[73] See Eaton, *Kingship*, 132; Johnson, *Sacral Kingship*, 123–128; Mowinckel, *Israel's Worship*, 1.181. Eaton points also to Ps 18 from which he deduces the ritual situation.

[74] See Dahood, 3.155. Allen (123) follows Dahood.

[75] Weiser, 724–727.

[76] See Gerstenberger ("Psalms," 212), who discusses the flexibility of a psalm and how it could easily be adapted to occasions other than what it had been originally composed for.

[77] See OT references to David's musical and poetic ability in 1 Sam 16.15–23; 2 Sam 1.17–27; 3.33; 6.5; 23.1; 1 Chr 16.7; 23.5–6; Neh 12.36; Amos 6.5. The headings that ascribe authorship to/for David, even though historically untrustworthy, at the least indicate the royal character of the particular psalms and therefore places them firmly in an interpretive context of royal ideology. For a comprehensive survey of views on

and singers, and invention of the instruments used, to the king.[78] Solomon is said to have authored 1005 "songs,"[79] and Hezekiah is credited with renewing the temple psalmody and music "according to the commandment of David" and with the "instruments of David." The burnt offering is accompanied by singing the "words of David."[80] This post-exilic witness of the Chronicler suggests that the Psalter was associated with royalty in general, and specifically with David as the founder of the dynasty. Even though the Chronicler acknowledges that not all the psalms were written by David (e.g., Asaph also is credited), they are linked to him.

Apart from the post-exilic OT witness there are other intertestamental sources that bear testimony to an association of the Psalter with royalty. Ben Sirach writes that David arranged the singing in the temple. Interestingly, he states that David also arranged the festival seasons throughout the year (Sir 47.8–10). The psalms are called "songs of the psalmist David" (4 Macc 18.15), the praise in the temple is carried out "according to the directions of King David" (1 Esd 5.60), and the temple singers conduct themselves according to the "arrangements made by David" (1 Esd 1.5, 15). In 2 Macc 2.13 the psalms are simply called "the writings of David." A similar association is found in the NT, where "David" is used as the equivalent of the Psalter, and there seems to be no concern with questions of authorship.[81] At Qumran David is credited with writing 4,050 psalms.[82] According to Josephus, David wrote the psalms, taught the Levites to sing, and made the musical instruments.[83] The evidence justifies Briggs' statement that "ancient Jewish opinion regarded David as the editor of the Psalter and the author of a great portion of the Psalms, so that David and the Psalter were essentially synonymous terms."[84] Although of later date, the following rabbinic statement illustrates what was probably a long-held and widely accepted view on Davidic authorship: "Who wrote the Scriptures? . . . David wrote the Book of Psalms, including in it the work of the elders,

---

Davidic authorship of the Psalms in Jewish literature see Daly-Denton, *David in the Fourth Gospel: The Johannine Reception of the Psalms*, 59–114. On his role as founder of the temple and cult see ibid., 72–79.

[78] 1 Chr 15.16–16.43; 25.1–31;; Ezra 3.10; Neh 12.24, 36, 45–46; Amos 6.5. Cf. 2 Chr 35.15.

[79] 1 Kgs 4.32. He is also credited, according to the headings, with Pss 72 and 127.

[80] 2 Chr 29.25–30. Hezekiah is also credited with a psalm in Isa 38.9–20.

[81] See Briggs (1.lv–lvi) for a list of citations and evidence showing interchangeability of David and references to the Psalter in the NT.

[82] See David's Compositions in 11QPs^a col. XXVII lines 2–11.

[83] *Ant.* 7.305–306. Briggs suggests that for Josephus, "David stands essentially for the Psalter" (1.lv).

[84] Briggs, 1.liv. For further discussion see A. M. Cooper, "The Life and Times of King David According to the Book of Psalms," 117–131.

namely, Adam, Melchizedek, Abraham, Moses, Heman, Yeduthun, Asaph, and the three sons of Korah."[85] At the least David was regarded as editor-in-chief, but as Eaton points out, all of these are "figures of royal dimensions or of royal appointment."[86] Thus the Psalter on the whole was associated with royalty. This would naturally accentuate the royal associations of those psalms which have clear royal themes, especially those with a complex liturgy in which the king has a central role, as Ps 118 does.

Rabbinic traditions show that this royal association was not lost on the Jewish mind. One is aware that rabbinic sources must be used with caution because of their late date. In this case there is obvious continuity between biblical, intertestamental, and rabbinic traditions. The Targum on Ps 118.22–29 shows in its divisions that Ps 118 is associated with David.

22) A youth was rejected by the builders. He was among the sons of Jesse and was entitled to be appointed king and ruler.

23) "This was from Yahweh," said the builders; "This is wonderful for us," said the sons of Jesse.

24) "This day Yahweh made," said the builders; "Let us rejoice and be glad in it," said the sons of Jesse.

25) "We pray you, Yahweh, save now," said the builders; "We pray you, give success now," said Jesse and his wife.

26) "Blessed is he who comes in the name of the Word of Yahweh," said the builders; "They will bless you from the temple of Yahweh," said David.

27) "God, Yahweh, illumine us," said the tribes of the house of Judah; "Tie the lamb with chains for a festival sacrifice until you have offered it and sprinkled its blood on the horns of the altar," said Samuel the prophet.

28) "You are my God and I will give thanks before you, my God, I will praise you," said David.

29) Samuel answered and said, "Praise (him), assembly of Israel, and give thanks before Yahweh for he is good, for his goodness is eternal."[87]

There is a similar division of the last part of Ps 118 in the Babylonian Talmud that is even more explicit in its Davidic association. It also involves David's brothers, Jesse, and Samuel.

---

[85] *b. B. Bat.* 14b–15a. Cf. *Eccl. Rab.* 7.19.4: "R. Huna said in the name of R. Aha: Although ten men composed the Book of Psalms, it is named after none of them but after David, king of Israel. . . . When the ten righteous men wished to compose the Book of Psalms, the Holy One, blessed be He, said to them, 'You are all pleasant, pious and worthy to utter hymns before Me, but let David utter them for all of you because his voice is sweet.' That is what is written, *The sweet singer of Israel* (2 Sam 23.1)."

[86] Eaton, *Kingship*, 21.

[87] *Tg. Ps.* 118. Translation is found in Snodgrass, "Christological Stone," 82–83. An alternate translation can be found in Werner, "Hosanna," 116–117; and I. Diez Merino, *Targum de Salmos*, 169.

> R. Samuel b. Nahmani said in R. Jonathan's name: *I will give thanks unto*
> *Thee, for Thou hast answered me* [Ps 118.21] was said by David; *The stone*
> *which the builders rejected is become the chief corner-stone* [Ps 118.22];
> by Yishai (Jesse); *This is the Lord's doing* [Ps 118.23], by his brothers;
> *This is the day which the Lord hath made* [118.24] by Samuel. *We beseech*
> *Thee, O Lord, save now!* [118.25] was said by his brothers: *We beseech*
> *Thee, O Lord, make us now to prosper!* by David; *Blessed be he that*
> *cometh in the name of the Lord* [118.26], by Jesse; *We bless you out of the*
> *house of the Lord* ([118.26], by Samuel; *The Lord is God, and hath given*
> *us light* [118.27], by all of them; *Order the festival procession with*
> *boughs,* by Samuel; *Thou art my God, and I will give thanks unto Thee*
> [118.28] by David; *Thou art my God, I will exalt Thee,* by all of them.[88]

The Targum and Talmud thus affirm, whether historicizing or not, a
royal interpretation of Ps 118. The setting may be the anointing of David
by Samuel. They also suggest that there is still the vestige of the king's
involvement in the procession which the psalm describes, possibly reflecting awareness of an earlier association of Ps 118 with kingship at the
autumn festival.

Messianic-Eschatological Interpretation of Stone Texts

A number of studies have pointed to a messianic and/or eschatological interpretation of the image of the stone in pre-Christian Judaism.[89] Snodgrass,
in his survey of Targum passages where "cornerstone" or "foundation
stone" appears, concludes that the words are generally interpreted, where
appropriate, as referring to rulers.[90] He argues convincingly, in light of
Qumran usage, the LXX rendering, and the Targum, that for Isa 28.16 "the
interpretation of the [stone] as referring to the promised Messiah is pre-
Christian".[91]   Other targumic passages associate the Messiah with the

---

[88] *b. Pesah.* 119a.

[89] See for example J. H. Elliott, *The Elect and the Holy: An Exegetical Examination*
of I Peter 2.4–10 and the Phrase βασίλειον ἱεράτευμα, esp. 32; Snodgrass, *Wicked*
Tenants; idem, "Christological Stone"; Jeremias, "λίθος, λίθινος," *TDNT* 4.268–280.

[90] Snodgrass, "Christological Stone," 76–77. See *Tg. Isa.* 28.16; *Tg. Jer.* 51.26; *Tg.*
Zech. 10.4; *Tg. Ps.* 118.22.

[91] Snodgrass, "Christological Stone," 78. He correctly notes that it is unlikely that
the Jews would introduce into the Targums messianic interpretations that could be applied
to Jesus, particularly in the case of passages that the church did interpret as messianic
and use in their apologetic against the Jews. For a list of Qumran passages related to Isa
28.16 see Elliott, *The Elect and Holy*, 27. Note the similarities between Ps 118 and Isa
28: reference to the stone; the danger from other nations who surround the land; both
passages focus on the theme that it is better to trust in Yahweh than to trust in men;
Ps 118.23 and Isa 28.29 both probably refer to the stone. Snodgrass ("Christological

stone.[92] Is it possible to link Ps 118.22 with this stream of thought? There is no extant pre-rabbinic interpretation of Ps 118.22 that is explicitly messianic or eschatological. The Targum on Ps 118 interprets "stone" as a youth,[93] implicitly identified as David. Jeremias has suggested that the Targum and Talmud passages quoted above relate the antiphonal divisions to the anointing of David as king in 1 Sam 16.13, raising the question, also explored by Snodgrass, of whether they represent a re-interpretation rising out of anti-Christian polemic.[94] Since Ps 118.22 was one of the two or three pre-eminent Scripture passages used in the early apologetic of the church, it would be a tempting target. It is possible that this verse was interpreted messianically prior to its use in the NT, and it would be somewhat surprising for it to gain such importance in the early apologetic if there was no messianic association to begin with; but as there is no clear evidence, it is difficult to draw firm conclusions.

Talmudic literature interprets Ps 118.22 in reference to several people, but especially David.[95] Apart from the antiphonal sections David is associated with Ps 118 several other times in rabbinic literature.[96] The Targum may or may not be reinterpreting Ps 118.22 in reference to David, but even if the Davidic connection was original it would by no means exclude a messianic or eschatological application, since David and kingship had definite messianic associations.[97] In addition, the messianic-eschatological

---

Stone," 47) suggests that Ps 118 may be dependent on Isa 28. However, if there is dependence, it could be in the opposite direction.

[92] Snodgrass, "Christological Stone," 78. In Zech 3.8 the stone is not the Messiah but "verification that the Messiah will be revealed." In Zech 4.7b the stone is interpreted as the Messiah.

[93] The word can also mean "lamb" or "servant."

[94] Jeremias writes, "The fact that it is nonetheless related to David shows the influence of the older Messianic interpretation" (*Eucharistic Words*, 259 n. 1). Snodgrass similarly concludes that "the targum, as it is preserved, refers to David. But . . . the present text of the targum appears to be a secondary reinterpretation necessitated by the Judaeo-Christian controversy" ("Christological Stone," 84–85; cf. 364).

[95] Of David: *Exod. Rab.* 37.1; *Midr. Ps.* 118.21; *b. Pesah.* 119a. As referring to the word of Abraham: *Pirque R. El.* 24. Of Jacob: *Midr. Ps.* 118.20. Of Israel: *Esth. Rab.* 7.10; *Midr. Ps.* 118.20,21. An anonymous individual: *Midr. Ps.* 118.21.

[96] For example, with Ps 118.4 in *Midr. Ps.* 118.8, which includes the Davidic covenant that will continue in the world-to-come. Also Ps 118.5, which is supposed to refer to David according to *Midr. Ps.* 118.9.

[97] Apart from expectations surrounding David, the Targum reveals an eschatological and messianic approach to the Psalms. S. Levey argues that messianic interpretations are found in several psalms (Pss 18.28–32; 21.1–8; 45.1–18; 61.7–9; 72.1–20; 80.15–18; 89.51–52; 132.11–18), but concludes that the Targum tends not to attribute messianic intentions to the Bible: "Of the wealth of Messianic possibilities in the Book of Psalms, the Targum utilizes only a choice few to interpret with reference to the Messiah" (*The Messiah: An Aramaic Interpretation: The Messianic Exegesis of the Targum*, 141).

interpretation of other OT stone passages and the description of the stone as a ruler/king raises the likelihood that similar associations would be made with Ps 118.22.[98]

3. The Significance of Ps 118's Royal Association

The title of a recent book, *Judaisms and their Messiahs at the Turn of the Christian Era*,[99] summarizes succinctly the view – that there is no uniform, widespread, or dominant messianic expectation – which has come to dominate scholarship. However, although the diversity within Judaism is unquestionable, and it may be more accurate to speak of Judaism in the plural, variation in details should not obscure the fact of an underlying core of widely held beliefs.[100] A detailed study of messianism in Second Temple Judaism lies beyond the scope of this study, but there is evidence supporting the expectation of a royal – sometimes Davidic – Messiah.[101] Although this is by no means uniform (even where the coming Messiah is king there is diversity), it nevertheless is a significant hope in several streams of Judaism, and it is unlikely that those groups which did not

---

However, the relatively small number of psalms seen to be messianic is related to the narrow way in which Levey defines messianism (ibid., xix). He does not develop the eschatological aspect of the Targum, which although a different issue than messianism would tend to encourage messianic speculation. Against glosses such as Jeremias and Snodgrass suggest, Levey concludes that there is little evidence for interpolation of messianic glosses where one would expect them, or deletion of messianic interpretations which may not be in harmony with mainstream exegesis (ibid., 144).

[98] Josephus' explanation of the Jewish revolt of AD 66–70 illustrates well the messianic-eschatological interpretation of the stone image (see *War* 6.312–315). It is clear that the Jews were expecting a leader – a king – who would rule over the world, as foretold in an "ambiguous oracle." N. T. Wright (*The New Testament and the People of God*, 314) plausibly suggests that it was Daniel in general and more specifically chs. 2, 7 and 9 to which the oracle refers. The stone of Dan 2.1–45 was interpreted as referring to the messianic kingdom that would destroy the Roman Empire. That this is true, in spite of Josephus' reinterpretation of the oracle in reference to Vespasian, is evident from his comments on Dan 2 (see *Ant.* 10.210), where he refuses to elucidate the meaning of the stone while at the same time suggesting it refers to a future event. He was understandably reticent to declare Rome's destruction. An alternate view is proposed by J. Blenkinsopp ("The Oracle of Judah and the Messianic Entry," 61), who argues that Josephus is referring to the Oracle of Judah in Gen 49. I find Blenkinsopp unconvincing.

[99] Edited by J. Neusner et al.

[100] Wright says it well in criticizing Neusner and others whose "proper concern for differentiated description can obliterate the equally proper task of overall synthesis" (*New Testament*, 244 and n. 4).

[101] See discussion in Wright, *New Testament*, 307–320; G. Vermes, *Jesus the Jew: A Historian's Reading of the Gospels*, 130–140. See further Schürer, *History*, 2.514–554.

espouse such a view would be unaware of its existence.[102] R. Horsley catalogs a number of populist messianic movements where a significant number of Jews would proclaim and follow someone as king in expectation of deliverance,[103] evidence that there was a relatively widespread hope that a royal figure would be God's agent of salvation. That kingship in general, and at times specifically Davidic kingship, was a widely known aspect of messianism is further supported by Bar Kochba's being hailed as *Son of David*, Herod's aspirations in building the temple to legitimate himself as the coming messianic king, the NT emphasis on the Davidic messiahship of Jesus, and the witness of intertestamental literature.[104]

The claim that messianic and Davidic hopes were often at the least intertwined and possibly inseparable in the ancient Jewish mind is not without merit,[105] yet some counter that although there is evidence supporting expectation of a Davidic Messiah, there was a more widespread dependence on the biblical model of popular/charismatic kingship, especially in popular messianic movements.[106] What is important is that *kingship, whether popular/charismatic in character or looking for the resumption of the Davidic dynasty, played a role in messianic*

---

[102] There may be less overt messianic expectation in Jewish writings than is sometimes assumed. For example, J. J. Collins ("Messianism in the Maccabean Period," 106) claims that traces of messianism are slight, and points only to two groups with a developed interest in the subject – the Qumran community and that which produced the *Psalms of Solomon*. Nevertheless, there can be little question that Judaism on the whole looked forward to a significant redemptive act of Yahweh, and that many expected a messianic figure to play a role.

[103] Horsley, "Popular Messianic Movements Around the Time of Jesus"; Cf. Horsley and J. Hanson, *Bandits, Prophets and Messiahs: Popular Movements at the Time of Jesus*, esp. 88–134.

[104] For references to Bar Kochba and Herod see Wright, *New Testament*, 308–309. For the Davidic king see 4QFlor 1.10–13; *Pss. Sol.* 17. For the Davidic Messiah see *4 Ezra* 12.10–35, and the royal Messiah in 1QSb 5.23–29.

[105] For example, Vermes concludes in a study of messianic speculation that the evidence demonstrates "unequivocally that if in the inter-Testamental era a man claimed or was proclaimed to be 'the Messiah', his listeners would as a matter of course have assumed that he was referring to the Davidic Redeemer" (*Jesus the Jew*, 134).

[106] So K. Pomykale (*The Davidic Dynasty Tradition in Early Judaism: Its History and Significance for Messianism*), in agreement with Horsley's emphasis on charismatic kingship ("Messianic Movements"; *Bandits, Prophets and Messiahs*). See S. Langston (Review of K. E. Pomykale, 30), who correctly cautions against relegating the idea of a Davidic hope during the Second Temple period to a minor status.

expectation.[107] Either kingship model would probably reflect many of the ideals associated with the Davidic king of the Psalms. The ideal of kingship in the Psalter is an issue deserving of a full length monograph and cannot be dealt with here,[108] but we accept that the idealized kingship of the Psalms inevitably gave rise to eschatological expectations of a figure who would live up to the ideal.[109] This may have been taken up in the prophetic literature, which affirms the election of the Davidic line but at times places the fulfillment in the future.[110] The removal of the dynasty in the exile no doubt served to fuel, in part at least, the expectations of a Davidic Messiah. Royal psalms, then, would provide a scriptural springboard for messianic speculation and expectation; and Ps 118, with its royal language and themes, a prominent place in the festival most emphasizing royalty, and links with David in Jewish literature, would not be least among these.

Conclusion

Psalm 118 was a king's psalm, associated especially with the Feast of Tabernacles, which during the monarchy was the royal festival *par excellence*, celebrating Yahweh's kingship and the king's role as Yahweh's representative. The psalm's royal themes and language strengthen its connection to the autumn festival. Psalm 118 was used in a procession, with the king playing the central role as leader and speaker. It centered on

---

[107] This would support moderate positions such as that of E. P. Sanders (*Jesus and Judaism*, 308), who suggests that one making claims of kingship would naturally be regarded as making messianic claims as well.

[108] For a thorough discussion of the royal ideal in the Psalms see Eaton (*Kingship*, 135–197); Johnson, *Sacral Kingship*; idem, "Conceptions," 205–213; Mowinckel, *Israel's Worship*, 1.50–61; K. Heim, "The Perfect King of Psalm 72: An 'Intertextual' Inquiry," 223–248.

[109] Rowley's view is representative of that of a number of scholars: "These psalms, therefore, are given both a present and a future reference, a present reference as an example, and a future reference as a promise of the day when the ideal will be realized" (*Worship*, 199–200). See further de Vaux, *Ancient Israel*, 110; Johnson, *Sacral Kingship*, 133–134; idem, "Conceptions," 234–235; Mowinckel, *Israel's Worship*, 1.59 and n. 65. M. de Jonge ("The Use of the Word 'Anointed' in the Time of Jesus," esp. 135, 147) recognizes the links between the use of the word "anointed" in the first century and expectations of Davidic kingship and the idealized king of the psalms.

[110] See Eaton, *Kingship*, 200; Kraus, *Worship*, 189–190; Mettinger, *King and Messiah*, 99, 100. Examples of prophetic literature pointing to a future fulfillment of idealized Davidic kingship include Isa 11; 32; Jer 23; Ezek 37. On the depiction of redemption in royal theology, including Ps 118, see M. Barker, *The Older Testament: The Survival of Themes from the Ancient Royal Cult in Sectarian Judaism and Early Christianity*, 176–178.

thanksgiving following the humiliation (military distress) and exaltation/ salvation of the king by the hand of Yahweh. This may have taken the form of a dramatic ritual including a mock fight with the nations with a humiliation and exaltation of the king, although this must be deduced from internal evidence. The precise role of the psalm in the temple cult remains unclear, but it would have emphasized and demonstrated aspects of the ideal kingship presented in the psalms. The psalm retained its association with kingship in intertestamental and late Judaism, through the Davidic association with the psalms in general, and more specifically as attested in the Targum and Talmud. Messianic interpretations of the OT stone passages as royal figures and widespread expectation of the Messiah coming as king, suggest interpretive horizons for Ps 118 in Second Temple Judaism and the NT.

II. Psalm 118 and the Feast of Tabernacles

A. *Tabernacles in the OT: Exilic and Post-exilic*

We have already suggested that the ideal of kingship gave rise to eschatological expectations, perhaps even before the removal of the monarchy. It is also possible that the autumn festival may have provided the impulse and themes for some of the eschatology in the Prophets, but more to the point is the question whether Tabernacles was associated with eschatological interpretation during the Second Temple period.[111]

Ezekiel's eschatological vision of the new temple detailing the renewal of the cult and festivals takes place at Tabernacles.[112] Kraus points out the

---

[111] Ezra and Nehemiah show that there is continuity of sorts in the celebration of Tabernacles in the First and Second Temple periods, although obviously the removal of the monarchy required adjustments. It is worth noting that in spite of the comment in Neh 8.17 that since the time of Joshua Tabernacles had not been celebrated "like this," Tabernacles was indeed celebrated during the monarchy and was the highlight of the cultic calendar. This may be an attempt to link the return of Ezra to the promised land with the initial settlement of the land under Joshua. For discussion see Rubenstein, *Sukkot*, 31–45.

[112] Ezekiel 40.1 places the vision "at the beginning of the year." This word string appears only here in the OT, leaving some uncertainty as to the month referred to. It could indicate that the vision took place in the first month (Nisan), or alternatively that the new year (Rosh Hashanah) is in view, which at the very least from the early post-exilic period (and up to the present) takes place in conjunction with Yom Kippur and Tabernacles. In support of the latter, the themes of the vision correspond to Tabernacles: the renewal of the temple most naturally is associated with the feast, and both the return

similarities between the eschatological message of Second Isaiah and the renewal of the cult in Ezek 40–48: "In this complex, too, an eschatological order is foreshadowed, down to the minute details of the sacral institutions. The Temple will become the redemptive centre of the world in the last days."[113] The central figure in the renewal of the cult is a royal figure – a prince – who represents the people, leads them in the cult, and joins them in procession to the temple at festivals.[114] It is during Tabernacles that Haggai proclaims the message that God will return and fill the temple with his glory, and that "the glory of this present house will be greater than the glory of the former house" (Hag 2.9).[115] Although the eschatological river of Ezek 47.1–12, which flows out of the temple, is not explicitly linked with Tabernacles in Ezekiel, Zechariah picks up on it and makes the association clear.[116]

The vision of Zech 14 is the passage most often used to support claims that Tabernacles had eschatological associations, as Yahweh's final victory over the nations culminates in the celebration of the festival at the restored temple. Several themes stand out in regard to Tabernacles, not least the repeated emphasis on the universal kingship of Yahweh, who "will be king over the whole earth" (14.9) and receive the worship of nations (14.16,17). Thus Tabernacles is associated with the day when Yahweh comes to reign as king over the earth.[117] It is also associated with judgment. Not to acknow-

---

of Yahweh to the temple, and the river that flows from the temple, are taken up again in the eschatological Tabernacles of Zech 14. Although he notes that the reference is ambiguous, L. C. Allen (*Ezekiel 20–48*, 229) suggests that a fall date would link well with Lev 25.9 and the proclamation of the year of jubilee, which takes place on the Day of Atonement. In support of a Nisan date for the vision see A. B. Davidson, *The Book of the Prophet Ezekiel*, 291–292. In any case, the vision also details the renewal of Tabernacles, which is referred to simply as "the Feast" (Ezek 45.25).

[113] Kraus, *Worship*, 231.

[114] This obviously recalls the role of the king in the Jerusalem cultus. On the procession see Ezek 46.9. For an examination of the prince's role and significance see D. Block, "Bringing Back David: Ezekiel's Messianic Hope," esp. 183–188.

[115] Note that the themes of election or re-election of Zion (Zech 2.10; 3.2; 8.3) and the Davidic king (Hag 2.23; Zech 4.9f.) are prominent in Haggai and Zechariah. See Kraus (*Worship*, 232–233), who argues for the prominence of these themes at the autumn festival.

[116] See *t. Sukk.* 3.3–10 where the river passages of Ezekiel and Zechariah are quoted for rituals at Tabernacles.

[117] The kingship of Yahweh, which formed a significant part of the autumn festival – the idea of Yahweh becoming King or coming to reign – is clear in Second Temple writings. In addition to Zechariah, note *T. Mos.* 10.1–10; 1QM 6.4–6; Wis 3.7. Note that although de Vaux accepts that Zech 14.16f. is devoted to the eschatological triumph or *Day* when Yahweh will be King over the earth, he argues that Tabernacles is mentioned only because it was the main feast of pilgrimage (de Vaux, *Ancient Israel*, 506). However, his eschatological interpretation can be used to support thematic ties with Tabernacles regarding Yahweh's future victory and universal kingship, which were

ledge Yahweh's kingship by worshipping at Tabernacles results in punishment, the withholding of rain.[118] Rubenstein points out that "the prophet envisions the celebration of Sukkot as the central festival of the restored temple,"[119] and plausibly suggests that the vision calls to mind the autumn festival of the first temple.[120] The status given to Tabernacles in the vision no doubt reflects on the importance enjoyed by the festival when Zechariah was writing.

It is not surprising that Zech 14 was assigned to be read on the first day of Tabernacles, although it is unclear when this became standard practice.[121] MacRae writes that "the feast appears already to have taken on messianic significance, and it is safe to assume that this characteristic entered into all future celebrations of it."[122] We will not assume this, but suggest that, whether solely or only partially dependent on its temple associations, Tabernacles was linked in Zech 14 with the eschatological restoration of Israel.[123] Two elements characteristic of the new age envisioned in Zech

---

characteristic of the proposed reconstructions of the autumn festival. Johnson not unreasonably adduces Zech 14 as direct evidence for some of the autumn festival emphases which depend generally on implicit evidence: "It seems reasonable to infer that such an eschatological picture is based upon what was already the established complex of ideas associated with this festival in the form which had been current in Jerusalem" (*Sacral Kingship*, 58–59).

[118] The association of Tabernacles with rain is widely attested in the Mishnah and rabbinic writings. For citations see Rubenstein, *Sukkot*, 47. With Rowley (*Worship*, 192), we find it unlikely that this is a newly invented association.

[119] Rubenstein, *Sukkot*, 46. Further, "On Sukkot, temple worship reached its apex as the people faithfully appeared to worship their God. Projected into eschatological time and universalized, Sukkot becomes the point at which all nations, not only Israelites, journey to the temple" (ibid., 46).

[120] See Rubenstein, *Sukkot*, 47: "The vision recalls the autumnal festival of first temple times and evokes the description of the mass gathering of all Israelites to celebrate the dedication of the temple under Solomon. . . . Despite the discontinuity in worship before the ascent of the second temple cult, celebration of Sukkot quickly took on its ancient character." W. Harrelson further suggests that Zech 14 "is reminiscent of the ritual of divine inthronization" ("The Celebration of the Feast of Booths According to Zech xiv 16–21," 91).

[121] See *b. Meg.* 31a. The passage contrasts the practice of reading Zech 14 on the first day with the contemporary practice of reading it on the first two days, which suggests reliance on earlier tradition.

[122] MacRae, "Tabernacles," 268. On the messianic-eschatological associations of Tabernacles in Judaism (and in the NT) see further S. Bergler, "Jesus, Bar Kochba und das messianische Laubhüttenfest."

[123] One would think that, because Tabernacles is the culmination of the eschatological vision of Zech 14, it would excite eschatological interpretations. However, Rubenstein argues that although the vision is eschatological, the focus is not on Tabernacles itself but rather on the restored city and temple, with the latter being the key eschatological concept. As a result Tabernacles' place in the vision is due to its status as the most

14 can be tied in with Tabernacles motifs.[124] The first is that of continuous light (Zech 14.7), which corresponds with the dominant motif of light in the Tabernacles celebration.[125] The second is the river flowing out of Jerusalem (Zech 14.8), which although not specified as coming from the temple clearly is reminiscent of Ezek 47. Tabernacles is associated with God's judgment concerning rain for the coming year, which probably forms the background to the prominence of the water libations and water-drawing ceremony at the festival. This would surely bring to mind the vision of the eschatological river of both Zechariah and Ezekiel – a continuous supply of water that would end dependence on rain. The vision therefore appears to emphasize Tabernacles motifs, which may indicate that the festival is not entirely dependent on temple links for its eschatological associations.[126]

---

important temple festival: "The prophet visualizes worship in that eschatological temple in terms of the acme of temple worship – the festival of Sukkot . . . hence the appropriate model for eschatological worship" (*Sukkot*, 49–50). Accordingly, only those groups which did not accept the validity of the present cult or priesthood would be inclined to entertain eschatological speculations at the festival. Thus, "the 'eschatological associations' of Sukkot are reflexes of the festival's deep temple associations. Zechariah 14 indicates that Sukkot was the temple festival *par excellence*, not that it possessed eschatological motifs" (*Sukkot*, 49–50). Rubenstein's argument can be challenged at several points. First, Zech 14 appears to emphasize Tabernacles more than temple. Second, although Tabernacles is closely associated with the temple, other themes such as kingship, Yahweh's coming to assume universal reign, and Yahweh's coming to judge both nature (rain) and man (Day of Atonement), are open to eschatological speculation. Since the ancient Tabernacles celebrated Yahweh's kingship, it is most appropriate that his universal rule be recognized by the nations at the festival. These association are linked with, but not dependent on, temple motifs. Third, even if Rubenstein is correct, individual Tabernacles motifs could take on an eschatological interpretation of their own over time with no conscious temple dependence. The best example of this is the highly developed eschatological interpretation of Tabernacles in the rabbinics. Fourth, to suggest that "those who celebrated Sukkot annually at the temple probably experienced no eschatological longings" denies to Second Temple Jews any sense of imagination. Last, it is suggested that to attempt to distinguish too finely between the complex of associations surrounding Tabernacles and temple may be an artificial exercise.

[124] Thackeray (*The Septuagint and Jewish Worship: A Study in Origins*, 66) writes that the LXX gives prominence to the festival and its dominant motifs in its emphasis on the cessation of winter (the allusion to cold and frost in Zech 14.6, and substitution of "spring" for "winter" in Zech 14.8). Presumably this is tied into the agricultural background of the feast, as Tabernacles signaled approaching winter.

[125] See *t. Sukk.* 4.4; *m. Sukk.* 5.1–4. MacRae ("Tabernacles," 269–270) suggests that the idea of continuous daylight is reflected in the candelabra ceremony.

[126] In addition, Zech 7.5 shows that the fast held in remembrance of the destruction of Jerusalem was observed not only in the fifth month but also in the seventh (probably

B. Tabernacles in Intertestamental Literature

Most scholars agree that Tabernacles was the highlight of the festal calendar in the OT. Zechariah 14 suggests that it was the temple festival *par excellence*, and Second Temple literature reveals that it continued to be the dominant pilgrimage festival.[127] Our interest is in those elements in the literature that suggest possible eschatological associations, and thus we will not cover exhaustively all references to Tabernacles.[128]

Pseudo-Philo and *1 Enoch*

Pseudo-Philo, dated to around the middle of the first century AD,[129] makes explicit the relationship between keeping the festival and the giving of rain (*L.A.B.* 13.7). He also highlights the judgment of man that takes place on the Day of Atonement, just prior to Tabernacles, a theme which appears often in the rabbinics and suggests the hope of restoration.[130] The Sin-Exile-Restoration cycle found in OT and intertestamental literature suggests that since the reason for the exile was sin, Israel's restoration is contingent on the removal of her sin guilt.[131] Surely the judgment of individual and nation regarding sin on Atonement would suggest eschatological expectations. Tabernacles, at least in the

---

at Tabernacles), and Zech 8.19 expands this to the fourth and tenth months as well. Had Israel thought of itself as restored it would have been redundant to continue this, yet the context and mood of Zech 7 indicates continuing disobedience and exile – the fasting has gone on for the past "seventy years." However, it also says that these feasts "will become joyful and glad occasions and happy festivals for Judah" (Zech 8.19). The passage that follows the prophecy presents an eschatological picture of the nations coming to Jerusalem to seek the Lord (Zech 8.20–23), prefiguring the ultimate fulfillment found in Zech 14, and thus providing another eschatological association for Tabernacles which would not easily have escaped the Jewish reader of Scripture.

[127] Josephus writes in paraphrasing 1 Kgs 8 that Tabernacles "is considered especially sacred and important by the Hebrews" (*Ant.* 8.100). Cf. *Ant.* 15.50: "This festival is observed by us with special care." He demonstrates its status in referring to it simply as "the Festival" (*Ant.* 13.372). G. F. Moore (*Judaism in the First Centuries of the Christian Era: The Age of the Tannaim*, 2.43) is justified in calling it the culminating festival of the year. Its importance is seen in Josephus' account of the war between Hyrcanus and Antiochus in 135 BC, where they suspend fighting so that Tabernacles can be celebrated (*Ant.* 13.240–244).

[128] For a comprehensive and technical study of references to Tabernacles in Second Temple literature see Rubenstein, *Sukkot*.

[129] D. J. Harrington ("Introduction to Pseudo-Philo," 299) suggests a date around the time of Jesus as most likely.

[130] *L.A.B.* 13.6. Note that all quotations of OT pseudepigrapha are from the Charlesworth edition unless otherwise specified.

[131] For citations from intertestamental literature see Wright, *New Testament*, 272 n. 12.

rabbinics, is when God declares the results of the judgment passed on Atonement, and forgives Israel. In the following passage (*L.A.B.* 13.10) Pseudo-Philo continues to link obedience with the blessing of rain and again points to the Sin-Exile-Restoration pattern and the future hope of salvation.[132]

The vision beginning in *1 En.* 60.1 is dated to the fourteenth day of the seventh month, deliberately associated with, and reflecting, Tabernacles motifs. The elements related to rain (lightning, thunder, the winds, reservoirs of water) are a point of main interest (*1 En.* 60.11–22). He sees millions of angels and the "Antecedent of Time was sitting on the throne of his glory." His vision is eschatological, pointing to the time of judgment and an eschatological renewal of the covenant.[133] The setting emphasizes the majesty and kingship of God, and if covenant renewal or celebration was part of the ancient festival (which is possible), this provides another festival link, as does the emphasis on judgment. Neither Pseudo-Philo nor *1 Enoch* make clear that Tabernacles itself is interpreted eschatologically. However, they do show that Tabernacles motifs and themes lend themselves to eschatological interpretation. If Tabernacles had not been interpreted eschatologically, its association with eschatological passages like these would at least have facilitated, and perhaps instigated, such interpretations.

Jubilees

Abraham is credited with being the first man on earth to celebrate Tabernacles (*Jub.* 16.21), a feast characterized by its emphasis on joy (*Jub.* 16.20, 25) and which he calls "the festival of the LORD." The cause of this rejoicing, and the reason the feast is instituted, is the promise made to Abraham that from Isaac would come a holy seed elected by God to become a special possession and people, a kingdom for God (*Jub.* 16.15–19). This is specifically linked to Tabernacles, since the feast begins immediately after Abraham receives the promise in the seventh month. A possible link to Ps 118 is suggested in the description of Abraham circling the altar with branches seven times every day, "praising and giving thanks to God" (*Jub.* 16.31). This points to a liturgical recitation that corresponds to the use of Ps 118.[134] Ps 118 is linked closely in the rabbinic sources with the ritual circling of the altar, and Ps 118.27 probably refers to the circling with branches. Whether intended as an allusion to Ps 118 or not,

---

[132] *L.A.B.* 13.10.

[133] *1 En.* 60.6.

[134] Cf. Rubenstein, *Sukkot*, 55.

those familiar with the contemporary practice of Tabernacles would no doubt have made this connection.

If the context of Abraham's Tabernacle observance suggests the possibility of eschatological applications, the vision Jacob has on the last day of the festival, in which Yahweh reveals to him that his seed will be kings and rule over all the nations for posterity, makes these explicit.[135] Clearly the vision refers not to the time of the monarchy but to the future. O. S. Wintermute argues that this section of *Jubilees* (23.9–32) is one in which the author looks beyond Moses (the historical context in which the author places himself) to what will happen in the "distant future."[136] The eighth day, which was added to the seven-day festival, is a response to this vision (32.27–29). There is no obvious reason why *Jubilees* should use Tabernacles in this way, unless it already had eschatological associations. The clearest connection with Tabernacles themes is that of kingship, and Zech 14 could at least have suggested the Tabernacles context of the eschatological kingdom where Israel dominates the nations. Whatever the antecedent associations which Tabernacles offered to the writer may have been, he chooses specifically to link his eschatological vision for Israel with a Tabernacles context.[137]

Josephus

Josephus provides a glimpse into the high ceremony surrounding Tabernacles in two passages that especially interest us. The first documents the rule of Aristobulus, who succeeded his father John Hyrcanus as high priest and also claimed the role of king, and the conflict with his brother Antigonus (104–103 BC).

> But on one occasion when Antigonus had returned from a campaign with glory, as the season of the festival during which tabernacles are erected to God was at hand, it chanced that Aristobulus fell ill, and Antigonus, arrayed in great splendour and with his heavy-armed soldiers about him, went up to the temple to celebrate the festival and to pray earnestly for his brother's recovery; thereupon the unscrupulous men who were bent on disrupting the harmonious relation between them, found in Antigonus' ambitious display and in the success he had achieved, a pretext to go to the king and maliciously exaggerate the pomp of his appearance at the festival, saying that everything that had been done was out of keeping with the

---

[135] See *Jub.* 32.17–19.

[136] Wintermute, "Jubilees: A New Translation and Introduction," 35.

[137] The promise of a seed from Abraham that would be like the Creator, which takes place during the Tabernacles celebration in *Jub.* 16.26–27, is explored more fully in ch. 8 of this study.

> behaviour of a private person and that his actions rather had the indications
> of one who imagined himself a king. (*Ant.* 13.304–306 [Marcus, LCL])

Aristobulus then orders the killing of Antigonus. That Antigonus could be accused of pretensions to royal authority because of the prominent role he took in the Tabernacles celebrations suggests how closely the feast was associated with the ruler. Aristobulus would have officiated had he not been ill, presumably in equally splendid clothing and show of ceremony. Rubenstein correctly discerns that "the display was not inappropriate for the festival, but inappropriate for a substitute high priest . . . so trouble-makers adduced the ostentatiousness as proof of disloyalty and ambition."[138] Antigonus, as the only brother whom Aristobulus had not killed, was in an especially delicate position and thus his actions could have been inter-preted as making a play for rule. The close association of rulership with a prominent role in the festival recalls the role of the king during the monarchy. It is apparent that the linkage had continued in the post-exilic period, and that leading a procession to the temple at the feast could be interpreted as making a political statement. This is even more apparent in the second passage detailing Herod's intrigues occasioned by his envy of Aristobulus III (ca. 35 BC), which came to a head at Tabernacles.

> When Tabernacles came round – this is a festival observed by us with
> special care – he [Herod] waited for these days to pass, while he himself
> and the rest of the people gave themselves up to rejoicing. But it was the
> envy arising from this very occasion and clearly working within him that
> led him to carry out his purpose more quickly. For Aristobulus was a youth
> of seventeen when he went up to the altar to perform the sacrifices in
> accordance with the law, wearing the ornamental dress of the high priests
> and carrying out the rites of the cult, and he was extraordinarily handsome
> and taller than most youths of his age, and in his appearance, moreover, he
> displayed to the full the nobility of his descent. And so there arose among
> the people an impulsive feeling of affection toward him, and there came to
> them a vivid memory of the deeds performed by his grandfather Aristobulus.
> Being overcome, they gradually revealed their feelings, showing joyful and
> painful emotion at the same time, and they called out to him good wishes
> mingled with prayers, so that the affection of the crowd became evident,
> and their acknowledgment of their emotions seemed too impulsive in view
> of their having a king. (*Ant.* 15.50–52 [Marcus and Wikgren, LCL])

Herod, spurred by envy and feeling threatened by the popular response to Aristobulus, arranged to have him drowned. Although Aristobulus had earlier been appointed high priest, and would thus be associated with the post and known as such by the people, it was not until he officiated at

---

[138] Rubenstein, *Sukkot*, 80–81.

Tabernacles that he received the kind of acclaim that Herod would consider a threat to his own position. This suggests that whatever longing for a king the popular masses may have had was intensified or at least brought to the forefront at Tabernacles. This was the festival associated with kingship and authority during the monarchy, when the new king may have acceded to the throne. That some of the vestiges remained is confirmed further in 1 Macc, where Jonathan chooses Tabernacles as the time to assume the role of high priest.[139]

Rubenstein justifiably concludes that "Sukkot is the festival on which pomp, intrigue and political machinations take place."[140] No doubt the large number of people present at the festival, and the elaborate ritual and ceremony, were significant factors in this, but one should not discount the possibility that the prominent role of the king and other royal motifs associated with the festival during the monarchy may have influenced expectation surrounding the later festival. The prominent role of Ps 118 in the Tabernacles rituals and liturgy would have provided a high profile stage for the leader of the cult, who enacted the psalm in a procession.

C. Tabernacles Symbols: Coins, Lulab, Water

Two of the symbols most closely associated with Tabernacles, the *lulab* and *ethrog*,[141] appear on coins and a number of other objects, especially Jewish tombstones.[142] The lulab and ethrog appear on coins dating from the First Jewish Revolt, specifically the fourth year (AD 69–70), and are associated with the phrase "Redemption of Zion." They also appear –

---

[139] 1 Macc 10.18–21: "'King Alexander to his brother Jonathan, greetings. We have heard about you, that you are a mighty warrior and worthy to be our friend. And so we have appointed you today to be the high priest of your nation; you are to be called the king's Friend and you are to take our side and keep friendship with us.' He also sent him a purple robe and a golden crown. So Jonathan put on the sacred vestments in the seventh month of the one hundred sixtieth year, at the festival of booths, and he recruited troops and equipped them with arms in abundance." The passage suggests not that Tabernacles happened to be the time when Jonathan received his appointment, but that it was the appropriate occasion on which to assume the authority invested in the high priesthood. As Rubenstein notes, "Dedication of temples, altar, and priestly dynasties consistently gravitate to Sukkot" (*Sukkot*, 64).

[140] Rubenstein, *Sukkot*, 81.

[141] The lulab is composed of myrtle and willow twigs tied around a palm branch. The ethrog is fruit, and is also called a citron.

[142] E. R. Goodenough has collected these in his extensively detailed work, *Jewish Symbols in the Greco-Roman Period*. Although his interpretations of the evidence have been criticized, it is the evidence and not his conclusions that interest us. For criticism see Rubenstein, *Sukkot*, 97–99; M. Smith, "Goodenough's Jewish Symbols in Retrospect."

sometimes the lulab without the ethrog – on coins of the Second Jewish Revolt (AD 132–135). Goodenough credibly concludes that the Tabernacles symbols here served as "tokens of triumph,"[143] and a number of scholars have not implausibly discerned in them a messianic significance.[144] After all, one would expect symbols associated with deliverance to appear especially during such times of heightened Jewish hope.[145] There is evidence that the lulab was associated with victory and deliverance. After "the yoke of the Gentiles was removed from Israel" and Simon the Maccabee had entered Jerusalem the Jews celebrated with palm branches: "the Jews entered it *with praise and palm branches*, and with harps and cymbals and stringed instruments, and with hymns and songs, because a great enemy had been crushed and removed from Israel."[146]

Also suggestive is the account in 2 Macc 10.5–8, where the celebration of the cleansing of the sanctuary is patterned after Tabernacles: "Therefore, carrying ivy-wreathed wands and beautiful branches and also fronds of palm, they offered hymns of thanksgiving to him who had given success to the purifying of his own holy place (2 Macc 10.7)." It is a matter of conjecture whether the original impulse for the use of the lulab at the dedication had anything to do with its being a symbol of liberation, or depended simply on its liturgical use at Tabernacles. Since Dedication takes Tabernacles as its pattern, it would have been natural for it to incorporate the latter's more prominent symbols. In any case, even if the lulab had had no association with deliverance and victory prior to its use at Dedication, it could hardly have avoided acquiring them since the festival celebrated these very themes.[147]

---

[143] Goodenough, *Jewish Symbols*, 4.144–146.

[144] Rubenstein (*Sukkot*, 97–98) questions Goodenough's position. Among those Rubenstein lists as favoring a messianic interpretation of the symbols see L. Kadman, *The Coins of the Jewish War*, 84, 93–94; H. Ulfgard, *Feast and Future: Revelation 7.9–17 and the Feast of Tabernacles*, 134–137; M. Dacey, "Sukkot in the Late Second Temple Period," 105–106.

[145] Cf. C. Roth, "Messianic Symbols in Palestinian Archaeology," 151–152.

[146] 1 Macc 13.51; emphasis added.

[147] Consequently, Rubenstein's (*Sukkot*, 98) conclusion that the lulab and ethrog "seem to be either general symbols of nature and fertility . . . or symbols related to the temple that point again to conception of Sukkot as a temple festival," dismisses too easily the possibility that they are associated with themes which at the least seem to provide a satisfactory reason for their use on coins of the revolts. It is difficult to imagine why "general" agricultural symbols would feature prominently during the revolts, especially with the phrase "Redemption of Zion." As for the lulab and ethrog being symbols of temple worship, this does not preclude their being eschatological symbols, especially if there was eschatological speculation related to the temple. This would be true especially of the Second Revolt.

The lulab and ethrog are especially common on Jewish tombstones, and appear in catacombs and on other items related to funerary usage.[148] Rubenstein suggests that, beyond demonstrating that the lulab was a popular symbol for Jews, it is difficult to determine what this means;[149] but as Goodenough more convincingly argues, it probably is meant to indicate more than just "Here lies a good Jew." He offers that, "however mechanically a given Jew may have availed himself of the lulab and ethrog," they were a seal of immortality that "represented his Jewish hope, here and in the hereafter."[150] Although Rubenstein criticizes Goodenough's material, suggesting that it is not always obvious whether a lulab or "simply" a palm branch is used, there is evidence that little distinction was made between the lulab and the palm branch, with the result that they were interchangeable.[151] The palm branch, as the dominant element in the lulab, not only represented it but was also the primary symbol for Tabernacles. Although Goodenough's mystical approach to Tabernacles is questionable, it is likely that the palm branch was a symbol of immortality.[152]

Another Tabernacles symbol meriting attention is that of the water libations and water-drawing ceremony which featured so prominently in the festival liturgy. Part of their background is God's judgment, made at Tabernacles, concerning rain; but the water symbol probably had acquired eschatological associations as well.[153] The jubilation at this time was un-

---

[148] See Goodenough, *Jewish Symbols*, 4.147.

[149] Rubenstein, *Sukkot*, 99.

[150] Goodenough, *Jewish Symbols*, 4.147, 166.

[151] Rubenstein, *Sukkot*, 98 n. 19. In response to this criticism see for example the following instances where the palm branch and lulab are interchangeable and where the palm branch represents the entire lulab. In *m. Sukk.* 3.9: "shake (the *lulab*)"; "waved their palm branches"; "carry his *lulab* in the morning"; "the entire day is a suitable time for the palm branch." Danby (*Mishnah*, 176 n. 12) also points out in his notes to *m. Sukk.* 3.8 that he translates lulab for palm branch, even though it denotes the palm, myrtle and willow branches together.. Also, *b. Pesah.* 95b uses the palm branch as symbol of Tabernacles, not the entire lulab. Cf. *b. Sukk.* 37b: "R. Jeremiah inquired of R. Zerika, Why in the blessing do we say only 'To take the palm-branch'? [i.e., omitting mention of the others] – Because it towers above the others."

[152] Rubenstein questions Goodenough's claim that the lulab and ethrog are symbols of immortality, suggesting that his interpretation should be treated with skepticism because it "derives from his discredited thesis of a mystical, syncretistic, non-rabbinic Judaism" (*Sukkot*, 99 n. 194). However, Rubenstein also acknowledges that in later rabbinic literature they are associated with new life (e.g., *Pesiq. Rab Kah.* 27.3). He acknowledges finally that "on a grave, however, the motif may point to personal immortality" (*Sukkot*, 99 n. 194).

[153] Cf. Thackeray, *Septuagint*, 63. The Mishnah tractate *Ta'anit* is concerned especially with rain, much of it related to Tabernacles. For examples of the association

matched by any other occasion, so that it was said, "Anyone who has not seen the rejoicing of *bet hashshoebah* in his life has never seen rejoicing."[154] The eschatological river of Zech 14 and Ezek 47 was linked with this,[155] and the emphasis on light at the water-drawing is suggestive of the continuous daylight of the Zech 14 Tabernacles.[156]

To sum up: The depiction of the lulab and ethrog on coins of the revolts, their widespread use on tombstones and related items, and examples of their use in 1 and 2 Macc, suggests they were associated with the deliverance of Israel and personal – perhaps also national – eschatological hopes. This is especially true of the palm branch, which was the dominant component of the lulab.[157] The water and light ceremonies of the festival prefigured the eschatological Tabernacles celebration when Yahweh would restore Israel and establish his reign over the nations.

---

between Tabernacles and rain see *m. Ta'an.* 1.1; *b. Roš Haš.*16a; *t. Roš Haš.* 12–13; *t. Sukk.* 3.18.

[154] *m. Sukk.* 5.1. *Bet hashshoebah* refers probably to the place or act of water drawing (see Danby, *Mishnah*, 179 n. 12). Note that all quotations from the Mishnah are from Neusner's translation unless otherwise specified. Cf. *t. Sukk.* 4.5: "Said R. Joshua b. Hananiah, "In all the days of celebrating Bet hasho'ebah, we never saw a moment of sleep." See also the description of joyful dancing and celebration by R. Simeon b. Gamaliel in *t. Sukk.* 4.4.

[155] Although the earliest witness is the Tosefta, it is probable that it reflects similar associations made during the Second Temple period. See *t. Sukk.* 3.3–10. The Tosefta explains the ceremony in reference to Ezek 47.2–5 and Zech 13.1; 14.8, with further commentary on Ezek 47.8–10. The eschatological river is immense both in size and depth, and in the scope of life it gives. It also provides cleansing from sin. In *t. Sukk.* 3.18 the water libation is linked to the Zech 14.17–18 blessing of rain in the eschatological kingdom.

[156] See *m. Sukk.* 5.2–4 for a description of the light ceremony in the Court of the Women: "And there was not a courtyard in Jerusalem which was not lit up from the light of *bet hashshoebah*" (*m. Sukk.* 5.3). Goodenough (*Jewish Symbols*, 4.154) advances a rather implausible phallic association for the lights.

[157] MacRae is probably justified in concluding that in Judaism the lulab was "a messianic symbol par excellence" ("Tabernacles," 272). See also Roth's conclusion that the lulab/palm branch is "a token of Redemption" and a messianic symbol "emphasizing the daily expectation of the deliverance of Israel" ("Messianic Symbols," 154).

D. Psalm 118 and the Hallel at Tabernacles

The Hallel Psalms were sung on the seven days of Tabernacles as well as on the additional eighth day, a practice which the Mishnah[158] considers an obligation.[159] Although there are a number of connections between the Hallel as a unit and Passover themes so that the psalms are especially appropriate for that festival, this is not so obviously the case with their use at Tabernacles. Rather, it is Ps 118 that stands out. As MacRae points out, Ps 118 is "better suited to Tabernacles than to any other feast."[160] Although the Hallel Psalms are sung as a group, it is Ps 118's role in the temple ritual that is described in detail.

> The religious requirement of the willow branch: How so? There was a place below Jerusalem, called Mosa. (People) go down there and gather young willow branches. They come and throw them along the sides of the altar, with their heads bent over the altar. They blew on the *shofar* a sustained, a quavering, and a sustained note. Every day they walk around the altar one time and say, "*Save now, we beseech thee, O Lord! We beseech thee, O Lord, send now prosperity* (Ps. 118:25)." R. Judah says, "(They say), '*Ani waho, save us we pray! Ani waho, save us we pray!*'" And on that day [seventh] they walk around the altar seven times. (*m. Sukk.* 4.5)

---

[158] There is a question on the reliability of the Mishnaic traditions regarding temple liturgy and worship. For example, Neusner calls it a "work of imagination . . . a realm of made-up memories, artificial dreams, hopes, yearnings" ("Mishnah and Messiah," 269). In spite of Neusner's dismissive (and unfounded) claims, it is likely that the Mishnah does preserve temple traditions accurately, especially as liturgical practice is relatively stable. C. A. Evans correctly notes that one has to take into account the type of rabbinic material when evaluating reliability: "One might reasonably expect liturgical material (such as prayers) to remain more fixed than, say, exegetical traditions" ("Early Rabbinic Sources," 56). See further L. Finkelstein, "The Origin of the Hallel," 332; S. Zeitlin, "The Hallel: A Historical Study of the Canonization of the Hebrew Liturgy"; Segal, *Passover*, 260–269; S. Safrai, "Pilgrimage to Jerusalem at the End of the Second Temple Period," 13–14. Rubenstein's work strengthens this position, as he points out that in general the two bodies of evidence for Sukkot practice in the Second Temple (Tannaitic, *Jubilees*, Josephus, 2 Maccabees, Zechariah, Plutarch) are more complementary than in tension: "Given the general agreement with extra-rabbinic sources, it seems that the rabbinic materials acquire a presumptive plausibility once the obvious historiographic tendencies are filtered out" (Rubenstein, *Sukkot*, 159–160). See further Rubenstein's list of studies supporting the trustworthiness of rabbinic traditions in certain areas (*Sukkot*, 104–105).

[159] *m. Sukk.* 4.8. See also *m. Sukk.* 4.1, which specifies that the Hallel and rejoicing are for eight days, whereas the water libation, willow branch, and waving of the lulab are for seven days.

[160] MacRae, "Tabernacles," 264.

Psalm 118 is connected with the willow ritual which took place every day of Tabernacles. It is likely that there was a procession from Mosa to Jerusalem during which the Hallel was sung, with Ps 118 providing the climax as they circled the altar (the willow branches were placed beside and above it). The exact function of the willow ceremony is unclear, although some scholars have associated it with rain production – a distinct possibility as Tabernacles is linked with God's judgment concerning rain. The tradition of the circling of the altar preserved in the Mishnah finds support from other literature. The description in *Jub.* 16 parallels this, with Abraham holding palm branches and fruit as he circled the altar seven times daily for seven days, and taking willow branches from the stream.[161] Similarly, although not mentioning the circling of the altar, the dedication of the temple in 2 Macc 10.5–8 includes branches, ivy-wreathed wands, and palm fronds. The procession with palm branches in 1 Macc 13.51 provides an additional parallel. The description of praise and singing in both Maccabean accounts is probably an allusion to the Hallel Psalms, and *Jubilees* appears to assume their use.

The Mishnah preserves an early tradition, a debate between the Houses of Hillel and Shammai, which defines at what point during the Hallel the lulab should be shaken.

> And at what point did they shake (the *lulab*)? "At *O give thanks unto the Lord (*Ps 118), beginning and end; and at *Save now, we beseech thee O Lord* (Ps 118:25)," the words of the House of Hillel. And the House of Shammai say, "Also: At, *O Lord, we beseech thee, send now prosperity* (Ps 118:25)." Said R. Aqiba, "I was watching Rabban Gamaliel and R. Joshua, for all the people waved their palm branches, but they waved their palm branches only at, *Save now, we beseech thee, O Lord* (Ps 118:25)."
> (*m. Sukk.* 3.9)

The shaking of the lulab takes place during the recitation of Ps 118. This shaking of the lulab at first seems at odds with the willow ritual. Do the worshippers hold willow branches and/or lulabs as they circle the altar? It appears that both passages (*m. Sukk.* 3.9; 4.5) refer to the same ceremony, that the worshipers held lulabs while the willow branches were laid around and over the altar, and that if willow branches were carried it would be by the priests.[162] The waving of the lulab apparently took place at more than

---

[161] See *Jub.* 16.30–31. Although Abraham circled seven times per day every day, this probably reflects the interest in the number seven by the author of *Jubilees* rather than actual practice.

[162] The details are not of great importance to our discussion. See Rubenstein (*Sukkot*, 108–117, 156–157) for discussion.

one point of the psalm. The feast built towards a climax so that on the seventh day this would have happened seven times.

Clearly Ps 118 was prominent at Tabernacles. There are several points internal to the psalm that parallel Tabernacles and made it uniquely suited to its use in the festival. First, the processional character of the psalm is especially appropriate to the festival. Second, the mention of tents in Ps 118.15 evokes the most distinctive feature of the feast. Third, the psalm shares the emphasis on light (118.27) that characterizes Tabernacles.[163] Third, Ps 118.27 explicitly mentions a festival, and may allude to a procession around the altar with branches. It is significant that the procession involves entering the temple up to the altar, as does Tabernacles. Thackeray points out that the LXX translation of Ps 118(117).27 is especially appropriate, for in place of the obscure Hebrew "Bind the Hag with cords to the altar," it renders "Order the festival procession with boughs even unto the horns of the altar."[164] It may be that Ps 118 was translated with its role in the festivals in mind.

E. Rabbinics

The Festival of Tabernacles and its primary symbols are highly eschatologized in rabbinic writings.[165] The experience of the Jews following the destruction of the temple made the exodus especially relevant to the Tannaim, who connect the festival to the exodus. The Amoraic midrashim continue and develop this emphasis, with eschatological-messianic symbolism and associations appearing often.[166] The lulab is portrayed as an eschatological symbol of victory at the judgment, of praise to God who grants eternal life, and symbolizes the coming of the

---

[163] See *m. Sukk.* 5.1–5; *t. Sukk.* 4.4.

[164] The translation is Thackeray's (*Septuagint*, 75–76). Note G. R. Driver's ("Psalm 118:27: אסורי הג," 130–131) reading of Ps 118.27 in fragment E from 11QPsª, where against Y. Yadin he translates אסורי הג as referring to the "ordered band of pilgrims" standing beside the altar. Yadin argues that it refers to the sacrificial animals: "the festal animals are bound with ropes" ("Another Fragment [E] of the Psalms Scroll from Qumran Cave 11 [11QPsª]," 6–7). It is not impossible that the psalm describes an ancient form of crowd control.

[165] Note that although the word "rabbinic" applies to both Tannaitic and Amoraic sources, the former (Mishnah, Tosefta) are of overall greater reliability in the preservation of liturgical practice in the temple than those of the later Amoraic period.

[166] See the evidence gathered in Rubinstein, *Sukkot*, 239–271. Rubenstein points out that prior to the destruction of the temple Tabernacles was not associated to the same degree with the exodus. He is probably correct in this, as the link is not emphasized in *Jubilees*, Maccabees, Pseudo-Philo, Josephus, or Philo.

Messiah.[167] Rubenstein suggests that the ideas derive primarily from
two sources: Zech 14 and Tabernacles' place as the prime temple festival.
Zechariah 14 is notable as one of the clearest eschatological prophecies,
and, as Scripture, "it would inevitably inform rabbinic eschatological
thinking. In addition the prophecy was selected as the haftara for
Sukkot... *To give Sukkot an eschatological role was simply to read
scripture well.*"[168]

No doubt Second Temple Jews could read their Scripture equally well,
if not with the same sense of dislocation as interpreters post-AD 70.
Another suggestive association is that of Tabernacles as the time when
God comes to judge the nation (rain), but also in regards to sin, as
redemption/forgiveness/cleansing is found on the first day of the festival.
Tabernacles is closely associated with Rosh Hashanah, Yom Kippur, and
the themes of repentance and atonement for sin. The lulab is both a
symbol and a means of atonement, and the festival sacrifices are thought
to provide atonement for the nations of the world. From the evidence,
Rubenstein concludes that the festival anticipates "the ultimate redemption
from sin and the ultimate advent of God."[169] This association is not
explicit in pre-rabbinic literature, although it is likely that Rosh Hashanah
and Yom Kippur originated in the ancient Tabernacles. In any case, their
calendrical proximity to Tabernacles suggests that their primary themes
were linked to some degree with the festival. When this is placed in the
context of continuing exile it gains new significance. If sin was the cause
of exile, then forgiveness would mark the restoration of Israel.
Tabernacles' emphasis on the coming of God in judgment and his
pronouncing forgiveness could have excited hopes of restoration.[170]

F. The Hallel and Dedication

The Feast of Dedication (or Hanukkah), took Tabernacles as its model.
This is clear in 1 and 2 Maccabees where at first it is identified simply as
the festival of booths,[171] and the celebration is compared with[172] and

---

[167] For numerous examples see Rubenstein, *Sukkot*, 273–317.

[168] Rubenstein, *Sukkot*, 289. Emphasis added.

[169] Rubenstein, *Sukkot*, 316. For rabbinic citations see ibid., 290–301.

[170] Cf. Wright, *New Testament*, 272. The concept of continuing exile will be
discussed below.

[171] 2 Macc 1.9.

[172] 2 Macc 1.18.

conducted in the same manner as Tabernacles.[173]   There are several possible reasons for this borrowing from Tabernacles.   First is that the dedication of the temple and altar under both Solomon and Nehemiah took place at Tabernacles.   It is likely that the Hasmoneans thought of their festival as standing in line with biblical tradition, and therefore drew on Tabernacles as the paradigmatic temple-dedication festival.[174] Second, and closely related to the first, is that Tabernacles was the chief of the temple festivals.   Zechariah 14 has already made this clear, and one wonders if the eschatological associations found there did not impress themselves on the Hasmoneans.   Although 1 and 2 Maccabees show an awareness of continuing exile, they also suggest it is in its last stages, thus making the eschatological festival a most appropriate pattern to follow.   From early on Dedication became a feast characterized by light (Josephus calls it simply "Lights"),[175] perhaps not coincidentally reflecting the motif prominent both in the Tabernacles liturgy and the eschatological festival of Zech 14.[176]

Dedication also borrowed the Hallel, appointing it to be sung on each of the eight festival days.[177] The mention of light in Ps 118 probably ensured that this psalm especially stood out in the Hallel, as is suggested in a rabbinic tradition: "And why is the Hallel read [at Hanukkah]?   Because [it] declared The Lord is God, and hath given us light [Ps 118.27]."[178] Dedication was a celebration that commemorated a great deliverance and victory, a restoration of national freedom.   It would be surprising not to find, in a people under foreign domination, hope for a similar deliverance to take place once again, and in fact Josephus states that the festival

---

[173] 2 Macc 10.5–8; 1 Macc 13.51.   See also 1 Macc 4.50–59 where, although not explicitly stated, there are parallels with the number of days and it is assumed the pattern is that of Tabernacles.   See further S. Stein, "The Liturgy of Hanukkah and the First Two Books of Maccabees"; J. C. VanderKam, "Hanukkah: Its Timing and Significance According to 1 and 2 Maccabees."

[174] See 2 Macc 2.10–16. Kraus (*Worship*, 90) plausibly advances that the central act of the dedication of the temple may once have been part of Tabernacles, and may have been a ceremonial act that took place regularly.

[175] *Ant.* 12.325.   Cf. 1 Macc 4.40.

[176] There is no detail on Dedication practice in the Mishnah, but the witness of the Talmud confirms this emphasis. Cf. *b. Šabb.* 21b; *t. Sukk.* 3.2. For a description of the importance of light at the feast see Moore, *Judaism*, 2.50. For a detailed discussion of the feast see S. Zeitlin, "Hanukkah: Its Origin and its Significance." See further Bergler, "Messianische Laubhüttenfest," 179–182; H. Del Medico, "Le cadre historique des fêtes de Hanukkah et de Purîm."

[177] *b. Šabb.* 21b; *t. Sukk.* 3.2; *b. 'Arak.* 10a; *b. Ta'an.* 28b.

[178] *Pesiq. Rab.* 2.1. In this regard, note J. Meysing's suggestion ("A Text-Reconstruction of Ps 117[118].27," 136–137) that the ancient Tabernacles inspired both Ps 118 and the dedication of the first temple as described in 2 Chr 7.1–8.

continued to carry these associations in his time.[179] Psalms with a high profile at the event would no doubt become associated with its main themes, explaining at least in part the association of the Hallel with freedom, salvation and redemption in rabbinic writings.[180]

Conclusion

A number of witnesses suggest that during the time of Jesus Tabernacles was associated with eschatological interpretations. Ezekiel and Haggai anticipate an eschatological renewal of the cult, with the latter's message delivered at Tabernacles. Zechariah presents Tabernacles as the temple festival *par excellence*, which serves as the model of eschatological worship in a renewed temple and continues Tabernacles' emphasis on Yahweh's kingship and his coming in judgment. The festival is linked with future salvation (Pseudo-Philo) and identified with eschatological visions (*1 Enoch, Jubilees*). *Jubilees* links with Tabernacles both the promises to Abraham and those made to Jacob concerning Israel's future domination of the world. Josephus shows that the festival was a time when political aspirations came to the fore, both for rulers and the masses. The lulab/palm branch, the chief Tabernacles symbol, appears on coins of the revolts, was associated with victory celebrations and deliverance, and its widespread use on tombstones suggests it was linked with immortality. The water ceremonies probably recalled the eschatological river of Ezek 47 and Zech 14. Although we do not depend on rabbinic evidence, the eschatological and messianic interpretation of Tabernacles and its symbols in the rabbinic literature is in some cases continuous with prior traditions, is in none of the major themes inconsistent with pre-rabbinic testimony, and may well be an elaboration of trends already latent in earlier thought. Psalm 118 was the most prominent psalm in the Tabernacles ritual, a position ensured by its close link to the lulab both in the liturgy and internally (118.27), the light motif, and the pageantry of procession in which the preeminent leader probably played a significant role. With these close ties it is very likely that whatever eschatological expectations and speculations were associated with Tabernacles would inform the interpretation of Ps 118. The role of the Hallel in the Dedication celebrations would further associate Ps 118 with the themes of victory and deliverance.

---

[179] See Josephus' description of the reasons for the institution of Dedication: *Ant.* 12.323–325.

[180] *b. 'Arak.* 10b; *b. Meg.* 14a; *Pesiq. Rab.* 2.1.

III. Psalm 118 and the Feast of Passover

A. Continuing State of Exile

Second Temple religious literature, both OT and non-canonical, attests to a widespread and recurring theme of continuing exile.[181] Recognizing this provides an important interpretive context for the Passover as it was observed in the first century and establishes the background for the eschatological expectations with which the feast was linked. No doubt such an understanding helped to nurture a longing and desire for another great deliverance such as that commemorated at Passover. However, the relevance of this theme extends beyond Passover, as it would have contributed to the general yearning for God's intervening on behalf of his people and the hope for Messiah.

1. Continuing Exile: OT

The curse of exile as a consequence for sin, warned of in Deut 28, had taken place, but the prophets expected a restoration from exile as promised in Deut 30.1–10. J. A. Scott argues convincingly that this Sin-Exile-Restoration pattern is found often in the OT and intertestamental

---

[181] See especially Wright, *New Testament*, 269–272; J. A. Scott, "'For as many as are of works of the law are under a curse' (Galatians 3.10)"; M. A. Knibb, "The Exile in the Literature of the Intertestamental Period"; P. R. Ackroyd, *Exile and Restoration: A Study of Hebrew Thought of the Sixth Century BC*; E. P. Sanders, *Judaism: Practice and Belief 63 BCE – 66 CE*, 279–303. Although Wright is not the first to note a continuing-exile motif, his proposals have drawn the most attention. Many remain unconvinced. M. Casey, for example, dismisses the evidence as "spurious" ("Where Wright Is Wrong: A Critical Review of N. T. Wright's *Jesus and the Victory of God*," 99), and R. Hays ("Victory over Violence: *The Significance of N. T. Wright's Jesus for New Testament Ethics*," 147–148) asserts it is doubtful whether such thinking extended beyond Qumran. Support, however, is increasing. Scott claims a "growing consensus on the concept of the exile in many Jewish writings of the Second Temple period" ("Galatians," 213). "Consensus" may be too strong a word, but certainly there is a growing appreciation for the concept, even though there may be disagreement over the implications. See for example C. A. Evans ("Jesus & the Continuing Exile of Israel," 100), who collects a mass of evidence which he concludes, against Casey, "fully justifies" Wright's emphasis on exile theology; and contributions to J. M. Scott's collection on the exile (*Exile: Old Testament, Jewish and Christian Conceptions*). Others generally positive towards return-from-exile theology include P. R. Eddy, "The (W)Right Jesus: *Eschatological Prophet, Israel's Messiah, Yahweh Embodied*," 45; D. L. Bock, "The Trial & Death of Jesus in N. T. Wright's *Jesus and the Victory of God*," 117–119 (although he applies it differently to the NT); and, more cautiously, Blomberg, "The Wright Stuff: *A Critical Overview of* Jesus and the Victory of God," 28.

literature.[182] Because exile is the consequence of sin, restoration depends on the removal of this state of guilt. However, although there was a return granted under Cyrus, Israel remained under foreign domination and the reality of restored Israel was far different from the triumphant vision of Second Isaiah. The complete return prophesied in Ezek 39.21–29 had not taken place, and the second temple, though a cause of rejoicing, was hardly the glorious temple of Ezekiel's vision (chs. 40–48). According to Isaiah (52.8) and Ezekiel (43.1–7; 48.35), the glory which filled the temple in 1 Kings 8.10 and indicated the presence of God among his people is to return to the new temple following the return from exile that Yahweh will accomplish. Yet nowhere in Second Temple literature is it asserted that the glory of Yahweh has returned to the temple. The implication is that in spite of a partial return to the land, Israel remained under judgment for her sin. As a result, Israel's hope for restoration was projected into the future.[183]

Post-exilic OT writings support this position. In Haggai the promise of the glory of a new temple is clearly eschatological. There is disappointment with the temple that is under construction, but Yahweh declares that the glory of the temple – and his own coming – lies in the future (Hag 2.6–7). This is clear in Ezra 3.10–13, where those who had seen the former temple wept aloud in grief when they saw the foundation of the second temple being laid. Ezra's prayer acknowledges the exile as a result of sin. Only a remnant has returned, and this under foreign domination. Even though the temple is rebuilt and the walls of Jerusalem restored, the remnant is in "bondage": "we are slaves" (Ezra 9.8–9). Nehemiah similarly acknowledges that the exile was due to Israel's sin, alluding directly to Deut 28. He also refers to Deut 30 in reminding God of his promise to restore from exile, tacitly acknowledging that although there has been a return, the exile continues (Neh 1.5–9). Israel's communal confession in

---

[182] Scott, "Galatians," 195–213. Scott (ibid., 205–206) points to a penitential prayer tradition based on Dan 9 which acknowledges the Babylonian exile as the fulfillment of the curse of Deut 27–32 for violating the covenant, and looks for the forgiveness of Israel's sin as the condition for her restoration, also in line with the promise of Deut 27–32.

[183] R. Watts ("Consolation or Confrontation? Isaiah 40–55 and the Delay of the New Exodus") has proposed an interesting example of this in his study of Isaiah, arguing that chs. 40–55 represent an explanation for the failure to return from exile (Yahweh's New Exodus plan has been postponed because Israel rejected Yahweh's means of deliverance) and a description of how this plan will be realized in the future (ibid., 31). Chapters 55–66 "suggest a post-exilic setting where disappointment with the return is beginning to be felt but where nevertheless Yahweh's promises concerning Jerusalem-Zion are re-iterated" (ibid., 32), and are an appeal to Israel to continue to prepare for the New Exodus. Watts plausibly concludes that for Isaiah, "within the context of the book as a whole, the New Exodus is still future" (ibid., 59).

Neh 9 is explicit in acknowledging the exile as a direct result of their sin, an exile which for them continues: "we are slaves today, slaves in the land you gave our forefathers" (Neh 9.36).

Jeremiah's prophecy that the exile would last 70 years (29.10–14; 25.11) is reinterpreted in Dan 9.24–27 as "seventy sevens," or seventy weeks of years (i.e., 490 years), which will end only when God intervenes to restore his people, destroy their enemies, and establish his reign in Zion. Consequently Daniel understands the exile as a state of judgment that continues in spite of the returns under Cyrus and the construction of the second temple.[184] P. R. Ackroyd, in his study of the exile and restoration in Hebrew thought, summarizes this position well:

> It is in effect an exile lasting 490 years, and with this we reach an understanding of exile and restoration which takes us well beyond the consideration of the sixth century. Here the exile is no longer an historic event to be dated to one period; it is much nearer to being a condition from which only the final age will bring release. Though bound to the historical reality of an exile which actually took place in the sixth century, the experience of exile as such had become a symbol of a period, viewed in terms of punishment but also in terms of promise . . . The understanding of the exile is clearly enlarged far beyond the temporal considerations of seventy years and the precise period covered by Babylonian captivity in the stricter sense.[185]

Such a reinterpretation of the exile is evident in Zechariah, where Yahweh is asked how long he will withhold mercy from Jerusalem, "which you have been angry with *these seventy years*?" (Zech 1.12; emphasis added). Yahweh's answer is that he will return to Jerusalem, his house will be rebuilt, he will choose Jerusalem and restore her (Zech 1.16–17). He declares, "I am coming and I will live among you" (Zech 2.10). There are recurring themes throughout Zechariah of the exile's being a punishment for sin, and the promise that God will forgive and restore Israel and judge her oppressors. Until that future restoration they remain, effectively, in exile.

---

[184] Scott, "Galatians," 201.

[185] Ackroyd, *Exile and Restoration,* 242–243. Cf. Wright, "In Grateful Dialogue: *A Response,*" 259: "the Babylonian exile was simply the beginnning of a longer period of history, *one in which the same political and theological conditions applied and to which the same word –* exile *– could therefore appropriately be given*" (emphasis original).

2. Continuing Exile: Intertestamental Period

A brief look at a few second temple writings confirms the argument that many thought of themselves as still living in the time of exile. *Jubilees* begins with a prediction of sin and subsequent exile (*Jub.* 1.1–14). Repentance will follow, and God promises that he will restore (*Jub.* 1.22–25). It is clear that this restoration takes place not on the return from Babylon but in the future, for the accompanying rebuilding of the temple will take place at the creation of a new heaven and earth. This marks the end of history and the present world and the beginning of God's eternal reign.[186] Since this is inaugurated on the restoration from exile, until the eschatological vision is fulfilled then the exilic age is still in force.[187] Similarly, Goldstein concludes in his study of 1 and 2 Maccabees that many Israelites believed they were still living in the "Age of Wrath." Although in Maccabees there is confidence that at least some of the aspects of the Age of Wrath have ended, it is not yet completed.[188] There still has not been a complete return from exile, and the glory of God has not returned, although there is hope that this will soon happen.[189]

One of the clearest examples of the concept of continuing exile is found in Tobit. There will be a return from exile to rebuild the temple – not the second temple, but the one envisioned by the Prophets – followed by a conversion of all the nations and a gathering of the diaspora. This will not happen until "the times of fulfillment shall come."[190] Thus the historical

---

[186] See further *Jub.* 1.15, 17, 26–29. God will gather his people from the the midst of the nations, build his sanctuary and dwell with them. Repeatedly underscored is the continuing presence of Yahweh with his people, a longing that *Jubilees* indicates will be fulfilled only upon his future return.

[187] See further *Jub.* 25.21.

[188] See for example 2 Macc 1.27–29: "Gather together our scattered people, set free those who are slaves among the Gentiles, look on those who are rejected and despised, and let the Gentiles know that you are our God. Punish those who oppress and are insolent with pride. Plant your people in your holy place, as Moses promised."

[189] Cf. J. Goldstein, "How the Authors of 1 and 2 Maccabees Treated the 'Messianic' Promises", 74. See further 2 Macc 2.7–8, 18: "When Jeremiah learned of it, he rebuked them and declared: '*The place shall remain unknown until God gathers his people together again and shows his mercy. Then the Lord will disclose these things, and the glory of the Lord and the cloud will appear*, as they were shown in the case of Moses, and as Solomon asked that the place should be specially consecrated.' . . . We have hope in God that *he will soon have mercy on us and will gather us from everywhere* under heaven into his holy place, for he has rescued us from great evils and has purified the place" (emphasis added).

[190] Tob 14.5–7: "But God will again have mercy on them, and God will bring them back into the land of Israel; and they will rebuild the temple of God, but not like the first one *until the period when the times of fulfillment shall come*. After this they all will return from their exile and will rebuild Jerusalem in splendor; and in it the temple of

return in the sixth century has "only a provisional character."[191] Restoration from exile is no longer seen primarily as a return to the land, but as a spiritual state. There are numerous other examples that substantiate this view. Nickelsburg persuasively concludes that much of Jewish post-biblical theology and literature "was influenced and sometimes governed" by a hope for restoration.[192] E. P. Sanders similarly discusses at length the issue of whether there was an expectation of a new temple and restoration in Jewish literature, concluding that "all the main themes of prophetic expectation continued."[193] There is evidence that a number of streams in Judaism were dissatisfied with the temple and did not accept it as the promised restoration. The literature often anticipates either that it will be rebuilt, purified or made more glorious.[194] There is also a widespread anticipation of the gathering of Israel, which implies that they are still in a type of exile.[195] There may be a question whether the

---

God will be rebuilt, just as the prophets of Israel have said concerning it. Then the nations in the whole world will all be converted and worship God in truth. They will all abandon their idols, which deceitfully have led them into their error; and in righteousness they will praise the eternal God. All the Israelites who are saved in those days and are truly mindful of God will be gathered together; they will go to Jerusalem and live in safety forever in the land of Abraham, and it will be given over to them. Those who sincerely love God will rejoice, but those who commit sin and injustice will vanish from all the earth" (emphasis added).

[191] Knibb, "Exile," 268.

[192] G. Nickelsburg, *Jewish Literature Between the Bible and the Mishnah: A Historical and Literary Introduction*, 18. Nickelsburg observes that the hope centers on a return of the dispersed, the restoration of Israel's sovereignty, and a new and glorified temple.

[193] Sanders, *Jesus and Judaism*, 87. For primary sources and discussion on the expectation of a significant temple action see further C. A. Evans, "Jesus' Action in the Temple: Cleansing or Portent of Destruction?" esp. 248–256.

[194] This study is not concerned specifically with the complex of issues surrounding temple expectation (e.g., questions of a new temple, restored temple, whether the current temple will first be destroyed, etc.). We are concerned more with showing that there was a concept of continuing exile, however that is to be resolved in regard to the temple. Goldstein writes that although there were many who accepted the second temple as God's chosen place, there were also many who "held the Second Temple to be incompletely holy or even completely unfit for the offering of sacrifices" ("1 and 2 Maccabees," 70). Some dissatisfaction with the temple may have related to an expectation that the temple would be restored by a royal figure with Davidic credentials. As Wright suggests, "If the new age was not yet present, as it was not, any building that might happen to occupy the Temple mount could not possibly be the eschatological Temple itself. There was therefore a residual ambiguity about the second Temple in its various forms. Many Jews regarded it with suspicion and distrust" (*New Testament*, 225–226).

[195] On the hope for the gathering of the dispersed see Schürer, *History*, 2.530–531. Sanders summarizes these expectations: "In general, the visionaries looked forward to

longing for restoration/salvation can be translated into the concept of a continuing exile. However, the fact that the literature evinces a desire both for restoration and the gathering of Israel suggests that their contemporary situation was completely incompatible with the prophets' description of a restored Israel. Restoration would be unnecessary had the exile actually ended.[196]

To sum up: End-of-exile hope, whether it be for a renewed, restored, or rebuilt temple, for the restoration of the people of Israel, and/or for the beginning of God's reign on Mount Zion, is not limited to a few sectarian groups.[197] It is found in a wide variety of time periods (pre-Maccabean, pre-Roman, Roman), is geographically widespread (Palestine, diaspora), and is found in different genres of literature (apocalyptic,[198] psalms, pseudepigrapha, additions to Scripture, Scripture). It is found in sectarian writings such as Qumran[199] and in others which were representative of a wider readership. Although revealing wide variation in belief and emphasis in different groups and on the individual level, the literature nevertheless bears witness to a widespread view that Israel remained in a state of exile well after the sixth century, and that this would continue

---

the full restoration of Israel. Just what that meant would have varied from group to group and even from person to person, but there was a lot of common ground, and the main lines can be clearly discerned. The chief hopes were for the re-establishment of the twelve tribes; for the subjugation or conversion of the Gentiles; for a new, purified, or renewed and glorious temple; and for purity and righteousness in both worship and morals. . . . These four elements of the future hope were very common . . . The general hope for the restoration of the people of Israel is the most ubiquitous hope of all. . . . in any case the reassembly of the people of Israel was generally expected" (*Practice and Belief*, 289–290, 294; emphasis added).

[196] The fact that there is no festival mentioned in the OT or intertestamental literature to mark the end of the exile may reflect a perception that the restoration was incomplete. I recently became aware that P. Churgin advanced this observation many years before the current interest in the subject (see "The Period of the Second Temple: An Era of Exile"; cited in Eddy, "*Eschatological Prophet*," 45 n. 27).

[197] The evidence obviates L. T. Johnson's charge ("A Historiographical Response to Wright's Jesus," 210) that, although there are some Second Temple sources containing a theme concerning exile, it is a fallacy to impute such an understanding to the wider populace.

[198] See Scott ("Galatians," 206–207) for examples in the Apocalypse of Weeks in *1 En.* 91.11–17 and 93.1–10, and the Animal Apocalypse in *1 En.* 85–90.

[199] Knibb evaluates CD 1.3–11 as follows: "For the author the Jews had remained in a state of exile until the events in the second century which led to the foundation of the Qumran community; this, in turn, was to be the immediate prelude to the final judgement and the beginning of the Messianic era" ("Exile," 263). See also the Apostrophe to Zion in 11QPs[a] (text in Sanders, *The Dead Sea Psalms Scroll*, 123).

until Yahweh intervened decisively to inaugurate the eschatological era, restore his people and return to reign as king amongst them.[200]

B. Passover and Exodus

1. OT and Intertestamental

The Passover is inextricably linked with the exodus from Egypt, the latter providing a wealth of symbols related to deliverance from bondage that were taken up time and again in the OT and Judaism. There is little explicit evidence from OT and intertestamental literature pointing to an eschatological interpretation of Passover, although there are hints. The great eschatological vision of Ezek 40–48 that follows the promise of restoration in ch. 39 reinstitutes the festival of Passover in the purified temple (Ezek 45.21).[201] The Sin-Exile-Restoration pattern found in OT and intertestamental literature is linked with Passover in 2 Chr 30.1–9, where Hezekiah invites the remnant left in Israel to celebrate the Passover and by doing so to turn from their sin. Restoration from exile will follow for their brothers. Passover is associated with deliverance from distress, as seen in the joyful Passover celebration explicitly related to the favor the King of Assyria has shown the exiles (Ezra 6.22). The description of Passover in *Jub.* 49 associates the feast with healing, apparently providing protection for Israel until the comprehensive redemption that will take place at the final Jubilee.[202] Ezekiel the Tragedian's comments on Passover probably reflect a widespread association of the feast with a future hope of deliverance: "So keep this festival [Passover] unto the Lord; for seven days you'll eat unleavened bread. For there shall be

---

[200] Second temple writings that suggest continuing exile: CD 1.3–11; 1QM 2.2f.; 2.7f.; 3.13; 5.1; 11QT 8.14–16; 57.5f.; 29.8–10; Tob 13.5, 16–18; 14.4–7; Bar 1.13ff; 3.6–8; 4.5–5.9; 2 Macc 1.27–29; 2.7–8; 2.18; 3 Macc 6.10; Sir 35.11; 36.1–17; 48.10; *Jub.* 1.15–17, 24, 26–29; 25.21; *Pss. Sol.* 8.12, 34; 9; 11.2f; 17.28–31, 50; *L.A.E.* 29.4ff.; *Apoc. Ab.* 27; Pr Azar (LXX Dan 3.26–45); Philo, *Rewards* 94–97;162–172; *T. Jud.* 22.3; *1 En.* 63.3; 90.28f.; 91.13; *T. Mos.* 4.5; *T. Job* 4.11; *T. Benj.* 9.2; *T. Levi* 16.1–5; 17.10–11; 2 *Bar.* 68.5–7; *Sib. Or.* 3.702–20. Knibb argues that although the *Testaments of the Twelve Patriarchs* have been influenced by later Christian redaction, a pre-Christian pattern of Sin-Exile-Return can be determined in *T. Levi* 10; 14f.; 16; *T. Jud.* 18.1, 23; *T. Iss.* 6; *T. Zeb.* 9.5–9; *T. Dan* 5.4–13; *T. Naph.* 4.1–3; 4f.; and *T. Ash.* 7.2–4; 7.5–7. Knibb concludes: "The restoration to the land cannot, however, be understood in terms of the return from Babylon at the end of the sixth century, but was an event that lay in the future so far as the author of the Testaments was concerned" ("Exile," 264–265). On the gathering of the dispersed see Schürer, 2.530–531.

[201] See B. Bokser (*The Origins of the Seder: The Passover Rite and Early Rabbinic Judaism*, 17), who emphasizes the future aspect of the reinstitution of Passover.

[202] See especially *Jub.* 49.13, 15. Cf. Bokser, *Seder*, 20.

deliverance from these ills; a 'going forth' he'll grant you in this month, and first of months and years it e'er shall be."[203] This "going forth" and it being the "first" of months features prominently in rabbinic eschatological speculation.

2. Actualization of Passover

The traditions of the Passover celebration preserved in the Mishnah show that the original exodus experience was actualized for the present generation and relived by the participants.[204] The coupling of this pre-eminent biblical symbol of freedom and liberation with the hope (expectation) that Rome would be destroyed and the exile come to an end explains why the Passover feast was sometimes the stage for riots.[205] Josephus, in describing an uprising at Passover, shows that special military precautions were taken by the Romans at the feast: "A Roman cohort stood over the cloisters of the temple (for they always were armed and kept guard at the festivals, to prevent any innovation which the multitude thus gathered together might take)."[206] In addition to the symbolism surrounding Passover one should not neglect the emotive significance of pilgrimage. S. Safrai argues that most Jews did not make the pilgrimage to Jerusalem for the feasts regularly: "There were people who looked forward for years

---

[203] Ezek. Trag. 188–192 (emphasis added). R. G. Robertson ("Introduction to Ezekiel the Tragedian," 803–804) dates the writing to the first part of the second century BC.

[204] See *m. Pesah.* 10.5: "In every generation a person is duty–bound to regard himself as if he personally has gone forth from Egypt . . .."

[205] Cf. Sanders, *Practice and Belief*, 138; A. Finkel, "Comparative Exegesis: A Study of Hallel and Kerygma," 115. For NT examples of unrest at Passover see Jeremias, *Eucharistic Words*, 207. Bokser (*Seder*, 74–75) argues that aspects of early rabbinic Judaism which would not have been central to the pre-AD 70 Passover meal can be identified in the traditions preserved in Mishnah and Tosefta. These are the intellectual discussion of the celebration which moves from educating children to involving the participation of adults; the expounding of the text, which is in keeping with the growing importance of midrash and enables the participants "to relate more fully to the exodus experience and to see it as paradigmatic of their own situation"; the mention of redemption, which both highlights the destruction of the temple and raises the hope for change; and the recitation of seven blessings, which emphasizes the divine dimensions of the rite. However, against Bokser, there is no reason to believe that these emphases are somehow new innovations. Surely prior to AD 70 there was discussion at the meal, a realization by the participants that they were in need of a new deliverance, hope for change, and awareness of a deeper significance to the rituals. The rabbis may have built on these, but they were by no means necessarily new ways of thinking.

[206] *War* 2.224. For the larger context see *War* 2.223–227. See further the parallel in *Ant.* 20.105–117, with a fuller description of a second uprising following immediately after Passover.

to this pilgrimage, and the pilgrimage itself was a great spiritual experience for the individual and for his associates."[207] The modern-day Islamic *Haj* may provide an equivalent. No doubt the emotional aspect of pilgrimage intensified any expectations associated with the feast, making for a volatile mix.[208]

3. The Cup of Salvation and Coins

It is reasonable to suppose that Jewish coins minted at times of national independence or revolt are those most likely to include messianic and/or other symbols of restoration, for it is at these times that heightened expectation would have combined with the possibility of such minting.[209] Consequently, coins of these periods may be significant for discovering symbols with messianic associations. Roth points to a series of nine coins from the First Revolt which have a jeweled chalice on them. It is also found on two earlier coins issued by Simon Hasmonaeus. Significantly, this figure does not appear on any extant coins of other periods. As it is found only in periods of heightened messianic awareness this suggests it is a messianic symbol. Roth claims that the contemporary Jew would easily have identified the object and realized that it represented the "the classical Cup of Salvation so clearly associated with Redemption" and prompted by Ps 116.[210] The link with Ps 116 is likely, since the psalm includes the only biblical example of the phrase "cup of salvation." As one of the Hallel Psalms it was closely tied to Passover.

The cup of salvation also figures prominently in rabbinic traditions, where it is interpreted eschatologically and especially related to Passover symbolism.[211] This may continue what is already suggested by the pre-rabbinic messianic symbolism attached to the cup. In the rabbinics the

---

[207] Safrai, "Pilgrimage," 19–20. He points out that nowhere in the Tannaitic literature is it stated that every Jew must make the pilgrimage in person on each of the three feasts.

[208] Note that this is not limited to Passover. Tabernacles also attracted many pilgrims and eschatological speculation, so the same mix of emotion and hope for deliverance would be present.

[209] Cf. Roth, "Messianic Symbols," 160. Roth suggests that only at three periods may one anticipate such symbols on Jewish coinage: the Hasmonean revolt which issued coins under Simon after 142 BC; the First Jewish Revolt in AD 66–70; and the revolt led by Bar Kochba during AD 132–135.

[210] Roth, "Messianic Symbols," 160–161. Roth effectively counters arguments that identify the cup as a pot of manna, the covered cup used for the wine-libation, or as a symbol of high priestly dignity. He also finds support for a messianic interpretation of other symbols appearing on coins of the same period.

[211] See for example *Gen. Rab.* 88.5.

four cups of Passover are given an allegorical interpretation in terms of redemption, the final destruction of Israel's enemies, and the messianic salvation. The Ps 116 cup is most closely connected to future redemption and represents the salvation that God will give the righteous in the world to come.[212] In several passages it is part of the four cups, but usually is thought to be plural and thus represents two cups.[213] The four are the cups of deliverance that God will give Israel, the cups of consolation of the time-to-come.[214] The Talmud preserves a tradition of an eschatological banquet (possibly including Passover symbolism) where David takes the cup of salvation and pronounces the grace.[215] If this allegorizing reflects earlier traditions then it would substantiate Jeremias' argument that the elements of the meal "combine a looking back over the history of God's saving activity in the past with a looking forward to the saving event of the Messianic future."[216] It is not clear whether the eschatological interpretation of the four cups witnessed in the rabbinics depends on previous traditions, although this is possible.[217] What one can plausibly suggest is that the cup of salvation of Ps 116 probably had eschatological-messianic associations in Second Temple Judaism. Its special link with Passover would only enhance the inherent themes of liberation already present in both psalm and feast.

---

[212] *Exod. Rab.* 25.9.

[213] As a note of interest, it is usually last, representing the third and fourth cups. The second part of the Hallel, which includes Ps 116, was sung following the third and fourth cups (cf. *m. Pesah.* 10.7).

[214] Respectively, *Midr. Ps.* 11.5 and *Midr. Ps.* 75.4.

[215] See *b. Pesah.* 119b: "R. Awira lectured [in the name of R. Ammi and/or R. Assi]: . . . The Holy One, blessed be He will make a great banquet for the righteous on the day He manifests His love to the seed of Isaac. After they have eaten and drunk, the cup of Grace will be offered [in turn, to Abraham, Isaac, Jacob, Moses, and Joshua, that one of them recite Grace, but they all turn it down for a variety of reasons]. Then David will be asked: 'Take it and say grace.' 'I will say Grace, and it is fitting for me to say Grace,' he will reply, as it is said, *I will lift up the cup of salvation, and call upon the name of the Lord* [Ps 116.13]."

[216] Jeremias, *Eucharistic Words*, 259. He also argues that there was an eschatological interpretation of the bread. Although rabbinic traditions do substantiate this claim, there is no evidence – apart from the cumulative case being made that Passover had eschatological association – showing that this depends on pre-rabbinic traditions. For eschatological interpretations of bread see *Gen. Rab.* 88.6; *Song Rab.* 1.7.3.

[217] The Ps 116 cup may have led to similar eschatological associations with the four cups of Passover, the dependence may have been reversed, perhaps there was no dependence in any direction, or possibly in both. Certainly Passover themes of liberation would have supported an eschatological/allegorical interpretation, and the rabbinics may simply develop these.

C. The Hallel and Passover

1. The Sacrifice and Evening Meal

The singing/repetition of the Hallel was an integral part of the liturgical experience during Passover, so much so that the feast would be incomplete without it. In a discussion over why the Hallel must be sung at the sacrifice on both the first and second Passovers, even though there are different requirements for the second, the rhetorical question is asked, "What is the reason? ... is it possible that Israel should sacrifice their Passover-offerings or take their palm-branches without reciting *Hallel*!"[218] The answer obviously is no. The Mishnah preserves the function of the Hallel at the Passover sacrifice performed on the afternoon of the fourteenth of Nisan.

> The Passover (offering) is slaughtered (by people divided into) three groups ... (When) the first group entered, the courtyard was packed, (then) the doors of the courtyard were locked. . . . An Israelite slaughtered (the Passover lamb) and a priest received the blood, hands it to his fellow, and his fellow to his fellow (each one) receiving a full basin and handing back an empty one. The priest nearest to the altar tosses (the blood) in a single act of tossing, toward the base. The first group went out and the second group came in. The second group went out and the third group came in. In accord with the rite of the first group were the rites of the second and third. (The Levites meanwhile) proclaimed the Hallel psalms (113–118). If they completed (the recitation), they repeated it, and if they completed it the second time, they repeated it for a third – even though they never in all their days had to repeat it a third time. R. Judah says, "In all the days of the third group they never even reached the verse, I love the Lord because he has heard my voice (Ps 116:1), because its numbers were small." (*m. Pesah.* 5.5–7)[219]

Thus the Hallel was closely associated with the sacrifice and preparation for the evening feast. It was at this time that tens of thousands would fill the Temple Court under the watchful eye of Roman soldiers. One of the main themes of the Hallel is thanksgiving for national and personal deliverance, and Ps 118 depicts a royal figure who has emerged victorious in battle against the nations. Sung in the Passover context, these psalms could not have failed to bring to mind thoughts of hope and redemption.

---

[218] *b. Pesah.* 95b. The second Passover is held a month after the first, specifically for those who were unable to celebrate due to ceremonial uncleanness or travel. Cf. *m. Pesah.* 9.3.

[219] Cf. parallel in *t. Pesah.* 4.10–11.

The Hallel also figured prominently in the evening meal,[220] the night of
the fifteenth, also preserved in the Mishnah.

> To what point does one say (Hallel)? The House of Shammai say, "To *A
> joyful mother of children* (Ps. 113:9)." And the House of Hillel say, "To *A
> flintstone into a springing well* (Ps. 114:8)." And he concludes with
> (a formula of) Redemption. R. Tarfon says, "'. . . who redeemed us and
> redeemed our forefathers from Egypt.' And he did not say a concluding
> benediction." R. Aqiba says, "'. . . So, Lord, our God, and God of our
> fathers, bring us in peace to other appointed times and festivals, rejoicing
> in the rebuilding of your city and joyful in your Temple worship, where
> may we eat of the animal sacrifices and Passover offerings,' etc., up to,
> 'Blessed are you, Lord, who has redeemed Israel.'" They mixed the third
> cup for him. He says a blessing for his food. (And at) the fourth, he com-
> pletes the *Hallel* and says after it the grace of song.
> (*m. Pesah.* 10.6–7)

The Hallel was led by one person with the other participants responding.
Several different options are found in the literature, but it is most likely
that, when an adult led, every phrase was followed by the repetition of
Hallelujah. The practice at the temple was probably similar, with the
Levites leading, and would apply to Tabernacles as well as Passover. However, it is possible that the leader and respondents alternated phrases.[221]
The placing of the Hallel in the meal may be significant in suggesting
eschatologizing tendencies. The recitation of Hallel begins immediately
following, and is considered the appropriate response to, the prayer that
actualizes through the Passover meal the exodus for the present generation: Because of the redemption God has accomplished, "We should
say before him, Hallelujah."[222] The first part of the Hallel is then recited

---

[220] For support that singing (i.e. Hallel) closes the Passover meal see further 2 Chr
30.21; Wis 18.8–9 (possibly also 10.18–20); Philo, *Spec. Laws* 2.148; *Jub.* 49.6.

[221] *m. Sukk.* 3.10; *m. Sotah* 5.4; *t. Pesah.* 10.6; *t. Sotah* 6.2–3; *b. Sotah* 30b; *b. Sukk.*
38a. The Tosefta offers several options. When a child leads every line has to be repeated. When an adult leads everyone responds with either "Hallelujah," with the leading
phrase/word of each psalm, or by alternating phrases. It seems likely that the hallelujah
practice was prevalent, but the latter option explains the division of Ps 118 into antiphonal parts in the Targum, Midrash, and Talmud (*b. Pesah.* 119a). The Hallel in the
Tabernacles temple practice would also be recited responsively, and with the repetition
of verses.

[222] See *m. Pesah.* 10.5: "In every generation a person is duty–bound to regard
himself as if he personally has gone forth from Egypt, since it is said, *And you shall tell
your son in that day saying, It is because of that which the Lord did for me when I came
forth out of Egypt* (Ex. 13:8). Therefore we are duty-bound to thank, praise, glorify,
honor, exalt, extol, and bless him who did it for our forefathers and for us all these
miracles. He brought us forth from slavery to freedom, anguish to joy, mourning to
festival, darkness to great light, subjugation to redemption, so we should say before him,

(Ps 113 and possibly 114). Psalm 113 opens with *Praise Yahweh, O servants of Yahweh*, a phrase that in rabbinic traditions is associated with deliverance: "We were Pharaoh's servants and Thou didst redeem us, and make us Thy servants. Therefore it is said *Praise, O ye servants of the Lord*, and not 'Praise, O ye servants of Pharaoh.'"[223]

A similar association is found in a rabbinic discussion over where it is appropriate to say Hallel and where not (i.e., outside of Israel): "There is a good reason in that case (of the Exodus from Egypt) because it says (in the Hallel), *Praise ye O servants of the Lord*, who are no longer servants of Pharaoh. But can we say in this case, Praise ye, servants of the Lord and not servants of Ahasuerus? We are still servants of Ahasuerus!"[224] Subsequently they give the ruling that the Hallel should be sung only in the land of Israel (in freedom), but it is also permissible to sing it in exile. Thus the Hallel's beginning phrase was most appropriately sung as *servants of Yahweh* and not of another power. For those in bondage the phrase would stimulate the hope of redemption, when they would be able to sing as servants of Yahweh with no self-conscious inconsistency. The following psalm (114) would only emphasize this as it recalls the exodus, the crossing of the Red Sea, the election of Israel at Sinai, and the entry to Canaan. The recitation of Pss 113 and 114 ends with a prayer of redemption,[225] so that "the retrospect invites the prospect of future deliverance."[226] Perhaps there is a hint of this in the joy associated with Passover. "There was (only) as much as an olive of the Passover-offering, yet the Hallel split the roofs!"[227]

The disagreement between the schools of Hillel and Shammai over whether the first part of the recitation of the Hallel included Ps 114 may support such a reading. Finkel suggests that the Hillelites looked at Pss 113 and 114 as remembering saving acts of the past, and separated them from the rest of the Hallel (Pss 115–118) as the latter "came to dramatize the future redemption." Thus the real reason for the division is an eschatological interpretation of the second half of the Hallel (especially

---

Hallelujah." Note that Danby translates the last phrase as "so let us say before him the *Hallelujah*," understanding it as a clear reference to begin the Hallel.

[223] *Midr. Ps.* 113.1.

[224] *b. Meg.* 14a. Cf. *b. 'Arak.* 10b; *Pesiq. Rab.* 2.1. There is no reason to think that Ps 113 was understood differently in pre-rabbinic Judaism. Surely singing as "Servants of Yahweh," and following this with Ps 114's summary of God's redeeming acts on Israel's behalf in the past, would have highlighted the present sad state under Roman rule.

[225] See *m. Pesah.* 10.6.

[226] Moore, *Judaism*, 2.42.

[227] *b. Pesah.* 86b. In other words, the Hallel was sung with great gusto. Passover is associated with an emphasis on joy in *Jub.* 49 as well.

Ps 116) by the Hillelites.[228] The Hillel school did interpret Ps 116 es-chatologically, as shown in the argument with the House of Shammai concerning the day of judgment,[229] and rabbinic writings bear witness to a widespread eschatological interpretation of all the Hallel psalms, especially those of the second half of the Hallel. However, apart from the early example of Ps 116, the evidence for a division on eschatological grounds is complicated by the late date of the sources. Three rabbinic passages seem to support a move within the Hallel from past to future focus. The Hallel tells of "God's wondrous works in days gone by, in present times, in the days of the Messiah, in the times of Gog and Magog, and in the time-to-come."[230] References to the past stop after Ps 114, and most interpretations with a future emphasis are found in Ps 116 and Ps 118. It is not clear that Finkel's argument is sustainable, as there may be other reasons for the division,[231] but it offers a possible and plausible solution.[232]

2. The Hallel and Internal Passover Themes

While Ps 118 is especially appropriate to and linked with Tabernacles, the Hallel as a group is most closely associated with Passover.[233] This is true not only functionally, as seen in the liturgy, but also thematically. The most obvious thematic link is Ps 114's evocation of the exodus, wilderness, and conquest experience. The last two verses (114.7–8) allow for a repetition of these acts in a new exodus.[234] Ps 115 suggests a time of distress for Israel, with the assertion that God will deliver his people and vindicate his name. Psalm 116 remembers a great deliverance from bondage (exodus?),

---

[228] Finkel, "Comparative Exegesis," 116.

[229] *b. Roš Haš.* 16b–17a; *t. Sanh.* 13.3.

[230] *Midr. Ps.* 26.6. See parallel in *Pesiq. Rab.* 51.7. Also *Lev. Rab.* 30.5.

[231] For example, Finkelstein ("Hallel," 327) argues that the different traditions of the Shammai and Hillel schools display the influence of political considerations during the years of changing Seleucid and Ptolomeic control.

[232] In support of Finkel, the focus of eschatological interpretations of Hallel Psalms in rabbinic writings centers on Pss 115–118. The internal relationships of the Hallel group support this trend, as they do move from celebrating God's acts in history towards the exaltation and vindication of God's servant. Thus it is not implausible that "the separation of Pss 115–118 from the Passover meal served the celebrants in the dramatization of future redemption" (Finkel, "Comparative Exegesis," 117).

[233] Cf. Kissane, 522–543; Mays, 361–381; and R. Hammer, "Two Liturgical Psalms: Salvation and Thanksgiving."

[234] Cf. Kissane, 525. Kissane (523) suggestively argues that that Ps 113.9, with its figure of a barren wife who is made fruitful, parallels Isaiah's use of the image to describe the contrast between Israel in exile and the eschatological new Zion of Isa 54.1 and 56.8. Cf. Mays, 362–363.

and Ps 117 recalls the mercy of Yahweh, perhaps related to his election of Israel. Whether these psalms were written specifically for Passover or not, they contain themes (e.g., election, deliverance from bondage, salvation) and imagery (e.g., cup of salvation, exodus) which make them especially appropriate for use at the festival.

3. Psalm 118 and Exodus Themes

Psalm 118 provided the climax to the Hallel and the high point of the liturgy and ritual of the Passover meal. It was common practice to repeat a second time either from Ps 118.21–29 or Ps 118.25–29.[235] This accentuates the importance of Ps 118 in the liturgy, and if there were any eschatological interpretation of the psalm, especially of the last verses, this section would have received heightened emphasis and provided a climactic experience for the celebrants. Although Ps 118 is most closely linked to Tabernacles, it contains a number of exodus parallels and associations which make it very suitable to a Passover context.[236] This is most clearly seen in connection to the Song of the Sea sung by Moses and Israel after they had escaped Pharaoh's army (Exod 15.1–18), of which Mays writes, "The psalm is understood as a text that speaks of the salvation on which the existence of the community is based . . . the exodus and all that symbol represents."[237] Strongest is the verbal connection: Exod 15.2a is quoted directly in Ps 118.14 and alluded to in Ps 118.21, and the psalm concludes with an allusion to Exod 15.2b in Ps 118.28. R. Hammer not implausibly argues that the central section of Ps 118 is deliberately patterned after the Song in its use of anachronistic language and the "rhythm and sound" of its short verses, reflections which were confirmed to the reader through the clear verbal similarities between the passages. In this regard he plausibly suggests a further echo – a paraphrase – of Exod 15.6 in Ps 118.15–16.[238] Mays further shows that Ps 118 speaks of salvation in language that also appears in the introduction leading up to the Song, and points to shared themes such as God's prowess in defeating the enemy and confidence in God's salvation even in the face of hostile nations. He justifiably concludes, "All these repetitions and relationships can be taken as directives that Ps 118 is to be read and understood

---

[235] *b. Pesah.* 119b.

[236] Note that although the exodus is connected with Passover in Exod 23–24, Tabernacles represents the exodus in Lev 23.43. Thus the exodus parallels are very appropriate for a psalm that was originally associated with Tabernacles.

[237] Mays, "Psalm 118," 137.

[238] Hammer, "Two Liturgical Psalms," 491–492, 495. Mays ("Psalm 118," 141) suggests that Ps 118.15–16 echoes Exod 15.6 *and* 15.12.

in light of the situation of Israel and of Israel's song in Exodus 14–15."[239]

The result of this intertextual linkage is to define one of the psalm's hermeneutical horizons.[240] Apart from Ps 118's links to Exod 14–15, a point of interest is the use of *Yah* as God's name. It appears in 42 verses in the OT, of which 25 are in chapters or psalms with exodus links. Of the 27 chapters referring to *Yah*, 15 have an exodus echo or association, giving a similar percentage in its distribution.[241] It appears that Yah is used around sixty percent of the time in passages related to the exodus. The fact that Ps 118 includes a disproportionate amount of these bolsters its exodus links.[242]

D. Passover, New Exodus and the Hallel in the Rabbinics

Although one is inclined to agree with Jeremias' claim that the Passover celebration is both retrospect and prospect, "a looking forward to the coming deliverance of which the deliverance from Egypt is the prototype,"[243] he is open to criticism because of heavy (almost exclusive) dependence on rabbinic evidence.[244] This study has attempted to build a cumulative case, without resorting to rabbinic statements, for the plausibility of eschatological interpretations being linked to Passover pre-AD 70. The eschatologization of Passover in the rabbinics may not provide a mirror image of pre-70 interpretation, but neither is it complete innovation. The roots from which it grew were already well planted in the fertile soil of intertestamental expectations. In some areas, such as the continuing state of exile and the use of exodus imagery to symbolize deliverance, there is clear continuity with earlier traditions. Speculation concerning the

---

[239] See Mays, "Psalm 118," 140–141. The similarities in the introduction to the Song and salvation language in Ps 118 are in Exod 14.11, 30–31 and Ps 118.7, 14, 17, 21, 24–25.

[240] Cf. J. L. Mays, "The Question of Context," 19. Brueggemann, commenting on Mays' intertextual approach, acknowledges that "these poems – cultic or instructive – live in the world of Israel's memories and Israel's rhetoric. . . . Such allusions and connections are what we would expect in this on-going act of re-symbolization" ("Response to Mays," 36).

[241] Exod 15; 17; Isa 12 (quotes Exod 15); Pss 68; 77; 105; 106; 113; 115; 116; 117; 118; 135; 149; 150. The latter two do not deal specifically with the exodus, but they do echo language from the Song.

[242] It has 7/46 of the total occurrences of the word, and 5/42 of the verses in which it is found. The Hallel on the whole is also over-represented. Of the 15 "Yah" chapters with exodus links, five are Hallel psalms (Pss 113, 115–118).

[243] Jeremias, *Eucharistic Words*, 206.

[244] See for example his extensive list of references to rabbinic writings in *Eucharistic Words*, 206–207.

Passover as time for deliverance and Messiah's coming is not attested in pre-rabbinic literature. However, neither is it inconsistent with the direction of intertestamental thought. As such, although we do not submit rabbinic literautre as evidence for the intertestamental eschatologization of Passover, it may preserve earlier traditions and at the least suggests possibilities.

Recognition of a state of continuing exile is evident in the literature, expanding and confirming the theme found so often in biblical and intertestamental literature. In a discourse over why the exodus must be mentioned at night, there is a discussion of the prophecy in Jer 23.7, 8 where a new exodus is promised, one that will replace the exodus from Egypt as the paradigmatic deliverance for Israel. That this prophecy remained unfulfilled is obvious, and the rabbis place it in the future.[245] A state of continuing exile is also assumed in the following comment: "R. Nahman, R. Eliezer ben Jose and R. Aha, commented . . . My children, here in Egypt you are to have a new and unprecedented experience in redemption. And according to the others: Here you are to have a completely new experience *which you will have again only in the time-to-come.*"[246] The exodus from Egypt is the pattern for the exodus from the current exile. That this deliverance will take place only once besides the original exodus, and that it is in the future, supports the argument that Israel had not returned from exile. This expectation of a new exodus, and the fact that it is patterned after the first exodus, helps explain the swirl of eschatological interpretations associated with Passover.

Passover night is associated with great events, deliverances, and acts of salvation. In Nisan (the month of Passover and the exodus) the world was created and the patriarchs were born and died. "In Nisan they [Israel in Egypt] were redeemed and in Nisan they will be redeemed in the time to come."[247] Passover is the day Joseph was released from captivity, and on that night God saved Hezekiah, Hananiah and his companions, and Daniel

---

[245] See *b. Ber.* 12b: "Ben Zoma said to the Sages: Will the Exodus from Egypt be mentioned in the days of the Messiah? Was it not long ago said: [quotation of Jer 23.7,8]. They replied: This does not mean that the mention of the exodus from Egypt shall be obliterated, but that the (deliverance from) subjection to the other kingdoms shall take the first place and the exodus from Egypt shall become secondary."

[246] *Pesiq. Rab.* 15.22 (emphasis added). The redemption from Egypt and the redemption of the future are dealt with in the context of the phrase "This month shall be unto you the beginning of months" (Exod 12.2), which was a springboard for rabbinic speculation. The larger context is a comparison of things that will happen in the time-to-come as they did at the exodus.

[247] *b. Roš Haš.* 11a–b.

from the lion's den.[248] On that night Abraham fought against Og and the four kings.[249] Since God acted precisely at midnight on Passover, and this is when miraculous deliverances for Israel took place, David chose to rise at that time to study Torah and thank God for the judgments that he carries out on that night.[250] It is also the time that God will choose to punish Rome, even as he punished Egypt.[251] This highlights what Braude calls "the recurring rhythm in Jewish history of deliverance at the midnight of Passover."[252]

Underlying this excitement surrounding Passover seems to be the Jewish expectation that the way God has worked in the past is the way he will work in the future, so that the Passover meal eaten before the exodus from Egypt prefigures the Passover meal which will precede the final redemption. The Targums on Exodus preserve a tradition of four nights, linked to Passover, on which God acts.

> It is a night reserved and set aside for redemption to the name of the Lord at the time the children of Israel were brought out redeemed from the land of Egypt. Truly, four nights are those that are written in the Book of Memorials. . . . The third night: when the Lord was revealed against the Egyptians at midnight; ... The fourth night: when the world reaches its appointed time to be redeemed: the iron yokes shall be broken and the generations of wickedness shall be blotted out, and Moses will go up from the midst of the desert and the king Messiah from the midst of Rome. One will lead at the head of the flock, and the other will lead at the head of the flock, and his Memra will lead between the two of them, and I and they will proceed together. *This is the night of the Passover to the name of the Lord: it is a night reserved and set aside for the redemption of all Israel, throughout their generations.*[253]

The new exodus is patterned on the exodus from Egypt. The exile motif is clearer in *Targum Pseudo-Jonathan*, where it is the night reserved for their deliverance "from their exiles throughout their generations."[254] It is hardly surprising, then, to find that the Messiah is expected on Passover night: "Then will Messiah who is called *'first'* come in the first month."[255] In

---

[248] *Exod. Rab.* 18.12. See also *Pesiq. Rab.* 17.4; 49.

[249] *Tg. Ps.-J.* Gen 14.13.

[250] *Pesiq. Rab.* 17.1

[251] *Pesiq. Rab.* 17.4; 49.9. See also *Tg. Neof.* Exod 12.41–42.

[252] Braude, "Introduction to Pesikta Rabbati," 1.13. See especially Piska 17 and 49. For a thorough discussion of this tradition see R. Le Déaut, *La nuit pascale: Essai sur la signification de la Pâque juive à partir du Targum d'Exode XII 42.*

[253] *Tg. Neof.* Exod 12.41–42 (emphasis added). Cf. the parallel passage *Tg. Ps.-J.* Exod 12.42. See also *Pesiq. Rab.* 15.3, 25.

[254] *Tg. Ps.-J.* Exod 12.42.

[255] *Exod. Rab.* 15.1.

fact, according to *Exodus Rabba*, the redemption will take place on that
night and no other.[256]

The Hallel Psalms, so closely linked to the themes and liturgy of
Passover, are associated with the first Passover as well. In comparing the
Passover in Egypt with contemporary practice, the Tosefta preserves that
"the Passover observed in Egypt requires song," namely the Hallel, even
as all the subsequent Passovers have required it.[257] Similar traditions
claim that when Pharaoh came to beg Moses and Aaron to take Israel and
leave Egypt he found that "they (the Israelites) were reciting the Hallel."[258]
Tradition also states that Moses and Israel recited the Hallel when they
came out of the sea. R. Jose settles a dispute over this matter by suggesting the unthinkable in a rhetorical statement: "Is it possible that Israel
slaughtered their Passover-offerings or took their palm branches without
uttering song!"[259] Although this is historicizing, the linking of the Hallel
with the first Passover and subsequent exodus probably reflects early
traditions and accentuates its significance both in the festival liturgy and
in the popular imagination.[260]

Conclusion

We have argued that many Jews understood themselves as living in a state
of exile that would not be lifted until God intervened to restore them and
establish his universal reign. In this context Passover, the paradigmatic
symbol of biblical deliverance, was looked at as the pattern for a new
exodus or liberation. Although in the OT (Ezek, Ezra, 2 Chr) there are
only hints of an eschatological interpretation of Passover, *Jubilees* and
Ezekiel the Tragedian reflect what was probably a widespread association

---

[256] See *Exod. Rab.* 18.11–12: "and on that night [Passover] Messiah and Elijah will
be made great; . . . So Israel has eagerly awaited salvation since the rising of Edom [i.e.,
Rome]. God said: 'Let this sign be in your hands: on the day when I wrought salvation
for you, and on that very night know that I will redeem you; but if it is not this night,
then do not believe, for the time has not yet come.'"

[257] *t. Pesah.* 8.22.

[258] *Exod. Rab.* 18.10.

[259] *b. Pesah.* 117a. Note the similarity between this and *b. Pesah.* 95b, where a
variant of the same argument is used to explain the requirement that Hallel be sung at the
sacrifices of both the first and second Passovers. I suggest that the interesting
conjunction of Passover and palm branches in both these passages does not reflect the
use of the branches at Passover. Rather, it rhetorically asserts that it is as inconceivable
for Passover to be unaccompanied by the Hallel as it would be to celebrate Tabernacles
without the Hallel and palm branches.

[260] For example, Wis 18.8–9 refers to the singing that accompanied Passover before
the exodus, and Wis 10.18–20 probably describes the singing of Hallel at the Red Sea.
See also *m. Sotah* 5.4; *t. Sotah* 6.2–3.

of the feast with a future hope of deliverance. Rabbinic literature represents a natural expansion of such traditions in portraying Passover as the occasion on which God has often acted on Israel's behalf, and expecting the future redemption and return of Messiah to take place at the feast. The Hallel was inseparably linked with Passover, both in the sacrifice and meal, and in the rabbinic literature was the feast's preeminent symbol. The sequence of the Hallel in the evening meal supports eschatologizing tendencies, since it is designated as the appropriate response to the prayer that actualizes the original exodus experience for the present generation. An example of this is the appearance of the cup of salvation, taken from Ps 116 and associated with Passover, as a symbol of restoration on Jewish coins of the First Revolt. Psalm 118, which contains a number of exodus parallels and allusions to the Song of the Sea (Exod 14–15), provided the climax to the Hallel and the Passover meal. It is difficult to imagine that the Hallel – and Ps 118 in particular – would not have been seen as symbols of future redemption.

IV. The Hallel

A. *Popularity in Judaism*

In the rabbinical writings Pss 113–118 are given the title "Hallel," although they are known also as the "Egyptian Hallel" in order to distinguish them from Ps 136 (sometimes called the "Great Hallel"), and from Pss 146–150.[261] They were recited on 8 days at Tabernacles, at the Passover sacrifice and meal, the first day of the Festival of Weeks (Pentecost), and 8 days at Dedication. They were recited at least 18 days a year, in some places 21 days, and in Babylon as many as 24 days plus on New Moons.[262]

---

[261] For the Hallel as "Egyptian" see *b. Ber.* 56a. For Pss 145–150 as Hallel see *b. Šabb.* 118b. For Ps 136 as "Great Hallel" see *b. Pesah.* 118a; *t. Ta'an.* 3.5. For a general introduction to the Hallel see L. N. Dembitz, "Hallel," 6.176–177.

[262] There are some differences in the practice of the Diaspora, where the Hallel is recited on nine days at Tabernacles, two days of Passover, and two days of Pentecost. The Babylonian practice added the recitation of the partial Hallel (the Hallel without Pss 115.1–11 and 116.1–11) on the days of the New Moon and for the last six days of Passover. See *b. 'Arak.* 10a; *t. Sukk.* 3.2; *b. Ta'an.* 28b. For discussion of the different practices see Zeitlin, "Hallel," esp. 22–28. On the partial Hallel of Babylon, Finkelstein argues that Pss 115.1–11 and 116.1–11 were additions to those psalms during pre-Maccabean and Maccabbean victories respectively. The Babylonian Hallel omits them because they resisted adding to the traditional temple liturgy, and thus sung them only on days when they were not sung at the temple: "They were willing to sing it in the

Their use at the major festivals, and in an especially prominent way at Tabernacles and Passover, is sufficient to show the importance they were accorded. Perhaps because of these associations they gained a place in the Jewish heart and imagination that few other Scripture passages could match.

It is likely that many Jews knew the Hallel by heart. Constant repetition no doubt helped to cement these psalms in the mind, and it is likely that first-century Jews placed a great deal more emphasis on memory than moderns do.[263] Wright is not far off when he suggests that the Hallel psalms "would have formed an important part of the mental furniture of the average Jew."[264] It is possible that the Hallel formed part of children's education in the schools. The Tosefta accepts as a matter of fact that children recite the Hallel: "How did they say that song? Like a child who recites the Hallel in school."[265] Commenting on the role of the scribe, M. Bar-Ilan writes that one of their main sources of income came from teaching, for which the scribe needed to provide his students with "teaching material." He did this by writing for them little scrolls that contained short passages from the Bible, among the more popular being Genesis, Leviticus, the Hallel (Pss 113–118) and the Shema (Deut 6.4–9; 11.13–21).[266] Thus the Hallel may have been a "textbook" to be studied. Zeitlin further suggests it was considered important in their education because of its emphasis on the election of Israel, the exodus, and redemption.[267] Although the evidence may be late, it is not implausible that the Hallel was considered significant enough to feature in children's education, and that the Hallel psalms were known from an early age.

---

synagogue only on those festive days on which it was not used in the Temple itself – namely, the New Moons and the last six days of Passover" (Finkelstein, "Hallel," 337).

[263] See Stanley, "Social Environment"; P. J. Achtemeier, "*Omne verbum sonat*: The New Testament and the Oral Environment of Late Western Antiquity." Finkelstein makes an important point in his assessment of the significant role that Scripture, the Psalms in general, and more specifically the Hallel played in shaping and forming the worldview of the society in which they were used: "When we recall that the lessons prepared for oral recitation on the Passover, and particularly the hymns, played a far more important part in the mental make-up of a people which had no access to printed books than similar selections might today, we will realize why every word was carefully weighed in these ceremonials. . . . It was important because the selections and poems recited on the Passover constituted what we would call effective adult education. The passages were recited again and again, the poems were sung and repeated throughout the country; and inevitably the ideas they conveyed became part and parcel of the people's thought" ("Hallel," 327).

[264] Wright, *New Testament*, 241.

[265] *t. Sot.* 6.2. See further Str-B 1.853–854.

[266] A. Demsky and M. Bar-Ilan, "Writing in Ancient Israel and Early Judaism," 23.

[267] Zeitlin, "Hallel," 27.

The Hallel was also very popular, apparently more so than the Torah or Prophets. A rabbinic passage gives strict rules on the number of people who can be involved in the reading and translation (i.e. of the Targum) of the Torah and the Prophets in public meetings: For the Torah, one can read and only one translate, and for the Prophets only one reads and at the most two may translate. In contrast, "As regards Hallel and the Megillah, even ten may read (and ten may translate). What is the reason? Since the people like it [lit. "it is beloved"], they pay attention and hear."[268] Apparently the Hallel stimulates enthusiastic participation, revealing not only familiarity with but also affection for these psalms. When R. Jose seeks to describe a state of blessedness he says, "May my portion be of those who recite the entire *Hallel* every day."[269] However, others question his statement on the grounds that, because the Hallel is instituted for special occasions, reciting it every day would be to treat it as common and diminish its dignity and status, so much so that "he who reads *Hallel* every day blasphemes and reproaches (the Divine Name)."[270] It is unlikely that the recitation of the Hallel was confined to the festivals, but this does show that while popular it was also considered sacred. Its unique status is confirmed by L. Rabinowitz in his comments on the Psalms and their use in rabbinic literature and liturgy: although there was a "gradual penetration" of the psalm into the liturgy, "In the talmudic period the statutory prayers included no psalms whatsoever on Sabbaths and weekdays, and the only psalms recited were the Hallel."[271] There were few Scripture passages that were recited as often as the Hallel, and none but the Hallel was specifically associated with each of the main festivals. All of this points to a high recognition factor for its psalms, assuring that allusions to them would resonate at a pitch that many could pick up on and appreciate, thereby effectively bringing into play a complex of associations and ideas already linked with them in the Jewish mind.

---

[268] *b. Meg.* 21b. Although this may be an anachronistic statement it would not be inconsistent with the attachment one could expect to find for a Scripture so often repeated and so significant in the liturgy of the major festivals.

[269] *b. Šabb.* 118b.

[270] *b. Šabb.* 118b. The critical note explains that because its recital was instituted for special occasions only, by reading it every day one treats it as a mere song.

[271] Rabinowitz, "The Book of Psalms: In the Talmud and Midrash and in the Liturgy," 13.1323.

Date

The date of the gathering of the Hallel is unclear. Finkelstein distinguishes between what he calls the "Egyptian Hallel" (Pss 113–114) and the "Complete Hallel" (including Pss 115–118), arguing that during the persecutions of Antiochus, when the Passover could not be celebrated in Jerusalem, the songs of pilgrimage which had been sung in the temple were used along with the traditional Passover psalms (i.e., Pss 113–114). When the temple was rededicated, the liturgy which had developed during the persecution was formalized as a unit and subsequently sung at all the feasts in celebration of the deliverance that had taken place.[272] However, he also suggests that the Hallel as a complete unit developed some time between the middle of the third century BC and 164 BC.[273] Zeitlin argues that the Hallel was composed during the Persian period or earlier,[274] and Goulder that the larger unit of Pss 107–118 was initially used for the Passover of Ezra 6.[275] It is, however, unlikely that the Hallel was composed as a unit. Much more probable is that individual psalms with compatible themes were brought together. As for when this happened, Finkelstein's suggestions, although plausible, are inconclusive, and it is possible that the unit was used at a much earlier date, as Goulder and Zeitlin claim. There is no clear date for the gathering of the Hallel, and little research has focused on the question, but at the latest it was well established as a unit by the Hasmonean period.

---

[272] Finkelstein, "Hallel," 333–334.

[273] Finkelstein, "Hallel," 322–323. Finkelstein argues that the recitation of the complete Hallel at Hanukkah furnishes a *terminus ad quem* for its origin. For a *terminus a quo* he argues that Ps 115 contains a theological argument over immortality which was at its height in the middle of the third century BC

[274] Zeitlin, "Hallel," 24.

[275] M. D. Goulder, *The Psalms of the Return (Book V, Psalms 107–150): Studies in the Psalter, IV.* He suggests the Passover of Ezra 6 as the initial use. B. Wacholder argues for an early date for the liturgical use of the Hallel unit, although he does not set a date for compilation: "Ezra-Nehemiah and Chronicles repeatedly employ the verb root *hll* in several interesting nominal and verbal formations such as in the formula *lehodot ulehallel.* This clause is all too often obscured by the English rendition of 'to thank and to extol.' It actually seems to signify 'to recite the *hodu* and the *hallel*'" ("David's Eschatological Psalter: 11Q Psalms^a," 30).

B. The Use of Ps 118 at Qumran

In spite of the extensive use of the Psalter at Qumran,[276] there are few manuscripts preserving portions of Ps 118.[277] This reflects more on the fragmentary state of the scrolls than the psalm's status, for the available evidence suggests that it played an important role in the liturgical life of the community. The scroll 11QPs[a] contains in col. XVI six verses from Ps 118 (1, 15, 16, 8, 9, 20), preceded by Pss 135 and 136, and followed by parts of Ps 145, with some additional inserts. Because of the non-canonical order of the Catena, it has been suggested that this is not in fact Ps 118 but rather a distinct composition that overlaps with previously existing material.[278] Whether or not the composer borrowed phrases from Ps 118 to form a new psalm, it appears that the Catena was a deliberate grouping liturgical in purpose, and therefore the fact that the psalm provides material for the liturgical complex suggests that it was well-known, adaptable, and played a significant liturgical role.[279] The occurrence of

---

[276] The work that has survived in the largest number of Qumran manuscripts is Psalms. Cf. Sanders, *Psalms Scroll*, 9; P. Flint, *The Dead Sea Psalms Scrolls and the Book of Psalms*, 220–221.

[277] For a reconstruction of all verses from the Hallel Psalms preserved at Qumran see M. Abegg et al., *The Dead Sea Scrolls Bible*, 549–551. Sections of Ps 118 are found in the following scrolls: Ps 118.25–29 (11QPs[a] frag. E I); Ps 118.1, 15, 16, 8, 9, 20 (11QPs[a] col. XVI); Ps 118.1, 5, 16 (11QPs[b]); Ps 118.1–3, 6–12, 18–20, 23–26, 29 (4QPs[b]). In addition note the possibility of Ps 118.1, 9 – in combination with Pss 147.18–20 and 105.1–11 – in 11QPs[a] frag. E III (see Sanders, *Psalms Scroll*, 164–165). Psalm 118.29 may be present in 4QPs[e]. Psalm 118.26, 27 and v. 20 may be quoted in 4QpPs[b] frag. 4 and 5 respectively. Snodgrass ("Christological Stone," 68) notes – yet admits that the evidence is inconclusive – a possible allusion to Ps 118.22 in 2Q23 1–11, in which the writer prophesies the demise of one of his enemies.

[278] See P. R. Ackroyd, "Some Notes on the Psalms," 398. Flint (*Psalms Scrolls*, 176 n. 21, 191) proposes that although the Catena in col. XVI contains verses found mostly in Ps 118, it cannot be a version of the psalm because of the fact that the psalm occurs elsewhere in the manuscript. Instead he suggests it forms a single psalm with Ps 136. Sanders similarly claims that the verses are not a "mutilated form of Psalm 118 but must be viewed as a coda to Psalm 136 made up of phrases familiar from Ps 118" (*Psalms Scroll*, 156).

[279] P. W. Skehan ("A Liturgical Complex in 11QPs[a]," 195–196, 202) argues that this is the clearest liturgical grouping in the scroll. On the liturgical function of Ps 118 see Skehan's discussion, (ibid., 196–200, esp. 197) and the more extensive comments by Wacholder ("Eschatological Psalter," 43–44, 48). On 11QPs[a] as a liturgical compilation that used psalms along with other compositions see M. H. Goshen-Gottstein, "The Psalms Scroll (11QPs[a]): A Problem of Canon and Text"; S. Talmon, "*Pisqah be'emsa' pasuq* and 11QPs[a] ." The use of Ps 118.25–29 in its traditional canonical order in Fragment E suggests that the arrangement of Ps 118 in the Catena is deliberate, and that rather than creating a new psalm without ties to Ps 118 it signals a liturgical role for Ps 118.

Ps 118.25–29 in Fragment E may indicate the use of the Hallel as a unit,[280] or alternatively may form part of another liturgical complex.[281] It is therefore possible that Qumran primarily provides examples of the liturgical use of Ps 118 rather than a straightforward copying of the psalm in its canonical sequence.

The most convincing explanation for the arrangement of 11QPs[a], which differs from the canonical order, is that it groups according to liturgical considerations and focuses on Davidic attribution.[282] There is general acknowledgement that the scroll emphasizes Davidic authorship of the psalms in general, and in particular of all the compositions found in the 11QPs[a] Psalter,[283] confirming the contemporary identification of the Psalter with Davidic kingship and indicating that at least in the Qumran community Ps 118 was attributed to David. This Davidic emphasis may suggest an eschatological reading of the 11QPs[a] Psalter. Wacholder argues that "David" should be understood as an allusion to the eschatological deliverer expected at the end of days.[284] As a result the scroll can be viewed

---

[280] For frag. E see Sanders, *Psalms Scroll*, 160–165. Such a sequence is plausible on the basis of spacing and restoration of the material missing between fragments D and E. See Skehan, "Liturgical Complex," 201 n. 24. For discussion see Flint (*Psalms Scrolls*, 189–191), who accepts that the entire Hallel was originally included in the manuscript. In his examination of 4QPs[b], Skehan ("A Psalm Manuscript From Qumran [4Q Ps[b]]," 320–322) notes in relation to Ps 118 (1–3, 6–12, 18–20, 23–26, 29) and the Hallel (there are fragments of Ps 115.2–3 and Ps 116.17–19, spaces for Ps 117, and apparently the beginning of Ps 113) that there are spaces where it is reasonable to expect that the majority of missing verses were originally present. M. Abegg et al argue that the Hallel "were most likely found together in 4QPs[b], 4QPs[e], and 11QPs[a], and possibly in 4QPs[o], although none of the four manuscripts still preserves all of them" (*Scrolls Bible*, 549).

[281] Ps 118.25–29 is followed by Pss 104, 147, 105 (all in frag. E), and then in the main text by Pss 146 and 148. Note that in frag. E III there appears to be an insertion of Ps 118.1, 29 between Pss 147 and 105. The sequence of these psalms is surprising.

[282] For a survey and evaluation of the various proposals to explain the structure of the scroll see Flint, *Psalms Scrolls*, 175–189.

[283] The last columns of the scroll end with an emphasis on David. The citation of 2 Sam 23.7 immediately precedes the prose note that credits David with 4,050 psalms (Compositions of David, col. XXVII 1–11). This indicates that the preceding material is understood to be David's (since here end the words of David), and the implication is that he composed not only all the material in this scroll but much more as well. Cf. Sanders, *Psalms Scroll*, 11; Wacholder, "Eschatological Psalter," 32. Flint additionally points out that Pss 151A and 151B emphasize Davidic authorship "by highlighting the achievements or career of David" (*Psalms Scrolls*, 193), and that the compiler has given a Davidic character to the entire collection by dispersing titled Davidic psalms among untitled ones (ibid., 194).

[284] Wacholder, "Eschatological Psalter," 23. Wacholder comments, "The use of the patronymic 'ben Jesse' seems to indicate that the historical monarch who bore this name was not the primary referent of that designation. Rather, it would seem that the designation 'David *ben Jesse*' refers to an idealized future deliverer who would lead Israel at the

as the eschatological liturgy that the Davidic deliverer will lead Israel in singing.[285] Both uses of Ps 118 in 11QPs[a] may support such a reading. First, in the Catena there is an addition to the traditional wording of Ps 118.9 (the phrase "It is better to trust in the LORD than to put confidence in a thousand people") that may allude to the final victory of Israel over the nations.[286] Second, Wacholder not implausibly explains the unusual placement of Pss 146 and 148 following Fragment E as the compiler's addition of angelic praise to the songs of David and Israel in the previous psalms.[287] Apart from this link, the combination of psalms in Fragment E would encourage eschatological hopes, since Pss 118, 104 and 105 have exodus allusions, and Ps 147 refers to the future gathering of exiles.

C. The Hallel in Legends

That the Hallel became associated with great deliverances is perhaps a natural development due to its content, themes of humiliation followed by exaltation, and probably most importantly its linkage with the feasts and their themes. R. Judah said, "the Prophets among them ordained that Israel should recite it at every important epoch and at every misfortune – may it not come upon them! – and when they are redeemed they recite it [in gratitude] for their redemption." Isaac bestowed his blessing on Jacob on Passover night, saying "tonight the whole world will sing the Hallel

---

End of Days" (ibid., 71). It appears that there has been a mixing of the historical and eschatological David that is retained by 11QPs[a], although the scroll "places its emphasis upon the future expectation" (ibid., 71).

[285] Wacholder writes, "An essential component of the future expectation is that this 'second David' will compose a fantastic number of psalms and hymns to be employed in the eschatological cultus. . . . The compiler was presenting a *halleluyah* for the End of Days that was attributed to David ben Jesse" ("Eschatological Psalter," 72).

[286] Cf. Wacholder, "Eschatological Psalter," 48–49. Against Sanders he translates "people" in the plural. For the text see Sanders, *Psalms Scroll*, 65. Because of the order of verses in the Catena and his view that this may be a separate composition, Sanders is not ready to classify the phrase as an addendum to Ps 118.9 (ibid., 19). Note that in any case the phrase parallels Ps 118.9.

[287] Wacholder, "Eschatological Psalter," 46: "The compositions contained in the preceding fragments emphasize that David and the people of Israel would offer thanksgiving hymns at the end of time. In the opinion of the compiler, however, one group was lacking from this roster of celebrants – the heavenly beings. This thought apparently inspired the joining of Psalm 146:10 to Psalm 148, which contains express mention of the angelic praise." Wacholder attributes the special role assigned by the compiler to Ps 118 to the fact that the psalm begin and ends with *hodu*, which he claims is especially associated with David (Ezra, the Chronicler), and with the eschatological son of Jesse in Isa 12 and Jer 33.11.

unto God."[288] Hezekiah and the people began to sing the Hallel Psalms and Sennacherib's Assyrian army was annihilated.[289] Moses composed the Hallel, and with Aaron and Israel recited Hallel the first Passover night. That night Pharaoh declared that Israel were no longer his servants but servants of God, an echo of Ps 113.1, and Israel responded with the Hallel.[290] Moses and Israel recited the Hallel when they ascended from the Red Sea, Joshua and Israel when the kings of Canaan attacked them. Hananiah, Mishael and Azariah recited it when Nebuchadnezzar had them thrown into the flames, and Mordecai and Esther when Haman rose against them.[291] It is no surprise then that Raba, seeking interpretation of his dreams, associates the Hallel with miracles: "In my dream I was made to read the Hallel of Egypt. He replied: Miracles will happen to you."[292]

The Hallel is associated with liberation and triumph. In *b. Meg.* 14a, deliverance from slavery to freedom, and from death to life, demands singing Hallel. It concludes that "the reading of Megillah is equivalent to Hallel" – i.e., both deal with salvation and redemption. Explaining why the Hallel is not read at Purim (Megillah is read) the rabbis teach "the Hallel is not read except on the overthrow of a kingdom".[293] This is contrasted with Hanukkah, celebrating God's destruction of the "kingdom of Greece," where the Jews proceed to voice the Hallel, saying "In times past we were servants to Pharaoh, servants to Greece; but now we are servants to the Holy One, blessed be He: *Praise, O ye servants of the Lord* (Ps. 113:1)."[294]

Although this kind of evidence exhibits the eschatological interpretation of the Hallel, it also highlights the problem that much of the material is found in rabbinic literature, and consequently cannot be used with confidence. This study has built a cumulative case from pre-rabbinic evidence that the Hallel probably was associated with eschatological and/or messianic themes and interpretations. This suggests that some of the eschatological interpretations in the rabbinics are not completely new

---

[288] See L. Ginzburg, *The Legends of the Jews*, 1.330.

[289] Ginzburg, *Legends*, 4.268; 6.362 n. 54.

[290] Ginzburg, *Legends*, 2.368–370; 5.435–436 n. 225, n. 228; 6.12–13, 418, 477.

[291] *b. Pesah.* 117a. See also *b. Pesah.* 95b. For the Hallel on the lips of Hananiah et al. after their rescue from the fire see *Midr. Ps.* 117.3. There is a disagreement in *b. Pesah.* 117a over whether Moses or David composed the Hallel. However, it is unlikely that the rabbis are ascribing authorship to the long list of people they say uttered the Hallel. The list rather associates the Hallel with times of trouble and deliverance.

[292] *b. Ber.* 56a. Cf. the parallel in *b. 'Arak.* 10b.

[293] *Pesiq. Rab.* 2.1. This is obviously not the case, but is intended to contrast Purim and Hanukkah. What stands out is that the Hallel is associated with triumph and victory.

[294] *Pesiq. Rab.* 2.1.

innovations and in fact reflect earlier traditions. Other statements may be developments of what was a pattern latent in earlier associations. At the very least pre-rabbinic speculation and interpretation must have served to suggest possibilities and provide a springboard for later reflection upon, and expansion of, proto-eschatological and messianic elements nascent in the Hallel. Thus it is worth examining the rabbinic interpretations of the Hallel.

D. *The Hallel and Rabbinics*

Each of the Hallel Psalms, except for Ps 117, is interpreted eschatologically at least once.[295] Apart from Ps 118,[296] the most heavily eschatologized is

---

[295] Psalm 113.2 is used to show that Israel will praise God forever in the world-to-come (*Midr. Ps.* 113.4). Psalm 114.4 is interpreted in a context of Tabernacles themes in the end times, where the past acts of God meeting his people will be continued in the eschatological age (*Midr. Ps.* 13.4). Psalm 115.1 is a prayer asking to be spared the distress ("pangs of Messiah") of the time preceding the coming of the Messiah, and is though to refer to the war of Gog and Magog (*b. Pesah.* 118a); Ps 115.5 refers to the judgment of the time-to-come, when the nations will be accused by the idols they worshipped (*Midr. Ps.* 31.3–4). For a list of rabbinic sources which contain eschatological and/or messianic interpretations of the Hallel see Jeremias, *Eucharistic Words*, 256–257; Cohn-Sherbok, "Jewish Note," 706. The list we have provided is more extensive, but Jeremias includes several additional citations: Ps 116.1 (*j. Ber.* 2.4d.48f); 116.9, 13 (*Exod. Rab.* 25.10); Ps 118.27b (*j. Ber.* 2.4d.49); Ps 118.28 (*j. Ber.* 2.4d.50).

[296] Psalm 118.1 is the praise given at Tabernacles when Israel is found righteous following the judgment, which will take place on the Day of Atonement (*Midr. Ps.* 118.2); Ps 118.7 confirms that at the final judgment God will be Israel's helper (*Midr. Ps.* 118.10); Ps 118.10 is a reference to the days of Gog and Magog (*Lev. Rab.* 30.5), and the wondrous works God will do then (*Midr. Ps.* 26.6; *Pesiq. Rab.* 51.7). The larger section Ps 118.10–12 applies to Gog and Magog's three attacks against Israel and their final destruction. The psalm is read in light of Zech 12–14, which is quoted seven times (*Midr. Ps.* 118.12–13). Psalm 118.15–16 describes the rejoicing at Israel's redemption in the time-to-come (*Pesiq. Rab.* 31.6), and Ps 118.19–20 the gates of the world-to-come (*Midr. Ps.* 118.17). The day of rejoicing in Ps 118.24 is interpreted as the day of the final redemption of Israel (*Midr. Ps.* 118.22). The day of redemption (presumably messianic) includes an antiphonal rendition of Ps 118.25–29, apparently the greeting for the coming Messiah (*Midr. Ps.* 118.22). Psalm 118.27a is a prayer requesting the light of redemption and redemption from bondage (*Midr. Ps.* 36.6). The light mentioned in the psalm will come when the time of redemption arrives and Jerusalem is built. God promises to send his light to Israel and bring darkness to the nations (*Midr. Ps.* 27.1). Psalm 118.27b concerns the festal procession that will celebrate the destruction of God and Magog (*Pesiq. Rab.* 51.7); Ps 118.28 is a reference to the future (*Lev. Rab.* 30.5) and the wondrous works God will do then (*Midr. Ps.* 26.5; *Pesiq. Rab.* 51.7). Finally, Ps 118.29 speaks of God's wondrous works in the life of the world–to–come (*Midr. Ps.* 26.5; *Pesiq. Rab.* 51.7).

Ps 116.[297] It is notable that they are the two Hallel psalms most quoted in the NT.[298] That the whole of Ps 116 was interpreted eschatologically at an early date, at least as regards resurrection and the final judgment, is attested by the argument between the Houses of Shammai and Hillel.[299] The fact that the NT quotes the two psalms so often in eschatological-messianic contexts suggests that some of the directions the rabbis took were not completely new. It is clear that the rabbinic exegesis of the Hallel – especially its second half – is predominantly eschatological and messianic, but the difficulty comes in determining what is innovation and what rests on prior traditions. It is unlikely that the Hallel would suddenly receive the widespread and heightened eschatological reading it does in the rabbinics without internal themes and external associations that would suggest and justify the attention. It is significant that none of the evidence we have gathered previously is contradicted in rabbinic interpretation. Rather, the rabbinic testimony confirms what we have identified as promising patterns and associations pre-AD 70. Consequently, although not to be adduced as evidence, rabbinic interpretations suggest that our conclusions are not without merit.

---

[297] The whole psalm is applied to salvation from Gehinnon at the final judgment. (*b. Roš Haš.* 16b–17a). The Midrash explains Ps 116.1 in reference to Deut 28.1, which is a passage associated with blessings and curses (i.e., the great curse of exile), and with the promise of Isa 58.9, an eschatological passage promising that God will hear Israel's cry (*Midr. Ps.* 116.1). Psalm 116.1 also refers to the days of the Messiah (*Lev. Rab.* 30.5), to God's wondrous works in the days of the Messiah (*Midr. Ps.* 26.6; *Pesiq. Rab.* 51.7), and is the prayer of David thanking God for his mercy at the judgment. It is read in light of Ps 116.3, 6 and assures that God will have mercy on Israel. These three verses are also associated with healing from sin and resurrection at the judgment (*b. Roš Haš.* 16b–17a; *t. Sanh.* 13.3). Note that this is an early interpretation assigned to the House of Hillel. Psalm 116.4 refers to the deliverance of the righteous from Gehenna (*b. Pesah.* 118a), and the salvation of children is adduced from Ps 116.6 (*t. Sanh.* 13.1); Ps 116.9 concerns the resurrection of the dead (*b. Pesah.* 118a), and more specifically the resurrection of the dead of the Land of Israel in the days of the Messiah (*Pesiq. Rab.* 1.4); Ps 116.13 speaks of salvation in the world to come (*Exod. Rab.* 25.9) and the feast of the time-to-come (*b. Pesah.* 119b). The "cup of salvation," found only in this verse, is the cup of salvation in the messianic future and in the days of Gog and Magog (*Gen. Rab.* 88.5); Israel's cup of deliverances (plural) in contrast to the cup of punishment given to the nations (*Midr. Ps.* 11.5); and the cup of deliverances, which is two of the cups of good and consolation God will give Israel in the time-to-come (*Midr. Ps.* 75.4).

[298] According to NA[27], the NT quotes Ps 116 once (116.10 in 2 Cor 4.13) and alludes to it twice (116.3 in Acts 2.24; 116.11 in Rom 3.4). In addition, Ps 116 may provide the background for Heb 5.7 (see Lane, *Hebrews*, 1.113), and Ps 116.4 for Mark 14.36 (see M. Kiley, "'Lord, Save My Life' as Generative Text for Jesus' Gethsemane Prayer").

[299] See above footnote.

E. Antiphonal Readings

Several rabbinic sources divide Ps 118 into antiphonal parts spoken by different groups.[300] This may reflect early practice, since the psalm's alternation of plural and singular presupposes such an arrangement internally. That both the Talmud and Targum divide Ps 118 between David and his contemporaries indicates a prior – and early – tradition associating the psalm with David.[301] Although this suggests possibilities for eschatological-messianic interpretations of the psalm, none are explicitly stated in either source. However, the antiphonal division in the Midrash on Psalms is interpreted messianically.

> *This is the day which the Lord hath made* (Ps. 118:24). After all the redemptions that came to Israel, enslavement followed, but from now on no enslavement will follow . . . *We beseech Thee, O Lord, save now!* (Ps. 118:25). From inside the walls, the men of Jerusalem will say, *We beseech Thee, O Lord, save now.* And from outside, the men of Judah will say, *We beseech Thee, O Lord, make us now to prosper!* (*ibid.*). From inside, the men of Jerusalem will say, *Blessed be he that cometh IN the name of the Lord* (Ps. 118:26). And from outside, the men of Judah will say, *We bless you OUT of the house of the Lord* (*ibid.*) From inside, the men of Jerusalem will say, *The Lord is God and hath given us light* (Ps. 118:27). And from outside, the men of Judah will say *Order the festival procession with boughs, even unto the horns of the altar* (*ibid.*). From inside, the men of Jerusalem will say, *Thou art my God, and I will give thanks unto Thee* (118:28). And from outside, the men of Judah will say, *Thou art my God, I will exalt Thee* (118:28). Then the men of Jerusalem and the men of Judah, together, opening their mouths in praise of the Holy One, blessed be He, will say: *O give thanks unto the Lord, for He is good, for His mercy endureth for ever* (118.29).[302]

---

[300] *Midr. Ps.* 118.14; 118.22; *b. Pesah.* 119a; *Midrash Hallel.* Note also *Tg. Ps.* 118.

[301] Cf. Werner, "Hosanna," 118; Snodgrass, "Christological Stone," 84–85. Concerning the dating of the Targum on Psalms, W. Bacher ("Targum," 62) argues it is Palestinian in origin and should be assigned an early date of composition (prior to AD 476). An earlier date is not implausible. Levey (*The Messiah*, 159) notes that *b. Šabb.* 115a mentions a ban placed on the Targum to Job by Gamaliel I (first half of the first century AD), and it is assumed that the Targum to Job and the Targum to Psalms had a common origin. For discussion see Daly-Denton (*David*, 16–17), who suggests that some oral traditions in the targum go back at least to NT times.

[302] *Midr. Ps.* 118.22. There is a parallel in *Midrash Hallel*: "For every redemption which we have been granted, servitude has returned upon us. After the first redemption we were once again enslaved (in Egypt) after the second also (in Babylonia), and so after the third; but after this redemption (the Messianic) there will be no exile, as it is said: 'And ye shall say on that day: O give thanks unto the Lord; make known His name among the nations' (Is 12.4) and there follows: 'Sing ye to the Lord, for He hath done excellent things' (Is 12.5), and it is said: 'Save now, O Lord, we beseech Thee!' (Ps 118.25). The men from Jerusalem say from within: 'Blessed by the name of JHVH be

The eschatological interpretation of Ps 118.24 sets the context within which the following verses are to be read. It is the day of redemption that ends enslavement forever, and this presupposes the coming of the Messiah. Thus it appears that Ps 118.25–29 is depicted as the antiphonal chorus that greets and accompanies the Messiah as he comes to Jerusalem at his *parousia*. Although the Midrash on Ps 118 is uncertain of date,[303] there is nothing that precludes Ps 118.24–29 being interpreted eschatologically and/or of the Messiah.[304] It is worth noting that it is precisely these verses that were repeated twice in the recitation of the Hallel at Passover and Tabernacles. The Targum and Midrash offer an antiphonal reading for Ps 118.22–29, the Talmud for 118.21–28. The options for doubling are given as Ps 118.21–29 or 118.25–29.[305] Therefore it is the verses which were singled out for the antiphonal reading that received a heightened emphasis, ensuring that Ps 118 provided the climax to the liturgy at both major festivals.

To sum up: The Hallel was one of the most beloved and recognizable portions of Scripture. It was repeated often and in liturgically prominent settings, and was probably studied and memorized from a young age.

---

he, that cometh' (Ps 118.26) and the men of Juda say from without: 'We bless you out of the house of JHVH' (Ps 118.27); the men of Jerusalem say: 'Thou art my God, and I will praise Thee' (Ps 118.28), the men of Juda say: 'Thou art my God, I will exalt Thee' (Ps 118.28). Both of them open their mouths in praise and intone: 'O give thanks unto the Lord, for He is gracious' (Ps 118.1)." Taken from Werner, "Hosanna," 114–115. Text can be found in J. D. Eisenstein, *Ozar Midrashim: A Library of Two Hundred Minor Midrashim*, 1.137.

[303] The date for the compilation of the Midrash on Psalms has been set as late as the ninth century. Braude, however, argues that although only an approximate date can be given, its start was probably in the third century, with development until the thirteenth century: "It seems that as early as the time of R. Judah I (d. ca. 220 CE) there existed, in an early form, a collection of homilies upon the Psalter" ("Introduction to the Midrash on Psalms," 1.xxv–xxvi). There is general agreement that the Midrash on Pss 1–118 is earlier than that on Pss 119–150. For discussion of the date see ibid., 1.xxv–xxx. Cf. Jeremias (*Eucharistic Words*, 260–261), who argues that such an interpretation of Ps 118 goes back to the time of Jesus. Our study suggests that Matthew and Luke may have used the psalm with such a sense. See ch. 3 of this study.

[304] See especially Jeremias' discussion in *Eucharistic Words*, 256–261. Cf. Snodgrass, "Christological Stone," 84–85; Cohn-Sherbok, "A Jewish Note," 706–708. It is interesting that although Ps 118 is used in procession at Tabernacles, the Talmud's antiphonal reading (apparently in procession) is found not in *Sukkah* but in the *Pesahim* tractate. Possibly this could be related to the expectation that Messiah would come at Passover.

[305] *b. Pesah.* 119b; *b. Sukk.* 39a; *m. Sukk.* 3.11; *t. Pesah.* 10.9. There is also an antiphonal reading of Ps 118.15–16, but it receives no special emphasis (cf. *Midr. Ps.* 118.14).

Although there is no clear date for its entry as a unit into the cult, it was well established at the time of Jesus. Rabbinic literature associates the Hallel with liberation and triumph and the great events of deliverance in Israel's history, interpreting the whole eschatologically, but especially Pss 116 and 118.

V. Psalm 118 in its Literary Context and in the Psalter

A. Approach

In recent years a new emphasis on reading the psalms within the context of the Psalter has gathered adherents in Psalms study.[306] Research has generally approached the psalms as individual units, showing little interest in the editorial activity that shaped the Psalter.[307] However, although the original setting of a psalm may have been the cult and/or a specific historical event, recovering the original setting may be an impossible task in many cases.[308] Consequently attention shifts to reading psalms in the literary context given by the editors of the Psalter, for it is plausible that their purposeful arranging of the psalms should provide insight into their interpretation in Judaism.[309] The historical and cultic settings of the

---

[306] Those who support an emphasis on the final shape of the Psalter include, among others, J. L. Mays, N. K. Gottwald, W. Brueggemann, P. D. Miller, B. S. Childs, C. Westermann, D. Howard, G. H. Wilson, J. C. McCann, and M. D. Goulder. For a survey of research and trends in approaching the psalms from a Psalter perspective see D. Howard, "Editorial Activity."

[307] Especially following Gunkel's work (*Die Psalmen*; *Einleitung*), which first proposed the classification of psalms according to type or genre, the standard approach to studying a psalm has been first to classify it, and then to compare it with other psalms in the same *Gattungen*. Until recently little attention was paid to interpreting the psalm in relation to its immediate literary context or a collection in which it might be included.

[308] Cf. Gottwald, *Hebrew Bible*, 525.

[309] As Goulder comments, "The earliest commentary on the psalms is the Psalter" (*Psalms of the Return*, 7). Cf. P. Miller, *Interpreting*, 3–28; E. Zenger, "New Approaches to the Study of the Psalms." J. P. Brennan summarizes well the approach: "A careful reading indicates that the Psalter has not developed in a haphazard and arbitrary way, but has been carefully woven together in such a manner that previously independent compositions, or smaller collections of such compositions, now comment upon or respond to one another. Hence, for a proper understanding of the Psalter it is not enough to study each of its 150 components in the historical context from which it originally sprang. They must all be studied in their relationship to each other, since all of them together convey more than they do if looked at separately" ("Some Hidden Harmonies in the Fifth Book of the Psalms," 126–127). See further Mays, "The Question of Context," 14.

psalms should not be ignored where these can be recovered, but as Mays correctly observes, "this final literary context is a setting that calls for study in its own right."[310] Most literary studies of the Psalter have approached the task in one of two ways: at the "higher" level, seeking organizing principles for the Psalter or larger collections; and at a "lower" level, focusing on links between adjacent psalms or a sequence of psalms.[311] There is also a readiness to admit that the final shape of the Psalter may include collections that were handed down as a unit.[312]

The Hallel may have been used as a literary unit prior to the final editorial activity on the Psalter, and thus would have come into the canonical book as a collection. The less likely alternative is that the Hallel was first recognized as a unit because of the order its psalms occupy in the Psalter. Whatever the case may be, since the Hallel had an established role in cultic settings of the Second Temple period, the cult provides the primary context within which the Hallel would be interpreted. However, its literary context provides an additional interpretive context both at the lower level, which includes internal connections within the Hallel and with surrounding psalms, and at the higher level, which situates the Hallel in a larger flow of themes.

---

[310] J. L. Mays, "Going by the Book: The Psalter as a Guide to Reading the Psalms," 121.

[311] I owe this characterization of higher and lower approaches to Howard, "Editorial Activity," 68. Among the studies which have focused on smaller units and sought to show that they are related by linguistic expressions, content, theology, or literary structure, see K. Seybold, *Die Wallfahrtspsalmen: Studien zur Enstehungsgeschichte von Psalm 120–134* ; D. Howard, "The Structure of Psalms 93–100"; P. Auffret, *La Sagesse a bâti sa maison: Etudes de structures littéraires dans l'Ancien Testament et specialment dans les Psaumes,* on Pss 15–24, 120–134, and 135–138; and B. Davis, a student of D. Howard, who applies this approach in his Ph.D. dissertation, "A Contextual Analysis of Psalms 107–118." Those who have done studies on the higher level include G. H. Wilson, *The Editing of the Hebrew Psalter*; and J. C. McCann, "Books I–III and the Editorial Purpose of the Hebrew Psalter." Goulder's studies on the Psalter (*Sons of Korah*; *Prayers of David*; *Psalms of Asaph*; *Psalms of the Return*) represent some of the most original and ground-breaking work on both of these levels.

[312] Howard notes that most scholars admit that "the final form of the Psalter incorporated fixed sequences of originally liturgical material" ("Editorial Activity," 65). This is in marked contrast to earlier Psalms research. Westermann, for example, points out that Gunkel had no interest in how the collection of psalms was handed down: "The possibility of partial collections bearing a materially unified character was excluded from the beginning" (*Praise and Lament in the Psalms,* 251). Westermann (ibid., 255–256) further suggests that one such collection was comprised of Pss 111–118. Cf. Westermann, *The Psalms: Structure,* 18–19.

B. The Hallel's Internal Connections

Barry Davis has produced the most detailed lower study of Pss 107–118, the literary division of which the Hallel forms the second half, focusing on lexical frequency and thematic analysis.[313] The Hallel was read as a unit in Judaism, but Davis' work shows that apart from the cultic institutionalization of these psalms that historically associated them together, they are also thematically and lexically very closely linked.[314] It is apparent that generally an individual psalm shares higher interconnection with the psalms closest to it in sequence. Each of the Hallel Psalms has stronger lexical and thematic links to others of the Hallel corpus than to non-Hallel psalms. The evidence also confirms that Ps 118 is the climax of the Hallel from a literary standpoint, as it summarizes and fulfills a number of themes from the previous psalms. Mays correctly concludes that "every one of the first five psalms in the cycle anticipates themes and motifs of Ps 118."[315] The implication of this is that a citation of Ps 118 would naturally lead the informed Jewish reader of Scripture to common themes shared with the other psalms, and vice versa. In the same way, eschatological associations or interpretations of one Hallel psalm would reflect on the unit as a whole.

C. The Hallel's Surrounding Context

The Hallel can also be interpreted in relation to the larger literary context of Pss 107–118.[316] P. D. Miller suggests in an unpublished paper that

---

[313] Davis, "Contextual Analysis."

[314] The percentage of lexical interconnection between Psalm 113 and others of the 107–118 unit shows that the closest links are to Pss 117, 115, 114, 112 and 118, in descending order. Psalm 114's closest connections come with Pss 113, 115, 118, 108, 116 and 110 in descending order. The highest percentage of links for Ps 115 are with Pss 117, 113, 118, 111, 112, 116, and 114; for Ps 116 the order is Pss 115, 117, 113, 118; and for Ps 117 it is Pss 113, 115, 111 and 118. For Ps 118, it is respectively Pss 117, 115, 113, 112 and 116. For detailed discussion of each psalm see the following page sections in Davis, "Contextual Analysis": Ps 113 (237–244); Ps 114 (253–259); Ps 115 (273–281); Ps 116 (286–290); Ps 117 (293–297); Ps 118 (301–304).

[315] Mays, 378. He states that "the cycle begins with Psalm 113 and its praise of the LORD as the God who reverses the fixed arrangements of human affairs by lifting up the lowly, needy, and helpless. Psalm 114 tells the story of the exodus as the manifestation of the LORD's rule in the world. Psalm 115 contrasts the LORD as Israel's help to the nations and their gods. Psalm 116 thanks the LORD for deliverance from death, and Psalm 117 calls on all nations to praise the LORD."

[316] Most scholars accept this division. For discussion see Davis, "Contextual Analysis," 7–11. G. H. Wilson ("Shaping the Psalter: A Consideration of Editorial Linkage in the Book of Psalms," 79) goes against the consensus by suggesting that Ps 118 is not part of the Pss 107–117 unit but is connected rather to Ps 135 as a frame for

Ps 109 is the cry of the oppressed David (to whom the psalm is ascribed), and Ps 110 is the "divine oracle to the needy king." Psalms 112–118 continue and develop Ps 111's direct response of praise and thanksgiving for the deliverance God has accomplished.[317] Davis similarly suggests that Pss 108–110 were juxtaposed to the Hallel Psalms as an encouragement to praise God for deliverance from enemies, "and because He offers the hope that He, one day, will establish His sovereign rule over all Israel's enemies."[318] J. Schaper has shown that Ps 110(109) was given a messianic interpretation in the LXX, which aids in confirming that it was the subject of eschatological interpretation in first-century Judaism.[319] There was thus a move from a plea for deliverance (Pss 108–109), to God's intervention (Ps 110), to praise and thanksgiving as a response (Pss. 111–118). As a result, the Hallel could be read as the praise that follows messianic deliverance.

Miller also suggests that Pss 111–118 "focus on Exodus but move to Zion," with Ps 118 providing the link between this exodus theme and the Zion-temple theme of Pss 120–134.[320] Apart from its place in the sequence of psalms which makes it a natural bridge, Ps 118 is especially suited to such a role as it is primarily associated with the temple cult of Tabernacles yet also contains a number of exodus themes.[321] It is possible then to read the Hallel as the song of praise that flows in response to deliverance – i.e., exodus – with Ps 118 forming the thematic bridge as the culmination of the exodus leading to an eschatological Zion. Mays plausibly suggests another eschatological connection, arguing that the Torah Psalms (Pss 1; 19; 119) are intentionally paired with psalms that can be read eschatologically (respectively, Pss 2; 18; 118), providing "an

---

Ps 119 and the Songs of Ascent. However, it is difficult to justify the separation of Ps 118 from its obvious literary unit.

[317] P. D. Miller, "Response to Erich Zenger, 'The Composition and Theology of the Fifth Book of Psalms, Psalms 107–145': 145–150."

[318] Davis, "Contextual Analysis," 317. Davis further argues that Pss 107–109 depict the distress of God's people and their cries for deliverance, and Ps 110 then declares that God is able to secure victory against powerful enemies ("Contextual Analysis," 162–163). See also Brennan ("Hidden Harmonies," 127–131), who suggests that Ps 110 was included in Book V to encourage hope in the people that God would fulfill his promises to David.

[319] Schaper, *Eschatology in the Greek Psalter*, 101–107.

[320] Miller, "Response." Miller observes, "The Exodus to Zion in Psalms 111–118 happens now as a kind of chiastic echo in the movement from Zion in Psalm 135 to Exodus in Psalm 136."

[321] Note that Pss 120–134, the Songs of Ascent, were sung on pilgrimage and at Tabernacles.

eschatological context for a piety based on Torah."[322] The shapers of the
Psalter are committed to Torah piety, believing that God will vindicate
even though they see the righteous suffer and do not see God's judgment
against the wicked. Nowhere in the final content of the Psalter is there
evidence that they surrendered this faith, the reason being "the eschatological context of Torah-piety – the hope for the coming kingdom of God."[323]
The danger in a literary approach to the Psalter is that it is based largely on
reader response. Mays correctly has cautioned of the danger "of overbidding
the material, of imagining connections,"[324] so that any conclusions must be
held cautiously. However, it is not implausible that first-century Jewish
readers would have discovered some of the same connections that modern
interpreters have, and with much less restraint if period exegesis is any
guide.[325]

D. The Eschatological Shape of the Psalter

The higher study of the Psalter, which looks for overall organizing
principles in the shaping and editing process, suggests that its final shape
has an eschatological orientation. In this regard the royal psalms play an
important role. First, the editors have historicized many of the psalms by
adding Davidic ascriptions, thus providing hermeneutical clues for how
they are to be interpreted.[326] Their message is that "it was primarily
David's voice that was to be heard in the Psalter ... the voice of the
promised king of Israel, the Messiah."[327] As a result of the removal of the
monarchy the royal psalms were eschatologized and invested with

---

[322] Mays, "The Place of the Torah Psalms in the Psalter," 33–34.

[323] Mays, "Torah Psalms," 34.

[324] Mays, "Going by the Book," 126–127. He continues, "Topics are so typical and
language so formulaic in the world of the psalms that it is difficult to decide whether
collocations and correspondences and contrasts are accidental or intentional, and if the
latter, what to make of them." See also G. H. Wilson ("Understanding the Purposeful
Arrangement of Psalms in the Psalter: Pitfalls and Promise," 48), who cautions on
applying a hypothesis which attempts to explain the final shaping of the Psalter.

[325] The use of chiasmus in period literature points to a sophisticated audience, so
there is no reason to deny them the ability to read/hear contextually. A literary approach
need not, therefore, be anachronistic.

[326] This ties them firmly to the history of God's relationship with Israel. See Childs'
comments: "Although the titles are relatively late additions, they represent an important
reflection of how the psalms as a collection of sacred literature were understood and how
this secondary setting became authoritative for the canonical tradition" (*Introduction to
the Old Testament as Scripture*, 520).

[327] Kraus, *Theology*, 176.

messianic significance.[328] As Childs perceptively questions, "At the time of the final redaction, when the institution of kingship had long since been destroyed, what earthly king would have come to mind other than God's Messiah?"[329] Second, the placement of royal psalms, some of which have been added or inserted into collections after they lost their place in the royal cult and acquired messianic interpretations, facilitates an eschatological reading.[330] For example, Mays suggests that the lament over the unfulfilled promises to David which closes Book III (Ps 89) receives its answer in Books IV and V, where the fulfillment of David's kingship is placed in the future, so that "a 'once and future' perspective is thus set on the psalmic presentation of the kingship of David."[331] Others have argued that the pairing of Ps 2 with Ps 1 as an introduction to the Psalter sets the tone for eschatological and messianic readings.[332]

Apart from the function of the royal psalms, some discern an eschatological stress brought to the Psalter through redaction. D. Mitchell argues that the Psalter was redacted to present an eschatological program like that of Zech 9–14,[333] and Becker that pre-exilic psalms were transformed into eschatological songs looking towards the deliverance and exaltation of Israel.[334] Whether these suggestions are sustainable or not, they are consistent with what appears to be a thematic movement in the Psalter that would encourage eschatological interpretations. For example, although Brueggemann does not deal explicitly with the eschatological shape of the Psalter, he discerns a general move from Ps 1 to Ps 150 of "obedience to doxology," of "urgent petition" to "glad confidence," and of

---

[328] Cf. Frost, "Ps 118," 156, 163; Mays, "Going by the Book," 127. Childs writes, "They were treasured in the Psalter . . . namely as a witness to the messianic hope which looked for the consummation of God's kingship through his Anointed One" (*Introduction*, 516).

[329] Childs, *Introduction*, 516.

[330] Cf. Westermann, *Praise and Lament*, 258.

[331] Mays, "Going by the Book," 125. See also Mays, "The Question of Context," 16–17.

[332] Several scholars have focused attention on the first two psalms as setting the tone for the rest of the Psalter. Among others, see Miller, "Beginning"; Mays, "The Question of Context," 16–17; Childs, *Introduction*, 516.

[333] Mitchell, *The Message of the Psalter: An Eschatological Programme in the Book of Psalms*.

[334] Becker, *Israel deutet seine Psalmen*. Cf. idem, *Psalmenexegese*, 93ff. Becker identifies four main ideas: the rule of God in Zion; deliverance from exile and return to the land; Israel's possession of the land for posterity; recognition by the nations of God's saving activity, followed by their judgment. Cf. Miller's summary of Becker in *Interpreting*, 14–15.

"suffering [complaint]" to "hope [praise]."[335] Others have recognized a
marked shift from private lamentation to public praise,[336] and both Wilson
and McCann have argued that the first three books of the Psalter express
the problem posed by exile and dispersion, with the last two books
responding to the problem by offering hope.[337] These kinds of patterns
lead Childs to the following plausible conclusion:

> However one explains it, the final form of the Psalter is highly eschatolo-
> gical in nature. It looks toward the future and passionately yearns for its
> arrival. Even when the psalmist turns briefly to reflect on the past in praise
> of the 'great things which Yahweh has done', invariably the movement
> shifts and again the hope of salvation is projected into the future. The
> perspective of Israel's worship in the Psalter is eschatologically oriented.
> As a result, the Psalter in its canonical form, far from being different in
> kind from the prophetic message, joins with the prophets in announcing
> God's coming kingship. When the New Testament heard in the psalms
> eschatological notes, its writers were standing in the context of the Jewish
> canon in which the community of faith worshipped and waited.[338]

Schaper's careful study of the Greek Psalter, in which he determines
that a number of psalms have received an eschatological or messianic
interpretation, adds a dimension beyond that of the eschatological *shaping*
of the Psalter, since he demonstrates convincingly that the *translation* of
many passages is interpretative.[339] It is possible that the LXX translation

---

[335] Brueggemann, "Bounded by Obedience and Praise: The Psalms as Canon," 202–
203, 212–213. Elsewhere Brueggemann comments, "It is then no wonder that the exilic,
post–exilic community appropriated old poems and hymns and liturgies in order to voice
both its faith and its unfaith. Such an act of appropriation continues through the exile to
be an act of daring, even a subversive act of symbolization, even if not done in a temple"
("Response," 41).

[336] See for example Gottwald, *Hebrew Bible*, 535; McCann, "Books I–III," 81.

[337]Wilson, *Editing*, 200–228; idem, "Shaping the Psalter," 75. McCann, "Books
I–III," 104. McCann is in basic agreement with Wilson in arguing that the answer (i.e.,
trust in God's kingship alone) to the "apparent failure of the traditional Davidic/Zion
covenant theology" is found in Books IV and V. However, departing from Wilson's
emphasis he also suggests that one can begin to find the answer in the first three books
as well.

[338] Childs, *Introduction*, 518.

[339] Schaper, *Eschatology*. For detailed study of individual psalms see his second
section, 46–127. LXX psalms that Schaper identifies as having an eschatological interpretation are Pss 1; 15; 21; 45; 47; 48; 55; 58; 72. Those with a messianic interpretation
are Pss 2; 8; 44; 59; 67; 71; 79; 86; 109. Note that Schaper's choice of psalms is representative rather than exhaustive, so that eschatological and messianic interpretations are
not limited to those above. He defines "eschatological" as material concerned with personal
afterlife, the resurrection of the dead, final judgment, and the world to come (ibid., 46).
On the translation as interpretative see ibid., 174.

of Ps 118 reflects an eschatological interpretation. In place of the MT's "the right hand of the LORD is exalted," the LXX translates Ps 118.16a as "the right hand of the Lord has exalted me," in what Wagner calls "a sharpening of the individual focus of the psalm."[340] This does not prove that the translators intended a messianic or eschatological meaning, but the wording is consistent with such an interpretation. The implication of the eschatological and messianic interpretation of LXX psalms is that the approach reflects the thought world of its Jewish translators. It suggests that royal as well as other psalms were probably given these kinds of interpretations prior to, and certainly following, the translation of the LXX. As Schaper plausibly summarizes, "The whole of the second century is a witness to a continual development of the formulation of eschatological and messianic hopes, with the Greek Psalter as one of its main monuments."[341]

To sum up: A number of internal movements, interconnections, and patterns suggest that the final shape of the Psalter at the least provided opportunity for, and perhaps encouraged, eschatological interpretations. It is possible that the Hallel in its immediate literary context was open to this kind of reading, with Ps 118 taking a particularly prominent role as the literary climax of the unit. In any case the flavor of the Psalter would have given it a general eschatological edge and association.

In this chapter special attention has been given to the various settings that influenced and mediated the understanding of Ps 118 in the first century. As a result it is now possible to evaluate the use of Ps 118 in the NT against the psalm's interpretive context in Judaism.

---

[340] Wagner, "Psalm 118," 160.
[341] Schaper, *Eschatology*, 160.

Chapter 3

Psalm 118 in the Synoptic Gospels

Although the main focus of this study is the presence and function of Ps 118 in the Fourth Gospel, there is value in examining its use in the Synoptic Gospels. In addition to providing a roughly contemporary application of the psalm, comparison of parallel or divergent use in the Synoptics could possibly bear on the difficult question of the latter's relationship to the Fourth Gospel. To investigate the Synoptic use of Ps 118 in more than a survey fashion lies beyond the scope of our research, so we will look briefly at each evangelist[1] and limit the discussion to the more obvious quotations and allusions (although a search for fainter echoes could prove fruitful). After summarizing the overall usage and the themes that Ps 118 supports in the Synoptics, it will be possible to compare these with John and consider any possible implications.

I. Psalm 118 in Mark

A. The Passion Prediction (Mark 8.31–33)

Mark's first clear allusion to Ps 118 takes place in the first passion prediction (8.31), a turning point in the Gospel that focuses attention on the

---

[1] There are several reasons for approaching each evangelist individually. First, although a number of the passages using Ps 118 are parallel, there is reason to believe that each evangelist was familiar with Ps 118, and that when Matthew and Luke drew on Markan passages that used the psalm they were aware of that use. In support, redactional changes on Markan passages that use Ps 118 show that there was conscious shaping of the narrative; Matthew and Luke each use Ps 118 in unique instances; and some parallel uses of Ps 118 are modified differently. Second, we have deliberately taken an approach that assumes the literary integrity of each Gospel. Accordingly, when material is appropriated from another source it is "owned" by the new source – i.e., it represents the views and theology of the appropriator. Third, looking at each separately will more clearly show the pattern of use within the particular Gospel. Although there is significant overlap, it is possible that each evangelist used Ps 118 a bit differently in service of particular emphases.

suffering that characterizes Jesus' mission.[2] Peter's climactic confession of Jesus as the Christ (Mark 8.27–30) is thus immediately qualified by a pre-view of the cross, which is set out as Jesus' goal and dominates the journey to Jerusalem.[3] The use of ἀποδοκιμάζω makes this an easily recognizable allusion, not only because of verbal correspondence with Ps 118 (117).22 but because of the recurrence of the rare verb in the quotation of Ps 118.22–23 in Mark 12.10–11. That Jesus' audience for the latter quotation is the chief priest, scribes, and elders (see Mark 11.27), the same group of leaders specified in 8.31, strengthens the connection.[4] It is possible that Ps 118.22 also underlies the prediction in Mark 9.12, as the verb ἐξουδενέω translates מאס and is used in the Acts 4.11 quotation of Ps 118.22 in place of ἀποδοκιμάζω.[5]

The allusion functions in several ways. First, Mark sought to explain the scandal of the cross by showing that the rejection of Jesus was necessary and according to God's will as revealed in Scripture. In this way the reverberations of Ps 118.22 become a subtle argument from Scripture, allowing the readers, as Juel comments, "to experience the scriptural character of the story (hence its 'necessity')."[6] The allusion functions as well to show that Jesus was consciously aware of his purpose and destiny: events could

---

[2] Mark's first allusion to Ps 118 may be in the Baptist's announcement of the one who comes after him (Mark 1.7). In Mark's account the Baptist does not explicitly identify Jesus as the one he had spoken of – that connection is left for the reader to discern. Making the allusion more subtle and less likely is the fact that unlike Matthew (11.2–6) and Luke (7.18–23), Mark does not record the Baptist's question to Jesus, thus leaving out an important step in the development of ὁ ἐρχόμενος as a title for Jesus. If there is an allusion to Ps 118.26 it is subtle and confirmed for the reader primarily by the literary link to the Entrance Narrative, the only place where Mark clearly applies the title to Jesus (Mark 11.9–10). Lane (51) notes possible reference either to Ps 118.26 or Mal 3.1f; 4.5f.

[3] On the critical place this pericope occupies in the framework of the Gospel see Hooker, 200; Taylor, 373. On the passion predictions in Mark see A. Feuillet, "Les trois grandes prophéties de la Passion et de la Resurrection des évangelies synoptiques."

[4] Among those who recognize the allusion to Ps 118.22 see Juel, 144; Gundry, *Mark*, 429; Lane, 301–302; Snodgrass, *Wicked Tenants*, 101. Hooker (202) says it is "perhaps an echo." Note that although Mark 8.31 is paralleled in Matt 16.21 and Luke 9.22, only the latter alludes to Ps 118.22.

[5] S. Kim ("Jesus – The Son of God, the Stone, the Son of Man, and the Servant: The Role of Zechariah in the Self-Identification of Jesus," 148 n. 51) suggests that ἐξουδενέω in Mark 9.12 may reflect both Isa 53.3 and Ps 118.22. Against this see Gundry's argument (*Mark*, 446) that only Ps 118.22 is in view. Snodgrass (*Wicked Tenants*, 100) bridges the two, advancing that it may be a case of "both . . . and," since both passages may have influenced the passion sayings. In any case, there is no evidence to affirm the verbal influence of Isa 53 on Mark 8.31 (cf. Marshall, *Gospel of Luke*, 370).

[6] Juel, 144–145. On Mark's purpose to show the divine will leading to the passion, see Hooker, 205; Lane, 301; Gundry, *Mark*, 431, 436.

not overtake him, for he understood that his ministry was being carried out in conformity with what had been predicted. Second, the context of the psalm serves to affirm Jesus' identity as Messiah, while at the same time underlining the suffering he must undergo.[7] Third, if there is a sense of scriptural inevitability attached to the prediction of rejection, the allusion carries an implicit – and equally inevitable – expectation that vindication must follow, as it does in the psalm. Fourth, it is possible, as Snodgrass argues, that with its rejection-exaltation theme Ps 118.22 "may be the basic form of the passion prediction."[8] Its use with the Son of Man sayings suggests the possibility that the rejected stone of Ps 118 may have contributed to the association of suffering with that figure.[9]

B. The Entrance to Jerusalem (Mark 11.1–11)

The first quotation of Ps 118 occurs in the context of Jesus' Entry to Jerusalem.[10] Mark has stressed that Jesus is a suffering Messiah, so although he enters Jerusalem to the sound of enthusiastic acclamation, the backdrop is one of looming confrontation. It is likely that Mark intended Ps 118, which is the only Scripture specifically quoted, to play a significant role in interpreting the action and framing the context of the narrative. It is readily apparent that the narrative is carefully crafted in its sequence, development, and highlighting of themes, to emphasize Jesus' identity as Messiah and reveal the character of his messiahship. First, in the immediately preceding account Bartimaeus publicly applied the title "Son of David" to Jesus (Mark 10.46–52). Second, the specific mention of the Mt. of Olives as the

---

[7] In Ps 118.22 the rejected stone is the king, who has undergone a period of intense suffering and humiliation, only for God to exalt and establish him. Although in its original context the Messiah is not in view, casting Jesus as a royal figure immediately following Peter's confession of him as Christ would surely be an obvious clue to an informed reader.

[8] Snodgrass, *Wicked Tenants*, 102. He suggests that at least in Mark and Luke "the dominant role in the formation of the passion predictions belongs to Psalm 118,22" (ibid., 101).

[9] To look closely at the Son of Man concept lies well outside our parameters. It is sufficient to note the possibility that Ps 118 may have aided in the association of the Son of Man with suffering. On the use of the rejected stone together with Son of Man see Kim, "Stone"; Snodgrass, *Wicked Tenants*, 101–102.

[10] The Synoptic use of Ps 118 in the Entrance Narrative provides the only clear parallel to the use of Ps 118 in the Fourth Gospel. Our primary concern is to highlight the main themes and purposes in so far as these can be ascertained in each of the Entrance Narratives, and examine where these diverge or agree with one another, especially with regard to John's account. The details – e.g., the difference of word order or word choice in each account – are well covered in the major commentaries and need not be reproduced here.

starting point for what is a deliberately staged symbolic act could easily evoke eschatological expectations (Mark 11.1; see Zech 14). Third, this careful staging, initiated by Jesus, is designed to associate him with kingship traditions.[11] Although Zech 9.9 with its coming king is not alluded to directly, Mark's emphasis on the acquisition and riding of the animal suggests that it implicitly underlies the Entrance.[12] At the same time, the lack of a clear citation of Zechariah brings focus to bear on Ps 118 and raises its profile as a royal processional pattern for the Entrance.[13] Other

---

[11] For a survey of examples of ancient formal entrances see D. R. Catchpole, "The 'triumphal' entry," 319–321; P. B. Duff, "The March of the Divine Warrior and the Advent of the Greco-Roman King: Mark's Account of Jesus' Entry into Jerusalem," 55–71. Duff (ibid., 58) argues that Zech 14, which depicts the return of Yahweh to reign, underlies the Entrance. By implication, Jesus is presented as acting in Yahweh's place. If this is the case – and I am not convinced – then it provides a thematic parallel to the New Exodus we propose in John.

[12] So Catchpole, 322; Beare, 414. Taylor (451) suggests it is probable, and Hooker (257), though less sure, leans in this direction. Mark has the most stripped down version of the Entrance, although the most emphasis on the acquisition of the animal. This probably is intended to indicate the fulfillment of Zech 9.9. In light of Mark's emphasis on the suffering of Messiah, the Zechariah passage could be especially appropriate with its characterization of the coming king as humble (see Moule, 87). Note the possible influence of the Oracle of Judah as well (see D. Krause, "The One Who Comes Unbinding the Blessing of Judah: Mark 11.1–10 as a Midrash on Genesis 49.11, Zechariah 9.9, and Psalm 118.25–26").

[13] For John's Entrance Narrative I note Tabernacles symbolism although arguing against a Tabernacles date. The same questions of dating and symbolism have been raised in Mark. In favor of a Tabernacles date see Schweizer, *Mark*, 228; C. W. F. Smith, "No Time for Figs"; idem, "Tabernacles in the Fourth Gospel and Mark." Based on the perceived necessity for a Tabernacles date, H. Patsch ("Der Einzug Jesu in Jerusalem: Ein historischer Versuch," esp. 16–26) argues for two traditions in the Gospel account, one of Jesus riding a donkey into Jerusalem and another one describing messianic acclamation. These may have been originally independent events but were joined in the Gospel tradition. Lane (390–391) leaves the question open, but notes that by not specifying that Jesus came to Jerusalem at Passover the Markan narrative allows for an extended ministry period in Jerusalem of approximately 6 months – from Tabernacles to Passover. There is little support for Nineham's (293) suggestion that the entry took place at the Feast of Dedication, although Hooker (256), who does not take a clear position, does not dismiss this possibility. Gundry (*Mark*, 629) and Mann (435) correctly question the redating of the Entry, which especially rests on the use of branches. Mark's στιβάδας (11.8) are more akin to straw/reeds than branches, and certainly far from John's palm branches (John 12.13). In favor of Tabernacles symbolism (although not dating) is that although all the main festivals share the liturgical use of Ps 118, the use of the psalm in procession is characteristic of Tabernacles. Tabernacles symbolism could therefore evoke a Ps 118 procession, and in turn the use of Ps 118 in an entrance context could evoke Tabernacles themes. If there is a Zechariah-Ps 118-Tabernacles complex in the Markan Entrance it is subtler than the Fourth Gospel's, because he lacks John's palm branches and a specific citation of Zechariah. For more on the Tabernacles festival see Str-B 2.774ff.

symbols that emphasize Jesus' royal dignity include his exercise of authority in requisitioning the colt, the fact that the colt had never been ridden,
riding as a dignitary rather than walking (as most pilgrims did) into Jerusalem, the honor shown by throwing garments on the colt to make a saddle
for Jesus, and the carpeting of the road with garments and foliage.[14] We
can affirm with Catchpole that there is "unmistakable kingly messianic
colouring" in the Entry Narrative.[15]

The way Mark describes it, a large crowd surrounding Jesus began to
cry out the words of Ps 118.25–26.[16] To this most familiar Scripture Mark
then adds, in parallel to Ps 118.26, the phrase Εὐλογημένη ἡ ἐρχομένη
βασιλεία τοῦ πατρὸς ἡμῶν Δαυίδ. In spite of the royal symbolism already
noted, some question whether Ps 118 is used messianically here. It is suggested that the cry was not suited to the person of a king,[17] that the words
were simply borrowed from the current liturgy and carried no explicit
messianic claims,[18] that Jesus' entry was subsumed in that of a group of
pilgrims whose enthusiasm was indistinguishable from that which normally

---

[14] Although not all of these are specifically signs of kingship, they are each appropriate to a king. The spreading of garments is reminiscent of the anointing and proclamation
of Jehu as king (2 Kgs 9.13). Cf. Hooker, 259; Sanders, "Ps 118," 179. As for the use
of foliage, Mann (436) argues that Mark's purpose in his unique use of στιβάδας, which
he translates as "mattress stuffing material from the fields" (cf. Dodd, *Historical Tradition
in the Fourth Gospel*, 155 n. 2), is "to defer any depiction of Jesus as king and deliverer,
and that he deliberately chose to mute the overtones of the occasion." It is true that
Matthew's – and especially John's – branches are more suitable for a religious procession,
but even if Mark's choice of words is more muted, he nevertheless indicates an abnormal
act of homage worthy of a royal figure. Against A. E. Harvey (*Jesus and the Constraints
of History*, 125), who advances the unlikely suggestion that the foliage was intended to
make "a steep and slippery path safe and more pleasant to ride on," the foliage does lend
itself to symbolic interpretation.

[15] Catchpole, "Entry," 323. Gundry (*Mark*, 626) misses when he states that Mark is
not interested in Jesus' kingship, although he acknowledges that the welcome to Jesus
has a Davidic messianic overtone (ibid., 630). It is worth pointing out that Mark's interest in a suffering Messiah does not require an emphasis on his humility and meekness,
nor is it incompatible with homage and royalty. In fact, an example of a suffering and
rejected – yet exalted – king is close at hand in Ps 118.

[16] Nineham (292) states that the ovation comes not from the multitude but from the
little band with Jesus. D. Bock (*Proclamation from Prophecy and Pattern: Lukan Old
Testament Christology*, 327) argues that Mark's account is the most indefinite about who
is acclaiming Jesus: those who encircle Jesus and use Ps 118 are his followers – presumably not a very large number. However, whether limited to followers or encompassing a
wider circle, far from suggesting a small group the text indicates it was a large and vocal
throng – the "many" and "others" who carpeted the road (11.8) now enthusiastically
shouting. Cf. Gundry, *Mark*, 630.

[17] Nineham, 292–293.

[18] Nineham, 293–294. He has in view the liturgy of the Feast of Dedication.

characterized such bands,[19] and that the addition is almost – but not quite!
– messianic, because it stops short of using the title Son of David. In short,
the words "are not full-throated Messianic homage."[20] I suggest, however,
that Mark intended something quite different from this in his use of Ps 118.

First, whatever the actual historical situation may have been, Mark does
not depict a pilgrimage procession.[21] Second, even if the words of Ps 118
had been borrowed from the liturgy of Dedication or Tabernacles, the context of these feasts would facilitate an eschatological and possibly messianic
interpretation of the psalm, especially when applied specifically to an individual in the circumstances Mark presents. Third, the addition to Ps 118.26
may be subtler but carries no less clear messianic implications than if Mark
had explicitly used the title Son of David. The phrase "kingdom of our father David" links back to Bartimaeus' confession of Jesus as Son of David
in Mark 10.47–48,[22] and is appropriate both in that David was connected
with the restoration of the kingdom,[23] and that Ps 118 was in some traditions
specifically associated with David.[24] Fourth, as the direct response to Jesus'
public symbolic action, the crowd's shouting of Ps 118 (in its unique Markan
form) indicates that they interpreted the event as heralding the imminent
restoration of David's kingdom.[25] In this sense the quotation is the crucial

---

[19] Lane, 393, 396–397.

[20] Taylor, 452 (also 457). W. Kelber (*The Kingdom in Mark: A New Place and a New Time*, 96–97) suggests that the intent of the addition is to lead the reader to be critical of Davidic messianic expectation. Crossan similarly asserts that the acclaim for the Davidic kingdom is "a function of Mark's polemic against Jerusalem in general and royal Messianism in particular" ("Redaction and Citation in Mark 11:9–10 and 11:17," 40).

[21] Mark's intent is at issue here. He does not specifically state that Jesus came to Jerusalem to celebrate a festival, there is no mention of pilgrims, and the behavior of the crowd surrounding Jesus was by any measure unusual and certainly not the average fare for pilgrim bands. Therefore to mute and even lose sight of the Entrance in a pilgrimage procession goes against the spirit and wording of the text.

[22] Catchpole ("Entry," 319) argues that Mark's plan is to link 11.1–10 with 10.46–52 in the same way as Peter's confession (8.27–30) is preceded by the healing of a blind man at Bethsaida (8.22–26). In effect, the Entry matches the confession and discloses Jesus' identity. Cf. Hooker, 257, 259–260. Although the phrase "father David" is rare, it is not unknown. See Acts 4.25; Str-B 2.26.

[23] See Lohmeyer, 231.

[24] The psalm's royal links would in any case have connected it to David in at least a general sense because of the widespread hope of a Davidic king. Harvey (*Constraints*, 127) offers the interesting suggestion that the word "blessed" would call to mind the Eighteen Benedictions, the fourteenth of which likely included a reference to the Davidic Messiah. Ps 118 is, however, a more immediate and likely parallel.

[25] Krause argues that the unbinding of the colt is a private symbolic act intended for the reader, who is supposed to recognize a "reversal" of the Gen. 49.11 oracle and therefore question whether Jesus has come "to restore Jerusalem to its Davidic glory" ("Blessing of Judah," 150). Whether Krause is convincing or not, it is clear that although

interpretive key for the Entrance Narrative, confirming and intensifying the various messianic and royal symbols and underlining their significance for elucidating Jesus' identity. Fifth, the use of Ps 118 together with the Davidic addition signals that the original royal context of the psalm should be read into the Entrance. The reader may have noted the possibility of a Davidic king as the primary actor in the psalm, especially since the addition interprets the psalm and associates it with Davidic expectations. The two greetings are parallel, proclaiming that the one who comes in the name of the Lord is the one who brings the long-awaited Davidic kingdom. Surely it would not be too difficult to connect that the one proclaimed Son of David on his approach to Jerusalem is the same one who ushers in the Davidic kingdom, and hence that the coming one is the Messiah.[26] The Hosannas accompany Ps 118.26 naturally, but they also add a flavor of acclamation and homage that is especially appropriate as an expression of the crowd's confident expectation (or hopeful anticipation) that Jesus is the coming one who will bring God's kingdom. Although the exact meaning of Hosanna is somewhat ambiguous here, at the least it illustrates Jesus' special dignity and status, and enhances the eschatological tone of the Entrance.[27]

More than the other Gospels, Mark evinces tension between messianic assertion and restraint that results in a degree of ambiguity.[28] It is not

---

Jesus accepted that the ascription of Davidic messiahship rightly applied to him, he did not approve all the expectations that went along with the identification.

[26] We agree with Gundry (*Mark*, 632–633) *contra* Lane (395–396) that the coming one in Mark 11.9 refers to Ps 118.26 and is not informed by Gen 49.10 (although the latter may be in view in Mark 11.1–6).

[27] The meaning of Hosanna is somewhat ambiguous in Mark. The phrase can easily carry an eschatological sense whether understood as an expression of jubilation or supplication. The majority of scholars state that it had lost its original Hebrew sense as a plea for salvation and become a term of greeting or acclamation (Nineham, 296; Gundry, 630; Hurtado, 173; Lane, 397; Taylor, 456), and in the Christian communities a liturgical acclamation (Mann, 437). However, this Christian use is less clear than in Matthew. It is less plausible than some scholars think that Hosanna was routinely applied to the average pilgrim as some kind of greeting, and certainly in Mark the context shows that it is not intended as a common greeting – at the least it is homage. Hooker's (256) suggestion that the pilgrims are celebrating the festival and not addressing Jesus with their Hosannas is unconvincing from a narrative point of view. It is more likely that at the time of Jesus the cry was still understood as a plea for God's intervention and salvation, and thus carried eschatological connotations. However, although Schweizer (*Mark*, 227) and Hooker (259) acknowledge this, they nevertheless argue that Mark understood it as a shout of praise. The second use of Hosanna (Mark 11.10: "Hosanna in the highest") is probably directed to God, either as an invocation for him to initiate the salvation and deliverance that will accompany the reinstatement of the kingdom (Lane, 398), or as a cry of acclamation for having inaugurated it through Jesus (Lagrange, *Marc*, 274).

[28] Cf. Lane, 393.

surprising, then, that the other Entrance Narratives state Jesus' kingship more explicitly, and perhaps more clearly elucidate the messianic import of the event.[29] However, Markan ambiguity should not be exaggerated. Whether or not the event was understood clearly at the time it took place, Mark invested the Entrance with messianic significance and intended for his readers to perceive in it the appearance of the Messiah.[30] More specifically, Mark portrays Jesus as the Davidic Messiah.[31] It is significant that the behavior of the crowd is directly related to Jesus' initial deliberate action. The implication, as Catchpole observes, is that Jesus silently endorses their actions as a proper response to his own: "The claims of others that he is a messianic figure are nothing less than his own claim to such a status."[32] There is, however, a subtle disjunction with the original context of Ps 118: it is easy to lose in the tumult of Mark's jubilant crowd, hailing the Davidic Messiah on his arrival to Jerusalem, that in the psalm it is the religious authorities who lead the way in recognizing and receiving the coming one. In Mark, the religious leaders are conspicuous by their absence.[33]

---

[29] Nineham (291) suggests that Mark "carefully avoids making the messianic character of the incident fully explicit." Lane (393) describes it as "remarkably restrained in its messianic assertion." Cf. Schweizer, *Mark*, 227.

[30] Against such an initial understanding see Hurtado, 168; Lohmeyer, 233; Lane, 393. On the messianic significance of the Entrance see Swete, 246–253.

[31] So Catchpole, "Entry," 334. Against the argument that Mark presents an anti-Davidic polemic, M. de Jonge points out that even though the term Son of David is not used in the Entrance, Jesus is nevertheless, in his own way, Son of David: "Mark does not make Jesus reject the term as such, but only as it functions in the expectations of the scribes as he describes them in his Gospel" ("Jesus, Son of David and Son of God," 98). It is possible that Mark intends to contrast the Davidic expectations of the enthusiastic crowd with Jesus' suffering messiahship (so Schweizer, *Mark*, 227), but although the Gospel does seek to correct expectations, this is not explicit in the Entrance, where the flavor is confessional.

[32] Catchpole, "Entry," 323. Lagrange (*Marc*, 274) similarly notes that Jesus accepts and even incites the acclaim.

[33] In Matthew (21.15–16), Luke (19.39) and John (12.19) the disjunction is more obvious, as the authorities are present at the Entrance and in clear opposition to Jesus. Although the primary point of reference is Ps 118, parallel entrances in the Greco-Roman world would magnify the failure of the authorities to welcome Mark's royal Messiah. Duff argues that Mark first creates and then subverts expectations of a triumphal entry so that readers will grasp the significance of Jesus' suffering messiahship ("Divine Warrior", 67, 71). Of course rejection by the leaders is at the core of the passion predictions, but although the distinction may be subtle, I suggest that the emphasis of the reversal of Ps 118 in the Entrance is on the failure of the leaders of Israel to receive their Messiah rather than on his suffering. Cf. Sanders, "Ps 118," 185.

C. The Parable of the Wicked Tenants (Mark 12.1–11)

In response to questions about Jesus' authority, Mark punctuates the end of the parable of the Wicked Tenants with a quote from Ps 118.22–23, identifying Jesus with the psalm's rejected stone.[34] Although some have questioned whether it makes sense in the context of the parable, an examination of the quote's function suggests that it was an intelligible and appropriate conclusion.[35] First, through a well-recognized wordplay the quotation identifies the psalm's rejected stone with the parable's son, thus facilitating Jesus' identification with the latter and interpreting the conflict in the parable in terms of that between Jesus and the religious authorities.[36] Second, the quotation underlines the rejection of Jesus by the religious establishment. Unlike Matthew and Luke, Mark does not specifically indicate the consequences this entails for the leaders, with the result that the emphasis falls to such a degree on their rejection of the son that Hooker suggests it is "the real turning point of the gospel, the moment at which the Jewish authorities reject their Messiah, and when his fate – and theirs – is sealed."[37] Third, although the beginning of the quote provides the scriptural frame for the rejection of Jesus, the citation goes beyond the dismal end of the parable and signals a reversal in keeping with the theme of vindication and exaltation that dominates the psalm. This in turn carries an unspoken yet clear warning to those who oppose Jesus: any victory they have will be temporary, for they cannot hope to thwart the divine plan.[38]

---

[34] The attention paid to the use of Ps 118 in the New Testament usually focuses on Ps 118.22, no doubt because stone *testimonia*, in which Ps 118.22 played a foundational and key role, were central to the church's early apologetic. However, if there are any traces of Ps 118.22 in the Fourth Gospel they are very faint, so we have not entered into the complex of issues that surround the subject. These have been treated in a number of theses, monographs, and articles. For bibliographical information on the voluminous secondary literature see Snodgrass, *Wicked Tenants*; Wright, *Jesus and the Victory of God*, 497–501.

[35] Nineham (313) argues that the main point of the quote – rejection – is at most of secondary importance in the parable. Hooker (275–277) in turn advances that the point of the parable is punishment (the indictment of Israel's leaders), which is at odds with the quote's emphasis on vindication. For this reason both classify it as a latter addition to the parable. Against this see Gundry, *Mark*, 689–690.

[36] On the wordplay see Snodgrass, *Wicked Tenants*, 113–118.

[37] Hooker, 278. Cf. Matt 21.43–44; Luke 20.18. There is no question that in Mark the rejection of Jesus carries serious consequences, but in this case they are not clearly spelled out. Note that the emphasis on rejection is in keeping with that predicted of the Son of Man in Mark 8.31.

[38] On the purpose of the quotation being to point towards exaltation after death see Kim, "Stone," 135; Lane, 420.

Fourth, the quote presents a shocking reversal of the psalm's original context, so that the leaders of Israel are cast as opponents of God's chosen king and thus enemies of God himself. A psalm of national hope and comfort becomes instead an indictment for treason.[39] Fifth, the exaltation of the stone affirms the status of Jesus' new community as the true Israel of God. By rejecting the stone the Jewish leaders have forfeited any claim they had to authority: the vineyard has been handed over to others.[40]

D. The Hymn (Mark 14.26)

Mark concludes his account of the institution of the Lord's Supper with reference to the singing of a hymn. This represents a liturgical allusion, as there is general agreement that the singing of the second half of the Hallel is in view, in keeping with the practice at Passover.[41] The allusion ensures that the Lord's Supper is interpreted in a Passover setting, with all the appropriate themes of eschatological redemption and hope the feast evoked. At the least, it contributes to viewing Jesus' actions and words as "a new passover rite."[42] Although Ps 118 is not directly quoted or alluded to, the reference could easily bring to mind the primary themes of the psalm and its role in the Passover liturgy. Considering the importance of Ps 118 in the self-identification of Jesus, the recitation of the Hallel may have been especially poignant that night, particularly considering that Ps 118 formed the climax to the Hallel. In this way the psalm became Jesus' own prayer before he went out to the Mount of Olives and the fulfillment of his mission.[43]

---

[39] In the psalm, it is the "nations" who fight against the king, and the religious authorities who affirm that the rejected stone comes with the authority of the Lord. There are examples of the scribes sometimes being identified as builders – in a positive sense – in Jewish literature: see Str-B 1.876; 3.379; Gundry, *Mark*, 663.

[40] Gundry (*Mark*, 663) suggests that a transfer of leadership from the Sanhedrin to Jesus and his disciples is in view. Hooker (277) notes that the transfer of the vineyard may signify that worship now centers on Jesus and not the temple, an idea remarkably close to that of the Fourth Gospel. On the new community see J. Marcus, *The Way of the Lord: Christological Exegesis of the Old Testament in the Gospel of Mark*, 127.

[41] See Hurtado, 227; Nineham, 387; Hooker, 344; Lane, 509. On the tradition of singing Hallel at Passover being current in the New Testament period see Gundry, *Mark*, 846.

[42] The phrase comes from Hooker (341), who suggests that, whether or not the original setting was a Passover meal, in a sense the events become a new Passover rite. Hengel (*Studies in Early Christology*, 237) observes that Ps 118 "marks directly the transition from the Jewish Passover liturgy to the early Christian eucharistic liturgy."

[43] See Lane (509) for a brief but effective example of how the significant themes of Pss 116–118 may have informed Jesus' prayer.

Summary

Mark uses Ps 118 sparingly but at critical points in the narrative (Mark 8.31; 11.9–10; 12.10–11). In the first passion prediction the allusion to Ps 118.22 helps introduce and define the suffering character of Jesus' messianic mission and shows that this was in conformity with Scripture. The quotation of Ps 118.25–26 is the interpretive key for the climactic Entrance Narrative, identifying him as the royal Davidic Messiah and hence affirming the eschatological import of his mission as the one who brings the kingdom and thus deliverance. Whereas in the passion prediction the use of Ps 118.22 emphasizes his suffering and rejection, the quotation of Ps 118.22–23 in the parable of the Wicked Tenants brings Jesus' ultimate victory and vindication to the forefront, casting his opponents as enemies of God himself and establishing his own authority as God's chosen one and therefore Israel's legitimate leader. Mark's use of the psalm is at its core bound up with the identity of Jesus – whether as rejected/exalted stone or royal coming one – and the failure of Israel's leaders to acknowledge their Messiah.

II. Psalm 118 in Luke

A. *The Baptist's Question (Luke 7.18–23)*

Luke first alludes to Ps 118 in the question that the Baptist sends two of his disciples to ask of Jesus: "Are you the one who comes (Σὺ εἶ ὁ ἐρχόμενος), or do we wait for another?" (7.19). The phrase ὁ ἐρχόμενος links back to the Baptist's preaching in Luke 3.16,[44] but also evokes Ps 118.26. If the connection to the psalm is not immediately obvious, it becomes so in Luke 13.35 and 19.38.[45] Both from the question and Jesus' response it is apparent that messianic expectation is at issue, and thus that

---

[44] Cf. Bock, 1.657; Nolland, 1.332; Wagner, "Psalm 118," 161.

[45] Nolland (1.329) contends that Hab 2.3 stands behind John's question. He is probably correct in maintaining that "the coming one" does not refer to any one figure in a specific strand of eschatological expectation, but rather the term "is a means of bringing to expression in a nonspecific manner the essence of all Jewish eschatological hope." However, that Luke twice draws the phrase from Ps 118 (in 13.35; 19.38) suggests a literary link to the use in this passage. Fitzmyer (1.666) too quickly dismisses the influence of the psalm here because he erroneously limits its application to festal pilgrims and ignores the psalm's royal links. Instead he advances that the phrase refers to Yahweh's messenger identified as Elijah (Mal 3.23), although Jesus rejects that role. For the different figures in Judaism seen as coming, see Fitzmyer, 1.666.

the term ὁ ἐρχόμενος, as in the Baptist's preaching, is invested with messianic significance.[46] Apparently Jesus' ministry had not followed the course John anticipated, so he seeks to clarify whether and what kind of Messiah Jesus is.[47] In response Jesus provides a demonstration of power that evokes a number of messianic prophecies in Isaiah, and signals their fulfillment.[48] Jesus does not explicitly state whether he is the coming one or not, but his message to John is nonetheless clear: he is doing the work of the eschatological age, in him the era of salvation has arrived. Therefore, even though Jesus does not conform to his expectations, John should recognize that Jesus is indeed the coming one whose way he was tasked to prepare.[49] Although the Baptist's question is reported in Matt 11.2–6, the repetition of the question by John's disciples is unique to Luke 7.20 and emphasizes Jesus' identification as the coming one.

B. The First Passion Prediction (Luke 9.22)

As in the Markan parallel (8.31–33), Luke's first passion prediction follows Peter's confession of Jesus as the Christ and alludes to Ps 118.22. Surprisingly, most commentators miss the allusion, and NA[27] does not list Luke 9.22 as alluding to the psalm, even though it does recognize the allusion in Mark 8.31.[50] The significant link to Ps 118.22 is the verb ἀποδοκιμάζω, which in its 9 NT occurrences always refers to the rejection of Jesus (with the exception of Heb 12.17), and six times quotes or alludes

---

[46] Marshall (*Gospel of Luke*, 290) concludes that we should see "vague messianic expectation" in the question. Cf. Bock, 1.657. On the identification of Messiah with the coming one in the Baptist's preaching see Marshall, *Luke: Historian and Theologian*, 126. On the coming one as an eschatological and messianic title see P. Grelot, "'Celui qui vient' (Mt 11, 3 et Lc 7, 19)," 276–277.

[47] For a summary of the various options advanced to explain the motivating reason for the Baptist's question see Fitzmyer, 1.664–665; Bock, 1.664–665. It is possible that he was not so much doubting Jesus' messianic identity as questioning the absence of vengeance and judgment that the Baptist had preached would be an aspect of the coming one's ministry (cf. Nolland, 1.327, 331; Grelot, "Celui qui vient," 278). This should not diminish, however, that he saw Jesus' ministry largely in positive terms (i.e., not primarily in terms of negative judgment).

[48] Behind the list in Luke 7.22 lie Isa 35.5–7; 29.18–19; 61.1; 26.19. Note that since these texts speak of the works of Yahweh, Jesus is announcing the fulfillment of Yahweh's works. Grelot ("Celui qui vient," 286–287) accordingly suggests that the coming of Yahweh can be seen in the works of Jesus.

[49] Cf. Marshall, 287, 292; Bock, *Proclamation*, 113; J. Lambrecht, "'Are you the one who is to come, or shall we look for another?' The Gospel Message of Jesus Today," 123.

[50] Exceptions include Marshall, *Gospel of Luke*, 370; Wagner, "Psalm 118," 162.

to the psalm.[51] It is therefore likely that Luke 9.22 and 17.25 also allude to Ps 118.22. The function of the allusion in Luke shares much in common with Mark. Now that Jesus' messianic identity has been established (Luke 9.20), the emphasis turns for the first time to the necessity of suffering in order to fulfill the divine plan for salvation.[52] Of course, vindication accompanies the promise of suffering. Again we note that the rejection motif draws heavily on Ps 118.22, and that Ps 118 may have aided in the synthesis of suffering with the Son of Man.[53]

C. The Lament over Jerusalem (Luke 13.34–35)

The first quotation of Ps 118 in Luke follows Jesus' resolute declaration to the Pharisees that he will proceed to Jerusalem regardless of threats to his life (Luke 13.31–33), for he expects to perish there (13.33). This leads to Jesus' lament over the city, for he knows that their obstinate refusal to respond to God and the violence with which they meet the messengers he sends (Luke 13.34) will bring tragic consequences – their house will be desolate (Luke 13.35a; see Jer 12.7; 22.5). Jesus then declares that the inhabitants of Jerusalem will not see him until they receive him, in the words of Ps 118.26, as the one who comes in the name of the Lord (Luke 13.35b). Since in Luke the phrase ὁ ἐρχόμενος has been invested with messianic significance, the sense here is that until Israel acknowledges Jesus as her messianic deliverer she will be unable to escape judgment.[54] Luke's wording is close to Matt 23.37–39, but whereas Matthew places the lament after Jesus' Entry to Jerusalem, Luke has located it in his Travel Narrative *prior* to the Entrance. As a result it is most natural to link it with the Entry as a conditional prophecy that offers Jerusalem an

---

[51] Four times it appears in quotations of Ps 118.22 (Matt 21.42; Mark 12.10; Luke 20.17; 1 Pet 2.7), and twice in allusions (Mark 8.31; 1 Pet 2.4). On the link between the verb and Ps 118.22 see Snodgrass, *Wicked Tenants*, 100. Note his list of other scholars who make the connection. The LXX use of the verb suggests that Ps 118.22 is the most appropriate contextual and verbal parallel to the passion predictions. The other five uses are in Jeremiah, four detailing the Lord's rejection of people (Jer 6.30; 7.29; 14.19; 38.35) and one showing people rejecting the Lord (8.9). None of these have a theme of exaltation after rejection.

[52] Cf. Marshall, *Gospel of Luke*, 367; Bock, 1.844; Nolland, 2.465; Fitzmyer, 1.780.

[53] On Ps 118 underlying the rejection motif see Nolland, 2.462. Bock (1.952–953) argues that the suffering royal figure of Ps 118 was one of three possible elements at the base of the synthesis, the other two being Isa 53 and the Psalter's (and early Judaism's) emphasis on the exaltation of the righteous.

[54] Bock (2.1243) claims that this is a turning point in the Travel Narrative: "The open door that Jesus mentioned in the previous parable is closing for this generation of Israel."

opportunity to receive her Messiah and avoid judgment.[55] Against this, the fact that there is a note of rejection in Luke 19.41–44, and that it is Jesus' disciples rather than the religious authorities and citizens of Jerusalem that cry out the greeting of Ps 118, leads the majority of commentators to dismiss the Entrance as the fulfillment of the prophecy and link it instead to the *parousia*.[56] However, Luke's point may be that the prophecy was fulfilled – albeit in an ironic and tragic way – in 19.37–40. Although Luke does not advance that God has abandoned Israel, neither does the prophecy unequivocally require that Israel receive her Messiah, either at the Entrance or the *parousia*.

The quotation performs several significant functions. First, it is the key christological use of the OT in the Travel Narrative, intensifying Jesus' messianic and eschatological significance: a result of judgment or salvation depends entirely on the nation's response to Jesus. Second, the quote ensures that the Ps 118 greeting and the title ὁ ἐρχόμενος are charged with eschatological expectation. Whether the prophecy is fulfilled in the Entrance or not, the failure of the majority to receive Jesus with the words of the psalm marks a definitive and tragic point in Israel's history. If Luke's intention is to hold out hope for a turning of the Jews, then the disciples' cries in 19.37–38 are a preview of the eschatological welcome that will be offered to Messiah at his *parousia*. In any case, Ps 118 is identified as the chorus that should have or will greet the Messiah. Third, the quotation also creates tension, for while it voices hope that Jerusalem will receive Jesus as Messiah, Luke has advanced the theological necessity for suffering to precede exaltation, and Jesus has just lamented the city's murderous treatment of God's servants. A possibly hopeful statement is therefore framed with sober declarations of rejection and death,[57] inevitably raising the

---

[55] D. C. Allison ("Matt 23:39 = Luke 13:35b as a Conditional Prophecy") argues persuasively for the conditional nature of the prophecy, and Wagner ("Psalm 118," 163) makes a strong case that the Entrance is in view.

[56] Marshall (*Gospel of Luke*, 577) acknowledges that this may refer to the Entry into Jerusalem in a heavily ironical way, but because of the parallel Matthean context he ultimately opts for the *parousia*. Bock (*Proclamation*, 326) rejects out of hand that Luke 19.38 is the fulfillment. Nolland (2.742) and C. A. Evans (216) maintain that the prophecy envisions a willing recognition of Jesus as Messiah at the *parousia*, and Bock (2.1251) that such a turning will take place before the second coming. Manson (*The Sayings of Jesus: As Recorded in the Gospels according to St. Matthew and St. Luke*, 128) and Geldenhuys (385) hold the opposite view, that rather than the second coming offering a last hope of salvation it signals final judgment. Recognition will then be forced. Plummer (353) takes the lonely position that the conversion of Jews throughout time is in view.

[57] A reader attuned to Luke's use of Ps 118 may have noted the use of Ps 118.22 in the passion predictions of Luke 9.22 and 17.25 standing on either side of Ps 118.26 in Luke 13.35b.

level of suspense for the reader who now waits to learn the fate both of Jesus and Jerusalem.[58]

D. An Additional Passion Prediction (Luke 17.25)

Luke inserts into a discourse on the coming days of the Son of Man (17.22–37) that Jesus must first suffer and be rejected (ἀποδοκιμάζω). It appears that Luke drew on the first passion prediction (Luke 9.22), and once again alludes to Ps 118.22.[59] Although Luke naturally uses Ps 118.22 – as he does elsewhere – in service of the themes of the theological necessity of the rejection and vindication of the Messiah, what stands out in this case is the threat of judgment. Whereas in Luke 9.22 it is the religious authorities who cause Jesus' death, responsibility is here extended to "this generation." That the days of the Son of Man are compared both to the catastrophic flood in the times of Noah and the fiery destruction of Sodom warns of dire consequences for those who reject Jesus. Wagner points out that although vindication is connected with resurrection in other uses of Ps 118.22 (e.g., Luke 9.22; 20.17; Acts 4.11), here it appears to come at the *parousia*.[60]

E. The Entrance to Jerusalem (Luke 19.28–40)

As the single clear reference to the OT in the Entrance Narrative, Luke's second quotation of Ps 118.26 can be expected to play a significant role in interpreting the event. This is especially true since Luke presents this as Jesus' first visit to Jerusalem, and the prophecy in 13.35 has raised the hope that the city will receive him as Messiah with the words of Ps 118. Although Luke's account differs from Mark's in some respects, they share a focus on Jesus' identity as king and Davidic Messiah that Luke's changes tend to highlight.[61] Immediately prior to the Entry Jesus implicitly

---

[58] On Luke's use of Ps 118 to create dramatic tension see Wagner, "Psalm 118," 163–164.

[59] This prediction is unique to Luke, with no Matthean parallel. On the possible link to Luke 9.22 see Nolland, 2.856, 859; Marshall, *Gospel of Luke*, 662. Wagner contends that although for the passion prediction in 9.22 Luke drew on Mark's wording (Mark 8.31), the repetition of ἀποδοκιμάζω in 17.25 suggests "both a recognition of and further exploitation of this intertextual echo of Ps 118" ("Psalm 118," 163). In other words, Luke recognized and intentionally used Ps 118.

[60] Wagner, "Psalm 118," 164.

[61] We will note Lukan changes where appropriate. Although we have argued that Mark is not disinterested in presenting Jesus as king in the Entrance, Luke is less subtle in underlining royal and messianic elements.

identifies himself with the nobleman in the parable of the Pounds (Luke 19.11–27), having already accepted the title Son of David (Luke 18.25–43). As in Mark, Jesus directs the acquisition of the animal, but Luke alone emphasizes the action of the disciples in mounting Jesus on the colt. For some, Luke's use of ἐπιβιβάζω is evidence that he recognized an implicit use of Zech 9.9 in Mark's account and sought to redactionally strengthen the link,[62] although the enthronement of Solomon (1 Kgs 1.33) provides a closer contextual and verbal parallel.[63] That Jesus rode on a specially selected colt indicates symbolic intent, as does the use of garments to make a saddle and carpet the path, and there may be some significance to the fact that Luke is the only evangelist who specifies that the cries of Ps 118.26 began at the descent of the Mt. of Olives.[64] In any case, it is Luke's use of Ps 118.26 that explicitly identifies Jesus as king and turns up the volume on what would otherwise be much more subtle evocations of Israel's kingship traditions.[65]

Luke's addition of the interpretative gloss ὁ βασιλεὺς (19.38) to his quotation of Ps 118.26 is especially significant because, although Jesus has been implicitly understood as a royal figure, this is the first time that he is specifically identified as king.[66] It is also the only unambiguously positive reference to his kingship, for although Jesus is elsewhere called king (Luke 23.2, 3, 37, 38) it is in a mocking rather than confessional sense. Psalm 118 is therefore the vehicle for Luke's most emphatic statement about Jesus' identity as king. Luke has also dropped Mark's addition to Ps 118 of "the coming kingdom of our father David," perhaps to avoid political misunderstanding,[67] and/or counter the impression that the kingdom of

---

[62] See Wagner, "Psalm 118," 165; Bock (2.1556). M. L. Strauss (*The Davidic Messiah in Luke-Acts: The Promise and its Fulfillment in Lukan Christology*, 313) argues that Luke's redaction emphasizes the oracle, although like Mark he leaves it an implicit allusion. Against the presence of Zechariah see Fitzmyer, 2.1244. Kinman (*Jesus' Entry Into Jerusalem: In the Context of Lukan Theology and the Politics of His Day*, 119–120) suggests that Luke may have avoided quoting Zech 9.9 because of political concerns.

[63] For parallels between the two narratives see Kinman, *Entry*, 94–95, 110; N. Fernandez Marcos, "La unción de Salomón y la entrada de Jesús en Jerusalén: 1 Re 1,33–40/ Lk 19,35–40," 89–97. Marshall (*Gospel of Luke*, 714) notes 1 Kgs 1.33 as a parallel to understanding that the act of mounting Jesus was a sign of kingship.

[64] Although it is by no means clear, this could evoke a Tabernacles-Ps 118-Zechariah context.

[65] Kinman (*Entry*, 101) correctly observes that Luke brings into play most features of OT royal entry narratives.

[66] Luke's redaction highlights and makes explicit Mark's implicit portrayal of Jesus as king in the Entrance. Cf. Strauss, *Davidic Messiah*, 316; Nolland, 3.927; Wagner, "Ps 118," 166; Bock, 2.1558.

[67] Cf. Kinman, *Entry*, 120; Strauss, *Davidic Messiah*, 315; Marshall, *Gospel of Luke*, 709. Luke also does not refer to the use of foliage/branches, perhaps for the same reason.

God should have been inaugurated on or shortly after Jesus' arrival to Jerusalem.[68] As a result the emphasis falls not on the arrival of the kingdom, which is not yet to appear (see Luke 19.11–27), but on that of the king who will rule that kingdom.[69] The fact that the first Lukan proclamation of Jesus as king specifically uses the words of a royal processional psalm, and occurs in the context of a procession that may evoke the enthronement of Solomon, may suggest that Jesus is coming to Jerusalem to be enthroned – or at least acknowledged and received – as king. In light of the prophecy in 13.35, which describes the use of Ps 118 to greet the Messiah, Ps 118 would then provide the pattern and context for the processional entry of the Davidic Messiah.[70] At the least, the addition of ὁ βασιλεὺς draws in the context of royal procession original to the psalm.[71]

The quotation of Ps 118 also functions as a rebuke of the nation's leadership and a portent of judgment. First, Luke's emphasis on Jesus' royal status stands in stark contrast to the failure of Jerusalem to receive him in a proper way: there is no mention of the citizenry of Jerusalem, for Luke has limited the acclaim to Jesus' disciples ("the whole multitude of the disciples," [19.37]), and the Pharisees' chorus is one of protest (19.39).[72] Jesus' answer to the Pharisees (Luke 19.40) should be interpreted against the backdrop of Ps 118 as a rebuke of the nation's leaders, for they neglected to fulfill the role that in the royal entrance liturgy was required of them, namely welcoming the king as the one who comes in the name of

---

[68] Cf. Evans, 289; Fitzmyer, 2.1245–1246.

[69] Luke omits Mark's initial and concluding Hosanna, perhaps because his readers would not have understood it (Marshall, 715; Fitzmyer, 2.1251). It is not clear that the couplet in 19.38 is Luke's paraphrase of Hosanna, as Plummer (448) claims. Our interest is that Luke's phrase may evoke the announcement of Jesus' birth as Messiah and Savior in Luke 2.10–14, therefore accentuating Jesus' identity as Messiah and savior in the Entrance. See Fitzmyer, 2.1251; Wagner, "Ps 118," 167.

[70] Although there is no mention of David in the Entrance, it is nonetheless clear that the king is Davidic. Luke identifies Jesus with David several times (Luke 1.27, 32, 61; 2.4; 18.38, 39) and it is clear that the Messiah is from the house of David (Luke 2.11).

[71] Marshall (*Gospel of Luke*, 715) notes that Ps 118.26 was originally addressed to the king, and that "this original force reappears in Lk." with the addition. Note that Luke compresses the narrative so that Jesus proceeds into the temple, as does the king in Ps 118, although Jesus' actions in disrupting the sacrifice would prove a reversal of the psalm.

[72] Unlike Mark, who leaves room for a wider spectrum of support, Luke has narrowed the scope of those who acclaim Jesus. Cf. Evans, 294; Nolland, 3.926; Marshall, *Gospel of Luke*, 715. This failure leads Kinman (*Entry*, 97, 143) to describe the Entry as a-triumphal in light of expectations surrounding Greco-Roman entries. On the development of the motif of the rejected king in the Lukan Travel Narrative see A. Denaux, "Old Testament Models for the Lukan Travel Narrative," 297.

the Lord. The extent of their failure is revealed in the charge that the inanimate stones of the temple would have been more responsive than they, if the disciples had not taken up the necessary cry.[73] The words of Ps 118.26 are therefore – for the religious leaders at least – both a mocking rebuke and a resounding indictment.[74] At the same time they are, second, words that signal judgment. Luke is the only evangelist explicitly to link predictions of destruction (19.41–44) with Jerusalem's failure to receive Jesus properly in his royal entrance.[75] Jesus' prophetic lament clearly evokes the earlier lament in Luke 13.34–35, suggesting that the latter has been fulfilled, albeit in an unexpected way with disastrous consequences: because Jerusalem did not recognize the time of its visitation and rejected its deliverer, it will be desolate.[76] For this reason Jesus weeps.

F. The Parable of the Wicked Tenants (Luke 20.9–19)

Jesus finishes the provocative parable of the Wicked Tenants with a quotation of Ps 118.22, although Luke, unlike Mark and Matthew, omits Ps 118.23.[77] The function here is similar to that of the quotation in Mark

---

[73] Wagner ("Ps 118," 168) suggests a number of additional allusions to Ps 118, arguing that there is a contrast intended between Jesus as the chosen cornerstone of Ps 118.22 and the stones of the temple and city, starting in Luke 19.40 and continuing in 19.44; 20.6, 17–18; 21.5–6. Although the echoes are somewhat faint, this not implausible suggestion would subtly underline the destruction that must inevitably follow the rejection of God's chosen stone.

[74] See Bock, *Proclamation*, 125; Sanders, "Ps 118," 187. Note that Jesus' answer makes clear that he approves of the disciples' understanding and acclaim, whereas in Mark this must be inferred.

[75] Kinman (*Entry*, 144) suggests that Luke's readers would have understood the connection, noting that not granting a proper entry to an important figure could have serious consequences in the Greco-Roman world.

[76] Fulfillment of Luke 13.35 is at least a possibility (cf. Wagner, "Ps 118," 167: "Lk. 19.37–38 *is* a fulfillment of 13.35, but in an unexpected and tragic manner.") The time of visitation refers to the entirety of Jesus' ministry (cf. Nolland, 3.932; Bock, 2.1558), but it is specifically the failure to recognize this in the Entrance that is in view here. Although the link between the two prophetic laments is clear (cf. Evans, 295; Fitzmyer, 2.1242; Bock, 2.1546), this does not always translate into support for the fulfillment of 13.35 in the Entrance. Marshall (*Gospel of Luke*, 715) argues that the significance of the Entrance scene is that the prophecy in 13.35 was *not* fulfilled at this point (cf. Bock, 2.1558). Since the prophecy in 13.35 does *not* state that Jerusalem must of necessity greet its Messiah, the city's failure to receive Jesus does not automatically call for fulfillment at some future time. In any case, whether the fulfillment of 13.35 is past or future, the failure of Jerusalem is not in doubt.

[77] Wagner ("Psalm 118," 164 n. 34, 175) argues that there is a "noteworthy" shift in focus from Ps 118.26 to Ps 118.22 following the Entrance, which he links to the failure of Jerusalem to welcome Jesus as the coming one. The implication is that this shift

12.10–11, except that Luke intensifies two motifs. First, the quote naturally looks back to the passion predictions and forward to the cross, but the fact that Luke particularly highlights the failure both of the religious leaders and the nation as a whole in the Entrance underlines more starkly the contrast between their rejection of Jesus and the psalm's promise of certain vindication. Second, the manner in which all the evangelists use Ps 118.22 carries an implicit note of warning for those depicted as opposing God's chosen cornerstone, but Luke 20.18 magnifies this to a declaration of impending judgment with allusion to a stone that will crush and destroy. While it is possible that Luke is alluding to Dan 2.34, 45f.,[78] it is in any case clear that ἐκεῖνον τὸν λίθον refers back to the rejected/exalted stone of Luke 20.17, and therefore that one's fate depends entirely on one's reaction to Jesus.

G. Peter's Sermon (Acts 4.11)

Luke's last reference to Ps 118.22 was pre-passion (Luke 20.17–18). Now Peter quotes from Ps 118.22 in his defense before the religious authorities, but the force of the text has changed from promise to proof of Jesus' exalted status: the rejected stone has, through resurrection, been thoroughly vindicated and exalted, and is now incontestably God's cornerstone. This makes clear that for Luke the psalm spoke of Jesus' death and resurrection. Luke explicitly identifies the religious leaders as the villains ("builders") of the psalm, but although this carries an implicit warning, the emphasis shifts from the earlier theme of retribution and judgment to the offer of salvation in Peter's preaching.[79]

---

confirms and is a result of Jesus' rejection by his people. There is indeed a shift, but this is rather a function of the Entrance Narrative, which depicts the arrival of the coming king to Jerusalem: after the coming one has come, there is no further need to emphasize his coming. Only Matthew speaks of the coming one after the Entrance, and this not to confirm that he was received but rather to highlight, as in Luke, the failure of Jerusalem's leaders. Therefore one should not read too much significance into the lack of references to Ps 118.26 following the Entrance.

[78] So Marshall, *Gospel of Luke*, 726.

[79] Although Ps 110 is more often given as a background for Acts 2.33 and 5.31, Wagner ("Ps 118," 172) plausibly argues that Luke's previous use of Ps 118 in the Gospel makes allusions to Ps. 118.16 likely. Cf. Dodd, *According to the Scriptures*, 99; Bruce, *Acts*, 66, 112–113. Especially on 5.31 see Daly-Denton, *David*, 46. Against this see Lindars, *Apologetic*, 43–44; Bock, *Proclamation*, 352 n. 89; Marshall, *Acts*, 78–79, 120; Longenecker, 279–280 (for Acts 2.33 only).

Summary

Of the three Synoptic evangelists Luke refers most often to Ps 118, and for the most part at significant points in the narrative.[80] Luke uses Ps 118.26 in the Baptist's questioning to establish Jesus' messianic identity and describe his works as those of the eschatological age (7.19–20). To the usual themes of rejection and vindication that accompany Ps 118.22 (see Luke 9.22) Luke adds a warning of judgment in 17.25 that he reiterates in the parable of the Wicked Tenants by turning the rejected stone into a crushing stone (20.17–18). In the post-resurrection preaching of Peter, Ps 118.22 becomes the definitive proof from Scripture for Jesus' vindication as the Christ (Acts 4.10–11). In the prophetic lament over Jerusalem (13.34–35) Luke creates dramatic tension as the possibility is held out that Jerusalem will welcome her Messiah with the words of Ps 118.26. The quotation also heightens Jesus' eschatological significance and underlines the determinative import of the Entrance for Israel's future. The most important use of Ps 118 is in the Entrance Narrative. First it interprets the event: Luke uses it to confirm Jesus' identity as king, turn up the volume on the royal traditions of Israel, and define the Entrance as the coming of the Davidic Messianic king to Jerusalem offering salvation. Second, it helps to shape the event. Because of the previous allusion to Ps 118.26 in Luke 13.35 the Entrance is interpreted as an enactment of a Ps 118 royal entrance that expects a proper welcome by the city. Third, the quotation signals Jerusalem's failure. Because the nation did not acknowledge Jesus' identity with the words of the psalm it missed its opportunity for deliverance and will now suffer the tragic consequences. Above all, Luke uses Ps 118 to underscore Jesus' absolute significance both in salvation and judgment.

III. Psalm 118 in Matthew

A. The Baptist's Question (Matt 11.2–6)

Matthew's only pre-Entrance use of Ps 118 is in the Baptist's question.[81] The function of Ps 118 in the passage is for the most part the same as in

---

[80] Wagner plausibly suggests a number of additional allusions and echoes to Ps 118. See the table of proposed quotation and allusion in his article "Psalm 118," 176–178.

[81] As in Mark 1.7 and Luke 3.16, the coming one of the Baptist's preaching (Matt 3.11) anticipates the use of the title in the Entrance (cf. R. Krüger, "Humilde, montado en un burrito: Mateo 21:1–11 y el recurso escriturístico," 81), and for Luke and Matthew links further with the question of the Baptist (Luke 7.19–20 ‖ Matt 11.2) and the prophetic lament (Luke 13.35 ‖ Matt 23.39). Although the Baptist does not explicitly

the Lukan parallel (Luke 7.18–23), except for a couple of unique Matthean details. First, Matthew states that the immediate cause of the Baptist's question is his having heard about "the works of the Christ" (Matt 11.2), thus signaling to his readers from the start that the question and Jesus' answer have messianic significance. The "works" refer both to Jesus' teaching (Matt 5–7) and his miracles (Matt 8–9), and interpret them as messianic. Whether the Baptist recognized the works as those of the Messiah is unclear; if he did, then Matthew is suggesting that John's personal doubts were less concerned with Jesus' identity as Messiah than the non-judgmental character of his messiahship, which was not in keeping with the Baptist's preaching.[82] Otherwise he is asking whether Jesus could indeed be the Messiah. In any case, in John's mouth the phrase "the coming one" is clearly a designation for Messiah.[83]

Second, unlike Luke's account where Jesus provides a demonstration of power for the Baptist's disciples, in Matthew Jesus points them back to what has already been accomplished. Although Matthew has prepared the reader to recognize the works that Jesus refers to as those of the Messiah, the allusion to several Isaiah passages in Jesus' answer significantly underscores this and interprets his entire ministry to this point as fulfilling eschatological and messianic prophecies.[84] The coming one therefore refers to the one who brings eschatological salvation. If up to now the "works of the Messiah" have been on display, the emphasis will now shift slightly – until Peter's confession (Matt 16.16) – to people's response to these works.[85] Third, Jesus' allusion to Isa 35.5–6 is especially significant in that Matthew alone notes the healing of the blind and lame in the temple following the entrance to the city, a sign that the coming one has brought eschatological salvation to Jerusalem.[86]

---

identify Jesus as the coming one at his baptism, Matthew's account most clearly implies this recognition as he is the only Synoptist who records John's reluctance to baptize Jesus (Matt 3.13–15). In Matthew the phrase is used as a term for Messiah, and in light of his Davidic emphasis should be understood as describing the Davidic Messiah. On this see Davies and Allison 1.312–314; Hagner, 1.51.

[82] On Jesus not meeting John's expectations of judgment see Davies and Allison, 2.241; Beare, 256–257; Morris, *Matthew*, 275.

[83] Cf. Hagner, 1.300. Against the coming one being a reference to Elijah see Hill, 197. Schweizer (*Matthew*, 255) suggests the Baptist left open the question in his preaching whether the coming one would be God himself or his emissary.

[84] Isa 26.19; 29.18; 35.5–6; 42.7, 18; 61.1.

[85] On this shift see Davies and Allison, 2.240; France, 191.

[86] Cf. Weren, "Jesus' Entry," 135. J. A. Brooks ("The Influence of Malachi Upon the New Testament", 30) argues that Malachi underlies the title of coming one in Matt 11.3‖Luke 7.19, although acknowledging that the idea is also found in Ps 118.26. However, the unique linking of this pericope with the quotation of Ps 118.26 in the Entrance Narrative suggests that the psalm is in view here.

B. The Entrance to Jerusalem (Matt 21.1–11)

Although Matthew depends on Mark 11.1–10, and like him quotes Ps 118.25–26, the changes on Mark and the addition of unique material gives his Entrance Narrative a distinctive coloring.[87] Of the Synoptists, Matthews account most clearly indicates that the Entrance is patterned after the kingship traditions of Israel. The central character is the Son of David, riding a royal animal into David's city. It is notable that the only entry accounts that mention the king's mount are Zech 9.9 and 1 Kgs 1, so by quoting the former, and punctuating it with words from Ps 118 used to greet ancient Israel's kings, Matthew makes plain that Jesus' Entry is that of the king of Israel.[88] Each of these details also highlights Jesus' eschatological import: the Son of David was the expected deliverer, Jesus fulfills a prophetic passage that depicts the coming of Israel's eschatological king, and the reader will soon learn that the cry on the lips of the crowd is the same that will greet the Messiah at his return.[89] It is possible, in light of his attention to Israel's royal traditions, that Matthew intends to present the Entrance as an enactment of the ancient Ps 118 processional with the Zechariahan king as its subject.[90]

---

[87] For a detailed list of differences between Mark and Matthew see Hagner, 2.591–592. The alterations are significant in underlining Matthew's creativity, and suggest that he was aware of his sources and used them intentionally. Regarding Ps 118, his addition to Ps 118.25 (Matt 21.9) and the repetition of this refrain in 21.15 are unique. On the use of Ps 118 in the Matthean Entrance see especially J. Nieuviarts, *L'Entrée de Jésus à Jérusalem (Mt 21, 1–17): Messianisme et accomplissement des Écritures en Matthieu*, 95–113. For a focused look at the use of the OT in the Matthew's Entrance see J. Miller, *Les citations d'accomplissement dans l'Évangile de Matthieu: Quand Dieu se rend présent en toute humanité*.

[88] Although Zech 9.9 may be implicit in Mark and Luke, only Matthew makes it explicit. For other examples of entries – none of which mention the hero's mount – see Catchpole, "Entry"; Duff, "Divine Warrior." France (297) suggests that Matthew may have intended to evoke the return of King David over the Mount of Olives following Absalom's rebellion (2 Sam 15.30), when he presumably rode a donkey. Matthew's mention of branches rather than Mark's straw or foliage is more fitting for a religious or royal procession. Note that Matthew does not refer either to the waving of branches or to palm branches in particular.

[89] Cf. Davies and Allison, 3.128. To this list one could add the Mount of Olives, which although not emphasized to the same degree as in Luke 19.37 would evoke eschatological associations.

[90] This is the most natural way of reading Zech 9.9 and Ps 118 together in the Matthean context. Ps 118 provides a royal processional (perhaps an enthronement ritual), and Zech 9.9 the specific royal figure coming to rule in Jerusalem. Davies and Allison (3.126) note the possibility of the psalm's ancient function – if it was known to Matthew and his readers – underlining the royal emphasis of the Entrance. However, they do not pursue the possible implications. Krüger ("Humilde," 80) points to a historical chiasm involving the purification of the temple by the Maccabeans and their celebration with

Looking specifically at Matthew's quotation of the psalm, he has completely dropped Mark's "coming kingdom of our father David" (Mark 11.10), and diverging from Mark and Luke quotes Ps 118.26 intact, focusing his modifications instead on Ps 118.25 by adding the phrase "Son of David" to the Hosanna. The majority of Matthean commentators assert that Hosanna is rendered as praise,[91] although this position has not gone unchallenged. Some argue that it retains its petitionary character,[92] and others correctly leave room for ambiguity, although this is less pronounced than in Mark.[93] In any case, none of these options detracts from the impor-

---

palms and branches with the entry of Jesus with palms and branches followed by purification of the temple. Perhaps the term "historical parallel" would be more correct than chiasm, since these are two separate sets of events and descriptions of them; but in any case Matthew does not mention palms, and it is questionable whether Jesus' goal in the Temple Action was to re-institute the sacrificial system.

[91] Morris (*Matthew*, 523 n. 13) suggests that people who used the word did so without a clear meaning in mind other than giving honor. It is a shout of praise and acclaim (Gundry, *Matthew*, 411; Beare, 414; France, 299; Keener, 492), directed to Jesus (Filson, 221; Hagner, 2.595–596) or Yahweh (Blomberg, 313). Alternatively it is a salutation (Weren, "Jesus' Entry," 134).

[92] Albright (252 n. 9) states strongly that the Hosanna "is a prayer for deliverance ('Save now!'); it is not in any way a cry of praise." C. C. Torrey (*The Four Gospels: A New Translation*, 45) argues that it is a cry to save the Davidic king. The difficulty comes in accounting for the dative following Hosanna. M. H. Pope ("Hosanna"; idem, "Hosanna: What it *Really* Means"; idem, "Vestiges of Vocative Lamedh in the Bible") has argued that Matthew wrongly translated his original Hebrew source which read "Hosanna *l-* the Son of David" and "Hosanna *l-* the highest," with the writer being unaware that *l-* can be used as a vocative. This would for Matt 21.9 render respectively "Help, please, O Son of David," and "Help, O Most High." Pope's argument stumbles on several points. First, it assumes a Hebrew original when it is more likely that Matthew depends on Markan Greek. Second, that *l-* is used with a vocative sense in the OT is still a point of debate (see P. D. Miller's negative evaluation in "Vocative Lamed in the Psalter: A Reconsideration"; and Pope's response, "Vestiges"). Third, although Pope states that "it is obvious that any Jew who knew even a little of the holy tongue and the sacred rites would know the original meaning of 'hosanna' and would not misconstrue it as meaning 'praise'" ("What it Really Means," 24), he denies such knowledge to Matthew. Against Pope see further Davies and Allison, 3.124–125. Sanders notes examples of Hosanna as a formula used when entering the presence of the king as judge (2 Sam 14.4; 2 Kgs 6.26), and interprets the Entrance cry as "recognition and acknowledgement of the king as judge in the city gate" ("Ps 118" 186). Pope ("What it Really Means," 22) is correct in noting against Brown (1.457) that 2 Sam 14.4 does not carry a sense of acclamation or greeting – it is a cry to the king to save.

[93] Davies and Allison (3.125) state that "it is reasonable to infer that in the first century 'hosanna' *could* mean 'praise.'" (Emphasis added.) This is a long way from asserting that Hosanna had lost its petitionary character. Hill (292) leaves room for interpretation, while Krüger ("Humilde," 80–81) suggests that it is difficult to establish definitively whether in Matthew the Hosanna is entirely petition or acclaim, or a mixture of both.

tant role the psalm plays in advancing Matthew's presentation of Jesus.[94] First, the addition to the quote facilitates and intensifies a christological interpretation of the event.[95] The focus is less on the coming kingdom than on the coming Son of David, who is God's instrument for bringing the kingdom. Although Jesus is not addressed explicitly as king, the identification of the Son of David as the royal coming one of the psalm makes clear his royal status and indicates to Matthew's readers that Jesus is the Davidic messianic king.[96] Second, the quote interprets the king of Zech 9.9 as the Son of David, and indicates that the crowd correctly understood Jesus' action as an enactment of the oracle. Third, the quote represents the first mass recognition of Jesus' messianic kingship, and Jesus says nothing that would contradict or correct the crowd's acclaim – quite the opposite, his actions are implicit claims to royal messianic status, and he defends the children's Davidic acclaim (Matt 21.16). Fourth, Matthew presents the quote as a confessional statement taken up by a very large crowd and shouted openly and enthusiastically for a long period of time.[97]

Of the Synoptics, Matthew's account underscores most clearly the messianic aspects of the Entry and in portraying widespread public support is the most positive and triumphalist in flavor.[98] The only clear opposition comes from the religious leadership, but although this foreshadows the

---

[94] The second Hosanna ("Hosanna in the highest") most naturally continues the allusion to Ps 118.25, although it is possible that Ps 148.1 is in view (so Blomberg, 313; Gundry, *Matthew*, 411). This does not resolve the question of the sense with which Hosanna is used in Matthew, for it could be a call for God to save the Son of David (Hill, 292), an ascription of highest praise to Jesus (Morris, *Matthew*, 523), or indicate a state of jubilation in heaven (Gundry, *Matthew*, 411).

[95] Cf. Schweizer, *Matthew*, 404; Hagner, 2.592; Davies and Allison, 3.113.

[96] The title of king is applied directly to Jesus in a positive sense only once (Matt 2.2). Matthew identifies him as the king of Zech 9.9 (21.5), but this is editorial comment. Otherwise the title is used mockingly (Matt 27.29; 27.42) or ambiguously (27.11; 27.37). In place of this Matthew emphasizes Jesus' status as Son of David, with a disproportionate 10 of the 19 NT occurrences of the title (1.1, 20; 9.27; 12.23; 15.22; 20.30, 31; 21.9, 15; 22.42). On Matthew's emphasis on the Davidic Messiah see P. W. Meyer, "Matthew 21.1–11," 181–182. T. Fahy (*New Testament Problems*, 136) renders each Gospel's use of the Ps 118.26 phrase "in the name of the Lord" as "with the title of Lord," but this ignores the psalm's original context.

[97] It is not impossible that Matthew's "very large crowd" (21.8) and the crowds that go before and follow after Jesus (21.9) are made up of disciples, but it appears that Matthew wanted to emphasize an overwhelmingly positive response by a great number of people in what was an impressive and important event. Cf. Gundry, *Matthew*, 410; France, 299; Morris, *Matthew*, 522 n. 11; Filson, 221. Morris (*Matthew*, 522–523) suggests that Matthew's use of the imperfect tense to describe the shouting indicates that it continued for some time.

[98] Cf. Albright, 253; Hill, 290; Davies and Allison, 3.123, 129.

intense conflict ahead, there is no wholesale sense of rejection by the nation.[99] Rather, as Matthew presents it, the majority have acknowledged Jesus' messianic kingship and received him properly.[100] Whatever the event and the quotation of Zech 9.9 may indicate about the character of Jesus' messiahship, and in spite of the rejection that follows the shattering of popular expectation, the primary focus of this passage is on the reception and recognition of Jesus as the Davidic Messiah, coming to Jerusalem as king.

C. *Jesus in the Temple (Matt 21.12–17)*

From a literary standpoint this pericope follows on and is a continuation of the first, so that Matt 21.1–17 should be approached as a textual unit. The use of Ps 118 especially links the entire passage together.[101] Several Matthean details also would harmonize with a re-enactment of the Ps 118 processional pattern.[102] Jesus' procession does not end at the city gates

---

[99] Luke also records a negative response from the religious leaders, but in contrast to Matthew there is no popular welcome, as Luke limits support specifically to the disciples. In Matthew it is the large crowd (including disciples) accompanying Jesus who acclaims him. There is no indication that the citizens of Jerusalem themselves joined in, for all that is said of them is that the city was "stirred" and asked who Jesus was (Matt 21.10). At the worst they are ambivalent, but the point is not their response, which is not listed, but that the reception was sufficiently large and vocal to stir the entire city. Mark does not specify any opposition, but he also does not clarify the size of the crowd nor how widespread the support was. The messianic element is not missing from either Mark or Luke, it is simply highlighted in Matthew.

[100] Matthew records the city asking who the cause of this excitement was, and "the crowds" responding with the title "prophet of Nazareth." It is unclear who "the crowds" refers to; it most naturally links to the crowds that had accompanied Jesus, but could also be the crowds in the city who recognize Jesus from Galilee. If the former, their answer is not necessarily an indication that they think him to be any less than Messiah, for otherwise their shouts of Son of David would be meaningless. Rather, it would mean, "the Son of David is Jesus, the prophet from Nazareth." Probably this does not refer to "the prophet" of Deut 18.15–18 (against France, 300; cf. Hagner, 2.596).

[101] Weren ("Jesus' Entry," 118) has argued this convincingly, pointing to a number of repetitions in the two passages. These primarily involve Ps 118: "Hosanna to the Son of David" is repeated in 21.9 and 21.15; in both cases it is preceded by κράζω and λέγω; there is a pattern of question and answer triggered by the cries of Hosanna, first those in the city answered by the crowds, second the religious authorities answered by Jesus.

[102] Mark and Luke both have Jesus enter the temple as the final step of the procession, although for Mark the actual cleansing of the temple is put off to the next day. Luke's account of the Temple Action is very abbreviated. Neither in Mark nor Luke is there any indication that the cries of Ps 118 continue into the temple. Although each of the Synoptics can be interpreted as a Ps 118 processional, and in each there is a disjunction with the psalm in terms of the reception Jesus should have received, Matthew's version

but proceeds into the temple, apparently accompanied by uninterrupted shouting of Ps 118.25–26 that at the least is taken up by children in the temple itself.[103] There is no mention of the religious authorities until Jesus enters the temple, and their opposition is specifically in reaction to the children's cries, more sharply underlining their failure to carry out what the occasion required of them. It is notable that their indignation is tied not to Jesus' provocative action in the temple, but to the healings and ascription of messianic status to Jesus by the quotation of Ps 118.

Matthew alone records the single Synoptic instance of Jesus healing in the temple, obviously evoking Matt 11.2–6, where in response to the Baptist's questioning whether Jesus was the coming one, Jesus had indicated that the healing of the blind and lame is a sign that the eschatological age prophesied by Isaiah has arrived. Now the coming one has entered the temple, acclaimed as the messianic king, and confirms his role as the one who brings eschatological salvation through the highly symbolic act of healing and including the excluded.[104] The healing of the blind especially underlines his identity as Son of David, for Matthew has twice before joined such healing with Davidic acclaim, and he does so a third time here.[105] The quotation of Ps 118.25 in Matt 21.15 performs several functions. First, it places the royal greeting of Ps 118 in the temple, where it should be: "*From the house of the Lord* we bless you" (Ps 118.26b).[106] Second, it sets the stage and is the immediate cause for the quotation of

---

provides the most links with the psalm's original context, which has a procession ending in the temple, presumably a Davidic king as the main character, the welcoming of the king into the temple with Ps 118.25–26, and continued jubilation in the temple. Note also the use of foliage in Matt 21.8 and Ps 118.27 (although Mark also mentions foliage, it provides a poor parallel to the psalm's), and the use of εἰσέρχομαι to describe the entry to the temple in Ps 118.19–20 and Matt 21.12 (cf. Mark 11.11 and Luke 19.45), and to Jerusalem in Mt 21.10.

[103] On the shouts continuing uninterrupted see Weren, "Jesus' Entry," 118.

[104] It may be that Matthew is showing the Son of David overturning the exclusion of the crippled and blind from participating in temple worship, an ordinance that was ascribed to David (2 Sam 5.8) although this completely ignores the context and intent of the king's words. Cf. Schweizer, *Matthew*, 408. Note that in Isa 56.1–8, from which Matt 21.13 quotes (in conjunction with Jer 7.11) immediately prior to the healings, inclusion of the excluded in temple worship is one of the signs that eschatological salvation is at hand. Although Gundry (*Matthew*, 400) is surely correct that Jesus provides an example to the church in serving the deprived, this is hardly the point in the temple healings and Jesus' defense of the children who praise him.

[105] Matt 9.27; 20.29–34; 21.14–15.

[106] Emphasis added. That the blessing comes from the children rather than the leaders presents a disjunction with the original context of the psalm that would call attention to, rather than obscure, the psalm's significance in the pericope. In any case, the Messiah has been properly welcomed, even if not by the right people.

Ps 8.3 (LXX) in Matt 21.16,[107] which in turn qualifies and interprets the quotation of Ps 118.25. First, Jesus' answer approves of the children's acclamation and thus explicitly confirms what were up to now implicit self-claims to be the Davidic Messiah. Second, the cries of Ps 118 are presented as the God-ordained praise that the infants in Ps 8 offer to Yahweh, an especially provocative intertextual play because here Jesus is the object of acclaim.[108] Third, since in the original context the children's praise is intended to silence Yahweh's enemies, the intertextual link makes the cries of Ps 118 a resounding rebuke to the religious authorities that designates them as the foes of Yahweh.[109]

D. The Parable of the Wicked Tenants (Matt 21.33–46)

Matthew quotes Ps 118.22–23 in the second of three parables, each of which declares guilty the religious authorities and warns of impending judgment. The function of the quotation is similar to that in the parallel passages, except that Matthew's shaping of the text brings into especially sharp focus the severe consequences of rejecting Jesus. First, Matthew states in 21.43 that the consequence of rejecting the stone will be the transference of the kingdom of God to another nation, and therefore that the religious leaders have forfeited OT Israel's privileged position as God's people (cf. Exod 19.5–6). This is not a wholesale rejection of the Jews, but rather the announcement of a holy nation that has expanded to include both Jew and Gentile, with acceptance of Jesus the determinative factor for inclusion.[110] Lest the leaders miss the gravity of their obstinate

---

[107] Gundry (*Matthew*, 414–415) plausibly suggests that the quotation of Ps 118.26 led Matthew to Ps 8: "The coincidences of the Lord's name ['O Lord, our Lord'; 'in the name of the Lord'] and the youngsters prove an irresistible magnet drawing the evangelist to his quotation." Davies and Allison (3.144) note the linking of Ps 8 with the song of Exodus 15 in Jewish tradition, suggesting that Matthew intends to make a connection "between the Christ event and the exodus" and also draw in the story of Moses. In this regard note in ch. 2 of this study the number of intertextual links between Ps 118 and Exodus 15.

[108] See Weren, "Jesus' Entry," 138; Blomberg, 316. France (302–303) suggestively asks whether Jesus is referring simply to the acceptability of the children's acclaim or is implicitly claiming a status higher than that of Son of David.

[109] Filson (224) and Hill (294) note the rebuke intended with the quotation of Ps 8, but miss the role of Ps 118. In a sense Ps 8 intensifies a rebuke that is already implicit in the children's use of Ps 118, for the latter had already shown that the leadership is unable or unwilling to recognize what even the young are able to discern.

[110] The addition of 21.43 is unique to Matthew. Cf. France, 310: "There is thus both continuity and discontinuity: the reign of God continues, and remains focused on a 'nation', but the composition of that 'nation' has changed." Keener (515) interestingly comments

behavior, Matthew personalizes the consequences in 21.44 with a return to the stone motif of 21.42: opposition to God's chosen stone leads to individual destruction.[111] Whereas the psalm emphasizes the rejection and vindication of the son, this turns the tables so that the rejecters become rejects. Although Matt 21.44 does not allude specifically to Ps 118.22 – the first line may allude to Isa 8.14–15, and the second to Dan 2.44–45 – [112] there is a strong intertextual linkage, for it is the psalm's rejected stone who becomes to any who reject him a stone that crushes and demolishes. The quotation provides an appropriate bridge between the leaders' rejection of Jesus in the Entrance and the harsh woes (Matt 23) that follow shortly after this encounter.[113]

E. The Lament Over Jerusalem (Matt 23.37–39)

Matthew takes up in the prophetic lament over Jerusalem the quotation of Ps 118.26 so recently heard in the Entrance. Unlike Luke's account, which allows the possibility that the lament was fulfilled in the Entrance,[114] there is general agreement that by placing it after Jesus' arrival to Jerusalem Matthew has excluded this option and points instead to the second coming as the time when the psalm will be used to acknowledge the Messiah.[115]

---

that the "nation" refers to "the holy 'nation' of a new exodus." See further Hagner, 2.624; Davies and Allison, 3.189–190.

[111] Although there is some textual uncertainty for Matt 21.44, there are strong reasons for accepting its authenticity. For discussion see Snodgrass, *Wicked Tenants*, 66–68; Metzger, *A Textual Commentary on the Greek New Testament*, 47. Unlike Luke (20.18), Mark does not preserve this tradition and hence any sense of judgment remains implicit and depends on the intertextual reading of Ps 118.22–23.

[112] See Gundry, *Matthew*, 431; Hagner, 2.623. Snodgrass (*Wicked Tenants*, 98–99) sees also the influence of Isa 28.16.

[113] Snodgrass presents convincing evidence showing that several "stone" passages – including those alluded to in Matt 21.44 and Ps 118.22 – were understood eschatologically in pre-Christian Judaism (see *Wicked Tenants*, 98–99; and his unpublished Ph. D. thesis, "Christological Stone"). This intensifies the eschatological tone at the end of the parable and underscores the ultimate significance of the rejected/vindicated son who is at the same time both the leader of the new inclusive community and the stone that crushes and excludes. As an interesting aside, Hagner (2.470) suggests a possible link between Ps 118.22 and Matt 16.18 where Peter is identified as a rock. If so, it is the faintest of echoes.

[114] Interestingly, Matthean commentators are more likely than Lukan to suggest that in Luke the Entrance is the fulfillment of Luke 13.34–35. See Filson, 249; Hill, 316; Beare, 461; Keener, 558; Gundry, *Matthew*, 474; Allison, "Conditional Prophecy," 81 n. 2.

[115] See for example Schweizer, *Matthew*, 437; Morris, *Matthew*, 592; Davies and Allison, 3.323–324; Filson, 249; Hill, 316; Blomberg, 351; Beare, 461; Keener, 558–559; Gundry, 474.

The main point of disagreement is whether speaking the words of the psalm is the *condition for* or the *result of* the Messiah's return; if the former, then Jesus' words signal the possibility of future repentance that will result in redemption.[116] Although the implication is that until that point of repentance they will remain under judgment, the tone is not one of condemnation but of hope. If the latter, the welcome could be either forced and therefore a sign of judgment,[117] or voluntary and accordingly hold out the hope of salvation.[118] Since Matthew does not clarify the attitude that will accompany the eschatological welcome, Jesus' words are somewhat ambiguous and therefore the sense of judgment more pronounced.[119] The best explanation is that Matt 23.39 expresses the condition for Israel to see her Messiah again, but does not promise or even necessarily expect that this condition will be met.[120]

The quotation of Ps 118.26 is all the more significant in that for Matthew it represents Jesus' last public words to his people and marks a critical change in Jesus' mission: his appeals to Israel are finished.[121] The phrase ἀπ᾽ ἄρτι suggests that a window of opportunity has closed and accentuates the judgment that the religious authorities must now remain under until they are ready to reverse their failure in the Entrance and wholeheartedly

---

[116] Allison comments, "The text then means not, when the Messiah comes, his people will bless him, but rather, when his people bless him, the Messiah will come. In other words, the date of the redemption is contingent upon Israel's acceptance of the person and work of Jesus" ("Conditional Prophecy," 77; see further 81). Cf. Davies and Allison, 3.323–324; D. J. Verseput, "Jesus' Pilgrimage to Jerusalem and Encounter in the Temple: A Geographical Motif in Matthew's Gospel," 116–117. Allison presents a strong and convincing argument for a conditional position, but the fact that recognition of the Messiah is the condition for Israel to see him again does not require that Israel actually fulfill said condition. As a result, against Davies and Allison (3.324), the lament offers not a *promise* but the *possibility* of redemption. Against Allison see Gundry, *Matthew*, 668; France, 332–333.

[117] So Hagner, 2.681; Fahy, *Problems*, 138–139; Manson, *Sayings*, 128.

[118] So Keener, 558–559; Gundry, 474; Blomberg, 351.

[119] This sense of ambiguity is apparent in several commentators who do not clarify whether redemption or judgment is in view. For example, without answering his own question Hill (316) writes, "But will they know him only as Judge, or is it being hinted that they will acknowledge him as King?" Cf. Morris, *Matthew*, 592; Filson, 249; Beare, 461.

[120] In support see France, 332: "Firstly, the words *until you say* are expressed in Greek as an indefinite possibility rather than as a firm prediction; this is the condition on which they will see him again; but there is no promise that the condition will be fulfilled."

[121] Note that the apocalyptic discourse is given not to the public but to the disciples. See France, 332: There is "a new situation now beginning, an eschatological change. Jesus is now leaving the scene of Jewish public life, in which he has made his unheeded appeal; the next meeting will be very different."

and unreservedly accept Jesus as their Messiah. [122] In turn, the eschatological interpretation of Ps 118 in this passage is then read back into the
Entrance, which becomes an anticipation of and pattern for the *parousia.*
The quotation also focuses attention on Jesus' symbolic withdrawal from
the temple, for it is his departure and absence that renders their house
"desolate."[123] Whatever glimmer of hope is offered by Jesus' deep concern for Jerusalem and by the possibility of a later repentance and redemption is tempered for the reader by the apocalyptic discourse, which drives
home the catastrophic consequences of Israel's failure.[124] Matthew's
last quotation of Ps 118 thus provides a fitting conclusion to his public
teaching and in a sense summarizes the themes which the psalm supports
throughout the Gospel: the history and fate of Israel turns on her reaction
to the coming one.

F. The Hymn (Matt 26.30)

Matthew includes Mark's reference to the singing of a hymn – a liturgical
allusion to the second part of the Hallel – as closure to the Last Supper.[125]
The meaning effects that the allusion brings to Mark apply here as well, except that Matthew's depiction of Ps 118 as the eschatological greeting that
will be offered to Messiah at his *parousia* and as the formula for inclusion
in Jesus' new community adds an anticipatory and perhaps confessional

---

[122] Davies and Allison (3.126) and Verseput ("Jesus' Pilgrimage," 116–118) suggest
that the contrast with the Entrance underlines the culpability of Jerusalem's citizens in
not receiving Jesus as Messiah. It is true that the citizens themselves do not clearly join
in the acclaim, but Matthew's focus seems to be on the grand scale of the reception that
did take place and the opposition specifically of the leaders. The woes are addressed
to the religious authorities, and as representatives of the nation responsibility for the
destruction of Jerusalem arguably is laid at their feet.

[123] Gundry (*Matthew*, 473) correctly notes, "The saying in v 39 explains the
desolation in terms of Jesus' absence." Cf. Blomberg, 351.

[124] Matthew's use of Ps 118 in the lament is more polemical than Luke's, although in
Luke 19.41–44 the tone of judgment is strong. Cf. Davies and Allison, 3.312–313. On
Matt 23.39 as a literary bridge between the denunciation of the religious leaders in ch.
23 and the explicit predictions of eschatological judgment in chs. 24–25 see France, 331;
Gundry, *Matthew*, 474; Hagner, 2.679.

[125] See discussion in Daube, *The New Testament and Rabbinic Judaism,* 192–195;
280; 330–331. Also France, 370; Morris, *Matthew*, 662; Gundry, *Matthew*, 529; Hagner,
2.774. Davies and Allison (3.483–484) suggest that first-century Christian readers may
have thought of Christian hymns that were sung along with the Eucharist rather than of
the Hallel. Although this is possible, one expects that many readers would have recognized from the context that Matthew is alluding to the Hallel. H. Rusche's ("Das letzte
gemeinsame Gebet Jesu mit seinen Jüngern. Der Psalm 136") claim that the hymn in
view is Ps 136 has little to commend it.

note to its singing at the meal. The disciples have acknowledged Jesus as their Messiah and participate in the new rites of his community. The relationship of the Last Supper to the Passover meal is especially significant in a New Exodus framework and bears on the interpretation of Ps 118, for in such a scheme the Supper symbolizes the new Passover rite, and the Hallel becomes the song of the New Exodus.[126]

Summary

Matthew concentrates his use of Ps 118 differently from Luke, referring to it primarily in and following the Entrance, and not alluding to Ps 118.22 in the passion predictions. His only pre-Entrance use is the allusion to Ps 118.26 in the Baptist's question (11.3), which itself links with the Entrance to prepare the reader to recognize the healings in the temple as a symbol of eschatological salvation. Apart from marking the end of the Galilean ministry and the journey to Jerusalem, Jesus' Entrance begins an extended section (Matt 21–23) set in the temple that is characterized by controversy and confrontation with the Jewish leaders and warnings of judgment and destruction that are taken up again in Matt 24–25. It is here that Matthew clusters his use of Ps 118, repeating in 23.39 the phrase from Ps 118.26 used in the Entrance and thus creating an *inclusio* that frames the passage. In addition, the repetition of Ps 118.25 in the Temple Action (20.12–17) links that pericope firmly with the Entrance, and the quotation of Ps 118.22–23 in 21.42, coming shortly after the Entrance, is the climax to one of three parables that illustrate the intensifying conflict. It appears that Matthew used Ps 118 in linking together and structuring this final encounter with the nation's leaders.[127]

---

[126] There is a great deal of secondary literature dealing with the Last Supper and its relationship to the Passover meal. See bibliographies in Hagner, 2.769–770; Davies and Allison, 3.478–481. For a comprehensive discussion of the issues see I. H. Marshall, *Last Supper and Lord's Supper*. On the significance of the Last Supper in a New Exodus framework see Wright, *Victory*, 554–563, 576–577, 605. Wright comments, "Passover looked back to the exodus, and on to the coming of the kingdom. Jesus intended this meal to symbolize the new exodus, the arrival of the kingdom through his own fate. The meal, focused on Jesus' actions with the bread and the cup, told the Passover story, and Jesus' own story, and wove these two into one" (ibid., 559). Cf. Davies and Allison, 3.478: "Jesus inaugurates a second exodus."

[127] On the structure of the passage see Hagner, 2.591; Weren, "Jesus' Entry," 119.

IV. The Relationship of John to the Synoptics

A comparison of John and the Synoptics reveals some differences in their use of Ps 118. The Synoptics tend to quote or allude clearly and focus their attention on the same few verses: Mark and Matthew refer to Ps 118.22–23, 25–26 and share a liturgical allusion to the Hallel, and Luke limits his use to Ps 118.22, 26. On the other hand, John's use of Ps 118 is both much more subtle and varied, drawing on the entire breadth of the psalm (118.5, 10–12, 19–20, 21, 24, 25–26, [117] 28c) yet at the same time ignoring Ps 118.22. A question is whether in spite of these differences their use of Ps 118 is thematically congruent. To anticipate the results of our study of John, some of the same meaning effects are achieved although at times with the use of different verses. This is to be expected, for each allusion to the psalm draws on the same literary context, and therefore depending on the context of the receiving text may evoke some of the same themes. In any case, since apart from the Entrance Narrative John does not record any of the Synoptic uses of Ps 118, it is most unlikely that he depends on the Synoptics or their sources for his use of the psalm outside of the Entrance.

As the only overlapping use of Ps 118 and also the focus of much of this study, it is the Entrance that primarily draws our attention. There are important details common to the evangelists which indicate that they all refer to the same event,[128] and some similarities that John shares uniquely with Luke and Matthew.[129] However, the differences of the Synoptic scene from the Johannine are much more numerous. The Synoptics do not mention a number of details that John includes: a crowd coming from Jerusalem to meet Jesus; the use of palm branches; the "finding" of the animal; the mounting of the animal following the cries of acclamation; comments about the later understanding of the disciples; Lazarus; and (apart from Matthew) the explicit quotation of Zech 9.9. Likewise John does not record many of the Synoptic details: Jesus coming from Bethpage, Bethany and the Mount of Olives; knowing about the animal in advance; sending two disciples to acquire the animal; sitting on the animal covered with garments; the carpeting of the path with garments and foliage; descending the Mount of Olives; the association of the Temple Action with the

---

[128] Each account includes the use of Ps 118.26, Jesus entering Jerusalem on an animal, and a formalized entry processional.

[129] Similarities include Luke's addition to Ps 118.26 of "the king," Matthew's quotation of Zech 9.9 (although in a different order, conflated with a different Scripture, and with important differences in the quoted text), and the opposition of the religious leaders recorded by both Luke and Matthew.

Entry; the different uses of Hosanna; and the Davidic additions to Ps 118.[130] In spite of these differences of detail there is a great deal of thematic overlap, for each emphasizes kingship and the royal traditions of Israel, has Jesus implicitly accept homage, makes claims about the identity of Jesus, to varying degrees evokes Tabernacles imagery, and assigns to Ps 118 a key interpretive role. But even as redactional changes add distinctive emphases to each Synoptic account, John's narrative introduces meaning effects that distinguish it sharply from the others, particularly in the area of Christology.

The vexed question of how to explain the relationship of John to the Synoptics is one not easily solved.[131] The consensus at the beginning of the twentieth century that John knew the Synoptics gave way to the view that he was perhaps ignorant of and certainly not dependent on them. At this point neither position can be taken for granted, for although the advocates of Johannine independence are in the majority, proponents of dependence have been growing in number.[132] It is important to locate our approach to the Fourth Gospel in this discussion, but we will not attempt to break new group, first because this is not our focus, and second because in any case it is impossible to decide the matter on the basis of an investigation of a very limited group of texts and quotations.

Much of the debate has focused on whether or not John knew one or more of the Synoptics and depended on them, but between the two poles lie a number of possible explanations. John may have known one or more of the Synoptics, but did not use them as a source in the traditional sense nor base his narrative on them. Alternatively, John may or may not have known the Synoptics, but one or more of them may have influenced the sources and traditions on which he drew. Similarities may be due to the independent Johannine and Synoptic use of a common stream of tradition, or the use of independent but similar traditions. Similarities may also reflect the development of oral tradition rather than a literary relationship to the Synoptics, be due to the influence of one or more of the Synoptics on an early stage of the redactional evolution of the Fourth Gospel, or reflect later redactional efforts to bring John into line with the Synoptics.

---

[130] Note that Matthew does not mention Bethany, and Luke does not make a Davidic addition to Ps 118 (although it is implicit) nor use Hosanna. The differences in detail justify Dodd's comment that the Synoptics and John "differ in every point where it is possible to differ in relating the same incident" (*Historical Tradition*, 155).

[131] For a comprehensive account of the discussion see D. M. Smith, *John Among the Gospels: The Relationship in Twentieth-Century Research*. See also M. Hengel, *The Johannine Question*.

[132] Smith comments, "In the twentieth-century discussion of the question of John and the Synoptics, the basic possibilities for explaining these relationships have been explored and perhaps exhausted" (*John Among the Gospels*, 180–181).

Perhaps John was aware of one or more of the Synoptics but disagreed with and therefore departed from them, or finally, he may have been completely ignorant of the Synoptics.

In spite of the divided state of opinion, it is possible to advance some limited suggestions. First, it is unlikely that the Fourth Gospel developed in complete isolation from other Christian communities and therefore in ignorance of the gospel traditions accepted by those communities.[133] Based on the assumption that Mark was the earliest and, at the time the Fourth Gospel was written, the most widely circulated of the Synoptics, it is reasonable to suggest that John may have at least been aware of Mark.[134] Second, knowledge of one or more of the Synoptics does not entail use and dependence, and in fact John's independence in developing his narrative and theological program is evident. Any influence of the Synoptics would be secondary to John's own distinct theological concerns and purposes, and therefore, as Smith advances, the Fourth Gospel "does not reflect them in any consistent and coherent way."[135] The position that seems most plausible to me is that John drew on a source(s) of tradition that was similar to, yet independent of, the Synoptic sources, and that he did not depend on the Synoptics or their sources.[136] Third, where there are divergences in parallel passages it is suggested that these should not be treated as a deliberate departure from the Synoptics. Applied to the Entrance Narrative, differences in detail and meaning effects should not be approached as a Johannine redaction or reworking of the Synoptic tradition.[137] We agree with Smith's statement that "exegesis of the Fourth

---

[133] In support see Brown, 1.xlvi; R. Bauckham, "John for Readers of Mark," 147.

[134] Since the chronological sequence for the writing of Matthew, Luke, and John is unclear, and there is no evidence that the former two had circulated widely at an early stage, it is possible but less likely that John was familiar with them. See M. D. Goulder ("From Ministry to Passion in John and Luke," 561–568) for an interesting yet unconvincing argument for Johannine dependence on Luke. Bauckham makes a strong case for Johannine awareness of Mark's Gospel, arguing convincingly that readers/hearers of the Fourth Gospel familiar with Mark could read the two narratives as "complementary" (see his discussion in "Readers of Mark," 155, 158–159, 170). Hengel (*Johannine Question*, 102) suggests awareness at least of Mark and Luke, with the Fourth Gospel developing in antithesis to the Synoptic tradition.

[135] D. M. Smith, "John and the Synoptics: Some Dimensions of the Problem," 171.

[136] See discussion in Brown (1.xliv–xlvii), who holds this position. Cf. Dodd, *Historical Tradition*, 152–162.

[137] Cf. Smith, "John and the Synoptics," 171; Marcus, 54. An example of misapplied Johannine redaction is E. D. Freed's claim (*Old Testament Quotations in the Gospel of John*, 69, 75–76) that John has taken Synoptic elements and inserted them into the Lazarus accounts, having very little interest in the Entrance itself which he uses only to highlight the theme of Jesus' kingship. Of course John is concerned with the kingship of Jesus, but the Entry helps to define his kingship, mediates and continues the emphasis on

Gospel will rightly not be dominated by redaction-critical questions of its relationship to the synoptics."[138]

This bears directly on the issue of how far John is responsible for the quotation and meaning effects of Ps 118 in the Entrance and its relationship to the other allusions to the psalm. Because the reconstruction of Johannine sources is long on imagination and short on evidence it is difficult to determine whether John went directly to the OT, quoted strictly from tradition, or followed the tradition back to the OT. There is sufficient agreement with the Synoptics to suggest that all draw on traditions that include reference to Ps 118, but this need not diminish Johannine creativity, for the comprehensive knowledge of the OT that John displays militates against wooden dependence on tradition. There is every indication that if he did draw on the OT in the tradition, he was inclined to, and capable of, expanding on or molding it to suit his theological purposes.[139] Since intentional appropriation of a pre-text makes the writer responsible for the quotation, at one level the question of responsibility is reduced to whether we may agree that John was familiar with the psalm, for if in taking up the tradition he was unaware of introducing the quotation and allusions into his text then he cannot be responsible for the meaning effects we suggest. Since whatever sources of tradition John may have used are extant only in, and are indistinguishable from, the text of the Fourth Gospel, and this displays knowledge of Ps 118, until contrary evidence is offered it is unwarranted to deny that John deliberately used Ps 118 and is responsible for its significance. Similarly,

---

kingship established earlier in the Gospel, and heightens the sense of expectation and tension as the reader approaches the climax of the kingship theme. John has so inter-twined the Entrance with the kingship theme that any attempt to separate them must be judged artificial. In a bout of circular reasoning, one of the primary proofs Freed offers is that John is different from the Synoptics, and thus the "changes" are proof of his dependence (ibid., 73–74). Against Freed's argument ("The Entry Into Jerusalem in the Gospel of John," esp. 329) that John is indebted to the Synoptics in his account of the Entry and his use of quotations see D. M. Smith's effective challenge ("John 12:12ff. and the Question of John's use of the Synoptics"), in which he convincingly demonstrates how improbable dependence is. Cf. Brown, 1.459–461; Schnackenburg, 2.378–379; Ridderbos, 422; A. Obermann, *Die christologische Erfüllung der Schrift im Johannesevangelium: Eine Untersuchung zur johanneischen Hermeneutik anhand der Schriftzitate* 187.

[138] Smith, "John and the Synoptics," 172.

[139] Following M. Menken's conclusions (*Old Testament Quotations in the Fourth Gospel: Studies in Textual Form*, esp. 13–14, 205–209), B. Schuchard also argues per-suasively that "John's citations are best explained in terms of his purposeful editing of extant versions of Old Testament passages" (*Scripture within Scripture: The Interrela-tionship of Form and Function in the Explicit Old Testament Citations in the Gospel of John*, xv–xvii). That is, they reflect authorial intent.

determining whether John developed layers of meaning for Ps 118 that were not present in the tradition depends on being able to reconstruct the original tradition. A more solid point of comparison are the Synoptics, which show that rather than contradicting or radically diverging from their primary themes, John's more advanced christological and soteriological interpretation of Ps 118 is a natural development of the Synoptic use.

Chapter 4

The Broader Context of John's Use of Ps 118

I. Introduction

The Fourth Gospel is not the most obvious – nor seems a promising – place to focus a study on the use and function of Ps 118. The only clear quotation is that of Ps 118.25–26 in John 12.13, with one ambiguous allusion, listed both by UBS[3] and NA[27], to Ps 118.20 in John 10.9. A number of important studies of the OT in John have focused on the more explicit citations, often but not always limited to the formula quotations, with questions of text form and source dominating the discussion. As a result John's use of Ps 118 is somewhat neglected.[1] Although all the major commentaries recognize the use of Ps 118 in the Entrance Narrative – its presence in such a central event guarantees some attention – its function and intertextual transformations are generally overlooked. Much more prominence is given to the formula quotation of Zech 9.9 in John 12.15 and to a number of issues incidentally related to Ps 118 (e.g., the significance of palm branches and liturgical meaning of Hosanna). A survey of commentaries shows that most deal with Ps 118 in passing, often in no more than a paragraph. An additional consequence of the predominant emphasis on explicit and/or formula quotations is that there has been little attention paid to identifying and examining other allusions to and echoes of Ps 118 which may be present in the text. Of course, there has been no attempt to examine whether the clear quote and the several allusions to Ps 118 connect and relate to one another.

Such relative neglect provides an opportunity to test the fruitfulness of an intertextual approach and address the imbalance that results from a focus on issues of source, text-tradition and form, to the near exclusion of

---

[1] For example, Menken (*Quotations*) does not treat the citation of Ps 118 in the Entrance Narrative because it has neither an introductory nor concluding formula. Schuchard similarly does not deal with the psalm, because John 12.13 "represents not a reference to the Old Testament *per se*, but simply a rendering of a popular Jewish festal greeting derived from Ps 118(117)" (*Scripture*, xiv). Freed's study (*Quotations*) is concerned more with text form and source than function.

questions concerning intertextual relationships.[2] Methodologically, I will begin with John's single explicit quotation of Ps 118 and examine whether an intertextual approach can yield new insights into its use and function in the Entrance. Beyond this, there are a number of clues in John's use of the OT which suggest that the search for further allusions and echoes may prove fruitful, and that his use of Ps 118 is more extensive than previously recognized. Because our study examines several allusions to the same immediate literary context scattered throughout one receiving text, it is possible to raise the seldom-asked question of whether there is coherence between the various references.[3] The promise in asking this question is suggested by R. A. Culpepper's observation that "little attention has been given to the integrity of the whole, the way its component parts interrelate, its effects upon the reader, or the way it achieves its effects."[4] If there are several allusions to Ps 118, we will be concerned not only with showing how each functions in its place, but also whether they are used to greater effect as a network of allusions.

Clarifications

Research on the Fourth Gospel has been dominated by questions of historicity, the sorting of layers of tradition, its composition history in relation to sources, the theology of the evangelist, and the development of the Johannine community. This study, on the other hand, is primarily concerned with the function and meaning of the text in its final canonical form and the inner coherence of the Fourth Gospel, and has no interest in discerning hidden layers of tradition, the development of the tradition(s), and in determining

---

[2] S. van Tilborg's complaint, although in reference to Matthean studies, applies equally well to the Fourth Gospel: "If one wants to find out what changes in meaning and in significance have been installed in Matthew's text by the specific use of scriptural allusions, translations and quotes, one searches in vain in the previous literature" ("Matthew 27.3–10: an Intertextual Reading," 159).

[3] The question is seldom asked, perhaps because few studies follow one pre-text through a later body of literature. Wagner ("Psalm 118," 157) observes in his study of Ps 118 in Luke-Acts that shorter studies which have dealt with one or more Lukan allusions to Ps 118 have not examined all of the quotations and allusions together. As far as I know, Wagner's is the only attempt to examine all citation of Ps 118 in an NT corpus and explore whether there is any connection between these. For a similar approach see W. Weren, "Psalm 2 in Luke-Acts: an Intertextual Study."

[4] Culpepper, *Anatomy of the Fourth Gospel: A Study in Literary Design*, 3. Culpepper's comment is in reference to what he perceives as deficiencies in the approach to the Fourth Gospel.

sources.[5] Anderson observes that the recent trend in Johannine studies is "a quest for the 'historical evangelist' and his socio-religious context."[6] We will take no position on a specific Johannine community, since the majority of proposed reconstructions are speculative and in any case are unnecessary to the task at hand.[7] We will not address the question of authorship, although as a matter of convenience and in keeping with the traditional name used we will refer both to the author and the Gospel as John. This is not intended to be a historical investigation, in spite of the emphasis on background issues as they relate to the historical context of Ps 118. We will use historical data as "aids to interpretation" rather than "using the gospel story for historical reconstruction."[8] Similarly, this is not intended to be a study on the life of the historical Jesus.[9] As such, when Jesus is referred to in this thesis, the meaning intended is "Jesus as the author of the Fourth Gospel presents him."

Before focusing on the quotation of Ps 118 in the Entrance it will be useful to examine the larger context of the use of the OT in John. Because a survey of the subject lies beyond the scope of this study, I confine myself to several important patterns that affect our approach to the psalm and that suggest the possibility of other allusions and echoes. These include John's

---

[5] Accordingly, for my purposes I will assume the literary unity of John. For an overview of source theories see P. N. Anderson, *The Christology of the Fourth Gospel: It's Unity and Disunity in the Light of John 6*, 33–47.

[6] Anderson, *Christology*, 31.

[7] See the convincing challenge, mounted by contributors to *The Gospels for All Christians: Rethinking the Gospel Audiences* (R. Bauckham, ed.), against the approach that assumes the primacy of a narrow, restricted and isolated community in the writing of the Gospels. The reconstruction of hypothetical communities can be highly speculative. For example, J. L. Martyn bases his construct on the "starting point" of John 9.22, which he calls a "secure point of correspondence" (*The Gospel of John in Christian History: Essays for Interpreters*, 92–93). The enthusiastic and uncritical acceptance of such reconstructions calls to mind M. Barker's warning that "subsequent theories can all too easily build upon such a patch [a gap in our knowledge], until it becomes so overlaid with expertise that the dubious foundations are hidden" (*The Older Testament*, 2). For a survey of major positions on the audience, purpose, and setting of the Fourth Gospel see R. Kysar, *The Fourth Evangelist and His Gospel: An Examination of Contemporary Scholarship*, 147–165. Contributions seeking to reconstruct a Johannine Community include: O. Cullmann, *The Johannine Circle*; R. E. Brown, *The Community of the Beloved Disciple*; J. L. Martyn, *History and Theology in the Fourth Gospel*; R. A. Culpepper, *The Johannine School: An Evaluation of the Johannine-School Hypothesis Based on an Investigation of the Nature of Ancient Schools*. For an example of these applied see D. Rensberger, *Overcoming the World: Politics and Community in the Gospel of John*, esp. 15–36.

[8] So Culpepper, *Anatomy*, 11.

[9] For detailed surveys on the subject see Wright, *Victory*, 3–124; Sanders, *Jesus and Judaism*, 1–58.

replacement theology, the way he uses Scripture, and the prominent role of the Jewish festivals in providing structure and thematic coherence. Following on this we will explore whether the Fourth Gospel reflects and develops the concept of continuing exile (along with its attendant themes) and how this might affect the interpretation of Ps 118.

II. Old Testament Use in John

A. Quotations

1. Formula Quotations

John's use of the OT has received increasing attention, both in his employment of direct quotations and OT themes, and as connections between John and Judaism are explored.[10] Since it is unnecessary to repeat these studies I will draw attention to some aspects which are suggestive for the investigation ahead. Lists of OT quotations in John have slight variations in them, as classification depends somewhat on how quotation is defined. For example, J. Painter and Freed each count 18 quotations, while Carson and Hengel propose 19.[11] There are 17 uses of quotation formulae in John: 1.23 (Isa 40.3); 2.17 (Ps 69.9); 6.31 (Ps 78.24)[12]; 6.45 (Isa 54.13);[13] 7.37–38; 7.42;

---

[10] See especially the commentaries of Hoskyns, Barrett, Brown, Carson, Beasley-Murray, and Schnackenburg. Also helpful is F.-M. Braun, *Les grandes traditions d'Israël et l'accord des Écritures, selon le Quatrième Évangile* (vol. 2 of *Jean le théologien*). See further C. K. Barrett, "The Old Testament in the Fourth Gospel"; D. A. Carson, "John and the Johannine Epistles"; C. A. Evans, "Obduracy and the Lord's Servant: Some Observations on the Use of the Old Testament in the Fourth Gospel"; Freed, *Quotations*; Menken, *Quotations*; Daly-Denton, *David*; Schuchard, *Scripture*; A. T. Hanson, "John's Use of Scripture"; idem, *The Prophetic Gospel: A Study of John and the Old Testament*; M. Hengel, "Old Testament." On the form of the OT citations see G. Reim, *Studien zum alttestamentlichen Hintergrund des Johannesevangeliums*, 3–55 (for the Entrance citations see esp. 26–32). For a useful survey of studies on the OT in John see Obermann, *Schrift*, 3–36.

[11] See the lists and categories in Carson, "John," 246; Freed, *Quotations*, 117–130; J. Painter, "The Quotation of Scripture and Unbelief in John 12.36B–43," 429–430; Hengel, "Old Testament," 392 (following NA[26]); Evans, "Obduracy," 225. Schuchard (*Scripture*, xiii) argues that there are 13 explicit OT citations; Daly-Denton (*David*, 34) identifies 16 quotations; Obermann (*Schrift*, 76) concludes that 14 passages cite Scripture; and C. F. Burney (*The Aramaic Origin of the Fourth Gospel*, 114–125) lists 20 quotations.

[12] Freed (*Quotations*, 118) argues that this is a combined or conflated quotation including Exod 16.4. So also NA[27].

[13] Freed (*Quotations*, 118) suggests that Jer 31.31–34 is also in mind together with the psalm. Similarly, NA[27] lists Jer 31.33.

10.34 (Ps 82.6); 12.14–15 (Zech 9.9);[14] 12.38 (Isa 53.1); 12.39–40 (Isa 6.10); 13.18 (Ps 41.9); 15.25 (Ps 35.19 and/or Ps 69.4); 17.12; 19.24 (Ps 22.18); 19.28; 19.36 (Exod 12.46 or Ps 34.20 or Num 9.12); and 19.37 (Zech 12.10). In addition, there is a clear quotation without a quotation formula in 12.13 (Ps 118.25–26). Introductory formulae in four of these passages (7.37–38; 7.42; 17.12; 19.28) clearly point the reader to the OT, yet no OT text is cited.

If one looks at explicit quotations as a measure of interest in the OT, then in comparison to the Synoptics John presents a bleak picture. Barrett lists the number of direct quotations from the OT according to Westcott and Hort's edition of the NT: Matthew has 124 (1.82 per page); Mark, 70 (1.67 per page); Luke, 109 (1.51 per page); but John trails with only 27 (.51 per page).[15] Unambiguous citations understandably do attract the most attention, but they are only the most obvious component of the intertextual relationship to the OT, as a comparison of Scripture quotations and allusions for Matthew and John in NA[26] shows: John has 19 unambiguous citations, and around 200 marginally noted allusions and parallels, while Matthew has 87 citations and about 400 allusions and parallels.[16] John's emphasis, it seems, much more so than Matthew's, is on allusion.

Examining in more detail the formula quotations as a group suggests that even here John's use of Scripture is allusive. First, no clear source is found for four of the quotations (7.38, 42; 7.12; 19.28), although scholars suggest a number of possibilities in a variety of combinations. Second, other quotations are not completely clear as to their source(s) (6.31, 45; 12.14–15; 15.25; 19.36). Even where there is a primary source (6.31, 45; 12.15), there is sufficient disagreement in determining a secondary source with which it may be combined to show a lack of precision in John's use. Third, a number of the quotations are a combination/conflation of more than one source (12.14–15; 19.36; most likely also 6.31, 45; 7.37–38, 42; 15.25; 19.36). Fourth, one of the formula quotations (7.42) is not a quote at all, although the fact that the crowd explicitly ties its messianic expectations to Scripture has sent scholars searching for a specific source. However, to find a distinct source based on verbal parallels seems beside the point, since the Jews were not "quoting" Scripture, but rather summarizing a current exegesis of Scripture which probably was not based on one single text.

It is apparent that one cannot always define and/or distinguish quotation from allusion very clearly – nor does John make such clear distinctions.

---

[14] Zech 9.9 is clearly in view, but may be combined with Zeph 3.16 or one of several Isaiah passages (35.5; 40.9; 41.10; 44.2). I find unlikely Carson's suggestion ("John," 246) of a primary combination of Ps 62.11 with Zech 9.9, with further influence by Isa 35.4 and 40.9. See discussion in ch. 5 of this study.

[15] Barrett, "Old Testament," 155.

[16] This is Hengel's count ("Old Testament," 392).

He uses quotation formulae to point the reader to Scripture, but these are not wooden attempts to proof-text. In reference to passages where John clearly uses the OT as background but does not indicate which, if any, specific passage he uses, Barrett perceptively comments, "Though John uses the O.T. he uses it in a novel manner, collecting its sense rather than quoting."[17] John's appeals to the OT are meant to evoke images, associations and patterns. As for the uncertainty of sources in combination quotes, this shows that John quotes or refers to Scripture with remarkable freedom and at times very loosely. He does not distinguish clearly between quotations, allusions, and echoes, even in those references which are introduced by a formula pointing to the OT. Consequently a formula quotation may be allusive; another is a subtle mixture of echoes; another an explicit quote intensified, expanded, modified by an added allusion or echo. The significant number of combination quotations also suggests that John intends to send the reader on a search. He gives clues as to where one should begin this search, but invites the reader to look beyond the specific citation to the surrounding context, to avoid the tunnel vision that narrows the view to a single verse, and to explore wider swaths of Scripture. It is worth noting that John's quotations are short and concise, what Menken calls "compressed,"[18] so that a few words are sufficient to launch the search.

2. Pattern of Quotation

Although it may be difficult to determine conclusively the source of several quotations, some patterns do emerge. The Psalter is quoted more than any other OT book. It is quoted singly at least 6 times (John 2.17; 10.34; 12.13; 13.18; 15.25; 19.24); in possible combination twice (John 6.31, in which the psalm is primary; 19.36); and is probably quoted singly in John 19.28, although there is disagreement over which psalm is in view (Ps 22.15 or 69.21). In addition, John quotes from Isaiah 4 times (John 1.23; 6.45; 12.38, 39; and possibly in combination at 12.14–15.), and from Zechariah twice (John 12.14–15; 19.37). Thus, John's choice of quotations comes almost exclusively from the Later Prophets and Psalms, following a general

---

[17] Barrett, "Old Testament," 156. As an example see Freed's discussion of the quotation in John 7.37, 38, where he concludes that "the exact source or sources of the quotation and the text used must thus far remain unknown. There is no single O. T. passage or combination of passages which satisfies the statement of Jn. . . . [He] simply adapts in a creative fashion his broad knowledge of the O. T. scriptures and Jewish tradition to suit his Christian theology" (*Quotations*, 37).

[18] Menken, *Quotations*, 80.

pattern observed elsewhere in the NT.[19] This preference for the Psalter – of the 18 explicit quotations as many as 9 may cite the Psalms – justifies asking whether its influence in the Gospel extends beyond the clear quotations.[20]

John's pattern of source selection – i.e., drawing repeatedly from texts that the early church interpreted messianically and eschatologically – also provides a window onto his orientation in using Scripture. That is, one may expect John to use the Scriptures eschatologically, and to draw most often from texts interpreted eschatologically. Furthermore, the extensive use of the Psalter may reveal something about the writer and perhaps about his audience as well. There can be little doubt about the Psalter's influence in shaping the expectation and worldview of Second Temple Judaism, justifying Wright's conclusion that "anyone whose spirituality and thinking had been even partially formed by regular use of the Psalms, and whose life was lived out under pagan oppression, would have no difficulty in making connections between the themes of the poems and their own situation."[21] It appears that John's worldview may have been shaped at least in part by the Psalter, and it is not unlikely that he may have participated in the Jewish liturgical use of the Psalms and been aware of various exegeses and interpretations surrounding them. At the least he was very familiar with the Psalter, and chose to use it more than any other OT book as a source. That he uses it so freely, subtly, and repeatedly, suggests as well that he expected his intended readers to have either some degree of familiarity with the Psalter, or access to those who did.

---

[19] According to Hengel's count of NA[25] ("Old Testament," 382–383), approximately 60% of all unambiguous OT citations are taken from Psalms, Isaiah, and Deuteronomy. Of special significance were Isa 53; Pss 22; 69; and 118; and Zech 12.10–12. Hengel (ibid., 392) gives the following pattern of quotation for John: Psalms (8); Isa (6); Pentateuch (3); Minor Prophets (2). On this general NT pattern see also Dodd, *According to the Scriptures*.

[20] F. W. Young ("A Study of the Relations of Isaiah to the Fourth Gospel," 222) makes a similar observation in reference to John's use of Isaiah. Daly-Denton (*David*, 28) suggests that Jn 7.38 is a composite citation of Ps 78.16, 20, which would increase to 10 the number of psalm quotations. Confusingly, she states first that 10 of the 16 quotations in John are from the psalms, and then that 76% of Scripture quotations in John are from the psalms (ibid., 34). According to her numbers, this should actually be 62.5% – still a noteworthy percentage!

[21] Wright, *Victory*, 586.

B. *Other Uses of the OT in John*

1. *Old Testament Themes, Motifs, Symbols*

The influence of the OT on the Fourth Gospel goes well beyond the explicit quotations. There are many OT themes, motifs, and symbols used throughout the Gospel, so much so that Carson comments, "The precise line of connexion with the OT is sometimes difficult to determine, not because of a want of OT evidence, but because of an overabundance."[22] The major commentaries and numerous scholarly works have dealt with these, so we will offer only a few examples: the Lamb of God (1.29, 36); the shepherd imagery and sheep (10.1–16); the vine and branches (15.1–8, 16); allusions to Abraham (8.33, 39, 40, 52, 53, 56, 57, 58), Jacob (1.51; 4.6, 12), Joseph (4.5), and Elijah (1.21, 25); the "I Am" sayings; the concept of wisdom; numerous references to Sabbath and the Law;[23] and titles for Jesus which have their conceptual roots in the OT, such as "king of Israel" (1.49; 12.13) and Messiah (1.41; 4.25).[24] In addition, Moses is mentioned thirteen times,[25] and there is an extensive exodus theme which we will examine below. It should be clear that the OT, in various forms and at different volumes, is woven throughout the Fourth Gospel.

2. *Literary Structure: Institutions and Feasts*

It is clear that John has a well-thought out literary structure and careful arrangement of narratives, but what especially interests us is the framework of Jewish institutions that underlies the Gospel. Following the prologue (1.1–18) and the beginning of his ministry (1.19–51), Jesus performs a sign at Cana, changing water to wine using purification vessels (2.1–12). In Jerusalem Jesus cleanses the temple (2.13–25) and has an extended discussion with Nicodemus, a Pharisee and leader in the Sanhedrin (3.1–21). The Samaritan discourse takes place at a sacred well (4.1–42). Of greater interest is the high profile of the Jewish festivals.[26] Passover is

---

[22] Carson, "John," 253.

[23] For Sabbath see 5.9, 10, 16, 18; 7.22, 23; 9.14, 16; 19.31. On the Law, 1.17, 45; 7.19, 23, 49, 51; 8.5, 17; 10.34; 12.34; 15.25; 19.7.

[24] Hengel notes that "Jesus' Jewishness is especially emphasized by John, because the messiah (only John uses the Aramaic word in the New Testament – twice) comes from Israel" ("Old Testament," 385).

[25] See 1.17, 45; 3.14; 5.45, 46; 6.32; 7.19, 22 (twice), 23; 8.5; 9.28, 29.

[26] On the use of the feasts in John see M. Moreton, "Feast, Sign, and Discourse in John 5"; D. Murray, "Jesus and the Feasts of the Jews"; and D. Williford, "A Study of the Religious Feasts as Background for the Organization and Message of the Gospel of John."

specifically mentioned as the setting for the Temple Action (2.13), and since Jesus remains in Jerusalem for the festival (2.23), the talk with Nicodemus may well take place in that context (3.1–21) – Jesus leaves Jerusalem only after this meeting (3.22). An unnamed feast is the setting for 5.1–47, where one also notes the conflict over Sabbath, another Jewish institution (cf. 9.1–41). Passover once again provides the context for 6.1–71, and Tabernacles for all of 7.1–9.41, except for the Adulteress Narrative (7.53–8.11) which is not part of the original text and interrupts the sequence. The Tabernacles context may also continue on through 10.1–21, with Dedication specified for 10.22–39. The Lazarus Narrative is not specifically tied in with a feast. However, one notes that the plot to kill Jesus in response to the Lazarus Sign ends with reference to the coming Passover, which provides the setting for 12.1–20.23 and includes the Anointing at Bethany, Entrance to Jerusalem, Last Discourse, and the Passion and Resurrection Narratives.[27]

It is noteworthy that John situates so much of his material specifically in the context of festivals. In commenting on the episodic character of the Fourth Gospel, Culpepper observes that the two-and-half years covered by the narrative are presented in scenes totaling only about two months, an important point when looking at the Gospel's plot development.[28] Most of these carefully chosen brief episodes take place at feasts (2.13–3.21; 5.1–7.52; 8.12–10.39; 11.45–20.23).[29] This suggests that John's intention in using the festivals as a structuring tool goes beyond an obsession with the calendar; in fact they dominate the movement of the story and are a primary clue for interpretation in each passage where they are prominently mentioned. It is probably not coincidental that in John the festivals, which were associated with eschatological interpretation, provide the context for much of the messianic speculation, questions regarding the identity of Jesus, and conflict with the religious authorities. They also form the backdrop to the principal public symbols of Jesus' ministry (the Temple Action and Entrance to Jerusalem), as well as the Last Supper and Discourse. The feasts provide structure and plot to the Gospel and, for the discussions and discourses which often follow an episode (most of the teaching material is in a festival setting), a context-appropriate source of themes, symbols and imagery.

In conclusion, the significance of this for our study is that, in the same way that the narratives and teaching sections allude to the main symbols

---

[27] The explicit Passover context ends with the burial of Jesus (19.38–42). However, the resurrection and appearances to Mary Magdalene and the disciples (20.1–23) take place on the first day of the week, which would still fall in the Passover week.

[28] Culpepper, *Anatomy*, 72.

[29] Episodes not in a festival context include 1.1–2.12; 3.22–4.54; 7.53–8.11; 10.40–11.44; 20.24–21.25.

and themes of the festival in which they are set, they may refer to liturgical practices and Scripture that played a prominent part in the feast. Psalm 118 – the entire Hallel – was inseparable in the Jewish mind from its liturgical and festival context. I have argued that John makes extensive, allusive, and subtle use of the OT, and that he deliberately uses the feasts to provide structure and a source of symbols. But the festivals do more than speak from their own context, also providing clues which can send the reader searching for related Scriptures. It may prove profitable to search for allusive and subtle uses of Ps 118 in the context of festivals where it would be on the lips and minds of worshippers, a ready and easily-recognizable source for John to draw on.

C. Replacement Theology

A number of scholars have noted that John's selection and distribution of formula quotations seems to be purposeful and carefully planned, shifting from correspondence with, to fulfillment of, Scripture.[30] The formula quotations show that Jesus' ministry (1.29–12.36) is foreshadowed in the OT, that it "conformed to scriptural expectations and requirements."[31] Those in the Passion Narrative (12.37–19.39), on the other hand, point to the fulfillment of Scripture and prophecy, as borne out by the consistent use of πληρωθῇ in each case. That the highest concentration of formula quotations is in chs. 12 and 19, respectively the end of Jesus' public ministry and his crucifixion/death, underscores John's intention to relate Jesus to the OT. However, although John presents Jesus as the fulfillment of Scripture and of Jewish expectations, he clearly shows that he is much more than this. John's Jesus consistently takes up significant elements and/or symbols in Jewish institutions and festivals, shows his authority over them, and replaces them with his work and person.[32]

John's replacement theology is replete throughout the Gospel, and especially evident in the feasts. At the first Passover Jesus can be seen replacing the temple (2.18–21), and at the second Passover (ch. 6) he performs the signs of Moses, replacing him and the wilderness manna. The multi-

---

[30] See for example Hengel, "Old Testament," 395; C. A. Evans, "On the Quotation Formulas in the Fourth Gospel," 79–83; idem, "Obduracy," 228; S. Porter, "Can Traditional Exegesis Enlighten Literary Analysis of the Fourth Gospel? An Examination of the Old Testament Fulfillment Motif and the Passover Theme," 403.

[31] C. A. Evans, *Word and Glory: On the Exegetical and Theological Background of John's Prologue*, 174.

[32] John's replacement theology is well-recognized. See for example Beasley-Murray, xci; G. Burge, *Interpreting the Fourth Gospel*, 76–77; G. Yee, *Jewish Feasts and The Gospel of John*, 16–17; Carson, "John," 254–256.

plication of the loaves and the walking on water also show him as the fulfillment of Passover. At the third Passover Jesus replaces the sacrificial
lambs offered at the temple. John portrays Jesus as the true source of
living water (7.37–38) and the light of the world (8.12), against the respective Tabernacles backdrop of the water-pouring ceremony and light as a
primary festival symbol. At Dedication Jesus is the one whom the Father
set apart as his very own (10.36). In addition, Jesus is the good shepherd
(ch. 10), a title that is identified closely with Yahweh in the OT (Ezek
34.11), and also the vine (ch. 15), most often identified with Israel (Isa 5).
Moses, Abraham, and other heroes of Israel function as antitypes for Jesus.[33]
W. D. Davies has convincingly advanced that Jesus replaces "holy space,"
including the temple (2.21), the pool of Siloam (9.7; Jesus is the true Sent
One), and Bethel, or the house of God (1.51).[34] Jesus renders obsolete the
dispute between Samaritans and Jews over the primacy of Mt. Gerazim or
Jerusalem as a place to worship God, pointing instead to himself as the
locus of worship (4.21–26). Thus John portrays Jesus not only as fulfilling
but also replacing holy space, the feasts, and other Jewish institutions. It
is of interest that one of John's most powerful tools in showing that Jesus
fulfills and completes God's plans for Israel is not the explicit use of
Scripture, but rather Jesus' replacing festal liturgical actions and symbols
that, even though they may not refer to any specific OT text, point clearly
to Scripture themes as a whole (e.g. light and water at Tabernacles). In
the same way, John will use some of the underlying symbols forming the
bedrock of Jewish expectations, concepts that may not necessarily point to
specific texts but are nevertheless clearly inspired by and inseparable from
Scripture (e.g. the true return from exile, the new exodus, the defeat of
evil, and the coming of God).

It has been suggested that John's replacement theology is an attempt to
take Jesus and the Scriptures out of Judaism,[35] and others point to it as a
sign of Johannine anti-Jewishness.[36] However, the replacement theme

---

[33] Cf. D. M. Smith, "John, the Synoptics, and the Canonical Approach to Exegesis,"
173.

[34] Davies, *The Gospel and the Land: Early Christianity and Jewish Territorial
Doctrine*, 288f.

[35] Hanson, *Living Utterances*, 129–130.

[36] For example, Yee (*Jewish Feasts*, 16–17) takes John's replacement theology as a
sign of his hostility to Judaism. However, her interpretation of replacement is colored
in that she does not differentiate between the different types of references to "the Jews,"
assuming that the phrase is always used in a hostile manner. For Yee, replacement
theology is a reflection of the conflicts between the Pharisaic Jewish and Johannine
Christian community following the destruction of the temple. This requires making
several assumptions – all of them open to question – which Yee accepts in building on
Brown's theory of evolving community: the Johannine community is primarily Jewish;

does not necessarily point to Jesus' discarding and abandoning Judaism. Actually, replacement is a somewhat crude term, used for lack of a better one. A more accurate understanding is that rather than canceling or making obsolete, Jesus is portrayed as fulfilling, embodying, giving new significance to and reinterpreting the story of Israel and its expectations in himself. Far from being anti-Jewish, Jesus systematically redefines the true Israel as those who believe in him. In any case, it is important to note at this point that there is a relatively clear replacement pattern in John, for this supports my contention that there is a subtler and more widespread replacement structure underlying the Fourth Gospel.

D. The OT and John's Audience

Scholars have offered a number of suggestions for the primary background of the Fourth Gospel – Gnosticism, Philo, the Hermetica, Qumran, Samaritanism, and various strands of Hellenistic and Palestinian Judaism.[37] There may be parallels to any of these, but increasingly the influence of the OT and Judaism is recognized as the fundamental background, "like the backcloth in a play."[38] It is the OT that John repeatedly quotes, its imagery and symbols with which he tells his story.[39] Consequently, the credibility of any source theory advanced at the expense of the principal influence of the OT must seriously be questioned.[40] Accordingly we will

---

they were involved primarily in the synagogue; and John reads polemic back into Jesus' ministry which was not originally present.

[37] See the summary of the most commonly proposed backgrounds in Beasley-Murray, liii–lxv; Carson, 58–63.

[38] The phrase is Hanson's ("Scripture," 365). B. D. Chilton summarizes the position well: "Each of the elements specified as possibly belonging to a second source of John is better appreciated, and seen as more vividly historical, within its Judaic environment. . . . the Fourth Gospel breathes the atmosphere of early Judaism so deeply, it cannot live outside that environment" ("[ὡς] φραγέλλιον ἐκ σχοινίων [John 2.15]," 335).

[39] For this reason Beasley-Murray (lv) can suggest that a thoroughgoing gnostic interpretation of the Fourth Gospel depends on "a scholarly minimizing of the Jewish relations that it exhibits."

[40] For example, Hengel argues that the Qumran finds have rendered implausible the credibility of theories that regard the Gospel as a half-gnostic work. Instead, "one thing remains certain: phenomenologically, despite its conflict with the Judaism of its time . . . . the Fourth Gospel is to be understood primarily from the Jewish sources of its period" ("Old Testament," 384). In contrast, C. Westermann bases his unfortunately mistitled book, *The Gospel of John in the Light of the Old Testament*, squarely on these shaky gnostic foundations. Although he states that the Fourth Gospel cannot be understood without considering the OT background (ibid., 76–77), he devotes most of his efforts to declaring what is gnostic in source and determining the different layers and sources of tradition. Any contrasts (above/below, Jesus/Jews, God/devil), conflict between Jesus

not enter further into this debate, but recognizing John's OT program is of obvious importance in establishing the plausibility of allusions and echoes.

The preponderance of OT links does not deny the possibility of other backgrounds. For example, R. Cassidy has argued that the Fourth Gospel's themes are especially appropriate for Christian readers facing Roman persecution and imperial claims, and that John intentionally emphasizes elements that would have a Roman resonance.[41] It is a matter of course that readers in a Roman context will find what van Tilborg calls "inter-ferences"[42] between the Johannine text and their own symbolic world. However, as true as it is that, for example, Ephesian readers would have Ephesian experiences and culture in mind when reading the Gospel, it is the text itself which determines and points to the co-texts or "interfering" text it is to be read against. In other words, whatever the initial sponta-neous reader response, the text creates its own referent world and leads the reader to understand the text in light of a different context – if the reader listens to the signs and clues the text gives. So for example, the Entrance Narrative could bring to the reader's mind the greeting for a Roman gover-nor or high official, but citation of Scripture and other signposts in the text should also lead him to the symbolic world of the OT. The Ephesian or Roman parallel may give the insider an additional referent, but this would be secondary, arrived at by result rather than intention. Where relevant I will examine other parallels, and every case must be taken on its own, but the Fourth Gospel's internal guideposts – i.e., the extensive reference to Scripture and Jewish practice – indicate that the OT is the fundamental and principal background against which it intends to be interpreted. As Schnackenburg puts it, "this gospel would be unthinkable without the O.T. basis which supports it."[43]

There is always the question whether the reader could have picked up on the interferences/relations John intended to establish with the OT,

---

and Jews, and Jesus' issuing warnings of judgment, are construed as later gnostic insertions. As a result, Westermann sheds much more gnostic than OT light on John.

[41] Cassidy, *John's Gospel in New Perspective: Christology and the Realities of Roman Power*, esp. 1, 28. He argues that the Fourth Gospel presents Jesus as fulfilling Roman titles (lord, savior of the world, lord and god) just as he does Jewish titles (ibid., 104 n22). See further Rensberger, *Overcoming the World*; S. R. F. Price, *Rituals and Power: The Roman Imperial Cult in Asia Minor*.

[42] S. van Tilborg, *Reading John in Ephesus*, 3–4: An interference is the "exchange which spontaneously originates between reader and text when a typical similarity or dissimilarity is seen . . . the mutual influence which two systems exercise on each other if they come together." In his analysis of the epigraphic material from Ephesus he examines the Fourth Gospel and the possible reader response in light of these inter-ferences.

[43] Schnackenburg, 1.124.

although this does not necessarily bear on authorial intentionality.[44] For example, Hanson writes in reference to an allusive use of Scripture that the readers would have been unable to recognize it, nor could John have expected anyone to appreciate it.[45]   However, if Hanson has indeed identified an allusion to the OT, it seems arbitrary to deny this same ability to earlier readers similarly attuned to the Scriptures.   Assuming intentional echo or allusion by the author, regardless of whether he expected everyone in his audience to recognize it, the reference would be there for the careful reader to mine. It is apparent that John was an OT master, a suggestion supported by the complexity of – and allusive combinations in – the formula quotations, and the extensive use of OT symbols and Jewish practice.   The pattern first of correspondence with and then fulfillment of Scripture in the formula quotations, the festival structure, and the programmatic replacement theology, reveal a writer who carefully and intentionally uses Scripture text and symbol to undergird and develop the plot of the Gospel. This carries important implications for what the intended readers may have known, what they would have recognized.

Old Testament symbol and allusion are woven into the Fourth Gospel to such a degree that one can plausibly conclude that John expected his readers to be familiar with the referent world he was pointing them toward – that is, he assumes a degree of competence in the Scriptures. The discourses in the festival contexts cannot be completely understood unless the reader is familiar with the principal themes and symbols of the feasts. Even if the Johannine community were not principally Jewish, one can assume that at least some Jews were present, and at the same time one cannot assume that Gentiles were ignorant of the Scriptures. Paul does not hesitate to use the OT when writing to primarily Gentile churches in Rome and Corinth. Culpepper credibly concludes that the narrator assumes that the intended

---

[44] The writer certainly intends to communicate to his reader, and accordingly would want to use references and symbols that the reader would understand. However, this does not completely govern his choices. Some echoes are audible only to a careful reader. In any case it is difficult to state with any degree of certainty what a reader could or could not understand, so that assumptions must be made primarily on the text itself and the clues it provides.

[45] Hanson, *Living Utterances*, 129. P. Rabinowitz writes, "If historically or culturally distant texts are hard to understand, it is often precisely because we do not possess the knowledge required to join the authorial audience" ("Truth in Fiction: A Reexamination of Audiences," 121–141; cited in Culpepper, *Anatomy*, 207). John's use of the OT indicates an expectation that his readers were familiar with Scripture. To paraphrase Rabinowitz, if historically or culturally distant echoes/allusions seem too hard to accept, it is often precisely because we do not possess the knowledge (familiarity with the OT) that the authorial audience did.

reader has a general knowledge of geography of the gospel story, an extensive knowledge of the OT, is familiar with the Jewish festivals, and has a general understanding of Jewish groups and beliefs.[46] If John wrote with a specific community in view, one can expect that the readers would be familiar with his use of Scripture;[47] and if he wrote for a wider audience it is still likely that the Gospel would reflect to some degree the concerns and emphases of his community, in which case it provides a window onto a group that was steeped in the OT.

It is important in the hunt for allusions to avoid the extreme of *echomania* – the hearing of echoes where none were intended – and the equally distorted extreme of *echo-skepsis*, which is reluctant to look beyond any but the most explicit quotations. The text – the clues and pointers it provides – should guide and determine the search for echo and allusions. In the case of the Fourth Gospel, its patterns and interweaving of OT text, symbol and theme are an invitation to look carefully and widely, and with sensitivity to more than verbal parallels.[48]

Conclusion

The conclusions drawn from this brief overview of John's use of the OT are important for the work ahead. The formula quotations show that even the most formal use of Scripture in John is allusive, that he refers primarily to those sections of the OT that were interpreted eschatologically, and that he appeals most often to the Psalms. Although not as obvious as formal

---

[46] For discussion see Culpepper, *Anatomy*, 215–222. It may also be significant that John consistently, although not exclusively, uses the LXX, or the Scriptures which would be most familiar to his readers. Menken (*Quotations*, 205–206) concludes that although John did occasionally use Hebrew, the large majority of his quotations are based on the LXX, a view which he suggests is now more or less standard. Cf. Schuchard, *Scripture*, xvii.

[47] Menken describes a number of exegesis techniques common in a Jewish milieu which John deftly uses, concluding that "the treatment of OT quotations in the Fourth Gospel suggests that this gospel has been written by a Jewish Christian within and for a group that was able to understand his use of Scripture" (*Quotations*, 208).

[48] Cf. Wright, *Victory*, 584. R. Kysar ("The Background of the Prologue of the Fourth Gospel: A Critique of Historical Methods") compares the studies of R. Bultmann and C. H. Dodd on the Prologue (1.1–18), focusing especially on their lists of possible parallels. Each offers more than three hundred parallels, but their overlap is only 7%. (Cited in Carson, "John," 59.) This demonstrates that a verbal parallel is not necessarily sufficient to establish relation/reference. Finding other pointers – e.g. liturgical context, a rare verbal correspondence, contextual clues – that *make sense* of the proposed allusion bolsters the claim.

quotations, the Fourth Gospel is also replete with OT themes, imagery, and symbols – an OT bedrock that is no less real for being subtle. John employs the feasts and other Jewish institutions to provide structure and plot development. The replacement theme situates John's Jesus firmly in Judaism, so that his ministry and identity are understood vis-à-vis Jewish practice and belief. It is plausible that John's audience was familiar with the OT and would have understood John's allusive use. Together these suggest, first and most obviously, that one should look to the OT as the principal backdrop against which John writes. Second, one can expect extensive and subtle allusion to Scripture, especially those texts that were interpreted eschatologically, and especially the Psalms. Third, one can expect to find in the festival narratives and discourses allusions to things closely identified with the relevant feast – e.g. liturgical imagery, symbols, themes, and perhaps Scripture. Fourth, since John has used the feasts as a structuring tool, it is possible that he also uses other themes and/or Scripture texts in his shaping of the Gospel. Fifth, the replacement theme provides a pattern that may extend beyond and be more fundamental to the theology of the Gospel than has so far been acknowledged.

The implications for Ps 118 are significant: it is a psalm interpreted eschatologically, used prominently at every Jewish feast, and thus is well-known by Jews and John himself, who quotes it clearly in 12.13. I will argue that John refers to it allusively a number of times, that in its repeated use it helps to provide structure and shape the plot of the Gospel, and that it plays a key supporting role in John's replacement scheme. It is to this replacement pattern, in the form of New Exodus, that we now turn.

III. New Exodus

A. Introduction

I have argued that in spite of a partial return to the land many Second Temple Jews saw themselves as living in a continuing state of exile, a view echoed in the post-exilic prophets and across a wide spectrum of intertestamental writings. Our survey suggests that the exile was not seen only – or even primarily – as a physical state, although this was certainly an aspect. The real exile – an extended time living under judgment as a punishment for sin – would not end until the inauguration of the eschatological era. The problem was a state of continuing exile; the hope was that

Yahweh would soon intervene and change this.[49]   The widespread and general hope of deliverance and restoration can be divided into three distinct yet interlinked categories which account for all of the expectations: the return from exile; the defeat of Israel's enemies; and the return of Yahweh to live and reign among his people.[50]   I will refer to this complex of restoration hope as the *New Exodus*, a phrase which although not specifically found in the ancient texts yet adequately describes the eschatological program presented by the Prophets and also ties these longings to the paradigmatic deliverance in Israel's past.[51]

It is only recently that the idea of New Exodus has gained attention in NT studies, possibly because the state of continuing exile had not been widely recognized.   Perhaps more than anyone else N. T. Wright has brought the idea to the forefront, arguing in *Jesus and the Victory of God* that Jesus' contemporaries could not help but see in his proclamation of the kingdom of God that he was announcing the end of exile: "Jesus was announcing that the long-awaited kingdom of Israel's god was indeed coming to birth . . . The return from exile, the defeat of evil, and the return of YHWH to Zion were all coming about."[52]   One need not agree with Wright's subsequent exegesis to recognize the strength of the New Exodus pattern he uncovers throughout the Synoptics.   Indeed, when one looks at the Gospels through the lenses of Jewish expectation, it makes sense that Jesus' messiahship is interpreted in light of restoration thought – it would

---

[49] More specific hopes included the re-establishment of the twelve tribes, the rise of a Davidic king, a significant temple event (either cleansing, rebuilding, or restoration), a decisive time for the Gentiles, and the establishment of Yahweh's reign. For a list of primary sources see Sanders, *Practice and Belief*, 289–294.   For the subjugation or conversion of the Gentiles see ibid., 79, 291–292. Cf. idem, *Jesus and Judaism*, 79–80, 214.

[50] Wright uses similar categories in *Victory*. For an evaluation of Wright's work see the contributions to *Jesus & the Restoration of Israel: A Critical Assessment of N. T. Wright's* Jesus and the Victory of God (C. C. Newman, ed.).

[51] As I use the term, New Exodus includes but is not limited to the return from exile. Since according to the Prophets the restoration from exile is accompanied by the return of Yahweh and the destruction of Israel's enemies, it is somewhat artificial to speak of the return from exile as a separate event or hope unless its inclusion in a larger complex of expectations is assumed.   In this sense to speak of the one is to speak of the whole. However, I will use New Exodus to refer to the entire complex of restoration hope, and the return from exile primarily in relation to that self-described specific longing.   It should be noted that the New Exodus includes but is not the same as a *second exodus*, a phrase which is used by some with a limited sense that does not include the larger pattern that we propose, and which in this study will correspond to release from bondage, return, and restoration of the twelve tribes.   Jesus does lead a new or second exodus, but this should be interpreted within a larger New Exodus context.

[52] Wright, *Victory*, 201.

almost seem strange if this were not the case. However, although the Synoptics have received some attention,[53] the Fourth Gospel has not yet been studied from a New Exodus vantage point.[54]

The main strands of New Exodus thought – the return from exile, defeat of Israel's enemies, and return of Yahweh – are at the core of the Fourth Gospel.[55] Wright's work in the Synoptics highlights by contrast that the New Exodus is even clearer in John, where there is already a replacement pattern to support Jesus' embodying aspects of the New Exodus and fulfilling them in his own person and ministry. Although he does not refer

---

[53] For the three Synoptic Gospels see Wright, *Victory*. For Matthew, see M. Rapinchuk, "The End of the Exile: A Neglected Aspect of Matthean Christological Typology." For Mark, see R. Watts, *Isaiah's New Exodus and Mark*. A number of studies on Luke draw out exodus parallels, especially in the Lukan Travel Narrative. D. Moessner (*Lord of the Banquet: The Literary and Theological Significance of the Lukan Travel Narrative*, 260) argues that the narrative presents a "drama of a New Exodus" in which the Prophet Jesus is the prophet like Moses. W. Swartley (*Israel's Scripture Traditions and the Synoptic Gospels*, 7) suggests that Israel's exodus and conquest traditions inform the Synoptic Travel Narrative, agreeing in general with C. F. Evans ("The Central Section of St. Luke's Gospel"), who interprets Luke's Travel Narrative as a Christian Deuteronomy. The most helpful study is M. L. Strauss' *Davidic Messiah*, which interprets the narrative as a new exodus patterned after Isaiah 40–55. It is noteworthy that each of these models, whether convincing or not as the organizing principle of the Lukan Travel Narrative, has exodus typology, motifs and themes as the main component. On the possibility of New Exodus theme in Acts, see D. Pao's recent study *Acts and the Isaianic New Exodus*.

[54] Others have recognized exodus typologies and parallels in John, but without developing these into, or interpreting them in a context of, a full New Exodus pattern. In other words, Jesus' ministry is interpreted against a backdrop of the exodus, but a new return from exile goes unrecognized. See for example J. Enz, "The Book of Exodus as a Literary Type for the Gospel of John"; R. Smith, "Exodus Typology in the Fourth Gospel." R. Morgan ("Fulfillment in the Fourth Gospel: The Old Testament Foundations," esp. 158–159) comes closest as he interprets Jesus' ministry specifically as a "New Exodus." However, although he uses the same phrase as this study, the sense is more that of a second exodus which does not include the eschatological program that we advance. Among the major commentaries Beasley-Murray recognizes a second exodus motif but does not develop it.

[55] There may be a question whether John approaches Exodus directly or goes back through Second Isaiah. It is clear that the original exodus story was taken up and reinterpreted in the Prophets as the paradigmatic deliverance that provides the pattern for all subsequent deliverances. Denaux ("Lukan Travel Narrative," 291) points out in surveying Lukan studies that describe Jesus' journey to Jerusalem as a New Exodus that the link to the first exodus can be made either with reference to Exodus-Deuteronomy or to Second Isaiah. John may go straight to Exodus, but it should be clear that in any case he looks through the lenses of the Prophets and therefore interprets the first exodus in relation to the eschatological new exodus. In this regard it is noteworthy that John quotes explicitly from Second Isaiah three times, and possibly a fourth (if used in combination with Zech 9.9 in John 12.14–15).

as such to the New Exodus, a careful examination of the Gospel's themes and symbols will show that it is at the center of John's plot development. It is to this that we now turn, looking first at the return from exile.

B. Return from Exile

1. Exodus Typology

a. Passover

For those Jews who longed for the real return from exile, the exodus was the paradigmatic deliverance from God which they hoped to see repeated. What God had done before he would do again – he would bring his people out of bondage and be their king. This story, "the classic Jewish meta-narrative,"[56] was repeated and brought to life every year at Passover, a feast whose primary purpose was to evoke the exodus. To celebrate Passover was to re-tell the exodus story, and in a sense to enact proleptically the return from exile. It is no accident that John emphasizes Passover, men-tioning it more than any other NT book does, and having Jesus celebrate it three times.[57] The Passover theme is developed throughout the Fourth Gospel. At the beginning of his ministry Jesus is singled out as the Lamb of God who will take away the sins of the world (1.29, 36). Although there are several possible backgrounds to the lamb, internal connections in the Fourth Gospel suggest that here the Passover lamb is most likely in view.[58] At the first explicit mention of Passover Jesus replaces the temple with his body, and by implication challenges the sacrificial system which was focused there, specifically the Passover sacrifices.[59] That it was his intention to replace the Passover sacrifice, and in some sense Passover itself, is bolstered by the emphasis on Passover in John 6, and at the trial and crucifixion.

---

[56] Wright, *Victory*, 577.

[57] John refers to Passover ten times (2.13, 23; 6.4; 11.55 [twice]; 12.1; 13.1; 18.28, 39; 19.14), and it is implied in 4.45. The unnamed feast in 5.1 may or may not be Passover. Luke mentions it seven times, Matthew and Mark four times each. In contrast to John the Synoptics record only the Passover which coincided with Jesus' last week in Jerusalem. On Passover in John see Porter's comprehensive overview of the theme ("Traditional Exegesis"). See further G. L. Borchert, "The Passover and the Narrative Cycles in John"; B. Gärtner, *John 6 and the Jewish Passover*.

[58] There are several possible backgrounds, and it may be that John does not intend to single only one out, but has two or three in view. See Brown (1.58–63) for a summary of the three main options.

[59] Cf. Porter "Traditional Exegesis," 412.

John relates the Jews' action and timing in taking Jesus before Pilate to Passover (18.28). Pilate also mentions the practice of releasing a prisoner at Passover in an attempt to free Jesus (18.39). The references to Passover in 11.55, immediately following Caiaphas' "prophecy," and in 12.1, preceding the anointing at Bethany, both anticipate Jesus' death, so that Jesus is "depicted as the Passover victim being prepared for sacrifice."[60] Although there are questions regarding the chronology of the passion week, it appears that Jesus is condemned to death at the same time as the priests are preparing to slaughter the Passover lambs in the temple (19.29). The vinegar given to Jesus to drink on the cross is lifted up to him on hyssop (19.29), clearly an allusion to the use of hyssop to smear the blood of the Passover lamb on the door frame (Exod 12.22). That none of Jesus' bones were broken (19.36) is interpreted as a fulfillment of Scripture, most probably referring to the injunction of Exod 12.34 not to break any of the sacrificial lamb's bones (cf. Num 9.12).[61] Instead Jesus' side is pierced (19.37), in another fulfillment of Scripture (Zech 12.10) which helps to invest the Passover death of Jesus with New Exodus significance. In the original Zechariahan context it is Yahweh himself who is pierced, and there follows a cleansing from sin and impurity for Jerusalem, a purifying of the land, and the return of Yahweh to reign as king. The Passover theme that began at the outset of Jesus' ministry closes with him replacing the Passover lamb as the ideal sacrifice. It is significant that Revelation, which has a controlling New Exodus theme, depicts Jesus as the Lamb whose slaughter led to the creation of a new people for God (Rev 5.6, 9–10). Just as the initial Passover sacrifice brought redemption for Israel in Egypt and was the defining moment preceding the exodus, in the Fourth Gospel Jesus' sacrifice redeems the new Israel and provides a new or second exodus.

b. Other Parallels Evoking the Exodus

The Passover theme is the most prominent but by no means the only exodus parallel in the Fourth Gospel. John invites readers to interpret Jesus' ministry and works in the light of the first exodus by weaving exodus allusions and symbols throughout the Gospel.[62] The Baptist

---

[60] Porter, "Traditional Exegesis," 416. Cf. M. Davies (*Rhetoric and Reference in the Fourth Gospel*, 234–235), who points to parallels in Jesus' death and the Passover lamb.

[61] Beasley-Murray (lix) suggestively points out that if there is also a conscious echo of Ps 34.20, then the "Righteous Man of the Psalms who by his death brings about the second Exodus" is in view.

[62] We agree with O. Piper that the Fourth Gospel "considers Exodus as its type" ("Unchanging Promises: Exodus in the New Testament," 20).

conducts his ministry in the wilderness, and in announcing that God's plan to restore Israel is now underway cites a passage of Scripture replete with New Exodus imagery (Isa 40.3 in John 1.23).[63] Much of the dramatic imagery of the paradigmatic exodus is found in John. Through the incarnation Jesus comes to dwell among his people even as Yahweh's presence dwelt among them in the wilderness tabernacle. John emphasizes the glory of Jesus in his "tenting" (1.14),[64] in the same way that God's glory is at the forefront when he visits his people at Mt. Sinai, at the tent of meeting (Exod 33.7–23) and in the tabernacle (Exod 40.34–38).[65] Jesus' claim to be the light, made in the context of the Tabernacles festival which officially remembers the wilderness period (8.12), calls to mind the pillar of fire that burned brightly and guided Israel. Significantly he invites people to follow him so they will not walk in darkness. In the same context Jesus evokes the water-giving wilderness rock (7.37–38), claiming he is the source of life-giving water. At Mt. Sinai God gave the Torah to Israel to obey as the first covenant. Jesus gives a new command – a new Torah – to his disciples, that they love one another as he has loved them (13.34).[66] Israel was the vineyard that God planted at the exodus: "You brought a vine out of Egypt; you drove out the nations and planted it" (Ps 80.8). Now Jesus claims to be the new vine (15.1), and those who want to be part of the new Israel must be branches in this vine.[67] The use of γογγύζω to describe the response of the Jews and even of his own disciples to Jesus (6.41, 43, 61; 7.12) deliberately evokes the reaction of Israel to Moses in the wilderness, where they murmured and grumbled against him (Exod 15.24; 16.2, 7–9, 12; 17.3; Num 14.2, 36; 16.41; 17.5). The significance of the disciples' crossing the Sea of Galilee, and Jesus' walking upon it (6.16–21), lies in part in re-enacting the Red Sea crossing. The surrounding literary context places this event in an exodus setting, making more plausible Beasley-Murray's suggestion that the Ἐγώ εἰμι that Jesus utters as he appears to the disciples on the sea (6.20) recalls Ps 77.16–20, where God comes to the aid of his people and leads them through

---

[63] See Schuchard's suggestive comment that to respond to the Baptist's exhortation "involves first recognizing that the coming of Jesus is the coming of God" (*Scripture*, 13).

[64] Note the use of ἐσκήνωσεν, which is associated with the tent of meeting and the wilderness, and celebrated in the feast of tents, or Tabernacles.

[65] Cf. C. R. Koester, *The Dwelling of God: The Tabernacle in the Old Testament, Intertestamental Jewish Literature, and the New Testament*, esp. 102; J. McCaffrey, *The House with Many Rooms: The Temple Theme of Jn. 14, 2–3*, 222–224.

[66] Cf. Wright, *Victory*, 159. Wright argues convincingly that Jesus institutes a new covenant with his disciples in the celebration of the Last Supper. However, the words of institution are not included in the Fourth Gospel.

[67] Cf. Wright, *Victory*, 162.

the sea at the exodus.[68] Similarly, in John Jesus appears and leads his disciples through the sea, evoking a new or second exodus.

There is widespread agreement that Jesus' ministry, at least in part, is related and contrasted to that of Moses.[69] John mentions Moses 13 times, more than any of the Synoptics.[70] The Law was given through Moses, but grace and truth – a superior covenant – was given through Jesus (1.17). If Moses has seen the "back" of God, only Jesus has seen God himself (1.18). He is the fulfillment of the Law that Moses wrote (1.45), and Jesus, the only one who has gone into heaven, has received a superior revelation to that of Moses (3.13).[71] The bronze serpent that Moses lifted up in the wilderness provided healing; when Jesus is lifted up (crucified), he will bring eternal life (3.14–15). To set one's hope in Moses is misplaced; in fact, those who do will find Moses himself as their accuser, since he pointed to Jesus (5.45, 46). Jesus goes up on a mountain specifically near the time of Passover (6.3–4) and then feeds the multitude in the wilderness (6.5–15). This leads to a discourse on the bread of life, where Jesus claims to be the true bread of heaven in contrast to the manna given by Moses (6.32). The religious authorities invoke the Law of Moses to stone the adulterous woman, but Jesus defends and forgives the woman instead (8.1–11). They also contrast their discipleship (as followers of Moses) with that of the blind man whom Jesus healed (9.28). John presents with irony their argument that Moses spoke with God (9.29), when the reader knows that Jesus is the Word of God.

c. Structural Parallels – Works and Signs

Some scholars have suggested that the very structure of the Fourth Gospel follows an exodus pattern. For example, Enz systematically compares sections of John to sections of Exodus, arguing that their content is par-

---

[68] Beasley-Murray, 89. Note that Jesus' walking on the water parallels God's control over the sea.

[69] For example, W. Nicol (*The Semeia in the Fourth Gospel*, 48–91) argues that the basic typology of the Signs Source was Moses and the exodus, so that Jesus is portrayed as a second Moses. On Moses in John see T. F. Glasson, *Moses in the Fourth Gospel*; W. Meeks, *The Prophet-King: Moses Traditions and the Johannine Christology*; Martyn, *History and Theology*, 102–135; M.-É. Boismard, *Moïse ou Jesus: essai de christologie johannique*.

[70] The count for Matthew is 7; for Mark, 8; and Luke, 10.

[71] This is in contrast to speculation of Moses having ascended to heaven to receive revelation. See further P. Borgen, "Some Jewish Exegetical Traditions in the Fourth Gospel," 243–258; Meeks, *Prophet-King*, 295–301.

allel,[72] and H. Sahlin claims that John is constructed according to typology drawn in large part from Exodus (with some use of Josh and 1 Kgs).[73] B. Stather Hunt points to an Exodus typology whereby Jesus duplicates the miracles which Moses did in the wilderness,[74] and some have compared the speeches of Moses in Deuteronomy with Jesus' Farewell Discourse.[75] R. Smith argues that the signs of Jesus are parallel to those of Moses bringing plagues in Egypt.[76] However, although references to signs most often pertain to the events leading up to the exodus itself, they also describe God's continuing actions on Israel's behalf up to the entry to Cana, thereby evoking the complete exodus experience.[77] Thus Smith, because he limits the signs parallels to the plagues, proposes some improbable correspondences, so that for example the plague of locusts is parallel to the feeding of the five thousand, when a much more appropriate background would be

---

[72] Enz, "Exodus," esp. 209–211. Enz offers a number of plausible isolated parallels, but although they support a deliberate literary pattern in which the career of Jesus is interpreted in the light of the ministry of Moses, they are insufficient to sustain his hypothesis that the larger structure of Exodus and John are parallel.

[73] Sahlin, *Zur Typologie des Johannesevangeliums*. A number of his parallels seem fanciful. For evaluation and criticism of Sahlin see Smith, "Exodus Typology," 330–333. W. Roth argues for a "veiled, narrative-thematic correspondence" of each festival section in John to one of the five books of the Law and to the Elijah-Elisha Narrative ("Scriptural Coding in the Fourth Gospel," 7): John 5.1–47 corresponds to Deuteronomy; 6.1–71 to Numbers; 7.1–10.21 to Leviticus; 10.22–11.54 to Exodus; 11.55–20.29 to Genesis; 1.19–4.54 to 1 Kgs 17–2 Kgs 13. Parallels there are, but the evidence is not compelling.

[74] Stather Hunt, *Some Johannine Problems* (cited in Smith, "Exodus Typology," 331–332). Stather Hunt finds parallels for the wedding at Cana (2.1–11 = Exod 15.23–26, the waters of Marah); the feeding of the five thousand (6.1–14 = Exod 16.11–26, the provision of manna); Jesus' claim to be living water at Tabernacles and in the Samaritan Discourse (4.7–42 and 7.37–38 = Num 20.7–13, waters from the rock at Meribah); and the death of Jesus (ch. 19 and 3.14–15 = Num 21.8–9, the bronze snake).

[75] For example A. Lacomara, "Deuteronomy and the Farewell Discourse (Jn 13:31–16:33)." See Brown's favorable comments, 1.lx.

[76] Smith, "Exodus Typology," 334–338. Jesus' 7 signs compare to 7 of the 10 plagues: the water turned to blood (Exod 7.14–24) = water turned to wine (John 2.1–11); plague on animals (Exod 9.1–7) = healing of official's son (John 4.46–54); disease of boils (Exod 9.8–12) = healing of the lame man (John 5.2–9); hail and thunderstorm (Exod 9.13–35) = stilling of the storm (John 6.16–21); onslaught of locusts (Exod 10.1–20) = feeding of the multitude (John 6.1–15); darkness upon the land (Exod 10.21–29) = healing of the blind man (John 9.1–41); death of the first–born (Exod 11.1–12.32) = raising of Lazarus (John 11.1–44) and death-resurrection of Jesus.

[77] For example, in Deuteronomy signs refer to the events in Egypt (4.34; 6.22; 7.19; 11.3), and other times includes events up to the entry (26.8–9; 29.1–3). Sinai is identified as a sign (Exod 3.12), and Num 14.11, 22 also points to all of God's actions – in Egypt and the wilderness – as signs.

the provision of manna in the wilderness.[78] Nevertheless, although some
of the parallels offered are overstretched and in some cases fanciful, and
none of the studies successfully establishes that John and Exodus share the
same structural pattern, there is sufficient substance to point to an exodus
pattern in the Gospel, specifically in the signs and works of Jesus. Brown
effectively argues that the Johannine use of ἔργον, with which Jesus describes his miracles and ministry as a whole, finds its OT background in
the work(s) that God has accomplished on behalf of his people in creation
and salvation history, and specifically in the exodus.[79] In this way Jesus
is reproducing the past salvific acts of God, and placing his ministry in an
exodus context. It cannot be coincidence that Moses was a man powerful
ἐν λόγοις καὶ ἔργοις (Acts 7.22).

The signs in the Fourth Gospel find their most natural background in
the events of the exodus, and are most often associated by scholars with
the signs of Moses.[80] However, although Moses does figure prominently
in John and was inseparably linked to the exodus and events in the wilderness, it is of interest that the great majority of "sign(s)" references from
Exodus through Deuteronomy point specifically not to Moses but to God.[81]
Thus when Jesus takes the first exodus as a model for much of his ministry,
he may be intent not so much on reproducing the signs and works of Moses

---

[78] Smith, "Exodus Typology," 336. Smith questions Stather Hunt's wilderness
typology, asking why, of all the beliefs circulating in Judaism at the time, John would
have singled out one which expects the Messiah to reproduce the wilderness miracles
(ibid., 333). Smith bases his own plague parallels on what he argues was a prophetic
expectation that the eschatological event that would establish God's reign would
"constitute a cosmic repetition of the afflictions which God sent upon Egypt" (ibid.,
340–341). Arranging Jesus' miracles in parallel to the plagues would therefore present
the fulfillment of these eschatological prophecies in Jesus' life. I suggest that the New
Exodus approach better explains why – if John did indeed do so – the Fourth Gospel
would show Jesus repeating the wilderness miracles or even paralleling the plagues: this
would identify him as leading a new/second exodus. As for Smith's proposal, if the signs
are parallel to the plagues (which I find unlikely), I suggest that it would be more
appropriate to view Jesus' death as the Passover which signals the exodus than as a sign
parallel to the death of the first-born.

[79] Brown, 1.526–527.

[80] For example, Smith ("Exodus Typology," 334) argues that the σημεῖα have as their
background the tradition of Moses' signs and wonders; Enz ("Exodus," 210) suggests
that the Moses sign group is a parallel to the Johannine group; and Brown (1.lx) also
highlights the parallels to Moses.

[81] Moses is mentioned in relation to signs in Exod 4.8, 9, 17, 28, 30; Deut 34.11. God,
with no reference to Moses, is linked to signs in Exod 3.12; 7.3; 8.23; 10.1, 2; 12.13;
13.9, 16; Num 14.11, 22; Deut 4.34, 6.22; 7.19; 11.3; 26.8–9; 29.1–3.

as on associating his work with that of Yahweh.[82] Consequently, although it is appropriate to speak of Jesus as a second Moses, this is only in a secondary sense. In fact, he surpasses Moses in every sense, not only in signs and works, but also in primacy of identity and the role he plays in the new exodus – and Moses himself is called as a witness to this. Jesus does not only repeat, but also invests with a new significance all the symbols he takes up. Jesus is the true water, evoking not only the wilderness rock but also the eschatological water that would come from the temple. He is the life-giving light to the entire world, and whereas manna nourished Israel in the wilderness, Jesus is the bread that gives eternal sustenance. The bronze serpent brought healing, Jesus provides eternal life.

In evoking the works/signs parallels to Moses it was no doubt John's intention to take the reader back to the exodus and portray Jesus as the leader of a new or second exodus. However, the Johannine Jesus associates his ministry principally with the Father, not with Moses. Jesus is bringing to completion the works his Father began long ago (4.34); he and the Father do the same work (5.17), so that Jesus will give life, raise the dead (5.21), and judge (5.22) – all activities reserved to God. Jesus does the works of the Father (9.3; 10.25, 37), and the Father does the works of Jesus (14.10).[83] Relating this to the exodus, Jesus' signs show his glory (2.11; 12.37, 41), much as God's signs demonstrated his own (Num 14.22). In spite of his signs, many do not believe in Jesus (12.37), echoing the unbelief God encountered in spite of his many signs (Num 14.11). In many of the exodus parallels to Jesus' ministry it is the works of Yahweh that Jesus reproduces: It is Yahweh who opened the Red Sea, guided Israel with the pillar of fire, gave the Law, instituted the first covenant, healed those who looked at the serpent, and provided bread and water in the wilderness. If the people grumbled against Moses, they did so even more against God.

Jesus' ministry in this sense makes it clear that one greater than Moses has come, one whose works and signs are those of the Father. The signs and works terminology evokes primarily the salvific acts of God on behalf of his people and presents Jesus as the one who will bring about a new deliverance and salvation, leading his people from bondage, through the wilderness, to a new promised land. Evoking Moses, the leader of the first exodus, and the exodus events themselves, reveals how John interprets the

---

[82] Note that one of the primary reasons given by John for the Jews' seeking to kill Jesus is because of his claims associating himself and his ministry with God. See for example 5.18; 8.58; 10.33, 36; 19.7.

[83] Other references to the works of Jesus: 5.36 (twice); 7.3 (said of Jesus); 7.21; 9.4; 10.32 (twice); 10.38; 14.11, 12; 15.24; 17.4. Interestingly, the "works" of Abraham are to accept Jesus (8.39).

significance of Jesus' ministry. In the first exodus Moses was an instrument of God's pleasure. But Jesus is the Ἐγώ εἰμι (cf. Exod 3.14) who is
one with the Father, has authority in himself, and reproduces the signs and
works of Yahweh.

2. Regathering the Exiles

a. The Twelve Tribes

One of the most persistently held hopes in Second Temple Judaism was
for the reassembling of the twelve tribes of Israel. Their restoration – the
complete return of the exiles – would mark the end of exile. It is against
this backdrop that the significance of the twelve disciples should be understood. Although John does not emphasize the Twelve to the same degree
as the Synoptics do, referring to the disciples in this way only four times
(6.67, 70, 71; 20.24), he was nevertheless speaking a symbolic language
whose meaning could hardly be missed. As Sanders observes, "The expectation of the reassembly of Israel was so widespread, and the memory of
the twelve tribes remained so acute, that *'twelve' would necessarily mean
'restoration'*."[84]   Through his symbolic actions Jesus is consciously announcing the regathering of Israel.   Jesus deliberately chose the Twelve
(6.70), and three of the references to the Twelve are in the very suggestive
context of the Bread of Life Discourse, which connects them in an unmistakable way to the exodus.   The twelve baskets (6.13) are gathered after
the feeding of the five thousand, where Jesus has recreated the exodus
miracle, feeding "Israel" and providing "manna" in the wilderness.

However, even as Jesus signals the regathering of the tribes he is redefining Israel. The Johannine emphasis on the Twelve is set in contrast to
those who have retreated from and rejected Jesus. Jesus has given bread
to the crowd, but they do not want to eat the Bread of Life, thus rejecting
Jesus' invitation to the New Exodus banquet and continuing in exile even
as their fathers wandered in the wilderness.[85]   It is only after this rebuff

---

[84] Sanders, *Jesus and Judaism*, 98; emphasis original. Sanders concludes that the
emphasis on the Twelve and the Temple Action herald the restoration of Israel, so that
"[what] we know with almost complete assurance – on the basis of facts – is that *Jesus is
to be positively connected with the hope for Jewish restoration*" (ibid., 118; emphasis
original).

[85] D. Swancutt ("Hungers Assuaged by the Bread From Heaven: 'Eating Jesus' as
Isaian Call to Belief: The Confluence of Isaiah 55 and Psalm 78[77] in John 6.22–71,"
235 n. 56) argues that Isaiah 55, which describes God's new covenant that will be
celebrated in a messianic banquet at the return of Israel from exile, was a significant
influence on the discourse in question. If so, then it is possible that when Jesus issues
the invitation to eat the bread of heaven (i.e. himself), he is echoing God's call to Israel

that John mentions that Jesus had chosen the Twelve (6.70), in this way identifying them – in contrast to the unbelieving Jews – with the true Israel. It is a reconstituted twelve tribes, the new community he is intent on forming, that Jesus will gather and lead out of exile.

b. Gathering the True Israel

A brief survey of John shows how pervasive the return-from-exile theme of gathering God's people is. From beginning to end the Gospel is intent on giving shape to the community of faith that represents the true Israel. At the start God has redefined the family, with inclusion determined not by blood ties or descent, but by belief in Jesus (1.13). Jesus came to his own, only to be rejected, but those who do receive him become children of God (1.11–12), and it is to this group that the eschatological blessings of the kingdom and the restored Israel – life, forgiveness, salvation (3.15–17; 5.21–27) – belong. In contrast, those who do not accept Jesus are condemned and under wrath – i.e., they remain in exile (3.18, 36; 5.23, 29). According to the testimony of the Father (5.37), the Scriptures (5.39), Moses and the prophets (1.45), and the Baptist (1.34; 5.33), the community of Jesus is the true Israel. As a result, to oppose Jesus is to oppose Moses and the Scriptures (5.45–47). It is no coincidence that one of Jesus' first disciples is identified as "a true Israelite" (1.47).

The architect and builder of the new Israel is the Father, who draws (6.44) those he has chosen to be his people and gives them – teaches them to go – to Jesus (6.37, 39, 45). The Father once again has provided bread from heaven, this time a bread that gives eternal life and salvation (6.44, 47–51). It is Jesus' death (sacrifice, flesh and blood) that affords entry to eternal life and forgiveness (6.53–58). That is, his death leads to a new or second exodus, liberating the exiles from their bondage. In contrast, those who grumble against Jesus do not have life (6.53) and are not part of God's family, for the simple reason that God has not chosen them (6.65). The religious leaders will die in their sin (8.21) – a stark way of saying they will remain in exile. However, if they join Jesus' community, then they can go where he goes (8.23–24).

---

to come eat and drink at the new exodus (Isa 55.1, 2) and thereby announcing that the New Exodus and salvation, presented in Isaiah as delayed (see R. Watts, "Consolation or Confrontation?"), have finally arrived. When this is combined with reference to the extended wilderness sojourn of rebellious Israel (Ps 78.24 is quoted in John 6.31) it highlights Jesus' invitation as "a new Exodus promise for hungry wilderness-wanderers" (Swancutt, ibid., 246).

Again John is at pains to point out the continuity of the new people of Yahweh with the old, as Jesus redefines the true children of Abraham as those who believe in him. When the Jews argue that they have not been slaves to anyone, in the sense that they belong to God, Jesus answers that those who reject him are owned not by God, but by sin. In contrast, Jesus' disciples will hold to his teaching and be set free from the sin that has kept them in exile (8.31–32). Submission to Jesus, joining his community, participating in the exodus he leads, is what releases from sin and bondage and makes one a true child of Abraham and therefore of God (8.31–41). To those who think they belong to Israel but reject him, Jesus insists that not only is Abraham not their father (8.39), but in fact they are children not of God but of the devil (8.42–47). Similarly, the authorities who reject Jesus by claiming to be disciples of Moses are blind and remain in exile, the guilt of their sin unrequited. On the other hand, the blind man whom Jesus healed and they excommunicated is included in Jesus' community, and sees (9.28–29, 35–41).

Jesus' community is continuous with Yahweh's true flock (cf. Ezek 34), which is formed by those sheep who listen to the voice of Jesus (10.1–21). In turn, those who reject Jesus are not his sheep, have not been given by the Father, will be excluded, perish, and not have life, and are not identified with God's people/flock (10.22–31). The new Israel includes the scattered children of God, whom Jesus will unite with the Jewish nation through his death (11.51–52) as he draws all men to himself (12.32). The quotations of unbelief show the division of the true people of God from unbelievers, for the new community of Israel does not include the leaders of the synagogue, to whom the quotations principally apply (12.37–43). John concludes Jesus' public ministry with a reiteration of his mission to restore Israel: Jesus has come to save, speaking the words of God and leading his people to eternal life. Those who refuse God's means of deliverance will remain in darkness, be condemned and judged (12.44–50).

The Last Discourse is replete with language that confirms the status of Jesus' community as God's true people. The disciples are Jesus' "own" (13.1) – his chosen (13.18), his children (13.33) – who will follow later to where Jesus is going (13.36) and live in the Father's house (14.2). In knowing Jesus they know not only the way to the Father (14.4, 6) but the Father himself (14.9), who loves them and will give them his Spirit (14.16–17, 20–21), and with whom they will dwell (14.23–24). Those who do not join Jesus' community will neither receive the Spirit nor dwell with the Father, and furthermore will be cut off from the true vine and destroyed (15.5–6). Moreover, those who persecute Jesus and the disciples hate the Father and remain guilty of sin (15.18–20, 23–24; 17.14, 16), but Jesus grants eternal life to those given him by, and also belonging to, the Father

(17.2, 6, 9). They are to be one – a new family of faith – even as Jesus and the Father are one (17.11), and the benefits of the renewed Israel are extended to those who will believe based on their testimony (17.20–21, 24). The Jews' cry that they have no king but Caesar (19.15) reveals their true identity and seals their exclusion from the true Israel, in contrast to those who in accepting Jesus affirm that Yahweh is their king. As for the disciples, they are still called the Twelve (20.24) even though only eleven are left, underlining their significance as a symbol of the restoration of Israel. The Gospel ends with the reinstatement of Peter and a call to discipleship (21.15–24), a reminder that in the new tribes of Israel there is room for latecomers returning from exile.

To sum up: The Fourth Gospel depicts Jesus gathering God's people into a new community of faith that – although a new Israel – stands in continuity with and is in fact the true Israel. It is Yahweh himself who created this new family and makes inclusion contingent on belief in Jesus. The true children of Abraham and the true disciples of Moses are those who follow Jesus. Furthermore, the heroes of Israel (Abraham, Moses, the prophets), the Scriptures, and Yahweh himself, all bear witness that the true Israel has gathered around Jesus. Consequently those who oppose him cannot truly be part of Israel, and remain in exile. On the other hand, those who believe in Jesus are Yahweh's eschatological flock for whom all the benefits of the covenant and the New Exodus are reserved. The repeated contrasting of belief and unbelief in Jesus' discourses, and the contrast between those who reject and those who believe or are at least more open to Jesus, draws attention to the disciples' symbolic role as the true Israel. His death, by providing forgiveness and redemption, inaugurates the return from exile. Jesus' message – that he was gathering the family of God and leading them to salvation and life – was a clear announcement that the restoration of Israel had commenced.

c. Forgiveness

Together with the symbolic regathering of the children of God, Jesus' message of forgiveness would have resonated loudly in hopeful ears. Forgiveness was essentially an eschatological blessing.[86] The Sin-Exile-Restoration pattern examined earlier shows that Israel went into exile due to her sin, and that the prerequisite for her coming out of exile was the removal of her guilt through forgiveness. Jesus does not specifically use the term except when he commissions his disciples with the message of

---

[86] See for example Isa 1.25–27; 4.3–4; 53.4–12; Jer 31.31–33; Ezek 36.24–29, 33; 37.23–28.

forgiveness (20.23). However, since he indicates that he is sending them as the Father had sent him (20.21), this implies that their ministry of forgiveness finds its pattern in the earlier ministry of Jesus. Several points suggests this is the case. First, when Jesus claims the authority to commission his disciples with this charge it implies that he himself has the authority to forgive. Second, Jesus called sinners to follow him. It appears that the lame man responded negatively (5.14), and the woman caught in adultery, whom Jesus explicitly refused to condemn, positively (8.11).[87] Third, it appears that Jesus had authority to identify people as sinners. Jesus warned the lame man not to continue sinning, and stingingly rebukes the religious leaders who are obviously not without sin (8.7). In addition he warns harshly that those who oppose him will die in their sin (8.21), are slaves of sin (8.34), will remain in their sin (9.41), will be without excuse for their sin (15.22), and that the Holy Spirit will convict of guilt (16.8–9). All of these present the opposite of forgiveness, bringing to mind the obvious consequence – remaining in exile. They also highlight by contrast the benefits which are applied to the members of the community, which in turn is the fourth signal that Jesus had a ministry of forgiveness. Jesus is after all the sin-removing Lamb of God (1.29), whose death, "like that of the Passover lamb, inaugurates a new community, united in love of God and humanity."[88]   Thus when Jesus forgives it is an effecting of the restoration. When he speaks of forgiveness, he is speaking the language of the return, a language the exiles understand well.

d. New Ownership

The claims Jesus makes on the members of his community are consistent with return-from-exile theology. In Jewish understanding and practice, redemption – i.e. the recovery of one who has fallen into another's power – leads to a change of ownership and authority.[89] The newly-freed person is not independent; he is now under a new master. In the first exodus God redeemed Israel from bondage in Egypt with the purpose that they would serve him. In reference to the second exodus Yahweh declares, "Fear not,

---

[87] Note Sanders' comment that "Jesus did not call sinners to repent as normally understood, which involved restitution and/or sacrifice, but rather to accept his message, which promised them the kingdom. This would have been offensive to normal piety" (*Jesus and Judaism*, 210).

[88] Davies, *Rhetoric*, 234–235.

[89] See Daube, *Rabbinic Judaism*, 273: "Liberation by God, in analogy to 'recovery' prescribed by the social laws, means, not liberation pure and simple, but a change of master. It means a passage from a distressing, foreign and arbitrary yoke to contentment and security under the rightful authority."

for *I have redeemed you*; I have called you by name, *you are mine*" (Isa 43.1). The Fourth Gospel applies this concept of recovery to Jesus, not least in that the exodus, understood as redemption, played a prominent role in the liturgy and celebration of Passover, which is in turn one of the more prominent themes in John.[90] When Jesus announces the return from exile, provides forgiveness and redeems the exiles from the bondage of sin through his death, he becomes their new master. The correlate of redemption from exile is submission to new authority. It is on this basis that Jesus calls to discipleship, that membership in the restored community is contingent on allegiance and loyalty to him. As he leads the exiles, recreating the works of Yahweh, he receives the obedience and ownership due to Yahweh, and is entitled to be the locus of the new Israel.

e. *Signs of Deliverance*

Evidence from several uprisings in the Second Temple period suggests that when Jesus acted and spoke in ways that recalled the exodus it would have meant something to the average Jewish reader of the Fourth Gospel. The "Egyptian" came to Jerusalem claiming to be a prophet, and led many people out into the wilderness, promising that at his command the walls of Jerusalem would fall down.[91] Theudas persuaded many to follow him to the river Jordan, which he claimed would part on command.[92] Other prophet figures led many into the wilderness, "as pretending that God would there show them the signals of liberty."[93] What these movements have in common, other than suffering defeat at Roman hands, are the signs promised by their leaders. Theudas and the Egyptian intended through their signs to recall the exodus and conquest. The movements also had in common what Wright describes as a "stylized symbolic entry into the land,"[94] with Theudas crossing the Jordan, and all going out into the wilderness. The signs themselves, although they would have been impressive, were not in themselves especially eschatological, so that in

---

[90] Daube plausibly suggest that "it is surely against the background of the Jewish concept of redemption, 'recovery', and in particular against that dominating the Passover-eve liturgy, that the New Testament references to a change of master acquire their full meaning" (*Rabbinic Judaism*, 282). He cites John 8.32 as an example.

[91] Josephus, *Ant.* 20.169–172; *War* 2.261–263 specifically states that he led them into the wilderness. Cf. Acts 21.38.

[92] Josephus, *Ant.* 20.97–98: "Theudas persuaded a great part of the people to take their effects with them, and follow him to the river Jordan; for he told them he was a prophet, and that he would, by his own command, divide the river, and afford them an easy passage over it; and many were deluded by his words." Cf. Acts 5.36.

[93] Josephus, *War* 2.259–260.

[94] Wright, *Victory*, 155.

fact they gained their significance – and brought a measure of popularity to the leaders – because of the events they alluded to. R. Webb concludes, "These prophetic figures called the people to gather together and participate in a symbolic action reminiscent of their past religious heritage, especially the events associated with the Exodus and Conquest."[95] The crowds were drawn because they expected God once again to intervene dramatically as he had at the first exodus. Sanders has argued persuasively that in general these groups did not actually believe they could defeat the much stronger and better equipped Roman army. Rather, because many believed that the time for restoration was near and that soon God would intervene and deliver them as before, they hoped that by taking actions that put them in danger and demonstrated their trust in God they could prompt him to act.[96] The "signals of liberty" expected by the people who followed these prophet figures into the wilderness were those that God had performed during the exodus, including the wilderness period and conquest.

It is in this context that the symbolic actions of Jesus must be interpreted. The Johannine Jesus was performing the "signs of deliverance" that the crowds expected would herald the new exodus, signs they actually expected Yahweh to work. This is why people saw miraculous signs and believed in his name (2.23; 6.14–15), associated him with the Christ, and put their faith in him (7.31). The work that Jesus was carrying on for the Father testified to his identity and task (6.36), a task which, to the discerning, would be clear. As Wright succinctly states, "The praxis of the prophet invited the interpretation."[97] The symbols – gathering the twelve tribes, offering forgiveness, performing the exodus works of Yahweh – all invited the interpretation that the exile had ended, and that the New Exodus, the great deliverance, was underway.

---

[95] R. L. Webb, *John the Baptizer and Prophet: A Socio-Historical Study*, 347. Cf. Sanders, *Practice and Belief*, 286. For a detailed study with numerous examples see also Horsley and Hanson, *Bandits, Prophets and Messiahs*.

[96] See Sanders' survey (*Practice and Belief*, 35–43) of the major instances of Jewish uprisings and conflict between 63 BC and AD 74. There are numerous examples of individuals and groups placing their lives at risk, apparently with the hope that doing so would encourage God to intervene on their behalf. These include the teachers and students who tore down Herod's offending eagle (Josephus, *War* 1.650), the men who faced Petronius during the crisis precipitated by Caligula (*Ant.* 18.261–272; 305–309), and the crowd that opposed Pilate's introduction into Jerusalem of standards with the bust of Caesar (*War* 2.169–174; *Ant.* 18.55–59).

[97] Wright, *Victory*, 194.

3. Conclusion

John depicts Jesus as replacing Passover and its sacrificial system. He is the new Passover lamb, his sacrifice brings redemption to Israel, and provides a new or second exodus. Jesus has brought the exile to an end, but he does not only initiate the return through a second exodus, he himself *is* the new exodus. The extensive Johannine exodus typology ensures that Jesus' ministry and work is interpreted in light of the first exodus, is related and contrasted to that of Moses, and understood as leading a second exodus. Jesus' actions are therefore understood as providing the "signs of deliverance" that proclaim the end of the exile. However, Jesus is not so much reproducing the works and signs of Moses as those of Yahweh, with whom he associates his ministry. His signs and works evoke the salvific acts of God. Through several symbolic actions Jesus proclaims the return from exile. He chooses the Twelve and gathers to himself a community of faith that represents the new and true Israel and will receive the benefits of the eschatological age. These are the true children of Abraham and interpreters of Moses, a new Yahweh-chosen people. By proclaiming forgiveness Jesus is making an eschatological statement and providing the conditions for a return from exile, removing the sin that kept Israel in bondage. According to the practice of redemption this entitles him to make claims of ownership and authority, demand obedience and loyalty, and be the focal point of the new Israel, as was Yahweh in the first exodus. In addition Jesus replaces the temple with a new center of worship – himself – and thereby fulfils the expectation of temple renewal. By enlarging the community to include Gentiles, and making the offer of salvation universal, Jesus gives another sign of the end of exile.[98] All of these – his actions and speech – communicated in a powerful symbolic language that Jesus was bringing the exile to an end and that the long-awaited restoration of Israel was imminent.[99]

It is true that some of these, for example the formation of a new Israel and the proclamation of forgiveness, are themes that do not require a New Exodus interpretation. However, such an approach gathers cumulative force when the points are treated as an interconnected whole rather than isolated subjects, and serious attention is paid to the Jewish background of

---

[98] The issue of the judgment and/or inclusion of the Gentiles as part of the New Exodus will be dealt with in the following section, although it would be equally appropriate under a return-from-exile discussion.

[99] In his study of the Synoptics, Wright identifies a number of the same restoration and end-of-exile signs. Some of the symbolic acts that we have not touched on in John include healing, renewal, open commensality, and feasts replacing fasts. See Wright, *Victory*, 436.

the Gospel.[100] I suggest that *these themes are a complex or configuration for whose collection together the most plausible common denominator is a return-from-exile motif.* Of course, if the exiles were being gathered, and a new/second exodus was taking place, then the defeat of Israel's enemies and the return of God to establish his universal reign must follow. The former entailed the latter, without which the New Exodus would be incomplete.

C. The Defeat of Evil

According to the Prophets and their interpreters, the return from exile would involve the defeat of Israel's enemies. This is a matter of course, for if God is to reign supreme, then those who have oppressed his people must be brought into submission. John presents the ministry of Jesus as carried out in conflict with the enemies of Israel and concluding in their decisive defeat. However, the villains are not the usual suspects, for Jesus has redefined who Israel's true enemies are. The principal enemy is Satan, and Jesus' ministry, from the beginning until the final confrontation, is an assault on the prince of this world who rules with the power of darkness. Jesus is the light come to dispel the darkness that keeps the world in its grip (1.5, 9; 3.19; 8.12; 9.5, 39; 12.35, 46). It is from the Evil One that the disciples will need protection (17.15). The world is in darkness (12.47), and it is this world that loves evil and thus will hate the disciples as it has hated Jesus (7.7; 15.18, 19; 17.14), that cannot receive the Spirit (14.7), will be convicted of sin (16.18), and has been overcome by Jesus (16.33).[101] It is the devil that inspired Judas (13.2), and then entered and led him out to betray Jesus (13.27). Judas is called a "devil" because he will betray (6.70), and the devil is the father of those who attack Jesus (8.44). Painter, in his study of the quotations of unbelief in 12.36–43, convincingly concludes that they are related to the power of darkness and the defeat of Satan. Jesus' signs have played a principal part in the spiritual conflict, but although influential they have not been decisive, for the prince of this world has blinded and hardened people so they will not respond.[102] However, the decisive battle will take place when Jesus is lifted up in death, bringing judgment on the world and driving out its prince, freeing all men

---

[100] That is, the theory is plausible in so far as it offers a coherent explanation for all the various data according to a credible interpretation of the most likely background for the Gospel.

[101] In John the "world" can be positive, neutral, or, as the above examples show, negative. In the case of the world that hates Jesus and his disciples, John underlines that it is under Satanic domination: it is the world that is under the prince of this world.

[102] Painter, "Scripture and Unbelief," 457–458.

from the darkness Satan has held them in and drawing them to himself, and thus setting the captives (exiles) free from bondage (12.31–33). This has been proleptically symbolized in the raising of Lazarus from the dead (11.1–44), where Jesus defeats the power of death, Satan's most potent weapon. Even as the prince of this world joins the conclusive battle and pushes him towards the cross, he has no power over Jesus (14.30). The prince of this world is judged/condemned (16.11), unable to overcome Jesus (1.5; 16.33).

Another enemy to defeat is the power of sin, which is a weapon of darkness that keeps God's people in bondage and exile. The Fourth Gospel presents slavery as bondage to sin, and Jesus as offering freedom from this slavery. It is sin that has kept the children of Abraham in bondage (8.34–38). Jesus is the Lamb of God who takes away the sin of the world (1.29), linked in the Fourth Gospel with the Passover lamb that Jesus replaces. However, the lamb symbol may also call to mind the apocalyptic warrior lamb who destroys evil in the world (cf. *T. Jos.* 19.8; *T. Benj.* 3). Such a combination of motifs would not be inconsistent with Johannine usage, for in Revelation the Lamb has redeemed (Rev 5.9–10) and shepherds God's flock (Rev 7.17), and also overcomes the enemies of the kingdom (Rev 17.14). First John similarly indicates that Jesus appeared to take away sins (1 John 3.5) and that his purpose was to destroy the devil's work (1 John 3.8).[103] Thus Jesus is the Passover lamb who comes to be lifted up in death, but he is also the warrior lamb, who through this sacrifice decisively defeats the power of darkness and sin and thereby destroys evil (3.14–15; 12.32).[104]

It is ironic that Jesus also sees the conflict against evil as taking place in his struggle with the religious authorities, "the Jews." The primary spiritual battle is against Satan, who represents the darkness that stands behind those who oppose Jesus. Although "the Jews" is used many times either neutrally or with positive connotations, when it is used negatively it almost always refers to the religious leaders or establishment, who are

---

[103] Cf. Brown, 1.60. Beasley-Murray (25) comments, "The Baptist has in view the Lamb who leads the flock of God, and who delivers them from their foes and rules them in the kingdom of God."

[104] It is unnecessary to insist on only one background for the lamb motif when there is the possibility of considerable overlap and when themes in John can be multifaceted. Wright argues that Jesus in his death, as symbolized in the Last Supper, "draws on himself the judgment he had predicted for the nation and the Temple, intending thereby to defeat evil and accomplish the great covenant renewal, the new exodus" (*Victory*, 615). This view is untenable for John, where Jesus dies neither to take the wrath of the Roman war machine upon himself, nor to defeat the evil embodied in the rebellious spirit of "violent" resistance to Rome. Rather, his death is intended to defeat the power of Satan and the sin that keeps his people in exile, and to offer universal salvation.

often portrayed as acting in a hostile way towards Jesus.[105] They parallel Satan in their opposition. The Jews plot to take Jesus' life (11.53), but it is Satan who is orchestrating this attack (13.2, 27). They are in sin and will remain guilty of sin (8.7, 21; 15.22, 24), under the devil's influence. The prince of this world keeps people in darkness, aided by the religious leaders who oppose those who want to confess belief in Jesus (9.34; 12.42). Their hostile opposition of Jesus is due to sin (8.34–38) and proof that they are blind in sin (9.39–41), placing them in league with Satan (8.42–47). In the ultimate betrayal they choose Caesar as king rather than Yahweh (15.15). Thus the religious leaders are cast as the flesh-and-blood visible enemies who in their opposition to Jesus and his message are doing the work of the devil.[106]

What is most striking is that the enemy of Israel is not the Roman Empire. In fact, there is no anti-Gentile polemic – quite the opposite, salvation in John, although from the Jews (4.22), is universal and open to all who believe. Whatever their fate – whether subjugation, destruction, or conversion – that God would deal decisively with the Gentiles was one of the primary expectations in Jewish restoration theology.[107] John does not present the Gentiles as the enemy to be subdued or destroyed. Rome may be an enemy of the Jewish people, but if John is interested in communicating this, he does so very subtly. Rather, Jesus brings light to every man (1.9), he comes to remove the sins of the whole world (1.29).

---

[105] This is in agreement with the conclusions of U. von Wahlde's article, "The Johannine 'Jews': A Critical Survey" (see esp. 45–46, 54), which surveys the positions adopted by eleven scholars. Cf. J. Ashton's argument that the phrase cannot be confined to a handful of highly placed officials (against von Wahlde), but that they are rather an "archetypal symbol of the sinfulness of mankind" ("The Identify and Function of the ΊΟΥΔΑΙΟΙ in the Fourth Gospel," 68). See further R. Pietrantonio, "Los 'ioudaioi' en el Evangelio de Juan." R. Leistner (*Antijudaismus im Johannesevangelium? Darstellung des Problems in der neueren Auslegungsgeschichte und Untersuchung der Leidensgeschichte*, 64–67) provides a useful summary overview of the issue in German scholarship.

[106] Wright (*Victory*, 606–607) argues that Jesus understood his fight against evil to include conflict with the religious leaders because they were bent on resisting Rome and saw violence as the answer to end domination, while in contrast his own message was one of non-violence. However plausible this may be for the Synoptics – in my view Wright's suggestion provides a partial yet insufficient explanation for the intensity and extent of opposition there – the Johannine account presents the conflict not as an issue of non-violence but as resistance to Jesus' identification of his work with the Father, his claims to authority, and the creation of a new community of faith.

[107] For a list of representative non-biblical Jewish sources showing the three main positions see Sanders, *Practice and Belief*, 291–292. There is a clear stream of thought in the Prophets that looked forward to the inclusion of the Gentiles in the salvation God would bring to his people. See for example Isa 25.6–7; 45.21–22; 51.4–5; 52.10–11; 56.3–4; Jer 3.17; Zeph 3.8–9; Zech 8.20–21; 14.9.

The coming of the Greeks signals that the final battle is at hand (12.20–21), and the title on the cross is written in Hebrew, Latin and Greek, so all can understand its significance. John's Jesus enlarges the kingdom (3.16, 17; 4.42; 6.33, 51; 8.12, 26; 9.5, 39; 12.19, 46–47), including in the expanded family of God – the new Israel – children whose sonship depends not on blood or racial ties to the Jewish nation, but on loyalty to Jesus (1.12; 11.52).

As a result the Gentiles are not the enemy. Their inclusion in the kingdom is a sign that the exile is ending and that the reign of God is dawning. Israel's great enemies are Satan, sin, and those Jewish leaders under the control of darkness. These are the enemies that have held Israel in bondage. Jesus destroys the power of the prince of this world to blind and keep in darkness, the power of sin that keeps people in exile, and the leaders who resist his calls to the exiles and keep them from being the liberated people of God they are meant to be. He has engaged in battle with all these enemies, and defeated them decisively. This is the defeat of evil.[108]

D. The Coming of God

The return of God was inseparable from – in fact was the bedrock upon which was built – the hope of full restoration. As Eichrodt states, *"The religious core of the whole salvation-hope . . . is to be found in the coming of Yahweh to set up his dominion over the world."*[109] The expectation was that Yahweh would return to reign in Jerusalem, gathering the exiles and once again living amongst them. The Prophets looked to the coming of God for the judgment of the wicked and deliverance of his people, with the post-exilic prophets especially emphasizing the coming for salvation.[110]

---

[108] Mettinger ("Fighting the Powers of Chaos and Hell – Towards the Biblical Portrait of God") has pointed out that the conception of God as King and the emphasis on his sovereignty is closely linked in the OT with a battle motif. The motif shows that "victory over evil is not to be achieved by human agents, and that the powers which are hostile to God will first be eradicated by God's ultimate eschatological victory" (ibid., 36). This informs the interpretation of passages in John (and elsewhere in the NT) that describe Jesus' confrontations with the powers of death, hell, and Satan. On God's destruction of Israel's enemies in intertestamental literature, and the role of the Messiah, see Schürer, *History* 2.526–529.

[109] W. E. Eichrodt, *Theology of the Old Testament*, 1.499; emphasis original. Cited in G. Beasley-Murray, *Jesus and the Kingdom of God*, 24 (cf. 348 n. 22, where he lists a number of scholars supporting a similar view). On the general expectation of the coming of Yahweh in the OT see further Beasley-Murray, *The Coming of God*, 7–20.

[110] Note that in the Prophets the coming of God is often combined with the return of the exiles: Isa. 24.23; 25.9; 31.4; 33.17–24; 35.2–10; 40.1–5, 9–11; 42.13–16; 43.1–5;

This emphasis is also found in the Day of the Lord passages which figure so prominently in OT eschatological expectation and are indistinguishable from the coming of Yahweh.[111] For Wright this is the key for interpreting the announcement of the Kingdom of God in the Synoptic accounts of the ministry of Jesus. The kingdom message would communicate that Yahweh was returning, the exile was over, and that he would destroy the enemies of Israel: "It cannot be stressed too strongly that the 'kingdom of god', as a theme within second-Temple Judaism, connoted first and foremost this complete story-line."[112]

Wright argues that Jesus presented his journey to Jerusalem as the symbol and embodiment of the return of Yahweh to his city and his temple. This climaxes in two events: the Temple Action, which is a symbolic enacting of Yahweh's judgment on the temple; and the Last Supper, where Jesus defeats evil and accomplishes the new/second exodus by drawing on himself the judgment he predicted for the temple.[113] Whether or not the argument as Wright presents it is sustainable for the Synoptics is a separate issue, but in John, even though we may arrive at some similar conclusions, the road traveled is very different. For one, the kingdom of God is mentioned only twice in John (3.3, 5). Moreover, John does not elaborate the Last Supper in the passion as do the Synoptics, and he describes the Temple Action as taking place early in Jesus' ministry. As it is not the coming to Jerusalem alone, but *its conjunction* with these two symbols on which Wright depends for his symbolized return of Yahweh, his proposal does not work for John. Instead of a journey to Jerusalem followed by two significant symbolic actions, what is left in John is the Entry, the importance of which as symbol Wright misses.

There is also the question of the role Jesus takes upon himself. Wright proposes that Jesus was conscious of a vocation "to enact in himself what, in Israel's scriptures, God had promised to accomplish all by himself. . . .

51.4–5, 11–12; 52.7–12; 54.1–8; 59.19–20; 60.1–4; 62.10–12; 63.1; 66.10–16.; Jer 3.17–18; Ezek 43.1–7; Joel 2; 3.1–2, 16–21; Mic 4.1–7; Zeph 3.14–20; Hag 2.6–9; Zech 1.16–17; 2.4–13; 8.2–3, 8–9; ch.14; Mal 3.1–5. Examples of a similar combination in other Jewish writings include *1 En.* 1.3–10; 25.3–5; 90.15; 91.7; *T. Mos.* 10.1–10; Wis 3.7; *Jub.* 1.26–28; *T. Levi* 8.11; *2 En.* 32.1; 11QT^a 29.3–9; 1QM 6.4–6; 1QS 3.18; 4.19; CD 7.9; 8.2–3; 1QH^a 3.

[111] See further Beasley-Murray, *Kingdom of God*, 11–16. These passages many times culminate in Yahweh's coming to execute judgment (e.g. Isa 13.4–5; 35.4; Ezek 7).

[112] Wright, *Victory*, 206. See further Beasley-Murray's argument (*Kingdom of God*, 17–25) that the kingdom of God in the OT is the coming of Yahweh.

[113] For Wright's discussion of the Temple Action see *Victory*, 405–428, 477–493; for the Last Supper, 553–563, 615. In Wright's own words, "We should see his final journey to Jerusalem, climaxing in those two events and in that which followed from them, as the symbolic enacting of the great central kingdom-promise, that YHWH would at last return to Zion, to judge and to save" (ibid., 631).

He would embody in himself the returning and redeeming action of the covenant God."[114]   How a young Jewish prophet could come to such a conclusion is a question that Wright struggles mightily to answer, with mixed results. Questions regarding the role of the Messiah in the coming kingdom can be complicated because of the variety of views in the ancient literature, but Beasley-Murray is correct in concluding that, on the whole, the outstanding messianic passages of the Old Testament "proceed on the principle that the subjugation of the evil powers in the world, the submission of the nations to God, and the establishment of the new order of the saving sovereignty are the effect of the working of Yahweh, and that the task of rule in the kingdom of God is given to the Messiah."[115] The OT places the primary emphasis on Yahweh: it is Yahweh who comes to judge, Yahweh who brings salvation and deliverance. In support, Webb has argued persuasively that around the time of the Baptist the figure most eagerly expected to come as deliverer was Yahweh.[116] As for the Messiah, he is Yahweh's unique representative, the mediator through whom he rules.[117] Such an understanding would be consistent with Jesus' fulfilling the Messiah's role as *"the future, eschatological realization of the ideal of kingship."*[118] Beasley-Murray would like to go beyond this, arguing that

---

[114] Wright, *Victory*, 653. Elsewhere Wright claims that Jesus intended "to enact, symbolize and personify" the return of Yahweh (*Victory*, 615). Although Wright's terminology is not completely clear, what is apparent is that he does not use the word *embody* in an incarnational sense. For example, he can state, "Am I then saying . . . that Jesus, in one sense, embodied Israel in making the true response to YHWH and, in another, embodied YHWH in returning at last to Israel? Yes" ("Dialogue," 277). Jesus understands his mission as one where he would be "the agent or even the viceregent of Israel's god" (Wright, *Victory*, 630). However, as Eddy correctly observes, this would constitute "a relationship of representation as opposed to personal identity" (*"Eschatological Prophet,"* 58). As suggestive as Wright's assertions about Jesus' embodying Yahweh's return may be, they are not ontological claims. Accordingly C. C. Newman observes, "Wright appears to have dissolved all the potential ontological elements of Christology into narrative" ("From [Wright's] Jesus to [the Church's] Christ: *Can We Get There from Here?*," 287). These categories are inadequate to account for John's new exodus program, where Jesus' embodying of Yahweh is not representational or symbolic but incarnational, and where the justification for his mission flows from his ontological claims.

[115] Beasley-Murray, *Kingdom of God*, 22.

[116] Webb, *John the Baptizer*, ch. 7.

[117] Cf. Beasley-Murray, *Kingdom of God*, 23: "In the Old Testament prophetic teaching *the Messiah is uniquely related to God and man, and as the representative of Yahweh he is the instrument of his rule."* Emphasis original. For others who follow this view see further ibid., 22 n. 19.

[118] So S. Mowinckel, *He That Cometh: The Messiah Concept in the Old Testament and Later Judaism*, 156; emphasis original.

"the Messiah is the form of the appearance of Yahweh the Lord."[119] The question is whether one can make the leap from the Messiah as ideal king and vice-regent to substituting in some way for the coming of Yahweh, and whether the Synoptics themselves support this. We will examine whether these kinds of claims are sustainable for the Johannine Jesus.

Several steps point the way forward. John presents Jesus as the ideal eschatological king and mentions the kingdom of Jesus three times (18.36), while at the same time stressing neither the kingdom of God nor, by implication, the kingship of Yahweh. It may be profitable to examine whether John reinterprets the concept of Messiah, contrasting Jesus to some of the prevalent Jewish expectations with the view that these are insufficient to explain his identity and ministry. This bears directly on the question of the coming of Yahweh, for whereas the focus in the Synoptics tends to be on Jesus as the Messiah ushering in the reign of God, in John it is arguably on the unity of Jesus with the Father and how this is in fact the real presence of God in the midst of his people. A difficulty is that the coming of Yahweh is not specifically stated as taking place, perhaps explaining in part why this is such a neglected subject. However, the Fourth Gospel's programmatic replacement motif may contribute to a solution. Jesus does not only lead a new/second exodus; he *is* the new exodus, effecting deliverance and salvation. He also defeats evil, forgives, performs the signs and works of the exodus, and gives resurrection life and salvation, in all of this equating his works with those of Yahweh. What is yet lacking for the full restoration of Israel, for the kingdom of God to be established, is for Yahweh to come and institute his universal rule. The New Exodus motif in John suggests that those with eyes to see will discern the coming of Yahweh.

E. Conclusion

The Fourth Gospel presents Jesus acting in ways that evoked traditions pointing to a New Exodus, and announcing that this would take place in his own person and ministry. When Jesus offered forgiveness, announced salvation, expanded the kingdom to include the nations, replaced the temple, called the Twelve, pronounced the formation of a new people of God, and proclaimed the defeat of evil, he was speaking a symbolic language that powerfully declared the end of Israel's exile and communicated an eschatological message of redemption. John mobilizes an extensive network of OT symbols and allusions to advance this program, so that even though the New Exodus itself is not specifically mentioned, it nevertheless can be

---

[119] Beasley-Murray, *Kingdom of God*, 24; emphasis original.

clearly heard. The attentive reader can discern the end of exile, the defeat of evil, and the coming of God, all realized in Jesus. This suggestion seems not to have been made previously in relation to the Fourth Gospel. Our study further suggests that there may be agreement between John and the Synoptics on a deeper level than has previously been recognized, for although there are important differences in the way and degree to which each Gospel develops the New Exodus, the basic pattern is arguably present in all.

John presents Jesus as the focal point of the New Exodus, but it is spiritualized in a way that many would not have expected at that time. Jesus does not literally gather the twelve tribes and restore them to the land. Rather, he calls a new Israel out of exile, and gathers twelve new tribes around himself. The return itself is spiritual, a release from the guilt of sin. In the person and ministry of Jesus the kingdom of God has broken into this world, but instead of a restored Jerusalem ruling over the nations, the kingdom is distanced from its earthly material manifestation. Jesus is the king of Israel, but his kingdom is not of this world. It is to this new promised land that Jesus leads the exiles. There is indeed a new/second exodus, but it is to the kingdom of the Father he loves that he leads them, a kingdom where only those who know the way – that is, Jesus – can go. In the same spiritualized way, membership in the new Israel is based on faith, not bloodlines or race. This is nevertheless the true Israel that Moses wrote of, Abraham expected, and the prophets looked for. The defeat of Israel's enemies is spiritual as well, for the battle is fought not against the Romans, but the darkness that enslaves men, the religious leaders who oppose the message of Jesus, and Satan who stands behind them. However, according to John the spiritual rather than physical understanding makes the New Exodus no less real: it is real people who constitute the new community, Jesus has won a real victory over Evil, and he leads them to a real kingdom.[120]

---

[120] Note the contrast to Wright's interpretation of the Synoptics, where although Jesus is not aiming at a nationalistic victory over the Gentiles, his kingdom plan is very much bound up with the political situation of Israel in this world. Jesus sees his vocation as taking upon himself the "wrath" (i.e., hostile military action) which was coming upon Israel "*because she had refused his way of peace*" (*Victory*, 596; emphasis original). In this he acts as Israel's representative, calling them away from nationalism and rebellion. Jesus was invoking the martyr-tradition of Israel, and his death would prove the climactic turning point in Israel's history: "This would be the new exodus, the renewal of the covenant, the forgiveness of sins, the end of the exile. It would do for Israel what Israel could not do for herself. It would thereby fulfill Israel's vocation, that she should be the servant people, the light of the world" (ibid., 597). In effect, Israel would no longer be nationalistic nor resort to force of arms to gain her independence, which in turn would prompt God to intervene and restore her.

John's replacement motif continues in the New Exodus, with Jesus taking the central role in the return from exile and defeat of evil. However, the Fourth Gospel goes a step beyond Wright's interpretation of the Synoptics, in which, he argues, "Jesus believed that he was embodying, and thus symbolizing in himself, the return of Israel from exile."[121] This portrays Jesus as the Ideal Returnee: he returns from exile and thus symbolizes Israel's return. But in the Fourth Gospel Jesus does not take on the role of Israel, symbolically enacting their return – he himself is Israel's new/second exodus. This points to a significant aspect of the replacement theme in which Jesus takes the place of Yahweh, performing in the New Exodus those things that were expected of God himself. It is Yahweh who was to forgive Israel and thereby bring the exile to an end, who would regather the exiles, who would defeat her enemies. In this sense, John's Jesus is different from Wright's picture of the Synoptic Jesus: *Jesus not only symbolically enacts, he in reality effects the New Exodus in his person and ministry.* To anticipate the work ahead, I will argue that John depicts Jesus as the eschatological ideal king, but going beyond this also portrays Jesus as embodying the coming of Yahweh so that in his Entrance to Jerusalem he actualizes Yahweh's return to Zion. This parallels in part Wright's conclusion, although it differs significantly in some important aspects. Wright generally neglects the symbolic significance of the Entry, and does not provide the bridge for Jesus to cross from being a king to embodying the redeeming action reserved to Yahweh. One of our tasks is to find this bridge in the Fourth Gospel.

---

[121] Wright, *Victory*, 481.

Chapter 5

Psalm 118 in the Entrance Narrative

I. Introduction

The Entrance to Jerusalem appears in each of the Gospels in what seems to be a pivotal role. However, if full-length studies are an indication, it has received relatively little attention in NT scholarship.[1] Of course all commentaries on the Fourth Gospel deal with the Entrance, but the coverage is restricted, perhaps due to space limitations or to the abbreviated nature of the Johannine narrative. Other related issues have also suffered from neglect. For example, surprisingly little attention is given to exploring the various alternatives that could form the principal background to the Entry. On some subjects the majority view comes close to consensus and is ripe for challenge. In this category, it is commonly held that the quotation of Zech 9.9 is meant as a corrective to the nationalistic ambitions of the crowd, and furthermore that the disciples' misunderstanding was in missing the significance of this quotation and not realizing that Jesus came as the Prince of Peace. Some topics remain unsettled: Did Jesus accept or deny the acclaim of the crowd? Were they responding with true belief? Had Hosanna lost its eschatological associations, only to be shouted without understanding as a liturgical praise? This study cannot fully redress the neglect of these areas or deal comprehensively with all related issues, as its primary focus is the use and function of Ps 118. However, a closer look at the intertextual play of Ps 118 in the Entrance Narrative may shed light on a number of these, contribute to their resolution, and bring some clarity to a passage that Sanders calls "one of the most puzzling in the Gospels."[2]

Psalm 118's importance and the significant role it plays in the Entrance has generally been overlooked, with most commentators addressing it in a cursory way, at most in one or two paragraphs. However, a closer look

---

[1] Kinman, whose Ph.D. thesis (*Entry*) focused on the Entrance in Luke, writes that in 1995 he was aware of only two other studies dedicated to the topic: A. Martin, "The Interpretation of the Triumphal Entry in the Early Church"; and D. Carr, "Jesus, the King of Zion: A Tradition-Historical Enquiry into the so-called Triumphal Entry of Jesus." To this short list can be added the recent work of J. Nieuviarts, *L'Entrée de Jésus à Jérusalem*.

[2] Sanders, *Jesus and Judaism*, 306.

will show that the Entrance is a symbolic action that, at the end of Jesus' public ministry, serves to define his identity and his work in an unexpected way. Although it is quoted only once, Ps 118's influence on the structure of the narrative extends beyond John 12.13, underlying the Entrance and providing the model for an enacted liturgy. It is against the psalm that other proposed backgrounds must be evaluated, for while the festival theme so central to John contributes imagery and context to the Entrance, the clues to interpreting it are found in Ps 118. In addition, the quotation of Zechariah has generally been misunderstood as a corrective rather than as intricately woven with, and in supporting role to, Ps 118.

In the chapter ahead we will explore first the immediate literary context of the Entrance and the explicit citation of Ps 118, before looking at various options for the background of the event and suggesting what role the psalm may have played. Several specific elements – the Hosanna, the palm branches, the addition "king of Israel," and the relationship of Ps 118 to the Zechariah quote – require attention. We will examine the Gospel's complex of allusions to "the coming one" separately, before returning to the Entrance to offer an interpretation of the function of Ps 118 in light of these factors. Ultimately the definitive standard of plausibility is whether the function of Ps 118 as proposed makes sense of the passage, provides a reasonable explanation for its peculiar emphases, and is in accord with John's theological emphases.

II. The Textual Unit

A. Macro Context

The Entry quotation of Ps 118 falls in the chapter that brings to conclusion the public ministry of Jesus, summarizes the content and effect of his teaching, and provides the transition linking ch. 11 to ch. 13 and on a larger scale the Book of Signs (chs. 2–11) with the Book of Glory (chs. 13–20). The context is shaped by the Lazarus Sign and its immediate consequences – the belief of many, and the plot by the religious leaders to kill Jesus. The approaching Passover provides the setting for much speculation and interest in Jesus amidst the threats of the religious establishment (11.55–57). Chapter 12 consists of two narratives (vv. 1–11, 12–19), a discourse (vv. 20–36), and two sections that conclude the chapter and the Book of Signs (vv. 37–43, 44–50). The opening scene of ch. 12 is the Anointing at Bethany, which anticipates Jesus' death but also his upcoming entrance to Jerusalem as king (12.1–8). Again the reader is reminded of the plot to kill Jesus, with a clear impression that it is a minority – albeit a powerful one – opposing the one in whom the crowds are putting their faith (12.9–11). The next day Jesus enters Jerusalem, acclaimed with such widespread support as the coming king of Israel that the Pharisees lament that the whole world has gone after him (12.12–19). This observation is confirmed by the coming of the Greeks (12.20ff.), which signals to Jesus that his hour of glorification – through death – has arrived. His being lifted up shows not only the means of his death but also its effects: this is the decisive battle when the world will be judged, the prince of this world will be driven out, Jesus will be exalted and return to the Father, the world will be drawn to him, and liberation won for the people of God. The theme of this unit (12.20–36) is the struggle between light and darkness, and the coming victory of Jesus.[3]

John then offers an apologetic from Scripture for the unbelief Jesus encountered, but the point is not so much to show mass rejection as to expose the underlying cause of this opposition, which is the power of darkness.[4] Thus the necessity of the "lifting up," where the definitive contest between light and darkness will take place. The apologetic is primarily oriented not towards a pessimistic interpretation of the effects of Jesus' ministry, but to highlighting the necessity of the conflict Jesus is soon to enter and the positive results that will flow from it. Accordingly John again underscores that many believed in Jesus (12.42), showing that the emphasis is on Jesus' purpose in the upcoming engagement.[5]

---

[3] See K. Tsuchido ("Tradition and Redaction in John 12.1–42") for observations on the linking of the raising of Lazarus, the Entry, and the coming of the Greeks.

[4] R. T. Fortna (*The Gospel of Signs: A Reconstruction of the Narrative Source Underlying the Fourth Gospel*), Martyn (*History and Theology*), and Nicol (*Semeia*), suggest that the Fourth Gospel should be read in the context of a debate between Jewish Christians and Jewish non-Christians in the synagogue. Consequently an explanation for the unbelief of the non-Christians is required. D. M. Smith ("The Setting and Shape of a Johannine Narrative Source," esp. 236–241) claims that the intent of the apologetic is to provide an explanation from the OT for the crucifixion that would be effective in evangelism and countering Jewish claims. These may indeed be the primary reasons for the inclusion of the apologetic section, but I suggest that John's purpose extends beyond these (see the following footnote).

[5] C. A. Evans argues that Jesus' ministry "resulted, for the most part, in unacceptance and unbelief" ("Obduracy," 223). Smith (233) similarly claims that "as the public ministry concludes, it is pronounced an apparent failure," although this is explained as the fulfillment of Scripture. However, John many times emphasizes belief following the signs, and especially at the close of Jesus' public ministry there is a widespread positive response. This is consistent with John's New Exodus theme, where Jesus goes to the cross to defeat the enemies of Israel (the power of sin and darkness, and the religious leaders in league with Satan) that keep them in bondage, and thus effects their return from exile and inclusion in Yahweh's extended new Israel. In this sense it is an apologetic of hope, for the defeat of Israel's enemies will result in an inclusive Israel

The chapter closes with a reiteration of Jesus' identity in unity with the Father, the significance of his ministry of redemption, and the conflict of light and darkness which defines his purpose and work. The literary context of the Entrance is thus focused on summarizing and interpreting the significance of Jesus and his ministry. The question of his identity is paramount, and each smaller unit foreshadows the coming conflict. Although this is the end of the public ministry, it marks the beginning of the consummation of Jesus' master plan and mission: Jesus enters Jerusalem acclaimed as king on his way to engage in a final decisive battle with the enemies of Israel, in which through being lifted up he will destroy the power of darkness and effect a New Exodus for the true children of God.

B. Micro Context

The Entrance Narrative is actually very brief, taking up only 8 verses (12.12–19). The Entry itself is conveyed with "a few bold strokes"[6] in 4 verses (12–15), followed by the reactions of the disciples, the crowd, and the Pharisees (16–19). Its length, however, is not commensurate to its pivotal role in the Gospel's structure and plot development. In comparison to the Synoptic accounts the Entry is concise, but it is common for John to compress narratives and expand discourses. This points to an economy of description where John concentrates in a few words only that which is useful to the purpose he is advancing. As a result, even brief details are not superfluous and may be pregnant with meaning.

The account begins with what appears to be a deliberate plan of action by the Passover crowd to welcome Jesus formally to Jerusalem (12.12), with which purpose they take palm branches and go out to meet him. This is accompanied by a considered and premeditated use of Ps 118.25–26, whose Hosanna is inseparably linked to palm branches. With the words of the psalm they shout acclamation to the one who is coming in the name of Yahweh, welcoming him as king of Israel (12.13). Jesus finds a donkey

---

with Jesus the object of universal belief. However, the reality of John's historical situation is that many Jews not only did not believe but were hostile in their opposition. According to the Gospel these opponents are in league with darkness, not true children of Israel, and thus the apologetic applies to them in its full negative force. I find partial support for this interpretation of the apologetic in Painter's argument in relation to the quotation of unbelief in 12.40 that "the purpose of this statement is to make clear that the decisive conflict is yet to take place, in the immediate future" ("Scripture and Unbelief," 458). Painter also correctly notes that many times the response to Jesus' ministry and signs is positive, and that belief is common in John (ibid., 445–446).

[6] The apt phrase is from Ridderbos, 421.

and sits upon it (12.14), intentionally enacting Zech 9.9 (12.15). The disciples do not understand "these things" at the time, but after Jesus is glorified they understand the meaning of the enacted Scriptures (12.16). The crowd that witnessed the raising of Lazarus bears witness to Jesus (12.17), as a result of which many go out to meet him (12.18), showing a wide cross-section of support from disciples, witnesses, and Jerusalemites combined with festival pilgrims. The religious leaders, in an example of Johannine irony, lament that in spite of their opposition to Jesus "the whole world is going after him" (12.19).

The Entrance serves several important functions. First, it underlines and elucidates Jesus' identity and origin, something which from the beginning John has been acutely concerned to establish.[7] The first chapter (1.19–51) systematically presents messianic titles, two of which – the coming one and king of Israel – culminate in the crowd's use of Ps 118 to acclaim Jesus. Although "king of Israel" is not original to Ps 118.26, John adds it to interpret who the coming one is, thereby distinctly presenting Jesus as a royal figure and clarifying the origin and authority of the coming one: he comes from Yahweh, for which reason the crowds bless him. The quotation of Zechariah also emphasizes his royal identity and is critical in interpreting the character of his kingship and mission. Second, as a structuring tool the Entry ties together the beginning of Jesus' public ministry with its conclusion and foreshadows the passion. Jesus started out acclaimed as king of Israel by Nathanael; now he climactically enters Jerusalem with large crowds affirming the same, and will shortly be tried and crucified as "king of the Jews." Third, in John the royal and messianic claims of Jesus rest much more on the Entrance than they do in the Synoptics. A number of scholars emphasize the royal and messianic implications of Jesus' Temple Action.[8] However, John does not include the Temple Action at the end of Jesus' public ministry, with the result that the Entrance takes on greater symbolic importance in establishing Jesus' royal credentials. Fourth, the Entry is a publicly dramatic, deliberate action that symbolizes the coming reign of God as part of the restoration of Israel, for "king of Israel" identifies not only the person but also the work he is expected to accomplish. Sanders argues that the coming kingdom was symbolized by three gestures – the Temple Action, Last Supper, and Entry – of which only one was publicly

---

[7] Cf. M. de Jonge's convincing argument that the first chapter is "meant to give a survey of messianic titles and designations and to emphasize that they find their true meaning and fulfillment in Jesus" ("Jewish Expectations about the 'Messiah' According to the Fourth Gospel," 248).

[8] For example, M. Hengel, *Studies in Early Christology*, 55–57; Wright, *Victory*, 413–428.

dramatic.[9] Although Sanders is referring to the Temple Action, in John the Entrance is the only one of these three performed at the end of Jesus' ministry, attracting considerable and favorable public attention in spite of the hostile stance of the religious authorities.

C. The Quotation

1. Verbal Parallels

There is no question that John 12.13 quotes Ps 118.25–26, reproducing the LXX, which in turn is an exact translation of the MT. This is the only clear quotation in John that is not either introduced or followed by a formula. Consequently it is sometimes classified as an allusion. However, the distinction is unimportant since the use of Ps 118 is not in doubt. In addition the context does not encourage the use of a formula – one can hardly expect the crowd to add an introductory formula to their repeated shouts. One suspects this is the reason why none of the Synoptics introduces the quote with a formula either. Several points are of interest upon a closer look at John and his sources.

John 12.13	*Ps 117.25–26 (LXX)*	*Ps 118.25–26*
	ὦ κύριε	אנא יהוה
Ὡσαννά·	σῶσον δή . . .	הושיעה נא ...
εὐλογημένος ὁ ἐρχόμενος	εὐλογημένος ὁ ἐρχόμενος	ברוך הבא
ἐν ὀνόματι κυρίου,	ἐν ὀνόματι κυρίου . . .	בשם יהוה
[καὶ] ὁ βασιλεὺς τοῦ		
Ἰσραήλ.		

First, Hosanna does not follow the LXX, but rather is transliterated from the Hebrew. Although John shares this feature with Matthew and Mark, I will suggest ahead that he uses it to different effect. Second, there is the unusual addition of "king of Israel," which is presented as part of the quote even though it is not original to the psalm in any known version. Each of the Gospel writers has taken unusual liberties in quoting Ps 118 in the Entrance, in each case intensifying Jesus' royal status and qualifying the identity and mission of the coming one. I suggest that Ps 118 uniquely leant itself to this kind of qualifying addition because of its multi-layered

---

[9] Sanders, *Jesus and Judaism*, 307. He suggests that the Entry did not attract large public attention (ibid., 308). Cf. R. J. McKelvey's description of the Entrance as "an acted parable of the coming kingdom of God" (*The New Temple: The Church in the New Testament*, 61).

historical and liturgical associations. This encourages a closer look at John's addition to Ps 118, as it may point to which specific layer or meaning-horizon he intended to bring into play and thereby provide an interpretive key both for Ps 118 and the Entrance.

2. *Thematic Parallels*

In quoting Ps 118.25–26 John deliberately sends the reader back to the entire psalm. An explicit citation signals that the text should be read in light of the earlier text – not the single verse, but the surrounding context that interprets and gives meaning to each verse. Although the verbal parallels may be the most explicit and obvious links, these in turn bring into play the underlying structure of the psalm and its major themes. That it was John's intention to allude to these becomes clearer when we look at the thematic parallels.

First, John is intensely interested in presenting Jesus as a royal figure. The addition of "king of Israel" to the quote forces the reader to question whether Jesus is coming to Jerusalem with plans of fulfilling the political hopes related to such phrases and imagery. But Jesus' expectation of re-jection, the Anointing at Bethany, and other references to his death, bring a heightened tension as this kind of humiliation and defeat is incompatible with the royal imagery and the acclaim he is receiving. However, a royal figure who goes through a period of suffering and rejection before being exalted is the main character in Ps 118. Second, in ch. 12 John is espec-ially concerned with the meaning of the death and resurrection of Jesus. It is notable that Ps 118 was used in the early apologetic of the church especially in relation to the death and resurrection of Jesus, with Ps 118.22 occupying a special role. Even though John does not quote from or spe-cifically allude to this verse, it is not implausible that the reader may have noted the obvious parallels in the psalm. Third, the pattern of conflict between Jesus and the Jews is heightened and intensified in chs. 11 and 12 as Jesus' public ministry comes to its climactic finish. Conflict between God's anointed king and the enemies of Israel is one of the principal themes of Ps 118. As we have seen, the Fourth Gospel portrays the ministry of Jesus as an assault on the powers of darkness. It is not implausible that John expected the reader to identify Jesus with the warrior king of Ps 118.[10] Fourth, Ps 118's context and royal figure would provide a number of parallels useful in elucidating Jesus' identity: the main character is a

---

[10] This is further intimated by the allusion to Ps 118.10–12 in John 10.24, which functions to compare the Jews surrounding Jesus to the nations that surrounded and attacked the king in Ps 118.

king; he will not die but live (118.17); he comes in the name of Yahweh (118.26) and proclaims salvation (118.14, 17, 21); he must suffer humiliation and rejection (118.5, 10–13), but God will exalt him (118.14); and his victory is described as God shining his light upon Israel (118.27). The king's identity entails his mission. In Ps 118 he battles the enemies of Israel, and is God's instrument to provide light, victory, and a salvation that directly alludes to the exodus (118.14).

To sum up: A brief overview of thematic links suggests that, far from quoting a couple of verses in a contextual vacuum, John is evoking an entire psalm rich in appropriate parallels. The reader would find in Ps 118 a paradigmatic royal figure who paradoxically undergoes great suffering and is humiliatingly rejected before God exalts him in triumph. He would also encounter a warrior king invulnerable to death emerging victorious from a titanic conflict with the enemies of Israel. The verbal and thematic parallels together are a powerful signal that the interferences or intertextual links between the two texts may be more significant than most scholars have previously recognized. There are clues indicating that the Entry as an event may be an extensive allusion to the liturgical procession internal to Ps 118. This would provide an unusual example of OT liturgical structure as intertext, although there is precedent for this on a smaller scale when John alludes to liturgical practices at Tabernacles in 7.37–38 and 8.12. It is to the various possible backgrounds of the Entry that we now turn our attention.

III. The Structure and Background of the Entrance

A. *Introduction*

Commentators generally agree that the Entry in John carries messianic significance and portrays Jesus as a royal figure. However, significant attention is rarely given to the possible backdrop(s) against which the actions of Jesus and the crowd are carried out. This is unfortunate, as John seldom serves up a narrative without subtly evoking a wider referent world. The Entry is the Johannine Jesus' principal – in fact, only – public act at the end of his ministry, and it is obviously intended as a symbolic action that will clarify his identity and the significance of his mission. John shows deliberate planning on the part of the crowd, an element that is missing in the spontaneous response of the Synoptics, and although John does not elaborate the procurement process as do the other Gospels, Jesus deliberately rides a donkey. Wright perceptively points out the importance of symbol in the first century world:

> It is events and actions, and the implicit narratives they disclose, that count
> within a world that knows the value of symbols. Modern westerners, who
> live in a world that has rid itself of many of its ancient symbols, and mocks
> or marginalizes those that are left, have to make a huge effort of historical
> imagination to enter into a world where a single action can actually *say*
> something.[11]

John has already demonstrated an adept touch at communicating through
symbol, in line with the best prophetic traditions of Israel. One recalls
Isaiah walking around stripped and barefoot for three years (Isa 20.3–4),
Jeremiah wearing a ruined linen belt (Jer 13.1–11), smashing clay pots
(Jer 19.1–14), and wearing a yoke (Jer 27.1–2), Hosea's marriage to an
adulteress (Hos 1.1–2.1), and the many actions and trials of Ezekiel,
including the death of his wife (Ezek 25.15–27).[12] John was well aware
that symbol communicates powerfully to those who perceive the world it
evokes. It is this thought world – a world towards which he pointed his
readers and that he expected them to recognize and appreciate – that we
now explore.

B. Options for the Background

1. Roman

John's readers, whether primarily Jewish or Gentile, would have been
aware of various types of entries accorded to political leaders under
Roman rule.[13] Kinman has identified three types of entry: the *parousia*,
which was a welcome for kings or other royal figures as they approached
the city; the entry of governors; and the Roman Triumph.[14] By the first
century AD the Triumph was awarded only to members of the imperial
family and those who were potential successors. It took place only in Rome,
and by NT times was a relatively rare event. As for the *parousia*, it had
become invested with significant political overtones and more closely
associated with the Caesars. Kinman suggests that because of the increasingly imperial dominance of the event, an entry patterned after this would

---

[11] Wright, *Victory*, 554.

[12] Other prophetic messages communicated through symbolized action include Jer
16.1–13; 18.1–12; 28.10–17; 32.6–15; Ezek 4–5; 12.1–7; 21.18–22; Hos 3.

[13] For example, see van Tilborg's discussion (*Reading John*, 210–212) of Hadrian's
visits to Ephesus.

[14] Kinman, *Entry*, esp. 25–47. There is no need to repeat his work in detail.

be interpreted as a challenge to Caesar.[15] Was Jesus, then, following a Roman Entry pattern when he came to Jerusalem? The memory of the seldom-repeated Triumph would probably not have been foremost in people's minds, and Jesus was obviously not welcomed as a governor. Of the three types of entry the *parousia* offers the best possibility, and indeed is the background Kinman suggests for Luke's account. However, the question remains whether John could have presented Jesus' Entry as a *parousia* without an accompanying violent response from the Roman authorities.

An enacted *parousia* would be inconsistent with the hints of a moderate political apologetic in John to indicate that Jesus' kingship did not seek to displace Roman rule by violent means.[16] For example, John does not include the inflammatory Temple Action after the Entry.[17] The Anointing at Bethany, even if subtly pointing to Jesus' anointing as king, clearly anticipates Jesus' death – hence the anointing of the feet and not the head.[18] Jesus' conflict is with Satan and the powers of darkness, not Rome; and although Jesus claims kingship, his kingdom is not of this world. Had the Entry been a *parousia*, one expects it would have played a key role in the trial of Jesus, but it is not mentioned, nor does Pilate place any importance on it.[19] Kinman answers the inevitable danger a *parousia* would pose by arguing for a political apologetic in Luke that presents Jesus' Entry as a *parousia* gone awry. The point then is the contrast between the triumph and glory of a *parousia* and the supposedly a-triumphal Lukan Entry

---

[15] Kinman, *Entry*, 30, 47.

[16] See for example Cassidy, *New Perspective*, 86. Schnackenburg (2.375) also suggests there is an attempt to clear Jesus "of the suspicion of being a political agitator."

[17] The Maccabean cleansing of the temple was surely remembered by nationalists (1 Macc 4.36–59; 2 Macc 10.1–8). If a temple action were preceded by Jesus' entering Jerusalem to acclaims of kingship from a group of followers it could reasonably be interpreted as seditious.

[18] Lindars (419) argues that the relocation of the Anointing is John's attempt to minimize the importance of the Entry into Jerusalem and refocus attention on the Lazarus Sign, which is given as the reason for Jesus' being killed and the large crowds greeting him. However, Lindars misses the crucial significance of the Entry, for which John has deliberately built expectation through repeated reference to the coming one.

[19] According to Barrett, "John knows that the charge on which Jesus was in fact executed was his claim, misinterpreted by the Roman governor, to be a king" (416), an issue introduced in the Entrance. However, Pilate does not in fact misinterpret Jesus' claim. Instead, he recognizes that Jesus is a king, yet appears not to be bothered by it in the least, correctly interpreting that it poses neither a political nor military threat. He crucifies Jesus because he fears the Jews, not because Jesus is seditious. J. Coakley ("Jesus' Messianic Entry into Jerusalem [John 12:12–19 par.]," 464 n. 13) notes that Pilate appears to have limited his intervention to disturbances where participants were armed, or were in the process of organizing themselves into an army.

where Jesus suffers rejection.[20] However, John portrays Jesus' Entry in a positive sense: an enthusiastic majority greet and acclaim him as king, with the only dissent coming from a small minority of religious leaders whom the reader knows to be blind and poisonous villains anyway. There is no attempt to minimize the event. To the contrary, Jesus has just recently accomplished his greatest sign, and now purposefully goes to be glorified.

A symbolic action patterned on the Roman *parousia* is incompatible with John's emphases and portrayal of the Entry.[21] John does not provide internal or other specific clues to point towards a Roman Entry, so that although the reader might notice Roman interferences – this is to be expected! – these are probably a matter of result rather than intention. When one considers the eschatological expectations surrounding the feasts and the ministry of Jesus, it seems unlikely that the Entry would set out to evoke imperial associations rather than those of an established Jewish eschatological figure.[22] In conclusion, there are other contexts that would be more immediately obvious to readers with an awareness of Jewish history and Scripture, especially as John points in that direction.

2. Jewish Entries

There is more Roman material describing entrances than is found in the OT and other Jewish sources. Kinman accordingly concludes that "the sort of formal protocol which characterized the Roman Triumph and other entries seems neither to be reflected in the Old Testament nor to have developed in the intertestamental era."[23] One reason for this may be that some entries seem to have been much more spontaneous and charismatic in nature than Roman ones. More important, however, is the large gap in the description of OT ceremonies, which very probably had an elaborate ritual and protocol. This suggests that the Psalms, and the reconstruction from these of the central role of the king in the cult, may provide promis-

---

[20] In Kinman's words, "Although he is the king, he is not received as one by Jerusalem. Jesus' entry is 'a-triumphal'. Seen in this light, Jesus' entry would, if anything, have stood as a modest embarrassment to those who might have hoped to see it in triumphalist colors" (*Entry*, 122).

[21] In support, John does not present the Entry as a *parousia*. No internal clues point to this, and the response one would expect from the Roman authorities in reaction to such a demonstration does not materialize. In addition, it would be incompatible both with John's limited political apologetic and his portrayal of Jesus as a king of a different kind of kingdom, to portray him as directly challenging Caesar.

[22] This does not deny that many would recognize Roman parallels, but I suggest that these would be secondary because of the clear signs that John gives pointing to his intended backdrop.

[23] Kinman, *Entry*, 48.

ing parallels that have generally not been explored. Indeed, whatever Roman interferences may resonate in the Entrance, John points the reader towards a Jewish background by appealing to Ps 118 and Zech 9, both of which were originally entry texts. Johannine scholars have usually focused their attention on the details of the festival imagery in the Entry and the character of Jesus' kingship in light of the Zechariah quote, in the process often ignoring the background for the Entrance itself even though this significantly affects the interpretation of the other elements. A brief survey of the possible Jewish options will be useful in setting the stage for the primary background that John intended.[24]

a. Pilgrimage

The pilgrimage processions provide a suggestive context for the Entry. Large crowds of pilgrims would make their way to Jerusalem for each of the three pilgrimage festivals, some of them no doubt approaching the holy city with songs and prayers. This has led some to claim that Jesus is greeted as a pilgrim, arguing that Ps 118.26 was used by the priests for a ritual blessing on the pilgrims entering Jerusalem.[25] Thus Schnackenburg sees the Entry as "a harmless procession of pilgrims" that was built up to serve a Christian messianic interpretation.[26] Against Jesus' Entry being a pilgrimage procession is the lack of a formal procession at Passover. Psalm 118 was used at the Passover sacrifice and the evening meal, but only at Tabernacles was it used in a ritual entry context. The symbolic importance given to mounting the donkey, and the singling out of Jesus, is also at odds with the corporate emphasis of the pilgrimages. It is true that the greeting from Ps 118.26, which originally applied not to the average pilgrim but to the king,[27] came to be used as a ritual blessing for participants in the Tabernacles processions and possibly for worshipers at other times. However, it is obvious that Jesus is not treated simply as a pilgrim, albeit a famous and popular one: he is acclaimed king of Israel, a title no ordinary pilgrim would have received.

Of the three pilgrimage feasts only Tabernacles provides a procession that could be a precedent for the Entry. Because of the prominent role of Ps 118 in the ritual, and other Tabernacles imagery in the Entrance,

---

[24] Kinman (*Entry*, 48–56) provides a useful survey of Jewish entrances. There is no need to repeat in detail the work he has done, so our interest will be primarily in responding to the various positions held by scholars.

[25] So, for example, L. A. Losie ("Triumphal Entry," 856), who argues that Jesus is greeted as a pilgrim. On Ps 118.26 as a blessing on the pilgrim see Hoskyns, 421.

[26] Schnackenburg, 2.524 n. 39.

[27] *Pace* Brown, 1.457; Schnackenburg, 2.375.

Lindars suggests that John uses the Tabernacles water-pouring procession as his pattern.[28] In the same way, because Dedication featured palm branches and in so closely resembling Tabernacles also shared some of its symbols, others have proposed it as the primary background.[29] Accordingly the Entry would intentionally evoke the Maccabean triumph over Syrian forces and the rededication of the temple (1 Macc 13.51; 2 Macc 10.7).[30] The primary difficulty with these positions is that John places the Entrance unequivocally in a Passover context. The Dedication context is much less appropriate in John than the Synoptics, as there is no temple-cleansing to parallel the Maccabean action. In addition, an entry patterned after a Maccabean triumph would appeal to nationalistic longings, something John is not seeking to do.[31] It is therefore unlikely, although there are possible interferences with a Maccabean procession, that John intends to signal this as precedent for Jesus. Regarding Tabernacles, John is not ignorant of the symbols associated with the feast, and intentionally sets

---

[28] Lindars, 422. He does not place the Entry at Tabernacles, but suggests it is "an equivalent of the Tabernacles procession for the water-pouring." Similarly, S. Temple concludes that the scene "must have represented an enactment of the Tabernacles ceremony by which the people showed that they accepted Jesus as the promised Anointed One" (*The Core of the Fourth Gospel*, 202). T. W. Manson ("The Cleansing of the Temple") goes the whole way and argues that the event originally took place at Tabernacles and was transferred to its present setting. Sanders and Mastin (287–288) suggest the entrance took place either at Tabernacles or Dedication.

[29] See for example B. A. Mastin ("The Date of the Triumphal Entry," esp. 82), who suggests that the nationalistic and liturgical background of Dedication favors it as background to the Entry. F. C. Burkitt ("W and Θ: Studies in the Western Text of St. Mark [Continued]: *Hosanna*," 142–143), although placing the Entrance at Passover and acknowledging parallels with Tabernacles, argues that "the behaviour of the Galilean crowd . . . was based on what was appropriate for *Hannuka*" and that the disciples shared the same sentiments.

[30] So Mastin, "Date," 80. Cf. W. R. Farmer, *Maccabees, Zealots, and Josephus: An Inquiry Into Jewish Nationalism in the Greco-Roman Period*, ch. 8.

[31] S. G. F. Brandon (*Jesus and the Zealots*, 324) has argued that Jesus' action was "obviously calculated to cause the authorities, both Jewish and Roman, to view him and his movement as subversive," in order to reveal his sympathies for the Zealot movement. However, this is foreign to John's purposes, and he does not in any way represent Jesus as leading a nationalistic uprising against Rome. Sanders (*Practice and Belief*, 35–43, 279–289) has argued persuasively that many Jewish movements did not resort to violence and did not expect the kingdom to come about by force of arms but rather by God's miraculous intervention. Jesus' Entry in John is consistent with this. In support see S. Freyne, *Galilee from Alexander the Great to Hadrian: 323 B.C.E. to 135 C.E: A Study of Second Temple Judaism*, 208–255. Kinman (*Entry*, 62–64) looks briefly at military welcomes as a possible precedent for the Lukan Entry (David in 1 Sam 17.58; Jehoshophat in 2 Chr 20.27–30; 1 Macc 4.19–25; 13.47–53), but correctly dismisses them since they do not place an emphasis, as the Entry does, on the animal ridden or on Jerusalem.

out to evoke its traditions. However, although it is a partial background and vital to the interpretation of the passage, the contemporary Tabernacles liturgy does not provide the principal model for Jesus' Entry.[32] In conclusion, although the festival context is essential for understanding the Entry, pilgrimage processions are of limited usefulness in determining the intended principal background.

b. Royal Entries

Intertestamental Jewish literature preserves a number of examples of formal entries to a city. Catchpole, focusing on Mark, has argued that Jesus' Entry conforms to "a family of stories detailing the celebratory entry to a city by a hero figure who has previously achieved his triumph."[33] These in turn find their precedent in an Israelite kingship ritual evidenced in 1 Kgs 1.32–40 and Zech 9.9.[34] There are a number of elements found in the welcoming of royals and other dignitaries that would commend this suggestion.[35] However, one must expect a degree of common practice, so that the question is not whether there are, for example, interferences (or points of correspondence) with the Maccabean accounts on which Catchpole depends so heavily, but whether these are the intertexts that John intends to point his readers towards. Even were Maccabean accounts to fit Mark's Entry, they do not correspond well to John's. In the same way, the use of εἰς ὑπάντησιν αὐτῷ in John 12.13, which elsewhere appears in reference to the reception of Hellenistic rulers into a city, does not necessarily signal that John is portraying Jesus in such light, although a formal greeting is obviously appropriate.[36] Instead, John clarifies his intentions by identify-

---

[32] See discussion below on John's use of Tabernacles.

[33] Catchpole, "Entry," 319.

[34] Catchpole takes his examples primarily from 1 and 2 Macc and Josephus. For example, see the entries of Alexander the Great (*Ant.* 11.325–339; 11.342–345); Apollonius (2 Macc 4.21–22); Judas Maccabeus (1 Macc 4.19–25; 5.45–54; *Ant.* 12.312; 12.348–349); Jonathan (1 Macc 19.86); Simon (1 Macc 13.43–51); Antigonus (Josephus, *War* 1.73–74; *Ant.* 13.304–306); Marcus Agrippa (*Ant.* 16.13–15); Archelaus (*Ant.* 17.194–239); and Alexander (*War* 2.101–110; *Ant.* 17.324–328).

[35] The pattern includes a victory and/or established status for the person, a formal/ ceremonial entry into the city, greetings and acclaim, and procession to the temple for a cultic act. Cf. Catchpole, "Entry," 321.

[36] See Brown, 1.461–462: "This was the normal Greek expression used to describe the joyful reception of Hellenistic sovereigns into a city." Brown suggests that the phrase gives some confirmation to the scene's carrying political overtones and the crowd's welcoming Jesus as a national liberator. However, note that this is also the phrase used to describe the two demoniacs and later the Gadarenes' coming out to meet Jesus (Matt 8.28, 34), neither of which were favorable receptions. I suggest that John used a common phrase, but also one that could be used to indicate a more formal

ing Jesus as the eschatological king of Israel, an appellation that manifestly does not apply to any of the intertestamental examples and instead sends one back to the OT.

Two passages stand out when one looks to the OT for a model, as they are the only ones showing Israel's king riding into Jerusalem. There are a number of parallels between Jesus' Entry and that of Solomon on his accession to the throne.[37] In 1 Kgs 1 Solomon mounts David's mule, is anointed and acclaimed as king, is then accompanied by a large celebratory crowd on his way to Jerusalem to sit on David's throne and, as in the Gospels, there is great anxiety among his opponents. However, against Solomon's accession being the precedent for the Entry is the lack of any clear reference to him in John. Likewise, when Jesus' identity is at issue the focus is on his relationship to the Father rather than David. The relevance of the Solomonic parallels comes not in their pointing to Solomon – they do not – but to the event they detail, which is the enthronement of the Israelite king. That is, to the extent that the Succession Narrative provides background to the Entry, John is interested not in Solomon but in the enthronement procession.[38]

The only other example is the coming of Zion's king in Zech 9.9, which in addition to the king's riding into Jerusalem also shares other elements with Solomon's enthronement procession. Both kings are linked to David (Solomon as his son; Zechariah emphasizing the city of David), are received with joy and acclamation, and their entries take place in Jerusalem. The riding of a royal mule or donkey is of special significance in the OT, closely associated with claims to kingship. Solomon's accession to the throne was secured – and symbolized – by mounting David's mule. Although there are no other examples of a king riding a mule to enthronement, there are instances of claimants to the throne doing so. Thus Absalom's riding on a mule as he led an army against David was symbolic of his claims to kingship (2 Sam 18.9). In the same way, after David fled from Absalom, Mephibosheth saddled his donkey, apparently

---

welcome such as Jesus received. Cf. Mastin ("Date," 81), who argues against Brown that in the Gospel the phrase is not a technical term.

[37] See for example R. Pietrantonio's interpretation of the Entry in light of 1 Kgs 1–2 and Targum Pseudo-Jonathan to Isa 9.5 ("El Mesías permanece para siempre: Juan 12:12–36").

[38] Kinman (*Entry*, 59–60) has examined the coming of the ark, detailed in 2 Sam 6.1–19, as a possible background. As with Solomon, there is no clear allusion to the ark of the covenant in John, so its relevance as a background procession lies in the ceremony it points to. If there was a yearly ceremony in ancient Israel that involved the ark's representing the coming and presence of Yahweh, then it would provide an especially appropriate conceptual background to the Entry if the latter in some sense represents the return of Yahweh to reign.

in hopes that the House of Saul would be restored to the throne (2 Sam 16.3; 19.26–29). Consequently the riding of such an animal by Zion's king distinctly signals his claim and right to kingship. It is less clear whether an enthronement procession is in view, since the text does not explicitly indicate such an event. However, it is very possible that the reader would have made the connection, seeing not only the parallels to Solomon's enthronement but also the significance of the animal and the role it would play in a coronation. Solomon was proclaimed king prior to entering the city, and thus entered as king on the way to sitting on David's throne. Zion's king also comes to Jerusalem already as king and, as does Solomon, enters the city as its ruler for the first time. It would not be unreasonable to expect the next step in the Solomonic paradigm to then be fulfilled – that is, a formal taking up of the throne or enthronement ceremony. It seems likely that Zech 9 alludes, if not specifically to Solomon's enthronement, then to the royal ceremonies and traditions which it reflects.

The OT royal processions thus provide a striking parallel to John's Entrance Narrative. When Jesus comes to Jerusalem he already is king (1.49). Although he has often come to the city, this is the first time he enters explicitly and publicly as king, and this to great acclamation and joy. The Entry is a prelude to his enthronement, which will be accomplished when he is lifted up and returns to his kingdom. John's appeal to Zech 9.9, and the addition of the title "king of Israel" to Ps 118.25–26, signals to the reader that Jesus' Entry finds its backdrop and precedents in the OT, specifically in the royal processions and rituals. John has intentionally evoked Israel's ancient enthronement traditions.

3. Conclusion

After briefly surveying the most prominent examples of entry processions several things become clear. First, there are many possible parallels. This is to be expected, as all entries will share some elements in common that set them apart from an ordinary citizen's visit to a city: a dignitary and/or special occasion is assumed; there is a formal greeting and/or ritual; and there may be symbolic actions indicating the nature and/or importance of the event. It is thus no surprise that John's Entrance Narrative resembles in different degrees every one of the possible parallels. However, the distinctives John employs in shaping the narrative indicate that he had definite purposes in mind and was not presenting a generic entry procession whose primary achievement is geographic – that is, moving Jesus from Bethany to Jerusalem. The challenge, then, is to determine which of the possible parallels are merely possible and which likely or probable.[39] This points to a second conclusion, namely, that John has signaled what precedent he has in mind. In quoting the OT twice and giving a central place to festival imagery, John indicates that a Jewish background – not Roman *parousia* conventions – is primary. For various reasons Zealot movements, Maccabean celebrations, and other processions preserved in intertestamental Jewish literature are not the most likely precedents. Likewise, although Jesus' Entry takes place at a pilgrimage festival, it is not patterned on a pilgrimage procession. Of all the Jewish examples, it is the royal entries of Solomon and Zion's king that provide the closest parallels. John does not specifically allude to Solomon's Succession Narrative, but in quoting Zech 9.9 he evokes ancient enthronement traditions that probably underlie both passages.[40]

It is surprising that commentators have not recognized the most obvious signal John gives for interpreting the Entrance:[41] John sets the context by quoting the ritual greeting from the most prominent processional psalm in Jewish liturgy. Psalm 118 was not only used in procession historically, but contains an entrance liturgy evident both in verbal allusion and its internal structure. John provides several signals that point the reader in this direction.

C. Psalm 118 as Structure for the Entrance

A quote suggests to the reader that the passage should be read in light of the earlier text, a signal that John conspicuously places at the beginning of the Entrance. I noted above a number of thematic parallels that make Ps 118 an especially appropriate source for John, but in addition the psalm

---

[39] An example of a possible but unlikely proposal is Evans' argument ("Obduracy," 232) that the entire section 12.1–43 is a midrash, at least in part, on Isa 52.7–53.12.

[40] The Succession Narrative certainly reflects enthronement traditions, and it is likely that Zech 9 does as well. Although 1 Kings 1 is not the parallel John has in view, it testifies to the ritual background he evokes. The same can be said for the coming of the ark, which although not the principal background nevertheless provides a relevant example of ritual processions involving the king.

[41] I am not aware of any study on John that has noted Ps 118 as the primary pattern for the Entrance. Kinman (*Entry*, 57–58), who has comprehensively surveyed all the relevant entrance parallels, does address Ps 118. However, he does so in only one page, concluding merely that the psalm is useful in showing Jesus' royal status. To my knowledge only Sanders ("Ps 118") has recognized Ps 118 as providing the pattern for the Entrance. Because his article is focused on the distinctives of the Synoptic accounts it is less directly relevant for John. Mastin also recognizes the potential: "The citation from Ps cxviii in the story of Jesus' Entry into Jerusalem supports the suggestion that the liturgy is in view here" ("Date," 80). Unfortunately he advances this in reference to the use of Ps 118 in the Dedication liturgy.

assumes a procession that corresponds to the Entry. The Entrance is obviously a symbolic action, something John takes pains to show by quoting not one but two prominent entry passages. However, several clues suggest that Ps 118 provides the precedent on which the Entrance is based and in whose light it should be read, with Zech 9.9 functioning to modify and explain the psalm's significance.

First, and not least, is the fact that John sets the context and designates the referent world of the Entrance by placing the Ps 118 quote at its head. Second, John's account suggests that the Entry was planned, which makes more likely a deliberate enacting of Ps 118. Unlike the Synoptics, it is not Jesus but the crowds who orchestrate the Entrance. The acquisition of palm branches, which were not in such abundant supply to be plucked easily in a spontaneous celebration, suggests that the crowd took a premeditated action to greet Jesus in a specific way. Third, the branches and the Hosanna, along with other parallels, evoke the liturgical setting of Ps 118. Of the Gospel writers only John clearly identifies the foliage used as palm branches, a detail that highlights the parallel to Ps 118.27.[42] Furthermore, only John parallels the psalm's internal procession with different groups accompanying and others receiving Jesus into the city. The crowd's use of Ps 118.26 also mirrors that of the liturgical procession in the psalm as it entered the city and proceeded to the temple. These suggest that John intends the reader to look beyond a formalized ritual greeting drawn from Ps 118.25–26, and is directing them instead to the psalmic procession as a whole. The welcome indicates that he is pointing beyond the present liturgical use of Ps 118, for Jesus is not greeted as an ordinary pilgrim. In taking the words from their contemporary liturgical setting and applying them to Jesus as king of Israel, the crowd is evoking the original royal associations of the procession reflected in Ps 118 and actualizing it in a messianic and eschatological sense.

A fourth clue is that the festival setting argues for and especially suits a significant role for Ps 118, which not only is associated closely with Passover liturgy, but also shares eschatological interpretive links.[43] There can be little doubt that the feasts had eschatological associations. They provided not only context but opportunity, attracting large crowds,[44] and were

---

[42] Van Bergen recognizes this, writing "Au v. 27 il y a un parallélisme frappant avec la procession triomphale des rameaux, qui est venue de Jérusalem à la rencontre de Jésus" ("L'entrée messianique de Jésus à Jérusalem," 17).

[43] In arguing that Ps 118 was interpreted eschatologically in Second Temple Judaism I did so without referring to the NT. It is apparent that the backgrounds elaborated in ch. 2 of this study complement the New Exodus ministry of Jesus as portrayed in John's realized eschatology.

[44] Sanders (*Practice and Belief*, 128) estimates between 300,000–500,000 participants, especially at Passover. Jeremias (*Jerusalem in the Time of Jesus: An Investigation into*

the occasion for intermittent uprisings, such that additional troops were on hand during Passover.[45] It is no surprise to see increased expectation at Passover, as it embodied the theme of national deliverance. But the other festivals, which in Jewish tradition were also related to the exodus, gave rise to eschatological expectations as well. Weeks commemorates the covenant and exodus (Deut 26.1–15), and even at this smallest of the three pilgrimage festivals there was an uprising.[46] Tabernacles, apart from its other multiple eschatological links, also commemorates the wilderness period (Lev 23.42ff.). Against the claim that Tabernacles had become a celebratory feast that had lost its supplicatory and eschatological bent, we should note that one of the most famous riots took place then, with many thousands killed, and that Jesus son of Ananus chose the feast to begin his prophecies of woe against Jerusalem before the revolt.[47] Josephus attests that the feasts commemorated not only the past, but looked to future acts of Yahweh: "Let them assemble in that city in which they shall establish the temple, three times in the year . . . in order to render thanks to God for benefits received, *to intercede for future mercies,* and to promote by thus meeting and feasting together feelings of mutual affection."[48] The relevance of this is that an eschatological setting encourages the use of other eschatological elements to communicate and emphasize its points. We have seen that John presents Jesus as the fulfillment of Israel's hopes, so it should not be surprising that in advancing his New Exodus agenda he chooses as precedent for Jesus' Entry the Ps 118 procession, which could both evoke ancient royal traditions and excite eschatological speculation.

Finally, in manipulating the festival setting John evokes Ps 118's ancient traditions. The festival context both communicates the intentions and interprets the actions of the crowd. Jesus' Entry to Jerusalem took place in a Passover context, the most suitable setting for highlighting his mission to effect a new/second exodus.[49] However, although John uses Passover as the controlling symbol of the passion, he also intentionally appeals to Tabernacles traditions in the Entrance, primarily through the

---

Economic and Social Conditions During the New Testament Period, 77–84) suggests a high of 180,000. Whatever the actual number, the city swelled to several times its normal population.

[45] For uprisings at Passover see Josephus, *War* 2.10–13; 2.224–227; *Ant.* 20.112. The latter shows the availability of extra troops.

[46] Josephus, *Ant.* 17.221–268; *War* 2.42–44.

[47] For the riot see *Ant.* 13.372; for Jesus son of Ananus, *War* 6.301–309.

[48] *Ant.* 4.203; emphasis added.

[49] See Wright's appropriate comment: "The controlling metaphor that he chose for his crucial symbol was not the Day of Atonement, but Passover: the one-off moment of freedom in Israel's past, now to be translated into the one-off moment which would inaugurate Israel's future" (*Victory,* 605).

use of specific Ps 118 elements that are closely associated with the feast. But this works both ways, for the Tabernacles-Ps 118 conjunction shares a complex of traditions such that each is inseparable from and affects the interpretation of the other. Consequently, although John points to Tabernacles through Ps 118, once he has done so the Tabernacles traditions in turn point to how Ps 118 is to be interpreted. This is not circular reasoning; it is liturgical intertextuality – that is, the two mutually support one another.

It is the links to Tabernacles that have led some to question whether the Entrance actually took place at Passover or was transferred to that setting at a later time.[50] One link is that Ps 118 is connected with a Tabernacles procession, whereas Passover does not have a formalized entry. In addition, although the Hosanna was said at every repetition of Ps 118, it was especially associated with the liturgical waving of the lulab at Tabernacles, so much so that the lulab was at times called a Hosanna. It is true that the palm branch had become a national symbol and its use was not restricted to Tabernacles. However, it was still most closely linked to the liturgical use of Ps 118 at the feast: the palm branch was first and foremost a Tabernacles symbol, not a Passover one. Accordingly, the fact that John places the psalm on the lips of a palm-waving crowd would trigger this common association.[51] John's specific allusion to palm branches therefore suggests several possibilities: 1) The Entry of Jesus originally had taken place at, or was closely associated with, Tabernacles. Alternatively, the Entrance took place at Passover, in which case 2) Jesus and the disciples transported large quantities of palm branches with them in anticipation of the crowd conducting a formal welcome; 3) the crowd, in frenzied excitement, grabbed/plucked whatever branches were at hand (in this case palms); 4) the crowd intentionally planned to acclaim Jesus and for some reason chose to do so with palm branches, underlying their symbolic significance since they were not associated with Passover. The first option is unnecessary once one understands John's purposes, the second is incompatible with the narrative, and the third is rendered unlikely by the lack of palm branches in this quantity in Jerusalem at the time of year. John's careful arrangement of detail suggests that the Tabernacles associations are deliberate, not because the Entrance historically took place then, but because of his theological agenda.[52] This in turn leads to the last link,

---

[50] For example, Manson, "Temple." Cf. Mastin, "Date"; Burkitt, "Studies."

[51] Against Carson (432), who in suggesting that the palm could have been used widely proceeds to discount its close association with Tabernacles.

[52] Ps 118 was distinctively associated with Passover through its prominent use in the festival's sacrifice and meal. It is possible then for John to tie firmly the psalm's use in

which is that a royal entrance would be much less appropriate to Passover than to Tabernacles, which is the feast associated with the ancient enthronement traditions of Israel.

John directs the reader towards Tabernacles through its shared links with Ps 118. His quotation of Zech 9.9 also draws the reader into this symbolic world, as it would naturally bring to mind the eschatological Tabernacles festival of Zech 14 where Yahweh comes to reign as king. The question is, Why does John point to Tabernacles? I have argued that John intends to evoke not the current festal liturgical use of Ps 118 but rather its royal associations. There is nothing to indicate that John has in mind the current water-drawing Tabernacles liturgy.[53] His interest is in those traditions that would indicate and support Jesus' royal status, and accentuate his eschatological significance. As J. Sanders puts it, "The symbols involved purposefully point to the ancient royal dimension of the reference."[54] If there was an enthronement ceremony in ancient Israel it probably took place at Tabernacles. Furthermore this is also the time when God would come to reign, both by proxy through his vice-regent the king, but also eschatologically, as in Zech 14. In evoking Tabernacles John brings these ancient enthronement traditions and eschatological expectations to the forefront and underlines them through the quotation of Zechariah. This in turn points back to and highlights Ps 118's royal connection, both ancient and eschatological. Psalm 118 preserves a ritual procession led by the king, and it is possible that it was used in ancient Israel at the (annual) enthronement of the king. Such a use would be consistent with the liturgical/ dramatic division of the psalm in the Talmud and Targum, and in the eschatological rendition of the Midrash where Jerusalem welcomes its messianic king.[55] However, even if such a ceremony did not exist in ancient Israel, these sources indicate that at least there were perceived links to a royal procession involving David, the paradigmatic king. In this case actual historical practice does not matter so much as what is *perceived* to have happened.[56]

The Entrance, then, is portrayed as a re-enactment of the royal procession preserved in Ps 118, which was part of a ritual complex

---

the Entry to a Passover setting, and at the same time evoke the psalm's Tabernacles links independently of an explicitly Tabernacles historical context.

[53] Against Lindars, 422.

[54] Sanders, "Ps 118," 180. Sanders is here referring specifically to the annual enthronement of the king (preceded by a ritual humiliation) at the New Year festival, where he argues Ps 118 would have been recited.

[55] See *b. Pesah.* 119a; *Tg. Ps.* 118; *Midr. Ps.* 118.22.

[56] It is not implausible that the attempts in rabbinic literature to elaborate the liturgical aspects of Ps 118 suggest how the psalm functioned in the pre-exilic temple ritual. Cf. Sanders, "Ps 118," 180–181.

celebrating the kingship of Yahweh's vice-regent. John points to this by subtly evoking liturgical and historical interlinks between related royal traditions. First, he emphasizes the psalm's royal connections, directing the reader beyond festival usage by clearly identifying the coming one as the king of Israel. Second, he underlines specific aspects of Ps 118 that summon to mind Tabernacles traditions – again, not contemporary but ancient ones – and confirms this with the Zechariah quote. As a result Ps 118 is interpreted in an ancient Tabernacles context, possibly evoking the role that the psalm was perceived to have played in the enthronement ceremonies of the king, and at the least linking it to a network of royal associations and expectations. All of this is done in service to Jesus' identity, for when Ps 118 is re-enacted with its original royal meaning it underscores and confirms his kingship: Jesus, the king of Israel, is coming to his enthronement. The reader is thus intended to recognize a re-enactment of the ancient liturgy, but one that is understood through the mediation of Jewish tradition and expectation. Even if one does not accept an early date for the traditions underlying the midrashic interpretation of Ps 118 as the ritual procession that will be re-enacted by the Messiah, John may be seen presenting it as such.[57]

The action of the crowd as portrayed by John indicates that Jesus is welcomed as the ideal eschatological king, for Passover did not provide an appropriate liturgical occasion to quote Ps 118 in procession – unless, that is, they were re-enacting the psalm with its original royal meaning.[58]

---

[57] This would provide another point of contact with the Synoptics, for it appears that both Luke (13.34–35) and Matthew (23.37–39) present Ps 118.26 as the eschatological welcome that will be offered to the Messiah at his *parousia*. It is noteworthy that Matthew and Luke provide an early tradition that interprets Ps 118 in much the same way as the later rabbinic literature (esp. *Midr. Ps.* 118.22). For further discussion see the relevant sections in ch. 3 of this study.

[58] It is not clear that each of the Synoptists intends to point the reader back to the ancient use of the psalm as John does, but neither would such an agenda be inconsistent with their presentation of the Entry. Each uses Ps 118 to develop the royal motif in the Entrance, and although the Tabernacles symbolism is muted in comparison to John, there is sufficient material to hint at such a connection, particularly in Matthew and Mark. See further the discussion of the Entrance for each of the Synoptics in ch. 3 of this study. Sanders correctly sums up the explosive implications of the psalm being used in the way I have suggested: "It would have been all right to recite it [Ps 118] as one among many psalms in celebration of a festival, but it would have been blasphemous to re-enact it with its original royal meanings to those not otherwise convinced of the claim. Such a re-enactment was surely not to be done until Messiah came to make his royal entry into city and temple when the authorities would by some grand re-enactment of the psalm receive and acknowledge their messianic king" ("Ps 118," 180). Sanders is not referring specifically to the use of Ps 118 in John, as he approaches the psalm and the Entrance in general and focuses primarily on the Synoptics.

Could John's readers be expected to make these connections? I suggest that the writer expected his readers to have the whole of Ps 118 in mind, and to be aware of its significance. In addition, the crowd makes clear that it is welcoming a king. As Bruce notes, although the psalm does not explicitly identify a king in the leading role, the crowd "spelt out plainly what the psalmist meant, and what they meant."[59] That is, they indicated that they were well aware of the royal connections and traditions behind the psalm.

D. Conclusion

Understanding the function of Ps 118 in the Entrance requires an awareness of the psalm beyond the verses quoted, for they are intended as a signpost pointing to the whole. Although the Entrance is obviously intended as a symbolic act, it is only when one looks at the complete psalm that the objective and significance – what exactly is being symbolized, and what it means – becomes clear. In addition to being the source of the cry on the crowd's lips, Ps 118 also supplies the precedent for the processional on the road into Jerusalem, so that the Entry is a re-enactment of the psalm according to its original royal meaning. The quote clarifies the identity of Jesus, and in calling into play the ancient ritual procession enacts the coming of Israel's king to his enthronement. A closer look at Ps 118 has thus revealed an extensive and significant function that no Johannine scholar or commentator seems to have recognized previously. It also provides a more appropriate alternative to the other precedents offered for the Entrance.[60] Although all of these are on target in identifying individual parallels, they also have serious disjunctions that make them less than ideal. On the other hand, Ps 118 supports *all* of the parallels and symbols.[61] The psalm has disjunctions as well, but these come into play only when significant parallels have been established and, as I will argue ahead, they serve to highlight John's theological emphases.

John has accentuated the ancient royal traditions associated with Ps 118 in part by appealing to Tabernacles and Zechariah. This complex of tradi-

---

[59] Bruce, 259.

[60] Those who propose other models generally have done so on the basis of parallel emphases or symbols. So, for example, it is true that Passover is a pilgrimage festival, that John evokes festal imagery, that Jesus' entrance could foreshadow a victory march, and that Maccabean exploits were high in the public mind. In the same way, the depiction of Jesus as universal king would be a great support and comfort to Christians in the face of Roman imperial claims, and as the king of Israel he has Solomon as a predecessor in the Davidic line.

[61] For example, it accounts for the Tabernacles and/or Dedication imagery, pilgrim usage, kingship theme, and any military imagery.

tions – interlinked in Jewish thought – suggests an additional interpretive dimension. In the pre-exilic royal ideology, where the Davidic king was Yahweh's vice-regent, the king's enthronement symbolized and re-affirmed Yahweh's enthronement. The primary Tabernacles emphasis was on Yahweh's coming, seen in its most explicit form in the eschatological festival of Zech 14 where Yahweh comes to reign as universal king. In quoting Ps 118 John intended to present Jesus as Yahweh's royal agent coming to enthronement. However, taken together with the Tabernacles imagery and the Zechariah quote, the expectations of Yahweh's coming to reign advance to the forefront. This fits John's New Exodus agenda, where Jesus effects the return from exile and identifies and defeats the enemies of Israel. The missing element has been the return of Yahweh, which in keeping with John's consistent pattern we can expect Jesus to fulfill as well. Passover is the appropriate time for exodus, and Tabernacles for the coming of Yahweh. In the Entrance both of these strands are brought together, so that the expectations of Yahweh's coming coincide with the festival celebrating and anticipating Yahweh's great deliverance.

John's larger agenda is becoming clearer. However, there is still the difficulty that Jesus' coming as Yahweh's vice-regent does not quite accomplish or fulfill the return of Yahweh. To consistently carry out his replacement and fulfillment theme and complete his New Exodus troika, John must set the stage so that Jesus' Entrance actualizes and consummates Yahweh's return. That is, there must be a move from symbol to reality. This leads us to examine specific aspects of Ps 118. Further exploration will provide support to the argument that Ps 118 is the model for the Entry, and show how the individual elements function in support of the whole. We turn now to the Hosanna and John's distinctive reference to palm branches.

IV. The Hosanna

The quotation of Ps 118 in the Entrance passages seems to be fairly straightforward. However, the Hosanna has especially attracted attention and been a point of disagreement as to its source (Hebrew or Aramaic), meaning, and function.[62] The difficulty stems from the form that Hosanna

---

[62] See especially Werner ("Hosanna"), who comprehensively summarizes and provides representative scholars for each of the principal positions taken up to 1946. For more up-to-date interaction see Fitzmyer, "Aramaic Evidence." See further W. F. Beck, "Hosanna"; Burkitt, "Studies"; Freed, "Entry"; G. F. Hawthorne, "Hosanna"; E. F. F. Bishop, "Hosanna: The Word of the Joyful Jerusalem Crowds"; J. S. Kennard Jr., "'Hosanna' and the Purpose of Jesus"; C. Burger, *Jesus als Davidssohn: Eine traditionsgeschicht-*

takes in the Gospels, an apparent change in the sense of the original cry
from supplication to jubilation, and questions concerning messianic
associations.   Accordingly we will examine the peculiarities of the
Hosanna translation, the original OT sense of the cry, and the alleged
change of meaning in Jewish and Christian usage, before applying our
findings to John's specific use.

A. The Form and Meaning of Hosanna

1. The Translation

The quotation from Ps 118.25–26 in John 12.13 mirrors the LXX, which
in turn is a faithful translation of the Hebrew.   However, whereas the
Hebrew הושיעה נא retains its sense of "save now" in the LXX's translation
σῶσον δή, the ὡσαννά on the lips of the crowd is found nowhere in the LXX,
nor in any Greek manuscripts prior to its occurrence in the NT, where it
appears only in the Entrance Narratives.   In other words, none of the evangelists depends here on the LXX, preferring instead a new word apparently
coined especially for this particular occasion.   The original הושיעה נא of
Ps 118.25 has been transliterated into Greek, so that ὡσαννά is a phonetic
citation.[63]   That is, the Hebrew word has remained untranslated, taking
on only the form of the Greek text in which it now stands.   It is possible
that this was mediated through the Aramaic הושע נא, which more closely
approximates ὡσαννα phonetically,[64] but this makes no difference in
determining the source of John's quotation, as the Aramaic is simply an
Aramaicized imperative form of the Hebrew found in the psalm.[65]   There
can be no question that Hosanna, whatever form and meaning it takes, is
a citation of Ps 118.   Although the imperative form of the verb does occur

---

liche Untersuchung, 47–51; B. Sandvik, *Das Kommen des Herrn beim Abendmahl im
Neuen Testament*, 41–43; E. Lohse, "Hosianna"; idem, "ὡσαννά," *TDNT* 9.682–684;
J. A. Motyer, "ὡσαννά."

[63] Weren suggests that "such a citation of sound is a phonetic repetition of a segment
from an earlier text in a later one *without repeating the meaning*" ("Jesus' Entry," 134;
emphasis added). I will take issue ahead with Weren's last phrase.

[64] Fitzmyer ("Aramaic Evidence"), followed by Weren ("Jesus' Entry," 134), argues
strongly for an Aramaic background. Brown (1.457) suggests it may be a transliteration
of both Aramaic and Hebrew. Against an Aramaic background see Coakley, "Entry," 474
n. 48. For discussion see Werner, "Hosanna," 101–105.

[65] See Fitzmyer ("Aramaic Evidence," 41), who may be correct in his grammatical
conclusions, but proceeds from these to make unsubstantiated claims as to the liturgical
use and meaning of Hosanna.

in the OT, the emphatic form with the precative particle נא appears only in Ps 118.25.

2. The Original meaning

The imperative הושיעה is always translated in the LXX by σῶσον (with the exception of Josh 10.6 where ἐξελοῦ is used), thus making clear its meaning of "save." In Ps 118.25 it is an appeal for salvation to Yahweh: the king has recalled a humiliating experience which he survived only with Yahweh's help. Yahweh has become his salvation (118.21), and has established the king as the capstone (118.22). However, although this has been completed, a call to rejoice in Yahweh's works (118.24) is immediately followed by the petition to save (118.25). This reveals the character of the Hosanna as a request that Yahweh in mercy confirm and preserve through the upcoming year the salvation he has already effected. The OT use of הושיעה supports this emphasis: twice it is used in appeals to the king for justice (2 Sam 14.4; 2 Kgs 6.26), but it is more often directed towards Yahweh (Pss 12.2; 20.10; 28.9; 60.7; 108.7). An overview of the other imperative uses of the ישע root confirms this pattern, for although used in appeals to Joshua (Josh 10.6) and by Ahaz to the king of Assyria (2 Kgs 16.7), overwhelmingly it is a plea directed to Yahweh.[66]

A careful look beyond the literal meaning of Hosanna suggests that it functions differently in the psalm than in other occurrences. The king has played the principal role in the liturgy, but then there is a break in the midst of the celebration with a seemingly out-of-place petition to Yahweh for salvation. This serves to affirm Yahweh's kingship and sovereignty over Israel, for the king's life, victory and throne are secured by and dependent on Yahweh's action. In the original royal procession preserved in the psalm, Hosanna, then, is the cry from the people – and perhaps the king – recognizing Yahweh's kingship and sovereignty, the primacy of which is represented in his earthly ruler. The people cry out for salvation (118.25), then the king who comes in the name of Yahweh (118.26) is identified as Yahweh shining his light upon them (118.27). The response is to take branches in celebration and join a festal procession. Therefore Hosanna is in its literal meaning supplicatory, but its function in the psalm is to recognize/confess Yahweh's sovereignty, and to relate the king's reign to Yahweh's kingship. This is an aspect that has remained largely unnoticed.

---

[66] See 2 Kgs 19.19; 1 Chr 16.35; Pss 3.7; 6.4; 7.1; 22.21; 31.16; 54.1; 59.2; 69.1; 71.2; 86.2, 16; 109.26; 119.94, 146; Isa 37.20; Jer 2.27; 17.14; 31.7.

3. Christian Changes

The supplicatory character of Hosanna continued in the festival use during the intertestamental period. At Dedication the cry would have given voice to the desire for a renewal of Israel, and at Tabernacles for the coming of Yahweh. At Passover it was repeated at the slaughter of lambs and the meal – both looking forward to Yahweh's redemption of Israel. Furthermore, Werner is correct in his observation that this supplicatory emphasis continued in rabbinic interpretation.[67] This seems at odds with the change that appears to have taken place in Matthew's – and certainly in the early Christian – use of Hosanna. Matthew 21.9 has Ὡσαννὰ τῷ υἱῷ Δαυίδ and Ὡσαννὰ ἐν τοῖς ὑψίστοις, with the children repeating the former phrase in Matt 21.15. The use of the dative most naturally indicates that the Hosanna is directed to Jesus as acclamation or praise. However, the near-consensus view that it had lost its original meaning is overstated. For one, Mark's use of the phrase is ambiguous and could support either option.[68] More importantly, although Matthew may use the Hosanna as praise, it does not follow that in the first century it always or even primarily carried this sense. A more defensible position is that of Davies and Allison who cautiously conclude that at the time Hosanna "*could* mean 'praise'."[69] By the time the *Didache* was written, it appears that at least in Christian circles Hosanna had acquired this sense of praise and become foremost an expression of exultation.[70]

B. The First-Century Meaning of Hosanna

The change of emphasis in the Hosanna has led most scholars to argue that its original supplicatory meaning had been lost by the first century.[71]

---

[67] Werner, "Hosanna," 121–122. See further the discussion of the eschatological interpretation of Ps 118 in rabbinic literature in ch. 2 of this study.

[68] See further the discussion in ch. 3 of this study.

[69] Davies and Allison, 3.125; emphasis added.

[70] *Did.* 10.6 reads " Ὡσαννὰ τῷ θεῷ Δαβίδ." See also Clement of Alexandria, *Paed.* 1.5.12; *Apos. Con.* 8.13. For a survey of the early Christian use of Hosanna see Werner "Hosanna." On Hosanna in the *Didache* see esp. Sandvik, *Das Kommen*, 37–40.

[71] For example, Lagrange, 325; Kysar, 191; Lightfoot, 250; Temple, *Core*, 203. A fairly typical example of this is van Bergen's description of an evolving Hosanna: "Dans les premiers temps c'était [Hosanna] une supplication . . . Dans la Bible, on l'utilisait pour s'adresser au Roi et demander son intervention . . . A la longue c'était devenu une acclamation qui s'adressait à Dieu ou à ses envoyés" ("L'entrée messianique," 17). Sanders and Mastin (288) appear to be exceptions among Johannine scholars, stating that Hosanna is used as a cry for help. Although one can reasonably expect that Ps 118 would come to be associated with the Eucharist through its use at the Last Supper, Sandvik

However, the evidence adduced to support such a shift of meaning is questionable and should caution against too quickly accepting this view. Although later Christian liturgy uses Hosanna with a sense of praise, the only early source that in a relatively clear way reflects such a meaning is Matthew. This has led some to look for evidence of a similar transformation in Jewish sources, arguing that Hosanna's significance was lost as it became a liturgical formula.[72] It is true that the multiple repetitions of the phrase in the liturgy, especially at Tabernacles, provided a natural means for it to become a liturgical formula. However, the fact that it became "a fixed formula in the procession round the altar of burnt offering"[73] is insufficient evidence to assume a "semantic shift."[74] In fact, an appreciation of liturgical practice and the evocative power of ritual may help explain why the evangelists chose to include a transliterated Hosanna. Although no doubt the transmission of Christian tradition played a part, this does not account for the initial phonetic citation.

Because the cry was known by every Jew, was repeated often in the festival liturgies, and had taken on a liturgical life of its own as the most recognizable refrain from the psalm, it should not be surprising if the phrase is transmitted in a way that would reflect it phonetically – that is, that would preserve how it sounded when spoken in the liturgies. Even though the LXX was widely used, since the liturgy was not conducted in Greek one would not expect the crowds to cry out σῶσον δή as they circled the altar. Hosanna had become so closely associated with the liturgy that even though the psalm as a whole might be translated, if in Greek the cry would actually sound strange to ears accustomed to hearing it in its old liturgical pronunciation. Familiarity with Hosanna would

---

certainly goes too far in arguing that "das 'Zitat' von Ps 118,25 mit dem Hosannaruf, das man in den Evangelien findet, der Eucharistieliturgie entstammt" (*Das Kommen*, 49).

[72] For example Hawthorne, "Hosanna"; Lohse, *TDNT* 9.682.

[73] Lohse, *TDNT* 9.682.

[74] So Fitzmyer, "Aramaic Evidence," 111. Following Lohse, he suggests that "the shift of meaning thus attested [by the association with Tabernacles] is clear" (ibid., 113). Lohse writes, "This sense [praise] must have been acquired already in pre-chr. Judaism, for when the Temple was still standing . . . hosanna was shouted out repeatedly as a fixed formula" (*TDNT* 9.682). Their logic is unclear, for there is no obvious link that justifies equating liturgical formulation with transformation of meaning. Jeremias makes the same unsupported assumption, dismissing the lack of Jewish evidence: "Der Bedeutungswandel des Hosianna vom Hilferuf zum Jubelruf bereits im vorchristlichen palästinischen Judentum erfolgt sei. Zwar haben wir für den Gebrauch des Hosianna als Jubelruf zufällig keinen direkten Beleg in der rabbinischen Literatur, wohl aber machen sachliche und sprachliche Erwägungen den Schluß unausweichlich, daß der Bedeutungswandel in Raum des Tempelkultus, also vor 70 n. Chr., stattgefunden hat" ("Die Muttersprache des Evangelisten Matthäus," 273).

ensure that intelligibility did not depend on translation.[75] One must not evaluate the transliteration only from a philological point of view – it also requires sensitivity to liturgical practice, an issue that is especially relevant in John. Nor should one assume that taking on life as a liturgical formula necessarily results in ossification and loss of meaning. Rather, the question is whether it is likely that a Jew would be ignorant of the meaning of one of the most oft-repeated Scripture passages.[76] Even for later Christians, many of whom rather quickly neglected the OT, discerning the original meaning of Hosanna was not an impossible task in spite of the change it had undergone in their liturgy.[77]

Furthermore, it is alleged that Tabernacles had lost its supplicatory character and emphasis, inevitably influencing the understanding of Hosanna. Thus Lohse states, "Wie sich die Bedeutung des Laubhüttenfestes wandelte und dieses vom Bitt- zum Freudenfest wurde, so wurde auch das הושענא aus einem Bittgebet zum Ausdruck des Jubels."[78] There is no doubt that Hosanna was closely identified with Tabernacles: the prayers uttered during the festival procession were given the name הושענות, the seventh day of the feast was called יום הושענא, and because the cry was accompanied by the shaking of the lulab, these were sometimes called הושענא.[79] Therefore, it is suggested, as goes Tabernacles so goes Hosanna. However, there is no indication either in rabbinic or earlier usage that Tabernacles had lost its supplicatory character. If anything, the opposite would be true. Were the conditions in the first century and following the destruction of the temple such to encourage a turn from expectant supplication to jubilant celebration?

It is also suggested that Hosanna "undoubtedly represents a cry that Jerusalemites used to greet pilgrims coming to Jerusalem for feasts like

---

[75] The extensive use of Hebrew at Qumran shows that it was far from being a dead language.

[76] To argue that the community in which the Gospel was written would be unaware of the original meaning of Hosanna is to assume an astounding ignorance on their part.

[77] Fitzmyer ("Aramaic Evidence," 111) gives the examples of Origen and Eusebius not understanding the transliterated Hosanna. However, a closer reading shows that in spite of this they both manage to understand the original meaning of the psalm. The same is true of Bar Hebraeus' reading, where he is aware of the original meaning of the Hebrew as well as the Christian tradition: "*Oshana* means in Hebrew redemption, and may be explained in Greek as Glory" (cited in Werner, "Hosanna," 120).

[78] Lohse, "Hosianna," 115. Jeremias argues similarly: "So kam es, daß das Hosianna seine ursprüngliche Bedeutung verlor, wie man daraus ersehen kann, daß es zur Bezeichnung des Laubhüttenfeststraußes wurde, und es hat nichts Überraschendes an sich, wenn der Ruf an dem Wandel des Wallfahrtsfestes vom Bittfest zum Freudenfest teilnahm und aus einem Hilferuf zum Jubelruf wurde" ("Die Muttersprache," 274).

[79] See for example *Lev. Rab.* 37.2 and *b. Sukk.* 37b.

that of Tabernacles and perhaps even Passover."[80] This is a remarkable assertion considering there is no evidence to show that it was applied to the average or even highly honored pilgrim. In any case, the greeting that would be applied to the processional crowd – although not to the individual, and not at Passover – would be that of Ps 118.26, not the Hosanna of 118.25. It is true that Matthew's Hosanna can be read as a jubilant greeting, but this is not the only possible interpretation. I am not aware of any Jewish source that preserves an example of someone greeted with Hosanna. It is more plausible to suggest that when the evangelists portray the crowd acclaiming Jesus with the Hosanna originally reserved to Yahweh in the psalm, it comments on the unique status and identify of Jesus rather than common pilgrimage practice.[81]

Celebration characterizes the Entrance Narratives, at least on the part of those acclaiming Jesus. This does not, however, necessarily indicate that the original sense of petition in the Hosanna is no longer understood. There is in fact no obvious contradiction between celebration and petition, praise and supplication, even though some scholars have been quick to make these an either/or option.[82] The festivals combined both, in celebration of what Yahweh had done but in supplication that he would do so again.[83] If it seems strange to have a supplicatory prayer in the midst of a celebration or thanksgiving, Ps 118 itself preserves such a mixture, one

---

[80] Among others see Fitzmyer, "Aramaic Evidence," 115. So also Hawthorne, "Hosanna"; Beasley-Murray, 210; Weren, "Jesus' Entry," 134.

[81] This bears on the messianic interpretation of Hosanna. It is clear that Matthew and Mark use Ps 118 in messianic contexts, but some argue this is a Christian interpretation that does not reflect contemporary Jewish views, so that consequently the Hosanna does not have a messianic interpretation in pre-Christian Judaism. For this view see Fitzmyer, "Aramaic Evidence," 115 and n. 46; Burger, *Jesus als Davidssohn*, 47–51. Against this see Werner, "Hosanna," 112, 119–121; Lohse, *TDNT* 9.683; Sanders, "Ps 118," 186. Lohse's comment is representative of the latter: "Wird gefolgert werden dürfen, daß in vorchristlicher Zeit mit dem Hosiannaruf der Ausdruck messianischer Erwartung verbunden gewesen ist" ("Hosianna," 116). Although there is no unambiguously messianic use of Hosanna in pre-Christian Judaism, my study of the intertestamental use of Ps 118 suggests that the phrase would be a natural vehicle for expressing eschatological and messianic hopes, thus supporting scholars such as Werner and Lohse who depend primarily on rabbinic evidence.

[82] For example, Werner argues that both Jews and Christians suppressed the traditional sense of the Hosanna as a "messianic supplication," the latter by making it a cry of jubilation, the former by stressing its supplicatory meaning ("Hosanna," 112–114). I fail to see how stressing the supplicatory character of the Hosanna would negate any messianic association. In fact Werner appears to contradict himself, for he appeals to rabbinic interpretations of Ps 118 to show that the Hosanna was understood messianically – rabbinics which had supposedly suppressed and then lost this original sense.

[83] Freed is correct in noting that the festivals were "festivals of joy as well as supplication" (*Quotations*, 73 n. 2).

that is not uncommon in the Psalter.[84] The original sense of Ps 118 is
jubilatory: the cry for salvation is a confession of Yahweh's victorious and
saving kingship and sovereignty, which is evidenced in his establishing
and preserving the king and is actualized by the king's ruling in Yahweh's
name.[85] In this sense the character of the Entrance Narratives mirrors that
of Ps 118, for there should be jubilation when the agent of God's blessing
and kingship arrives on the scene, signaling that Yahweh is establishing
his eschatological rule.[86] Accordingly, the different emphases and tones in
the Matthean and Jewish Hosanna traditions may not be so much contra-
dictory as parallel, reflecting their respective situations: the evangelists
celebrate the salvation that Yahweh has actualized in Jesus, and the Jew
petitions for the long-awaited and hoped for deliverance.

C. Hosanna in John

If Matthew reflects a change of meaning, John's use of Hosanna stands in
contrast. As Fitzmyer admits, "If we had only the Johannine form of the
tradition about Jesus' entry into Jerusalem, the debate [about the loss of

---

[84] Werner correctly observes that "in all Hebrew literature no passage in which
Hosanna expresses exultation occurs" ("Hosanna," 99). However, the context of Ps 118
encourages a celebratory understanding and use of Hosanna even if the literal meaning is
supplicative.

[85] Motyer captures this sense: "In this context [the royal procession] the cry 'O,
Save' would indicate an imploring cry to Yahweh to bring to reality that which the
liturgy has depicted" (*NIDNTT*, 1.100).

[86] It should be clear that the possibility that Hosanna can communicate a sense of
jubilation does not negate the possibility of retaining the original supplicatory character
at the same time. An example from the Hegesippus-Eusebius account of the killing of
James shows that the celebratory Hosanna could also be eschatological. James has been
asked by the Jewish leaders to disabuse the crowds at Passover of the widespread belief
that Jesus is the Messiah: "So the Scribes and Pharisees made James stand on the
Sanctuary parapet and shouted to him: 'Righteous one, whose word we are all obliged to
accept, the people are going astray after Jesus who was crucified; so tell us what is meant
by "the door of Jesus".' He replied as loudly as he could: 'Why do you question me
about the Son of Man? I tell you, He is sitting in heaven at the right hand of the Great
Power, and He will come in the clouds of heaven.' Many were convinced, and gloried in
James's testimony, crying: 'Hosanna to the Son of David!' Then again the Scribes and
Pharisees said to each other: 'We made a bad mistake in affording such testimony to
Jesus. We had better go up and throw him down, so that they will be frightened and
not believe him'" (*Eccl. Hist.* 2.23.10–15). Although the Hosanna is here is an
eschatological exclamation celebrating the future return of Jesus, one can also discern a
supplicatory tone. Indeed, eschatology always contains an implicit sense of supplication
that the consummation will come. A NT example is the numerous praise liturgies in
Revelation that are marked by a sense of heightened expectation as God's reign becomes
complete.

original meaning] would probably not arise."[87] John does not explicitly indicate what Hosanna means, and if he is aware of Matthew's possible change he at the least does not reflect it. However, this ambiguity does not mean he uses the Hosanna in ignorance or haphazardly. I suggest that John was well aware of the original meaning, and employed it to effect in his narrative.

Had John translated the Hebrew הושיעה נא he would have done so with σῶσον δή.[88] Instead he uses ὡσαννά, as do Matthew and Mark. Freed suggests that the Hosanna is transliterated precisely because the evangelist understood both the Hebrew and Greek to mean save, and wanted to avoided a suppliant sense that would be out of place in the joyful mood of the Entrance Narrative.[89] Against this, I have argued above that the transliteration may result from an attempt to preserve the liturgical links and associations that accompanied the Hosanna, and that it would tend to accentuate rather than lead to a loss of the original supplicatory meaning.[90] This would be especially true for John, who has shown not only an awareness of Jewish liturgy but also a marked tendency to allude to it. There is every reason to expect that John was aware of the original meaning and context of the Hosanna – how could he not have been? Every Jew knew

---

[87] Fitzmyer, "Aramaic Evidence," 113.

[88] Hoskyns (421–422) strangely argues that Hosanna is untranslatable into Greek. However, even though he is mistaken on this, the conclusion he draws is perceptive: "The importance of the occurrence of the word in the narrative of the Triumphal Entry is therefore not its accurate translation, but its marking of the fulfillment of an Old Testament citation and of a ritual practice among the Jews" (ibid., 422). Few recognize, as Hoskyns appears to, that the significance of the Hosanna in John is not primarily etymological.

[89] Freed, "Entry," 330. Freed argues that this was Matthew's intention, and that John depends on the Synoptics for his quote.

[90] *Pace* Brown (1.457), who argues that the transliteration indicates that Hosanna " is not a prayer of petition but a cry of praise." Even though Hosanna may, as Brown claims, already have entered the prayer formulae of the Christian community, John did not choose to reflect this usage although he easily could have. This objection applies also to Barrett (418), for although he notes that the "difficulties" in the Markan use do not arise in John, he concludes from this that "it may be that the word had already lost much of its original meaning and become little more than a jubilant shout of praise." The position that Hosanna had come to be a greeting or cry of praise is not an unpopular one among Johannine scholars. Cf. Schnackenburg, 2.375; Beasley-Murray, 210; M. de Merode, "L'accueil triomphal de Jésus selon *Jean*, 11–12," 55; Reim, *Hintergrund*, 26; Becker, 2.377; Daly-Denton, *David*, 179. Obermann's (*Schrift*, 193, 196) is a lonely voice, arguing that in John the Hosanna is understood as a cry for help just as it was in the OT.

this phrase by heart.[91] Even if it had been uttered without any other nod to Ps 118, every Jew would know where it came from, what it meant, and how it was used. Anyone with access to the Scriptures would know where to look if in doubt.[92] Specific clues also point to John being aware of and intending to evoke the meaning of the original psalm rather than Christian tradition. His simple and stark use is closer to the original processional sequence than that of Matthew and Mark, who add qualifiers to the Hosanna. Furthermore, John's Hosanna cannot be mistaken for a greeting.

It may be that John followed early Christian traditions when he transliterated Hosanna, but since he was aware of the translation options this represents an intentional choice. I have argued that John points the reader back to the original royal context of Ps 118. This makes an original reading of Hosanna more likely, but the transliteration of the phrase itself also serves to draw attention to the ancient royal ritual. First, it calls to mind Ps 118's most familiar sound/word, thus emphasizing the psalmic context for the Entrance. Second, as the most recognizable liturgical formula of Tabernacles, the Hosanna would especially evoke the complex of traditions shared by the festival and Ps 118. Third, it enhances the liturgical character and timbre of the Entrance. Fourth, it concentrates the reader's attention on John's purpose: a simple cry of σῶσον δή would communicate much more an urgency of supplication when John wants to evoke an ancient royal ritual. This bears not on what meaning Hosanna carries in John, but on how it functions.

The ambiguity of John's unqualified Hosanna allows a function and meaning more in line with the original context of the psalm. The principal options for the interpretation of Hosanna in the NT are that it was a plea that God assist/establish the Messiah; a supplication addressed to the Messiah; an exclamation of praise or jubilation; a greeting; or a marginal gloss referring to the palm branches.[93] However, none of these actually fit

---

[91] Morris (585) allows that John is aware of the meaning, but for some reason states that "it is not likely that the multitude used the term with a clear understanding of its etymological significance [i.e., save]."

[92] Burkitt ("Studies," 141) suggests that if the crowd did shout Hosanna in the Entrance, it was not because they remembered it from the psalm, but because the occasion of the Entry was "similar to that presupposed in Ps cxviii," which he takes to be Dedication. He has correctly hit on the importance of festival liturgy as signpost, but I suggest that it would be quite impossible to separate the liturgical Hosanna from the psalm itself – the one would evoke the other. Carson (432) acknowledges this last point: "Every Jew knew of its occurrence in Psalm 118:25." Similarly, Beasley-Murray, 210.

[93] Cf. Werner, "Hosanna," 106. Beck ("Hosanna," 128), points out that "save" can also mean "be victorious" in both Hebrew and Greek, and thus Hosanna expresses the wish that Jesus accomplish salvation. It is possible that John intends this as one of the layers of meaning for Hosanna – after all, Jesus is bringing salvation. This would be more plausible were the cry directed at Jesus.

either the original's or John's meaning and function exactly. In its original context Hosanna is not a plea for immediate salvation, as the hardship and danger have passed: the king has narrowly escaped death, but is now entering as a victorious conqueror. Rather, the cry is a celebrative suppli-cation, a confession of Yahweh's victorious and saving kingship actualized in the Davidic king ruling in Yahweh's name. The Hosanna is addressed not to the king, but to Yahweh. The king is then welcomed as Yahweh's vice-regent. Although the petition that Yahweh will assist the king is implicit, the primary function of the Hosanna is to indicate the relationship of the Davidic ruler to Yahweh, and link their kingships. John's account mirrors this pattern: the crowd is jubilant, celebrating Jesus' victory over death in resurrecting Lazarus; the Hosanna is addressed to Yahweh, not to Jesus; and the crowd, after invoking Yahweh, greets Jesus as the coming king of Israel, placing Jesus' kingship in the context of Yahweh's kingship. The supplication does not explicitly ask Yahweh to save King Jesus. Although this may implicitly be in view, the Johannine focus is not on Yahweh establishing the reign of Jesus, but on identifying Jesus' ministry with Yahweh.

John has retained the original meaning of the Hosanna in every sense. He has correctly discerned that the Hosanna is actually a confession of Yahweh's sovereignty in the form of a supplication. In addition, he has recognized the original function of the Hosanna in linking the kingship of Yahweh with the Davidic ruler. What then does Hosanna mean in John? On the lips of the crowd it echoes the cry to save, but it is not a plea that Yahweh save Jesus, nor is it a cry of abject desperation imploring the Messiah to deliver them.[94] Rather, it is a plaintive confession of Yahweh's sovereignty and kingship that is entirely appropriate in light of the following verse, where Jesus enters Jerusalem as king of Israel. Jesus' Entry thus corresponds to the entry of the Davidic king in Ps 118, and the Hosanna that precedes the entry to the city in both passages (pre-text and receiving text) performs the same function, identifying Jesus' kingship with Yahweh's rule.

This in turn is suggestive for the theme of the return of Yahweh. Because John preserves the original sense of the Hosanna, the emphasis then turns to the kingship of Yahweh, for the Hosanna is at heart a recognition of his

---

[94] Kennard ("Hosanna," 175) argues that the cry reflects the hope of the Galilean pilgrims that Jesus will perform a messianic act such as that of Judas Maccabeus in cleansing the temple. I suggest rather that the cry is the result of acknowledging Jesus' kingship, with the intent of linking his kingship to Yahweh's kingship and sovereignty. In any case, the use of Hosanna in company with Tabernacles symbols could bring to mind, as many scholars note, the Maccabean deliverance. What is less often noted, but naturally follows, is that such a context – the crowds longing for and crying out to God for a new deliverance – would accentuate the supplicatory character of Hosanna.

sovereignty. It implicitly calls for Yahweh himself to come and establish his kingship, not only through his vice-regent, but in his full eschatological reign.

D. Conclusion

It has been argued here that the shift of meaning for Hosanna in Christian liturgical usage, where the supplicatory sense is at least de-emphasized and perhaps lost, is not reflected in Jewish sources. There is no evidence to suggest that Hosanna had become a greeting for pilgrims or lost its original meaning in Judaism. Later Christian usage does not require that the Synoptic evangelists have been unaware of the meaning or original significance of the cry. In fact the original context of the psalm suggests that a celebratory use of Hosanna is appropriate, and that there is no necessary contradiction in its being used to communicate either a sense of jubilation or petition – or even both at the same time. To extrapolate from later Christian tradition – or even from Matthew's earlier use – and insist that Hosanna had lost its original meaning in all circles is therefore unwarranted. We have noted a generally unrecognized feature of the Hosanna peculiar to its original setting in Ps 118 that may explain its celebratory use in spite of the literal supplicatory meaning: although the literal meaning of Hosanna is supplicatory, it functions to recognize (confess) Yahweh's sovereignty, and to relate the king's reign to Yahweh's kingship.

John may not be ignorant of the possible shift of meaning in Matthew, but at the least he has ignored it for his own purposes. Because John does not qualify Hosanna with any additions, the meaning remains open and encourages the reader – if he is aware of the possible change in Christian liturgy – to look instead to the original context. Although it may do so unintentionally, the transliterated Hosanna evokes the Tabernacles-Ps 118 complex of royal traditions and emphasizes the character of the Entry as liturgical re-enactment. More clearly, John uses Hosanna in keeping with its original context. It is supplicatory in literal meaning, but confessional in function. It also functions structurally, bringing Yahweh to the forefront, and ensuring that Jesus' kingship is identified with Yahweh's rule.

V. The Palm Branches

The reference to palm branches in the Entrance is unique to John. Although Matthew and Mark mention foliage, agreeing that it was cut by members of the crowd and placed on the road as Jesus passed, the type is not indicated .[95] Only John specifies that the crowd took palm branches (τὰ βαΐα τῶν φοινίκων), and there is no explicit mention of cutting and placing them on the ground in a spontaneous gesture. Rather, although left unsaid, it is implied that they were waved in the air. The palm branches are a puzzling detail. Not only do they seem out of place at Passover, but John's choice of words to describe them is unusual. Both of these aspects require a closer look. I suggest that John intentionally specifies the branches as palm, and emphasizes them in service of his own purposes.

A. The Phrasing

John uses a remarkable phrase (τὰ βαΐα τῶν φοινίκων) to specify the kind of branches that the crowd used to welcome Jesus. Barrett summarizes as follows: "βάϊον is derived from the Coptic *ba(i)*, 'branch of the date-palm'. . . . φοίνιξ, sometimes used of palm-branches, will here mean 'palm-tree', so that the full expression, βαΐα τῶν φοινίκων, is pleonastic."[96] Hoskyns notes simply that this is "an awkward Greek phrase,"[97] and Brown calls it "somewhat tautological."[98] βάϊον is a relatively rare word: in the NT only John uses it, and it appears in the LXX only once, in 1 Macc 13.51, where the crowd praises καὶ βαΐων following Simon's expulsion of the Gentiles from the citadel in Jerusalem. Although the possibility of the phrasing is attested in the apocalyptic vision of *T. Naph.* 5.4, where Levi is given βαΐα φοινίκων δώδεκα as a sign of victory, the combination of βάϊον with φοῖνιξ is awkward, "a strange and obtrusive locution."[99] It is plausible that John intended to highlight the use of palm branches, and so, to ensure that they would draw attention, he chose a rare word and

---

[95] Matt 21.8 has branches from trees (κλάδους ἀπὸ τῶν δένδρων), Mark 11.8 identifies them as leafy branches/straw from the field (στιβάδας . . . ἐκ τῶν ἀγρῶν), and Luke omits mention of any kind of foliage, perhaps in service of a political apologetic.

[96] Barrett, 417.

[97] Hoskyns, 421.

[98] Brown, 1.456. Sanders and Mastin (287 n. 1) claim the phrase "is strictly redundant"; Bernard (2.424) that it is "superfluously precise." Lagrange (325) suggests that John used the unusual phrase to ensure against misidentification of the branches, as the Jews may have adopted the word βάϊον in a less precise sense.

[99] J. S. Hill, "τὰ βαΐα τῶν φοινίκων (John 12:13): Pleonasm or Prolepsis?" 133. The phrase in *T. Naph.* 5.4 appears without the articles.

seemingly tautological phrasing. Hill's questioning of Barrett therefore appears to be justified: "It seems rash indeed either to ignore it or to brush it aside as an inconvenient pleonasm."[100] Rather than being clumsy or betraying ignorance/confusion, it may be that John is signaling the symbolic importance of the palm branches, and cautioning the reader not to look at them merely as colorful detail.

The use of the palm branch in the Tabernacles and Dedication liturgies reflected and advanced eschatological associations, carrying a special significance in Judaism as a symbol of victory, resurrection, and authority.[101] This makes it especially appropriate for use in the Entrance where Jesus is celebrated as conqueror over death.[102] Jesus has recently raised Lazarus, and the reader is reminded throughout the narrative of this victory over death (12.1, 9, 17–18). However, although the palm branches are a reminder of the Lazarus Sign, they are primarily proleptic rather than analeptic in function – that is, they point forward to the decisive and final victory of Jesus. The death-resurrection theme that is intensified by the Lazarus allusions focuses on the upcoming passion, and frames the Entrance both in the Anointing and the discourse initiated by the coming of the Greeks. As a result Hill can credibly conclude that "this Johannine locution is properly a prolepsis in its own right – a linguistic signpost pointing forward to the death and resurrection of Christ."[103] Resurrection is victory, of course, but this takes on added significance when understood in the context of the upcoming battle with darkness. The palm branches then are a proleptic proclamation of triumph, anticipating Jesus' victory over the enemies of Israel.[104]

It appears that John intentionally uses the awkward phrasing to draw attention to the palm branches. One of his goals was to intensify the death-resurrection theme and proleptically point to Jesus' victory, but in addition I suggest that he intended to direct the reader to Ps 118 and highlight Tabernacles themes. The waving of branches would not necessarily call Ps 118 to mind, but the palm branch used in processional – and particularly in one that quotes Ps 118 – could not avoid this association. There are other

---

[100] Hill, "Pleonasm," 133.

[101] On the symbolic meaning of palm branches see the discussion in ch. 2/C above, and P. von Gemünden's useful background survey, "Palmensymbolik in Joh 12,13." See also Schnackenburg, 2.374; Davies, *Rhetoric*, 286–287; Kinman, *Entry*, 44.

[102] Cf. Davies, *Rhetoric*, 287.

[103] Hill, "Pleonasm," 135. Von Gemünden ("Palmensymbolik," 60–62) downplays the association with Tabernacles, suggesting that the palm is intended here primarily as a symbol of life and victory over death, which in post-Easter reflection underlines that the way to Jesus' death would be the way into life.

[104] Morris (584) is on the right track, arguing that "we must detect a reference to the triumph of Christ." He does not, however, relate it to the defeat of evil.

options. For example, Hill argues that the awkward phrasing is an allusion to the phoenix myth, pointing to Jesus as the true phoenix.[105] Others have suggested, because of the shared use of the rare βάϊον, that the phrase is an allusion to the entry of Simon the Maccabee (1 Macc 13.51).[106] However, the significant emphasis John places on death/resurrection makes the latter more unlikely, and as for the phoenix, although it provides a fascinating parallel there is no need for John to point to it, since palm branches are independently associated with victory and resurrection. Rather than drawing attention to the Maccabees or the phoenix, the pleonasm highlights the palm branches in the very context in which they stand – that is, a celebratory procession where Yahweh is invoked with Hosannas, and the king of Israel enters Jerusalem as the coming one. Psalm 118's king provides an appropriate parallel for the resurrection/victory theme, for he has emerged victorious from a severe conflict declaring "I will not die but live," and "[Yahweh] has not given me over to death" (118.17–18). The palm branches therefore function proleptically, but they also point back to a rich source (Ps 118) as the interpretive horizon for the Entrance.

B. Evoking Tabernacles Traditions

The waving of palm branches, especially in a processional context, is not traditionally associated with Passover. This is why Werner concludes that John's reference to palm branches is "confused" and an "entirely 'untimely' association with Tabernacles."[107] This reaction is understandable (even though misguided), for palm branches were primarily associated with Tabernacles and Dedication. Some scholars argue that because they had become a national symbol, the waving of palm branches was "no longer restrictively associated with Tabernacles,"[108] and thus they are not out of place in the Entrance. It is possible that palm branches were waved at other times, but this certainly was not the norm. For this reason scholarly interest in John's palm branches has focused primarily on questions of historicity – that is, the timing of the Entry, and the availability of palm branches at Passover. Both of these issues are important, for they point to

---

[105] Hill, "Pleonasm," 134.

[106] See Lightfoot, 238. W. R. Farmer ("The Palm Branches in John 12,13," 65–66) suggests that the use of βάϊον indicates that some of the palm-branch waving crowd may have looked on Jesus with expectations inspired by the Maccabees. Hill ("Pleonasm," 135) seems to accept that the Entry could look back to Simon's as a pattern.

[107] Werner, "Hosanna," 118–119 n. 53.

[108] Carson, 432. Morris (584) argues they could be used for general festal purposes, and it appears that Bruce (259) would agree with Carson. See further Farmer's argument ("Palm Branches," 62–66) that the branches were distinctive nationalist symbols easily recognized as such.

the function John intended for the palm branches when he intentionally highlighted them.

The use of foliage in processions is connected with both Tabernacles and Dedication, making it difficult to show decisively that one or the other is in view. In addition, Ps 118 was sung at both and each had a liturgical procession. Those proposing a Dedication background have thus depended principally on it being more suitable ideologically to the Entry than Tabernacles. For example, Mastin writes, "If one has to choose between Tabernacles and the Dedication, the nationalistic background of the latter seems far more suitable than the stay in the wilderness commemorated by the former as the inspiration for the behavior of the crowd."[109] This does not, however, take into account that in John the palm branches are framed by a resurrection theme, that he has no temple action following the Entrance, and no nationalist agenda. It further ignores that Tabernacles is associated not only with the wilderness – this exodus connection in itself would be sufficient to excite eschatological expectations – but also with kingship and the coming of Yahweh.[110] Accordingly, and in light of John's emphases in the Entrance, the Zechariah quote, and the very close links with Ps 118, it appears that Tabernacles is more appropriate than Dedication as a background. It should also be pointed out that a *liturgical* use of palm branches is most closely associated with Tabernacles.

This does not, however, indicate that the Entrance took place at Tabernacles. John explicitly and unequivocally places the Entrance at Passover, as is consistent with his New Exodus theological agenda. Brown is thus correct in concluding that "the theory that Jesus entered Jerusalem at Tabernacles rather than at Passover is interesting, but beyond the possibility of proof."[111] But even asking this question reveals a misplaced focus on an issue – the timing of the Entrance – that for John was settled, at the expense of the liturgical links and signs that underscore the palms' symbolic meaning. As such, questions of historicity can sometimes obscure those of function and meaning.[112] The question should be, With what

---

[109] Mastin, "Date," 82.

[110] Burkitt, among others, misses the point: "So long as *Hosanna* merely suggests to us a scene imitated from the Vintage-feast of Tabernacles, the whole account is puzzling" ("Studies," 142).

[111] Brown, 1.457.

[112] Because John has given a clear time setting (Passover), any evocation of a different festival should be seen as primarily symbolic. However, this is in no way a denial of the historicity of John's account. There is no necessary inconsistency in saying that palm branches are out of place at Passover, and affirming at the same time that they indeed were used in the Entry in an intentional re-enactment of the ancient Ps 118-Tabernacles liturgy. In the same way, the evocation of Tabernacles symbolism at Passover does not necessarily cast into doubt the historicity of the account: the former's

purpose did John emphasize the palm branches in a Passover context where he knew them to be out of place? John's previous allusions to festival practice show that he was well aware of the various symbols and imagery associated with each – that is, he did not use such symbols in ignorance or pointlessly. In part, then, the answer is that John highlights the palm branches in order to bring Tabernacles traditions into play.[113]

C. The Availability of Palm Branches

Jericho was famous for its palm trees, and it is likely that during Tabernacles great quantities of its palm branches were imported to Jerusalem for the building of the required shelters and use in the liturgy.[114] However, there is disagreement over whether – and if so, in what quantities – palms grew in Jerusalem and would have been available to the Passover crowds. Bultmann, for example, claims that "in Jerusalem there were no palm trees, from which the pilgrims would have had to cut the palm branches."[115] The evidence, however, is too unclear to make such a sweeping statement. For example, Pliny's comment that the town of Engedi was "second only to Jerusalem in the fertility of its land and in its groves of palm trees"[116] suggests that palm trees grew in the Jerusalem area. This is supported by the *Letter of Aristeas*, which in describing the Jerusalem area mentions the abudance of its "fruit trees and date palms" for which "no number can be given"[117] Since date palms prefer warm weather, Lagrange argues that palms grew in the warmer eastern valley through which Jesus passed, and were easily picked as they were lower in height. [118] On the other hand,

---

symbols would be the most appropriate for a crowd intent on recognizing a king of Israel. My point, therefore, it not to question the historicity of the account, but to note that an excessive focus on questions of historicity can at times miss the force of the symbols in question, as has happened with the palm branches. Such is the case with, for example, Brown, 1.457; Carson, 432; Bruce, 259; Morris, 584; and Burkitt, "Studies." Mastin ("Date"), although focusing on the question of the date of the Entry, has a rare appreciation for its liturgical context.

[113] Against Brown (1.461–462), who follows Farmer ("Palm Branches") in arguing that taking the palm branches evoked a Maccabean nationalist demonstration, I suggest that although the palm branches could evoke Maccabean precedents, John does not present his narrative with this in view.

[114] On the palms of Jericho see Pliny, *Nat.* 13.45. On the importing of palms from Jericho see Brown, 1.457.

[115] Bultmann, 417 n. 8.

[116] Pliny, *Nat.* 5.73.

[117] *Let. Aris.* 112.

[118] Lagrange (325) argues from the use of palm branches in the entry of Simon (1 Macc 13.51) that they must have been available. See further the interesting and credible suggestion by H. St. J. Hart ("The Crown of Thorns in John 19, 2–5") that the crown of

some doubts have been cast on this by a letter from Bar Kochba during the Second Revolt (AD 132–135) requesting that a large number of palms be brought from Engedi to Jerusalem for the celebration of Tabernacles: "I have sent you two donkeys . . . so that they [men] shall pack and send to the camp *lulavim* and *ethrogim*. . . . See that they are tithed and sent to the camp. This request is made because the army is big."[119] This suggests that at the time there was no large supply near Jerusalem, although this may be a result of deforestation by the Romans during the first war.[120] It is probably safe to conclude that there were palm trees growing in the vicinity of Jerusalem, although perhaps not in quantity. From the point of view of availability, we can agree with Jeremias that John's account "appears to be within the bounds of possibility."[121]

The availability of palms bears on the distinctives of John's account *vis-à-vis* the Synoptics. John does not indicate a source for the palm branches, and does not mention any cutting taking place. Whereas Matthew and Mark note that the crowd availed themselves of foliage by cutting from the fields and trees along the way as they accompanied Jesus, John indicates that the crowd came out from Jerusalem to meet Jesus *already carrying their palm branches*. Where did they acquire them? In the city itself there would have been very few – if any – palm trees,[122] and a large number are required for John's "great crowd" (12.12). It is possible that some cut branches en route or, together with this, possible but unlikely that the palm-carriers had gone outside Jerusalem to acquire branches some time earlier in anticipation of Jesus' arrival and, in a detail that John simply omits, kept them in the city as they waited. However, the suggestion most compatible with John's account is that the majority of the crowd acquired palm branches in Jerusalem. The most likely source would then be the lulabs used in the Tabernacles liturgy and kept in Jerusalem homes, easily available and in great quantity.[123] There is no inconsistency

---

thorns Jesus is made to wear came from the date palm. This may suggest that palms were available during Passover, perhaps growing in Jerusalem. In support he cites *b. Sukh.* 32b: "There are two palm trees in the valley of Hinnom, and a smoke goes up between them."

[119] J. Rousseau and R. Arav, *Jesus and His World: An Archaeological and Cultural Dictionary*, 50. See further ibid., 47–52; Y. Yadin, "More on the Letters of Bar Kochba," 89–92. There should be no question that Tabernacles is in view. Note that the palm is equated with the lulab.

[120] See Josephus, *War* 6.5–6: "After they [Romans] had cut down all the trees that were in the country . . . those places which were before adorned with trees and pleasant gardens were now become a desolate country every way, and its trees were all cut down."

[121] Jeremias, *Jerusalem*, 43.

[122] Jeremias, *Jerusalem*, 42–46.

[123] Cf. Bultmann, 417 n. 8; Schlatter, 265; Merode, "L'accueil triomphal," 54.

in this as the palm branch was the most recognizable component of the liturgical lulab, and the Bar Kochba letter shows that the one is equated with the other when he requests palm branches, but calls them *lulavim*.[124]

John's account therefore suggests a measure of premeditation on the part of the crowd. In Matthew and Mark the branches appear to be used in spontaneous acclaim as Jesus passes by, the celebrants cutting whatever happens to be on hand. John's crowd, however, specifically chooses the palm, and goes out with the intention of using it to greet the coming one. Barrett argues against premeditation, suggesting that ἔλαβον τὰ βαΐα τῶν φοινίκων can be "overtranslated as 'they took *the* palm branches', i.e., those that had been brought for the purpose." Instead the details are best explained, as in Mark, as a "spontaneous ovation."[125] However, it is difficult to understand the action of the crowd apart from some degree of planning, and whereas praise may be a spontaneous reaction, the acquisition of palm branches speaks of intentionality. One must agree with Farmer that "it is quite clear from St. John's account that the palm branches are not casually gathered from alongside the road nor cut down from trees just outside the city on the spur of the moment."[126] The premeditation apparent in the use of the palms suggests that the crowd recognized their symbolic significance and accordingly intended their own actions to be interpreted in that light.

D. *Implications for John*

The behavior of the crowd finds its inspiration in Ps 118 and Tabernacles. Because of the awkward phrasing, and because this was not normal behavior at Passover, the palm branches would have drawn the reader's attention, even as they have that of modern scholars. The branches were associated primarily with Tabernacles liturgy, and the readers could not

---

[124] On the palm branch representing the entire lulab and being indistinguishable from it see further the discussion in ch 2/C above. For the Bar Kochba letter see n. 119 above. See further Schnackenburg (2.374), who states that the lulab is named after the palm branch. Cf. Barrett, 417: "It is not impossible that John may have intended to represent the לולב (*lulab*, literally 'palm-branch') . . . used at the Feast of Tabernacles."

[125] Barrett, 417; emphasis original. So also Sanders and Mastin (287), and Morris (584), who calls it "a spontaneous expression of joy." Against this see Schnackenburg, 2.374: "There is no mention of a breaking or cutting off of the branches, and the definite article seems to imply that the pilgrims already had such palm branches." Lightfoot (250) similarly claims that "the Greek perhaps suggests that these [palms] had not been cut in passing, but had been previously prepared."

[126] Farmer, "Palm Branches," 65–66. In support see also Mastin, "Date," 78; Dodd, *Historical Tradition*, 155–156 n. 3.

have missed the significance of the Hosanna accompanying the palm branches, as these two were so closely linked in the Jewish mind that the lulabs were called Hosannas.[127] If the crowd were using the Tabernacles lulabs this would certainly heighten links to the festival liturgy. However, although John is evoking Tabernacles traditions, the shaking of the palm with the Hosanna is peculiar to the liturgy involving Ps 118, and thus the psalm would be primarily in mind.

Through the popular Tabernacles liturgy Ps 118 was indivisibly linked with the palm branch, but this is not a liturgical accident. The psalm itself preserves a liturgical use of branches (118.27),[128] which may or may not reflect the Tabernacle lulab. In any case, this makes it possible to point the reader beyond the current Tabernacles liturgy to the original Ps 118 procession, where Yahweh is acclaimed with Hosannas, and the king of Israel enters Jerusalem accompanied by jubilant worshippers carrying branches. It would not take a great leap of the imagination to equate the branches of Ps 118.27 with the palm branches of the Ps 118 liturgy at Tabernacles. In this way, even though the palm branch is not specifically mentioned in Ps 118.27, and therefore there is no verbal link to John 12.13, the palm functions as an example of liturgical allusion. When John highlights the palm branches he is thus reinforcing the original Ps 118 royal context for the Entrance. Accordingly the palms signify more than "a jubilant welcome accorded to a notable person."[129] The precedent is the ancient jubilant welcome with branches accorded the Davidic king, now repeated for Jesus, the ideal king of Israel.

E. Conclusion

While many note the peculiar pleonastic phrase John uses for palm branches, few have considered that it draws attention to itself, thereby inviting the reader to look at its symbolic meanings of victory, triumph, and resurrection. The palm branches function to remind the reader of Jesus' recent victory over death in the resurrection of Lazarus, and intensify the sense of anti-cipation surrounding Jesus' own death and resurrection. They function proleptically in pointing toward the decisive victory Jesus will win over

---

[127] The lulab was so closely linked to the Hosanna that it was called הושענא. Cf. Beasley-Murray, 210; Str-B 1.850; 2.789ff.

[128] This is, admittedly, a difficult passage, with some ambiguity in the intended meaning of הג and עבת. This is evident in the different translations, with NIV and RSV translating the former as "festal procession" and the latter as "branches" or "boughs." In contrast NASB and KJV translate as "sacrifice" and "cords." See discussion in Allen, 122.

[129] Barrett, 417.

the powers of darkness, thus anticipating the destruction of the enemies of Israel. The original context of Ps 118 would reinforce these functions, as the king has emerged victorious from battle, and has been preserved from death.

The palm branches also draw attention to themselves because they are out of place at Passover. They are not, however, a signpost to the timing of the Entrance, nor does John intend to evoke Maccabean nationalism. Instead, although the palm branches are not a part of the quotation as such, they signal an actualization of Ps 118, and evoke the complex of traditions shared with Tabernacles. Since the most likely source of the palm branches used at the Entrance was the lulab kept for Tabernacles, this would further accentuate the festival's symbolism. The palms function to emphasize Ps 118 as the context for the Entrance, and as a liturgical allusion to Ps 118.27 and the original royal procession of the psalm. When understood this way, the Entrance mirrors more closely the ancient procession preserved in Ps 118. The choice of palm branches is premeditated, in keeping with an intentional symbolic act by the crowd. Premeditation would also be consistent with a planned liturgical re-enactment of Ps 118.

VI. King of Israel

A. Introduction: Kingship in John

According to John the crowds acclaimed Jesus as ὁ ἐρχόμενος ἐν ὀνόματι κυρίου, [καὶ] ὁ βασιλεὺς τοῦ Ἰσραήλ. This presents a significant manipulation of the quote, as the title "king of Israel" is not original to Ps 118 yet is added in such a way that it is inseparable from the coming one. If the καί is read this aspect is particularly accentuated, making the two titles equivalent.[130] The coming one thus cannot be John the Baptist, Elijah,[131] or the Samaritan *Taheb*, for he is clearly identified as a *royal* eschatological figure. Apart from this important identification, the title, along with the use of Ps 118 and Zechariah, serves to accentuate the royal character of the Entrance.

---

[130] Barrett (418) notes that καί would then read "that is to say" and coordinate the two titles in one. Cf. Morris, 585 n. 42.

[131] Daube (*Rabbinic Judaism*, 23) offers the unlikely suggestion that the coming one may be Elijah.

Jesus' royal identity and function, also important in the Synoptics, is especially emphasized by John.[132] This in turn highlights the importance of the Entrance in developing the theme, for although Jesus' kingship dominates the flow of thought in the trial, outside these two narratives it receives little mention elsewhere in John. The word "king" appears 16 times, in every instance referring to Jesus or used in response to his claims.[133] However, only 4 of these occur outside the Trial Narrative. Of these 4, 2 identify Jesus as king of Israel (1.49; 12.13), and a third, the Zechariah quote in 12.15, is closely related to the title as it interprets it. Thus the title is used in three of the four non-trial identifications of Jesus as king. It is significant that from the beginning of his ministry Jesus is identified as the king of Israel, and that his ministry draws to a close with a reiteration of this status. In this way the title, which underscores Jesus' kingship at his transition into and out of public ministry, links the two and anticipates the climax of the Gospel.

In addition to its linking function the title is also used with special significance. "King of Israel" is used twice (1.49; 12.13), always in a positive sense, in contrast to the Synoptics where it is used mockingly of Jesus on the cross (Matt 27.42; Mark 15.32). John's other primary use of βασιλεύς is in the title ὁ βασιλεύς τῶν Ἰουδαίων, employed in contexts of rejection and unbelief (18.33, 39; 19.3, 19, 21 [twice]). βασιλεύς is also used negatively in the rejection of Yahweh as king (19.15), in the Jews' negative response when Pilate baits them by calling Jesus their king (19.14, 15), and several times in a more neutral sense (6.15; 18.37; 19.12). The only additional positive use is in 18.37 where Jesus affirms that he is a king, and in the reference to Zion's king (12.15), which interprets "king of Israel." It appears that when John wants to portray Jesus' kingship positively he uses the title "king of Israel." In both references the acclamation is born of belief, and accepted by Jesus as his rightful title.

---

[132] Kingship is an important motif throughout the Gospel: Jesus begins his ministry as king, enters Jerusalem as king, and is crucified as king. However, the obvious is sometimes overlooked, as Westermann (*John*, 71) demonstrates in asserting that "there are no extant royal features" in John other than the Entry, and that even this is diluted by the footwashing that follows. On Jesus' kingship in John see Hengel, *Early Christology*, 45–56; 333–357; J. Frey, *Die johanneische Eschatologie. Band 3: Die eschatologische Verkündigung in den johanneischen Texten*, 271–280. Hengel (ibid., 336) correctly observes that John "emphasizes the kingship of Jesus much more than the Synoptics."

[133] There are two references that do not specifically apply to Jesus. In 19.12 the Jews threaten Pilate by stating that he is no friend of Caesar if he lets Jesus go, for anyone claiming to be a king opposes Caesar, and in 19.15 the Jews say they have no king but Caesar. However, the first implicitly acknowledges Jesus' claim to kingship, and the latter equates rejecting Jesus' kingship with rejecting Yahweh's rule. On the rejection of Yahweh as king see Rensberger, *Overcoming the World*, 95–96.

Nathanael is ἀληθῶς 'Ισραηλίτης, an example of a true Israelite who has recognized the true king of Israel.[134] The Entrance likewise portrays the crowd responding with faith, and Jesus accepting their acclaim.[135] In sum, the special use of "king of Israel" and the rare non-trial emphasis on Jesus' royal status in the Entry suggests that the kingship of Jesus as presented in the Entrance has crucial implications for interpreting the theme's significance and function in the Gospel.

However, apart from widespread agreement that the title was intended messianically,[136] none of the major commentaries give it any particular importance. Given the importance of the kingship motif in John, and of the title for interpreting the Entrance, a closer look at the possible backgrounds for "king of Israel" is in order. Where is John pointing with the title? With what purpose? What is Ps 118's role and function in this? I suggest that the answer to these questions will cast new light on the Entrance. We will look first at the most promising backgrounds to the title before suggesting how John intended it to function.

B. Background Options for the title "King of Israel"

1. The Davidic Messiah

At first glance, the most obvious background for "king of Israel" is the Davidic Messiah. The Davidic descent of the Messiah was a standard feature of Messianic expectation, well-established both in the OT and in intertestamental Jewish literature.[137] Psalm 118 would also invite such an interpretation, as Jewish traditions appear to have associated it with the anointing of David by Samuel,[138] and the psalm assumes a royal figure in

---

[134] Note that this is the only use of 'Ισραηλίτης in John, in contrast to the often (but not always) negative use of 'Ιουδαῖος. Davies (*Rhetoric*, 210) argues that Nathanael recognizes Jesus as a true Israelite who is Israel's king. Against this I suggest that John's primary purpose is to introduce Jesus as king of Israel, and Nathanael as an example of the faith response the true Israel gives to its true king, in keeping with John's redefinition of Israel according to the New Exodus theme.

[135] See argument in ch. 7 below.

[136] For example, Bultmann (104 n. 7) states that "king of Israel" means essentially Messiah. So also Barrett (185–186): "[That Jesus is the Messiah] is certainly the meaning of 'king of Israel'." Cf. ibid., 418. This is a common position. See among others Beasley-Murray, 210; Bruce, 61.

[137] For example, 2 Sam 7.12–16; Pss 18.50; 89.3–4; Isa 9.7; 11.1, 10; 55.3. See further the discussion in ch. 2/C above. Cf. Kinman, *Entry*, 68–73. Accordingly, Sanders and Mastin (288) assert that the cry indicates the crowd's longing for Jesus "to restore the kingdom of David."

[138] *Tg. Ps.* 118; *b. Pesah.* 119a.

the liturgy, a king from the House of David. Upon encountering the title, it would be natural for the reader to think of the paradigmatic Davidic king as pattern for the eschatological king. The great difficulty with this is that John has little explicit emphasis on David, so that Anderson correctly writes, "John is nearly devoid of Davidic messianic motifs."[139] In fact, the only mention of David comes in a dispute over Jesus' messianic identity, where some in the crowd argue that he is disqualified because not descended from David nor born in Bethlehem (7.42). Some have seized on the fact that John does not answer this objection to advance questionable arguments. For example, Meeks argues that the Bethlehem tradition was manufactured,[140] and that John contains a polemic against the Davidic ideology of the eschatological redeemer.[141] Bultmann claims that "the evangelist knows nothing, or wants to know nothing of the birth in Bethlehem."[142] However, it is likely that John was aware of Jesus' descent from David and birth at Bethlehem, and expected his readers to know this as well.[143]

---

[139] Anderson, *Christology*, 229. He argues that to desire a king represented the abandonment of a pneumatic/charismatic model of theocracy based on God's promise to raise up prophets like Moses (Deut 18.15–18). Jesus accordingly objects to the idea that he is setting up a kingdom of power as a Davidic king, and is rather a prophet like Moses (ibid., 229–230). Davies also points to the Deuteronomy passage, arguing that "Jesus' life is so unlike that of David . . . that the connexion which the Synoptics make could be misleading" (*Rhetoric*, 212). Meeks (*Prophet-King*, 17, 20) reasonably suggests that the lack of attention paid to the title by scholars comes because "king of Israel" is usually thought to be equivalent to the Davidic Messiah, and since Davidic ideology appears to be played down in John, it is therefore thought not to be very significant. For a brief survey of views on the role of David in the Fourth Gospel, and of explanations offered for the apparent lack of emphasis on him, see Daly-Denton, *David*, 102–110.

[140] Against Dodd (*The Interpretation of the Fourth Gospel*, 91), Meeks writes, "That the tradition may have been Christian from the start and based on the historical fact that Jesus was born in Bethlehem cannot be maintained. On the contrary, it is much more probable that the motif of birth in Bethlehem, at whatever point it came to the attention of Christians, raised formidable difficulties in the light of the firm recollection of Jesus' origin in Nazareth of Galilee" (*Prophet-King*, 35). Meeks further denies that Jesus was from the seed of David. What Meeks fails to realize is that in the Middle East a person's place of origin is many times counted as the place from where his family historically originates. It is not unusual for a Middle Easterner, when asked where he is from, to give the family's original home even though he may have been born in a different place, lived all of his life in a different location, and perhaps never even visited his "home." Thus Jesus can be from Nazareth and still also be from Bethlehem by birth and family link.

[141] Meeks, *Prophet-King*, 41. See also Burger (*Jesus als Davidssohn*, 153–158), who argues that John is rejecting Jesus' Davidic birth in Bethlehem.

[142] Bultmann, 306 n. 6.

[143] Not least is the fact that another Johannine writing (cf. Rev 3.7; 5.5; 22.16) shows no hesitation in identifying Jesus with David. In support, see Hoskyns, 324; Beasley-Murray, 118–119; Barrett, 330; Brown, 1.329–330; Schnackenburg, 2.158 (more cautiously); and Carson, 329–330. One can hardly imagine that John or other members of his community

Why then does John not answer the objection? For one, it is likely that he is writing in his usual ironical style,[144] exposing unbelief as unwarranted with the expectation that his readers will recognize that all the objections advanced against Jesus' messiahship actually prove his identity. However, the use of subtle irony does not completely account for the lack of Davidic emphasis in John. A credible possibility is that John wants to refocus the question from Jesus' earthly origin to his heavenly origin.[145] In any case, although I suggest that John intentionally de-emphasizes David, this does not represent an anti-Davidic polemic.[146] The reader recognizes the irony that Jesus did indeed descend from David and was born in Bethlehem, but because Davidic ideology is not prominent throughout the Gospel, and Jesus is not programmatically compared to David, John can more easily re-direct the reader towards other backgrounds. When Jesus enters Jerusalem acclaimed as king of Israel John does not point the reader away from David – how could the Davidic Messiah not come to mind? However, he also does not identify Jesus explicitly with David, which he could have done were this his intention. The Gospel's relative silence on David supports the suggestion that the title is not intended primarily to evoke Davidic associations.

---

had never interacted with other Christians who would be aware of these traditions, although some scholars appear to assume such an isolated group.

[144] Cf. Barrett, 330; Brown, 329–330; Carson, 329–330; and Beasley-Murray, 118–119. Schnackenburg (2.159) tentatively concludes it may be irony. On irony in John see P. Duke, *Irony in the Fourth Gospel*.

[145] So, for example, Schnackenburg, 2.159. Meeks (*Prophet-King*, 41) similarly argues that John downplays Jesus' Galilean origin.

[146] Against Meeks (and others), the playing down of Davidic ideology need not indicate an anti-Davidic polemic. John's purposes may be more functional than theological. That is, he does not want Davidic ideology – which in any case Jesus fulfills – to distract the reader from the New Exodus motif of the coming of Yahweh. In a recent study Daly-Denton has argued for a more robust and positive Davidic presence in John than is usually recognized. Although acknowledging that "it seems that David *per se* is not important to John" (*David*, 103), she contends that the Fourth Gospel draws significantly on the figure of David for its portrayal of Jesus, and suggests a number of similarities between Johannine and biblical Davidic passages that function as "subtle recollections of the remembered and expected David" and whose cumulative effect is "a strong impression of his latent presence in the Fourth Gospel" (ibid., 315). It is not impossible that Daly-Denton has uncovered some legitimate Davidic parallels, but if so they are extremely subtle (see esp. ibid., 289–315). I concur that John does not repudiate Davidic Christology, but remain unconvinced that he intended to emphasize David in any special way, and certainly not to the extent that Daly-Denton argues for.

2. Other Kings of Israel

The title "king of Israel," although associated most naturally with the paradigmatic kingship of David, would also have applied to later kings. In this regard David's most famous son, Solomon, would provide a parallel to the messianic Son of David. Some scholars explore the links between Solomon and Jesus as sons of David,[147] and Solomon and Wisdom, which is especially relevant in John as a possible background to the prologue.[148] Sahlin, for example, argues that Jesus is portrayed as a second Solomon in his Entrance to Jerusalem.[149] No doubt there are a number of credible parallels, but it is unlikely that John intends to point with the title to Solomon or any one specific Hebrew king for that matter.[150] In support, other than the argument over Jesus' Davidic identity (7.42), no king is specifically mentioned in John,[151] and John does nothing to indicate that any is in view. Another option is the ancient Israelite tradition of non-dynastic popular charismatic kingship that Horsley argues continued in and inspired peasant messianic movements around the time of Jesus.[152] In this case the title would identify Jesus as a charismatic king anointed by a popular messianic peasant movement to lead them in a "liberating action."[153] Against popular charismatic kingship, whether John accurately represents contemporary views or not, he portrays Jewish messianic ideology as expecting a king from the line of David born in Bethlehem. Even if John were thought to advance an anti-David polemic he does not re-orient the

---

[147] For example, Burger, *Jesus als Davidssohn*, 16–24.

[148] Thus Beasley-Murray suggests that "king of Israel" in John 1.49 recalls Solomon. See further K. Berker's exploration of Solomon as son of David and possible wisdom connections ("Die königlichen Messiastraditionen des Neuen Testaments," 3–13).

[149] Sahlin, *Typologie*, 47–48. He argues that 1 Kgs 1.33–53 provides a typological parallel to John 12.12–19. Kinman (*Entry*, 49–54, 107–115) and N. Fernández Marcos ("La unción de Salomón") note the parallels for a Solomonic background, but this is in a Lukan context.

[150] For further discussion see section III above. The closest parallel to 1 Kgs 1 is Zech 9, which shares in common with the former passage a king of Israel riding on a donkey and entering Jerusalem as king for the first time, perhaps to be formally enthroned. Since John quotes the Zechariah passage it is plausible to assume, first, that the Succession Narrative informs the background of the Entrance, and second, that Jesus is more likely to be identified with Zion's king than with Solomon. Saul is certainly not in view, in spite of Daube's suggestion (*Rabbinic Judaism*, 18–19) that we think of him as "an ideal king" and background to Jesus' kingship.

[151] The exception is a reference to a temple porch bearing Solomon's name in 10.23. Solomon has a higher profile in Matt (1.6, 7; 6.29; 12.42 [twice]), and Luke (11.31 [twice]; 12.27).

[152] Horsley, "Messianic Movements," 471–495.

[153] Horsley, "Messianic Movements," 495.

reader to look for a charismatic king. In conclusion, it is unlikely that John has any specific Israelite king in view.

3. Moses

If the title does not point specifically to David or one of the other ancient Israelite kings, this leaves very few likely options. Even though John is probably contrasting Jesus' kingship with that of the Emperor, it is most unlikely that the title "king of Israel" was ever applied to Caesar, or that John is intentionally evoking Caesar as a model of kingship.[154] The title would point rather to an OT or other Jewish figure associated with eschatological expectations. Accordingly, Meeks argues that Moses traditions "provided for the Fourth Gospel not only the figure of the eschatological prophet, but the figure who combines in one person both royal and prophetic honor and function."[155] There does appear to be expectation of an eschatological prophet in John (1.21, 25; 4.19; 6.14; 7.40), Jesus is referred to as a prophet (4.19; 4.44; 6.14; 7.40; 9.17), and a function of his kingship appears to be testifying to the truth (18.37). Although it is left unclear exactly what background is in view, the speculation may well allude to the prophet like Moses mentioned in Deut 18.18–19, even though John does not explicitly identify Moses as a prophet and refers to him primarily as giver of the Law (1.17, 45; 5.46; 7.19, 22, 23; 8.5). It is possible that Jesus is a prophet like Moses, and since Jesus is also a royal figure, therefore a prophet-king.[156] But in any case, Dodd is correct in stating that the title ὁ προφήτης is "an inadequate, or even misleading, description

---

[154] The title does serve to highlight the different sources of their kingship and authority, as one is based on Yahweh's sovereignty and the other is a completely human system extended by military power. However, this is probably a result rather than the intention of John's use of the title. John is certainly evoking Yahweh's authority rather than Caesar's.

[155] Meeks, *Prophet-King*, 29. On Jesus as a prophet like Moses see further Anderson, *Christology*, 229–230; Reim, *Hintergrund*, 110–154. Elsewhere Reim ("Nordreich–Südreich. Der vierte Evangelist als Vertreter christlicher Nordreichstheologie") points to the lack of Davidic emphasis as a sign of John's Northern Kingdom theology, with an emphasis on Moses and Elijah.

[156] Meeks argues that Jesus' kingship is "identical to the office of a *prophet*" (*Prophet-King*, 81; emphasis original). He also makes much of "*the* false prophet" (Deut 13.1–6; 18.18–22; 34.10–12), so that the issue in John 7.15–24 is whether Jesus is the false prophet or the prophet like Moses. Meeks further applies this to the questioning of Jesus before the High Priest (18.19–24), so that it is a trial of the false prophet, asking whether he has led others astray. However, there were many false prophets, and it is not necessarily the case that one eschatological false prophet was expected.

of the real status of Jesus."[157] There is a sense, of course, in which Jesus is the prophet *par excellence*: the Law was given through Moses, but grace and *truth* through Jesus (1.17). But unlike a prophet, who communicates the words of God, Jesus' revelatory message points to and actually *is* himself.

Granted that Moses provides a likely background to Jesus' prophetic status, it is much less clear that he is the model for Jesus' kingship. Meeks exhaustively examines Jewish and other literature to show that Moses is the prototypical prophet-king. However, his own research works against him. Meeks admits that there is "little" in Josephus' portrayal of Moses that "directly suggests the 'prophet-king' of the Fourth Gospel."[158] Ezekiel the Tragedian relates a dream that Moses had where he is appointed God's vice-regent. However, Meeks provides no evidence of a prophet-king conjunction, and finds no other passage in apocryphal and pseudepigraphic writings to support his argument.[159] Qumran shows a clear expectation of an eschatological prophet like Moses based on Deut 18, but "there is no hint of Moses' kingship."[160] Only Philo supports Moses' kingship. It is not until the rabbinics that Moses' kingship is more clearly in view, with the tradition that he was king of Israel during the wilderness sojourn (based on Deut 33.5). However, although he is "the model for all subsequent prophets," Meeks admits that in the rabbinic sources "it is David who is the king par excellence."[161] Furthermore, a survey of Samaritan literature leads to the conclusion that "Moses is almost never called 'king'."[162] This is somewhat misleading, however, for although his unequalled prophetic status is emphasized, in none of the Samaritan examples Meeks provides is Moses called king. On the whole Meeks finds very little evidence – and what he does offer is not very obvious – to support a Mosaic prophet-king or the ideal of Mosaic kingship in Jewish circles.[163]

---

[157] Dodd, *Interpretation*, 239. Dodd continues, arguing that the title is not an appropriate one, although "it may represent a stage towards a true estimate of the status of Jesus. It has no further significance for the development of his distinctive teaching" (ibid., 240). Note that Jesus is greater than the prophets (8.52, 53).

[158] Meeks, *Prophet-King*, 145.

[159] Meeks, *Prophet-King*, 148.

[160] Meeks, *Prophet-King*, 173–175.

[161] Meeks, *Prophet-King*, 214.

[162] Meeks, *Prophet-King*, 227.

[163] It is of interest that Ps 118 echoes the Song of the Sea with its Mosaic association, and figured prominently at Passover. The exodus imagery in the Hallel would also heighten the connection with Moses. However, the royal figure of the psalm is not identified with Moses, although it could provide, for the sensitive reader, an opportunity to associate royal and Mosaic themes.

In the end one has to question whether Meeks has truly succeeded in uniting the prophet-king in Moses. Although John has many Moses parallels and allusions, I question whether Jesus' kingship is best understood as a Moses parallel. The Jewish (and Samaritan) sources do not support Moses as king except in a marginal sense in the rabbinics, neither does the ideal kingship portrayed in the psalms and prophets have much to do with him, nor does Christian tradition represent him as a king. This suggests that other referent points would more naturally come to mind.[164] Consequently, it is unlikely that Moses provides a parallel for Jesus as the king of Israel in the Entrance.

C. Psalm 118 and the King of Israel

In adding the phrase "king of Israel" to the quotation, John ensures that Ps 118 is interpreted royally, identifies Jesus with the royal figure in the psalm, and thus evokes the original liturgy as model for the Entry.[165] This, however, identifies in part the function of the title, but not specifically the subject it points to. I suggest that John intends to call into play the ancient institution of kingship. The ancient royal ideals and the later eschatological associations that developed alongside them in Judaism were well known, so that there was a widespread and immediate connection to passages like Ps 118.[166] M. Huie-Jolly's examination of the divine warrior myth, which she argues informs a number of the OT passages (including Zech 9–14 and Ps 118) used as *testimonia* in the early church, highlights the importance of the dramatic enactment of liturgy in the ancient Near East.[167] Although the New Exodus pattern I advocate in this study better explains the Fourth Gospel and is closer to the OT, Huie-Jolly is nevertheless correct in pointing out that ancient backgrounds "provided a framework for retelling the story [of Jesus' life]."[168]

---

[164] Note that the prophet-king combination is found in David and Saul. For David as prophet-king see Ginzburg, *Legends*, 6.249 n. 24. For Saul, see 1 Sam 10.1–12; 19.23–24.

[165] The addition also renders moot (i.e. "purely academic") the question of whether Ps 118's original setting was understood as royal.

[166] Barker (*The Older Testament*, esp. 1–7) argues that Christian proclamation was readily and widely understood because it built upon and evoked an already existing mythological framework. Although the direction she takes from this leads to some implausible conclusions, I suggest that her initial observation is credible and borne out by our study.

[167] Huie-Jolly, "Threats Answered by Enthronement: Death/Resurrection and the Divine Warrior Myth in John 5.17–29, Psalm 2 and Daniel 7," 191–217.

[168] Huie-Jolly, "Threats," 216. She suggests the framework is the divine warrior myth. Jesus' Entry to Jerusalem foreshadows his later victory procession (ibid., 208–209). When her proposal is applied, Jesus is a divine warrior king going into conflict with chaos/darkness before he achieves victory and subsequent enthronement. Note however

I have argued that neither Davidic expectations, nor any specific Israelite king, nor charismatic popular kingship is the intended background for "king of Israel." The Ps 118 king would naturally be associated with the Davidic line, but although expectations of a messianic Davidic king must inform to some degree the psalm's interpretation, John chooses not to make the connections explicit. Instead of evoking any of the royal identities mentioned above, the Ps 118 liturgy would have highlighted the office and role of the king in general, and evoked the ceremonial complex that celebrated his vice-regency and Yahweh's kingship at the ancient Tabernacles festival. The title summons up the institution of kingship in ancient Israel, whose ideals were eschatologized and laid the base for messianic expectation. In this sense, "king of Israel" evokes the ideal of kingship, providing the "framework" for identifying Jesus as the eschatological ideal king.[169] Psalm 118 has thus provided a model of the ideal king, and along with Tabernacles frames the Entrance in a context rich with royal traditions and possible enthronement links. Mirroring the ideal of kingship in the OT, Jesus' kingship is thus bound up in Yahweh's kingship. This is important for John's readers since, as van Tilborg points out, in the Roman Empire kings were kings only in so far as the Emperor allowed them to be, so that "kingship is linked with the question on whose authority one is a king."[170] As the one who comes in Yahweh's name, Jesus' kingship originates and finds its authority in Yahweh. However, I suggest that John was intending something deeper in the use of *king of Israel*, for he shows Jesus transcending the category of the ideal vice-regent.

This is consistent with the Johannine pattern of programmatically taking popular Jewish expectations concerning the Messiah and showing

---

that although the OT provides numerous examples of warrior kings, unlike their ANE neighbors none of them are thought of as divine. This does not preclude Jesus' fulfilling the divine warrior myth, but a better parallel is found in *Yahweh, who is the OT and Israel's only divine warrior king.* In addition to Huie-Jolly, for general background see F. M. Cross, *Canaanite Myth and Hebrew Epic: Essays in the History of the Religion of Israel.* Other studies that purport to have found the divine warrior motif in the NT include, for Revelation, A. Y. Collins, *The Combat Myth in the Book of Revelation*; J. Day, *God's Conflict with the Dragon and the Sea: Echoes of a Canaanite Myth in the Old Testament.* For Mark: Duff, "Divine Warrior." For the Gospel narratives: F. R. McCurley, *Ancient Myths and Biblical Faith: Scriptural Transformations.* And for John: J. L. Kovak, "'Now shall the Ruler of this World be Driven Out': Jesus' Death as Cosmic Battle in John 12:20–36."

[169] Note that the Tabernacles imagery in the Entrance would intensify this association.

[170] Van Tilborg, *Reading John*, 52.

that they are essentially inadequate to describe and explain Jesus.[171] The Jews argue that when Messiah comes no one will know where he is from (7.27), but they know that Jesus is from Nazareth and Galilee (1.45, 46; 2.11–13; 4.54; 5.1; 7.9, 10; 8.5, 7; 19.19). The irony is that they do not know his true origin, which is from the Father. They expect the Messiah to come from the line of David and be born in Bethlehem (7.42), and of course he was, although they do not realize it. They also believe the Messiah will abide forever (12.34), which disqualifies Jesus as he is going to be "lifted up" from the earth. Again ironically, it is precisely his being lifted up that secures eternally the benefits of his victory, so that his followers may abide with him. I suggest that John intends to show that *Jesus is the Messiah of Jewish expectation, but he is also much more than this.* Any approach that denies or treats as insignificant Jewish messianic expectations would make nonsense of the Gospel's stated purpose to persuade that Jesus is the Christ (20.31).[172] Rather than using them simply as a foil, John takes up Jewish messianic criteria and shows Jesus fulfilling them, but also transcending and transforming them, for they are insufficient to account for his person and function.[173]

The addition "king of Israel" is another example of this. The title would necessarily evoke the messianic Davidic king, and indeed Jesus fulfills this expectation: he is the messianic king from the House of David.[174] However, it appears that John does not want to present Jesus primarily as the Davidic king, for although he is that, he is also much more.[175] Similarly, the title functions to evoke the ideal eschatological king of the Psalms and the Prophets, but there is a disjunction: although Jesus comes as the ideal

---

[171] My interest lies not in determining whether these were actual Messianic expectations current at the time of Jesus, but what John intended to do when he presented them as such. For a more detailed discussion of the passages in question see Dodd, *Interpretation*, 87–93; de Jonge, "Jewish Expectations."

[172] Dodd concludes that John "is developing his doctrine of the person and work of Jesus with conscious reference to Jewish messianic belief." However, "while formally the evangelist claims for Jesus the Jewish title μεσσίας, in fact the Jewish conception of Messiahship is set aside, and his doctrine of the Person of Christ is mainly worked out under other categories" (*Interpretation*, 92). Similarly, Schnackenburg, 2.158: John "has no desire to establish the legitimacy of his Christ by the criteria of Jewish messianic expectation." It is true that John does not depend on these criteria, but this does not mean that he does not present Jesus as fulfilling them.

[173] As Beasley-Murray notes, "there is no category known to man in which Jesus can be placed. 'Messiah' only dimly describes the reality, unless one fills the term with the attributes of the risen, exalted and returning Lord" (*Coming of God*, 63).

[174] Cf. Rev 3.7; 5.5; 22.16, where this is not in doubt.

[175] Against Dodd (*Interpretation*, 229), who correctly notes Jesus' exalted kingship, but sees too much of an "implicit polemic" against current Jewish interpretations of kingship.

king, the reader must recognize that Jesus' kingship is of a higher order. I suggest that the title "king of Israel" primarily points to Yahweh, and provides a bridge between the eschatological ideal king of Ps 118 and Yahweh's kingship that links Jesus' royal entry to Jerusalem with the coming of Yahweh.

VII. Psalm 118 and the Zechariah Combination Quote

Important support for the proposed bridging function comes from the quotation of Zech 9.9 that immediately follows – and thus interprets – the reference to the king of Israel. As he often does when quoting, John abbreviates his source, and in replacing the first line's call to rejoice (χαῖρε σφόδρα) with μὴ φοβοῦ, which is not found in any version of Zech 9.9, signals a combination with another passage of Scripture.[176] It is this unidentified Scripture that is of first importance. The phrase μὴ φοβοῦ (or μὴ φοβεῖσθε) occurs a number of times in the LXX,[177] but the most likely sources for the quotation are limited to Isa 35.4; 40.9; 41.10; 44.2; and Zeph 3.16.[178] In the Zephaniah citation the LXX deviates in translating the combination of the form ירא with אל as θάρσει,[179] which suggests that if John did use Zephaniah he translated from the Hebrew.[180] We will look briefly at the most promising passages and highlight possible correspondences with John before coming to any conclusions as to his intended source.

One should keep in mind that although John uses only a short phrase this calls into play the immediate literary context from which it was drawn. First, Isa 35 presents an extended description of the return from exile, encouraging those who are afraid not to fear for "God will come . . . He will come and save," destroying their enemies (Isa 35.4) so that "the ransomed of the LORD shall return" (Isa 35.10).[181] A sign of this will be the healing of the blind, deaf, and lame (Isa 35.5–6), which the Synoptics

---

[176] Matt 21.5 quotes Zech 9.9 at greater length, and also combines it with a line from Isa 62.11.

[177] It appears especially in Isaiah. E.g., Isa 10.24; 35.4; 40.9; 41.10, 13; 43.1, 5; 44.2; 51.7; 54.4; Jer 46(26).27–28.

[178] None of the major commentaries or articles on the quotation in John 12.15 argue strongly for a passage other than these five.

[179] That is, instead of "do not fear" (MT) the LXX translates "be confident/courageous."

[180] Freed (*Quotations*, 78) notes that the four words "fear not" and "daughter of Zion" do not occur in the same context anywhere in the LXX, but do occur in the MT of Zeph 3.14–17.

[181] NA[27] lists Isa 35.4 as quoted in John 12.15. Smith (236) lists Isa 35.4 as influencing the addition, along with Isa 40.9 and Zeph 3.14–20.

show as fulfilled in Jesus in answer to the Baptist's question whether he is the coming one.[182] In an exodus motif, water will gush forth in the wilderness, streams in the desert (Isa 35.6), a suggestive parallel to the Johannine Jesus who is the source of streams of living water (John 7.37–38). Second, Isa 40 comforts exiled Israel with the hope of restoration, for their sin has been forgiven and paid for (Isa 40.2). Those bringing the message are encouraged not to fear. The reason? "Behold, the Lord GOD comes with might" (Isa 40.10).[183] The Baptist's ministry is defined according to Isa 40.3–5 (Matt 3.3; Mark 1.3; Luke 3.4–6; John 1.23), where the one preparing the way does so for Yahweh, not for the Messiah. This is a sign that precedes Yahweh's universal reign, when "the glory of the LORD shall be revealed, and all people shall see it" (Isa 40.5). Third, Isa 41.10 similarly encourages Israel not to fear, because Yahweh is with them.[184] He promises to destroy Israel's enemies (Isa 41.11–12), and reveals himself as their Redeemer (Isa 41.14) in a clear allusion to the end of exile. The one offering this hope is ὁ βασιλεὺς Ιακωβ (Isa 41.21), or in other words, the King of Israel. Fourth, the call not to fear in Isa 44.2 also comes in a context of redemption.[185] Yahweh has swept away Israel's sin and redeemed them (Isa 41.22, 23, 24). This Redeemer is ὁ βασιλεὺς τοῦ Ισραηλ (Isa 44.6), the only occurrence in the LXX of the exact phrase found in John 12.13.[186] And last, Zeph 3.14 parallels Zech 9.9 with a call to rejoice: χαῖρε σφόδρα θύγατερ Σιων κήρυσσε θύγατερ Ιερουσαλημ. The reason for this call is that the condition for return from exile has been met: Yahweh has taken away their punishment, defeated their enemies, and has returned to reign as βασιλεὺς Ισραηλ (Zeph 3.15). Because Yahweh is in their midst Zion is not to fear (Zeph 3.16–17). Yahweh will gather "the outcast," restore and return them to their home (Zeph 3.19).

---

[182] Matt 11.5; Mark 7.37; Luke 7.22.

[183] Barrett (417–418) suggests Isa 40.9 as a possible source for the combined quotation. So also Carson, 433; Bruce, 277 n. 11; Obermann, *Schrift*, 207; M. C. Tenney, "Literary Keys to the Fourth Gospel: The Old Testament and the Fourth Gospel," 303; and Sanders and Mastin (289), although they unnecessarily describe it as an "unconscious conflation of prophetic testimonies." Reim (*Studien*, 30) argues for a combination of Isa 40.9 and 62.11. Others who refer to the passage include Weren, "Jesus' Entry," 126–127; R. Longenecker, *Biblical Exegesis in the Apostolic Period*, 155; Haenchen 2.277 n. 11.

[184] Schlatter (266) is one of the few to propose this as a viable option. Bultmann (418 n. 4) lists it as a possibility.

[185] Barrett (417–418), Hoskyns (422), and Bultmann (418 n. 4) suggest this source as a possibility. Bauer (155) points to both Isa 44.2 and Zeph 3.16.

[186] Because of this, Schuchard (*Scripture*, 76–78) argues that Isa 44.2 is the most likely source for the combined quotation. See however Menken's dismissal (*Quotations*, 84) of the presence of the two articles as "casual," and his suggestion that the ὁ in John 12.13 and the τοῦ in Isa 44.6 (LXX) are questionable from a text-critical point of view.

What is striking about these passages is that they each point to Yahweh's return or presence as the reason not to fear. Each offers the hope of return from exile and pictures the destruction of Israel's enemies. Notably it is not the Messiah but Yahweh who does this – he is the one forgiving sins and thus marking the end of exile, who in power saves Israel and vanquishes her foes, who gathers the scattered, and who is either present or coming to establish his reign. Three of the passages explicitly identify Yahweh as King of Israel (Zeph 3.15; Isa 41.21; 44.6). It may not be possible to identify with certainty the source John intended, and in one sense it is not necessary, as they all share the same principal New Exodus theme and thus would function similarly in John. However, because of the phrase that it shares with Zech 9.9 ("rejoice daughter of Zion"), and because of its explicit use of "king of Israel" which connects it to the quotation of Ps 118 in John 12.13, Zephaniah is to be preferred.[187] It is possible that Zeph 3.15 provides the title "king of Israel" to Ps 118, and if not, at the very least a firm link that ensures each will interpret the other.[188]

With a minimum of words John has created a network of OT allusions. First, the addition of "king of Israel" to Ps 118 sends the reader searching for the royal figure's identity. Immediately following, John introduces a combined quote, the first phrase of which opens a window onto several passages that each contain *in nuce* the New Exodus. Each heralds the coming of Yahweh, and several identify Yahweh as King of Israel. The reader could thus make the connection: the King of Israel is Yahweh. This is not an implausible identification, for it is the kingship of Yahweh that dominates the OT. Although the monarchy is presented positively and flourished, there are glimpses of tension with the kingship of Yahweh, so that the demand for a king could be seen as a rejection of his rule (1 Sam 8.5–7). It is in the Psalter and the later Prophets that Yahweh's kingship is most emphasized, developing into an intense longing for him to return to

---

[187] Others who opt for Zeph 3.16 include Schnackenburg, 2.376; 2.525 n. 46; Brown, 1.458; Freed, *Quotations*, 78; Lindars, 424; Losie, "Triumphal Entry," 858; P. C. Mateos, "Uso e interpretación de Zacarías 9,9–10 en el Nuevo Testamento," 5. Becker (2.378) prefers this, but does not rule out Isa 40.9. Others list it as a possibility: Barrett, 417–418; Hoskyns, 422; Bultmann, 418 n. 4; Braun, 2.19; C. März, *"Siehe, dein König kommt zu dir . . .": Eine traditionsgeschichtliche Untersuchung zur Einzugsperikope*, 161. Menken argues that a choice between Isa 40.9 and Zeph 3.16 "is hardly possible, nor is it necessary" (*Quotations*, 84). It is of interest that Justin (*1 Apol.* 35.11) quotes Zech 9.9 as from Zephaniah. Freed (*Quotations*, 78 n. 4), however, notes that Justin at other times misidentifies OT sources. On the possible influence of Zephaniah on Deutero-Zechariah see Mateos, "Zacarías," 475.

[188] Few note the possibility that Zeph 3.15 provides the title. See however Brown, 1.462; Lindars, 424; Mateos, "Zacarías," 5.

reign.[189] Intertestamental literature also bears witness to the ultimate kingship of Yahweh, expressed succinctly in 2 Macc 1.24: "O Lord, Lord God . . . who alone art king."[190] Meeks observes that at Qumran only God is regularly called king,[191] and as for the rabbinics, their hope "knows God primarily as the King of Israel."[192] Although I do not wish to diminish the importance of messianic expectation in these sources, it is the hope of Yahweh's coming to reign that dominates.[193]

While many scholars note the change introduced to the Zechariah quotation, attention has generally focused on determining the source of μὴ φοβοῦ rather than on explaining the reason for the change. Some of those who do look to its function seem generally to have missed the principal themes of the pre-text. For example, Menken concludes that "do not fear" is intended to correct the misunderstanding of the crowds that Jesus was "a national king who does frightening things."[194] His suggestion is puzzling, as most scholars who think the Zechariah quote is a correction of the crowd's nationalistic expectations point instead to the mounting of the donkey and the "gentle" king of Zion (as does Menken himself), and the crowd does not seem to be exhibiting any fear that would require calming. Freed is truer to the original context of Zeph 3, suggesting that μὴ φοβοῦ is used in the Entrance in a joyful sense to indicate that "the coming of the messianic king is a time for rejoicing without fear."[195] However, he qualifies this by noting that the passage is applied to Jesus although "in Zeph 'king' refers to Yahweh himself rather than to the messiah as 'king of Israel'."[196] But this is precisely the point! John does not allude to Zeph 3 *in spite* of the

---

[189] For example, Exod 15.18; Num 23.21; Pss 5.2; 22.28; 24.7–10; 47; 93; 96; 97; 99; 146.10; Isa 6.5; 24.23; 33.22; 43.15; 52.7; Jer 8.19; 10.10; 46.18; 48.15; 51.57; Obad 21; Mic 2.13; 4.7; Zech 14; Mal 1.14. As von Rad observes, "Hope is set on the fact that Yahweh will show Himself to be the King. [This does] not question the present kingship of Yahweh. There is expectation merely of the final manifestation of His total kingly power" ("מלך and מלכות in the OT," *TDNT* 1.569). On kingship in general see also B. Klappert, "βασιλεία," *NIDNTT* 2.372–390.

[190] For further examples see Jdt 9.12; Tob 13.6–7, 10–11, 15; Wis 51.1; 1 Esd 4.46; 2 Macc 7.9; 13.4; 3 Macc 2.2; 5.35; *Pss. Sol.* 5.19; 17.1, 46. In *Pss. Sol.* 17.34 the Lord is the Messiah's king.

[191] Meeks (*Prophet-King*, 165) comes to this conclusion after searching the literature for the kingship of Moses.

[192] K. G. Kuhn, "מלכות שמים in Rabbinic Literature," *TDNT* 1.574. See also Str-B 1.172–175.

[193] For a survey of Yahweh as King in Jewish literature see Moore, *Judaism*, 1.226–232; 401; 431–434; 2.195; 209–210; 303; 371–375.

[194] Menken, *Quotations*, 86. Lagrange (325) similarly suggests it was added to demonstrate the peaceful character of the king. Cf. Schuchard, *Scripture*, 76–80.

[195] Freed, "Entry," 336.

[196] Freed, "Entry," 336 n. 39.

King of Israel being Yahweh, he does so *because* of that identification. In Zeph 3 Yahweh has forgiven, the exile is finished, the scattered exiles will be gathered, and the enemies of Israel have been defeated. All of these John shows as accomplished in the ministry and person of Jesus, a fact which is reinforced and brought into sharp focus by the combined quotation. However, although the entire New Exodus theme is called into play, above all else μὴ φοβοῦ points to Yahweh's kingship. Israel will never fear harm because "the King of Israel, the LORD, is in your midst" (Zeph 3.15). Zephaniah 3.16, the verse specifically alluded to, reiterates this: "Do not fear, O Zion . . . The LORD, your God, is in your midst, a warrior who gives victory."[197] In other words, John's crowds are not to fear – that is, they should rejoice – because Yahweh has come.

Only a few have recognized the implications of the Zephaniah intertext. Brown argues that it should correct the people's acclaim of Jesus as an earthly king instead of as "the manifestation of the Lord their God who has come into their midst."[198] Similarly, Losie recognizes that "the implication is that the 'King of Israel' is no earthly leader, but indeed 'the Lord . . . in your midst.'"[199] However, although they come to the verge, they apparently cannot see beyond an alleged correction of nationalism in the Entrance, and thus do not recognize that John portrays Jesus as actually fulfilling the coming of Yahweh. To start, John presents the Entrance as the re-enactment of an ancient royal liturgy at Tabernacles. The actualization of the liturgy transforms the royal figure of the psalm from an original OT king to the eschatological ideal king, a change mirrored in the eschatological interpretation of Ps 118 in early Judaism. The Tabernacles imagery evokes the ancient royal ceremonies (perhaps enthronement) that celebrated the kingship of Yahweh and that of his vice-regent, but which after the exile underwent a change of focus onto the eschatological coming of Yahweh's universal reign. In this way John has already introduced links with Yahweh's kingship before the identity of the king of Israel – which in turn identifies the eschatological king of Ps 118 – is finally established. The allusion to Zeph 3.16 then clarifies that the king of Israel is none other than Yahweh. We thus see a transformation in the Ps 118 quote from first evoking the original OT king, to evoking the eschatological ideal king, and then finally

---

[197] It is remarkable that this holds true not only for Zeph 3.14–20 but also for the other four preferred sources for μὴ φοβοῦ. Each pictures the New Exodus, and the reason given for Israel not to fear is specifically Yahweh's presence and/or imminent return.

[198] Brown, 1.462. Mérode notes that "Jean présente Jésus davantage comme le roi d'Israël au sens où *Yahvé* est le roi d'Israël en So 3, 15" ("L'accueil triomphal," 57).

[199] Losie, "Triumphal Entry," 858. See also Lindars (424), who notes that the Zephaniah passage describes the time "when God is present in the midst of the people as their King." The following criticism applies to him as well.

to providing the bridge for Yahweh's coming as King. Jesus does not only symbolize the return of Yahweh, nor as his vice-regent reign representatively. Instead, even as he has systematically filled and performed the role reserved for Yahweh in the defeat of evil and gathering of the exiles, Jesus enters Jerusalem as the presence of Yahweh. This was the missing – and most critical – part of the New Exodus, now shown as completed when Jesus comes to Zion as the true King of Israel.

On its own this network of OT allusions and transformations plausibly sustains the conclusions drawn, although some may think the bridge cannot support such weight. However, I suggest that the intertextual transformations in the Entrance are both the apex and result of a carefully constructed theological scheme to identify Jesus with Yahweh that includes at its core a network of allusions to the coming one of Ps 118. This network sets the stage so that the reader, when s/he comes to the Entrance, will more readily recognize the connections that I have proposed. It is to this that we now turn, before applying the results to interpreting the Entrance as a whole.

Chapter 6

The Coming One

As J. Schneider has correctly noted, "the significance of Jesus and the nature of His mission are brought out in sayings concerning His coming."[1] Since this bears directly on the Entrance and its use of Ps 118, it is necessary to look more closely at the function of the concept in the Gospel, with an interest in following its development as the reader would see it. Our approach will be to examine in sequence the evidence in John before suggesting what the literary and theological function of the ἔρχομαι network is, how this affects the interpretation of the Entrance, and its relationship to Ps 118.26. The reader should bear in mind that if this "re-telling" of John to highlight the pattern seems repetitious, it only reflects Johannine emphasis and structure. Furthermore, although descent-ascent and sending-returning schema have been noted in the Fourth Gospel, to my knowledge there has been no study of the coming-sent motif as we will approach it.[2] For the sake of convenience I have divided the material in John into six smaller sequential sections. The large number of "coming"

---

[1] J. Schneider, "ἔρχομαι," *TDNT* 2.671. Frey (*Eschatologie*, 203) notes that in John one encounters the title "als Chiffre für Jesus selbst."

[2] There are a number of significant studies on the *Sendungsformeln* in the Fourth Gospel. Their focus, however, is different from ours. Some concentrate primarily on the background of the sending motif. Thus, for example J. A. Bühner concludes that "die ursprünglich jüdisch-esoterische und rabbinisch nachwirkende Verbindung von 'Prophet' und 'Engel' ist damit die grundlegende religionsgeschichtliche Voraussetzung der johanneischen Christologie vom 'Weg des Gesandten'" (*Der Gesandte und sein Weg im 4. Evangelium: Die kultur- und religionsgeschichtlichen Grundlagen der johanneischen Sendungschristologie sowie ihre traditionsgeschichtliche Entwicklung*, 427). J. P. Miranda's equally detailed work (*Der Vater, der mich gesandt hat: Religionsgeschichtliche Untersuchungen zu den johanneischen Sendungsformeln: Zugleich ein Beitrag our johanneischen Christologie und Ekklesiologie*) also centers on background issues, concluding that all paths lead to the eschatological prophet like Moses. Others focus on the ascent-descent and/or coming-returning schema and its significance for Johannine theology (e.g., G. C. Nicholson, *Death as Departure: The Johannine Descent-Ascent Schema*; W. Meeks, "The Man from Heaven in Johannine Sectarianism," esp. 50–68), or on how the sending motif underlies the Gospel's Christology (e.g., J. Kuhl, *Die Sendung Jesu und der Kirche nach dem Johannes-Evangelium*, esp. 58–129; R. Schnackenburg, "'Der Vater, der mich gesandt hat': Zur johanneischen Christologie"; E. Haenchen. "Der Vater, der mich gesandt hat"). None of these emphasizes nor surveys the coming-sent motif, nor am I aware of any study that develops specifically the coming-sent motif as this chapter does.

references – and our purposes – require that this be a general survey. Consequently we will not be detained by the large number of issues that, although appearing in passages we will examine, ultimately are not determinative for the question at hand.

I. Survey of the Coming One Motif

A. *The Prologue and Testimony of the Baptist*

From the beginning Jesus is identified at least in part as one who comes. Jesus was the true light who "was coming into the world" (1.9), who "came to his own" but was not received (1.11). The first witness the Baptist bears concerning Jesus is that "he who comes after me" is greater in rank (1.15). Those who do receive the coming one are given right of membership in the new family of God (1.12). It is the coming one who is greater than Moses (1.17), and is in some sense God himself (1.18).[3] However, John has not identified Jesus specifically at this point, with the result that the reader knows the agent of salvation only as ὁ λόγος and ὁ ἐρχόμενος. This prepares the reader – before even meeting Jesus – to think of him as the coming one, one whose unity with the Father has been established from the beginning in the most remarkable terms (1.1, 18).

John introduces eschatological/messianic speculation early on when the Jews of Jerusalem send representatives to question the Baptist, who denies being any of the eschatological figures they suggest. Who is he, then? The Baptist answers with the words of Isa 40.3, which describes one who will raise his voice to proclaim the end of exile and the return of Yahweh (1.23). When questioned about his authority to baptize, he answers in a way that signals his authority comes from the one for whom he prepares the way (i.e., as his agent he has authority): among them stands one whom they do not know, "the one who is coming after me" (1.26–27). The Baptist refocuses the eschatological/messianic questioning on an unnamed figure who is identified primarily as the one who comes after him, which for anyone familiar with the Isaianic passage that the Baptist has used to interpret his ministry would call to mind the coming of Yahweh.[4] The

---

[3] On the textual issues for this admittedly difficult verse see Metzger, *Textual Commentary*, 169–170. Also M. J. Harris, *Jesus as God: The New Testament Use of Theos in Reference to Jesus*, 73–103.

[4] J. A. T. Robinson ("Elijah, John, and Jesus: an Essay in Detection," esp. 264–270) advances the idea that the Baptist saw himself as preparing the way for Elijah, and that Jesus for a time accepted the Elijah role. In support, Brown (1.44) suggests that the phrase "the one who is to come" may have been a title for Elijah, whom the Baptist

Baptist's witness continues when he recognizes Jesus as the one whose coming he anticipated, clearly identifying the sin-removing Lamb of God (1.29) as the coming one of 1.27: "This is he of whom I said, 'After me comes . . .'" (1.30).[5] Jesus is then identified as Son of God for the first time (1.34), and as the one who will bring the eschatological blessing of the Holy Spirit (1.33).

To sum up: John has highlighted the coming one title by creating a sense of anticipation surrounding the person's identity, until he finally and clearly identifies him with Jesus. In the process John has associated the coming one with the Isaianic coming of Yahweh, and has assigned to the coming one a function that was Yahweh's alone to accomplish – the removal of Israel's sin, which has kept them in exile.

B. Nicodemus, the Baptist, and the Samaritan Woman

Nicodemus identifies Jesus, because of his signs, as a teacher "who has come from God" (3.2). Jesus points out the inadequacy of Nicodemus' view of the kingdom (God's new family, which requires a new birth), and identifies himself as the one God has sent into the world (3.17). He then immediately describes himself as the light that has come into the world and is in conflict with darkness (3.19, in reference to 1.9). Several observations are in order. First, John is establishing a new pattern. This is

---

expected to come. In his comment on John 6.14, Brown (1.235) then states more categorically that he has already pointed out that the phrase is "a description of the prophet Elijah." Whether this was true in Jewish circles at the time, and even if for 6.14 it were a possible background rather than Deut 18, it is difficult to believe that John systematically presents the coming one as Elijah. I suggest there has been a widespread failure to recognize that the Baptist is portrayed by John as the Isaianic herald preparing the way for Yahweh, whose coming Jesus is qualified to fulfill as the enfleshment of Yahweh. This seems the most natural reading of the Isa 40 passage, and it is consonant with John's presentation of Jesus' completing the New Exodus works reserved to Yahweh.

[5] At least as far as the Fourth Gospel is concerned, this answers what J. D. G. Dunn calls the "tangled" question of whom the Baptist envisaged the coming one to be. Dunn argues that according to the Synoptics (Matt 11.3 = Luke 7.19) the Baptist had no clear idea who the coming one was to be, so that "a search for particular scriptural precedents at this point may be wrong-headed in assuming that 'the one coming' was more clearly delineated in the Baptist's mind" ("John the Baptist's Use of Scripture," 50). According to the Johannine Baptist the function of the coming one is clear: Jesus has come to inaugurate the New Exodus. As for a clear scriptural background, I will argue that this is a proleptic allusion to the Entrance and the use of Ps 118 there. Interestingly, Dunn suggests Mal 3.1 and Ps 118.26 as the most likely backgrounds before discarding them. If Mal 3.1 is the intended background, it is notable that the messenger prepares the way for the coming of Yahweh.

the first of many times in the Gospel that Jesus is identified as the sent one (πέμπω and ἀποστέλλω are used interchangeably), and the first time it is used in the same context with the coming one. It is generally accepted that John makes use of descent-ascent and sending-returning schema in his Christology.[6] However, I suggest there is also a coming-sent pairing that few have considered, perhaps because these are not so much contrasting concepts as two sides of the same coin. They are used interchangeably at times, and on other occasions there appears to be a deliberate switch from one to the other. The Nicodemus passage may provide the first example of Jesus responding to an inadequate understanding of his identity by applying to himself the opposite of the title used to identify him.[7] Nicodemus says Jesus is the one who came; Jesus corrects him and says he is the sent one. In the texts ahead I will highlight the coming-sent pattern in the same sequence that the reader would have become aware of it. Second, John is continuing and building on an earlier pattern in which he highlights the unique relationship of the Son and Father in the same context in which he mentions Jesus' identity as the one who comes. Salvation is through believing "in the name of the only Son of God" (3.18), although in the OT it is the revelation of the name of God – by God himself – that is associated with salvation.[8]

The Baptist again testifies to Jesus' identity as "the one who comes from above" and "the one who comes from heaven" (3.31). He then refers to him, with no obvious change of meaning, as "the one whom God has sent" (3.34), and underlines the relationship of the Father and Son that puts everything – authority and eternal consequence – into Jesus' hand. The Samaritan woman refers to the coming of the Messiah: "I know that Messiah is coming . . . when he comes he will proclaim all things to us" (4.25).[9] Jesus promptly identifies himself as the coming Messiah (4.26),

---

[6] So Nicholson, "The story of the Gospel is set between these two actions of descent and ascent and is dependent upon them" (*Death as Departure*, 21). Cf. M. L. Appold, *The Oneness Motif in the Fourth Gospel: Motif Analysis and Exegetical Probe into the Theology of John*, 29. See further J. W. Pryor, "The Johannine Son of Man and the Descent-Ascent Motif," 341–351; R. Kysar, *The Fourth Evangelist*, esp. 185–199; J. Comblin, *Sent from the Father: Meditations on the Fourth Gospel*, 1–19.

[7] "Send" is not opposite to "come," but rather a correlate, for the coming is contingent on and the result of being sent. However, for convenience I refer to it as opposite, with the intended meaning of "the other title."

[8] Cf. Young, "Isaiah," 223.

[9] It is unclear whether John is suggesting that Jesus is the fulfillment of the Samaritan *Taheb* expectation. Meeks (*Prophet-King*, 318 n. 1) argues that the title "Messiah" has been placed in the mouth of the Samaritan woman and is a "clear sign of the levelling of different terminologies." This finds support in J. Macdonald's similar suggestion that "Messiah is hardly the right term in the Samaritan case, for their concept of the one who is to come is not quite like that of Judaism and Christianity" (*The Theology of the Samar-*

and then later to the disciples as the sent one who completes Yahweh's
work (4.34).

To summarize so far: Jesus is described as the coming one, especially
by those who believe in him (the Samaritan woman, the Baptist). He
accepts the designation and identifies himself as the coming one. The
coming one is associated with the works and person of Yahweh in a
number of situations. Gradually the coming one and sent one are being
linked together, so that when the reader encounters Jesus as the sent one,
he associates this naturally with Jesus as the coming one.

C. The First Sabbath Confrontation and the Bread of Life Conflict

Jesus' healing of an invalid on the Sabbath results in conflict with the
religious authorities. However, the argument focuses not on his alleged
Sabbath-breaking but on the question of his identity. Jesus justifies his
Sabbath work by identifying his works with those of the Father, a claim
which scandalizes the leaders because, in calling God his own father, he is
"making himself equal with God" (5.17–18). Jesus then embarks on a
lengthy discourse that confirms the narrator's explanation for the Jews'
opposition: Jesus is indeed equating himself with Yahweh and claiming to
reveal him (5.19–47). He does exactly as the Father – that is, he does the
works of Yahweh, and their actions are inseparable (5.19). The Son raises
the dead and gives life, even as the Father does (5.21), and is entrusted
with all judgment (5.22). No distinction is made in the honor that should
be given equally to Father and Son (5.23). At this point Jesus describes
himself as the sent one, reinforcing the link between Son and Father. Not
to honor Jesus is to dishonor the Father who sent him (5.23), and to hear
Jesus' word and believe the one who sent him leads to eternal life (5.24).
Throughout, his claims to unity with the Father are peppered with
references to his identity as the sent one: the Son has life in himself (that
is, it is innate to him, even as to the Father [5.26]), has authority to
execute judgment (5.27), and will inaugurate the resurrection and
judgment (5.28–29), all in relation to pleasing "him who sent me" (5.30).

---

itans, 361). Whether the intention is to show Jesus fulfilling both Jewish and Samaritan
expectation (so de Jonge, "Jewish Expectation," 268) or not (see K. Haacker, "Samaritan,
Samaria," *NIDNTT* 3.462), the title is applied to Jesus only after he has shown that
Samaritan categories do not adequately account for his function and identity (i.e., Jesus
has not come to restore worship on Mt. Gerazim, but rather to replace both Jewish and
Samaritan centers of worship). This underscores John's program to reinterpret eschatological and messianic titles applied to Jesus, for although Jesus is usually reticent to
acknowledge to the Jews that he is the Messiah, he does so to a Samaritan, although he
has qualified its meaning first. This qualification is reiterated in the suggestive use of
ἐγώ εἰμι in Jesus' response (4.26). See further the discussion in Brown, 1.172–173.

Jesus states, "The Father has sent me" (5.36), and it is "the Father who sent me" (5.37) who is a witness to his unique status. His opponents do not know God because they do not believe "him whom he has sent" (5.38). Jesus then summarizes his discourse succinctly: "I have come in my Father's name" (5.43).

The questions in this major conflict revolve around Jesus' identity and authority, with Jesus equating his work with that of Yahweh, and identifying himself completely with the Father. To know Jesus it to know the Father, for their actions, words, and mission are the same. Jesus repeatedly defines the relationship as sender/sent one, and this is equated with coming in the Father's name: the one who comes in the Father's name is the sent one, and the one whom the Father sends is the one who then comes in his name, revealing him and completing his works. Up to now the reader has had hints of the coming-sent one being equated in some way with Yahweh. From now on, the reader knows Jesus as the coming-sent one who is one with Yahweh.

Conflict erupts again shortly after the miraculous feeding of the five thousand, which encourages the crowd to speculate that Jesus was "the prophet who is to come into the world" (6.14). Jesus withdraws as the crowd wants to make him king by force (6.15), motivated by the thought of securing material provisions (6.27–28). Their inadequate understanding and wrong motives are exposed, and Jesus tells them instead to do the work of God, which is to believe "in him whom he has sent" (6.29). This contains an implicit correction of the crowd, for while they have identified Jesus as the eschatological coming one, he refocuses their attention on his status as the sent one. The correction is reinforced and continued when the crowd asks him to reproduce the works of Moses, in response to which Jesus describes himself as the true bread come down (καταβαίνω) from heaven (6.33, 38, 41, 42, 50, 51, 58). In refocusing their attention Jesus has not denied that he is the coming one, but he has re-interpreted the concept, for he is much more than an eschatological coming prophet.[10] He is the bread of heaven whose mission is to do the will of "him who sent me" (6.38) – that will being that Jesus gather the new Israel and give resurrection life to those who believe in the Son (6.39–40). It is remarkable that belief in the Son and the Father are not distinguished. Jesus answers their grumbling by saying that no one will come to him unless the Father "who sent me" draws him (6.44). In a reference to Isa 54, which pictures the return from exile and destruction of Israel's enemies, Jesus

---

[10] John's interest is not in precisely identifying eschatological figures but in showing that Jesus transcends all of these categories. Thus "prophet" and "king" are linked together in 6.14–15, and in 7.40–41 prophet is distinguished from the title "Christ."

says that its fulfillment is for those who come to him (6.45). Only Jesus has seen the Father, he surpasses the first exodus provision of manna, and because his life is wrapped up in that of the living Father who sent him he is able to give life to others (6.57).

In summation, when speculation about a coming eschatological figure is applied to Jesus, he refocuses the crowd on his being sent and descending from heaven. Unlike the previous conflict, where Jesus identifies himself as the coming one, in the present confrontation he avoids accepting the title. This is a corrective intended to clarify that his identity transcends anything they expect of their eschatological figures. The reader, however, recognizes that the sent one is also the coming one. Jesus' claims as to his identity and source of authority lead to controversy and discontentment, which he answers by highlighting his fulfillment of the New Exodus. As before, John's focus is on explaining the unity of Son and Father, and Jesus' unique identity as correlated with Yahweh's. And once again the discussion is peppered with the coming-sent identification.

D. Tabernacles Conflicts

As Jesus expounds on his unity with the Father the conflicts intensify. At Tabernacles Jesus defines his teaching as not his own but the Father's, "who sent me" (7.16). Jesus is true and there is no unrighteousness in him, because he seeks the glory of the one "who sent him" (7.18). Speculation about Jesus being the Christ follows. The crowds claim to know where Jesus is from, yet "when the Christ comes" no one will know where he is from (7.27). Jesus responds that although they know his origin in one sense, in reality he has come from the Father: "I have not come on my own" (7.28). Instead, it is the Father who "sent me" (7.28), and whom they do not know. In contrast, Jesus knows him because he is from him, and "he sent me" (7.29). The crowds continue to speculate about Jesus being the Christ. Some in the crowd believe, suggesting that "when the Christ comes" surely he will not perform more miraculous signs than Jesus has (7.31). Jesus responds by identifying himself again with the one "who sent me," and to whom he will soon return (7.33). The third round of speculation results from Jesus' claim to give living water (7.37–38). Some think he is the prophet, others the Christ. Still others point out that surely the Christ "does not come" from Galilee, but "the Christ will come" from David and Bethlehem (7.41–42). It is notable that each of the three instances of speculation explicitly characterizes the Messiah as one who comes. In his first response Jesus identifies himself as one who has come, but he points to his unique relationship to the Father. He continues this emphasis by identifying himself with the Father who "sent" him, thus countering their misunderstanding and exposing Jewish messianic categories as insufficient to explain or describe him.

Jesus' answer to the third messianic question follows later, when conflict with the Pharisees resumes over his identity and claims. Jesus can testify on his own behalf because "I know where I have come from . . . but you do not know where I come from" (8.14). He identifies himself as one who has come, but he immediately sets out to qualify what this means: Jesus is not alone in his judgments, for he stands with the Father "who sent me" (8.16). His testimony is confirmed by the Father "who sent me" (8.18), and he is one with the Father, for to know Jesus is to know the Father (8.19). The identification with Yahweh is intensified when he warns his opponents that they will remain and die in sin (i.e., remain in exile) if they do not believe that ἐγώ εἰμι (8.24). This catches their attention, and they ask him who exactly he is. Jesus answers that he has already told them from the beginning, that he speaks the words of "the one who sent me" (8.26), again that he is ἐγώ εἰμι (8.28), that all he does and says reflects the Father, that "the one who sent me is with me" (8.29).

A new conflict erupts when Jesus suggests that the Jews are in bondage to sin, and that their rejection of Jesus entails rejection of Yahweh so that he is not their true father: if God were their father they would love Jesus, "for I came from God and now I am here. I did not come on my own, but he sent me" (8.42). They do not belong to God, for although Jesus speaks in Yahweh's place they reject him (8.47). They do not know the Father, but Jesus knows and is glorified by him (8.55). Then, for the third time in Tabernacles conflicts, Jesus identifies himself as ἐγώ εἰμι (8.58).

To sum up: In each of the three Tabernacles episodes Jesus acknowledges that he is the one who has come from Yahweh (7.28; 8.14, 42).[11] However, he is intent on defining what this means, and showing that he is much more than – and transcends – the categories of any coming messianic/prophetic figure they have expected. The conflicts thus revolve around questions of Jesus' identity and function, with Jesus making a variety of statements that all point to his unique identity in unity with the Father. Especially in the first two episodes, after the initial identification as the coming one Jesus speaks of himself as the sent one. However, as we have noted previously, this is not so much a redefinition as a refocusing of his identification with the Father away from categories that could easily be misunderstood (i.e., coming one). In 8.42 we see the interchangeability of the designations coming/sent. In each of the conflicts Jesus points to his identification with Yahweh, claiming to speak his words and equating knowledge of himself with knowledge of Yahweh. If that were not

---

[11] Tabernacles may run from 7.1–10.21, but for convenience I have separated the section 7.1–8.58 from the second Sabbath conflict.

enough, Jesus refers to himself as ἐγώ εἰμι three times, a claim significant enough to elicit stoning (8.59). As a result, the reader continues to recognize Jesus as the coming-sent one whose function and identity, although subordinate to the Father, are increasingly difficult to distinguish from Yahweh's.

E. The Second Sabbath Conflict, Dedication, and Lazarus

The second Sabbath conflict, like the first, revolves around Jesus' identity. He does the works of Yahweh "who sent me" (9.4), bringing sight to the blind man. His "sent" status is underlined with the reference to the pool of Siloam, which John identifies as meaning "sent" (9.7).[12] Although Jesus is not explicitly identified as the coming one at this point, the approximate meaning is communicated in speculation over his identity, since the unbelief of the religious leaders is definitively expressed in their declaration that they do not know where he is from (9.29), as is the belief of the healed man in recognizing that Jesus must be from God (9.30, 33). Jesus' response to the blind man's belief and his rejection by the Jews confirms this: "I came into this world for judgment" (9.39). In the Shepherd Discourse Jesus says that "all who came before me are thieves and robbers" (10.8; cf. 5.43), probably alluding to messianic pretenders. He further contrasts his coming for redemption with that of the messianic pretender who "comes" only to bring destruction: Jesus "came that they may have life" (10.10). Again Jesus is thoroughly identified with the Father (10.15, 17–18).

Eschatological-messianic speculation again surrounds Jesus at Dedication, when the Jews ask if he is the Christ. Jesus answers that he has told them, but they have not believed. What has he told them? He makes clear that it is his unity with the Father that is in view: "I and the Father are one" (10.30). According to John, the Jews interpret this to be a blasphemous claim, "making yourself God" (10.33). Jesus defends his statement by pointing out that he is the one whom the Father "sent into the world" (10.36). They need to understand that "the Father is in me and I in the Father" (10.38). The Jews again understand Jesus' self-identification with the Father as blasphemous (10.39). A correct appraisal of Jesus is found in Martha's response to his claims to be the resurrection and life: she believes that he is the Christ, the Son of God, "the one coming into the world" (11.27). As the last reference to the coming one before the climactic Entrance, her

---

[12] Siloam may be a play on the name Shiloh in Gen 49.10, perhaps also drawing into John its possible intertextual use in Isa 8.6. Cf. Hanson's suggestion ("Scripture," 364) that it is an example of Johannine allegory.

confession clarifies that messianic expectations surrounding the coming one were justified: the coming one is the Christ. But unlike previous occasions where Jesus responds to the Jews with a corrective when their speculation involves the coming of Messiah, he accepts the designation from Martha because it is born of belief and a truer – albeit still incomplete – understanding of his identity. The resurrection of Lazarus has as its goal the glorification of God and that people "may believe that you sent me" (11.42), a statement that must be understood in reference to the coming one in whom Martha has professed belief.

In conclusion, speculation about Jesus involves and/or is answered by his status as the coming-sent one. True belief involves recognizing Jesus as the coming one. He thoroughly identifies himself (person and works) with the Father, so much so that he is accused of claiming to be God (10.34, 39). John has ensured that as the reader approaches the Entrance narrative there can be no question that Jesus' claims go beyond those expected of a messianic figure – indeed, that they are understood in some sense to claim equality with Yahweh. Lest the reader miss this, John has the Jews accuse Jesus of this very charge four times (5.17–18; 8.58; 10.33, 38–39). Therefore, as Jesus enters Jerusalem acclaimed with the words of Ps 118.26, the reader recognizes that this is the same coming one who has been so thoroughly identified with Yahweh that to explain the precise relationship results in charges of blasphemy.

F. Post-Entry Teaching

1. The Epilogue

The coming-sent one nexus appears again in Jesus' summary discourse that both brings together the primary strands of his teaching and functions as a last call to belief. In the original Isaianic quotes explaining unbelief, it is Yahweh who will heal Israel, but in John it is Jesus who will heal, taking the role of Yahweh.[13] Following these quotations Jesus cries out that whoever believes in him actually believes in "him who sent me" (12.44) and to see him is to see "him who sent me" (12.45). Furthermore, "I have come as light into the world, that whoever believes in me may not remain in darkness. . . . I did not come to judge the world but to save the world" (12.46–47). He concludes by declaring that all of his words were the words of the Father "who sent me" (12.49). It is significant that this summary, which distills in a short paragraph those things that John developed through the gospel and most wanted to highlight, contains *en nuce* the

---

[13] Cf. Painter, "Scripture and Unbelief," 446.

coming-sent theme: Jesus the sent one is completely identified with Yahweh, and Jesus the coming one is the source of light and salvation, bringing us full circle to the coming one of the prologue (1.9, 12).[14]

2. The Last Discourse

We have seen that John uses conflict situations as a forum to reveal Jesus' unique identity and fill with new meaning the eschatological categories of Judaism. The coming one has already entered Jerusalem and been identified with Yahweh, so any subsequent encounters with the phrase will point the reader back to the Entrance and the definitive coming of the King of Israel. Lest the reader have missed the point of the coming-sent motif, the Last Discourse takes up much of the content and main thrust of the conflict discourses and repeats it as teaching for the disciples, confirming and elaborating on what John intended to communicate, only in a friendlier context. The scene in the upper room begins with a reiteration that Jesus had come from God (13.3), which leads to the footwashing. Once again the unity of Son and Father are at the fore: to accept Jesus is to accept "the one who sent me" (13.20), and Jesus calls for his disciples to "believe in God, believe also in me" (14.1). He explains to the disciples his unity with the Father, something they had not yet understood and would not completely grasp until after the resurrection. "If you had known me, you would have known my Father also; henceforth you know him and have seen him" (14.7). Again, anyone who has seen Jesus has seen the Father (14.9), and Jesus repeats the remark which the Jews thought blasphemous in 10.38: "I am in the Father, and the Father is in me" (14.10; again in 14.11). Jesus' words are those of the Father "who sent me" (14.24), and the world, because it does not know "the one who sent me" (15.21), will hate the disciples. If Jesus "had not come" (15.22) they would not be guilty, but whoever hates Jesus also hates the Father (15.23). Jesus acknowledges that at this point the disciples do not understand what he is saying, but promises that in the near future he will explain his teaching about the Father (16.25). For now it is sufficient for them to know that the Father loves them because they have believed "that I came from God. I came from the Father and have come into the world" (16.27–28). The disciples do not yet understand clearly,

---

[14] That the coming-sent motif features so prominently in this summary of Jesus' message and significance confirms it as one of the core themes of the Fourth Gospel. Note Dodd's insightful remark on 12.44–50: "[The verses] form a *résumé* of the leading themes of the discourses in chs. ii–xii. No new theme is introduced; yet the passage is no mere *cento* of phrases from the earlier chapters. It rings the changes afresh upon the themes of life, light and judgment, restating the central purport of what has already been said on these themes, in a series of concise, epigrammatic propositions" (*Interpretation*, 380).

even though they think they do, but what they do affirm – that is, their sufficient confession of faith – is that they "believe that you came from God" (16.30).

3. The Prayer

Jesus' prayer is a last statement and summing up of sorts. Eternal life is to know the only true God, and "Jesus Christ, whom you have sent" (17.3). Jesus shares God's glory (17.5), and describes the paradigmatic faith of the disciples in coming-sent terms: they "know in truth that I came from you; and they have believed that you sent me" (17.8). The "blasphemous" phrase declaring that Jesus is in the Father and the Father in Jesus (17.21) is repeated, Jesus as the sent one is emphasized (17.21, 23), and the knowledge that Jesus was sent is what separates believers from the world (17.25). After the discourse there is only one mention of Jesus as coming, although suggestively it is linked to his kingship: "For this I was born, and for this I came into the world," to testify to truth (18.37). Jesus is identified as the sent one only once more in an actualization of 17.18 where he sends the disciples out even as he was sent (20.21).

To sum up: It is apparent that the coming-sent motif is less ubiquitous than in the pre-Entry discourses. However, it is still scattered throughout the last discourse, is key to explaining Jesus' relationship to the Father, and is central to the belief of the disciples. Jesus three times in sequence tells them he came from God, and the disciples then make this their statement of faith. In Jesus' prayer, belief in him as the coming-sent one is crucial to discipleship and inclusion in the new community. It is also noteworthy that the unity of Jesus and the Father is not yet clear to the disciples. The true identity of Jesus is the most basic and most important misunderstanding in the Fourth Gospel, for we have seen that presenting Jesus as the embodiment of all that Yahweh is forms the core of John's agenda, an objective confirmed by the primary focus of the last discourse as it reiterates in detail what Jesus repeatedly taught in public.

II. The Function of the Coming-Sent Motif

A. Literary Function

The above survey shows that by the time the reader reaches the Entrance Narrative the coming one is a mind-numbingly familiar figure. But apart from ensuring familiarity, the network of coming one allusions functions as a literary tool in three principal ways: it builds towards a climax and arouses dramatic interest, helps to develop the Gospel's plot, and prepares the reader for the Entrance.

The entire public ministry of Jesus points resolutely to the passion, but there are several recurring themes that stand out in this. For example, the repeated journeys of Jesus to Jerusalem, each involving an increasingly longer stay and rising hostility, build suspense that culminates in the final climactic Entrance.[15] This is mirrored in the public ministry of Jesus, where conflict seems to increase from episode to episode, creating a growing sense of danger and anticipation that finally reaches its climax shortly after the Entrance.[16] The previous confrontations foreshadow and show the necessity for this final and decisive conflict for which Jesus specifically has come to Jerusalem. The coming one theme similarly builds towards a climax, first introduced in the prologue, then framed in the major conflicts with the opponents of Jesus, until finally culminating in the Entrance, which is the apex of the coming one network. John also builds dramatic interest in the coming one from early on, with his identity generating a sense of anticipation that continues until the Baptist identifies the enigmatic figure as the exile-breaking Jesus. Eschatological speculation among those Jesus encounters swirls around a coming eschatological figure, but Jesus is a coming one different from – or at least more than – the one they expect, a recurring theme that draws attention to John's progressive and repetitive revelation of Jesus' identity. When the coming one is discussed the reader does not know exactly what to expect: Jesus' reactions are somewhat unpredictable, and although on some occasions true belief follows, the encounters are increasingly characterized by opposition, contention, and accusations of blasphemy. All of this builds interest and anticipation that accompanies Jesus to the Entrance and the conflict where the New Exodus will reach its denouement.

In the most important study of John as a literary work, Culpepper correctly recognizes that "plot development in John . . . is a matter of how Jesus' identity comes to be recognized and how it fails to be recognized."[17] The previous survey shows both that the exposition of Jesus' identity is the heart of the coming-sent motif, and that the coming-sent motif is at the heart of the entire program, so that it functions as a vehicle for plot development. "Coming" is the primary catchword for messianic and other eschatological speculation, for the misunderstanding of Jesus' origin and authority, and is often at issue in the controversies, revealing the ignorance of the religious establishment that opposes Jesus. The coming-sent nexus

---

[15] Cf. F. Segovia, "The Journey(s) of Jesus to Jerusalem: Plotting and Gospel Intertextuality," 539.

[16] Cf. Culpepper, *Anatomy*, 129.

[17] Culpepper, *Anatomy*, 129.

also reveals John's careful arrangement of the Gospel, for he introduces it early and develops it as a theme through repeated and consistent use. As a result the motif becomes instantly recognizable and acquires significant meaning, and thus functions to establish "internal coherence"[18] and advance the primary arguments with which it has become associated. This constant repetition of the coming-sent motif is an important – perhaps obvious – signal arguing for its significance. As Culpepper notes, "the more repetition there is in a work the more evident it is that the author is using repetition to make a point."[19] However, the coming-sent motif has been largely ignored, so that at least in respect to the Entrance some of its more subtle meaning effects have escaped attention.

One of these meaning effects is the linking of belief and rejection with the coming-sent motif in what may be a subtle and probably unintentional parallel to Mark's messianic secret. True belief is marked by recognition of Jesus as the one come from the Father (so the disciples, Martha, the Baptist, the Samaritan woman, the blind man, the crowd at the Entrance). This is the paradigmatic statement of faith, the sign of discipleship and the key to inclusion in the new family of God. It is also the most basic statement of faith, which can be made even by those who are not yet aware of the full implications of what they are saying – they are speaking better than they know. Yet Jesus' opponents are befuddled and continually misunderstand that the coming-sent one is one with Yahweh. When they do have insight into what Jesus is claiming they respond with threats and attempts to kill, thus showing the face of obstinate unbelief. It is apparent that Jesus' unique relationship to Yahweh is somewhat hidden from his opponents, and only partially understood by believers until his glorification, partly because – although the reader may not see this – Jesus has not spoken clearly in explaining his relationship to the Father (16.25).

The coming-sent theme also prepares the reader for later developments. First, John has linked the coming of Jesus with his being sent. This is not the "stereoscopic" perspective that Culpepper and many others have noted in the descent-ascent and coming-return pairs, because they are correlates rather than opposites. However, they share a similarity of function with that which Culpepper assigns to the above pairs: "Only when these perspectives [his origin and destiny] are combined can Jesus be understood. This stereoscopic perspective conditions . . . the gospel's entire characterization of Jesus."[20] Jesus the coming one is also presented as Jesus the sent one. Identifying himself as the sent one refocuses attention on the sending one (the Father), which serves to identity him more closely with Yahweh.

---

[18] The phrase comes from Culpepper, *Anatomy*, 85.

[19] Culpepper, *Anatomy*, 87.

[20] Culpepper, *Anatomy*, 33.

This is the program – to point from himself to Yahweh, ground his coming and authority in Yahweh's sending, and further identify himself with Yahweh in person and ministry. The combination and interchangeability of the two phrases thus conditions the reader to think of Yahweh, and of Jesus' complex unity with him. John also prepares his readers to understand Jesus' coming not simply as the arrival of an expected eschatological figure – Messiah, prophet, or other – but as the return of Yahweh to defeat Israel's enemies, gather the exiles, and reign amongst his people. To ensure that this happens John repeatedly uses the coming one along with expositions of Jesus' identity, and continues to reinforce the same following the Entrance. Let the reader understand.

B. Theological Function

Since John's literary structure functions in service of his theological agenda it is difficult, and for the most part unnecessary, to try and separate one from the other. However, in this mix the coming-sent nexus does at times function in a more overtly theological way. The motif is central to understanding John's characterization of Jesus, who is identified as a coming one 40 times, and as the sent one 41 times.[21] As it is used so often not only to identify Jesus but also in discourses explaining his relationship to the Father, it is inevitably of theological import.

1. Characterization of God

The Fourth Gospel's characterization of God is inseparable from its characterization of Jesus. To know Jesus is to know the Father (8.19; 14.7), to see Jesus is to see the Father (12.45; 14.7, 9), to hear Jesus is to hear the words of the Father (7.16; 8.26; 12.49–50; 14.10, 24), to believe in Jesus is to believe in the Father (12.44; 14.1), and the works of Jesus are the works of the Father (5.19; 14.10). Thus it is not primarily the

---

[21] The references listed for Jesus as one who comes include his own statements and the speculation of others (whether negative or positive) where it specifically relates to his identity and/or function. ἔρχομαι: 1.9, 11, 15, 27, 30; 3.2, 19, 31 (twice); 4.25 (twice); 5.43 (twice); 6.14; 7.27, 28, 31, 41, 42; 8.14 (twice), 42; 9.39; 10. 8, 10; 11.27; 12.13, 15, 27, 46, 47; 15.22; 16.28; 18.37. In addition, ἐξέρχομαι: 8.42; 13.3; 16.27, 28, 30; 17.8. In regard to the use of ἐξέρχομαι, which means "to come forth," note Brown's (1.357) observation that this refers to the mission of the Son and not necessarily the internal life of the Trinity with Jesus proceeding from God. However, although Brown may be correct, it is difficult to separate the two, as the Son's mission is grounded in his unique ontological relationship to the Father. For references to the sent one see footnote below.

Father who speaks and acts in John, but Jesus who does so in his stead. John identifies God most often as Father, perhaps as many as 115 times.[22] What stands out for our purposes is that this title points beyond the Father to Jesus, who is identified as Son (of God or of the Father) 27 times, thus refocusing the reader on the unique relationship he shares with God.[23] The other primary characterization of God is that he has sent Jesus: He is, in Jesus' words, ὁ πέμψας με or ἀπέστειλέν με. Again, although this serves to identify the Father, in all 41 occurrences it is inseparable from the coming-sent combination focused on revealing Jesus' identity.[24] Culpepper concludes correctly that "God is characterized by Jesus and . . . having understood the gospel's characterization of Jesus one has grasped its characterization of God."[25]

2. Characterization of Jesus

The sending of the Son – which is the correlate to coming in the name of the Father – accentuates Jesus' agency. He is the one whom God sent, he comes not in his own name but that of the Father (5.43; 12.13), he does the will of the one who sent him (4.34; 5.30; 6.38–39), speaks his words, and fulfills his mission. The Father commissioned and sent the Son, who came, and completed the Father's works. The characterization of Jesus appears to be that of God's agent, a function/identification not infrequently noted. Davies, for example, suggests that the Sabbath conflicts encouraged the reader to recognize Jesus "as God's agent,"[26] and Meeks argues that John's frequent portrayal of Jesus as envoy or agent is modeled on Moses traditions.[27] P. Borgen provides a comprehensive discussion of Jesus as agent, arguing that John's Christology and soteriology are molded

---

[22] The count is according to G. Schrenk, "πατήρ," *TDNT* 5.996. Culpepper (*Anatomy*, 113) alternatively suggests it is used 118 times, but textual issues make determining an exact number a difficult task.

[23] This does not include the 13 times Jesus is identified as Son of Man.

[24] In effect, it reveals Jesus as the sent one. See 3.17, 34; 4.34; 5.23, 24, 30, 36, 37, 38; 6.29, 38, 39, 44, 57; 7.16, 18, 28, 29, 33; 8.16, 18, 26, 29, 42; 9.24; 10.36; 11.42; 12.44, 45, 49; 13.20; 14.24; 15.21; 16.5; 17.3, 8, 18, 21, 23, 25; 20.21.

[25] Culpepper, *Anatomy*, 113.

[26] Davies, *Rhetoric*, 228.

[27] Meeks (*Prophet-King*, 301–305) wants to show the correlation between Jesus and Moses as God's commissioned agents (cf. J. P. Miranda, *Die Sendung Jesu im vierten Evangelium: Religions- und theologiegeschichtliche Untersuchungen zu den Sendungsformeln*, 47–51). However, there is nothing unique to Moses' commissioning that applies to Jesus. Jesus' commissioning is not especially presented as that of a prophetic agent, but more that of Son, so that he is more than God's representative.

on Jewish rules for agency as found in halakhic sources.[28]   There are striking similarities between the Jewish principles of agency and the Fourth Gospel's portrayal of Jesus.[29] Paralleling these, and probably a more appropriate background considering John's interest in presenting Jesus as king, is the institution of kingship in the OT where the king functioned as Yahweh's representative – that is, a royal agent.

However, although Jewish categories of agency are enlightening, I suggest that they do not adequately explain Jesus' identity and function. Moses certainly acted and spoke in Yahweh's name as the paradigmatic prophet, but his claims would probably never have resulted in the charge of blasphemy. The king functioned as Yahweh's vice-regent and could symbolize and represent Yahweh's reign; but he was always other than Yahweh, in Israel never thought of as divine, and could not actually claim to fulfill Yahweh's reign. As for the agent in halakhic literature, although he could legitimately claim to represent his sender this would be a forensic rather than ontological claim. It is questionable whether agency can actually apply, at least in the sense that Borgen suggests where the one sent is like the sender, to Yahweh and his emissaries. His agents – angels, prophets, kings – are not like him. They may speak and act for him, but there is no comparison or identification of the agent with Yahweh, and they do not function as Yahweh. In contrast, although Jesus is clearly subordinate to the Father and appears to be his agent, he identifies himself with God to the degree that he is accused of blasphemy five times.[30] It is apparent that Jesus is not simply presenting himself as an authorized envoy, but is actually making claims that in some sense portray him as equal to the Father in

---

[28] Borgen, "God's Agent in the Fourth Gospel," 138: "The basic principle of the Jewish institution of agency is that 'an agent is like the one who sent him.' This relationship applied regardless of who was the sender. . . . Consequently, to deal with the agent was the same as dealing with the sender himself." For a detailed examination of Jewish legal sending formulae and the application of these categories to John see Bühner, *Der Gesandte*, 181–267. For a comprehensive and convincing argument against gnostic-Mandean influence on the sending formulae of the Fourth Gospel see Miranda, *Der Vater*, 132–304. Cf. Borgen (ibid., 148), who argues that the influence flows in the opposite direction.

[29] Borgen ("God's Agent," 143–144) notes the unity between agent and sender (in spite of the subordinate role of the agent), the obedience of the agent, the mission of the agent, the return and reporting back to the sender, and the agent appointing other agents as an extension of his own mission. Arguing in support of rabbinic categories of agency as background, C. Bryan correctly observes that this is a legal rather than "mystical" concept: the agent has a commission "and it is in relationship to his commission that the Agent is as the Sender" ("Shall We Sing Hallel in the Days of the Messiah? A Glance at John 2:1–3:21," 35).

[30] Apart from the four previously mentioned occasions (5.17–18; 8.58; 10.33, 38–39), this is also implicit in the charge that the Jews bring against Jesus in 19.7.

function and person. Consequently, although Jewish agency models provide a useful point of reference to understand his mission and identity, Jesus transcends these in the same way that he does Jewish messianic and eschatological categories. His is not the agency of the OT king or the prophet. As God's coming-sent one his agency is unique and unparalleled, so that in some way that is neither clearly nor completely explained Jesus not only represents and symbolizes Yahweh (which he does) but is the actual reality of what he symbolizes and represents.[31]

John accentuates this in the development of the coming-sent motif. The use of symbolism, irony, misunderstanding, and the subtle use of the OT, has signaled to the reader that he must look beyond the surface of the text, and that the meaning of a recurring theme – the coming-sent motif being one of the most pervasive – may expand and grow. This is precisely what happens with the coming-sent theme: John has developed and "grown" it, weaving it into the fabric of eschatological expectation and the exposition of Jesus' identity in such a way that the motif is reinterpreted and invested with new meaning and significance. There is linear development in that, although from the beginning John has shown that the coming-sent one is unlike any agent the reader has heard of, new perspectives come to light over the course of the Gospel that confirm and enrich the understanding of Jesus' identity. The often repeated coming-sent theme ties these different contexts together so that "they resonate simultaneously, thereby allowing the sensitive reader to grasp the whole with increasing appreciation."[32] At the same time, every one of the episodes in which the coming-sent motif functions so concentrates on revealing Jesus' unique identity that each is a reiteration of the same core message.[33] In this way the coming-sent theme is repeatedly reinterpreted only to be filled anew with the same meaning and significance, functioning as a rhetorical sledgehammer that pounds home over and again that Jesus is the very presence of Yahweh.

---

[31] Although Jesus is distinct from, and as Son subordinate to, the Father, he is nevertheless one with him. He is not an agent who represents and even symbolizes his master, but the actual physical revelation of God.

[32] Culpepper (*Anatomy*, 201) makes the comment in relation to recurrent symbols in the Gospel.

[33] This observation is in some ways similar to Dodd's argument that the Book of Signs is constructed so that each of the seven main episodes (according to his proposed division) "contains in itself the *whole* theme of the Gospel" (*Interpretation*, 386; emphasis original).

C. Function in the Entrance

As the coming-sent motif has grown and expanded in meaning, and through constant repetition become inextricably linked to the unique identity of Jesus, it brings to every new episode the meaning it has previously acquired. Although the motif functions in a localized way in each scene, John is also building the network with a larger program as its goal. We have noted that the direction of Jesus' public ministry is very much headed towards and reaches its climax in the final journey to Jerusalem and the attendant events. Not surprisingly the coming one network culminates there as well: what precedes the Entrance anticipates and prepares, what follows reiterates and reinforces. Jesus enters Jerusalem as the one who comes in the name of Yahweh, in a procession reminiscent of the ancient royal liturgies involving the enthronement of Yahweh's vice-regent. However, although the immediate literary context provides the primary interpretive horizon, the transformations, reinterpretations, associations and new meaning acquired by the coming-sent motif reverberate in the reader's ear. The quotation of Ps 118.26 in the Entrance thus is the climax of, and is invested with the meaning carried by, the entire network of allusions.

John has carefully prepared the reader to recognize the coming one not as a Jewish eschatological figure but as the very presence and embodiment of Yahweh. Without the systematic reinterpretation of the coming one theme, the transformation from Jesus as eschatological king to Jesus as the coming of Yahweh in the Entrance depends on the use of the title "king of Israel" in conjunction with the combined Zephaniah/Zechariah quotation – a plausible yet difficult intertextual reading. However, the coming-sent motif has made it not only a plausible but actually the most natural reading, with the coming one providing the bridge, and the addition "king of Israel" and the Zephaniah allusion playing a supporting and confirming role. One might attempt a paraphrase of John: "I have come in the name of the Father. If you have seen me come, then you have seen the coming of my Father. Do you not know that I am completing the works of the Father who sent me? Even as the Father fulfills his New Exodus promises, the Son came to regather the scattered exiles, to defeat Israel's enemies, and to reign as king of the true Israel." In other words, Yahweh, the true King of Israel, has returned to Jerusalem in the person of Jesus.

Such a reading is consonant with John's New Exodus agenda. It is notable that many times the coming of Yahweh in the OT is to do battle with Israel's enemies, especially in New Exodus passages.[34] The return from exile is contingent on Yahweh's coming to destroy Israel's enemies,

---

[34] See especially the passages offered as possible background to the Zechariah combination quote in the previous chapter.

thus providing the circumstances necessary for Israel to live free from fear and under his rule. Yahweh must return, and then accomplish the salvation that gathers the scattered exiles. This is exactly the sequence that John follows, for although the defeat of Israel's enemies and the gathering of the true Israel has been symbolically presented throughout Jesus' ministry, this is in anticipation of his actually translating these into accomplished fact in his being lifted up. The Gospel thus has built towards this climactic week when Yahweh will return to Jerusalem, go into battle to decisively and conclusively defeat Israel's enemies, and by so doing gather the scattered exiles to live under his universal reign. It is entirely consistent with John's high Christology for Jesus to perform these functions which were originally the exclusive province of Yahweh.[35]

III. The Coming-Sent Motif and its Relationship to Ps 118

I have argued that the Entrance forms the climax to the coming-sent motif and is central to John's New Exodus agenda, whose very core is the coming of Yahweh. The prologue has already affirmed the enfleshment of God the *logos* in the person of Jesus, so that the coming of God is more properly seen first in the incarnation. However, from a dramatic and plot-development point of view the promise and implications of the incarnation are realized in the symbolic Entrance to Jerusalem, which signals that the fulfillment of the New Exodus is at hand. It is with the words of Ps 118.26 that Jesus is identified as the coming one in the Entrance, so that even though the function of the quotation depends in large part on the previously developed coming-sent network of allusions, in using it as the locus of the network John is signaling that the quote is of some importance. However, although there can be no serious question that Ps 118 is the source of ὁ ἐρχομενος in the Entrance, there is some question whether Ps 118 was an influence for some of the previous ἔρχομαι allusions. We will now take a closer look at Ps 118's relationship to the coming-sent motif and suggest that its role is more significant than has been previously recognized.

---

[35] His actions do not symbolize those of Yahweh, they *are* those of Yahweh. Jesus has consistently taken Yahweh's place in John. Among other examples, Jesus takes away the sin that has kept Israel in exile (1.29), the Baptist prepares the way for his coming (1.23), he is the one who would heal Israel if only they would turn to him (12.40), he gives life and raises the dead (5.21), all judgment is entrusted to him (5.22), he receives the same honor as the Father (5.23), and is equally the object of saving belief (12.44; 14.1). Eternal life is to know the one true God, and Jesus who came in his name (17.3).

The use of the participial phrase with the definite article (ὁ ἐρχόμενος) suggests that "the coming one" is intended as a title, and it appears to function as such where found in this form (1.15, 27; 3.31; 6.14; 11.27; 12.13). Whether or not it was a technical term for the Messiah,[36] in John it is applied to an eschatological figure(s) (6.14), and used in messianic speculation (4.25; 7.27, 31, 41–42; 10.8, 10; 11.27). Even when the explicit title is not used, if the distinctive of coming describes or defines the character in question, then the title is implicit, for coming is the action of the coming one. Other than Ps 118, the most likely backgrounds for the coming one include Gen 49.10–12, Zech 9.9, and Deut 18.15, 18. In favor of the Oracle of Judah is its intertextual relationship to Zech 9.9, which is partly dependent on Gen 49.[37] Speculation in John (1.21, 25; 6.14; 7.40) about an eschatological prophet is probably based – at least in part – on Deut 18,[38] and Zech 9.9 is of course quoted in the Entrance.[39] In addition, the Zechariah and Genesis passages share with Ps 118 the important ἔρχομαι catch word. It is possible, then, that any – or all – of these may have been in John's mind as he wrote.[40] However, some factors weigh in favor of Ps 118 as the dominant background.

In the LXX ὁ ἐρχόμενος appears only twice (2 Sam 2.23; Ps 118[117].26), and only in the psalm is it used in reference to an individual, and in any

---

[36] N. Hillyer ("λῃστής," *NIDNTT* 3.378) suggests it is a technical term for the Messiah, as do Daly-Denton (*David*, 182) and Moloney, "The Fourth Gospel's Presentation of Jesus as 'The Christ' and J. A. T. Robinson's *Redating*," 249. Schneider likewise states that "in the Messianic dogma of Judaism the Messiah is the coming One" (*TDNT* 2.668). For a contrary view see Meeks (*Prophet-King*, 90), who argues that this cannot be demonstrated. It is noteworthy that in Matthew and Luke the title is invested with messianic significance apart from its Entrance usage. See discussion in ch. 3 above.

[37] See Fishbane, *Biblical Interpretation*, 501–502. Cf. Obermann, *Schrift*, 211. Blenkinsopp, based on the paraphrase of the title "Shiloh" in the Targum, amazingly argues that the "liturgical cry for the one to come . . . whatever its original meaning in the liturgy which Ps 118 contained . . . could hardly have been understood apart from the one that is to come of the Judah Oracle" ("The Oracle of Judah," 59). I question whether the oracle was as dominant as Blenkinsopp suggests. Furthermore, Blenkinsopp does not convincingly demonstrate that Josephus' mention of an oracle (*War* 6.312–315) has Gen 49 in mind, nor that the "Man of the East" in the *Sibylline Oracles* (see references in Blenkinsopp, ibid., 62–63) refers to the Oracle of Judah.

[38] So Meeks, *Prophet-King*, 90; Freed, *Quotations*, 32. Reim (*Hintergrund*, 248–249) assigns a significant role to the expectation of the prophet like Moses for both the coming and sending formulae. Against this see Wright, *Victory*, 163: "The great bulk of the relevant evidence does not point to Jesus being seen in terms of Deuteronomy 18."

[39] I suggest, however, that it plays a supporting and interpretive role to Ps 118. It is thus more likely that the shared coming one motif would depend more on Ps 118.

[40] Krause ("Blessing of Judah"), for example, argues that in Mark's Entrance Narrative the three passages are connected in a meaningful way.

way approximating a title.[41] This does not negate the possibility that the other passages are in view, for Genesis and Zechariah each speak of a figure who will come (i.e., the action of one who comes), but the title provides a unique, and thus striking, parallel to Ps 118. Another verbal parallel is found in 5.43, where Jesus states, "I have come in my Father's name." This is a first person rendition of Ps 118.26, with Jesus substituting the preferred "Father" for "Lord."[42] The combination of ὄνομα and ἔρχομαι is unique to Ps 118(117).26 in the LXX. This suggests that at least in 5.43a it provides the background, and as Jesus' coming in the name of the Father is contrasted with another coming in his own name in 5.43b, that it is also in view there. This same contrast of coming ones is paralleled in 10.8, 10, with Jesus declaring that, unlike earlier messianic pretenders, he came to bring life. This, together with a possible allusion to Ps 118.20 in 10.7, 9, enhances the preference for Ps 118.26 as the background to the coming one in the passage.

The special emphasis in the Fourth Gospel on the name of God is also suggestive, because only in John does Jesus specifically claim that he came in God's name (5.43), and Jesus' mission is characterized by making known the Father's name (17.6, 26), working in the Father's name (10.25), and keeping the disciples in the Father's name (17.12). The three "I Am" statements in John 8 (vv. 24, 28, 58) seem to indicate that God has given his name to Jesus, a suggestion apparently confirmed in Jesus' prayer, "keep them in the name you gave me" (17.11).[43] Because Jesus bears Yahweh's name, only those who believe in his name become children of God (1.12) and find salvation (3.18; cf. 2.23), the Holy Spirit is sent in his name (14.26), there is life in his name (20.31), and the disciples can ask in his name (14.13, 14; 15.16; 16.23, 24, 26). That a number of these citations are closely connected with coming-sent passages, and thus subtly parallel

---

[41] In 2 Sam 2.23 it is used in a plural general sense.

[42] S. H. Blank ("Some Observations Concerning Biblical Prayer," 79) argues that a correct translation of Ps 118.26 is "Blessed be he that cometh, Blessed in the name of the Lord." That is, the coming one is blessed, but does not come in, the Lord's name. Although Blank's translation is not impossible, John 5.43 makes clear that in the Fourth Gospel it is preferable to render the psalm as "Blessed, the one who comes in the name of the Lord." See Dodd's suggestion that to Christian readers the phrase "might suggest the meaning 'May the Coming One be praised *as* κύριος'" (*Historical Tradition*, 154 n. 2).

[43] See further Young, "Isaiah," 223; Dodd, *Interpretation*, 94–96. Note also Brown's (1.457) observation on the importance of the phrase from Ps 118: "In John 'he who comes in the Lord's name' has particular significance, since according to xvii 11–12 the Father has given Jesus the divine name." For a thorough study of the significance of the giving of the name to Jesus see G. F. Shirbroun, "The Giving of the Name of God to Jesus in John 17:11, 12." Among other functions, it authorizes Jesus' ministry and establishes his oneness with the Father (ibid., 282).

the name/coming pairing unique to Ps 118.26, supports my suggestion that the reader would most naturally think of Ps 118 as background. In addition to verbal links, other thematic and liturgical factors also favor Ps 118. The psalm's liturgical use was well known, and its prominent role at each of the main festivals is a factor especially telling in light of the fact that many of the coming-sent allusions occur in a festival context. There are therefore credible reasons for suggesting that Ps 118 formed the primary backdrop for many of the coming one allusions.

In any case, Ps 118's links to the coming-sent network of allusions are not contingent on establishing clear dependence in every case, for intertextual influence flows in both directions: the prior network influences the reading of the coming one in the Entrance, but the strategic placement of the coming one in the Entrance results in a re-reading of the theme. The coming one network is now understood as a series of proleptic allusions to the quotation of Ps 118.26 in 12.13, a literary role that can only be appreciated with hindsight, after the reader has reached the climactic Entrance. All previous coming one allusions refer to Jesus, who as the coming one in the Entrance brings to fulfillment in a formal and dramatically enacted sense the expectation of Yahweh's return. Is 5.43 then a freestanding allusion to Ps 118.26, or is it a proleptic allusion to the Ps 118.26 quote in the Entrance, or is it both? Is the coming one of 1.15 or 11.27 an allusion to Ps 118.26, or to some other passage, or to the Entrance? I suggest it is pointless to try and force a distinction between allusions to OT "coming" passages – whether Ps 118.26 or others – and repeating internal prolepses to the quotation of Ps 118.26 in the Entrance.[44]

Barrett has pointed out that John contains themes that are based on the OT but not upon one single passage, so that the evangelist "seems to have collected the sense of the O. T. and applied it in one vivid phrase, or picture."[45] Although I argue that Ps 118 is a suitable and likely primary background, it is possible that the coming one could be one of these themes used repeatedly in John without a clear indication of what passage it refers to. There is after all a web of eschatological expectations and OT passages that points to a coming figure, and it is possible that some of these inform John's use of the motif and/or specific allusions, thereby adding another resonant background. But although Ps 118 is probably not the single background to every coming one allusion, and regardless of whether or not one can show conclusively that Ps 118 is the background to

---

[44] This is a paraphrase of Culpepper, *Anatomy*, 62: "It is pointless to force a distinction between suggestive allusions and explicit repeating prolepses." Although Culpepper's comment is not in reference to the use of the OT, it can be adapted and applied in that direction.

[45] Barrett, 162.

many of the specific allusions (it unquestionably is to some), the Fourth Gospel's structure places the Ps 118.26 quote in 12.13 at the head of the coming one network, tying and binding it together and providing its primary interpretive point of reference. In this sense it does not matter what the OT background to each individual coming one allusion is, for the internal links in John relate them one to another and all as a group to Ps 118, so that they function in a proleptic sense prior to the Entrance, and analeptically when following it.[46] Once the coming one is clearly identified in the direct quotation of Ps 118.26, its strategic placement ensures that – if they were not related before – the network of coming one allusions will be read in light of and associated with the Entrance use of Ps 118.

Conclusion

The Ps 118.26 coming one is linked to a network of allusions to the coming-sent one that is at the heart of John's program to identify Jesus with Yahweh. The coming one is linked with the sent one, and the terms and concepts are sometimes used interchangeably and usually in close proximity, so that when the reader encounters Jesus as the sent one s/he naturally recognizes him also as the coming one. John programmatically takes up Jewish speculation about an eschatological and/or messianic coming one, shows these categories to be inadequate, and gives an exposition of Jesus' true identity, with the result that the reader identifies Jesus as the coming-sent one whose function and person are equated with Yahweh. The designation of coming-sent one has thus been reinterpreted and filled with new meaning, so that when Jesus enters Jerusalem the reader understands this as the coming of Yahweh, for Jesus is the embodiment of all that Yahweh is. The coming-sent motif functions as a literary tool to arouse dramatic interest and build towards the Entrance climax, to help develop the Gospel's plot, and to prepare the reader for the Entrance. It functions theologically in the Gospel's characterization of Jesus and of the Father, and in advancing John's New Exodus agenda. John's systematic reinterpretation of the coming one provides the bridge for the coming of Ps 118's eschatological king to be transformed into the coming of Yahweh. The psalm's influence extends beyond the climactic Entrance, since the extended network of coming one allusions, regardless of what original OT Scripture each may have as background, function either as proleptic or analeptic allusions to the Ps 118.26 coming one.

---

[46] This also parallels their literary and theological function, which first prepares the reader and establishes the unique identity of Jesus (proleptic), and then confirms and reiterates the latter (analeptic).

I have argued that Jesus' Entrance to Jerusalem not only symbolizes and represents but actually is the New Exodus coming of Yahweh to end the exile and defeat Israel's enemies. Up to now we have looked primarily at Ps 118's role and function in John's agenda, but the thesis advanced also has a number of implications for the reading of the Entrance following the Ps 118 quote. It is to this we now turn.

Chapter 7

Re-reading the Entrance

I. Introduction

A crowd has come out from Jerusalem, joining with witnesses to the Lazarus sign in acclaiming Jesus with the words of Ps 118.25–26. In response to their ovation Jesus finds and sits upon a donkey in fulfillment of Zech 9.9, and then proceeds into the city as the crowds continue the jubilant welcome. The disciples do not understand until after the resurrection that "these things were written of him, and that they had done these things to him" (12.16). In response to the widespread support Jesus has attracted, the Pharisees lament that "the world has gone after him" (12.19). It is when one compares the Johannine and Synoptic accounts that this apparently straightforward and simple sequence of events takes on greater significance. The explicit mention of the disciples' misunderstanding is unique to John. In addition, although John's quotation of Zechariah is both shorter and combined with a different Scripture than Matthew's, it is the different sequence in mounting and acclamation that is determinative for most scholars' interpretation of the passage. The Synoptics highlight the acquisition of the mount, signaling Jesus' intention to enact the coming of Zion's king, so that the mounting of the donkey precedes and is the cause of the accompanying crowd's acclaim and use of Ps 118.[1] In John this sequence is reversed, as the crowd's jubilant welcome precedes and apparently is the immediate cause for Jesus' finding and mounting the donkey. Jesus' action is thus a response (or reaction), and as such interprets both the action of the crowd and the character of the Entrance.

---

[1] This is clear in Matthew, and implicit in Mark and Luke where Zech 9.9 is not explicitly cited. Krause sees in Mark's account of the acquisition of the colt a reversal of Judah's blessing (Gen 49.10–12) so that the reader is prepared for a portrayal of Jesus "as less than peaceful and less than traditionally messianic" ("Blessing of Judah," 151). Although in John the coming of Jesus is positive (there is no cursing of the fig tree, no Temple Action, and the vineyard is not given to others), her argument provides an interesting parallel to mine, for John has prepared his reader to see Jesus as much more than any expected messianic figure, and, as I will argue ahead, a warrior king.

Although the cause for Jesus' mounting the donkey is fairly straight-forward (i.e., the acclamation of the crowds), his purpose in doing so is less clear. In addition to determining the function of the Zechariah quote, this also bears significantly on interpreting the crowd's use of Ps 118. We will look first at the explanation for the Johannine sequence supported by the great majority of scholars before challenging it and proposing an alternative reading. Following this we will examine the function of the Zechariah quote and the misunderstanding of the disciples.

II. Mounting the Donkey: Correction or Affirmation?

A. *Survey of Scholarship*

The majority of scholars interpret Jesus' action in mounting the donkey as a correction of the crowd, who in waving palm branches and acclaiming Jesus as king are displaying nationalistic expectations. It is only after the crowd has expressed these expectations that Jesus gets the donkey and sits on it, so that his action is a "protest" against the nature of the welcome,[2] "an acted parable designed to correct the misguided expectations of the pilgrim crowds,"[3] a "subtle correction of the people's nationalistic inter-pretation of messiahship,"[4] and a "prophetic action designed to counteract" nationalistic misunderstanding.[5] As a result of his action, the nationalistic expectations of the crowd supposedly are dampened down.[6] It is not only the sequence of the action but also the mount Jesus chooses that signals this correction. Zechariah's king is peaceful, humble and gentle, and thus

---

[2] Hoskyns, 422.

[3] Bruce, 259–260.

[4] Lindars, 420–421, 423. According to Morris (586) the action is intended "to sym-bolize a conception of messiahship very different from that of the crowds." Similarly, Beasley-Murray (210) argues that Jesus aimed "to correct a false messianic expectation."

[5] Brown, 1.462–463. Lightfoot (250) argues that κραυγάζω (12.13) caries an "especially sinister" sense in John, where it is used four times to describe the crowds crying out for Jesus' death: "This is probably sufficient evidence that the cries of the crowd are to be understood here also as having an unfavourable – perhaps we may say fanatical – character."

[6] So Carson, 433. Cassidy also suggests that "such a startling step could only serve to dampen any nationalist expectation on the part of the crowd" (*New Perspective*, 51–52). Coakley advances the unusual and unconvincing suggestion that "*Jesus did not intend to ride the donkey at all but was made to do so by enthusiastic followers*" ("Entry," 479; emphasis original). According to Coakley the gospel writers aim to minimize aspects which would represent Jesus as being not in control of events, and therefore present the account as they do: "At best we may imagine resignation on his part: he was not going to escape this time, and events would have to take their course" (ibid., 482).

riding a donkey shows that Jesus comes as Prince of Peace.[7] The donkey was also the animal used by merchants, businessmen, and men of peace.[8] Had Jesus come as a conqueror or warrior he would have used a war horse, but he chose its antithesis – a donkey – which therefore functions as a symbol of peace and a rejection of nationalistic expectations,[9] for Jesus will not accept the acclaim of the crowd until they correctly understand his peaceful mission.[10]

Aspects of this misunderstanding-correction scheme have been challenged occasionally.[11] Barrett, for example, accepts that the selection of the donkey may be a correction of nationalistic enthusiasm, but suggests it is "equally possible that he [John] is simply straightening out the story in terms of its Old Testament components: Jesus is greeted as the coming King in the language of Ps. 118; next he finds an ass and so fulfills Zech 9."[12] Whatever the original sequence, the majority view assumes that the crowd's action was nationalistic, that Jesus' action would serve – i.e., be understood – as a corrective, and that Jesus' intentions were completely peaceful. I suggest that each of these assumptions is open to question and that a different reading makes better sense of the Entrance: Jesus is affirming rather than correcting, the crowd is expressing true belief rather than a misguided sense of nationalistic messiahship, and Jesus is coming as a warrior king.

---

[7] See Lindars, 420–421; Tenney, 127; Morris, 586; Kysar, 192.

[8] Tenney, 127; Morris, 587.

[9] So Beasley-Murray, 210; Carson, 433; Bruce, 260; Losie, "Triumphal Entry," 859; and Cassidy, *New Perspective*, 51–52. Schnackenburg (2.376) comments: "The riding on a donkey, as opposed to the war-chariots and horses of a king, is a symbol of this [the peaceful character of the saving king]." Cf. van Bergen: "Il rejetait les conceptions messianiques du peuple" ("L'entrée messianique," 23).

[10] Others who subscribe to variations of the misunderstanding-correction view include Bultmann, 412–413; Becker, 2.378–379; Lightfoot, 238; Sanders and Mastin, 288; Kysar, 191; Malina and Rohrbaugh, 209; Schnackenburg, 2.375; Stibbe, 133–134; Davies, *Rhetoric*, 215; Menken, *Quotations*, 86, 87 n. 29; D. Moo, *The Old Testament in the Gospel Passion Narratives*, 182; Schuchard, *Scripture*, 77; Daly-Denton, *David*, 177–178; and W. A. Visser 't Hooft, "Triumphalism in the Gospels," 502–503.

[11] See März, *Siehe*, 43; Meeks, *Prophet-King*, 87; M. de Mérode, "L'accueil triomphal de Jésus selon *Jean*, 11–12," 51–52; Ridderbos, 424.

[12] Barrett, 418.

B. Affirmation and True Belief

1. Jesus' Response to the Crowd's Acclaim

The argument for misunderstanding and subsequent correction rests in large part on the assumption that the crowd's acclaim for Jesus is nationalistic in character. We will look at the action of the crowd below, but Jesus' actions – rather, what he did not do – suggest that correction is not in view. First, there is no indication that Jesus verbally corrected the crowd. Were the intentions and character of the crowd's acclaim unacceptable to Jesus, his silence would break with the pattern established in the survey of the coming-sent motif where Jesus has not hesitated to deflect verbally and reinterpret eschatological and messianic speculation about the coming one. Instead it fits the pattern of Jesus' accepting the title of coming one when used by those who believe.[13] Since the acclaim is specifically in reference to *the coming one*, the patterns developed earlier in the Gospel thus help to interpret Jesus' response in a more positive sense. In fact it appears that Jesus accepts the homage offered the coming one by those who witnessed or have heard of the Lazarus Sign.[14] Accordingly, Jesus' finding and mounting the donkey is a direct response to the crowd, but his intention is to accept and affirm their acclaim of him as the coming one, the true king of Israel.[15] Second, although the Entrance shares some features with the attempt to make Jesus king after the feeding miracle (6.14–15), unlike that occasion Jesus makes no attempt to flee.[16] His specific action, coupled with lack of action in other areas (not correcting and not fleeing), is therefore consistent with how he has responded to belief in the past, and completely out of character if the crowd's acclaim is nationalistic in character.

---

[13] True belief is marked by recognition that Jesus has come from the Father: so the disciples, Martha, the Baptist, the Samaritan woman, and the blind man.

[14] Cf. van Bergen ("L'entrée messianique," 13 and n. 8), who argues for a crowd composed of disciples along with those who witnessed the resurrection of Lazarus, joined by a group made up of pilgrims and youths. However many different groups the crowd was composed of, the issue is how their actions are portrayed.

[15] Cf. Ridderbos, 424: "In the Johannine context Jesus' 'finding' and mounting the donkey is his direct response to the acclamation of his kingship by the people and his acceptance of it – in keeping with the salvific kingship of God over Israel pictured in prophecy and the reign of the humble king of peace and justice."

[16] Against this, Schnackenburg (2.374) suggests that the attitude of the crowds is similar, and Beasley-Murray (210) that the scene is "uncomfortably reminiscent of the attempted messianic uprising mentioned in 6.14–15." So also Malina and Rohrbaugh, 209.

2. The Crowd

The crowd's use of "the coming one" parallels positively that of true believers who have used the title for Jesus. In another link to true belief the crowd interprets the coming one as the king of Israel. Jesus has earlier declared Nathanael to be ἀληθῶς Ἰσραηλίτης (1.47), and he in turn responds by calling Jesus the Son of God and the King of Israel (1.49), a paradigmatic confession of faith that Jesus accepts as true belief (1.50). It is the true Israelite who believes in Jesus and acclaims him as the true king of Israel.[17] There is probably a contrast intended between Nathanael the true Israelite and the unbelieving Jews, just as Jesus is positively identified as king of Israel, and derided as king of the Jews. Carson and Ridderbos argue that Nathanael is not a prototype of true and complete belief, and no contrast is intended with unbelief.[18] However, Jesus affirms his belief and promises that more will be revealed, and the fact that his belief is incomplete is of little consequence, for it is axiomatic that no one can truly understand completely the identity and function of Jesus until after the resurrection. Therefore, even though their understanding is not completely informed, the crowd in their recognition of Jesus as king of Israel represent the true Israel of God, for it is belief that determines the true Israelite. In this way Jesus' public ministry ends with the same confession of faith with which it began, now stated by a crowd that has initiated the enthusiastic welcome in a context of mass conversion, as many were putting their faith in Jesus on account of the Lazarus Sign (12.10–11). The Entrance crowd, rather than being a nationalistic mob, thus joins Nathanael as true Israelites – that is, disciples of Jesus.[19]

This characterization of the crowd as exhibiting belief receives support from the wider context of the Entrance with its emphasis on the growing popularity of Jesus. John wants to show that Jesus has a considerable following among the people, in contrast to the growing antagonism of the religious authorities. As Passover approaches the pilgrims expectantly look for Jesus (11.55–56) even as the leaders seek to arrest him, but this opposition does not deter the crowds who come to Bethany to see Jesus,

---

[17] So also Brown, 1.87: "It is Nathanael, the genuine Israelite, who hails him; and therefore 'the king of Israel' must be understood as the king of those like Nathanael who believe." Cf. Bultmann, 104 n. 4; Schnackenburg, 1.316; Barrett, 184–185. Davies (*Rhetoric*, 210) strangely suggests that Nathanael recognizes Jesus as a true Israelite.

[18] Carson (160) argues that Nathanael is not a convert in any sense. If he became a disciple he still had to pass through a lengthy period of misunderstanding. Jesus is referring to him as an Israelite in the sense that Palestinian Jews commonly referred to one another. Nathanael is thus a certain kind of Israelite, in whom there is no guile. Similarly Ridderbos, 89–90.

[19] Meeks (*Prophet-King*, 87) argues for the same parallel that I have presented. Cf. Schnackenburg, 2.376: the crowd "represents Israel as the people of salvation."

and the many who put their faith in him (12.9–11).[20] Whether or not these were permanent conversions is not the point.[21] It is true that their belief is primarily in response to the Lazarus Sign (cf. 2.23; 4.45, 48; 6.2, 14; 11.45), and that sign-belief has not always met with Jesus' approval (2.24–25; 6.14–15; 4.48). However, the Lazarus Sign is not presented in a negative light in the Entrance, and John's focus is decidedly on the crowd's acclaim of Jesus and that he entered as king. Of the four Gospels, John is the clearest in showing broad support for Jesus, with the crowds – in number great enough to cause the Pharisees to despair – joining the disciples.[22] The Entrance is the highpoint of the belief motif that John repeatedly emphasizes in chs. 11–12, showing that the majority openly believe and it is a minority – albeit a powerful one – that rejects.[23]

An objection to this is that following the Entrance the motif of rejection and unbelief resurfaces (12.37), apparently revealing that the crowd did not truly believe. It is possible that the statement of unbelief refers to the Entrance crowd, but if so their negative response would be to Jesus' predicting his death (12.23–33), and not the result of any corrective action he took in the Entrance. In any case, it is not clear that the statement of unbelief (12.37) – and the quotations of unbelief that follow it (12.38–43) – refer specifically to the Entrance crowd or, if they are the same, to the crowd that heard Jesus' death-prediction. The section 12.37–50 is chronologically separate from the preceding incidents, and the unbelief section is a summary of the unbelief that Jesus encountered throughout his ministry specifically *in spite of all the miraculous signs*, none of which took place in or following the Entrance. Admittedly there is tension between the motifs of belief and unbelief, seen here in that immediately following the quotations of unbelief John again highlights widespread belief, for even many among the leaders – the prototypes of unbelief – believed in him (12.42).[24] It is thus reasonable to argue that widespread belief is the dominant characteristic in the Entrance, with the only clear unbelief being that

---

[20] Ridderbos (412) notes that the crowds "no longer allow themselves to be intimidated by the authorities."

[21] Carson (431) correctly observes for the conversions in 12.10–11 that "the calibre of their faith is not assessed."

[22] Luke limits the acclaim to the band of disciples. I suggest that Matthew and Mark are best understood as portraying widespread support for Jesus in the Entrance, but some interpreters have argued that this is limited to the disciples. In any case, there is no ambiguity in John about the composition of the crowd extending beyond the circle of disciples.

[23] See Painter, "Scripture and Unbelief," 442–443.

[24] Painter ("Scripture and Unbelief," 445–446) points out that even though their belief is qualified (12.43), John does not hesitate to say they believed.

of the religious authorities.[25] The crowd is "the world" that has gone after Jesus, the true Israel who acknowledge him as their king, in sharp contrast to the unbelieving Pharisees, who in rejecting the king of Israel end up repudiating Yahweh's kingship (cf. 19.15).

In addition to the belief motif, the contrasting of the crowd with the unbelieving Pharisees, and the Nathanael parallel, two other factors point away from Jesus' action being corrective. First, it is never explicitly stated that the Entrance crowds misunderstood Jesus as a nationalistic Messiah. Only the disciples' misunderstanding is highlighted, and they certainly were not expecting armed insurrection. Second, if mounting a donkey was intended to dampen the crowd's enthusiasm, then Jesus utterly failed to accomplish his aim, for the crowd's acclamations continued unabated. If they had intended a messianic uprising, and Jesus' action failed to communicate his resistance to this, then they would have continued on to make him king and revolt against Rome. However, since their enthusiasm remained undiminished, and they did not proceed to insurrection, this suggests that their intentions were not revolutionary to begin with. Furthermore, it is very difficult to explain how Jesus' mounting of the donkey in John could function as a corrective, when this was the very action that precipitated the enthusiasm and acclaim depicted in the Synoptic accounts. In the Synoptics the mounting intensified expectation, and there is no reason to think that this powerful symbol would have accomplished any less in John.[26]

III. The Warrior King

Much is made of Jesus' choosing to enter Jerusalem on a lowly donkey instead of a war horse, and how this supposedly corrects the nationalist expectations of the crowd and symbolizes the coming of a gentle and peaceful king. However, a closer look at the Zechariah quote and its form in John, and a re-evaluation of the donkey, raises some questions about this interpretation.

---

[25] Against Carson (435), who argues in regard to the Entrance that John "does not accord a very high place to the crowd's positive response to Jesus," and that unbelief is the dominant motif.

[26] Although many scholars argue that the mounting in John was a corrective, there has been no explanation offered that adequately accounts for how the symbolic function could differ so dramatically from that of the Synoptics.

A. The Original Context of Zech 9

The original literary context of Zech 9.9 does not portray the coming of
Zion's king as a completely peaceful and non-violent event. The chapter
begins with an oracle of judgment promising destruction to a list of
Israel's enemies (Zech 9.1–8). The Lord will take away Tyre's possessions,
destroy her power, and consume with fire – and no better fate awaits
Damascus, Sidon, and other places (Zech 9.1–4). Ashkelon will fear and
be deserted, Gaza will writhe in agony and lose her king, Ekron's hope
will wither, Ashdod will be occupied, and the pride of the Philistines will
be cut off (Zech 9.5–6). Those who are left will belong to Yahweh, who
will defend his people against all oppressors (Zech 9.7–8). The coming
of Zion's king precedes what Bruce understatedly calls "a disarmament
programme" that will bring peace.[27] However, if the chariots are removed
from Ephraim and the war horses from Jerusalem, and the battle bow is
broken (Zech 9.10), it is not because hostilities have ceased, but because
Yahweh will never allow their enemies to oppress them again (Zech 9.8).
As for Israel's enemies, their disarmament is neither optional nor voluntary. The king's proclamation (read: command) of peace to the nations and
Yahweh's extension of his rule over the entire world (Zech 9.10) is by
force: the prisoners are released (Zech 9.11–12), Judah will be his bow,
and the sons of Zion will be like a warrior's sword against the sons of
Greece (Zech 9.13). Then Yahweh will appear, shield his people, and they
will destroy and overcome (Zech 9.14–17). In conclusion, the original
context of Zech 9 shows that the coming of Zion's king, as gentle/humble
as he may be, is that of a warrior whose kingdom will be extended by
conquest and force.

An intensification of the king as warrior is evident in the LXX rendition
of the Hebrew Zech 9.9. The Hebrew makes a clear distinction between
Yahweh (Zech 9.1–8, 10) and Zion's king (Zech 9.9), with Yahweh as
warrior and defender of Israel. As for Zion's king, the Niphal participle of
ישע, which is passive in meaning, suggests that he enters as one saved by
Yahweh.[28] The LXX, however, translates with the present active participle
of σώζω, so that it is Zion's king who comes saving. As Weren notes, "the
king himself is a saviour or liberator, he fulfills the same role that in the
Hebrew text is God's due."[29] The blurring of their roles continues in Zech
9.10, for while the Hebrew has Yahweh speaking in the first person as
warrior ("I will cut off the chariot . . . and the war horse"), followed by a
switch to the third person for the king's proclamation of peace, the LXX

---

[27] Bruce, 260.

[28] It can, however, also carry the sense of being victorious in battle, as preferred by
the RSV.

[29] Weren, "Jesus' Entry," 128.

continues in the third person from Zech 9.9, with the result that Zion's king takes the active role in removing the threat to Israel before announcing peace and extending his rule. If any of John's readers were able to compare the Greek of Zech 9.9 with the Hebrew, they would have noted this suggestive link between Jesus and Yahweh. More important for our purposes, every reader of Zechariah – and especially those familiar with the LXX – would see that to secure the New Exodus the king of Zion comes as a warrior.[30]

B. The Warrior in John

Since John has considerably shortened the quotation of Zech 9.9, it is remarkable that the single characteristic that remains to describe Zion's king is his riding on a donkey. Had John intended – as many scholars argue – to stress the humility or gentleness of Jesus as a corrective to the crowd, he could have quoted further and used the word πραΰς, as Matthew did (Matt 21.5).[31] However, it is not John's primary intention to emphasize Jesus' humility, which in any case is not stressed in the original Zechariah context either.[32] I suggest rather that one of the functions of the Zechariah quote is to show Jesus as a warrior. The quote is compressed to the point

---

[30] Menken (*Quotations*, 82–83) claims that it is impossible to decide whether the Hebrew text or the LXX underlies John's quotation of Zech 9.9. The LXX gives a correct translation of the Hebrew in all elements that are quoted in a recognizable way. Μὴ φοβοῦ, as I have suggested, comes from Zeph 3.16. The last phrase, καθήμενος ἐπὶ πῶλον ὄνου, matches neither the Hebrew nor LXX exactly. This may be due, as Barrett (419) suggests, to John rewriting simply and clearly the difficult Hebrew parallelism of Zech 9.9b, "caring more for the sense than for verbal accuracy." Or, more likely, the changes are intended to evoke Gen 49 and Israelite traditions of kingship. In any case, since most of John's readers probably used the LXX it is especially likely that they would recognize Zion's king as a warrior.

[31] The fact that John does not include πραΰς does not mean that Jesus' humility/ gentleness is not in view. However, we can reasonably suggest that had John wanted specifically to emphasize his humility then the easiest and clearest way to do so would be to quote as Matthew did. What must be kept in mind is that although Zion's king is presented as humble/gentle, this is in a context of military prowess. The OT context underlines his gentleness in regard to his people, and his warrior character as revealed against their enemies, a portrayal not inconsistent with the Johannine Jesus. In support see Brown, 1.462: "It is not an action designed to stress humility, for John omits the line of Zechariah cited by Matthew." Menken (*Quotations*, 87 n. 29) makes essentially the same observation, although he argues that the intention is to show that Jesus is not a king in the limited national-political sense but the king of peace whose victory will not come by violence. So also Schuchard, *Scripture*, 79. The three, however, interpret Jesus' action as corrective.

[32] Meeks (*Prophet-King*, 87) is one of the few who notes this aspect of Zechariah's original context.

that the mounting of the donkey signals a fulfillment of Zech 9.9 and its surrounding context, which in turn shares its principal themes with the Zeph 3 passage with which it is combined, thus emphasizing that the two passages illuminate each other. As we have seen, Zeph 3 portrays Yahweh as a mighty warrior coming to save his people from exile and defeat their enemies. Zechariah 9 is also a New Exodus passage, depicting Yahweh (and/or the king) destroying Israel's enemies and restoring the prisoners. There follows the promise – surrounded by exodus imagery – that Yahweh will gather and redeem his scattered people (Zech 10.6–12), and the climactic return of Yahweh to reign as king (Zech 14). The two passages thus draw the reader deep into the New Exodus theme, and provide a backdrop against which Jesus' Entrance and mission must be interpreted.

One can agree with a number of suggestions put forward by scholars who interpret Jesus' mounting action as correcting the crowds. For example, Carson argues that the Zechariah quotation presents Jesus as a gentle king, so that "he could never be reduced to an enthusiastic Zealot."[33] It is also true that the humble king is associated with the proclamation of peace to the nations and not strictly to Israel – he is not a nationalistic king. However, what many have failed to recognize is that the Prince of Peace is also a warrior king, and that there is no fundamental contradiction in this. Our characterization of Jesus as warrior corresponds to that other Johannine writing, the Revelation, where Jesus is to his own a gentle king, but to his enemies the Lamb who is a Lion, the fearsome warrior King of kings who implacably and utterly destroys all his foes (Rev 5.5; 19.11–21).[34] That the two works share the same portrayal of Jesus makes it more likely that John's community of readers would recognize the warrior motif in the Fourth Gospel. The text of Zechariah describes Zion's king coming on a donkey, in contrast to the war horse, because he hates war, and his goal is to establish peace for the nations. However, to achieve this he must first go into battle. Indeed peace will result, the prisoners will be released, and his reign will be established universally, but this happens only after the powers are disarmed. Even as Yahweh comes as a warrior in Zechariah and Zephaniah, in the Fourth Gospel's New Exodus program Jesus must defeat the powers of darkness and sin if he is to restore the scattered people of God.

When Jesus mounts the donkey as Zion's king the reader recognizes that he is coming as a warrior, and that his humility/gentleness neither contradicts this function nor is primarily in view, just as it is not the emphasis

---

[33] Carson, 433.

[34] This is consistent with the OT tendency to present the Kingship and sovereignty of God as especially manifested in the context of battle against his enemies. It is possible, as Watts suggests (*New Exodus*, 137–169), that Mark applied a Yahweh-Warrior motif to Jesus. Cf. Marcus, *Way of the Lord*, 23.

of the Zechariah passage. John first introduces Jesus as the warrior king of Ps 118 who has returned triumphant from battle, and then as Zion's king, whose mission of peace is extended by war. Jesus thus enters Jerusalem as a warrior king whose victory is proleptically celebrated by his people. Paradoxically the way to triumph and glory passes through death and apparent defeat, but the blood Jesus will shed is that of the new covenant which secures release for the prisoners (cf. Zech 9.11), and gains the decisive and final victory.[35] Although the conclusive battle looms ahead, the outcome is never truly in doubt – how could it be? For the distinction of roles between Yahweh and Zion's king, which was already blurred in the LXX, has been obliterated in John and is another signal to the reader that the warrior king is none other than Yahweh enfleshed.

C. The Donkey

Many scholars have assumed that mounting the donkey was a sign of humility and a correction of nationalistic conceptions of messiahship. Jesus certainly rejected the latter, but as we have argued, the donkey, even if contrasted with the war horse, should be read in light of the entire Zech 9 passage, which portrays Zion's king as a warrior who commands and establishes peace. Apart from this, rather than a sign of humility, the donkey – lowly animal that it may be – functioned symbolically in Jewish thought in a way more powerful than words to emphasize kingship and authority.[36] Earlier I suggested that the symbolic riding of the donkey was a claim to and/or a confirmation of kingship (so Absalom, Mephibosheth, and Solomon), and the mount of choice in the ancient coronation ceremony.[37] In addition, it appears that in taking the donkey which he "found" (12.14),

---

[35] Ps 118 may provide a thematic parallel that functions as a subtle balance, for while Jesus is acclaimed as the royal coming one of Ps 118.26, the reader may also be drawn back to 118.22 and the rejection/suffering that must precede exaltation. Jesus is acclaimed as a liberating king, but the discerning reader knows that the path to glory passes through rejection and humiliation and ultimately the cross. Thus Ps 118 functions to heighten Jesus' royal status, and even though it does not do so verbally, it may also subtly recall the rejected stone, providing tension and an ominous forewarning of a process not yet completed.

[36] In any case, it is not clear that riding a donkey would indicate a sense of humility, especially in a festival context where one typically proceeded on foot into Jerusalem. See Bernard, 426: "It is not to be thought that there is any suggestion of *humility* in riding upon an ass."

[37] See discussion in ch. 5/IIIB above. The use of καθήμενος in 12.15 to describe Jesus' sitting on the donkey may also evoke the enthronement ceremony. Schuchard points out that the verb "is characteristically used in the OG, with Josephus, and in the New Testament to describe a king (or God) sitting on his throne" (*Scripture*, 81). He points then to 1 Kgs 1 as especially significant in this regard.

Jesus was claiming the right to impress (i.e., take temporary possession of) another's animal, a royal prerogative rooted in Jewish social history and also practiced by Roman authorities.[38] Although unlike the Synoptics John does not emphasize the acquisition of the donkey, Jesus' action is nevertheless consistent with a claim to authority as the true king of Israel.[39] Such a claim would be intensified if through the quotation in 12.15 John intends to evoke Gen 49.10–11, since the phrase he uses to designate the donkey (πῶλον ὄνου) is used in the LXX only of the coming ruler's mount in Gen 49.11.[40] This is a plausible although subtle allusion that, apart from connecting the three primary OT coming one passages,[41] would accentuate the eschatological implications of Jesus' coming and his authority over Israel. The expected ruler is powerful, owning the "obedience of the peoples" (Gen 49.10), and oversees a time of prosperity and, presumably, peace (Gen 49.11). Significantly, Kinman notes that "a clear example of a Jewish king riding a horse is not to be found in the LXX."[42] Perhaps to a Roman the mount Jesus chose would not be a cause for excitement, but for those familiar with the donkey as symbol in the OT, Jesus' action confirmed his authority and kingship, and proclaimed that he was the king who would secure Israel's peace and prosperity.

In conclusion, the donkey is a symbol not of humility but of authority and kingship. Jesus' mounting of the donkey intensifies his claims to kingship, evokes the ancient enthronement liturgies with which Ps 118 is associated, and facilitates the transformation of Ps 118's king to the eschatological king. Those who argue that riding the donkey entails a rejection of the crowd's allegedly nationalistic claims have not given due attention to the context of Zech 9 which the quote evokes. As Ridderbos points out,

---

[38] For a description of how this act would have been understood by Jews and others see J. Derrett, "Law in the New Testament: The Palm Sunday Colt."

[39] Cf. Derrett, "The Palm Sunday Colt," 257–258. There is an interesting rabbinic use of Zech 9.9 that compares Moses and the Messiah: "R. Berekiah said in the name of R. Isaac: As the first redeemer was, so shall the latter Redeemer be. What is stated of the former redeemer? *And Moses took his wife and his sons, and set them upon an ass* (Ex. 4.20). Similarly will it be with the latter Redeemer, as it is stated, *Lowly and riding upon an ass* (Zech. 9.9)" (*Eccl. Rab.* 1.28). I agree with Barrett (419) that although in the Midrash the Messiah is compared to Moses, there is no such comparison intended in the Entrance.

[40] Menken (*Quotations*, 94–95) argues that John borrowed the phrase from Gen 49.11 to connect the passage with Zech 9.9. Cf. Schuchard, *Scripture*, 82–83.

[41] As noted earlier, Zech 9.9 is already linked intertextually to Gen 49.11 in the OT, so that John's quotation of Zechariah could subtly evoke Gen 49 regardless of whether this was John's specific intention. See Menken (*Quotations*, 88 n. 33) for a list of Jewish and Christian texts that interpret the Genesis passage messianically.

[42] Kinman, *Entry*, 52.

"in the prophecy riding a donkey serves not as a criticism of and warning against nationalistic monarchy but as a message of salvation."[43] Accordingly, there is no indication that the riding of the donkey is perceived by the crowd as a correction to their enthusiastic acclaim. Jesus, well aware of the donkey's symbolic significance in Jewish history and prophecy, could not have chosen a mount that would more clearly evoke the New Exodus traditions he was coming to Jerusalem to fulfill.

IV. The Function of the Zechariah Quote

The combined quotation of Zechariah provides the vehicle for John to introduce the Zeph 3.16 passage which may have provided – and at the least interprets – the "king of Israel" title added to the immediately preceding quotation of Ps 118.25–26. As in the original Zephaniah passage, the Gospel's call not to fear, which replaces Zechariah's original call to rejoice, is exultative because Yahweh has removed the cause of Israel's fear: he is returning to defeat their enemies, gather the scattered, and reign as king. Both Zephaniah and Zechariah share similar New Exodus themes that support and underscore John's design in the Fourth Gospel, and because of the LXX's blurring of the functions of Yahweh and Zion's king, the Zechariah quotation also helps to establish Jesus as functioning in Yahweh's place.[44] The addition of Zephaniah provides a linking function that intensifies Zechariah's traditional ties to Ps 118,[45] and further indicates John's intention to connect closely the two principal OT quotations in the Entrance and have them illuminate each other, a function of the Zechariah passage that becomes clear in its reiteration of several Ps 118 themes. I have argued that the fulfillment of the Zechariah prophecy functions as an affirmation of the acclaim offered by the crowd. As a result, Zechariah, although it deepens and expands several central themes, plays a supporting role to Ps 118, attesting that Jesus the coming one is indeed the king of Israel.

---

[43] Ridderbos, 424.

[44] This characterization of Jesus is not dependent on the Zechariah quote, for it has already been established repeatedly in John. Even without the LXX change, the fulfillment of the Zechariah passage would still depict Jesus as functioning in Yahweh's place, for Jesus not only announces peace (the original function of Zion's king in the Hebrew), he also provides the means to achieve it (i.e., Yahweh's role).

[45] I have previously shown the connections between Ps 118 and Zechariah through the Tabernacles Festival in ch. 2 above. In addition see Kim's ("Stone") exploration of the links between Ps 118 and Zechariah and his argument that they are foundational and determinative in Jesus' self-identification.

John's characterization of Jesus as a warrior king begins with the original Ps 118 coming one, a warrior king who has endured and emerged victorious from battle, a depiction supported by Zechariah's peace-loving warrior king. The Zechariah quote intensifies the eschatological and saving character of Jesus' kingship, who as Zion's king comes with salvation and the blood of the covenant in his mission to save the world (cf. 11.52; 12.19, 20; 12.32). This salvation has already been anticipated in Ps 118: in the Hosanna, in the coming one's proclamation of the salvation Yahweh has accomplished (Ps 118.14, 21), and in his arrival to Jerusalem which is accompanied by the shining of God's light upon his people (Ps 118.27). The two passages are therefore mutually supportive and interpretive. Taken together with John's emphasis on and knowledge of Jewish liturgy, this suggests that in combining Zechariah and Ps 118 he may have had one other significant connection in mind: the ancient enthronement festival.

I have argued that the enthronement of the OT king was both implicitly and explicitly an affirmation of Yahweh's absolute kingship. The Festival of Tabernacles, which was so closely connected with royalty, projected the eschatologization of the ideal of kingship onto the coming of Yahweh to reign universally, a hope most succinctly preserved in Zech 14. It is likely that Ps 118 was used in the ancient festival, and certainly the link is clear in the Tabernacles water liturgy performed in the time of Jesus. On each of the seven days of Tabernacles a procession went to the pool of Siloam and drew water, returned to the temple, and poured it in one of the silver bowls placed on the altar. These are the bowls mentioned in Zech 14.20 at the eschatological Tabernacles where Yahweh's universal kingship will be celebrated every year.[46] It was at this water libation ceremony that Ps 118 was sung, the lulab shaken, and Hosanna shouted. It is likely that John's readers would be aware of this Ps 118-Zechariah-Tabernacles complex, for he appears to expect knowledge of the ceremony, which provides at least in part the background to Jesus' claim to be the source of living water (7.37–38) in fulfillment of the eschatological river of Zech 14.8 and Ezek 47.1–5 that marks Yahweh's return.[47]

When Jesus enters Jerusalem acclaimed as the royal coming one of Ps 118, and does so symbolically on a donkey, the scene evokes the ancient royal enthronement festival. Jesus is not becoming king, for from the beginning the reader has known him as king of Israel (1.49), but the Entrance is the symbol-laden ceremony that affirms his reign publicly. The title "king of Israel," the use of Ps 118, and the Tabernacles symbols John has empha-

---

[46] See *m. Sukh.* 4.9.

[47] See rabbinic expectation of the eschatological water in *m. Šeqal.* 6.3; *m. Mid.* 2.6; *t. Sukh.* 3.3–9.

sized, would invite an interpretation of the Entrance as the enthronement of Yahweh's vice-regent, which would axiomatically celebrate Yahweh's kingship. However, the reader knows that to recognize Jesus' kingship is not simply a vicarious acknowledgment of Yahweh's kingship. The royal Entrance at a deeper level is not ancient Israel's kingship celebration re-enacted, but its eschatologized manifestation – the Tabernacles of Zechariah celebrating Yahweh's return and his universal kingship.[48]

V. The Disciples' Misunderstanding

One significant question remains in the Entrance passage: What is it that the disciples misunderstood? John reports in 12.16 that at first the disciples did not understand "these things" (ταῦτα οὐκ ἔγνωσαν αὐτοῦ οἱ μαθηταὶ τὸ πρῶτον). Because this immediately follows the riding of the donkey and the Zechariah quote, most scholars have interpreted the statement in reference to Jesus' action. However, John continues on to inform the reader that it was only when Jesus was glorified that the disciples remembered that these things were written about him and they had done these things to him (ἀλλ' ὅτε ἐδοξάσθη Ἰησοῦς τότε ἐμνήσθησαν ὅτι ταῦτα ἦν ἐπ' αὐτῷ γεγραμμένα καὶ ταῦτα ἐποίησαν αὐτῷ). This suggests that John could be referring to the use of Ps 118 together with or separate from Zechariah, since they both were "written about" Jesus, and only the use of Ps 118 actually involves a deliberate action taken by someone other than Jesus.[49] The interpretation turns on what "these things" refers to, with three main lines of argument most frequently advanced. The first suggestion is consistent with the interpretation of Jesus' action as corrective: the disciples misunderstand the peaceful nature of his kingship;[50] along with the crowd they do not recognize that Jesus is rejecting political and nationalist aspi-

---

[48] John's community of readers would later recognize this Tabernacles celebration in Rev 7.9, where the throne of Yahweh has become the throne of Yahweh and the Lamb (Rev 5.6; 7.17; 22.1, 3), and the coming of Yahweh, who in Revelation is ὁ ἐρχόμενος (Rev 1.4, 8; 4.8), becomes the coming of Jesus (Rev 1.7; 2.5, 16; 3.11; 16.15; 22.7, 12, 17, 20).

[49] Unlike the Synoptic tradition where the disciples procure the donkey and put Jesus on him, John does not record that the disciples actually did anything to Jesus. It is possible that John assumes knowledge of the Synoptic account or, as Brown (1.458) suggests, that "they" should be understood as equivalent to a passive. The RSV translates with this passive sense.

[50] Beasley-Murray, 210. Lagrange (326) suggests they did not understand the fulfillment of the prophecy of Zechariah. Cf. Patsch, "Der Einzug Jesu," 14. Schlatter (266) adds that the Jerusalemites were as unaware of the fulfillment as the disciples.

rations and refusing to stir up insurrection against the Romans,[51] nor realize that his kingship is one of peace and humility, not war.[52] The second option is that the disciples did not recognize that Jesus was Messiah. Barrett, for example, suggests that John was unaware of the contradiction he introduced in that the crowds recognize Jesus as Messiah but the disciples do not understand what the crowds do.[53] The third position argues for a theological misunderstanding. Brown maintains that the disciples did not understand the theological insight that the Zechariah passage affirms, namely, that universal kingship will not be achieved until Jesus is lifted up in death and resurrection.[54] Ridderbos similarly claims they did not realize that in taking up kingship Jesus had to be "lifted up,"[55] and Dodd that they did not recognize the Entry as a sign of Jesus' death and resurrection.[56]

Each of these positions is significantly flawed. There is some truth in the argument for theological misunderstanding, since the disciples did not understand until after the resurrection the significance of Jesus' being "lifted up" and his universal kingship. On two other occasions, both concerned with the death and resurrection of Jesus, John reports that the disciples did not understand the Scriptures until later (2.22; 20.9). However, these insights are misapplied to the Entrance, for although the use of the palm branches does proleptically and subtly celebrate Jesus as conqueror of death, that is not the main point of the procession, and it is difficult to see how Jesus' action signals his being "lifted up." As for the most prevalent interpretation, it is unnecessary to argue again that the mounting of the donkey was intended not to correct misunderstanding but to affirm the crowd's action. It is also extremely unlikely that the disciples failed to recognize Jesus as the Messiah when they had previously confessed him as

---

[51] Carson, 434; Kysar, 192.

[52] Cf. Morris, 588. Brown (1.463) also suggests they did not recognize Zechariah as counteracting nationalism. Hoskyns (420) claims that the disciples misunderstood not only Jesus' action but also the misunderstanding of the crowd, and thus joined ignorantly in the welcome.

[53] Barrett, 419. Lindars (420) appears to support Barrett.

[54] Brown, 1.463. According to Borchert ("Passover," 312), the disciples failed to understand "the real nature of glory."

[55] Ridderbos, 424. He argues further, "That it was specifically the humility of the donkey-riding king over which his own should rejoice – *that* they would understand only in the light of Scripture. And then they would understood (*sic*) it in the profound sense that Jesus had given to that humility: he was welcomed into the city by the crowd not only as the prince of peace but also as the one to be crucified there as 'the king of the Jews'" (ibid., 425). Cf. Daly-Denton, *David*, 187.

[56] Dodd, *Interpretation*, 370. He argues that in a symbolic sense the Bethany Anointing was Jesus' burial, so that in the Entrance Jesus rides on the donkey as symbolically dead and risen. Von Gemünden ("Palmensymbolik," 62) suggests that what became clear is that the way to Jesus' death would be the way into life.

such. Accordingly we can suggest what the disciples did know, and what they did not expect. John portrays the disciples as being aware that Jesus was king (1.49), albeit unlike any king they had expected. In addition, Sanders has argued persuasively that they did not expect a political kingdom established by force of arms.[57] The lack of response from the Roman authorities confirms that they did not regard Jesus or his disciples as a political/military threat. The disciples were not rounded up and executed as insurrectionists, and the Entrance was not a factor in the trial. It is true, as Marshall comments, that "the title of king was perhaps politically dangerous, certainly open to misunderstanding."[58] This does not, however, mean that in being called king Jesus would necessarily be seen as a rival to Caesar – that would depend more on the nature of his claims to kingship and whether or not he undermined Roman rule. That this is the case is apparent from Pilate's reaction to Jesus' acknowledgment that he is king, for if his statement were seen as a claim to rival Caesar then Pilate would have made no attempt to free him.[59] It is telling that the acclamation of Jesus as king of Israel provokes not the anger of the Romans, but that of the Pharisees. Therefore it is very unlikely that the disciples misunderstood Jesus as the leader of a rebellion, or that in acclaiming him as king of Israel they somehow did not recognize he was Messiah. In fact there is a much more promising explanation for the misunderstanding.

Throughout the Fourth Gospel the most consistent misunderstanding has to do with Jesus' identity as being one with the Father. In the survey of the coming-sent motif I showed that this is the principal issue in the majority of the controversies.[60] Whenever Jesus answers speculation (whether nationalistic, eschatological, and/or messianic) it is always in terms of his unique relationship to the Father. Jesus deflects comparison to any notable figures – the Davidic Messiah, Moses, the eschatological prophet – because as the enfleshed presence of Yahweh he utterly transcends all of these categories. Throughout the Gospel the most consistent misunderstanding of the dis-

---

[57] Sanders, *Jesus and Judaism*, 231: "It is now virtually universally recognized that there is not a shred of evidence which would allow us to think that Jesus had military/ political ambitions, and the same applies to the disciples. . . . They knew, in wandering around Galilee, that an army was not being created . . . They expected *something*, but not a conquest. Thus, except for the especially dense, *their expectation throughout must have been for a miraculous event which would so transform the world that arms would not be needed in the new kingdom*." (Emphasis original.)

[58] Marshall, *Historian and Theologian*, 161.

[59] Cf. Kinman, *Entry*, 103; E. Bammel, "The *titulus*," 353–364; Cassidy, *New Perspective*, 51.

[60] In support of my position, see Carson's detailed chart ("Understanding Misunderstandings in the Fourth Gospel," 91) of misunderstandings in John, which shows that misunderstanding almost always concerns Jesus' identity and/or mission.

ciples also concerns the identity of Jesus. Significantly, the exposition of
his identity underpins and is the principal subject of the Last Discourse, but
even then the disciples, who more than any others have repeatedly heard
this most essential truth, do not yet truly understand, for although they are
examples of true belief, it is axiomatic that until Jesus is glorified their
understanding is partial. I suggest that at its core this is the misunderstanding of the disciples in the Entrance. Each of the three OT citations in the
Entrance (four if we accept an allusion to Gen 49.11) deals with the coming
of a king. Zephaniah describes the King of Israel – Yahweh – coming to
his people; the Zechariah quote centers on the coming of Zion's king to
institute Yahweh's universal kingship; and Ps 118 provides the coming
one that bridges the gap between the eschatological king and Yahweh. It is
thus most likely that the misunderstanding has to do with the significance
and character of the coming king.

I suggest there are three levels of understanding in play. First, both the
crowds and the disciples understood that Jesus entered Jerusalem as the
coming eschatological king. Their belief is true although incomplete, as is
the case with every other example of true belief in the Fourth Gospel. John
signals the second (delayed) level of understanding with the historical
prolepsis of 12.16: it was only later, after the resurrection, that the
disciples (and other believers) understood the full import of the coming of
Jesus in light of his unity with the Father. That is, they recognized that
Jesus' coming signaled the completion of Yahweh's eschatological plan
for Israel (to redeem them from exile, defeat their enemies, and reign as
their universal king), since Yahweh's coming was actualized in Jesus. For
the reader, however, the incarnation makes this clear from the beginning,
and it is subsequently developed and confirmed through the programmatic
exposition of Jesus' identity in the confrontations with the Jews and in the
contrasting context of true belief. The reader stands above the disciples,
privileged with information that became fully obvious to them only later.
At this third level, the reader recognizes that when Jesus enters Jerusalem
as the coming one it is no less than the coming of Yahweh. Accordingly,
what the disciples failed to understand at the time was that Jesus' Entry to
Jerusalem was the actual return of Yahweh to inaugurate the New Exodus,
a misunderstanding that results from not yet recognizing that Jesus is the
physical presence of Yahweh in this world.[61]

---

[61] This is a significant point of disagreement with Wright, who argues that Jesus
came "as the representative of the people of YHWH, to bring about the end of exile, the
renewal of the covenant, the forgiveness of sins" (*Victory*, 539). I have argued that the
New Exodus agenda must be carried out by Yahweh, and that Jesus is portrayed as the
physical presence of Yahweh amongst his people. The strength of my suggestion
concerning the disciples' misunderstanding is that it is consistent with the greater

To sum up: Our development of the coming-sent motif and a consequent application of the findings to the Entrance has resulted in a re-reading that brings into question some of the most prevalently held interpretations of the passage. First, our conclusions challenge the argument that in mounting the donkey Jesus intended a correction of the allegedly nationalistic expectations of the crowd. Instead, Jesus' action is an affirmation of the crowd's acclaim as an expression of true belief. Second, rather than being a sign of humility intended to dampen the enthusiasm of the crowd, riding the donkey is a symbol of authority and kingship that evokes the ancient enthronement liturgies of Israel. Third, a closer examination of the original context of Zechariah supports our suggestion that Jesus enters Jerusalem as a warrior king. It has further been argued that the quotation of Zechariah invites the reader to interpret the Entrance in light of the eschatological Tabernacles celebration of Zech 14, where Yahweh returns to reign. Fourth, the misunderstanding of the disciples has to do with their failure to recognize Jesus' Entry to Jerusalem as the actualization of Yahweh's return to inaugurate the New Exodus.

---

misunderstanding theme in the Gospel, and with the misunderstanding exhibited by the disciples earlier in the Gospel and in the Last Discourse. It also is consistent with the New Exodus theme, and makes sense of the Entrance without resorting to a dubious correction of nationalism.

Chapter 8

"Abraham rejoiced . . .": Ps 118 in John 8.56

I. Introduction

Jesus' enigmatic statement in 8.56 that Abraham rejoiced to see his day
has puzzled commentators and remains somewhat unclear despite the
variety of backgrounds suggested. I suggest that Ps 118 provides a partial
background to this passage, and that such an understanding resolves some
of the passage's difficulties. The verse comes towards the end of the larger
literary unit 8.31–59 that is marked by growing controversy and hostility
and held together with references to Abraham.[1] The larger unit is often
divided into three smaller literary sections, although they can be read
together as a unified discourse.[2] In the third section the Jews accuse Jesus
of being possessed by a demon (8.48), interpreting his statement that those
who keep his word will not see death (8.49–51) as a claim to superiority
over Abraham and the prophets – clearly evidence of demonic possession
(8.52–53)! In response Jesus declares that it is the Father who glorifies
him, and that Abraham rejoiced to see his day (8.54–56), an assertion met
with mocking incredulity (8.57) that in turn elicits the dramatic ἐγώ εἰμι
statement from Jesus in 8.58. Incredulity turns to indignation as the Jews
attempt to stone Jesus, but he hides and escapes from the temple. Our
attention will focus primarily on the literary subsection 8.56–59 which
forms the climax to the chapter.[3]

The first task is to establish the plausibility of an allusion to Ps 118.24
in 8.56,[4] after which several questions need to be answered: What event is

---

[1] The ten references to Abraham, who is not mentioned elsewhere in the Fourth
Gospel, hold together the dialogue. See further C. H. Dodd, "A l'arrière plan d'un
dialogue johannique," 4–17.

[2] See W. Kern, "Die symmetrische Gesamtaufbau von Joh. 8, 12–58," 451–456. He
suggests that the discourse 8.31–59 can be broken into three smaller strophes, dividing
the third as 8.49–58. Whether one divides at 8.48 instead, as many do, the section is recognizable as a unit. For a literary overview of the passage see R. Robert, "Étude littéraire
de Jean VIII, 21–59."

[3] Although Bultmann (325) unnecessarily classifies 8.31–59 as a fragment, he recognizes 8.56–59 as a unit in the last of his three sections (8.48–59).

[4] Dittmar (*Vetus Testamentum*, 339) notes the parallel of Ps 118.24 to John 8.56 and
Rev 19.7, but does not treat the former as an allusion. Similarly, R. Mörchen ("Johanne-

Jesus referring to? Can the statement "Abraham rejoiced" be connected directly to this event? Why does Jesus assert that Abraham has seen his day? Why does Jesus state, "Before Abraham was, I am" (8.58), and what, if any, is the connection to 8.56? In addition to these last two questions of function, one must ask whether Ps 118 can be connected with Abraham.[5]

II. Establishing the Allusion: Ps 118.24 in John 8.56

John 8.56	*Ps 117.24 (LXX)*	*Ps 118.24*
Ἀβραὰμ ὁ πατὴρ ὑμῶν <u>ἠγαλλιάσατο</u> ἵνα ἴδῃ <u>τὴν ἡμέραν</u> τὴν ἐμήν, καὶ εἶδεν καὶ <u>ἐχάρη</u>.	αὕτη <u>ἡ ἡμέρα</u> ἣν ᾽ποίησεν ὁ κύριος <u>ἀγαλλιασώμεθα</u> καὶ εὐφρανθῶμεν ἐν αὐτῇ	<u>זה־היום עשה</u> <u>יהוה נגילה</u> <u>ונשמחה בו</u>

Apart from its startling claim about Abraham, the text provides several clues that should send the reader back to the OT. First is the rare verb ἀγαλλιάω, whose use is confined to the Bible and the early church,[6] and which appears infrequently in the NT.[7] Second, the unique combination of words in this verse also suggests that rather than being merely descriptive they are intended to draw attention to a pre-text. The combination of ἀγαλλιάω and χαίρω appears in the NT only four times, with two of these in the Johannine literature.[8] The NT combination of these verbs with ἡμέρα is also rare, the noun appearing only once with ἀγαλλιάω (John

---

isches 'Jubeln,'" 249) lists several LXX texts, including Ps 117.24, as paralleling the rejoicing in John. There is, however, no indication that an allusion has been identified.

[5] Several of these questions are the same as those asked by L. Urban and P. Henry in their article, "'Before Abraham was I am': Does Philo Explain John 8:56–58?" However, our answers are quite different.

[6] See Bultmann, "ἀγαλλιάομαι," *TDNT* 1.19. He argues that there is one single exception, and this possibly under Christian influence. This suggests that if one does look for a background, the most obvious source is Scripture.

[7] Bultmann notes that ἀγαλλιάω (and its more popular middle voice) is a new construct from ἀγάλλω or ἀγάλλομαι. In the NT it occurs only in 11 verses: Matt 5.12; Luke 1.47; 10.21; Acts 2.26; 16.34; John 5.35; 8.56; Rev 19.7; 1 Pet 1.6, 8; 4.13.

[8] Matt 5.12; 1 Pet 4.13; Rev 19.7; John 8.56.

8.56) and twice with χαίρω (John 8.56 and Luke 6.23).[9] The combination of the three key words – ἀγαλλιάω, χαίρω, and ἡμέρα – is unique in the NT to John 8.56. Third, these two verbs of rejoicing were especially associated with cultic settings.[10] For example, the OT antecedents of ἀγαλλιάω were "almost entirely restricted to the Psalms and the poetic parts of the Prophets."[11] This suggests that rather than Jesus' second phrase in 8.56b being tautological or unnecessary repetition of the first,[12] one should consider the possibility of intentional parallelism, one of the characteristic features of Hebrew poetry.

The wording of 8.56 has attracted some attention, although not in the areas that we have pursued. For example, Brown notes that it is "strange" for the first verb to be stronger than the second, when one would expect the joy at fulfillment to be stronger than that at the initial promise.[13] At least some of the proposals for mistranslated Aramaic originals underlying the text are driven by the difficulties scholars encounter in explaining the passage and the choice of words.[14] It is not unreasonable to suggest that unusual language patterns call attention to themselves, and possibly to precursors. However, the search for possible backgrounds has focused almost entirely on locating an appropriate event, to the exclusion of verbal parallels.[15] A search of the OT suggests that some of these difficulties –

---

[9] It is also used with εὐφραίνω twice (Luke 16.19 and Acts 7.41), which would parallel the LXX wording for Ps 118(117).24.

[10] The OT most often uses χαίρω "in a cultic relation, joy as festal joy and its expression" (H. Conzelmann, "χαίρω κτλ.," TDNT 9.363). Note that in the NT the combination of the two verbs in Rev 19.7 conforms to this, and I suggest that John 8.56 does as well.

[11] Bultmann, TDNT 1.19.

[12] Kysar (146), for example, calls it "redundant."

[13] Brown, 1.359.

[14] For example, Burney (Aramaic Origin, 111) suggests that ἠγαλλιάσατο means "to long." C. C. Torrey argues that 8.56 contains a tautology that could not have been present in the original Aramaic, suggesting that ἀγαλλιάω is a mistranslation of the Aramaic through haplography. Instead, Abraham "desired, or prayed, to see my day" ("The Aramaic Origin of the Gospel of John," 329; cf. idem, Our Translated Gospels, 144, 148). Boismard ("Importance de la critique textuelle pour établir l'origine araméenne du quatrième évangile," 48–49) arrives at a conclusion similar to Torrey's, although by different means: the original Johannine text preserved "to desire" rather than "to rejoice." It is not necessary, however, to resort to Aramaic mistranslation. See Moulton's (A Grammar of New Testament Greek, 2.475–476) evaluation of Burney and Torrey and his conclusion that an Aramaism in the ἵνα clause is "needless." For further argument see Urban and Henry, "Philo," 163–164; Barrett, 352; Schnackenburg, 2.494 n. 139.

[15] Identifying an occasion (as most scholars attempt to do) when Abraham explicitly "rejoiced" is obviously informed partly by verbal considerations, but for the most part the possibility that the unique verbal combinations (not just the act of rejoicing) are a signpost has been neglected.

the sequence and choice of words – may find a solution in acknowledging an allusion to Ps 118.24.

The MT combines the verbs גיל and שמח a number of times (27), most often in the Psalms (12), including Ps 118.24. However, their use with יום is restricted to two verses: Ps 118.24 and Isa 25.9. The combination found in Ps 118.24 is therefore extremely rare, just as that in John 8.56 which, if alluding to the psalm, translates the Hebrew words faithfully.[16] Although 8.56 most closely reflects the Hebrew, I suggest it is possible that John used the LXX. The problem is that where Ps 117.24 (LXX) uses εὐφραίνω, John uses χαίρω. The most natural way of identifying an LXX pre-text to 8.56 would be to search for combinations of ἀγαλλιάομαι and χαίρω, but the three occurrences are not relevant to John's use of the words, and most importantly are never combined with the critical noun ἡμέρα.[17] In the other direction, if looking for verbal allusions to Ps 117.24 (LXX) in the NT, the combination of ἀγαλλιάω and εὐφραίνω is found only once, in an Acts 2.26 quotation of Ps 16.9, again without ἡμέρα .[18] The combination of ἀγαλλιάω and ἡμέρα, which is used only once in the NT (John 8.56), may be sufficient to link Ps 117.24 (LXX) with 8.56, for although the combination appears four other times in the OT,[19] none of these corresponds contextually to John's use.

Significantly strengthening the verbal parallel is the correspondence between Ps 118.24's "be glad in *it*" (i.e., in the day), and John's "rejoiced to see my day." In both cases the important connection is that of rejoicing and the day. More precisely, the day is not simply the date, time, or occasion on which ones rejoices, but rather is, because of its nature, the object in which one rejoices.[20] This is a critical distinction, because in each of the above-noted NT and OT parallels where a verb of rejoicing is linked with "day," the latter is used as a temporal marker rather than with a causal

---

[16] Although Ps 117.24 (LXX) translates שמח with εὐφραίνω, the usual Hebrew equivalent for χαίρω is שמח (see Conzelmann, *TDNT* 9.363). As for ἀγαλλιάω (or rather, its antecedent equivalent ἀγαλλιάομαι and its derivatives), it is most often used to translate גיל. Accordingly, the words used in 8.56, if an allusion to Ps 118.24, would represent an accurate translation of the Hebrew. Obviously the same could be said for the verbal combination in Isa 25.9, but there are other reasons why it can be discounted as a plausible parallel.

[17] See Tob 13.15; Ps 95.12; Hab 3.18. It appears also in *Odes Sol.* 4.18.

[18] ἀγαλλιάω and εὐφραίνω are combined 31 times in the LXX, with most of these in the Psalms: Pss (21); Isa (7); others (3). However, it is of interest that they are found only three times with ἡμέρα: Ps 90(89).14; Isa 25.9; and Ps 118(117).24. The wording of Ps 117.24 (LXX), just as that of the Hebrew Ps 118.24 and John 8.56, is very rare.

[19] Isa 25.9; Pss 59.16(58.17); 89.16(88.17); 90(89).14.

[20] I owe this observation to Prof. I. H. Marshall.

sense.[21] As a result, in spite of verbal similarity none of these provides a plausible parallel for either the psalm or John's text. It is probably not coincidental that Ps 118(117).24 and John 8.56 are the only passages that combine the very rare verbal pairing along with the causal sense of ἡμέρα.

This would still leave the question of why John, if alluding to Ps 117.24 (LXX), would use χαίρω rather than the original and (at least in NT times) more distinctive εὐφραίνω. Several observations make such a change less problematic. First, χαίρω and εὐφραίνω are interchangeable and both are used to translate שמח. Although the LXX uses εὐφραίνω most often to translate שמח (especially in the Psalms), it also employs χαίρω a number of times, and there is little to differentiate their meanings.[22] Of the 39 OT canonical verses that use χαίρω, 17 translate שמח.[23] Second, patterns in the use of εὐφραίνω and χαίρω in the LXX show that over time the latter came to be preferred over the former. A comparison of their frequency of use in the LXX shows that εὐφραίνω is employed in 229 verses (OT:187; Apocrypha: 42) and χαίρω in 72 (OT: 39; Apocrypha: 33). Although εὐφραίνω has the greater number overall, when it comes to the Apocrypha χαίρω is proportionally much better represented.[24] Mirroring this, it is striking that nearly half the total number of occurrences of χαίρω are in the Apocrypha, although it is in volume much smaller than the OT. This suggests a shift in preference for χαίρω whereas the use of εὐφραίνω

---

[21] In Luke 6.23 the disciples are told to rejoice on that day (temporal), not because of the nature of the day. In Luke 16.19 the rich man feasts rejoicing every day (temporal). In Acts 7.41 Stephen recalls the Israelites making a calf "in those days" (clearly temporal), and in any case it is not clear that the subsequent rejoicing is directly linked to this. Although Isa 25.9, which shares with Ps 118.24 the closest verbal correspondence to John 8.56, is eschatological in tone, the day on which one rejoices is nevertheless a temporal marker. The three citations from the Psalms are also temporal: in 59.16(58.17) God has been a refuge in the day of trouble; in 89.16(88.17) the worshippers will rejoice all day long, and in 90(89).14 they will rejoice all their days.

[22] On their somewhat synonymous meanings see Bultmann, "εὐφραίνω," *TDNT* 2.773: "The alternation in translation and the combination with other verbs shows that εὐφραίνεσθαι does not have a specific meaning sharply differentiated from other expressions for joy."

[23] Prov 2.14; Jer 31(38).13; Exod 4.14; 1 Sam 19.5; 1 Kgs 4.20(2.46); 5.21; 8.66; 2 Kgs 11.14; 11.20; Esth 8.15; Hos 9.1; Jonah 4.6; Zech 4.10; Isa 39.2; Ezek 7.12. In Jer 7.34, χαίρω translates שמח, and immediately following, εὐφραίνω translates from the שוש root (another "rejoice" synonym), indicating that εὐφραίνω is not always preferred for שמח. In Zech 10.7, שמח is translated by χαίρω and then immediately following is translated a second time by εὐφραίνω, showing that they are synonymous and interchangeable. See also Conzelmann (*TDNT* 9.364), who provides examples from Qumran showing evidence of interchangeability between χαίρω and other verbs translating the Hebrew.

[24] In the OT, εὐφραίνω is preferred almost 5 to 1 over χαίρω, whereas in the Apocrypha they are almost equal in frequency of use.

appears to be on the decrease. Third, this trend is confirmed in the NT, which uses χαίρω in 68 verses and εὐφραίνω only in 14, thus lending credence to Bultmann's observation that in the NT εὐφραίνω does not play any great part.[25] Fourth, Johannine literature on the whole, and the Fourth Gospel in particular, favors the use of χαίρω.[26] Therefore, it is not impossible that if alluding to Ps 117.24 (LXX) John may have substituted the synonymous and much more widely used χαίρω in place of εὐφραίνω. Admittedly, the allusion would be stronger without such a change, but there are plausible explanations for how such an alteration could have come about without obscuring the intended allusion. In any case, one should consider that the liturgy of Ps 118, which was so prominent in the Tabernacles setting that John 8 reflects, probably would have been uttered in Hebrew or Aramaic. If John is echoing the liturgy and/or translating from Ps 118.24, then a preference for χαίρω would be understandable.[27]

In addition to the strong verbal links between 8.56 and Ps 118.24, several other factors strengthen the case for an allusion. First, by now it should be apparent that John was familiar with the psalm. Second, it is more likely that John would make use of a prominent and/or distinctive pre-text than one that is obscure, and Ps 118 was among the most memorable and oft-repeated texts in Jewish liturgy. Third, John's use of Ps 118 elsewhere suggests that recurrence is more likely. Fourth, it is generally accepted that 8.12–59 is placed at or near the Feast of Tabernacles and draws on its symbols. As one of the Scripture texts most prominently associated with Tabernacles, Ps 118 would be a recognizable and promising source. Furthermore, the verbs ἀγαλλιάω and χαίρω had a liturgical flavor and would especially evoke the cult.[28] In this light one should not underestimate the fact that Ps 118 was at the heart of the most prominent Tabernacles liturgy. Three

---

[25] Bultmann, *TDNT* 2.774: "Theologically [it is] overshadowed by the far more significant χαρά."

[26] Of the 68 verses that use χαίρω, the Fourth Gospel has 9, and other Johannine literature 6. This means that John uses almost one fourth of the total (15/68). John does use εὐφραίνω three times in Rev (11.10; 12.12; 18.20), but not in the Fourth Gospel. Luke (Gospel and Acts) accounts for most of the other uses, with 8 out of the total 14.

[27] If one is to defend an allusion to Ps 118.24 in Rev 19.7, similar reasoning would be necessary as it uses ἀγαλλιάω and χαίρω. If the writer is translating from Hebrew then a tie to Ps 118.24 is possible, although there would also be other plausible backgrounds. What makes the allusion in John 8.56 much stronger is the use of ἡμέρα, which considerably narrows the number of options. Although an allusion to the psalm in Rev 19.7 is weaker from a verbal angle, there are other factors which would argue in favor of Ps 118.24 as the preferred background, if there is indeed an allusion.

[28] This is especially true when words of rejoicing are found in combination. For example, of the 31 times ἀγαλλιάομαι is combined with εὐφραίνω, 21 are in the Psalms.

other important tests – thematic coherence, satisfaction, and historical plausibility – will be dealt with ahead as we examine the function and meaning effects of the allusion.

To sum up, the unique verbal combination shared by Ps 118.24 and John 8.56 suggests that an allusion is plausible. Their unique use of "day" in a causal sense with these verbs of rejoicing further increases the degree of coincidence between the passages. Although the verbal combination in 8.56 is an exact translation of the Hebrew of Ps 118.24, it is not impossible that John is alluding to Ps 117.24 (LXX). The interchangeability of χαίρω and εὐφραίνω, and the growing preference for the former in the Apocrypha and the NT (a preference also reflected in John), suggest reasons for a possible substitution. Whether John alludes to the Hebrew or LXX, in either case there are strong and unique verbal ties that support the likelihood of allusion. Such an allusion would also explain the order and parallelism of the verbs in 8.56 as reflecting the psalm.[29]

III. Establishing the Event

A. Difficulties in the Text

Although the words used to describe Abraham's experience may draw on Ps 118.24, it is still unclear what precise event Jesus is referring to. The general agreement over what he asserts – that Abraham has seen his day and rejoiced – quickly fragments into a variety of views on the specifics, the most important revolving around *when* this seeing took place (during Abraham's life or after?), on *which* occasion, and *what* he saw. These questions arise in part because John does not clearly identify his source, but also because of the "very peculiar"[30] Greek. The ἵνα clause can be interpreted in several ways, with some arguing that ἠγαλλιάσατο ἵνα ἴδῃ is forward-looking, expressing purpose and/or result, thus rendering the phrase "he longed with desire, rejoiced that he was to [see]."[31] Close to

---

[29] The proposed allusion falls short on the "history of interpretation" test, since I am unaware of anyone else who has identified an allusion to Ps 118.24 in John 8.56. However, of all the tests this is perhaps the least important in determining plausibility.

[30] So W. Milligan and W. F. Moulton in *The Gospel According to John*, 211 (cited in Urban and Henry, "Philo," 190 n. 11).

[31] Blass, Debrunner and Funk, *A Greek Grammar of the New Testament and Other Early Christian Literature*, 392.1a. The RSV also translates this way. Bruce (204) suggests it is a purpose clause, and Brown (1.359) translates "at the prospect of," suggesting it is "literally a purpose clause, but there is a tacit idea of desire and hope." See also Bultmann, 326 n. 1. Torrey's suggestion that ἀγαλλιάω is a mistranslation of the Aramaic, which would render "Abraham prayed that he might see," yields a similar result ("Aramaic Origin," 329). Against Torrey see Schnackenburg 2.494 n. 139.

this is the suggestion that it is anticipatory.[32] The other primary view is that the phrase is explanatory, so that it elucidates the content and grounds for Abraham's rejoicing. In other words, he rejoiced in what he saw, or "in that he saw."[33] Similar in result is Turner's view that ἵνα is causal, so that Abraham rejoiced *because* he saw.[34] The discussion of ἵνα is therefore very much about the *when*.

Jesus first states that Abraham rejoiced to see his day, and follows this by asserting that he saw it and was glad (καὶ εἶδεν καὶ ἐχάρη). If ἵνα is future in orientation then it would point to two distinct actions, distinguishing the promise of the first clause from the second, where it is fulfilled. Interpreting it this way, a number of scholars have suggested that the first clause refers to an event during Abraham's lifetime, and the second to Abraham in Paradise (or wherever).[35] It is possible that Jewish thought would give room for Abraham to experience or view in Paradise events on earth,[36] but although Abraham's joy as being contemporaneous with Jesus' life can be defended, it is unlikely in this passage for several reasons. First, the fact is that the verbs in the second clause are in the past tense. Second, the response from the Jews in the following verse indicates that they are thinking of Abraham's experience as past rather than present.[37] Third, the emphasis in 8.56–58 is on Jesus as both contemporary of and pre-existent to Abraham, not on Abraham as contemporary of the historical Jesus.[38] A somewhat neglected but much more plausible second option with the

---

[32] See Schnackenburg, 2.494 n. 139; cf. Bernard, 2.320: "seems to mean 'exulted *in the anticipation of* seeing,' which is not far removed from 'desired to see.'" Lagrange (255) renders it as "dans l'espérance de"; Schlatter (219) as "jubelnd nach etwas verlangen."

[33] Hoskyns, 347. See also Morris, 417 n. 107; Bauer, 131; M. Zerwick, *Biblical Greek Illustrated by Examples*, #410; Barrett, 351; Urban and Henry, "Philo," 163.

[34] N. Turner in Moulton, *Grammar*, 3.102. Zerwick (*Biblical Greek*, #429) notes the possibility that ἵνα ἴδῃ may stand for ὅτε εἶδεν, rendering "when he saw".

[35] So Bernard, 2.321: "This seems to say that Abraham in the other world was joyfully conscious of Christ's appearance in the flesh." Bauer (127) suggests that Abraham, in Paradise, watches the work of Jesus. Thus, as Bultmann (362 n. 2) argues, Abraham's is a present joy. See also W. Michaelis, "ὁράω," *TDNT* 5.343 n. 147; T. Vargha, "'Abraham . . . exultavit, ut videret diem meum': Ioh. 8, 56"; Lindars, 335; Haenchen, 2.29; Sanders and Mastin, 234.

[36] J. Derrett writes, "[Abraham] is the father of the Jewish people, but is also their patron. He is still alive. He watches the performance of his seed in the land promised to him and to them for ever, *haggadah* tells that he is interested in them both on earth and in whatever life there is after death" (*Law in the New Testament*, 86; note his references to Jewish literature in 86 n. 4–5).

[37] Cf. Schnackenburg, 2.222–223. Those who question this position include Hoskyns, 347; Brown, 1.360; Beasley-Murray, 139; Westcott, 140.

[38] Ridderbos says it well: The emphasis in John is "on the contemporaneity with the *historical* Abraham, not on that of the heavenly Abraham with the *historical* Jesus." (Emphasis original.)

forward-looking ἵνα is that while the second clause refers to the fulfillment of the promise, the two separate events both occur in Abraham's lifetime.[39] The other main possibility is that the second clause reiterates the grounds first given for the rejoicing, so that the two refer to the same single event during Abraham's earthly life.[40]

It appears that the most natural reading of ἵνα is as explanation, which implies that one should look for an event associated with Abraham's earthly life to elucidate Jesus' statement. However, it is possible that ἵνα is future-oriented, in which case I suggest that both the promise and later fulfillment take place in Abraham's lifetime. Either of the two positions is plausible.[41] Accordingly, it appears that Jesus is referring to an event(s) in Abraham's lifetime that in some way allowed him to see the "day" of Jesus.

B. Options for the Event

Genesis is the most obvious place to look for an event to match Jesus' statement. The difficulty is that at no point in the OT is there an explicit example of Abraham rejoicing. However, interpretations and expansions of Scripture in Jewish literature provide a number of possible parallels, so that the majority of scholars agree that recourse must be made to this body of contemporary Jewish thought. Most of the Jewish sources have been well-covered or at least recognized in the commentaries, and although there is some overlap they can be divided generally into two main areas: Abraham's vision(s) of the future, and expansions of Isaac material.

Rabbinic traditions of Abraham having a vision of the future world are an attractive alternative to explain 8.56.[42] Genesis 15 was interpreted as God showing to Abraham every generation, and one tradition mentions Abraham's joy in recognizing Akiba's knowledge of the law.[43] Elsewhere

---

[39] Schnackenburg (2.222) acknowledges the possibility of this in relation to Isaac: "We can think of the rejoicing at the promise of Isaac and the fulfillment of that joy at his birth."

[40] According to Brown (1.360) this was the view most widely held up to the 16th century. Lindars (334–335) dismisses the suggestion as "a redundant repetition."

[41] Westcott (139) attempts to solve the difficult phrase by proposing a somewhat unclear alternative that argues for a partial vision: "The peculiar construction may be explained by considering that the joy of Abraham lay in the effort to see that which was foreshadowed. It lay not in the fact *that* he saw, nor was it *in order to see*; but partial vision moved him with the confident desire to gain a fuller sight." (Emphasis original.) Although it is not clear how this solves the problem, it would fit well with two separate events occurring in Abraham's lifetime.

[42] For the primarily rabbinic idea of Abraham seeing the future see Str-B 2.525–526; Evans, *Word and Glory*, 162–164.

[43] *b. Sanh.* 38b. See also *4 Ezra* 2.14, where God shows Abraham how the world will end.

Akiba argues against Johanan ben Zakkai that God revealed to Abraham
not only this world but also the world to come.[44] A similar disagreement
arises from the interpretation of the phrase "entered into the days" in Gen
24.1, with Abraham seeing to the end of this world (R. Johanan) or into
the future world (R. Eliezer).[45] A difficulty with such texts is that they are
for the most part rabbinic and written after the Fourth Gospel, although
they probably reflect earlier traditions that may have been widespread and
known to John.[46] However, at no point do these sources indicate clearly
that Abraham had a vision of the Messiah's "day," and it appears that the
rabbis were more interested in Abraham's vision than in his reactions to it,
as there is no example of Abraham rejoicing.[47] What these traditions do
suggest is that it would not have been a strange concept for Jews of the
time that the future had been revealed to Abraham. As such they provide
an informing background to the passage.

Most scholars, even if they accept the possibility of a widespread
tradition of Abraham having a vision of the future, point to one of three
Isaac-related accounts – the announcement, the birth, or the *Akedah* – as the
event that Jesus is referring to.[48] In the first century there are examples of

---

[44] *Gen. Rab.* 44.28a. Presumably this would include the days of the Messiah. Hengel
("Old Testament," 387) argues for rabbinic traditions based on Gen 15 as the informing
background (cf. Schlatter, 220), and appeals to *Apoc. Ab.* 19–31. On the Palestinian
Targum to Gen 15 as background see Burney, *Aramaic Origin,* 111–112; M. McNamara,
*Targum and Testament: Aramaic Paraphrases of the Hebrew Bible: A Light on the New
Testament,* 144–145. For an overview of the relevant texts see H. Lona, *Abraham in
Johannes 8: Ein Beitrag zur Methodenfrage,* 295–304. A. Guilding (*The Fourth Gospel
and Jewish Worship: A Study of the Relation of St. John's Gospel to the Ancient Jewish
Lectionary System,* 109) argues that Isa 43 formed the background for the discourse in
John 8, and suggests that in 8.56 Jesus was referring to Isa 43.12, which as read in the
Targum to Isaiah mentions God declaring to Abraham what was to come. In support of
Guilding see D. Ball *'I Am' in John's Gospel: Literary Function, Background and Theo-
logical Implications,* 196–197. S. Cavaletti implausibly argues that Jesus is referring to
Abraham having a vision of the temple: "Non potrebbe – ci domandiamo – l'affermazione
di Gesù essere interpretata in base alla visione del tempio da parte di Abramo? Gesù si
identifica con il tempio; Abramo ha veduto il tempio 'costruito, distrutto e ricostruito'.
Se traduciamo questo testo in termini messianici, troviamo che Abramo ha visto il Messia
nato, morto e risuscitato" ("La visione messianica di Abramo," 181).

[45] *Tanh. B.* 6.60a. See Lightfoot, 195.

[46] See Barrett's (27–28) comments on John's relationship to rabbinic literature,
where he suggests probable awareness of oral teaching.

[47] Abraham's joy at the learning of Akiba is hardly relevant.

[48] An exception is M. K. Deeley ("Ezekiel's Shepherd and John's Jesus: A Case
Study in the Appropriation of Biblical Texts," 258–259), who argues that Ezek 33.23–29
lies behind the passage. Note that the two – a vision of the future and Isaac traditions –
are not incompatible, although there is no clear example of the two being combined in
Jewish literature. Lona (*Abraham,* 293–295) does, however, argue for a combination of
the two in this passage, claiming that there is no doubt that Gen 17.17 lies behind

Jewish interpretation that would not permit Abraham's laughter in Gen 17.17 to be read as scorn or unbelief and instead treated it as joy at the prospect of a son.[49] The connection most often suggested is to the birth of Isaac in Gen 21.1–7, and the play on the meaning of Isaac's name, "laughter."[50] Bruce argues that Abraham rejoiced when he spoke the words of Gen 22.8 ("God will provide himself with a lamb for the burnt-offering") to Isaac on their way to the place of sacrifice.[51] The latter two positions, however, fail to tie the phrase "Abraham rejoiced" to the event, and their connection to the Messiah is more easily read into than out of them. It is of course possible that, rather than referring to any specific event, John points to a general attitude of joy that Abraham possessed with a view towards the fulfillment of the promises made to him,[52] and/or that the mention of Abraham is no more than a functional tool to enlist him as a witness to Jesus along

---

Abraham's rejoicing, and that another strong influence is his vision in Gen. 15.12ff. See further Carson, 357; Lindars, 334.

[49] See especially Philo, *Mut.* 131, 154–169, 175; *Jub.* 15.17. For discussion of Jewish interpretation of Gen 17.17 see Lona, *Abraham*, 305–310. Reim (*Hintergrund*, 100–101) claims this as the background to the Johannine ἠγαλλιάσατο. Cf. Bauer, 127. Barrett (352) gives the example of *T. Levi* 18.14 where the patriarchs rejoice in the days of the "new priest." See further Ridderbos, 320. Hanson suggests that John 8.39–59 refers to the visit of the three angels to Abraham: "One of them is identified with the pre-existent Word. It is because of this that Jesus can claim to have seen Abraham" ("Scripture," 366). Boismard (*L'évangile de Jean*, 245) similarly points to Gen. 18.1–15 and a spiritual vision of the pre-existent Christ. Note however that, first of all, Jesus does not claim to have seen Abraham, and second, that what Abraham saw was "my day," which does not require a pre-incarnate vision of the *logos*.

[50] See Ridderbos, 321; Schnackenburg, 2.222–223; Carson, 357; Loisy, 581; Lagrange, 254–255; Zahn, 432. C. Brown represents the position well: "When Isaac was born, Abraham prophetically and in faith already saw in the day of his birth the birth of the Messiah . . . whose coming was heralded by the birth of Isaac" (*Het Evangelie naar Johannes*, 231; cited in Ridderbos, 321). The joy of Abraham in *Jub.* 16.19 is misapplied by some to the announcement of the birth (Morris, 418; Hoskyns, 348), and misunderstood as referring to the birth itself (so Carson, 357). In actuality the joy is directly linked to the promise, given after Isaac's birth, of a holy seed that will come from Isaac.

[51] Bruce, 205. Westcott (140) holds a similar position (i.e. the offering of Isaac). Bruce (207 n. 19) notes that in *T. Levi* 18.56 "Levi foretells the coming of a 'new priest' for whom 'the heavens shall be opened, and from the temple of glory shall come upon him sanctification, with the Father's voice as from Abraham to Isaac' (presumably a reference to Gen. 22:8, the only words spoken by Abraham to Isaac anywhere in the Bible)." See Schnackenburg's arguments (2.493 n. 133) against the sacrifice of Isaac prefiguring the passion as the day of Jesus, a view which was popular with the church fathers.

[52] So Morris (418–419), who points out that Jesus does not refer to any specific occasion. The uncertainty of a precise reference leads Hoskyns (348) to suggest that "the joy of Abraham may have as vague an Old Testament background as the joy of Adam [who rejoiced over Akiba's knowledge of the Torah]."

with Moses and Isaiah.[53] Although the latter may be factors to some degree, I suggest that John intended more than this, and that the *Book of Jubilees* presents the most plausible alternative.[54]

C. *The Argument for Jubilees*

I submit that Jesus is alluding to Abraham's rejoicing at the promise of a future exalted seed of Isaac which takes place at the celebration recounted in *Jub.* 16.20–31, with previous promise texts in *Jubilees* providing the immediate informing background.[55] Although based on Genesis accounts, in mediating and interpreting these *Jubilees* adds details that make it especially suitable because of context and subject matter to John 8.56. Before examining the texts themselves, it will be helpful in building a case to apply some of the tests used in evaluating echoes and allusions. First, in its predominant concern for ritual law and Jewish piety *Jubilees* portrays the patriarchs as paradigmatic examples to be emulated. Much of the book is a re-telling of Genesis (explaining its alternative title as "The Little Genesis"), with a significant section devoted to Abraham stories (chs. 11– 23).[56] It is more likely that an allusion to Abraham would come from a source where he features prominently. Second, on several occasions *Jubilees* characterizes Abraham specifically as rejoicing at the promise(s) of future blessing, providing an important verbal parallel that is all the

---

[53] On Abraham's role as witness see J. Derrett, "Exercitations on John 8," 449; J. Tuñí, "Personajes veterotestamentarios en el Evangelio de Juan," 279–292; Davies, *Rhetoric*, 136. See Lona's argument (*Abraham*, 327–332) that the description of Abraham is driven by Christology and not tradition.

[54] Urban and Henry ("Philo") argue strongly for Philo's exegesis of God's promise of Isaac to Abraham in Gen 17 (in *Mut.*) as the background, noting that the event is located in a biography of Abraham, and that Abraham rejoiced. However, they are not entirely convincing in arguing that Philo actually presents Abraham as having had a previous vision of the Logos and tying this to the "I am" of 8.58. In addition to *Jubilees* probably being read more widely than Philo, the former provides a better parallel and one that is much more easily arrived at than the very complex contortions required for Philo. For a summary of others who argue in favor of a Philo connection see Urban and Henry, ibid., 179–184.

[55] This suggestion, arrived at independently, is similar to that of P. Grelot, ("Jean 8,56 et Jubilés 16,16–29"), whose work I encountered later in my research. Other than Grelot, I am not aware of anyone who advances a similar position. Although the background I propose is similar to Grelot's, my approach and emphasis differ, as does the function I suggest. (Grelot is especially interested in exploring links between *Jubilees* and Qumran.) Even though a number of scholars note the parallel to *Jubilees*, this is generally in passing and without detail. See for example Bultmann, 326 n. 3 (he mentions *Jub.* 14.21; 15.17); Carson, 357; Morris, 418; Hoskyns, 348; Brown, 1.360.

[56] See Wintermute's comments in "Introduction," 35–41.

more significant because of its rarity. Third, *Jubilees* was available and accessible prior to the writing of the Fourth Gospel. Its date is relatively early, with most scholars agreeing that it was written sometime in the second century BC.[57] That other early writers refer to and/or quote from *Jubilees* suggests that in some circles at least it was regarded as an important source,[58] an observation bolstered by the interest in translating *Jubilees* and the knowledge of the book that R. H. Charles finds in early patristic writings.[59] If Charles' list of NT passages which he argues are connected to *Jubilees* actually depend on or presuppose it, then this would be additional evidence pointing to the book's prominence and probably widespread availability.[60] It appears that *Jubilees* was a well-known, distinctive, and prominent text, and that it is not implausible that it may have been accessible to John.

Although its early date, importance, and apparently widespread availability make it more likely that John was aware of *Jubilees*, there is no evidence of him referring to the book anywhere else. However, it is possible that John provides a clue in the Jews' mocking answer to Jesus in 8.57: "You are not yet fifty years old." We will look more closely at the function of this misunderstanding below, but what interests us at this point is the reference to fifty. The options most often suggested are that the Jews are indicating Jesus' approximate age (i.e., he was close to fifty), or else that they are aware that Jesus is not close to fifty but

---

[57] See discussion in Wintermute, "Introduction" 43–45. He suggests a date between 161–140 BC. This early date removes one of the difficulties encountered when arguing for rabbinic parallels, as *Jubilees* was written and in circulation before the time of Jesus and John.

[58] Wintermute notes the use of *Jubilees* by CD 16.2–4 and that it is probably a source for the *Genesis Apocryphon*: "The fact that two separate first-century [BC] writers treat Jubilees as an authoritative source indicates that Jubilees was already sufficiently established to warrant that status" ("Introduction," 44). There are also possible connections to Ethiopic Enoch (*1 En.*), Wisdom, and *4 Ezra* (see R. H. Charles, *The Book of Jubilees or The Little Genesis*, lxxx). See also Wintermute's list of other Qumran documents that "use expressions or ideas which are also found in Jubilees" ("Introduction," 50).

[59] See list in Charles, *Jubilees*, lxxvii–lxxii. His references to Samaritan literature and later patristic writings are of little relevance to this argument because of late dating, but there are a number of early examples. On the use of *Jubilees* in Christian circles see Schürer, *History*, 3.315–316. *Jubilees* was available at least in Hebrew, Greek, Latin, Syriac, and Ethiopic. On the various translations see Wintermute, "Introduction," 41–43.

[60] See Charles (*Jubilees*, lxxxiii–lxxxvi) for a list of passages "where the New Testament is dependent on our text, or presupposes it, or presents a close parallel" (ibid., lxxxiii). Wintermute accepts Charles' evidence: "On the basis of the evidence which he provided, it is clear that Paul and the authors of Luke-Acts, James, Hebrews, and 2 Peter were familiar with expressions and ideas that appear in Jubilees" ("Introduction," 49). However, although some passages seem very close, there is no undisputed reference to *Jubilees*.

used the number as a round figure that marked the end of a full working life.[61] Alternatively, M. Edwards credibly suggests that the word can be interpreted as a reference to the fifty-year Jubilee period.[62] The Jubilee was the fiftieth year that concluded the cycle of seven "weeks" of seven years instituted in Lev 25, when property was returned to the original owners, the farmer was not to sow or reap, and servants and slaves were released.[63] It is also the unit that the *Book of Jubilees* uses (hence its title) to calculate the age of the patriarchs and in its goal of calendrical reform. The book's concern for the Sabbath, and the fact that even Abraham did not complete four Jubilees before dying, would make the Jews' taunt especially appropriate for Jesus, the Sabbath-breaker who had in fact not yet completed even one Jubilee. This would be especially true if they had recognized an allusion to *Jubilees* in Jesus' immediately preceding claim. In any case, John's disinterest in dates, coupled with an apparent interest in the number seven, makes it more likely that he is using the number fifty symbolically than indicating the age of Jesus.[64] It is at least possible that John included the reference as another sign pointing the reader to *Jubilees*.[65]

A look at the text of *Jubilees* highlights the thematic coherence with the event Jesus describes and other elements that make it especially promising as a background. The first reference to Abraham's rejoicing follows the

---

[61] See G. Ogg ("The Age of Jesus When He Taught") for discussion of the various options and an apparent defense of Irenaeus' position that Jesus was in his forties when he taught. That it is a round number is more convincing. See for example Beasley-Murray, 139; Hoskyns, 348; Barrett, 352; Bauer, 127.

[62] Edwards, "'Not yet fifty years old': John 8.57," 451. G. W. Buchanan's ("The Age of Jesus") response to Edwards has missed the point of his argument and the criticisms are misdirected. Although Carson (356) questions the Jubilee link, at the same time he recognizes the possibility: "The verb rendered 'rejoiced' does not necessarily bear overtones of the Jubilee, but it is strong." In effect, the flavor of the event described would be consonant with the Jubilee.

[63] It is suggestive in the Tabernacles context of John 8 that the OT Jubilee started on the Day of Atonement, in the build-up to Tabernacles. As a year consecrated to "proclaim liberty throughout the land to all its inhabitants" (Lev 25.10), an allusion to it would have promising New Exodus connections.

[64] Note the number seven in the chronology of Revelation: seven seals of the scroll; seven trumpets; seven cups of wrath. Dodd (*Interpretation*) and Fortna (*Signs*) have suggested a series of seven signs in the Fourth Gospel. Schnackenburg (2.79) notes that there are seven metaphors combined with the ἐγώ εἰμι formula. Edwards is justified in writing, "It seems at least more probable that the text should be read in the light of the *Book of Jubilees* than that an author who ignored the birth of Jesus and assigns no dates to the stages of his ministry should have taken the opportunity, at this one point in the narrative, of throwing in a superfluous indication of his age" ("Fifty," 454).

[65] The proximity of the reference to "fifty," especially in this pregnant context where Abraham's rejoicing is underscored, strengthens the case for an allusion.

covenant of the pieces, which confirms God's promises to him of an heir ("seed"), many descendants, and possession of the land.[66] Abraham is given cause to rejoice again when the LORD appears to him, confirming and elaborating on the previous promises and the blessings to come for his seed. The rejoicing, however, follows the additional explicit promise of a son, and the promises God makes that will be fulfilled in this son, who is then identified as Isaac.[67] Sarah gives birth to Isaac a year later on the feast of first fruits, and he is circumcised. Following this, the angels who had announced the conception to Sarah return as promised, and announce to Abraham what is to come:[68]

> But from the sons of Isaac one would become a holy seed and he would not be counted among the nations because he would become the portion of the Most High and all his seed would fall (by lot) into that which God will rule so that he might become a people (belonging) to the Lord, a (special) possession from all people, and so that he might become a kingdom of priests and a holy people. (*Jub.* 16.17–18)

The significant development for our purposes is that the promise is related not to Isaac but to one of his sons, and that Abraham's joy is then specifically linked to the promise concerning the future son of Isaac: "And both of them [Abraham and Sarah] rejoiced greatly" (*Jub.* 16.19). More importantly, Abraham's response to this new promise is to build "an altar there to the LORD who . . . made him rejoice," and to institute a feast that is characterized as "a feast of rejoicing" (*Jub.* 16.20). There is no doubt that this is the Feast of Tabernacles.[69] Abraham is the first to observe this feast on the earth, and he does it "rejoicing with all his heart and with all his soul" (*Jub.* 16.25). Then the following elaboration of the promise is inserted into the midst of the details explaining the establishment of the Tabernacles celebration:

---

[66] "And Abram rejoiced and he told all of these things to Sarai, his wife. And he believed that he would have seed" (*Jub.* 14.21). Note that all quotation of *Jubilees* in this study is from Wintermute's translation.

[67] "'And I will bless her [Sarah] and I will give you a son from her. And I will bless him. And he will become a people. And kings of nations will come from him.' And Abraham fell on his face and he rejoiced" (*Jub.* 15.16–17). Following this Isaac is identified as the son who will be born a year later.

[68] There is a gloss in *Jub.* 16.15–16 that appears to place the return of the angels and their announcement prior to Isaac's birth rather than following it. However, this interrupts the natural flow of the passage and represents a corruption of the text. See Charles' and Wintermute's comments (loc. cit.) on the issue.

[69] It is identified as the Feast of Booths in *Jub.* 16.29. In addition, it takes place in the seventh month for seven days, and the liturgical details match Tabernacles.

And he blessed his Creator who created him in his generation because by his will he created him for he knew and he perceived that from him there would be a righteous planting for eternal generations and *a holy seed from him so that he might be like the one who made everything.* And he blessed and rejoiced and called the name of this festival "the festival of the LORD," a joy acceptable to God Most High.

(*Jub.* 16.26–27; emphasis added.)

The promise concerning the future seed of Isaac is the immediate cause for the institution and celebration of Tabernacles. Then, within Tabernacles itself, the promise identifies this future seed as one who in some way *will be like the Creator.*[70] It would not take a great deal of effort or imagination, especially for one so inclined, to interpret the seed as referring to an

---

[70] The most natural reading of this puzzling text is that it is the holy seed who will be like the Creator, although this is not beyond question. Wintermute's translation ("so that *he* might be like") leaves ambiguous whether it is Abraham or the holy seed who is compared. Charles' translation, on the other hand, is more easily applied to a community: "He knew and perceived that from him would arise the plant of righteousness for the eternal generations, and from him a holy seed, so that it should become like Him who had made all things." That is, "it" could refer to the holy seed, and/or to the plant of righteousness, the latter a phrase that sounds similar to that applied to the community in the Dead Sea Scrolls. (It is not clear whether the planting and the seed refer to the same entity or not.) There appear to be three main alternatives for interpreting the passage. 1. It may be that Abraham is compared to the Creator. In private correspondence Prof. Wintermute wrote, "One could argue that the simplest reading involves the memory that the Creator made a good (and holy) cosmos which humans messed up. The Creator made (planted?) a garden and placed in it holy (human) seed. The same sort of planting comes from Abraham. In that respect he could be regarded as like 'the one who created everything.'" However, although it would justify his translation, Prof. Wintermute concluded that this line of reasoning was not very satisfying to him. 2. It is possible to understand the planting as the community (which sounds like Qumran), and the holy seed as the members of the community. However, the idea of the community being like God is difficult to support. 3. The holy seed could be interpreted as an individual, and in a Christian context the passage could easily be applied to Jesus. As Prof. Wintermute wrote, "If Saint Paul had written this, I would understand that the seed was the one seed of Abraham, i.e. the Messiah 'so that he might be like the one who made everything.' I find it impossible to project such a view back into Jubilees." In the end, Prof. Wintermute concludes that the meaning of the passage remains unclear. Unclear as it may be, it is not difficult to see how this passage could be applied to a messianic-eschatological figure, although I am not aware of any such use (apart from the proposed allusion in John). Precisely because the meaning of the passage remains ambiguous it is ripe for exploitation, so that the question becomes not whether it is legitimate to attribute such a view back to the writer, but whether one can read such a view into the passage. After all, if one can imagine Paul writing, in reference to Jesus, of a holy seed who will be like God, then one can also imagine Paul – or John, as the case may be – recognizing the potential of a prior text that speaks of such a seed. It would not be the first time that a pre-text is interpreted differently from what the writer originally intended.

individual.[71] All along Abraham's joy has been linked to the promises, but his rejoicing culminates in this last promise, which is clearly tied to and explains the joyful character of Tabernacles. Consequently it is possible to link Abraham's rejoicing with the promise of an exalted seed and the Feast of Tabernacles.[72] The parallels to John 8.56 are striking, for the encounter takes place in a Tabernacles setting, refers to Abraham's rejoicing, and is concerned with the identity of Jesus and his "day."[73] It is remarkable that Abraham figures so prominently in John 8, a passage clearly placed at Tabernacles, while not being mentioned anywhere else in the Gospel.[74]

Jubilees also provides a link between Abraham and Ps 118. In describing Abraham's institution of Tabernacles, the writer of *Jubilees* portrays him celebrating the festival's most distinctive liturgy: "Abraham took branches of palm trees and fruit of good trees and each day of the days he used to go around the altar with branches" (*Jub.* 16.31). There is no serious question that the liturgical use of Ps 118 is being described.[75] According to *Jubilees*, Abraham's paradigmatic celebration of the Ps 118 Tabernacles ritual sets the pattern which Israel is then required to follow

---

[71] Grelot asserts that "Il est toutefois douteux que les *Jubilés* spéculent sur 'le descendant' d'Abraham par excellence" ("Jean 8,56," 625). However, whether Jubilees does so or not, the description of the future son makes it especially malleable for such use. CD 1.7 speaks of the community as a planting, and following shortly (1.11) of the raising up of the Teacher of Righteousness to lead this planting.

[72] Grelot correctly notes that the joy that characterizes Tabernacles is not linked to the traditional sojourn in the desert but to the promises: "l'auteur justifie et fonde le caractère de liesse qui caractérise la fête des tentes, sans aucune allusion au séjour d'Israël au désert, mais en liaison étroite avec les promesses d'avenir dont la descendance d'Abraham et d'Isaac est porteuse" ("Jean 8,56," 626).

[73] It is noteworthy that, shortly, Jesus will make a statement in which he appears to in some way claim to be like God, and which the Jews apparently understand as blasphemy. The celebration of Tabernacles is later associated in *Jubilees* with the *Akedah*, linking the seven days of Tabernacles to the seven days in which Abraham took Isaac, bound him, and then replaced him with a ram. After the provision of the ram Abraham returns to the Well of the Oath (the location where he first celebrated Tabernacles), and observes Tabernacles, which links festal joy with his going and returning in peace (*Jub.* 18.1–19). Another example of Abraham rejoicing is in response to Ishmael and Isaac's coming to him as he prepares to die, and as he sees their prosperity (*Jub.* 22.7).

[74] Cf. Grelot, "Jean 8,56," 627. Zahn (431) is one of the few commentators who notes that the Jewish tradition that Abraham founded Tabernacles is important for the understanding of the passage

[75] See further ch. 2 above. The lulab and ethrog are described here, and the distinctive waving of the palm with rejoicing marks the circling of the altar during the Ps 118 liturgy with the water-pouring. It is notable in this regard that Abraham's celebration takes place at the Well of the Oath, which would provide a ready source for the water-drawing ceremony.

(*Jub.* 16.28–30). We therefore have a pre-text that helps explain why John would find it appropriate to use the words of Ps 118 to describe Abraham's rejoicing.

D. Conclusion

A number of links suggest that *Jubilees* is a plausible background to the event to which Jesus alludes. It is an early, important, and widely read source that focuses significant attention on Abraham, is thematically coherent with the passage, and helps explain the passage. In addition, it provides one of the few examples of Abraham rejoicing, links him to Tabernacles, and suggests why the conjunction of Ps 118 with Abraham would have been especially appropriate.[76] The development of the initial vague promise of seed, on to Isaac, then to a future son of Isaac, and finally to a future exalted holy seed, provides John with a fertile background on which to draw. The former two tie the rejoicing clearly to the promise, whereas the latter two (and especially the last one) suggest – in a clearer way than the OT narratives that they expand upon – how Abraham could have at the least anticipated and perhaps in some way experienced the fulfillment of the promise and the coming of the exalted seed (i.e., Jesus) in the person of Isaac.[77] To sum up, we have suggested that the unique verbal combination in John 8.56 comes from Ps 118.24, that the event Jesus refers to is Abraham's rejoicing at the Tabernacles celebration of *Jub.* 16 in anticipation of the future exalted seed of Isaac, and that Abraham's enactment of the Ps 118 liturgy provides the link for John to describe the event in the language of Ps 118.24.

---

[76] In other words, it meets the majority of tests suggested for evaluating the presence of allusions and echoes.

[77] That is, in the promises of the angels and in the initial sign of their fulfillment through Isaac, Abraham anticipated and saw the day of Jesus, rejoicing in the future coming of the exalted seed who will be like God. Cf. Grelot, "Jean 8,56," 628: "Abraham a salué de loin le 'jour' où ce rejeton viendrait. . . . Ici, la vue du 'jour' due Christ se superpose à l'expérience de la naissance d'Isaac, qui en est la figure vivante."

IV. The Function

The question remains why Jesus asserts that Abraham had seen his day, as well as what he means by "my day." His statement is a direct response to the Jews' incredulous rhetorical question asking whether Jesus actually thinks he is greater than Abraham, and in calling Abraham as a witness Jesus implies precisely what they find so offensive: Abraham anticipated and longed for the day of Jesus. This is the springboard for the following verses, for provoked, the Jews' taunting remarks reveal misunderstanding that elicits clarification from Jesus – he is indeed greater than Abraham, existed before him, "I am." This they understand, for in claiming priority over Abraham, Jesus uses a title associated with Yahweh. This is what the passage says without recourse to the proposed Ps 118-Tabernacles-*Jubilees* allusion. However, bringing the meaning effects of the allusion into play draws out the purpose motivating Jesus' enigmatic statement, fine-tunes the development of the narrative, and highlights its coherence.

A. The Function of Ps 118

By using the liturgical words so familiar to the Jew, Jesus draws in the original context of Ps 118.24. The day of rejoicing and gladness is the day of vindication for the king, for Yahweh has saved him and established the rejected stone as the cornerstone (Ps 118.22). Yahweh's affirmation of the vice-regent becomes the cause of celebration, with the processional crowd bearing witness that this is the work of Yahweh (Ps 118.23). The close parallels to John 8.48–56 show what an appropriate choice the psalm is. The authorities have in large measure rejected Jesus, but he appeals to the Father as the one who has glorified him. Abraham is then called as a witness, using the same words that the Ps 118 processional cries out in support of the king, so that his voice joins their chorus in affirming that the rejected Jesus is God's chosen cornerstone. As a result of these parallels, the allusion functions, first of all, subtly to enlist Yahweh as a witness for Jesus, echoing his earlier appeals to the Father and reiterating that it is Yahweh who validates his words, ministry, and person (8.18, 28, 50, 54). It also casts Jesus in the role of the king vindicated and established by Yahweh. Second, it identifies Jesus' opponents with the builders who reject God's chosen king, contrasting them to Abraham, who along with the true Israel of the Psalms testifies that Jesus' words and works are Yahweh's doing.

Especially in view of the Tabernacles setting of John 8, I suggest that John also intends to evoke the Ps 118-Tabernacles complex, both in its ancient and more contemporary manifestations, and equate the day of Jesus with the day of Yahweh. We have already argued that Yahweh's kingship was probably celebrated with special emphasis in the ancient Tabernacles cult, and that Ps 118 formed part of this liturgy. This is not to say there was an enthronement or coronation ceremony for Yahweh, nor to equate without distinction the celebration of Yahweh's kingship to the day of Yahweh. At the same time, Yahweh's kingship as a description or expression of his sovereignty certainly played an essential part in the conceptual understanding of his day. Therefore, in its ancient festival setting the day of rejoicing in Ps 118.24 is not only the day of vindication for the king, but also one that primarily celebrates Yahweh's kingship – i.e., it is the day of Yahweh.[78] As a result, we see a blending of the person and kingship of Jesus with that of Yahweh, just as in the Entrance Narrative.

The exile precipitated a change in orientation for the prophets, so that the day of Yahweh came to be characterized by an expectation of decisive intervention on God's part that would result in salvation for Israel and destruction for her enemies. However, the association of the day of Yahweh with his kingship was not lost, but rather underwent a change of emphasis so that the focus was perhaps less on his present reign than on the time when he would come to establish conclusively his rule. The day of Yahweh therefore was characterized primarily by his coming. As Beasley-Murray observes, "This day of judgment upon evil men is viewed as the day of the Lord's *coming*, of his *appearing*, the day when he *draws near* for judgment. *The day of the Lord is the day of the coming of God.*"[79] The central role of Ps 118 in the contemporary Tabernacles festival ensured that the psalm kept pace with these developments, and suggests that the day of rejoicing of Ps 118.24 would have been associated with the day of Yahweh, when he would decisively intervene to save his people, destroy their enemies, and live amongst his people as king.[80] However, even though this back-

---

[78] This ancient cultic usage and association supports the observation that although the day of Yahweh often refers to his final and climactic intervention, it was not always thought of as a one-time date, or even necessarily God's final activity. See further G. von Rad, "ἡμέρα," *TDNT* 2.943–947; Beasley-Murray, *Kingdom of God*, 11–16, 43–45.

[79] Beasley-Murray, *Kingdom of God*, 15; emphasis original. Beasley-Murray quotes von Rad (*Old Testament Theology*, 2.119) in support: "There is something peculiar about the expectation of the Day of Jahweh, for wherever it occurs in prophecy the statements culminate in an allusion to Jahweh's coming in person."

[80] I have argued previously that in the first century Tabernacles would have been associated with the expectation of the coming of God to establish his reign. Mays ("Ps 118," 143–144) points out that the day in Ps 118.24 "is informed not only by the memory of salvation past but also by the hope of salvation to come." That is, for the later community there is an interplay of "psalmody and eschatological prophecy." In any case, the observant reader could note that the context of the psalm – the enemies of the king

ground has significant implications for interpreting Jesus' appropriation of Ps 118.24, most scholars do not appreciate that in calling it "my day" Jesus has laid claim to the day of Yahweh as his own.[81] Instead, Jesus' statement is generally interpreted in one of three ways: as being primarily a chronological reference to either his incarnation, his "era," or his glorification;[82] as specifying his function in salvation;[83] or as speaking to his identity and referring either to the day of the Son of Man or the appearance of the Messiah.[84]

Each of the three alternatives has some measure of truth, but each is also incomplete until placed in the proper context. Jesus does not say that Abraham saw "the day of the Messiah," the messianic age, or the day of the Son of Man. Rather, "day" should be interpreted in its immediate cultic context – the Tabernacles reading of Zechariah and the Ps 118 liturgy that evoked the day when Yahweh would return to reign as King.[85]

---

have been destroyed, Yahweh has saved his people, and he presumably lives amongst them in his temple – parallels the results expected from the eschatological day of Yahweh.

[81] Urban and Henry ("Philo," 185) argue against this being a reference to the day of Yahweh, noting that "day" is sometimes used in reference to daylight, the light of day, or the sunrise. They therefore suggest, very implausibly, that John means only "my light," in keeping with the Gospel's theme of light.

[82] Morris (418) suggests that a reference to the incarnation is most probable, and Bernard (2.320) that it is "the day of Christ's birth or appearance in the flesh." So also Zahn, 432. Ridderbos (320) and Michaelis (*TDNT* 5.343 n. 147) refer to it more generally as the "coming" of Jesus. G. Delling interprets the day as "the day of the definitive revelation of His glory" ("ἡμέρα," *TDNT* 2.951), Lindars (335) claims that it means "my time (era)," and Kysar (146) that "it stands for the whole Christ event." As Mays (137) notes, the day may have been associated with the resurrection of Jesus in the liturgy of the early church. Lagrange (255) refers to the period of "l'action du Messie."

[83] According to Barrett (353), "It is idle to ask whether by Jesus' 'day' John intended his ministry or the coming in glory of the Son of Man. He meant that the work of salvation, potentially complete in Abraham, was actually complete in Jesus." Beasley-Murray (138) points to "the day of salvation as the day of Jesus." Furthermore, the "day" refers to his ministry "as Revealer and Redeemer." Derrett ("Exercitations," 450 n. 56) suggests that "my day" implies the Day of Redemption. Interestingly, although he does not apply this specifically to John 8, Derrett lists Ps 118.24 as one of several examples in which he argues that "day" carries the meaning of "Day of Redemption."

[84] On the day as the day of the coming of the Son of Man see Bultmann, 326; Schnackenburg, 2.222; Odeberg, 307; Schneider, 185. As the day or time of the Messiah's appearance see again Schnackenburg, 2.222; Westcott, 139; Bauer, 127. Blank (176) suggests that the day points to both.

[85] In this context John's choice of the words from Ps 118.24 is especially evocative. The words of rejoicing, most often associated with the OT cult, are characterized by an eschatological flavor. As Conzelmann suggests "the roots are to be found in the connection between joy and kingship" (*TDNT* 9.363). Bultmann (*TDNT* 2.773) also observes that "since the joy of the last time is often depicted as the joy of cultic celebration," they

In harmony with John's New Exodus agenda, Jesus is portrayed as claiming the day of Yahweh as his own, identifying the two so that there is no distinction between them.[86] As Hengel correctly observes, "the day of Christ becomes thereby identical with the Day of Yahweh, God's eschatological epiphany."[87] This has obvious chronological and functional implications, for it follows that the eschatological coming of God is actualized in the coming of Jesus, and that this coming entails redemption and salvation for Israel. But ultimately the blurring of functional roles is bound up with and points to the ontological, so that the question of Jesus' identity is brought to the fore.[88]

B. The Function of Jubilees

Although the proposed function of Ps 118 does not depend on the presence of an allusion to *Jubilees*, the themes and context of the latter support and enhance the former. *Jubilees* does not indicate that Abraham saw the Messiah (either in a rabbinic-type vision of the future or a pre-incarnate appearance of the *logos*) or the messianic age, and it is neither the announcement nor subsequent birth of Isaac that stimulates Abraham's greatest joy. Rather, the most promising parallel in *Jubilees* characterizes Abraham's

---

(in this case specifically ἀγαλλιάω) naturally become eschatological terms. Therefore the use of the well-known Ps 118-Tabernacles liturgical phrase would easily link to the eschatological return of Yahweh in Zech 14. It is not insignificant that Tabernacles was the feast most characterized by rejoicing, and this was especially true for the water ceremony which included the Ps 118 liturgy (see Bultmann, *TDNT* 1.21).

[86] Although it is not possible to demonstrate conclusively that John intends to equate the day of Jesus with that of Yahweh, there are plausible reasons for advancing such an interpretation. To sum up, in its ancient festival context the psalm celebrated Yahweh's kingship, and thus the day of Yahweh. Also, the psalm's content shows the day of rejoicing as the time of Yahweh's decisive intervention. When interpreted in a Tabernacles context in the Second Temple period, this would encourage an interpretation of the day as that of Yahweh's eschatological intervention. Furthermore, the proposed function has explanatory power, and is consonant with John's identification of Jesus with Yahweh in the New Exodus. This interpretation depends somewhat on whether the allusion to Ps 118 is considered credible. Note, however, that Hengel and Carson (following footnote) arrive at the same conclusion without recognizing the allusion, nor, for that matter, providing any evidence for their claim.

[87] Hengel, "Old Testament," 387. Another who holds this minority view is Carson, 357: "the 'day' or the 'day of the Lord' becomes *Jesus'* day." Sanders and Mastin (234) point to the OT day of the Lord for reference, and it appears that they equate it with the day of Jesus.

[88] Note the similarity to Revelation, where the day of the Lord is the day of God and the Lamb (cf. Rev 6.16–17).

most extravagant rejoicing as a response to the promise of the future seed of Isaac that would in some way be like the Creator. The enigmatic statement makes it easier to explain how Abraham is to have seen the day of God's climactic intervention and coming actualized in Jesus. That the promise of this exalted seed is inserted into the midst of the Tabernacles festival which celebrates and expects Yahweh's return to establish his universal rule, and is actually given as the festival's *raison d'être*, provides another connection that John could have exploited to identify the day of Jesus with Yahweh's.[89]

C. The Misunderstanding

The Jews are portrayed as understanding Jesus to have declared that he saw Abraham. In this case their incredulous response is appropriate for one who is making claims, even if such a thing were possible,[90] that they believe are not commensurate with his age, experience and position.[91] However, Jesus claims neither that he saw Abraham, nor that Abraham saw him. His statement is that Abraham saw "my day." By concentrating on the *when* – i.e., the chronological impossibility of a young man having seen Abraham – the Jews have missed the point, which is *what* Abraham saw and *whom* he bears witness about. John's interest lies not in when Abraham saw the day, but in the day itself, and the implications this carries for the identity of one who claims the day of Yahweh as his own. This presents a familiar sequence in John, where Jesus makes an unclear statement, the response (positive or negative) reveals that the character(s) has missed the point, which in turn provides Jesus the opportunity to offer an explanation.[92] In this way Jesus' claim in 8.56 sets the stage for the

---

[89] Guilding raises the interesting possibility that the date of Jesus' birth may have been associated with Tabernacles (see the evidence she adduces in *Jewish Worship*, 100–103): "If the date of our Lord's birth was not known, it would probably come to be associated with that Jewish festival on which the thought of God's coming to dwell with his people was prominent, namely, the Feast of Tabernacles" (ibid., 100). Although this is speculative, the Fourth Gospel may connect the two in the use of tabernacling in 1.14.

[90] E. Delebeque ("Jésus Contemporain d'Abraham selon Jean 8,57," 85) argues that the Jews' question in 8.57 can be read as "Tu as vu Abraham *depuis moins de* cinquante ans?," which implies that they may be willing to accept that he had seen Abraham. Although the suggestion is unlikely, note Carson's (359) favorable comments.

[91] Bernard (2.321) argues in 8.57 against the strongly supported καὶ 'Αβραὰμ ἑώρακας; in favor of καὶ 'Αβραὰμ ἑώρακε σε; Although his position is defensible, this alternative appears to be an adaptation to 8.56. For discussion see Barrett, 352; Brown 1.360.

[92] On misunderstanding as literary technique see Culpepper, *Anatomy*, 152–165; Duke, *Irony*, 145. H. Leroy (*Rätsel und Missverständnis: Ein Beitrag zur Formgeschichte des*

dramatic "I am" pronouncement of 8.58. Although the precise background and meaning of the "I am" utterance is disputed, most commentators recognize that Jesus is appropriating a title or form of speech associated with Yahweh. This suggests that, more than claiming contemporaneity with and pre-existence to Abraham, Jesus is proclaiming his unity with Yahweh.[93] The Jews do not misunderstand this astounding assertion, for whatever the actual laws on what constituted blasphemy at the time, John indicates a reaction consonant with an unacceptable identification with Yahweh.[94]

Recognizing the pattern of misunderstanding has important implications for this study. First, Jesus' answer to the Jews in 8.58 makes more plausible the argument that the point of 8.56 is the identification of Jesus with Yahweh. Since the misunderstood statement affords the opportunity to clarify and explain an important theme or teaching, this entails that the subsequent explanation, in reiterating the original point, indicates what exactly was at issue. In effect, this leads to a re-reading of the first verse in light of the second. Such a reading is consistent with the pattern noted earlier, that the most prevalent misunderstanding in the Fourth Gospel –

Johannesevangeliums, 82–88) includes John 8.56–58 as one of the 11 misunderstandings he identifies. It should be noted that Leroy's system of classification is much too rigid, and it is also questionable whether these misunderstandings were riddles that only community insiders could understand. See further Carson, "Misunderstandings."

[93] Some argue that Jesus is not making claims to deity but only to pre-existence. So E. D. Freed, "Who or What Was Before Abraham in John 8:58?," 52; Sloyan, 111. Lindars (336) similarly suggests that the point is that Jesus "continues for ever." Bultmann (327 n. 5) also states that one should "reject the view . . . that the sentence identifies Jesus with God." It seems, however, that identifying Jesus with God is precisely what John intends to do. As Brown (1.367) states, "No clearer indication of divinity is found in the Gospel tradition." Note the build-up throughout John 8, with the confusion in 8.24 and 8.28 over Jesus' 'I am' statements clearing up in 8.58, where the ἐγώ εἰμι is grammatically absolute and stands alone. Cf. R. Robert, "Le malentendu sur le Nom divin au chapitre VIII du quatrième évangile." As Ball observes, "Surely it is this ἐγώ εἰμι more than any other which forces the reader to see Jesus' words as a claim to divinity. It is the reaction of the Jews to these words which confirm that the reader was correct to think that Jesus was equating himself with the words of Yahweh in the earlier uses of the phrase" (*'I Am' in John's Gospel*, 197).

[94] Although Derrett sees an allusion to Isa 43.13 in John 8.58 (i.e., *ani hu*), he contends that "whether this statement was 'blasphemous' would be a matter of opinion. 'I am' is hardly the Name" ("Exercitations," 451). However, whether it is the divine name or not, it is a formula that Yahweh used to declare his identity and sovereignty as the one true God, and as such would be inappropriately applied to anyone other than the God of Israel. The context would also aid in determining the intention of such speech, and since the Jews take up stones in response, this suggests they understood the utterance as a blasphemous claim to deity. See Carson, 358; C. Williams, *I am He: The Interpretation of "Ani Hu" in Jewish and Early Christian Literature*, 182.

for the disciples, for others who express true albeit incomplete faith, as
well as for those who do not believe – is Jesus' identification as one with
Yahweh and his fulfilling of Yahweh's redemptive role. Second, misunderstandings are a signpost to the reader that the passage requires a more
careful look. The confusion following 8.56 signals that there is more there
than may meet the eye at first glance. Since the explanation restates in a
clearer way what the former intended to teach, those backgrounds that
provide the most appropriate contexts to create these meaning effects are
magnified for the attuned reader, thereby increasing the likelihood that our
proposed allusions would be recognized. Third, the proposed function of
Ps 118 in 8.56 explains the reason for Jesus' "I am" statement in 8.58. Most
commentary finds no link between the statement that touched off the misunderstanding and that which follows it. For example, although Culpepper
classifies the passage as a misunderstanding, he concludes that a "precise
resolution of the misunderstanding is not given to the reader."[95]   It is
unlikely that John's primary purpose is to assert Jesus' chronological
precedence to Abraham (as startling as that would be), for any comparison
to Abraham is secondary to the primary objective of identification with
Yahweh. Accordingly, the proposed reading of 8.56 suggests that rather
than introducing to the passage an unrelated statement, Jesus' "I am"
declaration is an entirely appropriate development of the immediately
preceding claim. Our proposal therefore has the virtue of accounting for
the sequence and content of the material.

V. Other Echoes: Liturgical, Thematic, and Structural

A. *A Liturgical Echo: Ps 118.25 in John 8.58*

Identifying the allusion to Ps 118.24 in 8.56 suggests that the search for
other echoes in the surrounding literary context may be fruitful. For the
reader familiar with the practices at Tabernacles, and especially one who
had recognized the previous allusion to Ps 118, the ἐγώ εἰμι in 8.58
may well have stirred echoes of the Ps 118 liturgy. The background and
meaning of Jesus' "I am" statements raise a number of complex questions
into which we cannot go in detail, but at least in the case of 8.58 the
majority of scholars, despite disagreeing on the implications of such a
position, line up in support of either Exod 3.14 or the Isaianic אני הוא as

---

[95] Culpepper, *Anatomy*, 158.

the source on which the words draw.[96] Although there is some support for the Exodus parallel,[97] the arguments in favor of *ani hu* are more convincing.[98] The LXX consistently renders *ani hu*, an expression that Yahweh uses to declare himself (especially in Isaiah), by ἐγώ εἰμι. As Dodd correctly observes, it is used "as the equivalent of a divine name."[99] If one thinks of the dialogue in John 8 taking place in Aramaic or possibly Hebrew, then Jesus may well have voiced the words *ani hu* in reference to himself.

Of interest is a tradition preserved in the Ps 118 Tabernacles liturgy:

> Every day they walk around the altar one time and say, "*Save now, we beseech thee, O Lord! We beseech thee, O Lord, send now prosperity* (Ps 118:25)." R. Judah says, "[They say], *'Ani waho* {אני והוא}, *save us we pray! Ani waho* {אני והוא}, *save us we pray!*'" And on that day [the seventh day of the willow branch] they walk around the altar seven times. (*m. Sukk.* 4.5)[100]

In an apparent attempt to avoid explicitly pronouncing the divine name in Ps 118.25,[101] the liturgy replaces אנא יהוה with אני והוא,[102] which is a

---

[96] The use of "I am" without addition presents the most plausible parallel to the OT designation of Yahweh. See John 6.20; 8.24, 28, 56; 13.19; 18.5, 6, 8. The "I am" appears with predicate several times in the self-designations of Jesus: the bread of life (6.35, 48); the bread from heaven (6.41); the living bread (6.51); the light of the world (8.12); the door of the sheep (10.7, 9); the good shepherd (10.11, 14); the resurrection and the life (11.25); the way, the truth, and the life (14.6); the vine (15.1, 5). The standard study on the parallels to "I am" remains E. Schweizer's *Ego Eimi: Die religionsgeschicht-liche Herkunft und theologische Bedeutung der johanneischen Bildreden, zugleich ein Beitrag zur Quellenfrage des vierten Evangeliums.* For discussion see Schnackenburg, 2.79–89; Brown, 1.533–538;

[97] See for example Enz, "Exodus," 213; Odeberg, 307; Sloyan, 111; Schnackenburg 2.224; A. Probst, "Jésus et Yahvé," 45.

[98] See Carson, 343; Bernard, 2.322; Bruce, 206; Derrett, "Exercitations," 451; Dodd, *Interpretation*, 93–96. On the Isaianic *ani hu* as background for the sayings in John see Ball, '*I Am*' *in John's Gospel*, 177–203. Although arguing for an Isaianic background, Williams (*I am He*, 299, 301) suggests the possible additional influence of Deut 23.39. H. Zimmerman ("Das absolute Ἐγώ εἰμι als die neutestamentliche Offenbarungsformel") argues that *ani hu* provides the bridge between the OT use of *ani YHWH* and the NT ἐγώ εἰμι. Lindars (336) appears to argue against *ani hu* as a background primarily because he holds that "John never simply identifies Jesus with God." Bultmann (327 n. 5) objects to *ani hu* as well, but without argument.

[99] Dodd, *Interpretation*, 94. See for example Isa 41.4; 43.10, 13, 25; 45.18; 46.4; 48.12.

[100] Only the material in {} is not original to Neusner's translation.

[101] The text reads אנא יהוה הושיעה נה אנא יהוה.

[102] Danby (*Mishnah*, 178 n. 13) notes that "instead of the repeated 'We beseech thee, O Lord' (*ana YHWH*, which involves pronouncing the Sacred Name) they modify the

slight variation on אני הוא.[103] The phrase *ani waho* is therefore a reverent substitute for, and equivalent of, the divine name; and since it is function-ally equivalent to and only slightly different in form from the familiar *ani hu*, it would not require mental gymnastics for the reader acquainted with this tradition to hear the echo of a liturgical phrase in the ἐγώ εἰμι of 8.58. Although one cannot argue with certainty that the change in the liturgy took place before the writing of the Fourth Gospel (the earliest witness is R. Judah ben Ilai, ca. 130–160 AD), Qumran provides examples of a similar use of the third person singular pronoun as substitute for the divine name, and one especially close parallel to *ani waho*.[104] Furthermore, liturgy is generally less subject to rapid change than other forms of speech, and the avoidance of pronouncing the divine name by finding appropriate substitutes pre-dates the rabbis. Accordingly, it is not impossible that in this case the Mishnah reflects Second Temple practice.[105]

Several factors increase the plausibility of an echo. First, through the

---

sounds to *ani waho*." For others who support this interpretation see Rubenstein, *Sukkot*, 112. See William's detailed discussion of the use of the term in the liturgy of Taber-nacles (*I am He*, 205–213).

[103] A case can be made that *waho* is used simply as the third person singular pronoun, and therefore that *ani waho* and *ani hu* are functionally synonymous. See J. Baumgarten, "A New Qumran Substitute for the Divine Name and Mishnah Sukkah 4.5." On *ani hu* as the likely source for *ani waho* see Carson, 343; Stauffer, *Jesus and His Story*, 181. Williams (*I am He*, 213) argues that it is difficult to determine the nature of *ani waho*'s formal resemblance to *ani hu*, but concedes that the latter may have contributed to the formulation of *ani waho* as an interpretation of the divine name.

[104] See discussion and citations in Rubenstein, *Sukkot*, 112–113. The close parallel he notes is 4Q266. There is an enigmatic saying attributed to Hillel that appears to use *ani* in place of the divine name: "It was said that when he used to rejoice at the Rejoicing at the place of the Water-Drawing, he used to recite thus, 'If *ani* is here, everyone is here; but if *ani* is not here, who is here?'" (*b. Sukk.* 53a). The last phrase can also be translated as "If I am here . . . if I am not here," although the former ("If 'I' is here . . .") seems more likely (in support see Odeberg, 332–333; Stauffer, *Jesus*, 179–18). In any case the notes to the translation point out that *ani* was interpreted by some as referring to God. Significant for our purposes is that this tradition dates back to the Second Temple, uses *ani* to refer to God, takes place at the celebration of Tabernacles, and may be linked more explicitly to the water drawing ceremony in which Ps 118 played such a central role. It may thus provide an early parallel to the use of *ani waho* in *m. Sukk.* 4.5. Ball ('*I Am' in John's Gospel*, 37 n. 4) notes that if the *Sukkah* reference is correctly attributed to Hillel, then it is plausible that an understanding of *ani hu* and *ani waho* as standing for the secret name of God may have influenced John's use of ἐγώ εἰμι.

[105] Cf. Rubenstein's conclusion: "R. Yehuda's tradition thus reflects a divine cognomen popular during second temple times. The evidence of the Qumran scrolls demonstrates once again the reliability of the tannaitic traditions" (*Sukkot*, 113). Cf. Dodd, *Interpretation*, 95: "It is not impossible that the traditional interpretation of it may have had its beginnings during the period to which the Fourth Gospel belongs."

oft-repeated and thus familiar vocalization of the psalm in the festival, the *ani waho* formula links the ἐγώ εἰμι saying more closely to the Tabernacles context of the passage. Second, we have noted the structural links between 8.56 and 8.58; the former sets the stage for the latter, which in turn explains the former. The order is of interest because the proposed sequence of allusions parallels the flow of the psalm itself: the allusion to Ps 118.24 in 8.56 leads to the liturgical echo of Ps 118.25 in 8.58. A reader who had recognized the first allusion would be more likely to make the connection to a phrase which immediately follows it in the liturgy.

A third and much more subtle link may be John's emphasis on "the name." God has given his name to Jesus (17.11), whose mission it is to make the name known (17.6, 25–26). Dodd has argued that in rabbinic literature *ani waho* was taken to stand for "the intimate association or quasi-identification of God with His people."[106] Applied in John, he suggests that the divine name takes the form "not merely of אני הוא, ἐγώ εἰμι, but of אני והוא, ἐγώ καὶ ὁ πέμψας με."[107] If his argument is sustainable, then the revelation of the divine name in Jesus is connected with his being sent, a link that is strengthened by our argument that the coming-sent theme functions to identify Jesus with Yahweh. It is also suggestive that Jesus explicitly claims to come in the name of the Father (5.43; 17.3), a phrase that would evoke Ps 118 as it functions in the Entrance Narrative. Accordingly, it is possible that the links between the coming-sent theme and the name of God would increase the resonance of the liturgical echo.

I cautiously suggest that the liturgical phrase *ani waho* provides an informing background for Jesus' statement in 8.58. It is certainly not the primary background – that distinction most likely belongs to the Isaianic *ani hu* – but a credible argument can be made for the phrase being linked to, and thus informing the meaning of, the ἐγώ εἰμι sayings, especially those placed firmly in a Tabernacles context.[108] Such an echo would evoke

---

[106] Dodd, *Interpretation*, 94. Rubenstein (*Sukkot*, 112) confirms such an interpretation of *ani waho* (lit. "I and He") as current among the Palestinian amoraim, where God shares in the suffering of his people, and in saving them thus saves himself. Young ("Isaiah") points out that the particular use of the "name of God" in Isaiah is paralleled in John. Since Isaiah is the primary source for *ani hu*, the parallels are especially relevant.

[107] Dodd, *Interpretation*, 96. Carson (343) suggests that it is "not obvious that a similar association should be read into John." Although it may not be obvious, it also is not impossible.

[108] Beasley-Murray (140) assumes this in discussing the basis for Jesus' proclamations in 7.37–38 and 8.12: The ἐγώ εἰμι sayings of 8.24, 28, 58 "are linked with the festival celebrations through the 'I and he' formula in the Psalms singing each day, and form part of the background and meaning of Jesus' ἐγώ εἰμι utterances." Cf. E. Stauffer ("Probleme der Priestertradition," 147–148), who argues that the absolute ἐγώ εἰμι derives from the

not Ps 118 so much as the liturgical interpretation and practice of the psalm. As with the background, the meaning effects will come primarily from other sources, except that, because the festival liturgy in part underlies the saying, it contributes an additional layer of meaning and reference that evokes the Tabernacles-Ps 118 complex with its attendant historical associations and eschatological expectations. In this way, although it is not a dominant background, the liturgical phrase from Ps 118.25 may form part of the echo – the history and thought of Israel – that would reverberate both in Jesus' utterance and the ear of the Johannine reader.

B. A Thematic Echo: Ps 118.22 in John 8.59

There may be two further echoes of Ps 118 in John 8, although they are the faintest and most speculative of those suggested.[109] The first is a possible thematic echo to Ps 118.22 in 8.59, where the Jews pick up stones to stone Jesus. Barrett argues that some Synoptic *testimonia* are no longer present as such but have been worked into the thematic structure of the Fourth Gospel.[110] Particularly relevant for us is the rejected stone: "This was a very popular testimony in the early Church, and though the testimony itself is absent from John its sense is everywhere apparent, often in a more pregnant form than in the other Christian literature."[111] It is possible that John is evoking, in a most subtle way, the rejected stone theme in which Ps 118.22 played a dominant role. In support, first, the allusion to Ps 118.24 in 8.56 could easily draw in the psalm's surrounding context, of which v. 22 was one of the most familiar texts. In 8.56 Jesus has cast the Jews in the role of the builders who rejected God's chosen stone. In 8.59 Jesus is not identified as the stone, but one could see subtle irony in that the Jews reject

---

cultic theophany passages of the OT and lives on in the liturgy of the Jewish festivals of Passover and particularly Tabernacles. For a more detailed argument see idem, *Jesus*, 174–194. Ball (*'I Am' in John's Gospel*, 170–172), although preferring the Isaianic *ani hu* as primary background, notes that the only occasions in which a rabbinic interpretation – that is, in which *ani hu* has become a fixed formula the utterance of which would be considered blasphemy – could be brought into play is 8.58 and 18.5–6. However, since *ani waho* is probably dependent on *ani hu* it may not be necessary to make this an either/or distinction.

[109] Due to their dubious status I have been very uncertain about whether these should even be included in this study, but have proceeded to cover them as possibilities from a reader response point of view. See further n. 120 below.

[110] Barrett, 157–162.

[111] Barrett, 161. Note that John need not be dependent on the Synoptics for knowledge of stone interpretation, as it was widespread in early Christian circles, and was the subject of much Jewish speculation.

the true cornerstone by picking up stones from the temple.[112] The irony
would be even more poignant as these antagonists had perhaps even that
same day participated at the temple in the Ps 118 Tabernacles liturgy that
rejoices in God's chosen stone, although of course they would not have
recognized themselves as the builders. Second, a rejected stone echo would
thematically parallel the conflict in John 8, as the religious authorities'
opposition to Jesus becomes increasingly hostile and even violent.[113] It
may be more than coincidence that John mentions two attempts to stone
Jesus, and that each of these is the result of a confrontation between Jesus
and the Jews in which Ps 118 may be alluded to: The allusion to Ps 118.24
in 8.56 precedes the event in 8.59, and the stoning attempt in 10.31–33
follows an allusion to Ps 118.10–12 in 10.24.

C. A Structural Echo: Ps 118.27 in John 8.12

A very faint echo of Ps 118.27 may surface in Jesus' statement "I am the
light of the world" (8.12). Light is one of the more powerful symbols developed in the Fourth Gospel, and its background one of the more complex,
with a variety of roots suggested either in the OT, Judaism, festival practice
and themes, Hellenism, pagan religions, or a combination of any of these.[114]
The links to the festival of light celebrated at least on the first night (and
perhaps the other nights as well) of Tabernacles are especially suggestive,
since Jesus' statement takes place at Tabernacles. If we suppose that the
festivities evoked, among other Scripture texts, the unending light of the
eschatological Zechariahan Tabernacles (Zech 14.6), it is also possible
that Ps 118.27 would come to the celebrant's mind.[115] In favor of this, first
of all, it may be significant that John specifies the location of Jesus' statement

---

[112] Stones probably would have been available among the materials used in the on-going
construction of the temple. See Str-B 1.1008–1009; Bultmann, 328 n. 3; Brown, 1.360.

[113] Davies has suggested that Jesus' exit from the temple grounds in 8.59 represents
"the departure of the Divine Presence from the old 'Holy Space'" (*The Gospel and the
Land*, 296). The authorities' rejection of Jesus leads to Jesus' rejecting them – they will
remain in sin (8.21–24), in a state of spiritual exile.

[114] For discussion of a variety of options see Odeberg 286–292; Bultmann, 40–44;
343–344; Barrett, 335–338; Schnackenburg, 2.188–192; Dodd, *Interpretation*, 201–212;
Beasley-Murray, 126–129, 140. For the development of the light theme in John see
especially Culpepper, *Anatomy*, 190–192.

[115] M. Davies argues that Jesus' teaching is more obviously based on Zech 14 and
scriptural references to the light perpetually burning in the sanctuary than to knowledge
of ritual practice in Jerusalem at the Feast of Tabernacles (*Rhetoric*, 93; see also 226–227).
However, the close links between Zech 14 and the festival suggest that a combination of
the two is more likely.

as the temple, and more precisely the Court of the Women, which is where the light festival took place (8.20).[116] Descriptions of the festivities detail that the light comes from the place of water-drawing.[117] The water-drawing procession made its way every morning through the court on its way to the altar, singing the Hallel. Psalm 118.27 preserves what may be an ancient description of this processional repeating the phrase "The Lord is God, and he has given us light." It is not impossible that those who rejoiced in the evening would remember the words they had intoned that morning on their way through the very location from which the burning light now illuminated (shone upon!) them.

Second, the original context of the psalm provides an appropriate thematic parallel. The psalm links the one who comes in the name of the Lord (Ps 118.26) with the shining of Yahweh's light upon Israel, so that this one's coming either results in or perhaps actually personifies that light (Ps 118.27). As argued previously, by this point in the Fourth Gospel John has already used Ps 118 to identify Jesus as the one who comes in the name of the Father, providing an appropriate background for one who now claims to be the light for his people.[118] The literary unit of John 8 begins with an ἐγώ εἰμι statement (8.12), and reaches its climax in Jesus' ἐγώ εἰμι declaration in 8.58. It is tempting to see a parallel literary function at work in the use of Ps 118, with the "light" echo in 8.12 beginning the section, and the *ani waho* echo in 8.58 forming an inclusion.[119]

To sum up: Of the three echoes, the last two are especially faint and speculative, and indeed any parallels with Ps 118 may be attributable to mere coincidence. Stones need not carry any special significance since they are, after all, a useful weapon, especially if at hand. Psalm 118 also does not explain the mention of light, for which there are much stronger backgrounds. My claims of influence are of a much lower order, for these echoes fall in the area of reader response. Did John intend to evoke them?

---

[116] On the Court of the Women as the location of Jesus' proclamation, see Schnackenburg, 2.195–196; Brown, 1.344. For background see Str-B 2.805–807.

[117] See *m. Sukk.* 5.1: "He who has not seen the joy of the place of water-drawing has not seen joy in his whole life-time . . . There was no court in Jerusalem that was not bright from the light of the place of drawing [water]."

[118] There is little question that the saying points the reader back to the prologue, where the Baptist bore witness to the light that was coming into the world (1.7–9). It is not impossible that the informed reader may have noted the close connection of this first "light" saying with the development of the coming-sent theme.

[119] On the inclusion function of the ἐγώ εἰμι sayings see Brown, 1.367; Ball, *'I Am' in John's Gospel*, 81–82.

Perhaps not. Is it possible that an informed reader could hear these echoes, or read them into the text? Perhaps so.[120]

VI. Conclusion

John brings into play the Ps 118-Tabernacles complex of associations by describing Abraham's eschatological joy in 8.56 with the words of Ps 118.24, thus identifying the day of Jesus with the day of Yahweh. A possible allusion to *Jubilees* provides as background an occasion when Abraham anticipates with rejoicing the promise of a holy seed that will be like the Creator, linking this to the foundation of Tabernacles and the celebration of the Ps 118 liturgy. The meaning effects of the allusion are consonant with the New Exodus framework used to describe Jesus' ministry and person. In the process of redefining the true Israel, he has warned that even seed of Abraham can be excluded (8.31–47): the true children of Abraham are those who, like their father, rejoice at the day of Jesus. In claiming the day of Yahweh as his own – the day when Yahweh returns to accomplish the restoration of Israel, defeat their enemies, and establish his universal rule – Jesus indicates that he actualizes the day of Yahweh's kingship and eschatological rule. This serves to identify Jesus with Yahweh not only functionally (soteriology) but also ontologically. The ἐγώ εἰμι that follows in 8.58 confirms this identification, and is functionally equivalent to the claim in 8.56.[121] An echo in 8.58 of the

---

[120] In regard to the viability of more than one background informing a particular text or context, and more specifically the intention of the writer *vis-à-vis* the response of the reader, at least the following scenarios are possible. 1. The writer may intend to evoke a single background, and because of contextual indicators no other background is drawn in by the reader. 2. The writer intends one single background, although aware of other backgrounds closely associated with or perhaps inseparable from it that the attuned reader will recognize. 3. The writer intends one primary background, but leaves room for other backgrounds to play an informing role. For example, one expects that a Jew would naturally think of Zech 14 and the evening light festival when light is mentioned during Tabernacles, even if John points primarily to some other background. 4. The reader may draw in backgrounds which the writer never intended or perhaps was even aware of. Accordingly, it is not impossible that at times more than one background may be brought into play, even when one particular parallel is intended to be primarily in view.

[121] J. Blank says it well: "Es ist, als sagte Jesus hier: Die Offenbarung Jahwes, das bin ich. Ich bin die Stätte göttlicher Gegenwart und Offenbarung in der Geschichte. . . . So ist die Formel nicht nur 'Ausdruck' der Offenbarung, sondern sie sagt selber, was die Offenbarung ist und daß sie hier ist. . . . Diejenigen, die sich mit Jesus auseinandersetzen, haben es mit dem *Ego eimi* selber zu tun, mit dem geschichtlichen Offenbarer und Repräsentanten Jahwes, und also mit Jahwe selbst" (*Krisis: Untersuchungen zur johanneischen Christologie und Eschatologie*, 246).

liturgical phrase *ani waho* would underscore not only Jesus' unity with the Father, but also possibly "carry the further implication of Jesus as the representative of God's people binding them to the Father."[122]   The suggested function of Ps 118 in this passage discloses again the tension, so characteristic of the Fourth Gospel, between statements that identify Jesus with Yahweh and others that differentiate them from each other.[123]

---

[122] Beasley-Murray, 131; so also Bruce, 193.

[123] See Carson, 344: "This does not mean that Jesus and Yahweh of the Old Testament are identified without remainder . . . But this tension between unqualified statements affirming the full deity of the Word or of the Son, and those which distinguish the Word or the Son from the Father, are typical of the Fourth Gospel from the very first verse."

Chapter 9

The Door: Ps 118 in John 10.7–10

I. Introduction

The Shepherd Discourse is one of the more difficult passages in the Fourth Gospel, with wide-ranging disagreement on a number of issues. The passage begins with Jesus uttering an enigmatic παροιμία (10.1–5) and the statement that it was not understood by the audience (10.6). The following series of pronouncements are divided into two sections that continue and develop some of the main themes of the *paroimia*, centering on the close identification of Jesus with the door (10.7–10) and the shepherd (10.11–16). This is followed by a theological conclusion (10.17–18) and the reaction of the Jews (10.19–21). Although on the surface it appears to be straightforward, the interpretation of the text is dogged by a number of questions. Our primary interest in the passage lies in the possibility that Ps 118 serves as the background for the door sayings (10.7, 9), a suggestion made by a number of scholars.[1] However, the suggestion is generally made in passing, with no evidence put forward to support the allusion other than to note that the psalm was used messianically elsewhere in the Gospels. In addition, there has been little attention paid to examining what function the allusion

---

[1] See P. Stuhlmacher, *Biblische Theologie des Neuen Testaments*, 2.230; Schlatter, 235; E. Fascher, "Ich bin die Tür!: Eine Studie zu Joh 10:1–18," 43, 49; J. Beutler, "Der alttestamentlich-jüdische Hintergrund der Hirtenrede in Johannes 10," 31; Dittmar, *Vetus Testamentum*, 125; A. Simonis, *Die Hirtenrede im Johannes-Evangelium: Versuch einer Analyse von Johannes 10,1–18 nach Entstehung, Hintergrund und Inhalt*, 251; A. Reinhartz, *The Word in the World: The Cosmological Tale in the Fourth Gospel*, 81; Brown, 1.394; Carson, 385; W. F. Howard, *Christianity According to St. John*, 138; J. Velasco Arenas, "'Yo soy la puerta' (Jn 10,7.9): Trasfondo y sentido de la imagen cristológica de la puerta," 77; Ball, *'I Am' in John's Gospel*, 229; T. Kambeitz, "I Am the Door," 111. Beasley-Murray (169) identifies Ps 118.20 as "the most likely precedent for the figure." Hoskyns (374) lists Ps 118.19, 20 for reference along with examples of early Christian literature where the metaphor of the door or gate is applied to Jesus, although he does not explicitly say that it informs the use in this passage. Schnackenburg (2.290) writes that "the choice of door as symbol of the Saviour could have ties with the Messianic interpretation of Ps 118." However, he qualifies this by suggesting that the gnostic material for the door motif "is certainly much richer."

would perform in the passage.[2] Consequently this study will focus on examining the plausibility of the allusion and suggest what its intended function may have been. First, however, it is necessary to address some of the critical issues that affect one's approach to, and interpretation of, the passage.

II. Setting the Parameters

A. The Macro Context

Because 10.19–21 mentions the healing of the blind man some argue that these verses should immediately follow 9.39–41. In a similar reference to prior discourse, 10.26–29 refers to the shepherd and his flock although 10.22 appears to place it several months later than the Shepherd Discourse, leading to the proposal that 10.22–29 should also follow the relocated 10.19–21 (i.e., 10.19–29 precedes 10.1–18). As a result the entire narrative of ch. 10 would be located at the Feast of Dedication.[3] However, such a re-ordering of the text is unwarranted, not least because there does not appear to be a satisfactory explanation as to how such a dislocation would have come about in the first place.[4] In addition, the text makes sense as it stands, and as Carson points out, "the Evangelist favours returning to themes already brought up and exploring them a little further."[5]

We will therefore approach the text in agreement with recent scholarship, which has reached a general consensus that the present verse sequence is a purposeful arrangement and makes sense both internally and in its surrounding literary context.[6] This suggests, first of all, that the

---

[2] An exception to this is Velasco's work ("Puerta"), although our conclusions are somewhat different.

[3] See for example Schweizer, *Ego Eimi*, 110; Bernard, 2.343–344. J. D. Turner ("The history of religions background of John 10," 33) adopts 10.19–30, 1–18, 31–42 as the original order. Bultmann (360) rearranges the text as follows: 10.22–26, 11–13, 1–10, 14–18, 27–39. For a history of scholarly opinion see P.-R. Tragan, *La parabole du 'Pasteur' et ses explications: Jean, 10,1–18: La genèse, les milieux littéraires*, 55–172. For studies on the structure of the text see O. Kiefer, *Die Hirtenrede: Analyse und Deutung von Joh 10,1–18*; Simonis, *Die Hirtenrede*; J. Schneider, "Zur Komposition von Joh. 10."

[4] See Jeremias ("ποιμήν κτλ.," *TDNT* 6.494–495) for discussion of ancient writing techniques in relation to the possible confusion and re-insertion of pages which could have led to dislocation. He concludes that this is extremely unlikely.

[5] Carson, 380. See also Barrett, 367: "[John's] thought moves in spirals rather than straight lines." Cf. Brown, 1.388.

[6] The validity of the preserved order of John 10 is one of the areas of general agreement that emerged from the Johannine Writings Seminar's focus on the Shepherd Discourse (with the exception of Turner, "History of religions," 33–52). Another area of consensus

Shepherd Discourse is to be read as a continuation of the conflict between Jesus and the religious authorities in ch. 9 over his identity and authority, and in the context of exclusion from the synagogue. A second implication is that the Shepherd Discourse is intended to be read in a Tabernacles context, with 10.22 bringing to a close the Tabernacles sequence begun in ch. 7 and marking the shift to a new festival setting. If one accepts the present order of the text then clearly it is implausible to argue that the Shepherd Discourse takes place at or is primarily governed by the themes of the Feast of Dedication.[7] At the same time, since 10.1–21 is not specifically placed at Tabernacles it is possible that along with ch. 9 it acts as a chronological bridge, taking place between the two feasts. As noted above, the return to the shepherd theme in 10.26–29 links the two passages, and in any case the two feasts are uniquely suited to blur together and overlap, since they share some themes and motifs in common and were associated historically by the Jews.[8] Accordingly Brown is justified in suggesting a "twofold direction" and function for 10.1–21, so that both feasts inform its context.[9]

It is more likely, however, that the reader would have associated the narrative primarily with the last temporal setting mentioned (Tabernacles at 7.37), especially since there is a clear temporal marker following the Shepherd Discourse that would distinguish the new context from the former.[10] As a result, we will approach 10.1–21 as chronologically associated with the Feast of Tabernacles because of the sequence preserved in the Gospel, while at the same time affirming that it is interlinked themati-

---

is that chs. 9 and 10 are closely related (see J. Beutler and R. T. Fortna, "Introduction," 3–5). In agreement with these points are Brown, 1.388–390; Barrett, 367–368; Dodd, *Interpretation*, 354–357; Schneider, "Komposition," 220–225; Simonis, *Die Hirtenrede*, 38ff, 59–64; Beasley-Murray, 166–167; Ridderbos, 352; Schnackenburg, 2.276–278; Haenchen, 395–396.

[7] That a Dedication motif dominates the whole of John 10 is the implication of Guilding's (*Jewish Worship*, 129–130) argument that the change of subject from ch. 9 to 10 results from the lectionary readings which for the Sabbath nearest to the Feast of Dedication all contain the theme of sheep, shepherds and of God the Shepherd of Israel. This would indeed be a remarkable coincidence if one could determine with any certainty the lectionary system in use at that time. The question is not whether there were lectionary readings, which there clearly were, but which passages were stipulated for each Sabbath. For a critique of Guilding's triennial lectionary cycle see L. Morris, *The New Testament and the Jewish Lectionaries*; Schürer, *History*, 2.450–451. J. E. Bruns ("The Discourse of the Good Shepherd and the Rite of Ordination") argues for a predominance of Dedication motifs in 10.1–18 at the expense of Tabernacles themes.

[8] The purification of the temple is called a feast of Tabernacles in the month of Chislev (2 Macc 1.9). See discussion in ch. 2 above.

[9] See Brown, 1.388–389. Schnackenburg (2.278) suggests a similar sharing of contexts.

[10] Cf. Reinhartz, *The Word in the World*, 50 n. 6.

cally both with the following passage and the Feast of Dedication in which
the latter is set. This suggests that although one can expect John primarily
to evoke Tabernacles imagery and themes as the principal context (following
his pattern in the other festival narratives), there may be a secondary contextual layer from Dedication subtly called into play, especially where the
themes of the two festivals converge and complement each other.[11]

B. The Micro Context

A third area of general agreement is that 10.7–18 is an interpretation of the
paroimia. Consensus dissolves, however, when it comes to identifying
this relationship more precisely, and around the question of genre. The
paroimia itself could belong to any of a number of genres. Together with
παραβολή it translates the Hebrew מָשָׁל, which can refer to a wide variety
of literary forms.[12] More important is the bearing that genre may have on
10.7–10 and what this implies for how closely the latter text must conform
to the former. Here again there is a multiplicity of views,[13] much of it
owing perhaps to a lack of uniformity and precision in defining the various
terms of metaphorical language. In any case, the continuing discussion
and disagreement in determining the genre of the different sections of the
Shepherd Discourse suggests that it is a complex task which we will not

---

[11] Although there may be a question as to whether the audience would recall events
and teachings in chronologically-prior narratives, one should keep in mind that John's
primary audience was readers of the Gospel, who would have little problem with temporal distance between narratives or interpreting an earlier event (Shepherd Discourse) in
light of a later point in the text (Dedication) which the former has anticipated in some
way.

[12] Brown (1.390–393) identifies it as parabolic, Carson (380) as a "figure of speech"
that is "distinctly Johannine," Schnackenburg (2.285) as a "cryptic discourse," and Barrett
(367) argues that the entire discourse is neither parable nor allegory, although it is related
to both, preferring to describe it as a "symbolic discourse." Carson (383) points out that
the common feature in all of the literary forms is that "there is something enigmatic or
cryptic about them."

[13] For example, Brown (1.390–393) argues that 10.7ff. consists of allegorical interpretations of twin parables in 10.1–5; Beasley-Murray (167) labels it a "meditation" on
the parable; and Lindars (354–355) first argues that we have an expansion and development of the parables, and then calls it "a discourse in monologue form." Schnackenburg
sees it as "extensions of the imagery" from the *paroimia* (2.294), and "developments of a
revelatory kind" (2.280). J. P. Martin ("John 10:1–10," 171–172) argues that 10.7–10 is
not an explanation but rather a "restatement" of vv. 1–5, so that the whole text (vv. 1–10)
is a "symbolic saying." R. Kysar ("Johannine Metaphor – Meaning and Function: A Literary Case Study of John 10:1–18," 93) concludes that the different is between "implicit
and explicit metaphor."

be able to undertake in detail.[14] What is clear is that there is disjunction between the *paroimia* and the following text, and especially with the Door section.[15] Whereas in the *paroimia* Jesus is identified as the shepherd by entering through the door, in 10.7, 9 he *is* the door.[16] One would expect Jesus to declare "I am the shepherd of the sheep" rather than "I am the door," which departs so startlingly from the roles assigned in the *paroimia*. Although the dual identification of Jesus as door and shepherd is not a problem for Johannine Christology, it does pose a problem for the cohesiveness of the text, as there is some tension if Jesus is simultaneously both the shepherd and the door by which the shepherd enters.

Attempts by scholars to alleviate the undeniable awkwardness of the disjunction fall most often, although not always, in one of the following categories. First is the suggestion that the discourse is composed of a series of parables which were combined to make a literary unit.[17] A second approach presupposes that the *paroimia* is a parable, and is characterized by searching for underlying sources that would explain the subsequent expansion and interpretation in 10.7–18.[18] Third, some commentators see

---

[14] For a discussion of the different views of genre relating to 10.1–18 see Kysar, "Johannine Metaphor," 84–85, 96–101; J. Quasten, "The Parable of the Good Shepherd: Jn 10:1–21," 7–12, 151–153.

[15] In addition to the disjunction with the door, one notes that whereas the shepherd led the sheep out of the fold, now he leads them in and out (10.9); new actors are introduced – hired hands (10.12), sheep from other pens (10.16); the gatekeeper is not mentioned again; the death of the shepherd is introduced and becomes a focal point (10.15).

[16] There is not a complete disjunction between 10.7–10 and the *paroimia*, for although the identification of Jesus as the door is a departure from the former, the contrast between Jesus and those who come falsely continues in 10.8, 10, advancing the *paroimia's* contrast of Jesus the true shepherd over against the thieves. The tension apparent to most is not so to L. Schenke ("Das Rätsel von Tür und Hirt. Wer es löst, hat gewonnen!, " 85–87), for he argues that the door metaphor reflects a purposeful structure where Jesus as the door *to* the sheep (10.7–8) corresponds to 10.1–2, and Jesus as the door *for* the sheep corresponds to 10.3–5.

[17] So J. J. O'Rourke, "Jo 10.1–18: Series Parabolarum," 22–25. Bruce (225) argues that 10.7–9 is a short parable inserted into a longer one (10.1–5, 10–17), which accounts for the abrupt shift to the image of Jesus as the door. Cf. Temple, *Core*, 178. Note however that Bruce's unlikely suggestion would disturb the balance in the alternation of the door (10.7, 9) and subsequent comparison (10.8, 10). A. George ("Je suis la porte des brebis: Jean 10,1–10," 18) argues that there are three small parables (1–3a; 3b–5; 11b–13) which are then explained in vv. 7–10, 11a and 14–18.

[18] See J. A. T. Robinson, "The Parable of John 10.1–5." Robinson argues that 10.1–5 is a fusion of two simpler parables. Cf. Brown (1.391–393) and Lindars (354). Dodd famously describes 10.1–5 as "the wreckage of two parables fused into one, the fusion having partly destroyed the original form of both" (*Historical Tradition*, 383). Tragan (*La parabole*, 191ff.) argues that 10.1–2 is the original parable and vv. 3–5 an allegorizing commentary. Falling in the same general category is J. Derrett's ("The Good Shepherd:

no contradiction in Jesus being both door and shepherd at the same time. Morris, for example, notes that such statements "are not uncommon in the Gospel,"[19] and others put forward examples from Middle Eastern sheep farming where the shepherd fulfills the function of a door by sleeping in the opening to the sheep enclosure.[20] Fourth, it appears that early on the difficulty of the unexpected door saying led to what Metzger calls an "alleviation of the text,"[21] with ὁ ποιμήν replacing ἡ θύρα. Although they are in the minority, a surprising number of scholars have accepted ὁ ποιμήν as original.[22] Similarly, Torrey and M. Black argue, from a different vantage point, that mistakes in translation from the original Aramaic led to the reading of "door" instead of "shepherd."[23] It appears that, as with the copyist who first introduced the ὁ ποιμήν reading, its modern support rests

---

St. John's Use of Jewish Halakah and Haggadah," 50) fascinating but unconvincing suggestion that the discourse is based on a parable which the evangelist decoded by tracing back the biblical allusions and then subjecting them to Jewish interpretive techniques. In spite of some influential detractors, the majority of commentators do, however, view 10.1–5 as a single unit.

[19] Morris, 499. He continues, "Jesus is the bread of life (6:35), and He gives it (6:51). He speaks the truth (8:45f), and He is the truth (14:6). Throughout the Gospel He is depicted as showing men the way, and He is the way (14:6)."

[20] See E. F. F. Bishop ("'The Door of the Sheep' – John x.7–9," 308), who suggests this "may well answer the criticism that there is a 'harsh change' from the simile of the shepherd to that of the door or vice versa." Cf. K. Bailey's argument, based on his observations of sheep farming in the Middle East, that the door of the second "poem" (10.7–10) represents a different situation than that of the first "poem," where the sheep are kept within the courtyard of the family home. In 10.7–10 the setting is an enclosure in open pasture land: "There is no door and no door-keeper. . . . Once inside the enclose the sheep are safe as long as the open entrance is secured. There is no door. The shepherd sleeps across this entrance and thus *he is the door*" ("The Shepherd Poems of John 10 and Their Culture," 8; emphasis original). However, it is not obvious that such a distinction is intended in the transition from the *paroimia* to the Door section. In any case, there is clearly a door which the doorkeeper opens in the *paroimia*.

[21] Metzger, *Textual Commentary*, 229.

[22] See Schweizer, *Ego Eimi*, 142–143; Wellhausen, 48; U. Busse, "Open Questions on John 10," 10. P. Weigandt ("Zum Text von Jon X 7," 43–51) sees merit in the reading. For further discussion of the textual problem from this point of view see Tragan, *La parabole*, 182–190.

[23] Torrey (*Translated Gospels*, 112) argues that the original Aramaic was wrongly divided by the translator, thus rendering "I am the door of the sheep" instead of "I came as the shepherd of the sheep." The impetus for this argument is clear: "The interruption made by vss. 7 and 9 is intolerable" (ibid., 113). M. Black (*An Aramaic Approach to the Gospels and Acts*, 259 n. 1) arrives at a similar conclusion ("I am the shepherd of the sheep") although by slightly different means. Sanders and Mastin (249) adopt Black's suggestion of dittography, arguing that to accept "door" as the original reading leaves 10.7–10 "in an almost intolerable state of confusion." To remain consistent, Torrey (*Translated Gospels,* 113*)* argues that 10.9 is an addition to the text to support 10.7, a suggestion that Barrett (371) rightly dismisses as "unwarrantable." Cf. Bruce, 225.

less on the textual plausibility of the reading than in its ability to relieve the tension of the contrasting metaphors.[24] The great majority of manuscripts support the reading ἡ θύρα, it is clearly *lectio difficilior*, and should be retained.[25]

These solutions may be plausible to different degrees, but the awkwardness many see in Jesus' being identified both as door and shepherd may stem primarily from assuming that John has not moved away from the original picture of the *paroimia*, and thus expecting uniformity and formal coherence in the application of the metaphors. Certainly the section 10.7–18 is connected to the *paroimia*, and 10.6 implies that what follows is in some form intended as an explanation.[26] However, this is not the allegorical explanation of a parable which requires a direct and exclusive relationship between each element and its parallel, for here both door and shepherd apply to the same person.[27] Our passage may be a symbolic or cryptic discourse, a development and expansion of the *paroimia*, a change from implicit to explicit metaphor or from enigmatic speech to direct exposition – strict categorization is unnecessary. What is apparent is that in drawing on the main images of the *paroimia* John does not restrict himself to a singular correspondence of prior object to later object but instead uses the images within a wide range of meaning.

Accordingly, it is possible – actually preferable – to view the Door section not so much as an interpretation or explanation of the *paroimia* as an independent development of its metaphors.[28] We will approach 10.7–10 primarily as a distinct unit, in the same way that 10.1–5 should be considered on its own. This is not to say that they are isolated and unrelated to

---

[24] The reading is supported by various Coptic manuscripts and p[75], but in spite of the prestige that the latter enjoys, the variant appears to be an obvious correction.

[25] The majority of scholars are in agreement with this. See Schnackenburg, 2.288; Barrett, 370–371; Hoskyns, 373; Lindars, 358; Beasley-Murray, 164; Brown, 1.386; Morris, 505 n. 25; J. Painter, *The Quest for the Messiah: The History, Literature and Theology of the Johannine Community*, 296 n. 25; M. Rodríguez Ruiz, "El discurso del Buen Pastor (Jn 10,1–18): Coherencia teologico-literaria e interpretacion," 31; Velasco, "Puerta," 56; Jeremias, "θύρα," *TDNT* 3.179 n. 1.

[26] Schneider ("Komposition") suggests that the explanation develops three key words – the door (10.7–10), shepherd (10.11, 14), and his own sheep (10.11, 15, 17, 26–30).

[27] Against 10.7ff being an allegory see Kysar, "Johannine Metaphor," 93; Velasco, "Puerta," 62–64. Although in his commentary Brown (1. 390) suggests that 10.7–18 is allegorical explanation of the parable, in a later review he finds Kiefer (*Die Hirtenrede*) persuasive in arguing that the later sections are not an explanation or interpretation as one finds in the Synoptics, but rather a "development of the imagery" and pictures taken from the *paroimia* (Brown, Review of O. Kiefer, 100).

[28] See Schnackenburg, 2.281; Carson, 384; Painter, "Tradition, history and interpretation in John 10," 60.

one another for, to use Barrett's term, there is an "interpenetration"[29] of material and language. In this regard, Kysar's suggestion that one should look at the units that make up the discourse as a "continuation of imagery" in consecutive "images" or "word pictures" is attractive.[30] To sum up, the Door section draws on and is informed by the *paroimia's* metaphors, but is independent in its interpretation and application of them. That is, it borrows the language, but not necessarily the meaning and function. A number of the problems noted by commentators are easily resolved, or at least significantly eased, if one expects less coherence and strict correlation between 10.1–5 and 10.7–10.[31]

---

[29] Barrett, 370.

[30] Kysar, "Johannine Metaphor," 89–90. Accordingly, one should not expect strict coherence in such a series of word pictures, each of which is intended to imprint an image on the mind of the reader and create an impression of Jesus' identity and function.

[31] It is especially important that one note the approach advocated here, for it is critical to the interpretation of the passage ahead. Many of the objections that may be raised against my particular exegesis of the passage arise from a fundamentally different understanding of the relationship of the *paroimia* to the units that follow it. In this regard several points should be made. 1. Most of the problems that commentators note in the passages are a direct result of an expectation that the metaphors of the Door section should correspond to the *paroimia*, as though there were precise continuity between the two. Some thus labor mightily and creatively – although for the most part unsuccessfully – to create a coherent picture. The fact that there are disjunctions, however, favors an approach that does not link the units so closely. Indeed, if the Door unit were intended as an explanation of the *paroimia* on the lines of those found in the Synoptics, one would expect a greater degree of correlation and continuity between the two. The simplest solution is that the writer did not intend such continuity. 2. The logical mind may find difficult the use of a single metaphor in relation to apparently incompatible referents. Leaving aside the fact that, if the Door section is to be interpreted separately from the *paroimia*, there is then no logical inconsistency in such use, it may also be the case that John and his readers could more easily hold such "fuzzy" images in tension. 3. My exegesis follows – depends on – the approach that I adopt, in which the Door section is informed by previous metaphors, but independent in its development of them, with the result that there is not exact continuity. Although some of my conclusions as to the use of Ps 118 may be new, the approach that I have taken is not without precedent, since some scholars have separated 10.1–5 from 10.7–10 as I have done. I suggest, therefore, that this is a legitimate approach, even if not one that all will find convincing. See in particular Kysar, "Johannine Metaphor." Others who do not expect strict correlation include O'Rourke ("Series Parabolarum," 22–25) and Bruce (225), who argue that the unit was originally a separate parable; Brown, Review, 100 (see n. 27 above); Painter, "Tradition," 60; Schnackenburg, 2.280–281. Quasten rejects the idea that 10.7ff. is "a rigorous methodical interpretation of the parable" ("Good Shepherd," 154). Carson (382–384) comments: "The fuller explanation in these verses cannot easily be accommodated as long as we think of vv. 1–5 as a cohesive narrative parable, and the verses before us as a mere explanation of them . . . The tensions are largely alleviated when we recognize that the expansions in these verses are not predicated on a single narrative

Such an approach has several implications for the study of the passage. First, the Door section (10.7–10) is no more secondary to the *paroimia* or to 10.11–18 than the door metaphor is secondary to that of the shepherd.[32] Martin has correctly pointed out that generally the door sayings are over-shadowed or largely ignored in favor of the good shepherd sayings. This is understandable in that the former may appear to be inserted between two passages that emphasize the shepherd. However, the door plays a not insignificant role in the *paroimia*, and is important in its own right as central to the following section.[33] Second, the door in the *paroimia* may have a different function and degree of importance than that of the Door section.[34] Third, if John intended to evoke a specific background for the door sayings, then we are not limited to the language or context of the *paroimia* but can look beyond it for other possible referent sources.

III. Establishing the Allusion

A. The Background of the Door

It is clear that the door is a significant metaphor in the Shepherd Discourse, which mentions it in both 10.1 and 2 (and the doorkeeper in 10.3), before taking it up again as the main symbol of the section 10.7–10. Although θύρα is used especially in relation to the openings to houses, rooms, tombs, and, as in the *paroimia*, can be applied to the entrance of an enclosure for sheep, its double combination with an "I am" saying and the soteriological

---

parable, but are further metaphorical uses of the three dominant features of the shepherding language introduced in vv. 1–5."

[32] Kysar perceptively notes that "whatever the character of the metaphorical language of the second half of the passage, it is implicitly demeaned by speaking of it as allegory, interpretation, expansion, or some such term" ("Johannine Metaphor," 84).

[33] Martin, "John 10," 171. Cf. Brown, 1.392. See further P. W. Meyer, "A Note on John 10.1–18," 233: "There seems to be a certain consensus that the interest of vss. 7–10 in θύρα is secondary and represents a later interpretation of vss. 1–5 which missed the point of these verses and concentrated by mistake upon a secondary element within them, namely ἡ θύρα, rather than upon the central idea of the ποιμήν. All such solutions fail, however, to be satisfactory for the one decisive reason that they ignore the actual importance of the word θύρα in vss. 1–5. . . . That vss. [7 and 9] concentrate on ἡ θύρα is very far from indicating a misunderstanding of vss. 1–5 on the part of some editor; in all the textual uncertainty of these verses there is evidence only that such an editor (if there is one here at all!) 'got' the real point of vss. 1–5, not that he missed it."

[34] For example, M. Sabbe suggests that in the *paroimia* the door has a "subordinate function . . . to oppose the shepherd to the thief, the robber and the stranger. . . . The 'I am' sayings of Jesus of verse 7 and surely that of verse 9 are more important" ("John 10 and its relationship to the Synoptic Gospels," 90).

implications of its function within the passage suggest that John intended for his readers to look beyond the literal sheep pen and the noun's more mundane use. Indeed most commentators have gone on to propose some background that would enrich the metaphor. Barrett suggests that θύρα evokes a "very complicated background," including parallels in the Synoptics, the gate of heaven in Greek literature and in the gnostic mythologies which developed this thought, and similar phrases from OT and apocalyptic literature.[35] Some argue for gnostic influence as primary,[36] which Odeberg combines with Jewish mysticism.[37] A minority propose a strong Synoptic influence,[38] while others claim that the only background is the *paroimia* itself.[39] However, the majority of scholars look to the OT for parallels, and Ps 118.20 is often mentioned.[40]

---

[35] Barrett, 372–373. Note that he suggests John did not have this background either consciously or unconsciously in mind.

[36] Bauer, 134–135; Becker, 1.330; Schweizer, *Ego Eimi*, 142–143. Turner ("History of religions," 50) claims that although the shepherd motif is drawn especially from the OT, the Door section owes more to Gnosticism. Sabbe argues that the door is either directly inspired by Synoptic material or is "some echo of mythic gnostic symbolism" ("John 10," 90).

[37] Odeberg, 314ff. He explores Jewish mysticism and focuses heavily on Mandean literature. He also links 10.9 to 1.51, arguing that they "*refer to the same spiritual reality*" (ibid., 323; emphasis original).

[38] For example, Sabbe, "John 10," 90; Painter ("Tradition," 61–62) suggests the possibility of a development of gospel tradition.

[39] Jeremias indicates at first that the background to the door is most naturally the OT, specifically the messianic interpretation of Ps 118.20, and he is at times cited in support for this position. However, he goes on to conclude that "nearer the mark . . . is that it arose out of Jn 10:1–2" (*TDNT* 3.179–180). Cf. Painter, *Quest*, 293. Lindars (358) argues that "the primary reference of *the door* . . . is to specific words in the parable, i.e. verses 1 and 2. [The 'I am'] does not have the rich overtones of a revelation-formula, but is a pointer to the interpretation of the parable." Bailey ("Shepherd Poems," 8), while not explicitly advocating dependence on the *paroimia*, argues for a continuation of the sheep farming context, albeit in a different geographical setting from the first, as the primary background for the Door section.

[40] For those who suggest Ps 118 as a background see n. 1 above. Other suggested parallels from the OT include Derrett's ("The Good Shepherd," 42) argument for Mic 2.13 as background to 10.9. Velasco ("Puerta," 75–76) suggests parallels with Exodus, with specific emphasis on the door of the Tent of Meeting (Exod 29.33; 33.11) foreshadowing Jesus as the door that allows for meeting with the Father. For further discussion of the possible influence of door-speculation in Exodus see Simonis, *Die Hirtenrede*, 251–253. Against the OT background, Ashton (*Understanding the Fourth Gospel*, 187) states that the symbols used in the Fourth Gospel with the "I am" sayings are "abundantly attested in the Old Testament" with one exception, that being the "I am the door" sayings in John 10.7, 9. However, Velasco's ("Puerta," 39–50) survey of the use of "door" in the OT and Jewish literature through Josephus would suggest otherwise.

More so than suggesting a complex background, the diversity of parallels offered demonstrates that the metaphor of the door is a common one across a number of religions, cultures, and bodies of literature, not all of which are equally plausible as informing the Johannine use. That the Fourth Gospel is dependent on Gnosticism is with good reason rarely asserted in modern scholarship, and its influence here is unlikely.[41] Similarly, although it is possible that John drew on traditions common to or at the least parallel with the Synoptics, direct dependence on the latter has little to commend it. As for the *paroimia* providing the primary background, we have argued that the Door section borrows from it vocabulary but not necessarily its meaning or function.[42] Especially in light of the OT background that most scholars accept for the shepherding imagery, it is likely that John's other symbols and language – including the door – draw on the Scriptures of Israel.

B. Verbal Parallels

The background most often suggested for the door of 10.7–10 is Ps 118.20. The reasons for this are seldom given, other than that it seems appropriate and that Ps 118 is used elsewhere with a messianic sense. True yet insufficient, this type of assertion leaves the impression that the allusion rests more on assumption than careful argument. We will now take a closer look at the evidence for an allusion and examine whether it can be established with more certainty. John 10.7 and 10.9 will be treated as referring to the same door and thus sharing the same background, even though the latter is not modified explicitly by the phrase "of the sheep."

---

[41] Against those presenting gnostic or Mandean backgrounds as primary for the door metaphor see Velasco, "Puerta," 39–43. Jeremias (*TDNT* 3.179–180) judges gnostic influence here as being "rather dubious."

[42] Clearly the door in 10.7, 9 keys off of the noun in 10.1–3. However, whereas in the parable the door discriminates between the true shepherd and thieves, the picture changes in 10.7–10 where Jesus is identified as the door, and the contrast is between the true and false coming ones and their function. This picture is not necessarily coherent, in that a door cannot be described as the coming one, yet it is clearly intended not as the entrance for the shepherd (as in the *paroimia*), but to present Jesus as the single means of access to relationship with God and the eschatological blessings of his presence. We therefore disagree with Lindars that 10.7–10 is merely explanatory, and that the *paroimia* supplied both its vocabulary and meaning.

John 10.7b, 9	Ps 117.19–20 (LXX)	Ps 118.19–20
10.7 'ἀμὴν ἀμὴν λέγω		
ὑμῖν ὅτι ἐγώ εἰμι	19 ἀνοίξατέ μοι	פִּתְחוּ־לִי
<u>ἡ θύρα</u> τῶν προβάτων.	<u>πύλας</u> δικαιοσύνης	שַׁעֲרֵי־צֶדֶק
	<u>εἰσελθὼν</u> ἐν αὐταῖς	אָבֹא־בָם
	ἐξομολογήσομαι τῷ κυρίῳ	אוֹדֶה יָהּ׃
10.9 ἐγώ εἰμι <u>ἡ θύρα·</u>	20 αὕτη ἡ πύλη	זֶה הַשַּׁעַר
	τοῦ κυρίου	לַיהוה
δι' ἐμοῦ ἐάν τις <u>εἰσέλθῃ</u>	δίκαιοι	צַדִּיקִים
σωθήσεται καὶ	<u>εἰσελεύσονται</u> ἐν αὐτῇ	יָבֹאוּ בוֹ׃
<u>εἰσελεύσεται</u> καὶ		
<u>ἐξελεύσεται</u> καὶ νομὴν		
εὑρήσει.		

The initial difficulty in arguing for an allusion here is that the term John uses for "door" is θύρα, whereas Ps 117 (LXX) uses πύλη. Because neither John's most distinctive phrases ("door of the sheep"; "I am the door") appear in the OT, nor that of Ps 118.19–20 ("gate[s] of righteousness") in the NT, the verbal link cannot be said to be strong. The closest verbal link is the use of εἰσέρχομαι, which describes the movement of the processional through the gates and into the temple in Ps 117.19–20 (LXX), and is characteristic of the sheep in the discourse (10.1, 2, 9 [twice]).

This difficulty is alleviated by several factors. First, the Hebrew שער is translated by both πύλη and θύρα.[43] Second, the use of both nouns in the NT suggests that they are sometimes interchangeable, especially when applied to the temple gate.[44] Third, although both nouns are used frequently in the LXX,[45] the NT uses θύρα approximately four times as often as πύλη, and John does not use the latter at all.[46] Therefore if John were alluding to Ps 118 the verbal discontinuity could be accounted for if he translated from the Hebrew and used the more popular and equivalent

---

[43] For example, Ezek 46.12 translates the Hebrew once each with θύρα and πύλη, referring to the same gate. See further Velasco ("Puerta," 43–48), who notes that there are at least seven Hebrew nouns translated by θύρα. There is no need to replicate his study. See also Simonis, *Die Hirtenrede*, 98–99.

[44] Luke uses θύρα (Acts 3.2; 21.30) and πύλη (Acts 3.10) to describe the same temple gate. Matthew 7.13–14 uses πύλη whereas the parallel in Luke 13.24–25 uses θύρα. Jeremias (*TDNT* 3.173) suggests that the two are equivalent in their application to the temple gate.

[45] The number for πύλη is 288; for θύρα, 188 (these numbers are approximate, as there are discrepancies between the various LXX versions).

[46] In the NT θύρα is used 37 times and πύλη 9 times. More than 25% of the former's use is Johannine (7 times in the Gospel, 3 times in Revelation),

θύρα. There may, however, be another reason for using θύρα even if John depended on the LXX. Whereas πύλη is used most often to describe the gates of a city, the temple, or the entrance to the tabernacle court,[47] the semantic range of θύρα is wider, referring most often to the entrance of a room or house, sometimes to that of a prison cell or sepulcher, but also including the entire range of the narrower πύλη. Consequently John may have preferred to use θύρα, for this would permit him to describe appropriately the door of the sheep fold (10.1, 2) and, while maintaining a measure of continuity with the *paroimia* by using the same word in 10.7–10, yet retain the flexibility of the semantic range to apply it differently in evoking a separate context.

It may be significant that both in the discourse and Ps 118 the use of εἰσέρχομαι is on each occasion linked to the door. In fact, in the NT the emphasis on entering the door is especially Johannine. Of the 8 NT combinations of εἰσέρχομαι with either θύρα[48] or πύλη,[49] 6 accentuate entering the door. Of these, 2 are parallel (Matt 7.13 ∥ Luke 13.24) and 4 are Johannine. In the LXX the combination, although not rare, is not very frequent either.[50] More significant is that only 20 of the 43 occurrences underscore both the door and the entering, unlike the majority where these appear to be incidental factors.[51] It seems that the blending of the verbal combination together with the specific emphasis on entering the gate is less frequent than one would expect.[52] This increases the plausibility of connecting John with a prior passage that features the same verbal combi-

---

[47] The doors of the temple in Ezekiel's vision (chs. 40–48) are most often described with πύλη, although θύρα is also used (e.g., Ezek 40.11; 42.3, 11, 20; 46.12). Similarly, both nouns are used to describe the entrance to the court of the tabernacle and temple (πύλη: Exod 27.16; 37.13, 16, 20; 39.8, 19; Num 3.26; 4.32; Jer 43.10. θύρα: Exod 38.20; 39.19; 40.5, 6; 2 Chr 4.9; Ezek 42.9). Note that their use with αὐλή in these verses parallels John 10.1, 2. On the NT use of πύλη see Jeremias, "πύλη," *TDNT* 6.921–928. On the use of θύρα see Jeremias, *TDNT* 3.173–180. On the use of "door" in OT and Jewish literature see Velasco, "Yo soy la puerta," 43–53.

[48] Matt 6.6; 25.10; Luke 13.24; John 10.1, 2, 9; Rev 3.20.

[49] Matt 7.13.

[50] The verb εἰσέρχομαι is combined with θύρα 13 times; with πύλη, 30 times.

[51] The 20 are as follows: Obad 11, 13; Jer 17.25; 22.4; Lam 4.12; Esth 4.2.; 2 Chr 23.19; Pss 24(23).7, 9; 100(99).4; 118(117).19, 20; Isa 26.2; Ezek 43.4; 44.2, 3; 46.2, 9; Tob 8.13. A further search of ἔρχομαι in combination with πύλη and θύρα in the LXX shows that the specific entering of the door is not given prominence. The NT examples of ἔρχομαι in combination with θύρα (Matt 25.10; John 20.19, 26; 2 Cor 2.12) and πύλη (Acts 12.10) similarly do not share the combined emphasis on entering and the door, although this could be implied in Matt 25.10–11.

[52] One would expect that the verbs most commonly linked with doors would express entering and exiting. However, this happens less often than one would expect, and occurs especially in John and in Ps 118.

nation and emphasis, and since the 20 parallels are not all equally appropriate, the number of contextually promising pre-texts, which includes Ps 118.19–20, is actually not that large.

Other factors which would support an allusion to Ps 118.19–20 include the likelihood that OT passages underlie the images of the shepherd, sheep, and thieves, thereby increasing the plausibility that the door metaphor also has an OT background. More particularly relevant is that John is aware of and has used Ps 118 elsewhere in the Gospel, and specifically at a previous Tabernacles discourse (8.56–59). Therefore it is significant that the discourse is situated at Tabernacles, in which Ps 118 played a prominent liturgical role. Early Christian use of Ps 118 is also suggestive. Clement of Rome, at the end of the first century, in quoting Ps 118.19–20 refers to it as "that gate which is in righteousness, even in Christ."[53] It is possible that Clement is also alluding to John 10, which would connect the passage to Ps 118.[54] We have argued above that in spite of John's use of θύρα instead of πύλη, Ps 118(117).19–20 provides a plausible and fitting verbal parallel to the door in 10.7, 9. However, although all of these points are appropriately put to use as supporting evidence in defending the allusion, they may fall short of fully persuading that there is such an allusion to begin with. I shall now go on to suggest that John, far from simply flavoring the discourse with scriptural language absent any intention of evoking a specific passage, gave other clues that support what is otherwise a relatively weak verbal link to Ps 118.

C. Contextual Evidence

Kysar has proposed that 10.1–18 is composed of five interlocking images, each of which is contrastive in form, juxtaposing positive and negative images.[55] Applied to the Door section, Jesus as the door (10.7b) is con-

---

[53] *1 Clement* 48.3.

[54] Bernard (2.354) argues that the passage seems to carry an allusion to the door sayings of John 10, and suggests the same for Ignatius, *Phld.* 9.1: "He is the gate of the Father, through which enter Abraham and Isaac and Jacob and the Prophets and the Apostles and the Church." The latter appears to be an attempt to ease the potentially awkward "all who came before me" of John 10.8. However, although it attests that Jesus was identified as the door in early Christian circles, the citation in Ignatius does not connect the saying to Ps 118 as Clement does. Of interest is Hegesippus' tradition that James was executed as a result of his answer to a question reminiscent of John 10.7, 9, "What is the gate of Jesus?" After asserting Jesus' exclusive significance, James is thrown down from the temple and stoned to death (Eusebius, *Hist. Eccl.* 2.23.12–19). Whatever the historical reliability of this account, it affirms that Jesus was understood to have applied the title of "door" to himself.

[55] Kysar, "Johannine Metaphor," 86–89.

trasted with the thieves and robbers (10.8), and the pattern repeats (10.9, 10a) before ending with a positive declaration about Jesus (10.10b). I suggest that there is another underlying pattern within this alternation of positive and negative: identification as the door (A), and negative identification of coming ones (B1) in contrast to the true coming one (B2).

10.7b	A	Ἀμὴν ἀμὴν λέγω ὑμῖν ὅτι ἐγώ εἰμι ἡ θύρα τῶν προβάτων.
10.8	B1 B2 (implied in the statement "before me")	πάντες ὅσοι <u>ἦλθον</u> [πρὸ ἐμοῦ] κλέπται εἰσὶν καὶ λῃσταί, ἀλλ' οὐκ ἤκουσαν αὐτῶν τὰ πρόβατα.
10.9	A	<u>ἐγώ εἰμι ἡ θύρα·</u> δι' ἐμοῦ ἐάν τις εἰσέλθῃ σωθήσεται καὶ εἰσελεύσεται καὶ ἐξελεύσεται καὶ νομὴν εὑρήσει.
10.10	B1 B2	ὁ <u>κλέπτης</u> οὐκ <u>ἔρχεται</u> εἰ μὴ ἵνα κλέψῃ καὶ θύσῃ καὶ ἀπολέσῃ· <u>ἐγὼ ἦλθον</u> ἵνα ζωὴν ἔχωσιν καὶ περισσὸν ἔχωσιν.

The structure of the passage as outlined above reveals several patterns. First the Door section is characterized by movement – of the sheep, thieves and Jesus. However, whereas the sheep's activity is described with εἰσέρχομαι and ἐξέρχομαι, John uses ἔρχομαι to contrast Jesus and his rivals. Second, this "coming" is intended not to depict the activity of motion but rather to identify and legitimate. It is no longer entering by the door, as in the *paroimia*, that identifies the true shepherd – this is what now identifies the true sheep. Legitimacy and authority are now intertwined with being the true coming one. Third, the point of contrast in the unit is in opposing the true coming one with illegitimate coming ones. John does not juxtapose the thieves with Jesus the door, but rather with Jesus the coming one. Although Jesus identifies himself as the door, this is clearly separate from his function as coming one (a door cannot be depicted as one that comes). Fourth, it appears that it is precisely because he is and fulfills the function of the coming one that he, as opposed to his purported competitors, can declare ἐγώ εἰμι ἡ θύρα.

Each of these observations is relevant to the use of Ps 118 in this section.[56] We have seen that the use of ἔρχομαι to describe an individual's function and/or identity is reserved almost entirely to John's presentation of Jesus, especially in revelatory discourse and conflict situations. That same function is evident here, as Jesus' identity and authority are again at issue. In this case his identity is underlined by the twice-repeated contrast with who his rivals are not – i.e., they are not the coming one.[57] It is noteworthy that the intensely polemical contrasts that are evident in the Door section diminish in force as one enters the Shepherd section (10.11–16), so that the contraposition of identities is sharpest where the "coming one" is used.

The question of precisely whom Jesus is contrasted with has occupied much of the attention focused on this passage.[58] The suggestions proffered include the corrupt priests and kings respectively of the Hasmonean and Herodian dynasties,[59] false messiahs,[60] zealot nationalists,[61] the Jewish leaders at the time of Jesus,[62] Hellenistic and gnostic saviors,[63] Satan,[64] a combination of two or more of these,[65] or no one in particular.[66] There is

---

[56] We take these up in no particular order, especially as the points are interlocked and there is also a good deal of overlap between them.

[57] Although Jesus is not explicitly identified as the coming one in 10.8, this is clearly assumed as the point of contrast.

[58] For discussion and a summary of views see Quasten, "Good Shepherd," 9–12.

[59] Zahn, 444.

[60] Bernard, 2.353; Lagrange, 277–278; Fascher, "Ich bin die Tür," 36f.; Velasco, "Puerta," 69; Bruce, 226. Sanders and Mastin suggest this is "indicated by the absolute use of *came*, i.e., claiming to be the 'coming one,'" 249. H. G. Wood ("Interpreting This Time," 266) argues that false messianic leaders who are exponents of messianic war – violent revolutionary leaders like Judas the Galilean – are in view.

[61] Simonis, *Die Hirtenrede*, 139, 210–214.

[62] Kiefer, *Die Hirtenrede*, 51 (Pharisees in particular); Brown, 1.393 (Pharisees and Sadducees).

[63] Bultmann, 377. Against Bultmann see Haenchen, 2.47.

[64] Odeberg, 327–328; Reinhartz, *The Word in the World*, 92. In 8.44 the devil is characterized as a murderer, which parallels the killing and destruction that accompanies the thief in 10.10. Brown (1.394) comments, "the opposition between the thief and the shepherd is a reflection of the opposition between Satan and Jesus." If Satan is the primary antagonist then by implication "the Jews" are included in the description, for in the Fourth Gospel they are his agents and kin.

[65] Carson (385) includes despotic local leaders along with messianic pretenders. Beasley-Murray (170) suggests it is any "who claim to be mediators of salvation," including false messiahs, redeemer gods of the pagan world, and Pharisees who claim to hold the keys of the kingdom. Smith (206) points to messianic prophets and pretenders, and perhaps the present Jewish leaders.

[66] Barrett (371) claims that John's intention, rather than singling out particular persons, was "to emphasize the unique fulfillment of the Old Testament promises in Jesus." At the same time, if anyone is in view he suggests it may be messianic pretenders or "more probably the many 'saviours' of the Hellenistic world" (ibid., 369).

some textual uncertainty in 10.8 in that some sources omit πάντες and p⁷⁵ omits πρὸ ἐμοῦ. However, both of these have strong support elsewhere and their omission can be explained as an attempt to deflect possible criticism of OT figures.[67] In any case, ἦλθον is aorist and therefore could be applied to all figures prior to Jesus. At the same time, since the present tense is used in relation to these rivals in both 10.8 and 10.10, it is more likely that the contemporary opponents of Jesus are in view, especially considering the context shared with ch. 9. The use of "coming one" also suggests false messiahs and any who claim to have the authority to lead Israel to freedom. Since the Fourth Gospel presents Satan as Jesus' primary adversary and the hostile religious authorities as his henchmen – i.e., those who "come" as his agents – it is possible that they are at least partly in mind. As a result, the rivals here most likely include, but are not limited to, messianic pretenders past and present, the current religious authorities, and Satan. The point of the contrast is to assert Jesus' identity as the coming one to be unique in history. Hoskyns is therefore correct in observing, "[Any] limitation is foreign to the Evangelist. His horizon is nowhere limited, *all – before me – are*. Every claim in the past or in the present to give life except through Jesus is destructive of life; all who make the claim have been and are thieves and robbers."[68]

Inseparable from and mirroring the pattern that juxtaposes the identity of the different coming ones is that of the purpose/result of their coming: the implication of violence accompanies the false coming ones (10.8), in contrast to the true coming one who brings security of pasture (10.9); the violent intent of the thief who comes is then stated explicitly (10.10a), again contrasted with Jesus who came to bring life in abundance (10.10b).[69] The significance is that the function of the door presupposes and is contingent on the identity and function of the coming one. It is the coming one – not the door – who secures life, security, and abundant pasture for the sheep. At the same time, the task of the coming one is also to act as the door that

---

[67] On the variant πρὸ ἐμοῦ see discussion in Velasco, "Puerta," 56–57; Brown, 1.386. In addition to external reasons favoring inclusion (majority of documents, antiquity of support, and attestation in the four major families), one can easily imagine that later copyists would want both to defend the integrity of OT characters and to apply the contrast with Jesus not only to those who came before him but also to any contemporary pretenders, thereby leading to changes in the text.

[68] Hoskyns, 374. Cf. Bultmann, 376: "It is purely secondary to ask which particular historical figures might be referred to here as those who came before Jesus. The saying is of fundamental significance and refers to all pretended revealers, all pretended saviours who have ever called men to them, who have ever been followed by men."

[69] See further A. Bottino, "La metafora della porta (Gv 10,7.9)," 211. Lindars (359) claims that at 10.10 a new line of exposition begins. This is obviously not the case, not least since the verse provides the balance of contrasting pairs, as seen above.

provides access to the place of eschatological blessing and mediates membership in the true flock of Israel. The door, then, is firmly tied to the identity and function of the coming one, for it is the coming one, and only he, who can legitimately claim to be the door.[70]

The exclusiveness of the claim to be the coming one, together with the subsequent elaboration of the coming one's function, underscores the phrase's eschatological import and fixes the contrastive pattern of this section firmly in the larger coming-sent theme already identified in the Gospel. That Ps 118 (particularly 118.26) underlies this pattern would facilitate recognition of the allusion to Ps 118.19–20. This in turn brings to light a pattern of allusion, although in this case of congruent rather than contrasting pairs: the door (John 10.7b/Ps 118.19–20) alternates with the coming one (John 10.8/Ps 118.26), and then repeats in a second identical pairing of door (John 10.9/Ps 118.19–20) and coming one (John 10.10/Ps 118.26). The section's emphasis on the coming one increases the likelihood that John intended for the reader to note the parallel to Ps 118.19–20.[71]

---

[70] This connection is seldom noticed. Schnackenburg (2.290) hints at the link, although he sees it in the inverse way to mine: "As the exclusive revealer who exposes the non-salvation way of other 'bringers of salvation', he is the one door to the sheep. In this sense the first door-word contains Jesus's absolute but also 'critical' – that is, severing and judgment-delivering – claim to be God's eschatological envoy. Hence the appellation 'door' inherently implies Jesus's status as he who was sent or who has come – in antithesis to the way that thieves and robbers happen to come along." That is, according to Schnackenburg the door defines who is and who is not the coming one. It is true that in the *paroimia*, entrance by the door defines true and false shepherds, and it would probably distinguish between true and false coming ones if this motif were present in 10.1–5, which it is not. It is not until the Door section that Jesus and his opponents are contrasted as true and false coming ones, and since their entering is not at issue, it is difficult to see how the door is supposed to distinguish between them. (Although in the *paroimia* entering by the door characterizes the shepherd, in 10.7–10 only the sheep's entering is mentioned.) To think of the true and false coming ones entering, respectively, by the door and over the wall, is to extend the discriminatory function of the door in the *paroimia* to a section that has retained the metaphor of the door but applies it differently. Otherwise Jesus would, as the door, be in the position of permitting himself to enter as the true shepherd. The images of thief and shepherd may still be with us, but in this section John's interest is in establishing the legitimacy of the one who will act as the door. For this task there could be no better or more natural choice than the coming one, to whom the reader needs no introduction.

[71] Proximity of an additional allusion to the same pre-text is not an insignificant factor in determining the plausibility of intentional allusion, especially since it would serve as a signal to the reader.

IV. An Allusion to the Temple Door

Up to this point we have suggested evidence that may support an allusion to Ps 118.19–20. The psalm originally refers to the gate(s) of the temple through which the psalmic processional entered. The Targum attests to this, replacing the psalm's "This is the door to Yahweh" (Ps 118.20a) with "This is the entrance of the temple of Yahweh." As a result, if there is an allusion to Ps 118.19–20, then the Johannine door would most naturally point to the gate of the temple. Before discussing what function such an allusion might have, we will look for evidence that might suggest why it would be especially appropriate for this passage.

A. The Gates of Righteousness and Ps 118

In an article largely ignored by commentators, J. Morgenstern argues that the eastern gate of the temple was associated with Ps 118.[72] Evidence gathered from medieval Jewish and Muslim writers, as well as Christian pilgrims, appears to associate the Golden Gate with Ps 118. According to these traditions, this is the gate(s) at which the righteous and repentant sinners gathered to ask for pardon from God, and it was opened with the recitation of a phrase attributed to David that is very close in wording to Ps 118.19.[73] Arguing from rabbinic and early Christian tradition, Morgenstern further claims that this gate, which was known by various names at different times, was originally called the "Gates of Righteousness," as preserved in Ps 118.19.[74] Identifying the specific names of the temple gates throughout history is an uncertain task, for which reason Morgenstern's arguments may not be entirely convincing.[75] However, the prominent association of the eastern gate with Tabernacles suggests that a link with Ps 118 should not be dismissed out of hand. The Ps 118 processional took place shortly after the dawn ritual in which the eastern gate played the central role.[76] Since John accentuates the door in a Tabernacles context, it is pos-

---

[72] Morgenstern, "The Gates of Righteousness."

[73] See Morgenstern, "Gates," 10.

[74] For the evidence Morgenstern adduces see "Gates," 10–15. Other later names include "Golden Gate," "Gate of Mercy," "Gate of the Shekinah," "Eternal Gate," and "Gate of Repentance."

[75] See for example the various opinions and evident confusion in the identification of the different gates of the temple in Jeremias, *TDNT*, 3.175 n. 5. Morgenstern, however, concludes confidently, "In Ps. 118.19f., the psalm traditionally recited in the Jewish ritual upon the festivals, the Gates of Righteousness, the gate of Yahweh through which the righteous enter, are unquestionably, as tradition has held, this eastern gate" ("Gates," 36).

[76] *m. Sukk.* 5.4 details a ritual at dawn, following the Tabernacles celebration of lights, in which the eastern gate is central. Morgenstern also points to Esdras 5.47 and Josephus

sible that the temple gate most prominently connected with the feast could come to mind. This is particularly likely if, as rabbinic evidence suggests, it was principally through this gate that worshippers entered the temple on special occasions.[77] An interesting link with Ezekiel is that it was through the eastern gate that the glory of Yahweh departed the first temple (Ezek 10.18–19), and according to his Tabernacles vision it is through this same gate that the glory of Yahweh returns to the eschatological temple (43.1–5).[78] In any case, it is likely that because of its processional character and internal door liturgy Ps 118 was linked to one of the prominent gates, and even if one is unable to establish with certainty that the eastern door of the temple was associated with the psalm, it is the most obvious choice.

B. *Ezekiel, Tabernacles, and the Temple*

Two thematic currents underlying the passage provide a suggestive context for an allusion to the temple door. First, there is widespread agreement that the discourse draws on Ezek 34 as a background for the images of the shepherd (both true and false) and sheep.[79] This makes more likely the recognition of other themes and passages from Ezekiel, one of the most prominent being the vision of the eschatological temple that takes up much of Ezek 40.1–47.12. The ministry of and at the temple, its measurements and central role in the life of Israel, the eschatological river that proceeds from it, and the return of the glory to the temple, are the primary subjects, but there is also surprising attention focused on the doors of the temple. Πύλη is used approximately 288 times in the LXX, but a disproportionate 45 of these occur in Ezek 40–47, and all of these in reference to the

---

(*Ant.* 11.154), which record that the returning exiles gathered at the former eastern gate of the temple for the Tabernacles celebration. For discussion see Morgenstern, "Gates," 29–31. See also Neh 8.1, where at the beginning of Tabernacles the people gather at the Water Gate to hear the reading of the Law. Since elsewhere in Nehemiah this is identified as an eastern gate (Neh 3.26; 12.37) it is probably the same one referred to in the previous citations. This raises the question whether it was the gate out of which the priests issued at daybreak to begin the water-drawing ceremony and the subsequent Ps 118 processional. Beasley-Murray (113) and Carson (321–322) assert that the procession returns rather through the watergate on the south side of the inner court.

[77] See rabbinic evidence in Morgenstern, "Gates," 29 n. 46.

[78] Note that this gate was not to be opened again, for Yahweh had passed through it (Ezek 44.1–3). The inner door facing east was to be opened only on the Sabbath and New Moon (Ezek 46.1). However, it appears that in intertestamental practice the outer door was opened, despite the injunction in Ezekiel.

[79] Although the imagery of the shepherd and sheep draws on a wide OT background, the majority of scholars point to Ezek 34 as the primary background. For the OT background of the shepherd image see D. Mollat, "Le bon pasteur. Jean 10, 11–18. 26–30," 25–29; Deeley, "Ezekiel's Shepherd."

temple. Similarly, 7 of the 30 times that the LXX combines πύλη with εἰσέρχομαι are in Ezek 40–46.[80] There is no OT book or section with as high a concentration of these terms.

It is noteworthy that Ezekiel's vision of the eschatological temple takes place in a Tabernacles context, first because it provides another point of contact with the Shepherd Discourse, but also because it overlaps with and underscores the second thematic current, which is the close connection between the feast and the temple. Tabernacles is the setting for Solomon's dedication of the temple (1 Kgs 8; 2 Chr 7.8–10), and Haggai's proclamation of the return of Yahweh to the temple (Hag 2). It is therefore not surprising that Ezekiel's vision of the renewed cult and temple takes place just prior to the feast, and no accident that the Feast of Dedication, which commemorates the consecration of the altar following the desecration by Antiochus Epiphanes, is patterned after Tabernacles. In fact, because it is in their connection to the temple that the themes of the two feasts converge, a shared temple emphasis in the two sections of John 10 could explain in part the overlap scholars have noted in the passage. Tabernacles also features a daily processional liturgy, patterned on Ps 118, that enters the temple through one of the main gates. We have therefore a confluence of interlinked sources that highlight the temple and facilitate the association of the door in 10.7–10 with the door of the temple.

Several other factors lend support to this suggestion. First, aiding readers in recognizing a temple connection is the fact that much of John 7–10 is set in a temple and Tabernacles context. The word "temple" (either ἱερός or ναός) is used 14 times in the Fourth Gospel, but the majority of these are concentrated in ch. 2 (vv. 14, 15, 19, 20, 21) and chs. 7–10 (7.14, 28; 8.2, 20, 50; 10.23), outside of which it is used only three times (5.14; 11.56; 18.20). Second, of those LXX combinations of εἰσέρχομαι with either πύλη or θύρα in which the door and act of entering do not appear to be incidental, the majority have to do with entering the gates of the temple.[81] It is therefore more likely that the verbal combination in 10.7, 9 would evoke a temple context. Third, John's use of θύρα instead of πύλη, although in no way

---

[80] The combination appears in 30 verses, but πύλη is used in these a total of 60 times, 16 of which are in the 7 verses identified in Ezek 40–46. Clearly this is a disproportionate percentage. Θύρα is used much less often in Ezekiel, but this is to be expected since, even though it can be used in reference to the temple gates, πύλη is the preferred designation. Although he does not explain his reasons for doing so, Martin ("John 10," 173) suggests that the metaphorical background for the use of the door in John may include Ezekiel's prophecy of the new temple whose gate will be opened on the Sabbath (cf. Ezek 44.1; 46.1).

[81] The ratio is 13 (2 Chr 23.19; Pss 24(23).7, 9; 100(99).4; 118(117).19, 20; Isa 26.2; Ezek 43.4; 44.2, 3; 46.2, 8, 9) to 7 (Obad 11, 13; Jer 17.25; 22.4; Lam 4.12; Esth 4.2; Tob 8.13). The latter usually refer to entering the king's palace or the gates of the city.

indicating that the temple door is in view, would because of its wider semantic range facilitate such an application in the discourse. As Velasco correctly notes, "Podía, así, describir la escena habitual del pastor que entra al corral sin negar con ello la posibilidad de referirla a la puerta del Templo."[82] The combination of these factors suggests that an allusion to the door of the temple would not be incompatible with the themes of the passage, nor one that would be beyond the grasp of the attuned reader.[83]

V. The Function of the Allusion

A. *Replacing the Temple Door*

Alluding to Ps 118.19–20 in a context which accentuates the temple may indicate that John intends to identify Jesus with, and in a sense have him replace, one of the temple's main gates. This accords with the Gospel's replacement theme in which the primary institutions and symbols of Judaism find their fulfillment in Jesus. In this case the allusion would develop and reiterate the replacement of the temple – Jesus has already identified his body as the temple (2.18–22) and declared that he fulfills the function of the temple as the locus of worship (4.19–26) – while at the same time anticipating Jesus' consecration as the new temple during the Feast of Dedication (10.36). The purpose in identifying Jesus as the door reflects its original function in the psalm: the king approaches and calls out for the doors to be opened that he may enter and worship; the door-keepers then open the door for the king and the accompanying procession, and they enter the temple. The Hebrew describes the door as "the door to Yahweh," and the LXX as "this is the door of the Lord." In both, but especially in the Hebrew, the door of Ps 118 is the means of access to and

---

[82] Velasco, "Puerta," 77.

[83] It may be objected that the passage works uniformly with the image of sheepfolds, and that there does not seem to be any allusion in the text to the temple. It is also possible that the points adduced as evidence above do no more than make it possible that the door sayings contain an allusion to the door of the temple, or at most are compatible with such an allusion while not actually furnishing a positive argument that the allusion is present. There is no need to repeat the argument advanced above, except to point out that there is a remarkable confluence of a number of factors – verbal, liturgical, thematic, intertextual – that are compatible with such an allusion and thus lend support to the most obvious indicator, which is the fact that in Ps 118 the door refers to the temple entrance. An allusion to the temple door is plausible only to the degree that an allusion to Ps 118 is deemed credible.

encounter with Yahweh. As Velasco notes, "cerrar o abrir las puertas del Templo equivale a cortar o reanudar la relación con Dios."[84]

In appropriating the psalm Jesus is therefore establishing that it is his mediation that provides access to the presence of Yahweh and establishes communion with him. This is not stated explicitly, perhaps because John's message is that "what Jesus came to bring was nothing other than himself,"[85] so that it is Jesus who mediates life, salvation, and the eschatological benefits of the new exodus to the sheep. However, what is implicit here – i.e., that Jesus as the door gives access to Yahweh – is stated explicitly in 14.6.[86] As the door to the new temple, Jesus renders the old means of access obsolete. As F. Manns comments, "Jean leur montre que le véritable temple est venu: c'est le corps du Christ ressuscité, c'est par lui qu'on a accès désormais au Père."[87] This would be especially significant to the reader, for at the writing of the Fourth Gospel the Jerusalem temple had already been destroyed. Consequently Jesus, as the only remaining temple, has indeed completely "replaced" the central symbol of Judaism. A test of this suggestion is whether it makes sense in, and provides a meaning effect that harmonizes with, the passage.[88]

B. Three Primary Functions

The widespread agreement that the Shepherd Discourse is to be read in light of ch. 9 suggests that the contrast between shepherd and thief finds its immediate parallel in that of Jesus and the religious authorities, and that the focal point of the activity depicted in the *paroimia* – τὴν αὐλὴν τῶν προβάτων – is the temple and Jewish establishment.[89] This is signi-

---

[84] Velasco, "Puerta," 76.

[85] Ashton, *Understanding*, 187.

[86] The parallel with John 14.6 is often noted. See for example Bottino: "Gesù si proclama la *porta delle pecore* ma non dice a che cosa dà accesso questa porta, in quanto è in Lui che si trovano i beni salvifici. Il testo di Gv 14,6 indica chiaramenta dove conduce Gesù: al Padre" ("La metafora," 213).

[87] F. Manns, "Traditions Targumiques en Jean 10, 1–30," 156. Manns unconvincingly argues that the background to the passage, including the door, can be found in the Targums.

[88] The following suggestions as regard to function would still be the case if there were no allusion to the temple but simply to the saving function of Jesus as opposed to the false saviors. However, the proposed allusion to Ps 118 and the temple replacement function would accentuate and intensify the function of exclusivity, inclusivity, and security, in a way that would especially resonate with Jewish Christians.

[89] It is true that the noun αὐλη is not a technical term that would unambiguously indicate to the reader that the temple court is in view. For example, in the NT it is used 12 times, but only once (Rev 11.2) in an explicit reference to the temple court. (Otherwise it is used 7 times for the palace of the high priest; once each for a house, the praetorium, and twice for a sheepfold.) However, of the 157 verses in the LXX that use the noun, the

ficant because the three primary meaning effects of the door in 10.7–10 – exclusivity, inclusion, and security – are especially relevant when set in the context of the preceding conflict and exclusion from the synagogue, and each speaks to those facing a similar situation at the time of the writing of the Gospel.

1. Exclusivity

In his influential article Robinson argues that the main point of the original parable in 10.1–3a was to challenge the gatekeepers of Israel to open the door to Jesus: "While he is still with them the authorities have a last chance to fulfill their role as the watchmen of the house of Israel, to recognize and admit the master of the house of Israel."[90] In such a case Jesus' door statements would take on added meaning in light of the refusal of the authorities to receive him as they should have: Jesus does not need for them to open the door and permit entrance, for he himself is the door. But whether Robinson is correct or not,[91] the use of Ps 118 may provide this same meaning effect. In the psalm, v. 19 is the king's request for

---

great majority are concerned with the temple court(s), and a remarkable 31 of these occur in Ezek 40–47.2, all in reference to the temple. The setting of the discourse suggests that such a nuance is not implausible: the discourse can be read as a response to the events of John 9, and the confluence of Tabernacles (expecting the eschatological temple and including the prominent door/entrance liturgy of Ps 118), Ezekiel, the temple replacement theme, and Ps 118, would facilitate a temple allusion. In addition, the reader should recognize that Jesus is speaking metaphorically and is not truly concerned with a sheepfold – that is, the fold probably stands for something else. In support see Simonis (*Die Hirtenrede*, 125), who argues that αὐλή (10.1) is an allusion to the temple court. Cf. Reinhartz, *The Word in the World*, 67: "By default, the sheepfold . . . must be the temple, the Jewish community, or the Jewish theocracy." Velasco similarly states, "La interpretación de *thyra tês aulês* en Jn 10,1, como 'puerta del atrio del Templo' parece ahora perfectamente posible" ("Puerta," 76). Note that even though Velasco argues for the use of Ps 118.20 as the primary background to the door, and argues that John 10.1 refers to the door of the temple court, he does not specifically suggest that Jesus replaces or is the door of the temple. The closest hint comes in his statement that "es la persona de Jesús, no la puerta del templo, la única mediación que verdaderamente conduce hasta el Padre" (ibid., 79).

[90] Robinson, "Parable," 237. In support of Robinson see Dodd, *Historical Tradition*, 385. Cf. Simonis (*Die Hirtenrede*, 155–159), who interprets the doorkeeper as someone with a function in the temple, including perhaps Caiaphas, the high priests, and/or the Pharisees. Their duty was to open the door of Israel for Jesus, but failed to do so.

[91] Robinson ("Parable," 237) admits that as a result of the fusion he proposes with the parable of 10.3b–5, the dominant figure becomes the shepherd rather than the door-keeper. It is therefore less likely that readers would have recognized the doorkeeper's significance, and thus would not read 10.7–10 with this background in mind.

entry and v. 20 appears to be the response from the priests who guarded and determined access to the door. In opening the door to the king the doorkeepers recognize him as the coming one and once-rejected but now exalted stone. In the Fourth Gospel the religious authorities – i.e., the temple establishment – did not recognize the legitimacy of Jesus as the coming one and thus did not welcome him as required in the psalm. Jesus therefore dispenses with their services, declaring that they no longer have the keys of authority and are not the keepers of the door – he will determine to whom the door will open. With the door sayings Jesus claims the exclusive right to regulate entry to the sheep's locus of blessing: the new temple and the presence of Yahweh.

The door statements establish first the exclusivity of Jesus' mediatorial role, but the focus then shifts to those whom he mediates for and the exclusivity of the new community. One of the more disputed issues in the discourse is whether Jesus is the door *to* or *for* the sheep. The genitive in ἡ θύρα τῶν προβάτων (10.7) can be read as either subjective or objective, and because the door in 10.9 is not qualified by a following statement, its interpretation depends partly on how 10.7 is understood. This gives rise to four primary positions. First, both door statements may mean "door *for* the sheep."[92] Second, a uniform meaning of "door *to* the sheep" may be intended, so that Jesus mediates the pastoral office and provides the only legitimate access for the shepherds who will minister to the sheep.[93] Third, some suggest that 10.7 should be explained in favor of "*to* the sheep" and 10.9 in favor of "*for* the sheep," thus covering the shepherds and the larger community.[94] Fourth, some commentators make no distinc-

---

[92] So Stuhlmacher, *Biblische Theologie*, 2.230; Painter, *Quest*, 296; Simonis, *Die Hirtenrede*, 202–204; Rodríguez, "El discurso," 33; Bultmann, 377 n. 7; Beasley-Murray, 169–170; Velasco, "Puerta," 67. Jeremias writes, "The ambiguous v. 7 is to be interpreted solely in terms of v. 9, and the meaning of the expositor in both verses is that 'I am the door for the sheep'" (*TDNT* 3.179). However, he appears to contradict himself when in the same article he suggests that in 10.7 "the further thought is added that Jesus alone mediates the true pastoral office" (ibid., 3.180).

[93] So Lagrange, 277f; Howard, *Christianity*, 139–140. Quasten's statement is typical of this view: "Jesus . . . defines Himself as the only person through whom the pastoral office is legitimately bestowed in the kingdom of God. From Him every true vocation takes its origin" ("Good Shepherd," 158). Schnackenburg (2.289) suggests that the objective genitive tends to favor this interpretation, although he approaches the door as a symbol that points to the exclusive role of Jesus rather than that of pastors.

[94] See Fascher, "'Ich bin die Tür!," 48; Beutler, "Hintergrund," 31; Kiefer, *Die Hirtenrede*, 15–19; Schenke, "Das Rätsel von Tür und Hirt," 87; Brown, 1.393–394; Bauer, 135; Schneider, 200–201; Lightfoot, 210; George, "Je suis la porte," 21–22. Bernard (2.352) qualifies his position by suggesting it is the *primary* use for each verse, although in 10.7 it applies to both shepherd and sheep. Although the majority who hold this view see 10.7 as the legitimization of the leaders of the community, Morris (506–507) applies

tion and see the door as the means by which both shepherds and sheep enter.[95]

It is unlikely that the door in 10.9 refers to the mediation of the pastoral office, since the activity of those entering the door, and the resulting benefits, are understood more easily of sheep than shepherds. Although in 10.7 the door is more ambiguous, it is preferable not to view its primary function as distinguishing between false and true shepherds. The argument for the objective genitive assumes that the legitimizing function that the door plays in the *paroimia* continues in the Door section.[96] However, this ignores the change of context and the discontinuity between the two units.[97] Although the issue of Jesus' authority and legitimacy *vis-à-vis* his rivals does continue in the Door section, it centers not on entering by the door or on his being the door, but rather on his identity as the true coming one.[98] In addition,

---

it to Jesus' rivals as a challenge that if they are to bring sheep into the fold they must enter through him. In rejecting Jesus they show that they are impostors and not true shepherds. A minority view within this position holds that although 10.7 is the door "to the sheep," this relates to the access of Jesus to the fold rather than the mediation of the pastoral office. For example, Ridderbos (357) argues, "Because he is 'the door of the sheep,' he has access to the sheepfold, he exercises pastoral care over the flock, and no one else has the right to manage the flock." In a similar vein, Meyer argues that the door in the *paroimia* refers to the death of Jesus whereby he himself gains access to the fold, and sets the context for the doors in 10.7, 9: "What is at first the 'door' by which the true ποιμήν enters becomes the 'door' by which communion of the sheep with the shepherd is established; this in turn becomes the 'door' for the sheep" ("A Note," 234).

[95] So Westcott, 153; Hoskyns, 373. Barrett (371) argues for variety and ambiguity in meaning. Lagrange (282) allows for both although he had earlier emphasized the entry of shepherds. J. Bover expresses it well: "Pero a esta limitación, innecesaria, parece preferible la plenitud o complejidad de sentido. En la realidad *Puerta de las ovejas* es lo uno y lo otro" ("El símil del Buen Pastor [Jn. 10, 1–18]," 301).

[96] For example, Brown (1.393–394) suggests that this interpretation "lies very close to the parable itself."

[97] If the door in 10.7 functions the same way as in 10.1, 2 (i.e., as entry for the true shepherd), then one must explain why 10.9 departs from the pattern. For this reason George ("Je suis la porte," 24–25) argues that 10.9 was added by the final editor of the Gospel, because otherwise it is out of place in not corresponding to the use of the door that he alleges for 10.1, 2, 7.

[98] The function of the coming one in this passage is not recognized by most scholars. For example, although Rodríguez argues for a uniform interpretation of the door as "for the sheep," he accepts a continuation of its legitimizing function: "No se puede, pues, hablar de incoherencia de pensamiento en los vv. 7–8 con respecto a los vv. 1–2 ó a toda la parábola anterior. La aparente incoherencia se debe al carácter del discurso como discurso de revelación. La categoría semántica de 'legitimidad' estaba ya presente en los vv. 1–2, pero el evangelista ha querido subrayarla expresamente en los vv. 7–8 . . . En los vv. 7–10 aparece [Jesus] como la puerta, expresando el tema de la 'legitimidad' del verdadero pastor frente a los falsos pastores" ("El discurso," 32).

the *paroimia* contrasts Jesus with his adversaries, whereas the objective genitive would shift the focus to Christian shepherds and their opponents.[99] The objective genitive is an attractive option in that it would give legitimacy to the shepherds of the Christian community, but neither here nor anywhere else in the Fourth Gospel (with the exception of ch. 21) is any shepherd other than Jesus talked about. The contrast is between Jesus and all others who claim authority to mediate eschatological blessing to the sheep, not between Christian shepherds and the shepherds of Judaism. As Loisy points out, "Le Christ est pour les brebis l'unique porte du salut. Il n'est pas question, pour le moment, d'autres pasteurs que lui-même, et ceux qu'il associera à son ministère ne sont, par rapport à lui, que de simples brebis."[100] Consequently it is best to understand the door in both verses as providing entry for the sheep.

In conclusion, the door in 10.7–10 highlights the exclusivity rather than the legitimacy of Jesus' mediatorial role for the sheep. This function is accentuated by its combination with an ἐγώ εἰμι statement, as these are used in the Fourth Gospel to underline Jesus' unique and exclusive soteriological role.[101] In this context Christian shepherds do receive their legitimacy from entering through the door, but it is a legitimacy that comes from being sheep first. Any who do not enter through the door are not Jesus' sheep, and therefore cannot aspire to be shepherds of the church. The message to the disciple cast out of the synagogue and refused inclusion in the Jewish community is that the excluders are actually the excluded, for in refusing to enter through Jesus the Door they show themselves not to be true sheep. The disciple on the other hand is assured of full participation in the true flock of Israel and of all the accompanying eschatological blessings.

---

[99] On the door in 10.7 as "to the sheep" and in 10.9 as "for the sheep," Carson (384) comments, "This distinction is too clever; it assumes a continuation of the watchman motif from v. 3."

[100] Loisy, 611.

[101] Velasco highlights the contextual use of the Deutero-Isaianic ἐγώ εἰμι, which provides an appropriate parallel for its use here: "La finalidad sotereológica y la exigencia de exclusividad frente a los falsos dioses extranjeros son las dos notas centrales de este tipo de sentencias" ("Puerta," 65). Against any special significance for the ἐγώ εἰμι door sayings, Jeremias argues that they are not "a formula of revelation" but rather "simply an interpretative formula" (*TDNT* 6.496). However, he bases this on the assumption that what follows the *paroimia* is "simply an allegorising, paraphrasing interpretation controlled by the eastern love of colourful depiction" (ibid., 6.495).

2. Inclusion

A door is by nature discriminatory, restricting entry. The emphatic δι' ἐμοῦ
(10.9) underscores the message that Jesus alone mediates salvation and
membership in the eschatological flock of Israel.[102] If there is only one
door, then choice is reduced to entering by it or remaining outside. Ashton
claims that such exclusivity is a later development in the Johannine community, arguing that while the light saying in 8.12 is an invitation open to
all, the door sayings expose an inward-looking and isolationist community
that adds the condition of entry to the fold.[103] However, the door's discriminatory function is not a new development, for in a sense it summarizes the
conflict and choice underlying the whole of chs. 7–10. The claims of Jesus
throughout the Fourth Gospel are exclusive and absolute, for this is what
forms the basis for the community, and is the nature of what Bultmann
labels "the *intolerance of the revelation*."[104] Jesus possesses the authority
to open and shut the door (cf. Rev 3.7), and the closed door carries with it
a sense of inescapable judgment. Those who do not join his procession
(cf. Ps 118) will be denied entry. For them, Jesus is a closed door.

A door is also by nature inclusive, permitting entry. The message of
the door is that even as it is closed to some, it is open to all who recognize
the voice of the shepherd. They know his voice, and he knows them
(10.14). The context of Ps 118 aids in this function of inclusion, for there
the door is opened at the king's command, so that those who have joined
his procession gain entry with him to the presence of Yahweh.[105] In 10.7–
10 every explicit statement concerning the door has to do with its being
open to the sheep (i.e., inclusion), so that the strong flavor of exclusion,
although very real, is entirely implicit. That is, the emphasis is not on
who is *un*authorized to come in, but on who *is* authorized. The motif of
continuous and unimpeded movement in and out (10.9) through the door
to pasture underscores the openness of the door to all those who are Jesus'

---

[102] To "find pasture" (10.9) is an OT phrase associated with Israel's eschatological
deliverance and blessings (cf. 1 Chr 4.40; Ps 23.2; Ezek 34.12–15; Isa 49.9).

[103] Ashton, *Understanding*, 188.

[104] Bultmann, 378: "Jesus' ἐγώ εἰμι always means that there is only *one* who can
lead man to salvation, only *one* Revealer. There are not various possible answers to
man's quest for salvation, but only one. A decision must be made. This is the basis of
the *intolerance of the revelation*" (emphasis original).

[105] Jeremias points to Ps 118.19 (the gates of righteousness) as a parallel to God
opening "a door of faith to those who come to believe (Ac 14.27) by giving them the
possibility of believing" (*TDNT* 3.174–175).

own sheep.[106] This is the most open of doors because the only requirement for admittance is a willingness to enter by the appropriate door. There is no coercion to enter, nor is there forced exclusion. As in the psalm, the door is opened to those who cry out for entry. The full extent of this inclusivity becomes clear in its extension to those who were historically excluded from the flock of Israel: Samaritan and Gentile sheep will approach and enter together with the Jewish sheep through the one door, forming one flock under one shepherd (10.16).[107] The door is therefore simultaneously the sign of absolute exclusivity and of complete inclusion.

3. Security

The door sayings are essentially christological. They declare that Jesus fulfills the purpose of the temple and its gates in providing access to Yahweh. He is the mediator exclusive of all mediators, and his mission is universal, extending beyond the confines of Judaism. Out of this flows the fundamentally soteriological character of the door sayings. As noted above, in 10.7–10 the door no longer functions to legitimize the identity and authority of the shepherd, that role falling instead to the contrast of coming ones. Rather, the sayings summarize Jesus' soteriological import over against his opponents, and thus establish the basis of security for the sheep. He is the door of salvation (10.9), who secures life for the sheep and guarantees their well-being and safety. As the sheep enter the door they place themselves under his protection. Although they may have been cast out of the synagogue, the sheep retain the right of access to the new temple and the security it affords.

VI. The Door in New Exodus Context

The door sayings are informed by, and contribute to, the New Exodus context of the discourse. There is widespread agreement that the symbol of the

---

[106] Since the stress of the image is on the sheep's free access to pasture through the door, one should not read too much into the movement in and out. See Schnackenburg's (2.293) warning: "Once again we should not press the image too closely by interpreting in terms of the individual elements. The only thing that matters is the end in view: to reach the pasture of life."

[107] Martin argues that the historical reality behind the figure of the door should be understood as providing a contrast between the Jewish community, which defined itself so rigidly that Samaritans, Gentiles and Christians were excluded, and Jesus who provides an open door: "Against this the way of Jesus functions as an open door. . . . By his death and resurrection Jesus has become the door *to* an open community and the door *of* an open community [that includes Gentiles and Samaritans]" ("John 10," 172–173).

shepherd in John 10 draws in general on the OT depiction of Yahweh as
Shepherd, and particularly on Ezekiel's portrayal.[108] Although the shepherd
imagery is applied to the Davidic Messiah and to the leaders of Israel,[109] it
is Yahweh who is the Shepherd *par excellence*.[110] It is significant that the
references to Yahweh as Shepherd are concentrated especially in the Psalter
and the prophecy of the exile, with the result that they naturally acquire a
New Exodus flavor: Yahweh will gather the scattered flock and shepherd
them in safety.[111] A factor that makes Ezek 34 an especially appropriate
background is the dualism created in that both Yahweh and the Davidic
Messiah are depicted as the Shepherd of Israel. This has led some scholars
to suggest that Jesus is declaring himself both God and Davidic Messiah.[112]
However, we have argued that it is unlikely that John intends to emphasize
Jesus' Davidic connections. In fact Jesus' claims in the discourse mirror
much more closely the description of Yahweh's role in Ezek 34 than that
of the Messiah. There Yahweh removes the wicked shepherds and replaces
them as Shepherd, searches for and gathers the scattered sheep from their

---

[108] Bultmann (367) argues that the image comes from gnostic tradition. Against this
see Barrett, 374. See also Schnackenburg, 2.295: "Every derivation of the Johannine
shepherd scene that does not come from O. T. or early-Christian sources will . . . appear
questionable." Brown's (1.398) comment is representative of the majority opinion:
"Basically it would seem that Ezekiel's portrait . . . served as the model for Jesus' portrait
of himself as the ideal shepherd."

[109] For its application to the Davidic Messiah see for example Jer 23.35; Ezek 34.23–
24; 37.24; Mic 5.3. Jeremias (*TDNT* 6.489) notes that the leaders and teachers of Israel,
and in particular Moses and David, are "extolled as faithful shepherds."

[110] See Pss 23.1–4; 28.9; 68.7; 71.1; 77.20; 78.52; 79.13; 80.1; 95.7; 100.3; 121.4;
Isa 40.11; 49.9–10; 56.8; Jer 23.3; 31.9–10; 50.17–20; Ezek 34.11–20, 30–31; Mic 2.12;
4.6–8; 7.14; Zeph 3.19; Zech 9.16; 10.8.

[111] Jeremias notes, "Even in later Judaism, on the basis of the statements of the OT,
God was described as the Shepherd of Israel who led his flock out of Egypt, guides them
in the present, will one day gather again the scattered flock, and will feed them on the
holy mountain" (*TDNT* 6.489).

[112] See for example Bover, "El símil," 305: "En la profecía de Ezequiel existe cierto
dualismo: tanto Yahvéh como el Mesías son el Pastor de Israel, el único Buen pastor.
Pero este dualismo desaparece en el cumplimiento de la profecía. Jesús es a la vez el
Mesías, nuevo David, y es también el mismo Yahvéh, el Dios de Israel. . . . Conclusión
de todo lo dicho es que Jesús, bajo la imagen del Buen Pastor, se declara Mesías y
Dios." Deeley, who argues that Ezekiel 33–37 presents a broad plot outline which is
developed in John 8–11, suggests that "the appropriation of Ezekiel 33–37 makes it
possible for John to speak of Jesus as the 'good shepherd' in such a way and in such a
context that he emphasizes Jesus' unity with the Father as well as his authority to rule
and his rightful place as Davidic descendant. . . . In one sense, Jesus takes on Ezekiel's
role as prophet as well as the roles of Yahweh and David" ("Ezekiel's Shepherd," 264).

exile, and returns them to pasture on the mountains of Israel before appointing David to tend over them.[113] This follows the general pattern of New Exodus passages where the Messiah's role is secondary and dependent on Yahweh's prior decisive activity.[114] In John 10 it is Jesus who is contrasted with and replaces the false shepherds, who calls out and gathers his sheep by name, secures pasture for them, mediates salvation and guarantees abundant life. In light of the context of Ezek 34, and consonant with the programmatic replacement theme already identified in the Fourth Gospel, Jesus is thus depicted as fulfilling the New Exodus role reserved for Yahweh.[115] The dualism in Ezekiel is then especially appropriate, since John identifies Jesus as being one with the Father, yet also separate from him.

In characterizing himself as the door, Jesus has declared himself the sole means of access to the eschatological pastures that the Ezekielan flock – that is, the true Israel that Yahweh regathers from exile and shepherds – enjoys in abundance and complete safety (Ezek 34.13–16, 25–29). The startling discontinuity is that Jesus calls and leads out (10.3–4) the sheep from the fold (which signifies the temple), and thus out of the fold of contemporary

---

[113] R. Klein (*Ezekiel: The Prophet and His Message*, 122) emphasizes three actions of Yahweh: removing the bad shepherds, freeing the sheep from the control of the shepherds, and liberating the sheep from exile.

[114] Cf. Beasley-Murray, 179: "The prophetic allegory [Ezek 34] is one with OT messianic teaching generally in representing God as the Deliverer of his people, gathering them into their land, giving them salvation in his kingdom, and *then* providing them with the Messiah who shall act as Shepherd on his behalf."

[115] Jesus in effect claims the same authority over his flock that Yahweh does over Israel. Cf. Mollat, "Le bon pasteur," 30: "Par cette formule *Je suis le bon pasteur*, Jésus revendique en outre un droit plénier et exclusif sur le troupeau, comme Yahweh sur Israël." It is of interest that the NT does not apply the title of shepherd to God, even though it is characteristic of his portrayal in the OT. Jeremias (*TDNT* 6.491) notes that this may be explained by the christological application of the figure. Wright appears to miss the implications of the Ezekiel background and instead argues that Jesus is presented as greater than Moses: "Moses was the great deliverer of his people, the shepherd of God's flock, who led the nation out of slavery into the promised land. So Jesus leads the New Israel out of the bondage to sin into the pastures of new life and freedom (John 10:9)" (*Victory*, 159).

Judaism.[116] However, this is not so much a rejection of the institutions of Judaism as an insistence that these have found their fulfillment and locus of meaning in him.[117] Jesus uses the door sayings, in reference to the temple doors, to bring into focus his exclusive mediatorial and soteriological role, but in so doing he also proclaims that he embodies the reality of everything which the temple and its doors can only represent.[118] Inevitably this redefines the significance and function of the temple, both as it stands in Jerusalem and at the center of the newly regathered flock of Israel.

For John's purposes Ps 118 was an especially appropriate Scripture text to draw on. It highlights the central role of the temple in the cult, the mediatorial role of the doors in providing access to the presence of

---

[116] It is true that the metaphor implies going in and out of the one fold, not going out permanently from the existing fold. There are various ways that "fold" and "flock" can be interpreted, but we have argued that the fold signifies the temple, and the flock the members of the community of Jesus. Since Jesus is rejected by the contemporary religious establishment, he is in a sense calling and leading the sheep out of the fold of contemporary Judaism and the temple – they are an obsolete "fold." However, because it is the community of Jesus that constitutes the true Israel, and because the Scriptures, temple, and the other institutions of Judaism are fulfilled and consummated in Jesus, there is a sense in which they have never truly left the fold. It is not desirable to interpret every image of the discourse as applying singly and precisely to some action or state of the sheep. Rather, the metaphors together create the overall image, which is of a new flock that, under the protection of Jesus, has security, plenty, and continued and unimpeded access to the eschatological blessings of the new age. The image of leading the flock out is applied in the OT to God leading Israel to the promised land in the first exodus (e.g. Ps 78.52–55). The same image appears in the New Exodus (Mic 2.12–13), with Yahweh going out before the sheep, at their head. Cf. Carson, 383; Schnackenburg, 2.505 n. 29. I. de la Potterie ("Le Bon Pasteur," 941ff.) argues strongly for Exodus typology in the *paroimia* image. Simonis (*Die Hirtenrede*, 125, 177) advances that the αὐλή in the *paroimia* represents the temple forecourt, so that in leading the sheep out, Jesus is liberating them from Temple Judaism.

[117] John does not intend to show Jesus replacing a physical door in the temple, as if his purpose were to reinforce Jesus' earlier replacement of the temple in ch. 2. As with the other temple replacement statements, it is the function that stands out: Jesus replaces the sacrificial system centered in the temple, he replaces the holy space of the temple as the locus of worship, and by claiming to be the door he takes over the temple's role of providing access to God.

[118] See further G. Braumann: "Jesus is not only like a door. He is the door; this reality, this divine truth, applies to no one but him. . . . The 'I am' sayings are not to be regarded as parabolic pictures designed to illustrate the significance of Jesus, so that one could grasp the intended reality on the basis of the picture. It is rather the reverse. It is Jesus himself who determines the meaning of the picture" ("ἐγὼ εἰμί," *NIDNTT* 2.280–281).

Yahweh, and the community's entering of this place.[119] In conjunction with Tabernacles and Ezekiel it would bring to mind the eschatological temple to which the glory of Yahweh will return, which will be the seat of his universal reign, and to which the nations will come to worship. In light of the Fourth Gospel's underlying New Exodus theme and the coming-sent motif, it is evident that in Jesus the eschatological temple is actualized and the glory of Yahweh has returned. The community of readers would recognize the striking parallel in Rev 21.22: in the new Jerusalem there is no temple, "for its temple is the Lord God the Almighty and the Lamb."[120] Jesus as the door provides the means of access for the community that enters this temple and enjoys the eschatological benefits guaranteed in Ezekiel's vision.

To sum up: It has been argued here that the Discourse is to be interpreted primarily in the context of the Feast of Tabernacles although perhaps sharing thematic links with Dedication, and that even though 10.7–10 is informed by the metaphors of the *paroimia* in 10.1–5, it develops these independently. What is a relatively weak verbal link to Ps 118.19–20 can be explained by translation of the Hebrew, although reference to the LXX is not impossible. Additional support for the allusion comes from early Christian use of Ps 118 in reference to Jesus as the door, the Tabernacles setting, and the prominent use of the coming one theme that underlies the passage. It has further been suggested that the allusion is to the temple door. In favor of this is the original context of Ps 118, and a confluence of

---

[119] Admittedly there are some points of discontinuity with the psalm. For example, in Ps 118 it is the king (coming one) who leads the procession up to and then through the temple doors, but in 10.7–10 the focus is neither on Jesus entering the door as true shepherd nor on his leading the flock into the fold. However, such differences are present in almost every allusion, and there are more points of continuity than discontinuity: temple doors, guardians who permit or refuse entrance, the coming one, a procession that enters through the gate, the declaration of salvation following entry of the gate. Even where there is continuity – for example, the language describing the sheep entering through the door of the fold corresponds to that of Ps 118 where the righteous enter through the temple door, in each case resulting in salvation – this may miss the point of the allusion. In this case the emphasis is on the identity and significance of Jesus and his mediation of access to God – the benefits to the sheep are incidental, flowing from the former. Accordingly, the fact that Ps 118.19 presents the king entering the temple and Ps 118.20 speaks in turn of the righteous entering does not mean that John was alluding only to one or the other verse: his focus is not on drawing in a parallel that portrays either the coming one or the righteous entering, but on the door that provides access to the temple and thus to God.

[120] I am not claiming continuity with the shepherd imagery, in which case the parallel would be somewhat awkward, as the shepherd has become a lamb. The point is that the community of readers familiar with the Johannine writings would recognize that according to Revelation Jesus has indeed replaced the temple.

interlinked sources that highlight the temple and facilitate the association of the door in 10.7–10 with the temple door.[121] The effect of the allusion is to portray Jesus as replacing the temple door and thus fulfilling its function of providing access to Yahweh. This brings into focus Jesus' exclusive mediatorial and soteriological role as the sole means of access to Yahweh, to membership in the flock of Israel, and to the eschatological blessings of the new age. He thus provides the basis of security for the sheep. Furthermore the allusion accentuates the inclusiveness of the new Israel, for the door is open to any who will enter by it.

---

[121] The links are as follows: 1. Ezekiel is linked with the eschatological temple, an emphasis on the temple doors, and Tabernacles. 2. Tabernacles is linked with the temple and with its renewal, with the Feast of Dedication, and with the processional of Ps 118 that enters the temple doors. 3. John 10.7–10 is set at Tabernacles, is a bridge to Dedication, counts Ezekiel as a significant influence in its background, emphasizes the door, and is linked to Ps 118 through the coming one theme.

Chapter 10

Two Additional Allusions

I. "Then the Jews surrounded him . . .":
Ps 118 in John 10.24–25

A. Introduction

John moves the reader on from the Shepherd Discourse to a new setting
marked by the introduction of the Feast of Dedication in 10.22. The unit is
composed of two parts (10.22–30; 34–39) which are interrupted by an
attempted stoning (10.31–33), and ends with a return to the witness of the
Baptist (10.40–42). It is the first section that especially interests us. Jesus
is in the vicinity of the temple when the Jews surround him and ask for a
definitive statement clarifying whether he is the Messiah (10.24). He answers
that he has already made this clear with the miracles done in the Father's
name (10.25), but they have not believed because they are not his sheep
(10.26–29). This marks a return to the themes of the Shepherd Discourse,
underscoring the close ties the two units share, before the passage culminates
in Jesus' declaration of oneness with the Father (10.31). We will argue that
Ps 118.10–12 underlies the surrounding of Jesus in 10.24. A. T. Hanson
first proposed this allusion as an example of an "extremely unobtrusive"
use of the OT,[1] and indeed it has escaped the attention of most scholars.[2]
Unfortunately Hanson did little to support his suggestion, and spent only a
few lines examining the allusion's possible function. It is to both these
tasks – establishing the allusion more firmly and exploring its function –
that we now turn our attention.

---

[1] Hanson, *Living Utterances*, 127; cf. idem, *The Prophetic Gospel*, 254–255.

[2] Barrett and Lindars mention the verbal parallel only to dismiss the possibility of allusion. Barrett (380) writes, "It is very doubtful whether an allusion is intended." Lindars
(367) argues that an allusion is unlikely: "There is no hint of the psalm in the context,
and the word [ἐκύκλωσαν], though uncommon, is quite natural." Although Hoskyns
(386) cites Ps 118.10–12 for reference along with Pss 22.12, 16 and 109.3, and Daly-
Denton (*David*, 164) "draws attention" to Ps 117.10–12 as a parallel, neither suggests
that allusion or echo is in view.

B. Establishing the Allusion

Ps 117.10–12 (LXX)	John 10.24–25

πάντα τὰ ἔθνη
<u>ἐκύκλωσάν</u> με καὶ

<u>ἐκύκλωσαν</u> οὖν
Αὐτὸν οἱ Ἰουδαῖοι καὶ
ἔλεγον αὐτῷ, ἕως πότε τὴν ψυχὴν
ἡμῶν αἴρεις; εἰ σὺ εἶ ὁ Χριστός,
εἰπὲ ἡμῖν παρρησίᾳ. ἀπεκρίθη αὐτοῖς
ὁ Ἰησοῦς, εἶπον ὑμῖν καὶ οὐ
πιστεύετε· τὰ ἔργα ἃ ἐγὼ ποιῶ

<u>τῷ ὀνόματι κυρίου</u>
ἠμυνάμην αὐτούς
κυκλώσαντες <u>ἐκύκλωσάν</u> με καὶ
<u>τῷ ὀνόματι κυρίου</u>
ἠμυνάμην αὐτούς

<u>ἐν τῷ ὀνόματι τοῦ πατρός</u>
μου ταῦτα μαρτυρεῖ περὶ ἐμοῦ·

<u>ἐκύκλωσάν</u> με
ὡσεὶ μέλισσαι κηρίον καὶ
ἐξεκαύθησαν ὡσεὶ πῦρ ἐν
ἀκάνθαις
<u>καὶ τῷ ὀνόματι κυρίου</u>
ἠμυνάμην αὐτούς

John describes the surrounding of Jesus with κυκλόω, a verb that is emphasized dramatically in Ps 117 (LXX) and would fittingly evoke its context of conflict and victory. The word is used only four times in the NT, twice in reference to the hostile encompassing of a city (Luke 21.20; Heb 11.30) and twice for the encircling of an individual (John 10.24; Acts 14.20). Only in John does it indicate a possibly hostile gathering around an individual – in Acts it is Paul's friends that surround him. The use of κυκλόω in the NT is therefore rare, generally hostile in intent, and it is used only once in a context that mirrors that of the psalm. The specific form used in 10.24 (ἐκύκλωσάν) is unique in the NT and exactly as that of the psalm. If one starts with the psalm and proceeds to the NT, the verbal parallel could suggest an allusion. On the other hand, if one begins with John and returns to the OT there are many possible sources, since the LXX uses κυκλόω in 86 verses. However, the number of plausible parallels diminishes rapidly, as it is used less often of the encircling of an individual (30 times). These can be divided further into neutral,[3] positive,[4] and negative[5] instances, so that the surrounding of an individual by enemies is limited to 12 verses.[6] Of these not all are equally appropriate, as three specify the encircling of the place (Judg 16.2) or house (Judg 19.22; 20.5) where the individual is staying, and in one the agent is metaphorical and inanimate (2 Sam 22.6). The question is, To which of the figures from the remaining eight verses – Absalom, Jehoshaphat, David, or the coming one – would John want to compare Jesus? The first two options are unlikely, and although David would be a very appropriate choice he does not figure in the Fourth Gospel. It appears, then, that even though κυκλόω is used often in the LXX, there are very few plausible parallels to John 10.24, and of these the most likely is Ps 118(117).10–12.

Twice in the Fourth Gospel Jesus uses the phrase ἐν τῷ ὀνόματι τοῦ πατρός to answer his opponents in conflict situations.[7] In 5.43 it is used to establish that Jesus comes in the name of the Father, in what we have argued is an allusion to Ps 118.26. It is clear that the psalm's ὀνόματι κυρίου (vv. 10, 11, 12, 26) is synonymous with the Johannine ὀνόματι τοῦ πατρός. Jesus uses the phrase a second time in 10.25 where he deflects his opponents' question in the name of the Father, thus providing a fitting contextual parallel to the psalm which three times portrays the king as surrounded by enemies only to repel them in the name of the Lord. Thus, although the verbal parallels to Ps 118(117).10–12 are separated in 10.24, 25, they

---

[3] Jdt 10.18.

[4] Yahweh surrounds with songs of deliverance (Ps 32[31].7), and guards Jacob/Israel (Deut 32.10); the king is surrounded for protection (2 Kgs 11.8; 2 Chr 23.7); the assembly is called to surround Yahweh (Ps 7.7[8]); an individual is surrounded by pomegranates (Sir 45.9), worshippers at the altar (Sir 50.12), truth (Ps 91[90].4), and lovingkindness (Ps 31.10).

[5] Surrounding by people: Judg 16.2; 19.22; 20.5; 2 Sam 18.15; 22.6; 1 Kgs 22.32; 2 Chr 18.31; Pss 22.16(21.17); 109(108).3; 118(117).10, 11, 12. Surrounding by nature (sea, waves, rivers): Jonah 2.3(4), 5(6). Surrounding by non-persons: bitterness and hardship (Lam 3.5); iniquity (Ps 49.5[48.6]); snares (Job 22.10); arrows (Job 16.13); the terrors and wrath of Yahweh (Ps 88.17[87.18]); Yahweh is surrounded by the lies of Ephraim and deceit of Israel (Hos 12.1).

[6] It is used to describe the surrounding of the place where Samson was staying (Judg 16.2); the men of Gibeah surrounding the house where a traveler was staying (Judg 19.22; 20.5); the surrounding of Absalom (2 Sam 18.15); Jehoshaphat surrounded in battle by Syrian opponents (1 Kgs 22.32; 2 Chr 18.31); David surrounded by the cords of Sheol (2 Sam 22.6), by enemies with words of hate (Ps 109[108].3) and by enemies labeled as dogs (Ps 22.16[21.17]); and the coming one surrounded by enemies (Ps 118[117].10, 11, 12). Note that Boismard and Lamouille (274) suggest the possibility of an allusion to Ps 22.17 in John 10.24, and Schuchard (*Scripture*, 68 n. 38) points the reader to parallels in Pss 7.6–8 and 82(81).1, the latter being quoted (v. 6) in 10.34.

[7] The phrase is used only one other time in the NT, in Luke 1.59, in reference to the naming of the Baptist.

follow exactly the sequence repeated in the psalm.[8] The use of κυκλόω is rare enough, but when combined with acting in the name of the Lord it is unique to John 10.24–25 and Ps 117.10–12 (LXX).[9]

In addition to the verbal and contextual parallels, the prominent liturgical use of Ps 118 at the Festival of Dedication makes it an especially appropriate source for allusion in this passage. Allusion is all the more likely considering the significant use of Ps 118 in 10.7–10, for not only is the Shepherd Discourse in close proximity, it is also taken up again in 10.26–29, ensuring that the two passages will be linked in the reader's mind. When added to John's recognized use of the LXX to make allusions, his use of this psalm specifically, and the fact that the prior use of ὀνόματι τοῦ πατρός is most likely from the psalm, it seems credible that John intended an allusion to Ps 118(117).10–12.[10]

C. The Function of the Allusion

1. Setting the Context

The second half of ch. 10 is specifically placed at the Feast of Dedication. John mentions that it was winter, perhaps simply indicating familiarity with the feast and giving local color, or perhaps to explain why Jesus was walking in Solomon's Colonnade, as this would offer shelter from the biting wind.[11] For the reader the mention of the feast may, as Lindars suggests, contribute to "the sense of mounting climax" as the passion approaches,[12] and although surely more than a mere chronological marker, at the least it helps to move

---

[8] Note the contextual parallels: both the king and Jesus are surrounded by enemies; each rebuffs them in the name of the Lord; the psalm and Jesus' activity are placed in a temple context.

[9] We have seen that the use of κυκλόω is rare in the NT, so it is not surprising that its pairing with ὀνόματι τοῦ πατρός is unique to John. However, a search of even the less specific verbal pairing of ὄνομα (i.e., not limited to its use with κύριος) and κυκλόω in the LXX yields only three results apart from Ps 118(117).10–12: two have to do with the naming of rivers (Gen 2.11, 13), and one with David's inability to build the temple for the Lord because of the warfare with which his enemies surrounded him (1 Kgs 5.17).

[10] It is possible that John's use of the verb may not be a deliberate allusion that the reader is intended to recognize and see significance in. That is, the language of the psalm, with which John clearly was familiar, may have stimulated his choice of words without necessarily being significant. The same caveat could be voiced for most proposed allusions. Among other factors that militate against this possibility is the use in close proximity of the phrase "in the name of the Father," which most likely is drawn from the psalm and thus substantially increases the plausibility of deliberate allusion.

[11] Beasley-Murray (173) suggests that the weather may be a cryptic statement identifying the cold weather with the spiritual state of the Jews. Cf. Hoskyns, 386.

[12] Lindars, 366.

the narrative along. In addition, it has been noted that when John mentions other festivals by name they are significant in relation to Jesus' identity and mission,[13] so that it is very unlikely that the mention of this feast is incidental.[14]

In fact, Dedication furnishes a promising context for John to continue the systematic replacement of Jewish institutions and highlight Jesus' unique identity.[15] In 10.36 Jesus describes himself as the one whom the Father consecrated and sent into the world. In this pregnant context, which recalls not only the Maccabean consecration of the temple altar but also evokes the tabernacle and different temples that had stood in Jerusalem, John's choice of words points to Jesus as the ultimate fulfillment of the festival.[16] In light of the festival replacement theme, it is not implausible that the reader could recognize Jesus as the newly consecrated temple.[17] This would in turn complement and complete the theme of temple replacement that John had developed earlier and most recently had resurfaced with the allusion to Ps 118.19–20 in 10.7–10.[18] Accordingly it may be significant that John mentions Solomon's Colonnade as Jesus' specific location, for it was thought to be the only section to have survived the

---

[13] With the exception of the feast in 5.1, which he leaves unnamed, John relates major themes and/or symbols of the specified festival to Jesus. This is especially clear with Tabernacles (light, water) and Passover (e.g., the Last Supper, bread from heaven, sacrificial lamb).

[14] Schnackenburg (2.305) considers it to be of little importance. So also Barrett (379), who sees "no symbolical correspondence between the conduct of the feast and the ensuing discussion."

[15] On the customs of the festival and their explanation in rabbinic literature see Str-B 2.539–541; also O. S. Rankin (*The Origins of the Festival of Hanukkah: The Jewish New-Age Festival*), who argues that Dedication is the festival of the "New Age," which looks to the sovereignty of God's Messiah and the fullness of all messianic blessings.

[16] See Carson, 399; Beasley-Murray, 177; Hoskyns, 392. Hoskyns points out that variants on τὰ ἐγκαίνια are used in the LXX to describe the dedication of the altar in the Tabernacle (Num 7.10–11), Solomon's Temple (1 Kgs 8.63; 1 Chr 7.5), and following the return (Ezra 6.16).

[17] Others who suggest the replacement of the temple at Dedication include Brown, 1.411; Morris, 517; Smith, 210; H. Thyen, "Johannes 10 im Kontext des vierten Evangeliums," 131; Schuchard, *Scripture*, 65 n. 27. Westcott (157) comments: "Christ in fact perfectly accomplished what the Maccabees wrought in a figure, and dedicated a new and abiding temple." Guilding (*Jewish Worship*, 129) points out that Dedication would have been associated with two contrasting sets of ideas: the blasphemy of false worship and the defiled temple, over against the true worship of a regathered Israel and the return of the glory to a restored temple. This provides a fitting backdrop for John's temple replacement theme.

[18] The reader would recognize that Jesus had already replaced the temple with his body, taken its place as the locus of worship, and fulfilled the function of its doors in providing access to God.

destruction of Solomon's temple, and thus to provide the single physical link between the first and second temples.[19] It is noteworthy that following the confrontation at Dedication the Fourth Gospel does not picture Jesus returning to the temple again.[20] This informs the context within which the function of Ps 118 is to be interpreted.

2. The Question

The Jews gathered around Jesus in the temple area and asked that he tell them plainly whether he is the Christ. In the Fourth Gospel the Jews are often, although not always, depicted as opponents. In this case the uncertainty is important because the phrase Ἕως πότε τὴν ψυχὴν ἡμῶν αἴρεις; can be understood in a positive sense as expressing curiosity ("How long will you keep us in suspense?"), or more negatively as a display of impatience and annoyance. Although a number of scholars have argued for the former position, that the question demonstrates a desire to learn the truth – "an unsatisfied longing which seeks rest"[21] – is not very convincing. Although κυκλόω can be used in a neutral or positive sense, when ἐκύκλωσάν is used in the LXX for the surrounding of an individual it always carries a hostile or negative sense.[22]

---

[19] On the evidence for this view see J. C. VanderKam, "John 10 and the Feast of the Dedication," 205–206. In support he cites Josephus, *War* 5.185; *Ant.* 15.401; 20.221. Cf. Brown, 1.402. Carson (391) suggests that John's reason for including the detail may be that he saw in it an anticipation of where the believers would regularly gather together after the resurrection (Acts 3.11; 5.12).

[20] The concentration of temple vocabulary is in ch. 2 (where Jesus replaces the temple) and in chs. 7–10. After ch. 10, the temple is mentioned only twice, and in neither of these is Jesus physically present at the temple (11.56: Jews at the temple; 18.20: Jesus used to teach at the temple). That is, following the replacement of the doors and the consecration, Jesus has completed his involvement with the temple. Blank (178) has suggestively questioned, in reference to Jesus' departure from the temple in response to the Jews' attempt to stone him following the "I am" statement of 8.58, whether "verlässt vielleicht mit Jesus auch die göttliche *Schekhina* den Tempel?" If plausible, then this "departure" might best be placed after the confrontation in ch. 10. Cf. n. 39 below.

[21] Westcott, 157. Cf. Bernard 2.343; Bultmann, 361. Most translations favor a positive interpretation (e.g., NIV, NASB, KJV, RSV). Guilding (*Jewish Worship*, 132) suggests the Jews are merely asking for a clarification of the Shepherd Discourse in plain words. Sanders and Mastin (258) also support this position, yet later appear to qualify it when commenting that in the stoning attempt it is possible – though not the most obvious meaning – that the Jews were already carrying stones with the prior intent of stoning Jesus after eliciting an incriminating statement from him. Kysar (166) claims, as do others, that most commentators favor a positive interpretation. However, there appears to be a relatively even division between scholars on this issue.

[22] The sole exception is Sir 50.12.

The parallels with the earlier discourses at Tabernacles also suggest an ambiance of conflict.[23] Barrett gives examples of the idiom meaning "trouble, annoy, vex, pester,"[24] so that the question may betray the Jews' frustration with Jesus' enigmatic speech, as this deprives them of clear and explicit claims to use against him as a basis for attack.[25] Another option is that John intends a play on the literal meaning of the phrase. The noun ψυχή can mean *life* as well as *soul*, and αἴρω can be translated both as *to take away* and *to lift up*. The closest parallel is in 10.17–18 in reference to the death of the Good Shepherd, so that if one translates accordingly it would render, "How long do you take away our life?"[26] In that case John may mean that those who reject Jesus fall under his judgment and thus lose their lives.[27] It may also mark realization on the part of the Jews that Jesus' exclusive claims and the universal scope of his mission imply the death of the narrow Judaism they uphold, a threat to which they respond with hostility.[28] In the context of temple replacement and the exclusive claims of the Shepherd Discourse, it becomes more likely that the Jews could see Jesus as a threat to their institutions, and certainly this would not be impossible for the reader to recognize.

---

[23] In both settings Jesus is in the temple area (7.14, 28; 8.2, 20, 59), the Jews pressure him to declare his identity (8.25), there is speculation about his messianic identity (7.26–27, 31, 41f; 9.22), conflict and rising hostility, an attempt to stone Jesus arising from perceived blasphemy (8.59), and an identification of Jesus with the Father (8.58, among others).

[24] Barrett, 380. Beasley-Murray (173), following Barrett, thus renders the question "How long do you intend to *annoy* or *provoke* us?"

[25] Scholars arguing for a negative intent in the request include Carson, 393; Schnackenburg, 2.305; Beasley-Murray, 173; Painter, "Tradition," 67–68; Sabbe, "John 10," 76.

[26] Hoskyns (383, 386–387) is the main proponent of this position. Brown (1.403) supports Hoskyns' suggestion as possible, while also acknowledging that it could mean *annoy*. See also Lightfoot, 213.

[27] So Brown, 1.403.

[28] Note that neither Hoskyns nor Lightfoot (213) argue that the questioning is hostile. Rather the interrogation carries a sense of urgency, as the implications of Jesus' message require complete assurance that he is indeed the Messiah. See Hoskyns, 383, 386–387: "The Jews perceive clearly that the conclusion of the application of the parable of the Good Shepherd links the death of Jesus with the emergence of the new people of God, and they see also that this involves the destruction of Judaism as an independent political and religious organism. To the Evangelist Judaism is fulfilled and superseded, to the Jewish opponents of Jesus it is destroyed, its life is taken away—unless indeed Jesus be veritably the Christ of God. . . . The ministry and death of Jesus involve the destruction of Judaism, in order that the Scriptures may be fulfilled. The Jews understand the peril without perceiving that it is necessary in order that they may fulfil their true destiny. Jesus is taking away their life. It is this sense of peril that forces the question of the messiahship which alone could justify His behaviour."

This is especially suggestive considering the often-noted similarity between 10.24–25 and the Synoptic trial narrative.[29] It is not clear that this actually represents a reworked trial narrative,[30] but parallels include the question of messianic identity, the hostility of the religious authorities, the charge of blasphemy, the Jews' stubborn unbelief (cf. Luke 22.67–68), and the determined effort to find evidence with which to convict Jesus. Less noted is the pairing of the question concerning his identity with accusations involving the temple. In this light it may not be coincidental that temple replacement is an important theme in the Dedication Narrative, nor that the passage links back to the Shepherd Discourse and therefore Jesus' claims via allusion to Ps 118.19–20 to fulfill the mediatorial function of the temple doors. The emphasis on temple replacement in John 10 would therefore accord with the accusation in the Synoptic trial narratives that Jesus made threats against the temple, a charge eventually dispensed with when he utters what is deemed blasphemy.[31]

The purpose of the question, then, is not so that they can acknowledge his authority and follow him if he answers in the affirmative, but rather it is the insistent demand of men who have already decided that Jesus is not the Messiah and are seeking a statement that would provide a basis to discredit and attack.[32] The allusion to Ps 118.10–12 encourages the reader to recognize the interrogation as a continuation and heightening of the conflict theme. By framing the Jews' question in the context of Ps 118 John underlines their rejection of Jesus and intensifies the characterization of

---

[29] See Luke 22.67–68; Mark 14.55–64; Matt 26.59–66. See discussion in Dodd, *Historical Tradition*, 91ff.; Brown, 1.405; Schnackenburg, 2.306; Smith, 202. On the relationship of ch. 10 to the Synoptics, and specifically 10.22–39 as a reworked trial narrative, see Sabbe ("John 10," esp. 76). If John does indeed introduce traditional aspects of the trial narrative at this point, it is more likely that he drew on independent tradition than that he is directly dependent on one or more of the Synoptic accounts.

[30] Lightfoot (209) suggests that 10.22–39 plays the same role in John as the trial narrative does in Mark (14.55–64). Dodd (*Historical Tradition*, 91) similarly concludes that it is "an alternative formulation of material" also found in the Markan account, but an independent tradition. The question is unsettled as in the Gospels these kinds of confrontations and questions are not restricted to the trial narrative. On this see Beasley-Murray, 174.

[31] The theme of temple replacement followed by the attempted stoning in 10.31 is in accord with the Synoptic presentation of Jesus' Temple Action as decisive in the Jews' final action against him. Both in ch. 10 and the Synoptic trial account the reason for the subsequent violent action is the charge of blasphemy.

[32] Painter ("Tradition," 67–68) notes that the Jews' question ignores the fact that according to 9.22 there are already those who confess Jesus as Messiah and the decision has been made to exclude them from the synagogue. This implies that rather than being curious and positive, their request seeks an unequivocal declaration that could be used against Jesus.

their actions and approach to him as being decidedly hostile.[33] This depiction finds an appropriate parallel in the religious authorities who are united
in opposition to Jesus in the trial narrative. Also, although the connection
is very subtle, it is interesting that an allusion to Ps 118.19–20 is used to
introduce the temple replacement theme in ch. 10, and that in short proximity
a question framed in an allusion to Ps 118.10–12 may evoke the context
of the Synoptic trial narrative in which threats against the temple play a
significant role.

3. Identifying Jesus

As in the other conflict narratives, it is the issue of Jesus' identity that is
at the core of this passage. Two questions frame the discussion: whether
Jesus is the Messiah (10.24), and whether he claims to be God (10.33).[34]
We have noted that although in the Fourth Gospel Jesus does not deny
being the Messiah, he responds to messianic speculation by identifying
himself as the coming-sent one and refocusing attention on his unique
relationship to the Father. In none of the attacks on Jesus is the reason
given that he has claimed to be the Messiah. Rather, it is his declaration
of unity with the Father – understood as blasphemy – that inflames the
Jews and fuels their hostility. In the Dedication Narrative John does not
specifically use the coming-sent theme until 10.36, but the allusion to Ps
118.10–12 performs the same function. When the reader recognizes the
allusion, it becomes clear that it is the coming one whom the Jews have
surrounded. In the psalm the king battles against his opponents, facing
their furious attacks and repeated attempts on his life before gaining
victory. It is this same beleaguered yet triumphant king who then enters
the temple as the coming one.

Jesus' reply to the Jews (10.25), which is framed in an allusion to Ps
118.10–12, thus reiterates his identity as the coming one. In response to
their question he states that they should know the answer for he has already
told them, although in fact one cannot find an instance in the Fourth Gospel

---

[33] In any case, the Jews' violent response to Jesus' words in 10.30 confirm the motives
underlying their question.

[34] On the structure of the passage see E. A. Wyller, "In Solomon's Porch: A Henological Analysis of the Architectonic of the Fourth Gospel." Wyller argues that 10.22–38
is "the structural summit" of the Fourth Gospel and the high point of its dramatical development, of which 10.30 is the watershed declaration. Jesus' assertion of unity with the
Father is thus the central statement of the Gospel (ibid., 153). Although his structural
arguments are not entirely convincing, Wyller's observations on the climactic force of
the passage bring into focus the importance of the Jews' question and Jesus' answer in
setting the stage for and building towards what many consider the definitive statement of
Jesus' relationship to the Father.

when Jesus openly declares to the Jews that he is the Messiah.[35] Jesus is
not, however, claiming to have previously clarified his messianic status.
Their messianic speculation is first and foremost concerned with his identity, and on that subject Jesus' words and actions have been sufficient to
establish the redefinition of messiahship in the language of divine sonship
and to communicate what he unequivocally re-states in 10.30: his unity
with the Father.[36] Jesus deflects the Jews' belligerent demands "in the
name of the Lord," mirroring the Ps 118 king who three times recalls being
surrounded by his enemies only to "cut them off" in the name of the Lord.[37]
Those readers who recognized the allusion would identify Jesus with the
embattled king and therefore with the triumphant coming one. Although
the king is pushed to the point of death, his ultimate victory is as inevitable
as the assured routing of his enemies, so that the allusion leaves no question
as to who will emerge victorious in the continuing conflict between Jesus
and the Jews.

Jesus first suggests that the Jews should have recognized him by the
mission he carries out in the Father's name. He then declares that they
have not believed because they are not his sheep (10.26), thus directing
the reader back to the Shepherd Discourse with all the implications that
passage has for his identity. The resumption of Shepherd material in
10.26–29 parallels in several points the Door section of 10.7–10, which
describes Jesus as the only true coming one who constitutes the new flock
of Israel, leads them out of exile, and mediates eschatological blessing.
In concert with this subtle reverberation from 10.7–10, the allusion to
Ps 118.10–12 names Jesus as the coming one, a designation that so often
accompanies and facilitates the elaboration of Jesus' identity in John.
In this way, together with the evocation of the Shepherd Discourse, the

---

[35] Barrett (378) explains Jesus' unclear answer as a parallel to the Marcan theme of
the messianic secret. Accordingly his teaching should have left no doubt that he was the
Messiah (Barrett, 380). However, more likely than the messianic secret is a theme of
messianic redefinition in terms of unity with Yahweh. Jesus' teaching and actions more
closely parallel expectations of Yahweh's ultimate redemptive action than popular speculation about the Messiah.

[36] VanderKam perceptively argues that it is no accident that John locates what is one
of the strongest assertions of Jesus' divinity at the Feast of Dedication. Antiochus IV had
not only banned the temple cult but also required that he be worshipped in the temple as
a god. As a result, "Jesus' strong assertions [10.30, 36, 38] were uttered at a time when
the blasphemous pretensions of Antiochus IV to be a god would have been particularly
fresh in the minds of Jewish people" ("John 10," 211). Those who are not Jesus' sheep
would therefore see him as only another pretentious blasphemer. See further Smith, 212.

[37] The Hebrew (מול) actually means "to circumcise" (*Hiphil*: "to cause to circumcise").
The colorful picture of forced circumcision accentuates the king's total victory and the
utter defeat and humiliation of his opponents.

allusion to Ps 118 accentuates the question of Jesus' identity, anticipating and leading naturally to the dramatic pronouncement in 10.30.[38]

4. Identifying Jesus' Opponents

Even as the allusion intensifies the sense of conflict and aids in identifying Jesus, it brings into stark focus the true identity of the Jews who are intent on destroying him. In the psalm it is τὰ ἔθνη that surround the king, and although they direct their aggression specifically at him, in doing so they also oppose themselves to Israel and ultimately to Yahweh, whom the king represents. Here there is startling discontinuity with the psalm, for in identifying Jesus with the embattled king, John ensures that the Jews are cast in the role of his antagonists. Instead of joining, as did their ancestors, the shouts of joy and victory in the tents of the righteous (Ps 118.15) and the king's processional as it enters the temple, the present guardians of Judaism are revealed as the enemies of Israel. In their determined aggression against the coming one they have rejected the true hope of the Israel they claim to represent, and thus taken the place of τὰ ἔθνη. What they can expect is defeat by God's right hand (Ps 118.15–16) and to be "cut off." The return to the Shepherd Discourse in 10.26–29 reiterates this, for the Jews who earlier were portrayed as false coming ones are now identified as those who, not being Jesus' own sheep, are also not part of the true flock of Israel. There is thus an interplay of allusions to Ps 118, for it is the Door

---

[38] The exact nature of the unity of Father and son in 10.30 – whether functional and/or ontological – is much debated. For example, Busse ("Open questions," 15) argues that there is only functional unity, while Painter ("Tradition," 69) emphasizes the evidence for ontological equality and functional subordination. Dunn states that in the Fourth Gospel "we have not yet reached the concept of an ontological union between Father and Son, of a oneness of essence and substance" (*Christology in the Making: An Inquiry into the Origins of the Doctrine of the Incarnation*, 58). This is correct if Dunn means that the concept is not as developed as in later formulations, but if he means that the concept of ontological union is not present, then the evidence we have advanced would suggest that this is incorrect. On the interpretation of 10.30 in the early exegesis of the church, and its prominent use both by heretics and in defense of orthodox teaching, see T. E. Pollard, "The Exegesis of John X. 30 in the Early Trinitarian Controversies." See further M. Wiles, *The Spiritual Gospel: The Interpretation of the Fourth Gospel in the Early Church*, esp. 112–128. Pollard sums up well the paradox of Jesus' essential unity with the Father yet distinction from him, a tension which underlies the New Exodus and replacement themes set out in this study and that is crystallized in 10.30: "The Fourth Gospel, with its emphasis on the divinity of Jesus Christ—the central fact of the Church's faith—set the problem of fitting this fact into the framework of belief in 'one God'—the basic presupposition of the Church's faith. The evangelist himself was content to leave the problem in the paradox of *distinction-within-unity*" (ibid., 348). See further Ball, *'I Am' in John's Gospel*, 279.

section which defines inclusion in the flock and therefore highlights by contrast the exclusion of those who surround Jesus with hostile intent.[39] Psalm 118's function in the Dedication Narrative thus parallels the polemical contrasts of the Door section, establishing Jesus' complete command and denying to his enemies the prestige and authority they purport to have as Israel's religious leaders.

II. The Prayer of Jesus in the Lazarus Narrative:
Ps 118 in John 11.41b–42

A. Establishing the Allusion

1. Initial Issues

The Lazarus Narrative contains a number of complex issues which we cannot examine in detail.[40] Our attention will focus on the smaller section 11.38–44, and more specifically on the prayer of Jesus in 11.41b–42. Jesus arrives at

---

[39] The allusions to Ps 118 appear to be subtly interlinked. For one, they tend to surface in conflict situations. This is the case not only for the coming-sent complex, but also for the other allusions identified so far (8.56; 10.7, 9; and 10.24). The present allusion appears in a passage closely linked with the previous Door section, which itself established the temple replacement theme in ch. 10 that is taken up and underscored in the Dedication Narrative and thus helps to set the context for the hostility of the Jews. The contrast of coming ones in the Door section also continues in the present allusion, as the Jews are cast as the enemies of Israel's king. The stoning attempt in 10.31 explicitly recalls the previous attempt in 8.59 ("*again* they picked up stones"). Both violent reactions are occasioned by similar pronouncements, and both follow allusions to Ps 118. Last, Guilding argues that one of the principal Dedication themes is that "the restoration and dedication of the Temple must precede the return of the Shekinah" (*Jewish Worship*, 128). We have argued that in the Fourth Gospel Jesus replaces the temple proper and then its doors, is finally dedicated as the true temple, and in the Entrance to Jerusalem fulfills Yahweh's return. If one accepts this sequence as fulfilling Guilding's proposed Dedication theme, then we have allusions to Ps 118 in two of the critical passages, and a clear quotation of Ps 118 in the concluding and climactic Entrance. Psalm 118 would thus have a significant supporting role in developing this theme of a renewed temple and the return of Yahweh.

[40] We will not argue the historicity of the account. For that see W. B. Hunter's article, "Contextual and Genre Implications for the Historicity of John 11:41b–42," which summarizes and interacts with the primary issues involved. For discussion of the traditions underlying the Lazarus Narrative, its relation to the Synoptic accounts of resurrection miracles and specifically to the Lukan Lazarus Parable (Luke 16.19–31) see Dodd, *Historical Tradition*, 228–232; Brown, 1.427–430. R. Dunkerley ("Lazarus," 321–327) argues, not entirely convincingly, that the resurrection of Lazarus is an actualization of the Lukan parable.

Lazarus' tomb (11.38) and orders that the stone be removed. When Martha hesitates (11.39), Jesus challenges her to believe (11.40). Following the removal of the stone Jesus utters a prayer (11.41–42), after which he calls Lazarus out of the tomb (11.43–44). A. T. Hanson and M. Wilcox – independently of each other – proposed that 11.41b alludes to Ps 118.21.[41] However, perhaps because so few scholars have acknowledged the allusion, it remains largely undeveloped.[42] Although Hanson and Wilcox are to be commended for discovering the allusion, they fail to look seriously at its function. Wilcox is primarily concerned with isolating different levels of tradition, and Hanson limits his insights to a few lines. We will therefore look briefly at the evidence for the allusion, but concentrate our attention on examining its function in the passage.

2. Verbal and Contextual Evidence

John 11.41–42	Ps 117.5, 21, 28c (LXX)	Ps 118.5, 21
ἦραν οὖν τὸν λίθον. ὁ δὲ Ἰησοῦς ἦρεν τοὺς ὀφθαλμοὺς ἄνω καὶ εἶπεν, Πάτερ,	117.5 ἐν θλίψει ἐπεκαλεσάμην τὸν κύριον καὶ ἐπήκουσέν μου εἰς πλατυσμόν	מן־המצר קראתי יה ענני במרחב יה
εὐχαριστῶ σοι ὅτι ἤκουσάς μου.	117:21 ἐξομολογήσομαί σοι ὅτι ἐπήκουσάς μου καὶ ἐγένου μοι εἰς σωτηρίαν	אודך כי עניתני ותהי־לי לישועה
	117.28c ἐξομολογήσομαί σοι ὅτι ἐπήκουσάς μου καὶ ἐγένου μοι εἰς σωτηρίαν	
ἐγὼ δὲ ᾔδειν ὅτι πάντοτέ μου ἀκούεις, ἀλλὰ διὰ Τὸν ὄχλον τὸν περιεστῶτα εἶπον, ἵνα πιστεύσωσιν ὅτι σύ με ἀπέστειλας.		

---

[41] Hanson, "Lazarus"; Wilcox, "Prayer."

[42] The major commentaries do not note the allusion. Hunter ("Historicity," 68) mentions that Hanson's suggestion is not impossible, but dismisses it as having "difficulties." M. Cimosa ("La traduzione greca dei Settanta nel Vangelo di Giovanni," 49) accepts the allusion on the strength of Hanson's suggestion, yet offers no evidence in support. A. Finkel ("Hallel and Kerygma," 120) also appears to accept the allusion. Frey (*Eschatologie*, 441) notes the similarity of the thanksgiving form to that of Ps 118.21.

The phrase in 11.41b is, as Wilcox notes, "strikingly similar" to the LXX,[43] which through the addition of the string to Ps 117.28c emphasizes the original parallel in Ps 117.21.[44] The difficulty is that John's choice of verbs is different from the LXX. The NT uses the psalm's ἐπακούω only once (2 Cor 6.2 quoting Isa 49.8), and Wilcox notes that it is difficult to explain why John would change ἐξομολογέω to εὐχαριστέω, since the latter is not particularly Johannine. As a result he concludes that the allusion "is clearly not to the text of the LXX."[45] On the other hand, εὐχαριστῶ σοι provides an appropriate translation for אודך, so that it is possible, as Wilcox suggests, that John translated from the Hebrew.[46] However, one should not absolutely dismiss the LXX as a possible source. Although it is true that εὐχαριστέω is not particularly Johannine, he does use it 3 times in the Gospel (6.11, 23; 11.41; cf. Rev 11.17) while not using ἐξομολογέομαι at all. He thus preferred the former, in keeping with the general pattern throughout the NT.[47] Conversely, the LXX does not use εὐχαριστέω.[48] John similarly may have preferred the more popular ἀκούω to ἐπακούω. In any case, although exact verbal correspondence would make for a stronger allusion, the different words are equivalent in meaning. The Hebrew ענה most closely translates as "to answer" or "to respond," which is close to but not exactly the same as the LXX's choice of ἐπακούω, which carries the thought "to listen to someone with the implication of heeding and responding to what is heard."[49] This meaning of "to listen" corresponds exactly with ἀκούω.[50] The two words of thanksgiving – εὐχαριστέω and ἐξομολογέομαι – are also synonymous.[51] As a result the LXX string ἐξομολογήσομαί σοι ὅτι ἐπήκουσάς μου is semantically equivalent to John's εὐχαριστῶ σοι ὅτι ἤκουσάς μου. The two phrases are also recognizably parallel, and equally unique – the former

---

[43] Wilcox, "Prayer," 130.

[44] The original Hebrew does not include the phrase that the LXX adds in translating Ps 118.28.

[45] Wilcox, "Prayer," 130. The reason Hunter ("Historicity," 68 n. 51) gives for rejecting the allusion to Ps 118 is the verbal differences.

[46] Wilcox, "Prayer," 130–131. Hanson ("Lazarus," 254) points out that the use of the present tense in 11.41 instead of the LXX's future tense is closer to the Hebrew of Ps 118.21.

[47] The NT uses εὐχαριστέω 37 times, especially in the Pauline writings. In comparison it uses ἐξομολογέω 10 times, but only 4 times does it carry a meaning of thanksgiving/praise (Matt 11.25; Luke 10.21; Rom 14.11; 15.9).

[48] It is used 6 times in the Apocrypha, but not in the canonical books of the OT.

[49] So J. P. Louw and E. A. Nida, *Louw-Nida Greek-English Lexicon Based on Semantic Domains*, 24.60.

[50] The LXX may thus be slightly closer in meaning to John than the Hebrew. However, since the LXX provides an acceptable translation of the Hebrew, this does not weaken the plausibility of John using the Hebrew directly.

[51] See Louw and Nida, 33.349 and 33.351.

is found only in Ps 117.21, 28 (LXX), the latter only in John 11.41. The Hebrew string is also found only in Ps 118.21. In conclusion, the allusion may draw on the LXX, but also appropriately translates the Hebrew.[52]

In addition to the verbal parallels several other factors support the plausibility of the allusion. First, it is clear that Ps 118.5, 21, and the added phrase in v. 28c, are words spoken by the king. It is likely that the psalm was recited with some antiphonal divisions, with the verses in question representing the prayers of the coming one – that is, they are a prayer within a prayer. It is especially appropriate, then, for Jesus, who had recently been identified in 11.27 as the coming one, to echo the prayers of the psalm's coming one. Second, the allusion to the coming one in 11.27 finds its counterpart in the prayer itself, where Jesus voices his desire that the surrounding witnesses come to recognize him as the sent one (11.42). Third, although this is the first direct use of Ps 118 (excepting the development of the coming-sent complex) outside a festival context, because the reader has already encountered several allusions to the psalm he is thus more attuned to its presence and more likely to recognize it here. Familiarity with the ubiquitous psalm does not depend on a specific festival parallel. A closer look at the prayer itself will suggest other contextual parallels.

B. Examining the Prayer

1. Initial Characteristics of the Prayer

Several characteristics of Jesus' utterance indicate that it was a prayer and was intended to be understood as such. The reference to God as "Father," although unusual, is characteristic of how Jesus addresses God in prayer elsewhere, and underlines the intimate relationship between Father and son.[53] The utterance is quite short, beginning with an expression of thanksgiving. In this it is not unusual, for many Jewish prayers begin with and emphasize thanksgiving and/or praise.[54] In fact, an examination of Jewish

---

[52] Unlike Wilcox, Hanson ("Lazarus," 254) does not argue clearly for either the LXX or the Hebrew as the source.

[53] Other examples include John 12.27–28; 17.1, 5, 11, 21, 24, 25; Matt 11.25; Mark 14.36 (par. Matt 26.39; Luke 22.42); Luke 11.2. Jeremias argues strongly that Jesus uses the Aramaic אבא in addressing God: "We can say quite definitely that there is *no analogy at all* in the whole literature of Jewish prayer for God being addressed as Abba . . . . A new way of praying is born. Jesus talks to his Father as naturally, as intimately and with the same sense of security as a child talks to his father" (Jeremias, *The Prayers of Jesus*, 57; emphasis original). Odeberg (334) also argues that *Pater* corresponds to *Abba*.

[54] Note for example the opening of Paul's letters (Rom 1.8; 1 Cor 1.4; 2 Cor 1.3; Eph 1.3), and the Qumran Thanksgiving Hymns (1QH^a). See Brown, 1.436. Jeremias argues

prayer forms shows that 11.41b–42 shares the formal characteristics of the *hodayoth* and *berakoth* traditions.[55] The gesture of raising the eyes to heaven was not unheard of in Judaism,[56] although it appears to be rare in the later period.[57] It is "a natural prelude to prayer,"[58] and is Jesus' posture for prayer on several occasions both in John and the Synoptics.[59] Some scholars have suggested that the prayer originates in the evangelist's mind rather than Jesus',[60] and others that Jesus is incapable of prayer. Bauer, for example, asserts that "der johannische Christus überhaupt nicht wirklich beten kann."[61] However, whatever the source of the prayer, the Fourth Gospel portrays it as coming from Jesus, and whatever tension it may create or reveal in John's Christology does not change the fact that he depicts

---

that "thanksgiving is one of the foremost characteristics of the new age. So when Jesus gives thanks he is not just following custom . . . he is actualizing God's reign here and now" (*Prayers*, 78). In any case, the emphasis on thanksgiving in prayer would not be foreign to John's audience.

[55] For discussion of the *hodayoth* form of prayer, which became characteristic of Christianity, see J. M. Robinson, "Die Hodajot-Formel in Gebet und Hymnus des Früh-Christentums." His research demonstrates convincingly that John 11.41b–42 stands in the *hodayoth* tradition of prayer. For a number of examples of *hodayoth* and *berakoth* prayers see G. Lathrop, "The Prayer of Jesus and the Great Prayer of the Church," 158–173. Lathrop argues that at the time of Jesus only a loose distinction between the two forms can be made, so that in fact they represent the same prayer form (ibid., 159 n. 1), and lists 11.41–42 as an example of this form (ibid., 162–163). We will examine the form more closely ahead.

[56] Cf. Ps 123.1. Kysar (182) suggests that standing with eyes uplifted may have been the common posture for Jewish prayer. The tax-collector in Luke 18.13 specifically does not lift up his eyes, but this appears to emphasize his humility in contrast with the Pharisee who, it is implied, did raise his eyes.

[57] So Str-B 2.246–247.

[58] Brown, 1.427.

[59] John 17.1; Mark 6.41 (par. Matt 14.19; Luke 9.16); Mark 7.34.

[60] Fortna argues that Jesus' lifting of the eyes may have been thaumaturgic, and that "only to John does it suggest a prayer and so provide for his insertion" (*Signs*, 83). Schnackenburg (2.339) suggests that the prayer is an insertion to give the event a theological explanation, whereas the source had the removal of the stone followed immediately by Jesus' command to Lazarus. Hanson claims that John creates teaching, conversations, and incidents that conform to themes from Scripture, in order to show that Jesus' teaching and actions fulfill Scripture. Jesus' prayer in 11.41–42 is a "striking" example of this: "John feels justified, on the basis of [prayers in the Psalms] to tell us not only what Jesus prayed but also how. He was confident that it must have happened this way because so it was foretold in Scripture" (Hanson, "Scripture," 369). Cf. idem, *The Prophetic Gospel*, 245.

[61] Bauer, 149. Similarly, E. Käsemann (*The Testament of Jesus: A Study of the Gospel of John in the Light of Chapter 17*, 5) states that when the Johannine Jesus prays it is "proclamation" or "address, admonition, consolation and prophecy" – i.e., it is instruction rather than genuine supplicatory prayer. Becker (2.363–364) calls it a "Demonstrations-gebet," which he does for show.

Jesus as praying.[62] As far as the reader is concerned Jesus is recognizably engaged in prayer, and s/he has been made privy to its content.[63] Bauer's protestations notwithstanding, the question of where, when, and with what purpose Jesus uttered his prayer is therefore relevant.[64]

2. The Occasion and the Audience

The where and when of the prayer is an issue because Jesus thanks the Father "that you have heard me" (11.41b), yet what he may have said to the Father – presumably a request – is not explicitly stated. Scholars have dealt with this in several ways. First, some argue that Jesus is alluding to an unrecorded prayer. The aorist may refer to a previous prayer – spoken or unspoken – that is implied but not mentioned until this point,[65] or to a present prayer that is unrecorded. For the latter, John may want the reader

---

[62] There is at many points in the Fourth Gospel a sense of tension in that Jesus is one with the Father, yet not without differentiation. Prayer by Jesus is consistent with Johannine Christology in that the subordination of the son to the Father is never denied. See Schnackenburg, 2.339. Wilcox ("Prayer," 131) notes that the Targum to Ps 118.21 adds "I give thanks before thee that thou has received my prayer," which makes the act of praying explicit in the psalm. The Targum thus provides an appropriate parallel to 11.41–42 where John makes explicit through the characteristics listed above that Jesus' words are to be regarded as prayer. The use of a prayer from Ps 118 would also accentuate the utterance as prayer speech.

[63] Although Jesus' words are addressed to the Father, at a literary level they are meant to communicate to the reader/hearer. This leads to the suggestion that, since it is a medium of declaration to the reader/hearer, the prayer is not "real." In private correspondence Prof. Frey wrote, "Hier liegt eben doch weniger ein 'richtiges' Gebet vor als vielmehr eine Form der Verkündigung im Medium des erzälten Gebets." (See further Frey, *Eschatologie*, 441–442, esp. n. 129). It is of course important to distinguish between various levels of interpretation, but in this particular case questions of historicity do not bear on the function of Jesus' utterance, since at the literary level John presents it as a "real" prayer, and intends for the reader to understand it as such. No matter that the prayer form may be used as a literary device, the reader is told it is a real prayer and therefore at the level of reader response it is real. In any case, I suggest that a declaratory function is not foreign to biblical prayer (see argument in section B3 below).

[64] Bauer (149) suggests that because the Johannine Jesus is incapable of genuine prayer the question of where or when he had uttered a prayer is irrelevant.

[65] Beasley-Murray (194) and Bruce (248) suggest that the text assumes Jesus has already prayed concerning the raising of Lazarus. Other scholars try to locate the prayer more specifically. Sanders and Mastin (275) suggest a prayer was offered during the agony in 11.33, and E. Grubb ("The Raising of Lazarus," 407) points to either 11.33 or 11.38. Westcott (172–173) proposes that the prayer was made and the answer assured before 11.4, as does Bernard (2.937). Hunter argues for a private prayer that "surely . . . is to be placed at some point in the chronology prior to what is related in 11:11, perhaps even as early as 11:4" ("Historicity," 60 n. 22).

to think that Jesus prayed internally so that only God heard.[66] Second, others emphasize that no specific prayer is in mind because the continuous and unbroken communion that Jesus shares with the Father ensures that his requests are heard before he articulates or even formulates them.[67] A further step in this line is to argue that their unity of will obviates the need for request or intercession.[68] A third option is that the thanksgiving itself includes the request, so that Jesus thanks the Father for what he has anticipated in absolute faith. Because the result is assured he utters his request in the form of a thanksgiving.[69] In any case, the words recorded in 11.41b–42 are the only prayer occasion and prayer-speech that John places before the reader, and thus the only prayer that he intends for them to hear. A possibility so far overlooked is that by framing the beginning of the prayer with an allusion to Ps 118 John portrays Jesus as praying the psalm. That is, Jesus prays only once, but in doing so he adopts as his own a prior prayer. The thanksgiving prayer of 11.41b thus draws in and presupposes the context of Ps 118, where the king's grateful prayer follows his victory over death.

This raises the question of what, if anything, the crowd overheard. Bultmann strongly asserts that "it is obvious" that Jesus' words were not overheard – all they saw was the actions that indicated prayer.[70] This is far from obvious, but since John presents the words of Jesus for the benefit of

---

[66] So Morris, 560. The greatest difficulty is that John does not indicate clearly that a previous or present prayer – spoken or unspoken – is in view, although he easily could have if that were his intention.

[67] See Kysar, 182–183; Lindars, 401; Barrett, 402. Bultmann (408) argues that Jesus never needs to make a request in prayer. One problem with this view is that the Father's continuous hearing of Jesus is not emphasized until 11.42, suggesting that in 11.41b the aorist more likely refers to a specific prayer. In addition, these scholars are not completely consistent in their argument that no other prayer is in view, for their statements still assume an implicit request for the raising of Lazarus. Kysar (182) argues that Jesus' words reflect his confidence that "his desire to bring Lazarus to life has already been heard long before it is articulated." Lindars (401) suggests that "Jesus' communion with the Father is such that he need not actually formulate his request," and Barrett (402) that because of their constant communion the Father "has already 'heard' his petition for Lazarus." In other words, at some point in time Jesus' "request," "desire," or "petition," whether formulated or not, becomes known to the Father, thus allowing Jesus to thank the Father for the assured results.

[68] See for example D. A. Lee, *The Symbolic Narratives of the Fourth Gospel: The Interplay of Form and Meaning*, 214.

[69] See Jeremias, *Prayers*, 78; Haenchen, 2.67; Westcott, 173.

[70] Bultmann, 408. He provides no support for his statement. Morris (561) states that "we have no reason for thinking the crowd heard." Brown (1.436–437) suggests that the crowd may not have heard the prayer but only recognized the actions indicating prayer. Against this see Painter, *Quest*, 318; Sanders and Mastin, 275; Lindars, 401.

his readers,[71] what matters is that the reader "hears" the entire prayer quite clearly, and recognizes that the setting implies an audience to the prayer within the narrative. As far as the reader is concerned, Jesus prayed out loud and was overheard by the crowd. This brings us to ask what the prayer was intended to accomplish.

3. The Purpose of the Prayer

The majority opinion is that Jesus purposely prays (or at least adopts the posture of prayer) in a recognizable way in order that the subsequent miracle be interpreted in the context of his relationship to the Father.[72] Accordingly, praying may indicate to the crowd that far from being a magician or mere wonderworker, Jesus is completely dependent on the Father and has no authority apart from him.[73] Otherwise the prayer may simply show to the crowd the source of Jesus' power,[74] help them recognize the union of Father and son,[75] or establish that Jesus shares with the Father the divine prerogative of raising the dead.[76] Although most scholars assume that Jesus in some way requests the raising of Lazarus,[77] this does not translate into their arguing that the primary purpose of the prayer was to bring Lazarus back to life. Rather, it has to do with what the prayer says about Jesus.

Jesus does state in his prayer that he is praying for the benefit of those standing around him (11.42), and any of the above results would indeed benefit the crowd. However, what some find distasteful is that the prayer's

---

[71] Schnackenburg (2.339) writes, "The bystanders are meant to hear his words and . . . be exhorted to faith. This function makes Jesus' prayer not a demonstration. It is a stylistic device of the evangelist's, who is thinking more of his readers than of the crowd in Bethany."

[72] Painter (*Quest*, 318) argues that the prayer establishes the relationship of Father and son.

[73] See Sanders and Mastin, 275; R. H. Fuller, *Interpreting the Miracles*, 107–108; Barrett, 403; Bultmann, 408; Kysar, 182–183. Carson (418) emphasizes dependence, but unlike the scholars above does not connect it to a correction of a "wonderworker" image.

[74] Brown, 1.436–437. Malina and Rohrbaugh (201) claim that 11.41–44 is "clear patronage language. As God's broker, Jesus has complete confidence that the patron will provide." The resurrection of Lazarus confirms the status of Jesus, and the prayer is intended to make clear that God is the source of what is provided.

[75] Hoskyns, 406; Becker, 2.364. Smith (226) suggests the prayer is intended to clarify Jesus' knowledge of his relationship to the Father, Schlatter (255) that it shows their unity and that Jesus' work depends on the Father, and Frey (*Eschatologie*, 442) that it highlights the son's divine agency.

[76] Bruce, 238.

[77] Most scholars assume such a request, although they disagree on the when and where. As we have noted, the proposals most often advanced are that the request was explicitly stated in a prior or present unrecorded prayer, or in an unarticulated communication that proceeds out of the oneness of Father and son, or in an actualization of the thanksgiving phrase.

purpose therefore appears to be to affect – even impress – the bystanders. The assumption is that if Jesus prays primarily for the crowd to hear then the prayer is for show and therefore artificial.[78] Together with this, even if Jesus' prayer is genuine, it is intolerable and contrary to the nature of prayer that it become a vehicle to preach to the crowd.[79] Loisy thus suggests that Jesus' prayer – if it can be called that – [80] is only an action for the crowd, praying to the gallery: "le Christ ne parle à son Père que pour provoquer la foi en sa personne et en son rôle divin; et le discours est en peu gauche, parce que la situation n'est pas réelle."[81]

The problem seems to be the prayer's dual address – that Jesus speaks simultaneously to the Father and to the crowd. This draws a strong reaction from Loisy: "Mais cette combinaison de prière pour Dieu et de prière pour la galerie est tout ce qu'il y a de moins naturel au monde, et l'on peut ajouter de moins digne du Christ."[82] However, this fails to appreciate Jewish prayer forms, for many of the *hodayoth* and *berakoth* were public prayers that verge on and cross into proclamation.[83] In fact, dual address in prayer is not uncommon in the NT. One thinks of Stephen's prayer in Acts 7.59–60, and a number of Paul's letters begin with a *berakah* or *hodayah*[84] formulation that is intended to affect the reader. Surely many OT (and NT) prayers, while addressed to God, also served variously to instruct, to warn, or as confessions of orthodox belief that benefited the listener.[85] In this line, Mowinckel has argued that the purpose of postcanonical psalmography

---

[78] Thus Morris (561) writes, "This does not mean that His prayer was primarily for the crowd to hear. That would make it an artificial thing." See Fuller: "To the modern reader this prayer is irritating, if not offensive. The whole thing looks like a put-up show, anything but genuine prayer. Jesus knows he need not pray, but apparently stages a prayer to impress the by-standers!" (*Miracles*, 107). Ashton (*Understanding*, 327) emphasizes that the phrase in 11.42 is added to show that Jesus did not actually need to pray – i.e., it is a demonstration for the crowd.

[79] See A. R. George's comment: "If . . . we affirm that Jesus did in fact pray, there seems no reason to deny that He may have offered his thanksgiving *aloud* simply for the sake of the crowd; what is intolerable is that He should have used this very prayer to convey the fact. We are thus driven to regard these words as 'a comment or interpretive gloss of the evangelist,' which has somehow got into the text . . . If that is so, we can ignore it for our purpose" (*Communion with God in the New Testament*, 198–199; cited in Hunter, "Historicity," 55).

[80] Loisy comments, "si toutefois le nom de prière convient à des réflexions qui sont exprimées pour l'édification de l'assistance" (651).

[81] Loisy, 651.

[82] Loisy, 651.

[83] Cf. Lathrop, "Prayer of Jesus," 159.

[84] The singular of *hodayoth* is not found in biblical Hebrew, but is regularly rendered as *todah* in the Mishnah, and as *hodayah* in modern Hebrew.

[85] See for example Solomon's prayer when the ark is brought to the temple (1 Kgs 8.15–21) and at the dedication of the temple (1 Kgs 8.22–54).

was both to express the author's piety and to teach the disciples about the character and work of God: "A prominent feature of this type of psalm was the worshipper's testimony *coram publico* . . . In such a testimony something of a desire to win other people for God is always included."[86] The use of the Psalms in the temple cult yields a similar result, as the communal and public character of the liturgy functions to instruct the congregation. Psalm 118 itself preserves an early example of dual address, for although it is in its entirety a thanksgiving liturgy directed to God, it includes a call to worship, orders to different participants (118.19, 27), and consists primarily of the proclamation of Yahweh's deeds. It is therefore entirely appropriate for Jesus to pray in a way that challenges the listener to right belief.

What many detractors overlook is that Jesus is praying *for*, not *to*, the surrounding crowd. That is, rather than providing a lesson for the listeners, Jesus prays on their behalf. The prayer may reveal the unity of Father and son, identify Jesus as God's agent or representative, and/or highlight that God is the source of his authority and thus distinguish him from popular magicians and wonderworkers. Inevitably it will communicate content to the audience and thus potentially affect them in some way. However, none of these is Jesus' primary purpose in praying.[87] The chief object of Jesus' prayer is to intercede for the bystanders, that they recognize him as the sent one.

C. The Function of the Allusion

1. Preparation for Battle: Anamnesis

We have argued that Jesus' compressed expression of thanksgiving in 11.41b is composed almost entirely of an allusion to Ps 118.21. If this is the case then one function of the allusion is to provide the content of Jesus' prayer. By vocalizing the familiar verse from Ps 118 Jesus' prayer presupposes and evokes the entire content of the psalm that is applicable to the present context, so that Ps 118 becomes his prayer. The implications of this actualization of the psalm become clearer against the backdrop of the formal characteristics of the *hodayoth/berakoth* prayer form as applied to 11.41b-42. The pattern contains three primary parts

---

[86] S. Mowinckel, "Psalms and Wisdom," 218 (cited in Hunter, "Historicity," 66).

[87] Lindars (401) is one of the few who recognizes this, although he completely misses the implications of the coming-sent theme. He argues instead that the prayer intercedes for the bystanders to recognize the glory of God in the miracle (see 11.40).

that flow into each other: the naming of God, *anamnesis*, and supplication.[88]

Hodayoth *Prayer Form*	*John 11.41b–42*
1. The naming of God	Πάτερ, εὐχαριστῶ σοι
2. *Anamnesis*	ὅτι ἤκουσάς μου. ἐγὼ δὲ ᾔδειν ὅτι πάντοτέ μου ἀκούεις,
3. Supplication	ἀλλὰ διὰ τὸν ὄχλον τὸν περιεστῶτα εἶπον, ἵνα πιστεύσωσιν ὅτι σύ με ἀπέστειλας.

Jesus' prayer starts off with the familiar "I thank thee," along with the naming of God. He then remembers a past deed of God that is understood to have implications for the present situation, which leads to the supplication. It is the *anamnesis* that specifically evokes the psalm and upon which we will first focus our attention, for it carries a sense of implicit supplication separate from the explicit supplication that follows it. The prayer "recalls" the events of Ps 118, where the king thanks God for a resounding victory recently won. Since Jesus' battle lies ahead this is clearly anticipatory, so that the *anamnesis* contains the implicit request that the events of the psalm be actualized in his person and ministry. In this sense the prayer is first a preparation for battle, an image for which John has prepared the reader. The word that John uses to describe Jesus' emotions (ἐμβριμάομαι in 11.33, 38) expresses strong indignation, outrage, and anger,[89] which the context suggests are aroused by and directed at the power of death, and thus against Satan who kills and destroys. Barrett has argued that Jesus is angry that a miracle is almost being forced upon him,

---

[88] Cf. Lathrop, "Prayer of Jesus," 159; Hunter, "Historicity," 63. Lathrop defines *anamnesis* as "the expressed awareness that the truth regarding God remembered and acknowledged in the prayer is now in fact actively engaging and affecting the situation of the community . . . that the deed of God is still powerfully present" ("Prayer of Jesus," 158 n. 4). Note that my application of the prayer form to 11.41b–42 differs in some aspects from those of Hunter and Lathrop.

[89] The NIV, NASB, and RSV translate as though Jesus was deeply moved with grief or sympathy. Cf. Hoskyns, 404. Carson (415) notes that this is "lexically inexcusable." Others who interpret the text as indicating anger include Schnackenburg, 2.335; Brown, 1.425; Barrett, 399. A few implausibly suggest that Jesus' emotions have a thaumaturgic background. For example, according to Haenchen (2.66) Jesus is intensifying his inner preparation. Cf. C. Bonner, "Traces of Thaumaturgic Technique in the Miracles," 171–180; Bultmann, 407 n. 4.

for this will reveal the messianic secret and lead to his death.[90] More popular is the suggestion that Jesus is indignant at the unbelief of the mourners,[91] and closer to the truth that he is angry with the sin, sickness and death that produce such grief.[92] However, Brown is on the mark when he points out that the Synoptics depict similar displays of anger when Jesus is confronted with "manifestations of Satan's kingdom of evil" – in this case death – and suggests a possible parallel to Jesus' distress in the Garden of Gethsemane as he prepares for the final and decisive encounter.[93] Jesus therefore approaches the tomb to challenge Satan, his arch-enemy and the destroyer revealed in the death of Lazarus, in a pre-cursor to the conclusive battle they will later engage in. As Calvin perceptively comments, "Christ does not come to the sepulchre as an idle spectator, but like a wrestler preparing for the contest."[94] The psalm then provides an especially appropriate contextual parallel, for as Jesus prepares for warfare he utters the victory thanksgiving of the coming one, who is a warrior king.[95]

2. Conquering Death: The Thanksgiving of Faith

Proceeding from and closely tied to the implicit request that victory be granted in the upcoming struggle against his enemies (death and Satan) is a second implicit request for the resurrection of Lazarus, which will result from the conquest of death and prefigure that of Jesus himself.[96] In the psalm the king confidently affirms that "I will not die but live" (118.17), assured that however severe the trial Yahweh "has not given me over to death" (118.18). In fact, it is this escape from death that leads directly to

---

[90] Barrett, 399.

[91] So Bauer, 147–148; Loisy, 648. Schnackenburg (2.226, 337) adds that Jesus is moved by the inevitability of death. Hoskyns (404–405) notes also the half-belief of the sisters. Bultmann (406) advances the unlikely suggestion that Jesus' weeping in 11.35 is intended to provoke this unbelief in the Jews. Although unbelief is possible in 11.37, since Jesus himself weeps it is unlikely that John intends to portray the grief of the mourners as unbelief in Jesus' power.

[92] So Bruce, 246; Kysar, 180. Carson (416) combines this with anger at unbelief.

[93] Brown, 1.426. For the Gethsemane parallel see Brown, 1.435. Cf. Mark 1.43; Matt 9.30.

[94] Calvin, 2.13.

[95] We have noted earlier that the Fourth Gospel presents Jesus as a warrior who is intent on destroying the enemies of Israel. Ps 118 contributes to this image of the warrior king in the Entrance as well.

[96] A number of scholars note the parallels between the resurrections of Lazarus and Jesus. On the parallels/contrasts see J. P. Martin, "History and Eschatology in the Lazarus Narrative John 11.1–44," 332–343; Lindars, 400–401. Painter (*Quest*, 320) highlights the symbolic character of the story.

the victory thanksgiving in 118.21 which Jesus prays. Since it is the psalm's coming one who has defeated death, the prayer then becomes a testimony to the resurrection of Jesus – the ultimate conquest that is acted out and anticipated in the more immediate raising of Lazarus.[97] At no point does John explicitly state that Jesus prays for the resurrection of Lazarus, but the prayer calls into play appropriate themes in the psalm that indicate Jesus' intention. That is, the implicit request for resurrection rests on the identification of Jesus with the psalm's coming one, the conqueror of death, rather than to a specific application of the psalm to Lazarus. Lazarus does not escape death – it is Jesus' power over death that secures his return to life. The grounds for this are made explicit in Jesus' bold pronouncement that he is the resurrection and life (11.25–26), of which this is a more subtle echo.[98]

I have suggested that the *anamnesis* carries a sense of implicit request, in keeping with its character as the recollection of God's past actions with implications for the present situation of those praying. However, the overriding tenor of the prayer is one of such utter confidence that the sense of implicit supplication is subsumed and becomes a witness to the authority of Jesus. In the psalm the king recalls his anguish (118.5), the fierce attacks of his enemies (118.10–12), being pushed to the point of falling (118.13), and coming face to face with death (118.17–18). These, however, alternate with emphatic declarations of triumph and assurances of Yahweh's power and sovereignty in providing deliverance, for the battle lives only in memory whereas the victory is present reality. When Jesus echoes the king's prayer he inverts the original order: triumph followed by thanksgiving becomes the thanksgiving of faith followed by triumph. In doing so he indicates that the certain and inevitable result of his prayer is that, just as the coming one of the psalm did, he will completely defeat death and achieve total victory over all his enemies.[99]

---

[97] Hanson, in the single function he advances for the allusion, suggests that the prayer highlights the relation of the raising of Lazarus to the resurrection of Jesus: "Jesus, as he thanks his Father for the sign vouchsafed in the raising of Lazarus, also looks forward to his own resurrection" ("Lazarus," 255).

[98] In this regard, note that Martha's declaration of belief in Jesus' resurrection power includes a clear reference to him as the one "who was to come into the world" (11.27).

[99] Note that Ps 118.10–12 is used in 10.24–25 to characterize Jesus' confrontation with the Jews as a battle between the coming one and those who oppose themselves to Yahweh's rule. Here the psalm is used once again to frame Jesus' battle against a spiritual force – Satan and the tyranny of death. In both passages the psalm assures that the outcome is never in doubt.

3. The Supplication: Belief in the Sent One

The allusion also functions to ensure that Jesus' identity is clearly expressed to the crowd. Jesus first brings the psalm into play by alluding to it in 11.41b, after which he states that the reason he said[100] this (i.e., the thanksgiving in 11.41b) is so that the people standing around may believe that God sent him – that is, that he is the sent one.[101] Although a number of commentators advance that the purpose of Jesus' prayer involves a recognition by the crowd of his relationship to the Father, few have perceived that there is a petition that the witnesses come to faith. Although the *anamnesis* contains an implicit sense of supplication, this is not the formal supplication characteristic of the *hodayoth* prayer. In this case the purpose of the event and of the prayer, which John has made clear is "that they may believe," is also the result that Jesus prays for and expects.[102] The few who do recognize that Jesus prays for the listeners to come to faith have missed his emphasis on what exactly they are expected to believe – that is, that Jesus is the sent one.[103] For example, Brown suggests that Jesus "wishes only that his audience will come to know the Father who has sent him."[104] Ridderbos similarly argues that Jesus "wants to direct their eyes neither to the grave nor toward himself but to the 'whence' of his coming."[105] However, Jesus does not pray that the crowd come to know *the Father* who sent him – he wants them to know *that* the Father sent him. In other words, the emphasis

---

[100] Bernard (2.398–399) argues for the variant reading "because of the multitude standing by *I do it*, that they may believe that thou didst send me." However, this is poorly attested and, as Bernard himself admits, is "undoubtedly weak." See further Brown, 1.427.

[101] In other words, the allusion to Ps 118 in some way is supposed to indicate that Jesus is the sent one, a function that it fulfills through the coming-sent complex which renders synonymous the two designations of coming and sent one.

[102] Lathrop suggests that the supplication is implicit in Jesus' declaration that God has heard him – that is, Jesus' request to God is "continue to hear me" ("Prayer of Jesus," 162). He correctly points out that the purpose of the prayer (i.e., the belief of the crowd) underscores "the communical and proclamatory character of the prayer" (ibid., 162). However, he fails to recognize that the purpose/intention of the prayer is indistinguishable from the actual supplication.

[103] For example, although Hunter ("Historicity," 63) recognizes the supplication in accordance with the *hodayoth* prayer form, he misses the emphasis on the sent one as the object of belief.

[104] Brown, 1.436. According to Brown, Jesus' purpose is that through the exercise of his power, which is the power of the Father, they "will come to know the Father and thus receive life themselves" (1.436) and "believe in the source of his power" (1.437).

[105] Ridderbos, 405. He comes closer than anyone else to recognizing the importance of the sent one in this passage, although he interprets this primarily in the context of Jesus' agency rather than the coming-sent theme that is developed throughout the Fourth Gospel.

is on who Jesus himself is. John focuses the reader's attention not on the Father, but on the one whom the Father sent, with the result that the intended object of the crowd's faith is Jesus.

I have argued that John depicts Jesus' prayer as being uttered out loud. The implication is that the people standing around hear him say that he prays for their benefit, that they may believe in him. Jesus is not telling them how to interpret his prayer – i.e., that this shows his dependence on the Father, that he is not a wonderworker, etc. – , for his request that they come to faith is predicated not on the content of his prayer (as if they would believe because he prays in front of them) but on the action he is about to undertake. What the prayer does prepare the listener for is to interpret the miracle as a sign that Jesus is the sent one, with all the implications this carries in John. The reader knows that Jesus was recently identified as the coming one who grants life and resurrection (11.25–27), only to identify himself as the sent one immediately prior to acting this out in raising Lazarus. It would not be difficult to recognize the recurrence of the coming-sent pattern that so often accompanies the identification of Jesus with Yahweh, in this case through his assuming the Father's prerogative to raise the dead.

Whatever else the prayer may accomplish – and there is no reason to think that its effect is limited to one area – the single purpose that John clearly indicates is that people may know that Jesus is the sent one, a phrase that is tightly interwoven with the coming-sent theme and therefore with Ps 118.[106] One could paraphrase the prayer as follows: *"Father, I thank you that you have heard me. Just as the warrior king of Ps 118 did, I am now entering into battle, and I know that the result will be a resounding victory over this great enemy death, for it will not hold Lazarus nor will you allow death to hold me. I am confident of victory because I know that you hear me always. But I have said this on account of the people standing by, so*

---

[106] Wilcox ("Prayer," 131) suggests that Ps 118.21 may have been used because it preceded the well-known 118.22, and the latter's stone motif would have linked the psalm to the raising of Lazarus through the use of the keyword λίθον in 11.41a. The idea is interesting but misapplied to the stone, for the coming-sent theme is much more prevalent in John and present both in the prayer and its surrounding context. Wilcox also advances a possible connection in the use of the verb κραυγάζω in 11.43a and 12.31a, which "may be pure coincidence or it may reflect an underlying link of some kind between the two sections in which references to Ps cxvii are found. We may ask then whether what we have before us in John xi.41b may not be a trace of an early Christian 'stone'-midrash" (ibid., 131–132). Whatever the merits of the κραυγάζω connection, a much more obvious link than the stone *testimonia* is the coming-sent theme which appears in both passages. In any case, Wilcox asserts that the writer of the Fourth Gospel was unaware of the link. Because Wilcox focuses on distinguishing tradition from Johannine addition he does not explore the function of the Ps 118 allusion. This focus on tradition may also influence his pointing to the stone *testimonia*, which certainly figures in tradition but otherwise does not stand out in this particular passage or in the Fourth Gospel as a whole.

that, when I emerge victorious *they may believe that you sent me* and recognize that I am the one who comes in your name." This is precisely what John portrays as happening in the Entrance, for Jesus' request is fulfilled when those who witnessed the Lazarus resurrection, and others who have heard about it, enthusiastically welcome him as the coming one.[107] In this way the allusion to Ps 118 in Jesus' prayer subtly prepares the reader for the victorious Entrance and foreshadows the decisive battle towards which the conqueror of death resolutely moves.

---

[107] Hunter ("Historicity," 63) argues that the answer to Jesus' petition is recorded in 11.42 rather than 11.44. Although he is correct in noting that the raising of Lazarus was not Jesus' primary request, the fulfillment of the prayer actually comes in the subsequent belief of the witnesses, as recorded in 11.45 and 12.10. Even then, it is not until the Entrance that this is expressed as belief in Jesus as the coming-sent one.

Chapter 11

Conclusion

Throughout this study our attention has focused on the presence and function of Ps 118 in the Gospel of John, in light of the psalm's literary context and its interpretation in Judaism. It is now time to present a summary of the conclusions that have emerged.

I. Summary and Conclusions

While many have assumed an eschatological-messianic interpretation of Ps 118 in first-century Judaism, few have considered evidence other than rabbinic which would substantiate such claims. By examining in ch. 2 the various settings in which the psalm was used, and thereby establishing its hermeneutical horizons, this deficiency has been rectified. It was argued that Ps 118 was originally a royal processional psalm set in the temple cult of the autumn festival. The psalm's association with kingship continued during the intertestamental period, and its specific links to David, together with the messianic exegesis of stone texts in Judaism, facilitated messianic interpretation. Psalm 118's most important interpretive contexts are the Jewish festivals, a fact that is especially significant in the closer examination of the psalm in John, where the festivals feature prominently. Psalm 118 is first and foremost linked to Tabernacles, both in its high-profile liturgical role and by allusions internal to the psalm. This ensures that it shared the festival's eschatological interpretations, which are clear in period literature. The lulab and ethrog, inseparable from Ps 118 in the liturgy, became symbols of victory, deliverance and immortality, associations only intensified by the use of the Hallel at Dedication.

It was argued that post-exilic and intertestamental literature evinces a widespread belief that Israel remained in exile long after the sixth century BC, and would continue in this state until Yahweh intervened decisively to restore and come to reign among them. The use of Ps 118 at the Passover sacrifice and as the climax to the meal takes on added significance in such a context of continuing exile, for the feast looked to the future through the paradigmatic deliverance in Israel's past. Rabbinic material makes explicit the eschatological and messianic interpretation that pre-rabbinic sources imply, and in many instances appears to be in a direct line of development with earlier traditions. The Davidic context of Ps 118's liturgical use in 11QPs[a] may have facilitated eschatological interpretations, and the eschatological shape of the Psalter adds another layer to the understanding of Ps 118. As a result it is possible to suggest that when the NT writers used Ps 118 there was a wealth of motifs, themes, and interpretive contexts which made it especially rich in meaning and appropriate for messianic-eschatological use. This goes a long way toward answering the often neglected question of why specific OT texts prove so prominent in the NT.

The still open question of John's relationship to the Synoptic Gospels, as well as the fact that the latter represent a roughly contemporary use of the psalm, suggests the value of the survey of the Synoptic use of Ps 118 carried out in ch. 3. Although more properly the subject of a separate monograph, and even though limited to obvious quotations and widely recognized allusions, I am not aware of another study that looks at each Synoptic evangelist's use of the psalm, examines the possible coherence of the citations in each Gospel, and compares the results. This reveals that John's use of Ps 118 is both more subtle and varied, although, as can be expected when drawing on the same source, there is much thematic congruence. As in John, the Synoptic use of the psalm is essentially focused on expounding the identity of Jesus and exposing the failure of Israel's leaders to acknowledge their Messiah. Special attention was given to the Synoptic Entrance Narratives, which although differing a great deal in the details from John's, yet also share with it significant thematic overlaps: each emphasizes kingship and the royal traditions of Israel, has Jesus implicitly accept homage, evokes Tabernacles imagery in varying degrees, assigns to Ps 118 a key interpretive role, and it is arguable that in each the psalm can be understood as underlying the procession into Jerusalem.

Anticipating the conclusions of our focus in chs. 5–7 on the Johannine Entrance, it was further noted that John's narrative introduces meaning effects that sharply distinguish it from the Synoptics, particularly in the area of Christology. Whereas in the Synoptics Ps 118 turns up the volume on Davidic messianic kingship, in John's Entrance it points to Yahweh's kingship. This does not, however, indicate that John's Christology radically diverges from and contradicts the Synoptic Christologies. Again, this would require a thorough investigation, but I suggest that John makes explicit what is for the most part implicit in the Synoptics, that he does not so much depart from as develop what is already present in nascent form, that rather than being incompatible pictures, the more advanced Johannine Christology complements and expands that of the Synoptics. In regard to John's relationship to the Synoptics, although the matter cannot be decided on the use of one psalm, I find most plausible the position that he drew on a source(s) of tradition that was similar to, yet independent of, the Synoptic sources, and that he did not depend on the Synoptics or their sources. Furthermore, there is every indication that John, if he did draw on the OT in the tradition, was inclined to, and capable of, expanding on or molding it to suit his theological purposes, so that he is responsible for the quotation and meaning effects of Ps 118 in his text.

In ch. 4 a brief overview of John's use of the OT provided the context within which to approach in the following chapters the Entrance use of Ps 118 and the search for other allusions. It was observed that John tends to cite allusively, to draw on texts that were interpreted eschatologically, and to appeal most often to the Psalms. In addition to the citation of Scripture, a bedrock of OT themes, imagery and symbols underlies the Gospel, with the Jewish festivals given special prominence. Accordingly it was suggested that the OT forms the principal backdrop against which John writes, and that since Ps 118 was interpreted eschatologically, used prominently at every Jewish feast, and known by John, a search for subtle allusions might prove fruitful.

Special attention was also given to a replacement theme in which Jesus takes up and "replaces" elements of Jewish institutions with his person and work. In this vein we returned to the concept of continuing exile argued in ch. 2, suggesting that the widespread hope of restoration, referred to in this study as New Exodus, can be divided into three interlinked categories of expectation: the return from exile, the defeat of Israel's enemies, and the return of Yahweh to live and reign among his people. Further exploration revealed that these strands of New Exodus thought are at the core of the Fourth Gospel, an observation that seems not to have been made previously. First, it was argued that Jesus' actions and speech communicated that he was bringing the exile to an end and that the restoration of Israel was imminent. The offer of forgiveness, announcement of salvation, expansion of the kingdom to include Gentiles, the formation of a new people of God, the calling of the Twelve, the replacement of the temple and Passover along with its sacrificial system, his signs and works, all announced that a new exodus would take place in his own person and ministry. Second, Jesus is presented as engaging in battle and defeating the enemies that have held Israel in bondage: the prince of this world, the power of sin that has kept them in exile, and the religious authorities who resist Jesus' authority and keep Israel from being the liberated people of God they are meant to be. Significantly, Jesus takes the central role in the return from exile and defeat of evil, thus pointing to an overlooked aspect of the Johannine replacement theme in which Jesus performs in the New Exodus those functions that were reserved for Yahweh himself. It was suggested that the presence of these first two strands of restoration hope are promising indicators that the search for the third strand, the coming of God, will be fruitful.

Having established the necessary background, in chs. 5–7 our focus turned particularly to the Entrance Narrative, which contains the only explicit quotation of Ps 118 in John. Chapter 5 was devoted to examining the quotation and its function. A survey of the more prominent examples of entry processions in the ancient world led to the conclusion that the closest parallels are the royal entries of Solomon and Zion's king, and that John is evoking the ancient enthronement traditions which probably underlie these passages. It was suggested further that Ps 118, the most prominent Jewish processional psalm, provides the precedent on which the Entrance is based and in whose light it should be read, so that the Entry is a re-enactment of the psalm according to its original royal meaning. In evoking this ancient ritual procession the quotation thus points to the Entrance as the coming of Israel's king to his enthronement. The suggestion that Ps 118 underlies the Johannine Entrance procession has not been made previously. It was suggested that John has accentuated the ancient royal traditions associated with Ps 118 in part through his use of Tabernacles imagery and the quotation of Zechariah, evoking a complex of traditions interlinked in Jewish thought. In ch. 2 of this study the linking in pre-exilic royal ideology of Davidic kingship with Yahweh's kingship was discussed, as well as the Tabernacles emphasis on Yahweh's coming, which is seen most explicitly in Zech 14. In quoting Ps 118 John presents Jesus as Yahweh's royal agent coming to enthronement, but taken together with the Tabernacles imagery and the Zechariah quote the expectations of Yahweh's coming to reign advance to the forefront. In keeping with the New Exodus theme in which Jesus fulfills Yahweh's role in redemption, it was suggested that John intends to portray Jesus' Entrance as actualizing and consummating Yahweh's return.

Further exploration of specific aspects of the quotation of Ps 118 provided support for the psalm's underlying the Entrance and for the suggested New Exodus function of the Entrance. A generally unrecognized feature of the Hosanna peculiar to its original setting is that, although its meaning is supplicatory, it functions as a confession of Yahweh's sovereignty and links the king's reign to Yahweh's kingship. It was argued that John retains this original sense and function, thus ensuring that Jesus' kingship is identified with Yahweh's rule. Additionally, it was suggested that the transliterated Hosanna evokes the Tabernacles-Ps 118 complex of royal traditions and accentuates the character of the Entry as liturgical re-enactment. Although the palm branches are not a part of the quotation as such, they signal an actualization of Ps 118 and evoke the traditions it shares with Tabernacles. It is possible to see them as a liturgical allusion to Ps 118.27, in which case the Entrance mirrors more closely the ancient procession preserved in Ps 118. While many note the peculiar pleonastic phrase John uses for palm branches, few have considered that it draws attention to itself, inviting the reader to look at its symbolic meanings of victory, triumph, and resurrection. The branches remind the reader of Jesus' recent victory over death, intensify the sense of anticipation surrounding Jesus' own death and resurrection, and proleptically point toward the victory Jesus will win over the powers of darkness, thus anticipating the destruction of Israel's enemies.

A survey of the possible background options for the title "king of Israel," which John adds to the quotation of Ps 118, concludes that it identifies Jesus with the royal figure of Ps 118, thus evoking the psalm's original liturgy as model for the Entry. Evoking the ancient institution of kingship provides the framework for identifying Jesus as the eschatological ideal king. It was argued, however, that John shows Jesus transcending this category, and that the title points to Yahweh, providing a bridge between the eschatological ideal king of Ps 118 and Yahweh's kingship. Support for this bridging function is adduced from the immediately following combined quotation of Zeph 3.16 and Zech 9.9, the former of which contains *en nuce* the New Exodus and names Yahweh as King of Israel. The Ps 118 quote thus moves from first pointing to an OT king, to evoking the eschatological ideal king, and finally to providing the bridge for Jesus' royal entrance to be identified with Yahweh's coming as King. This provides the most critical element of the New Exodus – the return of Yahweh, now shown as completed when Jesus comes to Zion as the true King of Israel. It was suggested that these intertextual transformations in the Entrance are the high point and result of a carefully constructed theological scheme to identify Jesus with Yahweh, that includes at its core a network of allusions to the coming one of Ps 118.

It is to developing this network of allusions that we turned our attention in ch. 6. While many have noted the descent-ascent and sending-returning schema in the Fourth Gospel, in spite of its ubiquity the coming-sent motif advanced in this study has escaped previous attention. The titles of coming and sent one are linked together, used interchangeably, and often used in close proximity, so that the one implicitly assumes the other. John systematically takes up Jewish speculation about a coming one, shows their categories to be inadequate, and gives an exposition of Jesus' true identity. In the process the coming-sent motif is reinterpreted and filled with new meaning, so that the reader perceives Jesus as the coming-sent one whose function and person are equated with those of Yahweh. As a result, when

Jesus enters Jerusalem the reader is prepared to recognize this as tantamount to the coming of Yahweh, since Jesus the coming one is known to embody all that Yahweh is. The development of this motif provides the bridge for the coming of Ps 118's eschatological king to be understood as the coming of Yahweh. In addition to the psalm's critical role in advancing the New Exodus agenda, it was argued that its influence extends beyond its quotation in the Entrance, since the extended network of coming one allusions, regardless of what OT text(s) may stand behind each individual occurrence, function either as proleptic or analeptic allusions to the climactic arrival of the Ps 118 coming one in the Entrance.

Chapter 7 presents a re-reading of the Entrance Narrative in light of the conclusions arrived at in chs 5 and 6, for these carry a number of implications for the interpretation of the narrative that immediately follows the quotation of the psalm. Our study calls into question the widely held view that in mounting the donkey Jesus intended to correct the allegedly nationalistic expectations of the crowd. It is suggested instead that Jesus' action affirms the crowd's acclaim as an expression of true belief. Second, it is argued that the donkey's significance has been consistently misunderstood: rather than being a sign of humility intended to dampen the enthusiasm of the crowd, riding the donkey is a symbol of authority and kingship that evokes the ancient enthronement traditions of Israel. Third, a closer look at the original context of the Zechariah quote and its form in John supports this study's argument that Jesus enters Jerusalem as a warrior king, fulfilling Yahweh's warrior role. The quotation of Zechariah also invites the reader to interpret the Entrance in light of the eschatological Tabernacles of Zech 14, which celebrates Yahweh's return to reign. Fourth, it is argued that the suggestions most often advanced in explanation of the disciples' misunderstanding are flawed. What is in view is the disciples' failure to recognize Jesus' Entry to Jerusalem as the actualization of Yahweh's return to inaugurate the New Exodus, a shortcoming that results from not yet perceiving that Jesus is the physical presence of Yahweh in this world.

The Entrance use of Ps 118 is the most explicit and high-profile, and the coming-sent theme pervades the first 12 chapters of John. In chs. 8–10 of this study a search for additional allusions to the psalm proved fruitful. In ch. 8 a previously unnoticed allusion was identified in John 8.56, where Abraham's eschatological joy is described with the words of Ps 118.24. It was further suggested that the event Jesus refers to may be the narration in *Jub.* 16 of Abraham's rejoicing in anticipation of a future exalted seed who will be like the Creator. This celebration is linked specifically to the foundation of Tabernacles and the liturgy of Ps 118, providing the impetus for John's recounting the event with the words of the psalm. The study goes on to argue that the allusion functions to identify the day of Jesus with the day of Yahweh. That is, Jesus claims to actualize the day of Yahweh's kingship and eschatological rule, thus identifying himself functionally and ontologically with Yahweh. The pattern of misunderstanding in the Fourth Gospel suggests that the ἐγώ εἰμι that follows in 8.58 is intended to confirm this identification, and is functionally equivalent to the claim in 8.56.

An allusion to Ps 118.20 in John 10.9 has often been noted in passing, although without accompanying evidence in its favor or an examination of its possible function. This neglect has now been rectified in ch. 9 of this study. Departing from the approach most often taken, it was argued that even though the section 10.7–10 is informed by the metaphors of the *paroimia* in 10.1–5, it develops and applies these independently. We conclude that what is a relatively weak verbal link to Ps 118.19–20 in 10.7, 9 can be explained by a translation of the Hebrew, although reference to the LXX is not out of the question. Also in favor of the allusion is the early Christian use of Ps 118 in reference to Jesus as the door, and particularly the prominent use of the coming one motif in the passage. The more difficult and subtle argument is that the allusion is a reference to the temple door. In favor of this is the original context of Ps 118, and a confluence of interlinked sources – Ezekiel, Tabernacles, Ps 118, Dedication, and the setting of the Shepherd Discourse – that highlight the temple and facilitate linking the door in 10.7–10 with the temple door. The result is a continuation of the temple replacement theme, with Jesus fulfilling the function of the temple doors in providing access to Yahweh. This understanding of the allusion brings into focus, first, Jesus' exclusive mediatorial and soteriological role as the sole means of access to Yahweh and the eschatological blessings of the new age. Second, it underscores the inclusiveness of the community of Jesus, for the door is open to any who will enter, and third, it establishes the basis of security for the sheep.

Two additional allusions were addressed in ch. 10. First, the proposed allusion to Ps 118(117).10–12 in John 10.24 has escaped the attention of most scholars, warranting the attention given here to establishing it more firmly and exploring its function. The setting of Dedication and a possible allusion to Ps 118.26 in 10.25 strengthen the possibility of allusion. It was suggested that the Dedication setting furnishes a promising context for John to continue the replacement theme, with Jesus being consecrated as the new temple. The allusion to Ps 118 reiterates Jesus' identity as the triumphant coming one, and in accentuating the question of Jesus' identity, anticipates and leads naturally to the dramatic pronouncement in 10.30. The allusion further indicates that the Jews' question should be interpreted as hostile, and in a startling reversal of the psalm's original context reveals the religious authorities as the enemies of Israel, who in opposing the coming one are excluded from Yahweh's flock.

The function of a second neglected allusion (Ps 118[117].5, 21, 28c in John 11.41b–42) had not been explored prior to this study. It was suggested that Jesus' prayer shares the formal characteristics of the *hodayoth* tradition, an observation that in this particular case bears significantly on its interpretation, and that by framing the beginning of his prayer with an allusion to the psalm, John portrays Jesus as adopting the psalm as his prayer. The Ps 118 prayer functions as an implicit request for victory in the upcoming struggle, and is a confident declaration of Jesus' authority that proleptically points to his defeat of death. Recognition of the allusion aids in discerning an aspect that has been almost entirely overlooked, that the primary purpose of Jesus' prayer is to intercede for the bystanders, that they recognize him as the sent one as a result of the subsequent Lazarus Sign. That is, the intended object of the crowd's faith is Jesus. The prayer is fulfilled in the Entrance, when those who have witnessed the resurrection of Lazarus, and others who have heard about it, welcome Jesus as the coming one.

It is apparent that John has used individual allusions to Ps 118 in a relatively consistent and coherent way. For the most part they build towards the Entrance, and are often used in conjunction with the coming-sent motif and/or in close proximity to another Ps 118 allusion. They are also invariably employed in the task of expounding Jesus' unique identity, repeatedly aiding in equating the function and person of Jesus with those of the Father. The allusions are consistent with the New Exodus theme, and play a not insignificant role in its development, particularly in preparing the reader to recognize that when Jesus enters Jerusalem acclaimed as coming one, this is in reality the coming of Yahweh. It can safely be stated that the psalm's presence is wider, and its significance greater, than has been previously recognized.

II. Implications

A. Method

Three distinct methods were adopted at the outset of this study, each of which proved fruitful. First, the aim of the intertextual approach was to discern the influence of one text on another, and the meaning effects generated by the prior text's absorption by and subsequent interaction with the new context. Listening for these more finely tuned signals aided in identifying a previously unnoticed allusion to Ps 118 in John 8.56, and furthered the development of three allusions (in John 10.9; 10.24–25; 11.41–42) which had been noted briefly by others but whose function had not been examined. The attention paid to recovering the unstated material that resonates to one familiar with the literary context of the citation, together with an appreciation for intertextual transformations caused by continuity and discontinuity between texts, proved significant in the interpretation of these allusions and especially for the quotation of Ps 118 in the Entrance Narrative. The development of the coming-sent theme in John also benefited from an intertextual approach, shedding light on a significant yet neglected motif. It is suggested further that the criteria advanced for evaluating the plausibility of echoes and allusions proved their worth.

As for the second approach – the mediation of Scripture through intertestamental sources – the examination of Ps 118's use in the Second Temple cult repaid study, for it appears that the interpretations with which it became associated through its liturgical life in the festivals bears on its use in the NT. The psalm's links to Tabernacles traditions proved especially significant, particularly in the Entrance and in the allusions in the Abraham and the Shepherd Discourses.

Finally, the study of particular allusions to Ps 118 demonstrated that its use was consistent with respect for context, and that the allusion was best understood when the receiving text was examined in broad interaction with the entire psalm. This lends support to the argument in favor of the recognition of larger context fields in quotation. It is suggested that the combination of these approaches may be applied fruitfully in other studies.

B. Points for Further Exploration

A study such as this one will, because of its limited scope, touch on some areas only briefly, inevitably leaving gaps. A more detailed exploration of the Synoptic use of Ps 118, including a search for additional allusions and echoes, remains to be done. The same can be said for the psalm's presence and function in the NT outside the Gospels. This would allow for comparison across the various corpora to determine patterns of usage and whether there is coherence of meaning and similarity of function. Although our study has developed the New Exodus motif in John to some degree, in light of the growing attention this particular theme is receiving in NT scholarship, and in consideration of its apparent presence and importance in the Fourth Gospel, a more complete analysis is called for. A related question is to what degree the Johannine use of the New Exodus theme corresponds to and harmonizes with that proposed by others for each of the Synoptics, particularly in regard to Jesus' function and identity.

C. The Present Work in Relationship to Johannine Studies

We can only briefly address the question of how the findings of this thesis might be related to current trends in Johannine scholarship. First, it is now widely acknowledged that the Fourth Gospel must be read in light of the Old Testament and in interaction with the Jewish context from which it arose. A significant development which has only recently gained an audience in scholarship is the recognition of a concept of continuing exile in Judaism and the complex of restoration hope – what we have called the New Exodus – that accompanies it. The results of our study suggest that the New Exodus provides an important and viable model through which to read the Fourth Gospel. As such our work offers corroboratory support for the claims others have made regarding the presence of a New Exodus model in the Synoptics. Furthermore, our conclusions suggest that there may be a degree of correspondence and harmony between John and the Synoptics on a deeper level that has not been previously recognized, for although there are important differences in the way and degree to which each Gospel develops the New Exodus, the basic pattern is arguably present in all.

Second, it is often stated that the Fourth Gospel is anti-Jewish, advancing the displacement of the Jews as God's people. The results of our study call this into question, arguing instead that John sees the new community of Jesus not as a flock excluded from Judaism, but as the true Israel from which the religious authorities are excluded. We have noted that it is the religious authorities who are branded as the enemy (they are in league with Satan and are examples of unbelief), in contrast to the masses who respond positively to Jesus. A New Exodus reading suggests that there is not a wholesale rejection of Judaism – there is a wholesale redefinition of who the true Israel is. While I remain unconvinced that the Fourth Gospel was written *for* a specific community, it is likely that the community in which the Fourth Gospel took shape influenced its content and message to some degree. According to our results, it would appear that this community understood itself to be the true restored-from-exile Israel, continuous with the Israel of Abraham, Moses, and the Prophets.

Finally, the Christology of the Fourth Gospel has deservingly been the subject of many studies, to which we add only a couple of observations. First, our results not surprisingly show that John's Christology is firmly tied to the OT. However, although the stated intent of the Gospel is that people might believe that Jesus is the Christ (20.31), it was argued that there is relatively little emphasis on the fulfillment of "messianic" expectations and a great deal more attention paid to aspects that are more properly the province of Yahweh. This is reflected somewhat in the use and function of Ps 118. Whereas in the Synoptics it is usually applied messianically, in John the psalm consistently supports the comparison of

Jesus with Yahweh. It appears that in John there is a radical reinterpretation of what Messiah is and does, and there is reason to believe that this takes place under the influence of the OT portrayal (and its contemporary inter-pretation) of Yahweh's eschatological redeeming action. Second, the vantage point of the New Exodus sharply underscores the extent to which Jesus is identified both ontologically and functionally with the Father. Although he is subordinate to the Father as son, he carries out the work reserved to Yahweh, gathering the exiles, defeating the enemies of Israel, and embodying – not symbolically, but in reality – the return of Yahweh. His appropriation of Yahweh's role extends beyond occasionally taking up a divine prerogative, actually covering the entire complex of restoration hope, at the core of which was a longing for the abiding presence of God. What allows this complete identification of Jesus with Yahweh in the Johannine New Exodus – and accordingly may limit the theme in the Synoptics – is John's emphasis on the incarnation: in the person of Jesus, God has indeed come to reign and dwell among his people.

Bibliography of Works Cited

1. Primary Sources

Ante-Nicene Christian Library: Translations of the Writings of the Fathers Down to A.D. 325. Edited by A. Roberts and J. Donaldson. 24 vols. Edinburgh: T & T Clark, 1867–1872.

Abegg, M. Jr, P. Flint, and E. Ulrich, eds. *The Dead Sea Scrolls Bible.* San Francisco: Harper, 1999.

Allegro, J. M., ed. *Qumran Cave 4.I (4Q158–4Q186).* DJD 5. Oxford: Clarendon, 1968.

The Babylonian Talmud: Translated into English with Notes. Edited by I. Epstein et al. 34 vols. London: Soncino, 1935–1952.

Biblia Hebraica Stuttgartensia. Edited by K. Elliger and W. Rudolph. 4th corrected ed. Stuttgart: Deutsche Bibelgesellschaft, 1990.

Charles, R. H. *The Book of Jubilees or The Little Genesis.* London: Adam and Charles Black, 1902.

Charlesworth, J. H., ed. *The Old Testament Pseudepigrapha.* 2 vols. ABRL. New York: Doubleday, 1985.

The Dead Sea Scrolls Translated: The Qumran Texts in English. Translated by F. García Martínez. ET W. G. E. Watson. 2nd ed. Leiden: Brill, 1996.

Eisenstein, J. D. *Ozar Midrashim: A Library of Two Hundred Minor Midrashim.* 2 vols. New York: Eisenstein, 1915. Repr. in Israel: Beney Braq, 1990.

Eusebius. *Ecclesiastical History.* Translated by G. A. Williamson. Minneapolis: Augsburg, 1965.

The Greek New Testament. Edited by K. Aland et al. 3rd corrected ed. Stuttgart: United Bible Societies, 1983.

Josephus. ET H. St. J. Thackeray et al. 10 vols. Loeb Classical Library. Cambridge: Harvard University Press, 1926–1965.

Metzger, B. M., ed. *The Oxford Annotated Apocrypha.* Expanded ed. Oxford: Oxford University Press, 1977.

The Midrash on Psalms (Midrash Tehillim). Translated by W. G. Braude. 2 vols. Yale Judaica Series 13. New Haven: Yale University Press, 1959.

The Midrash Rabbah. Edited by H. Freedman and M. Simon. 5 vols. London: Soncino Press, 1977.

The Mishnah. Translated by H. Danby. Oxford: Clarendon, 1933.

The Mishnah: A New Translation. Translated by J. Neusner. New Haven and London: Yale University Press, 1988.

Novum Testamentum Graece. Edited by E. Nestle et al. 27th rev. ed. Stuttgart: Deutsche Bibelgesellschaft, 1993.

Pesikta Rabbati: Discourses for Feasts, Fasts, and Special Sabbaths. Translated by W. G. Braude. 2 vols. New Haven and London: Yale University Press, 1968.

Philo. Translated by C. D. Yonge. Peabody, Mass.: Hendrickson, 1997.

Sanders, J. A. *The Dead Sea Psalms Scroll.* Ithaca, N.Y.: Cornell University Press, 1967.

Septuaginta. Edited by A. Rahlfs. Stuttgart: Deutsche Bibelgesellschaft, 1935.

Targum de Salmos. Edited by I. Diez Merino. Bibliotheca Hispana Biblica 6. Madrid: Instituto Francisco Suárez, 1982.

The Tosefta. Translated by J. Neusner. New York: KTAV Publishing House, 1981.

2. Commentaries on John

Barrett, C. K. *The Gospel According to St. John: An Introduction with Commentary and Notes on the Greek Text*. 2nd ed. Philadelphia: Westminster, 1978.

Bauer, W. *Das Johannesevangelium*. HNT 6. Tübingen: J.C.B. Mohr (Paul Siebeck), 1925.

Beasley-Murray, G. R. *John*. WBC 36. Waco, Tex.: Word, 1987.

Becker, J. *Das Evangelium des Johannes*. 2 vols. ÖTKNT 4/1, 2. Gütersloh: Mohn; Würzburg: Echter, 1979–1981.

Bernard, J. H. *A Critical and Exegetical Commentary on the Gospel According to St. John*. Edited by A. H. McNeile. 2 vols. ICC. Edinburgh: T&T Clark, 1928.

Blank, J. *Das Evangelium nach Johannes*. Geistliche Schriftlesung 4/1b. Düsseldorf: Patmos, 1981.

Briggs, C. A., and E. G. Briggs. *A Critical and Exegetical Commentary on the Book of Psalms*. 2 vols. ICC. Edinburgh: T.&T. Clark, 1907.

Brown, C. *Het Evangelie naar Johannes*. Vol. 1. 3rd ed. Korte Verklaring, 1950.

Brown, R. E. *The Gospel According to John*. 2 vols. AB 29/29A. New York: Doubleday, 1966–1970.

Bruce, F. F. *The Gospel of John: Introduction, Exposition and Notes*. Grand Rapids: Eerdmans, 1983.

Bultmann, R. *The Gospel of John*. ET G. R. Beasley-Murray. Philadelphia: Westminster, 1971.

Calvin, J. *The Gospel According to St. John*. ET T. H. L. Parker. 2 vols. Calvin's New Testament Commentaries 4–5. Grand Rapids: Eerdmans, 1959–1961.

Carson, D. A. *The Gospel According to John*. Leicester: Inter-Varsity Press; Grand Rapids: Eerdmans, 1991.

Haenchen, E. *A Commentary on the Gospel of John*. ET R. W. Funk. 2 vols. Hermeneia. Philadelphia: Fortress, 1984.

Hoskyns, E. C. *The Fourth Gospel*. Edited by F. N. Davey. 2nd ed. London: Faber & Faber, 1947.

Kysar, R. *John*. Minneapolis: Augsburg, 1986.

Lagrange, M.-J. *Évangile selon Saint Jean*. 5th ed. Paris: Gabalda, 1936.

Lightfoot, R. H. *St. John's Gospel*. Edited by C. F. Evans. Oxford: Clarendon, 1956.

Lindars, B. *The Gospel of John*. NCB Commentaries. Grand Rapids: Eerdmans; London: Marshall, Morgan & Scott, 1972.

Loisy, A. *Le quatrième évangile*. Paris: Picard, 1903.

Malina, B. J. and R. L. Rohrbaugh. *Social-Science Commentary on the Gospel of John*. Minneapolis: Fortress, 1998.

Milligan, W., and W. F. Moulton. *The Gospel According to St. John*. International Revision Commentary on the New Testament 4. New York: Scribners, 1883.

Morris, L. *The Gospel According to John*. NICNT. Grand Rapids: Eerdmans, 1971.

Odeberg, H. *The Fourth Gospel*. Uppsala: Almqvist & Wiksells, 1929.

Ridderbos, H. *The Gospel according to John: A Theological Commentary*. ET J. Vriend. Grand Rapids and Cambridge: Eerdmans, 1997.

Sanders, J. N., and B. A. Mastin. *A Commentary on the Gospel According to St. John.* New York: Harper and Row, 1968.

Schlatter, A. *Der Evangelist Johannes: Wie er spricht, denkt und glaubt.* Stuttgart: Calwer, 1930.

Schneider, J. *Das Evangelium nach Johannes.* THKNT. Berlin: Evangelische Verlagsanstalt, 1976.

Sloyan, G. S. *John.* IBC. Atlanta: John Knox, 1988.

Smith, D. M. *John.* Abingdon New Testament Commentaries. Nashville: Abingdon Press, 1999.

Stibbe, M. *John.* Sheffield: JSOT Press, 1993.

Tenney, M. C. *The Gospel of John.* Vol. 9 of The Expositor's Bible Commentary. Grand Rapids: Zondervan, 1981.

Wellhausen, J. *Das Evangelium Johannis.* Berlin: Reimer, 1908.

Westcott, B. F. *The Gospel According to St. John.* London: J. Murray, 1882. Repr., Grand Rapids: Eerdmans, 1981.

Zahn, T. *Das Evangelium des Johannes.* Kommentar zum Neuen Testament 4. Leipzig: A. Deichertsche Verlagsbuchhandlung, 1908.

3. Secondary Sources

Achtemeier, P. J. "*Omne verbum sonat*: The New Testament and the Oral Environment of Late Western Antiquity." *JBL* 109 (1990): 3–27.

Ackroyd, P. R. *Exile and Restoration: A Study of Hebrew Thought of the Sixth Century BC.* Philadelphia: Westminster, 1968.

——. "Some Notes on the Psalms." *JTS* n.s. 17 (1966): 392–399, esp. 396–399.

Albright, W. F. and C. S. Mann. *Matthew.* AB 26. Garden City, N.Y.: Doubleday, 1971.

Alexander, P. S. "Retelling the Old Testament." Pages 99–121 in *It is Written: Scripture Citing Scripture: Essays in Honour of Barnabas Lindars.* Edited by D. A. Carson and H. G. M. Williamson. Cambridge: Cambridge University Press, 1988.

Allen, L. C. *Ezekiel 20–48.* WBC 29. Dallas: Word, 1990.

——. *Psalms 101–150.* WBC 21. Waco, Tex.: Word Books, 1983.

Allison, D. C. Jr. "Matt. 23:39 = Luke 13:35b as a Conditional Prophecy." *JSNT* 18 (1983): 75–84.

Amir, Y. "Authority and Interpretation of Scripture in the Writings of Philo." Pages 421–453 in *Mikra: Text, Translation, Reading and Interpretation of the Hebrew Bible in Ancient Judaism and Early Christianity.* Edited by M. J. Mulder. CRINT. Assen/Maastricht: Van Gorcum, 1990.

Anderson, A. A. *The Book of Psalms.* 2 vols. NCB Commentaries. London: Oliphants, 1972.

Anderson, P. N. *The Christology of the Fourth Gospel: It's Unity and Disunity in the Light of John 6.* WUNT2/78. Tübingen: J.C.B. Mohr (Paul Siebeck), 1996.

Appold, M. L. *The Oneness Motif in the Fourth Gospel: Motif Analysis and Exegetical Probe into the Theology of John.* WUNT 2/1. Tübingen: J.C.B. Mohr (Paul Siebeck), 1976.

Ashton, J. "The Identity and Function of the ΙΟΥΔΑΙΟΙ in the Fourth Gospel." *NovT* 27/1 (1985): 40–75.

——. *Understanding the Fourth Gospel.* Oxford: Clarendon, 1991.

Auffret, P. *La Sagesse a bâti sa maison: Etudes de structures littéraires dans l'Ancien Testament et specialment dans les Psaumes*. OBO 49. Freibourg: Universitäts-verlag; Göttingen: Vandenhoeck & Ruprecht, 1982.

Bacher, W. "Targum." 12.57–63 in *The Jewish Encyclopedia*. Edited by I. Singer. 12 vols. New York, 1925.

Baethgen, F. *Die Psalmen*. 2nd ed. Göttingen, 1897.

Bailey, K. "The Shepherd Poems of John 10 and Their Culture." *IBS* 15 (1993): 2–17.

Ball, D. M. *'I Am' in John's Gospel: Literary Function, Background and Theological Implications*. JSNTSup 124. Sheffield: Sheffield Academic Press, 1996.

Bammel, E. "The *titulus*." Pages 353–364 in *Jesus and the Politics of His Day*. Edited by E. Bammel and C. F. D. Moule. Cambridge: Cambridge University Press, 1984.

Barker, M. *The Older Testament: The Survival of Themes from the Ancient Royal Cult in Sectarian Judaism and Early Christianity*. London: SPCK, 1987.

Barnes, W. E. *The Psalms*. 2 vols. WC. London: Metheun, 1931.

Barrett, C. K. "The Old Testament in the Fourth Gospel." *JBL* 48 (1947): 155–169.

Bauckham, R., ed. *The Gospels for all Christians: Rethinking the Gospel Audiences*. Grand Rapids: Eerdmans, 1998.

_____. "John for Readers of Mark." Pages 147–171 in *The Gospels for all Christians: Rethinking the Gospel Audiences*. Edited by R. Bauckham. Grand Rapids: Eerdmans, 1998.

Baumgarten, J. "A New Qumran Substitute for the Divine Name and Mishnah Sukkah 4.5." *JQR* 83 (1992): 1–5.

Beale, G. K., ed. *The Right Doctrine from the Wrong Texts? Essays on the Use of the Old Testament in the New*. Grand Rapids: Baker, 1994.

_____. *The Use of Daniel in Jewish Apocalyptic Literature and in the Revelation of St. John*. Lanham: University Press of America, 1984.

Beare, F. W. *The Gospel according to Matthew*. San Francisco: Harper & Row, 1981.

Beasley-Murray, G. R. *The Coming of God*. Exeter: Paternoster, 1983.

_____. *Jesus and the Kingdom of God*. Grand Rapids: Eerdmans; Carlisle: Paternoster, 1986.

Beck, W. F. "Hosanna." *CTM* 23 (1952): 122–129.

Becker, J. *Israel deutet seine Psalmen: Urform und Neuinterpretation in den Psalmen*. SBS 18. Stuttgart: Katholisches Bibelwerk, 1975.

_____. *Wege der Psalmenexegese*. SBS 78. Stuttgart: Katholisches Bibelwerk, 1975.

Beker, J. C. "Echoes and Intertextuality: On the Role of Scripture in Paul's Theology." Pages 64–69 in *Paul and the Scriptures of Israel*. Edited by C. A. Evans and J. A. Sanders. JSNTSup 83. SSEJC 1. Sheffield: JSOT Press, 1992.

Berder, M. *"La pierre rejetée par les bâtisseurs": Psaume 118,22–23 et son emploi dans les traditions juives et dans le Nouveau Testament*. Études Bibliques, n.s. 31. Paris: Gabalda, 1996.

Bergen, P. van. "L'entrée messianique de Jésus à Jérusalem." *Les Questions Liturgiques et Paroissiales* 38 (1957): 9–24.

Bergler, S. "Jesus, Bar Kochba und das messianische Laubhüttenfest." *JSJ* 29/2 (1998): 143–191.

Berker, K. "Die königlichen Messiastraditionen des Neuen Testaments." *NTS* 20 (1973–74): 1–44.

Beutler, J. "Der alttestamentlich-jüdische Hintergrund der Hirtenrede in Johannes 10." Pages 18–32 in *The Shepherd Discourse of John 10 and its Context: Studies by Members of the Johannine Writings Seminar*. Edited by J. Beutler and R. T. Fortna. SNTSMS 67. Cambridge: Cambridge University Press, 1991.

_____, and R. T. Fortna. "Introduction." Pages 1–5 in *The Shepherd Discourse of John 10 and its Context: Studies by Members of the Johannine Writings Seminar*. SNTSMS 67. Edited by J. Beutler and R. T. Fortna. Cambridge: Cambridge University Press, 1991.

Bishop, E. F. F. "'The Door of the Sheep'—John x.7–9." *ExpTim* 71 (1959–1960): 307–309.

_____. "Hosanna: The Word of the Joyful Jerusalem Crowds." *ExpTim* 53 (1941–1942): 212–214.

Black, M. *An Aramaic Approach to the Gospels and Acts*. 3rd ed. Oxford: Clarendon, 1967.

Blank, J. *Krisis: Untersuchungen zur johanneischen Christologie und Eschatologie*. Freiburg: Lambertus, 1964.

Blank, S. H. "Some Observations Concerning Biblical Prayer." *HUCA* 32 (1961): 75–90.

Blass, F., A. Debrunner, and R. Funk. *A Greek Grammar of the New Testament and Other Early Christian Literature*. ET R. W. Funk. Chicago: University of Chicago Press, 1961.

Blenkinsopp, J. "The Oracle of Judah and the Messianic Entry." *JBL* 80 (1961): 55–64.

Block, D. I. "Bringing Back David: Ezekiel's Messianic Hope." Pages 167–188 in *The Lord's Anointed: Interpretation of Old Testament Messianic Texts*. Edited by P. E. Satterthwaite et al. Carlisle: Paternoster; Grand Rapids: Baker Books, 1995.

Blomberg, C. L. *Matthew*. NAC 22. Nashville, Tenn.: Broadman, 1992.

_____. "The Wright Stuff: *A Critical Overview of* Jesus and the Victory of God." Pages 19–39 in *Jesus and the Restoration of Israel: A Critical Assessment of N. T. Wright's* Jesus and the Victory of God. Edited by C. C. Newman. Downer's Grove, Ill.: InterVarsity; Carlisle: Paternoster, 1999.

Bock, D. L. *Luke*. 2 vols. Baker Exegetical Commentary on the New Testament 3A–B. Grand Rapids: Baker, 1994–1996.

_____. *Proclamation from Prophecy and Pattern: Lukan Old Testament Christology*. JSNTSup 12. Sheffield: JSOT Press, 1987.

_____. "The Trial & Death of Jesus in N. T. Wright's *Jesus and the Victory of God*." Pages 101–125 in *Jesus and the Restoration of Israel: A Critical Assessment of N. T. Wright's* Jesus and the Victory of God. Edited by C. C. Newman. Downer's Grove, Ill.: InterVarsity; Carlisle: Paternoster, 1999.

Boismard, M.-É. *Moïse ou Jesus: essai de christologie johannique*. BETL 84. Leuven: Leuven University Press, 1988.

_____. "Importance de la critique textuelle pour établir l'origine araméenne du quatrième évangile." Pages 41–57 in *L'évangile de Jean: Études et Problèmes*. Edited by M.-É. Boismard et al. RechBib 3. Louvain: Desclée de Brouwer, 1958.

_____, and A. Lamouille. *L'Évangile de Jean*. Vol. 3 of *Synopse des quatre Évangiles en français avec parallèles des Apocryphes et des Pères*. Paris: Cerf, 1977.

Bokser, B. M. *The Origins of the Seder: The Passover Rite and Early Rabbinic Judaism*. Berkeley: University of California Press, 1984.

Bonner, C. "Traces of Thaumaturgic Technique in the Miracles." *HTR* 20 (1927): 171–180.

Borchert, G. L. "The Passover and the Narrative Cycles in John." Pages 303–316 in *Perspectives on John: Method and Interpretation in the Fourth Gospel*. Edited by R. B. Sloan et al. Lewiston, N.Y.: E. Mellen, 1993.

Borgen, P. "God's Agent in the Fourth Gospel." Pages 137–148 in *Religions in Antiquity: Essays in Memory of Erwin Ramsdell Goodenough*. Edited by Jacob Neusner. Studies in the History of Religions. Supplements to *Numen* 14. Leiden: Brill, 1968.

_____. "Some Jewish Exegetical Traditions in the Fourth Gospel." Pages 243–258 in *L'Evangile de Jean: Sources, rédaction, théologie*. Edited by M. de Jonge et al. BETL 44. Gembloux: Duculot, 1977.

Bottino, A. "La metafora della porta (Gv 10,7.9)." *RivB* 39 (2, 1991): 207–215.

Bover, J. M. "El símil del Buen Pastor (Jn. 10, 1–18)." *EstBib* 14 (1955): 297–308.

Brandon, S. G. F. *Jesus and the Zealots*. New York: Scribner's, 1967.

Bratcher, R. G., and W. D. Reyburn. *A Translator's Handbook on the Book of Psalms*. Helps for Translators. New York: United Bible Societies, 1991.

Braude, W. G. "Introduction to the Midrash on Psalms." 1.xi–xxxvi in *The Midrash on Psalms*. Edited by W. G. Braude. 2 vols. Yale Judaica Series 13. New Haven: Yale University Press, 1959.

_____. "Introduction to Pesikta Rabbati." 1.1–33 in *Pesikta Rabbati*. Edited by W. G. Braude. 2 vols. New Haven: Yale University Press, 1968.

Braumann, G. "ἐγὼ εἰμί." *NIDNTT* 2.278–281.

Braun, F.-M. *Les grandes traditions d'Israël et l'accord des Écritures, selon le Quatrième Évangile*. Vol. 2 of *Jean le théologien*. 4 vols. Paris: Gabalda, 1959–1972.

Brennan, J. P. "Some Hidden Harmonies in the Fifth Book of the Psalms." Pages 126–158 in *Essays in Honor of Joseph P. Brennan*. Edited by R. F. McNamara. Rochester, N.Y.: St. Bernard's Seminary, 1976.

Brewer, D. I. *Techniques and Assumptions in Jewish Exegesis Before 70 CE*. TSAJ 30. Tübingen: J.C.B. Mohr (Paul Siebeck), 1992.

Breytenbach, C. "Das Markusevangelium, Psalm 110,1 und 118,22f.: Folgetext und Prätext." Pages 197–222 in *The Scriptures in the Gospels*. Edited by C. M. Tuckett. Leuven: Leuven University Press, 1997.

Brooks, J. A. "The Influence of Malachi Upon the New Testament." *SWJournTheol* 30/1 (1987): 28–31.

Brown, C., ed. *New International Dictionary of New Testament Theology*. 4 vols. Grand Rapids: Zondervan, 1975–1985.

Brown, R. E. *The Community of the Beloved Disciple*. New York: Paulist Press, 1979.

_____. Review of O. Kiefer, *Die Hirtenrede: Analyse und Deutung von Joh 10,1–18* and A. J. Simonis, *Die Hirtenrede im Johannes-Evangelium: Versuch einer Analyse von Johannes 10,1–18 nach Entstehung, Hintergrund und Inhalt*. *CBQ* 31 (1969): 98–100.

Bruce, F. F. *The Book of the Acts*. Rev. ed. NICNT. Grand Rapids: Eerdmans, 1988.

Brueggemann, W. "Bounded by Obedience and Praise: The Psalms as Canon." Pages 189–213 in *The Psalms and the Life of Faith*, by W. Brueggemann. Edited by P. D. Miller. Minneapolis: Fortress Press, 1995.

_____. "Response to James L. Mays: The Question of Context." Pages 29–41 in *The Shape and Shaping of the Psalter*. Edited by J.C. McCann. JSOTSup 159. Sheffield: JSOT Press, 1993.

Bruns, J. E. "The Discourse of the Good Shepherd and the Rite of Ordination." *AER* 149 (1963): 386–391.

Bryan, C. "Shall We Sing Hallel in the Days of the Messiah? A Glance at John 2:1–3:21." *SLJT* 29/1 (1985): 25–36.

Buchanan, G. W. "The Age of Jesus." *NTS* 41 (1995): 297.

Bühner, J.-A. *Der Gesandte und sein Weg im 4. Evangelium: Die kultur- und religionsgeschichtlichen Grundlagen der johanneischen Sendungschristologie sowie ihre traditionsgeschichtliche Entwicklung*. WUNT 2/2. Tübingen: J.C.B. Mohr (Paul Siebeck), 1977.

Bultmann, R. "ἀγαλλιάομαι." *TDNT* 1.19–21.

_____. "εὐφραίνω." *TDNT* 2.772–775.

Burge, G. M. *Interpreting the Fourth Gospel.* Grand Rapids: Baker, 1992.

Burger, C. *Jesus als Davidssohn: Eine traditionsgeschichtliche Untersuchung.* FRLANT 98. Göttingen: Vandenhoeck & Ruprecht, 1970.

Burkitt, F. C. "W and Θ: Studies in the Western Text of St. Mark (Continued): *Hosanna.*" *JTS* o.s. 17 (1916): 139–152.

Burney, C. F. *The Aramaic Origin of the Fourth Gospel.* Oxford: Clarendon, 1922.

Busse, U. "Open questions on John 10." Pages 6–17 in *The Shepherd Discourse of John 10 and its Context: Studies by Members of the Johannine Writings Seminar.* Edited by J. Beutler and R. T. Fortna. SNTSMS 67. Cambridge: Cambridge University Press, 1991.

Buttenweiser, M. *The Psalms: Chronologically Treated with a New Translation.* New York: KTAV Publishing, 1969.

Carr, D. "Jesus, the King of Zion: A Tradition-Historical Enquiry into the so-called Triumphal Entry of Jesus." Ph.D. diss., King's College, London, 1981.

Carson, D. A. "John and the Johannine Epistles." Pages 245–264 in *It is Written: Scripture Citing Scripture: Essays in Honour of Barnabas Lindars, SSF.* Edited by D. A. Carson and H. G. M. Williamson. Cambridge: Cambridge University Press, 1988.

_____. "Understanding Misunderstandings in the Fourth Gospel." *TynBul* 33 (1982): 59–89.

_____, and H. G. M. Williamson, eds. *It is Written: Scripture Citing Scripture: Essays in Honour of Barnabas Lindars.* Cambridge: Cambridge University Press, 1988.

Casey, M. "Where Wright Is Wrong: A Critical Review of N. T. Wright's *Jesus and the Victory of God.*" *JSNT* 69 (1998): 95–103.

Cassidy, R. J. *John's Gospel in New Perspective: Christology and the Realities of Roman Power.* Maryknoll, N.Y.: Orbis, 1992.

Catchpole, D. R. "The 'triumphal' entry." Pages 319–334 in *Jesus and the Politics of His Day.* Edited by E. Bammel and C. F. D. Moule. Cambridge: Cambridge University Press, 1984.

Cavaletti, S. "La visione messianica di Abramo." *BeO* 3/5 (1961): 179–181.

Charlesworth, J. H. "Biblical Interpretation: The Crucible of the Pseudepigrapha." Pages 66–78 in *Text and Testimony: Essays on New Testament and Apocryphal Literature in Honour of A. F. J. Klijn.* Edited by T. Baarda et al. Kampen: J. H. Kok, 1988.

_____. "The Pseudepigrapha as Biblical Exegesis." Pages 139–152 in *Early Jewish and Christian Exegesis: Studies in Memory of William Hugh Brownlee.* Edited by C. A. Evans and W. F. Stinespring. Homage Series 10. Atlanta: Scholars Press, 1987.

Cheyne, T. K. *The Book of Psalms.* London: Kegan Paul, Trench & Co.,1888.

Childs, B. S. *Introduction to the Old Testament as Scripture.* London: SCM Press, 1979.

Chilton, B. D. "(ὡς) φραγέλλιον ἐκ σχοινίων (John 2.15)." Pages 330–344 in *Templum Amicitiae: Essays on the Second Temple Presented to Ernst Bammel.* Edited by W. Horbury. JSNTSup 48. Sheffield: JSOT Press, 1991.

Churgin, P. "The Period of the Second Temple: An Era of Exile." *Horeb* 8 (1944):1–66.

Ciampa, R. E. "What Does the Scripture Say? An Analysis of the Presence and Function of Scripture in Galatians 1–2." Ph.D. diss., Aberdeen University, 1996. Published as *The Presence and Function of Scripture in Galatians 1 and 2.* WUNT 2/102. Tübingen: Mohr Siebeck, 1998.

Cimosa, M. "La traduzione greca dei Settanta nel Vangelo di Giovanni." *BeO* 39 (1997): 41–55.

Clements, R. E. "Interpreting the Psalms." Pages 95–121 in *A Century of Old Testament Study*. Rev. ed. Guildford: Lutterworth, 1983.

Coakley, J. F. "Jesus' Messianic Entry into Jerusalem (John 12:12–19 par.)." *JTS* 46 (1995): 461–482.

Coggins, R. Review of M. D. Goulder, *The Psalms of the Sons of Korah. ExpTim* 95 (1984): 56.

Cohn-Sherbok, D. M. "A Jewish Note on ΤΟ ΠΟΤΗΡΙΟΝ ΤΗΣ ΕΥΛΟΓΙΑΣ." *NTS* 27 (1981): 704–709.

Collins, A. Y. *The Combat Myth in the Book of Revelation*. Missoula: Scholars Press, 1976.

Collins, J. J. "Messianism in the Maccabean Period." Pages 97–109 in *Judaisms and their Messiahs at the Turn of the Christian Era*. Edited by J. Neusner, W. S. Green, and E. S. Frerichs. Cambridge: Cambridge University Press, 1987.

Comblin, J. *Sent from the Father: Meditations on the Fourth Gospel*. ET C. Kabat. Maryknoll, N,Y.: Orbis, 1979.

Conzelmann, H. "χαίρω κτλ." *TDNT* 9.359–372.

Cooper, A. M. "The Life and Times of King David According to the Book of Psalms." Pages 117–131 in *The Poet and the Historian: Essays in Literary and Historical Biblical Criticism*. Edited by R. E. Friedman. Chico, Calif.: Scholars Press, 1983.

Cross, F. M. *Canaanite Myth and Hebrew Epic: Essays in the History of the Religion of Israel*. Cambridge, Mass.: Harvard University Press, 1973.

Crossan, J. D. "Redaction and Citation in Mark 11:9–10 and 11:17." *BR* 17 (1972): 33–50.

Culler, J. *The Pursuit of Signs: Semiotics, Literature, Deconstruction*. London: Routledge & Kegan Paul, 1981.

Cullmann, O. *The Johannine Circle*. ET J. Bowden. Philadelphia: Westminster; London: SCM Press, 1976.

Culpepper, R. A. *Anatomy of the Fourth Gospel: A Study in Literary Design*. Philadelphia: Fortress, 1983.

———. *The Johannine School: An Evaluation of the Johannine-School Hypothesis Based on an Investigation of the Nature of Ancient Schools*. SBLDS 26. Missoula: Scholars Press, 1975.

Dacey, M. "Sukkot in the Late Second Temple Period." *Australian Journal of Jewish Studies* 6/2 (1992): 105–106.

Dahood, M. *Psalms*. 3 vols. AB 16–17A. Garden City: Doubleday, 1965–1970.

Daley-Denton, M. *David in the Fourth Gospel: The Johannine Reception of the Psalms*. AGJU 47. Leiden: Brill, 2000.

Daube, D. "The Old Testament in the New: A Jewish Perspective." Pages 1–39 in *Appeasement or Resistance and Other Essays on New Testament Judaism*. Berkeley: University of California Press, 1987.

———. *The New Testament and Rabbinic Judaism*. Peabody, Mass.: Hendrickson, 1956.

Davidson, A. B. *The Book of the Prophet Ezekiel*. Cambridge Bible for Schools and Colleges. Cambridge: Cambridge University Press, 1883.

Davies, M. *Rhetoric and Reference in the Fourth Gospel*. JSNTSup 69. Sheffield: JSOT Press, 1992.

Davies, W. D. *The Gospel and the Land: Early Christianity and Jewish Territorial Doctrine*. Berkeley: University of California Press, 1974.

———. "Canon and Christology in Paul." Pages 18–30 in *Paul and the Scriptures of Israel*. Edited by C. A. Evans and J. A. Sanders. JSNTSup 83. SSEJC 1. Sheffield: JSOT Press, 1992.

———, and D. C. Allison Jr. *A Critical and Exegetical Commentary on the Gospel according to St. Matthew*. 3 vols. ICC. Edinburgh: T&T Clark, 1988–1997.

Davis, B. C. "A Contextual Analysis of Psalms 107–118." Ph.D. diss., Trinity Evangelical Divinity School, 1996.

Day, J. *God's Conflict with the Dragon and the Sea: Echoes of a Canaanite Myth in the Old Testament.* Cambridge: Cambridge University Press, 1985.

Deeley, M. K. "Ezekiel's Shepherd and John's Jesus: A Case Study in the Appropriation of Biblical Texts." Pages 252–264 in *Early Christian Interpretation of the Scriptures of Israel: Investigations and Proposals.* Edited by C. A. Evans and J. A. Sanders. JSNTSup 148. SSEJC 5. Sheffield: Sheffield Academic Press, 1997.

Del Medico, H. E. "Le cadre historique des fêtes de Hanukkah et de Purîm." *VT* 15 (1965): 238–270.

Delebeque, E. "Jésus contemporain d'Abraham selon Jean 8, 57." *RB* 93/1 (1986): 85–92.

Delitzsch, F. *Biblical Commentary on The Psalms.* Translated from the 2nd German edition by D. Eaton. 3 vols. London: Hodder and Stoughton, 1889.

Delling, G. "ἡμέρα." *TDNT* 2.947–953.

Dembitz, L. N. "Hallel." 6.176–177 in *The Jewish Encyclopedia.* Edited by I. Singer. 12 vols. New York: 1925.

Demsky, A., and M. Bar-Ilan. "Writing in Ancient Israel and Early Judaism." Pages 1–38 in *Mikra: Text, Translation, Reading and Interpretation of the Hebrew Bible in Ancient Judaism and Early Christianity.* Edited by M. J. Mulder. CRINT. Assen/Maastricht: Van Gorcum, 1990.

Denaux, A. "Old Testament Models for the Lukan Travel Narrative." Pages 271–305 in *The Scriptures in the Gospels.* Edited by C. M. Tuckett. Leuven: Leuven University Press, 1997.

Derrett, J. D. M. "Exercitations on John 8." *EstBib* 52/2 (1994): 433–451.

_____. "The Good Shepherd: St. John's Use of Jewish Halakah and Haggadah." *ST* 27 (1973): 25–50.

_____. *Law in the New Testament.* London: Darton, Longman & Todd, 1970.

_____. "Law in the New Testament: The Palm Sunday Colt." *NovT* 13 (1971): 241–258.

Dimant, D. "Use and Interpretation of Mikra in the Apocrypha and Pseudepigrapha." Pages 379–419 in *Mikra: Text, Translation, Reading and Interpretation of the Hebrew Bible in Ancient Judaism and Early Christianity.* Edited by M. J. Mulder. CRINT. Assen/Maastricht: Van Gorcum, 1990.

Dittmar, W. *Vetus Testamentum in Novo: Die alttestamentlichen Parallelen des Neuen Testaments im Wortlaut der Urtexte und der Septuaginta.* Göttingen: Vandenhoeck & Ruprecht, 1903.

Dodd, C. H. "A l'arrière d'un dialogue johannique." *RHPR* 37 (1957): 5–17. Repr. as "Behind a Johannine Dialogue." Pages 58–68 in *More New Testament Studies.* Manchester: Manchester University Press, 1968.

_____. *According to the Scriptures: The Sub-Structure of New Testament Theology.* London: Nisbet, 1952.

_____. *Historical Tradition in the Fourth Gospel.* Cambridge: Cambridge University Press, 1963.

_____. *The Interpretation of the Fourth Gospel.* Cambridge: Cambridge University Press, 1968.

Donaldson, T. L. "Parallels: Use, Misuse, and Limitations." *EvQ* 55 (1983): 193–210.

Draisma, S., ed. *Intertextuality in Biblical Writings: Essays in honour of Bas van Iersel.* Kampen: J. H. Kok, 1989.

Driver, G. R. "Psalm 118:27: הג אסורי." *Textus* 7 (1969): 130–131.

Duff, P. B. "The March of the Divine Warrior and the Advent of the Greco-Roman King: Mark's Account of Jesus' Entry into Jerusalem." *JBL* 111/1 (1992): 55–71.

Duhm, B. *Die Psalmen.* 2ⁿᵈ edition. HKAT 14. Tübingen: J.C.B. Mohr (Paul Siebeck), 1922.

Duke, P. *Irony in the Fourth Gospel.* Atlanta: John Knox Press, 1985.

Duling, D. C. "Testament of Solomon: A New Translation and Introduction." 1.935–959 in *The Old Testament Pseudepigrapha.* Edited by J. H. Charlesworth. 2 vols. ABRL. New York: Doubleday, 1985.

Dunkerley, R. "Lazarus." *NTS* 5 (1958–1959): 321–327.

Dunn, J. D. G. *Christology in the Making: An Inquiry into the Origins of the Doctrine of the Incarnation.* 2ⁿᵈ ed. London: SCM Press, 1989.

_____. "John the Baptist's Use of Scripture." Pages 42–54 in *The Gospels and the Scriptures of Israel.* Edited by C. A. Evans and W. R. Stegner. JSNTSup 104. SSEJC 3. Sheffield: Sheffield Academic Press, 1994.

Eaton, J. H. *Kingship and the Psalms.* Studies in Biblical Theology. Second Series 32. London: SCM Press, 1976.

_____. *Psalms of the Way and the Kingdom: A Conference with the Commentators.* JSOTSup 199. Sheffield: Sheffield Academic Press, 1995.

Eddy, P. R. "The (W)Right Jesus: *Eschatological Prophet, Israel's Messiah, Yahweh Embodied.*" Pages 40–60 in *Jesus and the Restoration of Israel: A Critical Assessment of N. T. Wright's* Jesus and the Victory of God. Edited by C. C. Newman. Downer's Grove, Ill.: InterVarsity; Carlisle: Paternoster, 1999.

Edwards, M. J. "'Not yet fifty years old': John 8.57." *NTS* 40 (1994): 449–454.

Eichrodt, W. E. *Theology of the Old Testament.* ET J. A. Baker. 2 vols. London: SCM Press, 1961–1967.

Elliott, J. H. *The Elect and the Holy: An Exegetical Examination of I Peter 2:4–10 and the Phrase* βασίλειον ἱεράτευμα. NovTSup 12. Leiden: Brill, 1966.

Ellis, E. E. "Midrash, Targum and New Testament Quotations." Pages 61–69 in *Neotestamentica et Semitica: Studies in Honour of Matthew Black.* Edinburgh: T&T Clark, 1969.

Engnell, I. *Studies In Divine Kingship in the Ancient Near East.* 2ⁿᵈ edition. Oxford: Blackwell, 1967.

Enz, J. J. "The Book of Exodus as a Literary Type for the Gospel of John." *JBL* 76 (1957): 208–215.

Evans, C. A. "Early Rabbinic Sources and Jesus Research." Pages 53–76 in *SBL Seminar Papers, 1995.* Edited by E. H. Lovering. Atlanta: Scholars Press, 1995.

_____. "Jesus' Action in the Temple: Cleansing or Portent of Destruction?" *CBQ* 51 (1989): 237–270.

_____. "Jesus & the Continuing Exile of Israel." Pages 77–100 in *Jesus and the Restoration of Israel: A Critical Assessment of N. T. Wright's* Jesus and the Victory of God. Edited by C. C. Newman. Downer's Grove, Ill.: InterVarsity; Carlisle: Paternoster, 1999.

_____. "Listening for Echoes of Interpreted Scripture." Pages 47–51 *Paul and the Scriptures of Israel.* Edited by C. A. Evans and J. A. Sanders. JSNTSup 83. SSEJC 1. Sheffield: JSOT Press, 1992.

_____. *Luke.* New International Bible Commentary. Peabody, Mass.: Hendrickson, 1990.

_____. "Obduracy and the Lord's Servant: Some Observations on the Use of the Old Testament in the Fourth Gospel." Pages 221–236 in *Early Jewish and Christian Exegesis.* Edited by C. A. Evans and W. F. Stinespring. Atlanta: Scholars Press, 1987.

_____. "On the Quotation Formulas in the Fourth Gospel." *BZ* 26 (1982): 79–83.

_____. *Word and Glory: On the Exegetical and Theological Background of John's Prologue.* JSNTSup 89. Sheffield: JSOT Press, 1993.

_____, and J. A. Sanders, eds. *Paul and the Scriptures of Israel.* JSNTSup 83. SSEJC 1. Sheffield: JSOT Press, 1992.

_____, and W. R. Stegner, eds. *The Gospels and the Scriptures of Israel.* JSNTSup 104. SSEJC 3. Sheffield: Sheffield Academic Press, 1994.

Evans, C. F. "The Central Section of St. Luke's Gospel." Pages 37–53 in *Studies in the Gospels: Essays in Memory of R. H. Lightfoot.* Edited by D. E. Nineham. Oxford: Blackwell, 1957.

Fahy, T. *New Testament Problems.* Dublin: Clonmore & Reynolds; London: Burns & Oates, 1963.

Farmer, W. R. *Maccabees, Zealots, and Josephus: An Inquiry Into Jewish Nationalism in the Greco-Roman Period.* New York: Columbia University Press, 1956.

_____. "The Palm Brances in John 12,13." *JTS* n.s. 3 (1952): 62–66.

Fascher, E. "Ich bin die Tür!: Eine Studie zu Joh 10:1–18." *Deutsche Theologie* 9 (1942): 33–57, 118–133.

Fekkes, Jan. *Isaiah and Prophetic Traditions in the Book of Revelation.* JSNTSup 115. Sheffield: Sheffield Academic Press, 1995.

Feldman, L. H. "Use, Authority and Exegesis of Mikra in the Writings of Josephus." Pages 455–518 in *Mikra: Text, Translation, Reading and Interpretation of the Hebrew Bible in Ancient Judaism and Early Christianity.* Edited by M. J. Mulder. CRINT. Assen/Maastricht: Van Gorcum, 1990.

Fernández Marcos, N. "La unción de Salomón y la entrada de Jesús en Jerusalén: 1 Re 1,33–40/Lc 19,35–40." *Bib* 68 (1987): 89–97.

Feuillet, A. "Les trois grandes prophéties de la Passion et de la Resurrection des évangiles synoptiques." *RevThom* 4 (1967): 533–60; 1 (1968): 41–74.

Filson, F. V. *A Commentary on the Gospel According to St. Matthew.* 2nd ed. London: Adam & Charles Black, 1971.

Finkel, A. "Comparative Exegesis: A Study of Hallel and Kerygma." *Journal of Dharma* 5 (Jan/Mar 1980): 109–121.

Finkelstein, L. "The Origin of the Hallel." *HUCA* 23 (1950–51): 319–337.

Fishbane, M. *Biblical Interpretation in Ancient Israel.* Oxford: Clarendon, 1985.

_____. "Inner Biblical Exegesis: Types and Strategies of Interpretation in Ancient Israel." Pages 19–37 in *Midrash and Literature.* Edited by G. H. Hartman and S. Budick. New Haven: Yale University Press, 1986.

_____. "Use, Authority and Interpretation of Mikra at Qumran." Pages 339–377 in *Mikra: Text, Translation, Reading and Interpretation of the Hebrew Bible in Ancient Judaism and Early Christianity.* Edited by M. J. Mulder. CRINT. Assen/Maastricht: Van Gorcum, 1990.

Fitzmyer, J. A. "Aramaic Evidence Affecting the Interpretation of *Hosanna* in the New Testament." Pages 110–118 in *Tradition and Interpretation in the New Testament.* Edited by G. F. Hawthorne and O. Betz. Grand Rapids: Eerdmans; Tübingen: J.C.B. Mohr (Paul Siebeck), 1987.

_____. *The Gospel according to Luke.* AB 28/28a. Garden City, N.Y.: Doubleday, 1981–1985.

Flint, P. W. *The Dead Sea Psalms Scrolls and the Book of Psalms.* STDJ 17. Leiden: Brill, 1997.

Fortna, R. T. *The Gospel of Signs: A Reconstruction of the Narrative Source Underlying the Fourth Gospel.* SNTSMS 11. Cambridge: Cambridge University Press, 1970.

France, R. T. "The Formula-Quotations of Matthew 2 and the Problem of Communication." Pages 114–134 in *The Right Doctrine from the Wrong Texts? Essays on the Use of the Old Testament in the New*. Edited by G. K. Beale. Grand Rapids: Baker, 1994. Repr. from *NTS* 27 (1981): 233–251.

_____. *Matthew*. TNTC 1. Leicester: InterVarsity; Grand Rapids: Eerdmans, 1985.

Freed, E. D. "The Entry Into Jerusalem in the Gospel of John." *JBL* 80 (1961): 329–338.

_____. *Old Testament Quotations in the Gospel of John*. NovTSup 11. Leiden: Brill, 1965.

_____. "Who or What Was Before Abraham in John 8:58?" *JSNT* 17 (1983): 52–59.

Frey, J. *Die johanneische Eschatologie. Band 3: Die eschatologische Verkündigung in den johanneischen Texten*. WUNT 117. Tübingen: Mohr Siebeck, 2000.

Freyne, S. *Galilee from Alexander the Great to Hadrian: 323 B.C.E. to 135 C.E: A Study of Second Temple Judaism*. Notre Dame: University of Notre Dame Press, 1980.

Frost, S. B. "Asseveration by Thanksgiving." *VT* 8 (1958): 380–390.

_____. "Psalm 118: An Exposition." *CJT* 7 (1961): 155–166.

Fuller, R. H. *Interpreting the Miracles*. London: SCM Press, 1963.

Gärtner, B. *John 6 and the Jewish Passover*. ConBNT 17. Lund: Gleerup, 1959.

Geldenhuys, N. *Commentary on the Gospel of Luke*. NICNT. Grand Rapids: Eerdmans, 1951.

Gemünden, P. von. "Palmensymbolik in Joh 12,13." *ZDPV* 114/1 (1998): 39–70.

George, A. "Je suis la porte des brebis. Jean 10,1–10." *BVC* 51 (1963): 18–25.

George, A. R. *Communion with God in the New Testament*. London: Epworth, 1953.

Gerstenberger, E. "Psalms." Pages 179–233 in *Old Testament Form Criticism*. Edited by J. H. Hayes. Trinity University Monograph Series in Religion 2. San Antonio: Trinity University Press, 1974.

Ginzburg, L. *The Legends of the Jews*. 7 vols. Philadelphia: The Jewish Publication Society of America, 1968.

Glasson, T. F. *Moses in the Fourth Gospel*. Studies in Biblical Theology 40. Naperville: Allenson, 1963.

Goldstein, J. A. "How the Authors of 1 and 2 Maccabees Treated the 'Messianic' Promises." Pages 69–96 in *Judaisms and Their Messiahs at the Turn of the Christian Era*. Edited by J. Neusner et al. Cambridge: Cambridge University Press, 1987.

Goodenough, E. R. *Jewish Symbols in the Greco-Roman Period*. 13 vols. Bollingen Series 37. New York: Pantheon Books, 1954–1968.

Goshen-Gottstein, M. H. "The Psalms Scroll (11QPs^a): A Problem of Canon and Text." *Textus* 5 (1966): 22–33.

Gottwald, N. K. *The Hebrew Bible: A Socio-Literary Introduction*. Philadelphia: Fortress, 1985.

Goulder, M. D. "From Ministry to Passion in John and Luke." *NTS* 29 (1983): 561–568.

_____. *The Prayers of David (Psalms 51–72): Studies in the Psalter, II*. JSOTSup 102. Sheffield: Sheffield Academic Press, 1990.

_____. *The Psalms of Asaph and the Pentateuch: Studies in the Psalter, III*. JSOTSup 233. Sheffield: Sheffield Academic Press, 1996.

_____. *The Psalms of the Return (Book V, Psalms 107–150): Studies in the Psalter, IV*. JSOTSup 258. Sheffield: Sheffield Academic Press, 1998.

_____. *The Psalms of the Sons of Korah*. JSOTSup 20. Sheffield: JSOT Press, 1982.

Green, W. S. "Doing the Text's Work for It: Richard Hays on Paul's Use of Scripture." Pages 58–63 in *Paul and the Scriptures of Israel*. Edited by C. A. Evans and J. A. Sanders. JSNTSup 83. SSEJC 1. Sheffield: JSOT Press, 1992.

Grelot, P. "'Celui qui vient' (Mt 11, 3 et Lc 7, 19)." Pages 275–290 in *Ce Dieu qui vient: Études sur l'Ancien et le Nouveau Testament offertes au Professeur Bernard*

Renaud à l'occasion de son soixante-cinquième anniversaire. Edited by R. Kuntzmann. Lectio Divina 159. Paris: Cerf, 1995.

_____. "Jean 8,56 et Jubilés 16,16–29." *RevQ* 13 (1988): 621–628.

Grubb, E. "The Raising of Lazarus." *ExpTim* 32 (1921–1922): 404–407.

Guilding, A. *The Fourth Gospel and Jewish Worship: A Study of the Relation of St. John's Gospel to the Ancient Jewish Lectionary System.* Oxford: Clarendon, 1960.

Gundry, R. H. *Mark: A Commentary on His Apology for the Cross.* Grand Rapids: Eerdmans, 1993.

_____. *Matthew: A Commentary on His Handbook for a Mixed Church under Persecution.* 2nd ed. Grand Rapids: Eerdmans, 1994.

Gunkel, H. *Die Psalmen übersetzt und erklärt.* 4th ed. HKAT II/2. Göttingen: Vandenhoeck und Ruprecht, 1926.

_____, and J. Begrich. *Einleitung in die Psalmen: Die Gattungen der religiösen Lyrik Israels.* Göttingen: Vandenhoeck & Ruprecht, 1933.

Haacker, K. "Samaritan, Samaria." *NIDNTT* 3.449–467.

Haenchen, E. "Der Vater, der mich gesandt hat." *NTS* 9 (1962–1963): 208–216.

Hafemann, S. J. *Paul, Moses, and the History of Israel: The Letter/Spirit Contrast and the Argument from Scripture in 2 Corinthians 3.* WUNT 81. Tübingen: J.C.B. Mohr (Paul Siebeck), 1995.

Hagner, D. A. *Matthew.* WBC 33A–B. Dallas: Word, 1993–1995.

Hammer, R. "Two Liturgical Psalms: Salvation and Thanksgiving." *Judaism* 40 (1991): 484–497.

Hanson, A. T. "John's Use of Scripture." Pages 358–379 in *The Gospels and the Scriptures of Israel.* Edited by C. A. Evans and W. R. Stegner. JSNTSup 104. SSEJC 3. Sheffield: Sheffield Academic Press, 1994.

_____. *The Living Utterances of God: The New Testament Exegesis of the Old.* London: Darton, Longman & Todd, 1983.

_____. "The Old Testament Background to the Raising of Lazarus." *SE* 6 (1973): 252–255.

_____. *The Prophetic Gospel: A Study of John and the Old Testament.* Edinburgh: T&T Clark, 1991.

Harrelson, W. "The Celebration of the Feast of Booths According to Zech xiv 16–21." *Religions in Antiquity: Essays in Memory of Erwin Ramsdell Goodenough.* Edited by J. Neusner. Supplements to *Numen* 14. Leiden: Brill, 1968.

Harrington, D. J. "Introduction to Pseudo-Philo." 2.297–303 in *The Old Testament Pseudepigrapha.* Edited by J. H. Charlesworth. 2 vols. Garden City, N.Y: Doubleday, 1985.

Harris, M. J. *Jesus as God: The New Testament Use of* Theos *in Reference to Jesus.* Grand Rapids: Baker, 1992.

Hart, H. St. J. "The Crown of Thorns in John 19, 2–5." *JTS* n.s. 3 (1952): 66–75.

Harvey, A. E. *Jesus and the Constraints of History.* Philadelphia: Westminster, 1982.

Hawthorne, G. F. "Hosanna." 2.761 in *The International Standard Bible Encyclopedia.* Edited by G. F. Bromiley. 4 vols. Grand Rapids: Eerdmans, 1982.

Hay, D. M. *Glory at the Right Hand: Psalm 110 in Early Christianity.* SBLMS 18. New York: Abingdon, 1973.

Hays, R. B. *Echoes of Scripture in the Letters of Paul.* New Haven: Yale University Press, 1989.

_____. "On the Rebound: A Response to Critiques of *Echoes of Scripture in the Letters of Paul.*" Pages 70–96 in *Paul and the Scriptures of Israel.* Edited by C. A. Evans and J. A. Sanders. JSNTSup 83. SSEJC 1. Sheffield: JSOT Press, 1992.

_____. "Victory over Violence: *The Significance of N. T. Wright's Jesus for New Testa-ment Ethics.*" Pages 142–158 in *Jesus and the Restoration of Israel: A Critical Assessment of N. T. Wright's* Jesus and the Victory of God. Edited by C. C. New-man. Downer's Grove, Ill.: InterVarsity; Carlisle: Paternoster, 1999.

Heim, K. M. "The Perfect King of Psalm 72: An 'Intertextual' Inquiry." Pages 223–248 in *The Lord's Anointed: Interpretation of Old Testament Messianic Texts.* Edited by P. E. Satterthwaite et al. Carlisle: Paternoster; Grand Rapids: Baker Books, 1995.

Hengel, M. "The Old Testament in the Fourth Gospel." Pages 380–395 in *The Gospels and the Scriptures of Israel.* Edited by C. A. Evans and W. R. Stegner. JSNTSup 104. SSEJC 3. Sheffield: Sheffield Academic Press, 1994.

_____. *The Johannine Question.* ET J. Bowden. London: SCM Press; Philadelphia: Tri-nity Press International, 1989.

_____. *Studies in Early Christology.* Edinburgh: T&T Clark, 1995.

Hill, D. *The Gospel of Matthew.* NCB. Grand Rapids: Eerdmans; London: Marshall, Morgan & Scott, 1972.

Hill, J. S. "τὰ βαΐα τῶν φοινίκων (John 12:13): Pleonasm or Prolepsis?" *JBL* 101 (1982): 133–135.

Hillyer, N. "λῃστής." *NIDNTT* 3.377–379.

Hollander, J. *The Figure of Echo: A Mode of Allusion in Milton and After.* Berkeley: University of California Press, 1981.

Hooke, S. H., ed. *Myth and Ritual.* Oxford: Oxford University Press, 1933.

_____, ed. *Myth, Ritual, and Kingship: Essays on the Theory and Practice of Kingship in the Ancient Near East and in Israel.* Oxford: Clarendon, 1958.

_____, ed. *The Labyrinth: Further Studies in the Relation Between Myth and Ritual in the Ancient World.* London: SPCK, 1935.

Hooker, M. D. *The Gospel According to Saint Mark.* BNTC 2. Peabody, Mass.: Hendrick-son, 1991.

Horgan, M. P. *Pesharim: Qumran Interpretations of Biblical Books.* CBQMS 8. Washing-ton, D.C.: The Catholic Biblical Association of America, 1979.

Horsley, R. A. "Popular Messianic Movements around the Time of Jesus." *CBQ* 46 (1984): 471–495.

_____, and J. S. Hanson. *Bandits, Prophets and Messiahs: Popular Movements at the Time of Jesus.* Edinburgh: T&T Clark, 1985.

Howard, D. M. Jr. "Editorial Activity in the Psalter: A State-of-the-Field Survey." Pages 52–70 in *The Shape and Shaping of the Psalter.* Edited by J. C. McCann. JSOTSup 159. Sheffield: JSOT Press, 1993.

_____. "The Structure of Psalms 93–100." Ph.D. diss., University of Michigan, Ann Arbor, 1986.

Howard, W. F. *Christianity According to St. John.* Philadelphia: Westminster Press, 1946.

Huie-Jolly, M. R. "Threats Answered by Enthronement: Death/Resurrection and the Divine Warrior Myth in John 5.17–29, Psalm 2 and Daniel 7." Pages 191–217 in *Early Christian Interpretation of the Scriptures of Israel: Investigations and Proposals.* Edited by C. A. Evans and J. A. Sanders. JSNTSup 148. SSEJC 5. Sheffield: Sheffield Academic Press, 1997.

Hunter, W. B. "Contextual and Genre Implications for the Historicity of John 11:41b–42." *JETS* 28/1 (1985): 53–70.

Hurtado, L. W. *Mark.* San Francisco: Harper & Row, 1983.

Jacquet, L. *Les Psaumes et le coeur de l'Homme: Étude textuelle, littéraire et doctrinale.* 3 vols. Gembloux: Duculot, 1979.

Jeremias, J. "Die Muttersprache des Evangelisten Matthäus." *ZNW* 50 (1959): 270–274.

_____. *The Eucharistic Words of Jesus.* ET N. Perrin. London: SCM Press, 1964.
_____. *Jerusalem in the Time of Jesus: An Investigation into Economic and Social Conditions During the New Testament Period.* ET F. H. and C. H. Cave. Philadelphia: Fortress, 1969.
_____. "λίθος, λίθινος." 4.268–280 in *Theological Dictionary of the New Testament.* Edited by G. Kittel and G. Friedrich. ET G. W. Bromiley. 10 vols. Grand Rapids: Eerdmans, 1964–1976.
_____. "ποιμήν κτλ." *TDNT* 6.485–502.
_____. *The Prayers of Jesus.* SBT 6. London: SCM Press, 1967.
_____. "πύλη." *TDNT* 6.921–928.
_____. "θύρα." *TDNT* 3.173–180.
The Jewish Encyclopedia. Edited by I. Singer et al. 12 vols. New York and London: Funk & Wagnall, 1914.
Johnson, A. R. "Hebrew Conceptions of Kingship." Pages 204–235 in *Myth, Ritual, and Kingship: Essays on the Theory and Practice of Kingship in the Ancient Near East and in Israel.* Edited by S. H. Hooke. Oxford: Clarendon, 1958.
_____. "Old Testament Exegesis, Imaginative and Unimaginative." *ExpTim* 68 (1956–1957): 178–179.
_____. "The Psalms." Pages 162–209 in *The Old Testament and Modern Study: A Generation of Discovery and Research.* Edited by H. H. Rowley. Oxford: Clarendon, 1951.
_____. "The Role of the King in the Jerusalem Cultus." Pages 71–111 in *The Labyrinth: Further Studies in the Relation between Myth and Ritual in the Ancient World.* Edited by S. H. Hooke. London: SPCK, 1935.
_____. *Sacral Kingship in Ancient Israel.* Cardiff: University of Wales Press, 1967.
Johnson, L. T. "A Historiographical Response to Wright's Jesus." Pages 206–224 in *Jesus and the Restoration of Israel: A Critical Assessment of N. T. Wright's* Jesus and the Victory of God. Edited by C. C. Newman. Downer's Grove, Ill.: InterVarsity; Carlisle: Paternoster, 1999.
Jonge, M. de. "Jesus, Son of David and Son of God." Pages 95–104 in *Intertextuality in Biblical Writings.* Edited by S. Draisma. Kampen: J. H. Kok, 1989.
_____. "Jewish Expectations about the 'Messiah' According to the Fourth Gospel." *NTS* 19 (1972–73): 246–270.
_____. "The Use of the Word 'Anointed' in the Time of Jesus." *NovT* 8 (1966): 132–148.
Juel, D. H. *The Gospel of Mark.* Nashville: Abingdon Press, 1999.
Kadman, L. *The Coins of the Jewish War.* Corpus Nummorum Palaestinensium 3. Tel-Aviv: Schocken, 1960.
Kambeitz, T. "I Am the Door." *Bible Today* 27/2 (1989): 110–112.
Käsemann, E. *The Testament of Jesus: A Study of the Gospel of John in the Light of Chapter 17.* ET G. Krodel. Philadelphia: Fortress, 1968.
Kasher, R. "The Interpretation of Scripture in Rabbinic Literature." Pages 339–377 in *Mikra: Text, Translation, Reading and Interpretation of the Hebrew Bible in Ancient Judaism and Early Christianity.* Edited by M. J. Mulder. CRINT. Assen/Maastricht: Van Gorcum, 1990.
Keener, C. S. *A Commentary on the Gospel of Matthew.* Grand Rapids: Eerdmans, 1999.
Kelber, W. *The Kingdom in Mark: A New Place and a New Time.* Philadelphia: Fortress, 1974.
Kennard, J. S. Jr. "'Hosanna' and the Purpose of Jesus." *JBL* 67 (1948): 171–176.
Kern, W. "Die symmetrische Gesamtaufbau von Joh. 8, 12–58." *ZTK* 78 (1956): 451–456.
Kiefer, O. *Die Hirtenrede: Analyse und Deutung von Joh 10,1–18.* SBS 23. Stuttgart: Katholisches Bibelwerk, 1967.

Kiley, M. "'Lord, Save My Life' as Generative Text for Jesus' Gethsemane Prayer." *CBQ* 48 (1986): 655–659.

Kim, S. "Jesus—The Son of God, the Stone, the Son of Man, and the Servant: The Role of Zechariah in the Self-Identification of Jesus." Pages 134–148 in *Tradition and Interpretation in the New Testament*. Edited by G. F. Hawthorne and O. Betz. Grand Rapids: Eerdmans; Tübingen: J.C.B. Mohr (Paul Siebeck), 1987.

Kimball, C. A. *Jesus' Exposition of the Old Testament in Luke's Gospel*. JSNTSup 94. Sheffield: JSOT Press, 1994.

Kinman, B. *Jesus' Entry Into Jerusalem: In the Context of Lukan Theology and the Politics of His Day*. AGJU 28. Leiden: Brill, 1995.

Kinzer, S. M. "All Things Under His Feet: Psalm 8 in the New Testament and in other Jewish Literature of Late Antiquity." Ph.D. diss., University of Michigan, 1995.

Kirkpatrick, A. F. *The Book of Psalms*. 3 vols. The Cambridge Bible for Schools and Colleges. Cambridge: Cambridge University Press, 1903.

Kissane, E. J. *The Book of Psalms*. Dublin: Browne and Nolan, 1964.

Kittel, G., and G. Friedrich, eds. *Theological Dictionary of the New Testament*. ET G. W. Bromiley. 10 vols. Grand Rapids: Eerdmans, 1964–1976.

Klappert, B. "βασιλεία." *NIDNTT* 2.372–390.

Klein, R. *Ezekiel: The Prophet and His Message*. Columbia: USC Press, 1988.

Knibb, M. A. "The Exile in the Literature of the Intertestamental Period." *HeyJ* 17/3 (1976): 253–272.

Knowles, M. *Jeremiah in Matthew's Gospel: The Rejected Prophet in Matthean Redaction*. JSNTSup 68. Sheffield: JSOT Press, 1993.

Koester, C. R. *The Dwelling of God: The Tabernacle in the Old Testament, Intertestamental Jewish Literature, and the New Testament*. CBQMS 22. Washington, D.C.: Catholic Biblical Association, 1989.

Kovak, J. L. "'Now shall the Ruler of this World be Driven Out': Jesus' Death as Cosmic Battle in John 12:20–36." *JBL* 114 (1995): 236–247.

Kraus, H.-J. *Psalms 60–150*. ET H. C. Oswald. Minneapolis: Fortress, 1993.

_____. *Theology of the Psalms*. ET K. Crim. Minneapolis: Augsburg, 1986.

_____. *Worship in Israel: A Cultic History of the Old Testament*. ET G. Buswell. Oxford: Blackwell, 1966.

Krause, D. "The One Who Comes Unbinding the Blessing of Judah: Mark 11.1–10 as a Midrash on Genesis 49.11, Zechariah 9.9, and Psalm 118.25–26." Pages 141–153 in *Early Christian Interpretation of the Scriptures of Israel: Investigations and Proposals*. Edited by C. A. Evans and J. A. Sanders. JSNTSup 148. SSEJC 5. Sheffield: Sheffield Academic Press, 1997.

Krüger, R. "Humilde, montado en un burrito: Mateo 21:1–11 y el recurso escriturístico." *RevistB* 54/2 (1992): 65–83.

Kuhl, J. *Die Sendung Jesu und der Kirche nach dem Johannes-Evangelium*. Studia Instituti Missiologici Societatis Verbi Divini 11. St. Augustin: Steyler, 1967.

Kuhn, K. G. "מלכות שמים in Rabbinic Literature." 1.571–574 in "βασιλεύς κτλ." *TDNT* 1.564–593.

Kysar, R. "The Background of the Prologue of the Fourth Gospel: A Critique of Historical Methods." *CJT* 16 (1970): 250–255.

_____. *The Fourth Evangelist and His Gospel: An Examination of Contemporary Scholarship*. Minneapolis: Augsburg, 1975.

_____. "Johannine Metaphor—Meaning and Function: A literary Case Study of John 10:1–18." *Semeia* 53 (1991): 81–111.

Lacomara, A. "Deuteronomy and the Farewell Discourse (Jn 13:31–16:33)." *CBQ* 36 (1974): 65–84.

Lagrange, M.-J. *Évangile selon Saint Marc.* Paris: Gabalda, 1911.

Lambrecht, J. "'Are you the one who is to come, or shall we look for another?' The Gospel Message of Jesus Today." *LS* 8 (1980–81): 115–128.

Lane, W. L. *The Gospel According to Mark.* NICNT. Grand Rapids: Eerdmans, 1974.
_____. *Hebrews.* 2 vols. WBC. Dallas, 1991.

Langston, S. Review of K. E. Pomykale, *The Davidic Dynasty Tradition in Early Judaism: Its History and Significance for Messianism. JBL* 115 (1996): 529–530.

Lathrop, G. "The Prayer of Jesus and the Great Prayer of the Church." *LQ* 26/2 (1974): 158–173.

Le Déaut, R. *La nuit pascale: Essai sur la signification de la Pâque juive à partir du Targum d'Exode XII 42.* AnBib 22. Rome: Pontifical Institute, 1963.

Lee, D. A. *The Symbolic Narratives of the Fourth Gospel: The Interplay of Form and Meaning.* JSNTSup 95. Sheffield: JSOT Press, 1994.

Leistner, R. *Antijudaismus im Johannesevangelium? Darstellung des Problems in der neueren Auslegungsgeschichte und Untersuchung der Leidensgeschichte.* Bern and Frankfurt: Herbert Lang, 1974.

Leroy, H. *Rätsel und Missverständnis: Ein Beitrag zur Formgeschichte des Johannesevangeliums.* BBB 30. Bonn: Hanstein, 1968.

Levey, S. H. *The Messiah: An Aramaic Interpretation: The Messianic Exegesis of the Targum.* Monographs of the Hebrew Union College 2. Cincinnati: Hebrew Union College Press, 1974.

Lindars, B. *New Testament Apologetic.* London: SCM Press, 1961.

Lohmeyer, E. *Das Evangelium des Markus.* KEK. Göttingen: Vandenhoeck & Ruprecht, 1963.

Lohse, E. "Hosianna." *NovT* 6 (1963): 113–119.
_____. "ὡσαννά." *TDNT* 9.682–684.

Lona, H. E. *Abraham in Johannes 8: Ein Beitrag zur Methodenfrage.* Europäische Hochschulschriften 23/65. Bern: Herbert Lang; Frankfurt/M: Peter Lang, 1976.

Longenecker, R. *Biblical Exegesis in the Apostolic Period.* Grand Rapids: Eerdmans, 1975.
_____. *The Acts of the Apostles.* Vol. 9 of The Expositor's Bible Commentary. Grand Rapids: Zondervan, 1981.

Losie, L. A. "Triumphal Entry." Pages 854–859 in *Dictionary of Jesus and the Gospels.* Edited by J. Green, S. McKnight, and I. H. Marshall. Downers Grove, Ill.: Inter-Varsity Press, 1992.

Louw, J. P., and E. A. Nida, eds. *Louw-Nida Greek-English Lexicon Based on Semantic Domains.* 2nd ed. New York: United Bible Societies, 1988.

Macdonald, J. *The Theology of the Samaritans.* London: SCM Press, 1964.

MacRae, G. W. "The Meaning and Evolution of the Feast of Tabernacles." *CBQ* 22 (1966): 251–276.

Maiburg, U. "Christus der Eckstein: Ps. 118,22 und Jes. 28,16 im Neuen Testament und bei den lateinischen Vätern." Pages 247–256 in *Vivarium.* FS T. Klauser. JAC 11. Münster: Aschendorff, 1984.

Mann, C. S. *Mark.* AB 27. Garden City: Doubleday, 1986.

Manns, F. "Traditions Targumiques en Jean 10, 1–30." *RevScRel* 60 (1986): 135–157.

Manson, T. W. *The Sayings of Jesus: As Recorded in the Gospels according to St. Matthew and St. Luke.* London: SCM Press, 1949.
_____. "The Cleansing of the Temple." *BJRL* 33 (1950–51): 271–282.

Marcus, J. *Mark 1–8.* AB 27. New York: Doubleday, 1999.

_____. *The Way of the Lord: Christological Exegesis of the Old Testament in the Gospel of Mark*. Louisville: Westminster/John Knox, 1992.

Marshall, I. H. "An Assessment of Recent Developments." Pages 1–21 in *It is Written: Scripture Citing Scripture: Essays in Honour of Barnabas Lindars*. Edited by D. A. Carson and H. G. M. Williamson. Cambridge: Cambridge University Press, 1986.

_____. *The Acts of the Apostles*. TNTC 5. Inter-Varsity Press: Leicester; Grand Rapids: Eerdmans, 1980.

_____. *The Gospel of Luke: A Commentary on the Greek Text*. NIGTC. Grand Rapids: Eerdmans, 1978.

_____. *Last Supper and Lord's Supper*. Biblical and Theological Classics Library 20. Carlisle: Paternoster, 1997.

_____. *Luke: Historian and Theologian*. Exeter: Paternoster, 1970.

Martin, A. W. "The Interpretation of the Triumphal Entry in the Early Church." Ph.D. diss., Vanderbilt University, 1971.

Martin, J. P. "History and Eschatology in the Lazarus Narrative John 11.1–44." *SJT* 17 (1964): 332–343.

_____. "John 10:1–10." *Int* 32 (1978): 171–175.

Martyn, J. L. *The Gospel of John in Christian History: Essays for Interpreters*. New York: Paulist Press, 1978.

_____. *History and Theology in the Fourth Gospel*. New York: Harper & Row, 1968.

März, C.-P. *"Siehe, dein König kommt zu dir ...": Eine traditionsgeschichtliche Untersuchung zur Einzugsperikope*. ETS 43. Leipzig: St. Benno, 1980.

Mastin, B. A. "The Date of the Triumphal Entry." *NTS* 16 (1969–70): 76–82.

Mateos, P. C. "Uso e interpretación de Zacarías 9,9–10 en el Nuevo Testamento." *EstAg* 7 (1972): 471–493; 8 (1973): 3–29.

Matthewson, D. L. "The Meaning and Function of the Old Testament in Revelation 21.1–22.5." Ph.D. diss., University of Aberdeen, 1998.

May, H. S. "Ps 118: The Song of the Citadel." Pages 97–106 in *Religions in Antiquity: Essays in Memory of Erwin Ramsdell Goodenough*. Edited by J. Neusner. Supplements to *Numen* 14. Leiden: Brill, 1968.

Mays, J. L. "Going by the Book: The Psalter as a Guide to Reading the Psalms." Pages 119–127 in *The Lord Reigns: A Theological Handbook to the Psalms*. Louisville: Westminster John Knox Press, 1994.

_____. "The Place of the Torah Psalms in the Psalter." Pages 128–135 in *The Lord Reigns: A Theological Handbook to the Psalms*. Louisville: Westminster John Knox Press, 1994. Repr. from *JBL* 106/1 (1987): 3–12.

_____. "Psalm 118 in the Light of Canonical Analysis." Pages 136–145 in *The Lord Reigns: A Theological Handbook to the Psalms*. Louisville: Westminster John Knox Press, 1994. Repr. from pages 299–311 in *Canon, Theology, and Old Testament Interpretation*. Edited by G. M. Tucker et al. Philadelphia: Fortress, 1988.

_____. *Psalms*. IBC. Louisville: John Knox Press, 1994.

_____. "The Question of Context in Psalm Interpretation." Pages 14–20 in *The Shape and Shaping of the Psalter*. Edited by J. C. McCann. JSOTSup 159. Sheffield: JSOT Press, 1993.

McCaffrey, J. *The House with Many Rooms: The Temple Theme of Jn. 14, 2–3*. AnBib 114. Rome: Pontificio Instituto Biblico, 1988.

McCann, J. C. "Books I–III and the Editorial Purpose of the Hebrew Psalter." Pages 93–107 in *The Shape and Shaping of the Psalter*. Edited by J. C. McCann. JSOTSup 159. Sheffield: JSOT Press, 1993.

McCullough, W. S. *The Book of Psalms*. Vol. 4 in *The Interpreter's Bible*. Edited by G. A. Buttrick. 12 vols. New York: Abingdon-Cokesbury, 1953.

_____. "Israel's Kings, Sacral and Otherwise." *ExpTim* 68 (1956–1957): 144–148.

McCurley, F. R. *Ancient Myths and Biblical Faith: Scriptural Transformations*. Philadelphia: Fortress, 1983.

McKelvey, R. J. *The New Temple: The Church in the New Testament*. London: Oxford University Press, 1969.

McNamara, M. *Targum and Testament: Aramaic Paraphrases of the Hebrew Bible: A Light on the New Testament*. Shannon: Irish University Press, 1972.

Meeks, W. A. "The Man from Heaven in Johannine Sectarianism." *JBL* 91/1 (1972):44–72.

_____. *The Prophet-King: Moses Traditions and the Johannine Christology*. NovTSup 14. Leiden: Brill, 1967.

Menken, M. J. J. *Old Testament Quotations in the Fourth Gospel: Studies in Textual Form*. Contributions to Biblical Exegesis and Theology 15. Kampen: Kok Pharos, 1996.

Mérode, M. de. "L'accueil triomphal de Jésus selon *Jean*, 11–12." *RTL* 13 (1982): 49–62.

Mettinger, T. N. D. "Fighting the Powers of Chaos and Hell—Towards the Biblical Portrait of God." *ST* 39 (1985): 21–38.

_____. *King and Messiah: The Civil and Sacral Legitimation of the Israelite Kings*. ConBOT 8. Lund: Gleerup, 1976.

Metzger, B. *A Textual Commentary on the Greek New Testament*. 2nd ed. Stuttgart: Deutsche Bibelgesellschaft, 1994.

Meyer, P. W. "Matthew 21:1–11." *Int* 40/2 (1986): 180–185.

_____. "A Note on John 10.1–18." *JBL* 75 (1956): 232–235.

Meysing, J. "A Text-Reconstruction of Ps 117(118).27." *VT* 10 (1960): 130–137.

Michaelis, W. "ὁράω." *TDNT* 5.315–367.

Michaels, J. R. *1 Peter*. WBC 49. Waco, Tex.: Word, 1988.

Michel, D. "Studien zu den sogennanten Thronbesteigungspsalmen." *VT* 6 (1956): 40–68.

Miller, J. *Les citations d'accomplissement dans l'Évangile de Matthieu: Quand Dieu se rend présent en toute humanité*. AnBib 140. Rome: Pontificio Istituto Biblico, 1999.

Miller, O. and M. J. Valdes. *Identity of the Literary Text*. Toronto: Toronto University Press, 1985.

Miller, P. D. Jr. "The Beginning of the Psalter." Pages 84–92 in *The Shape and Shaping of the Psalter*. Edited by J. C. McCann. JSOTSup 159. Sheffield: JSOT Press, 1993.

_____. *Interpreting the Psalms*. Philadelphia: Fortress, 1986.

_____. "Response to Erich Zenger, 'The Composition and Theology of the Fifth Book of Psalms, Psalms 107–145': 145–150." Unpublished paper presented to the Book of Psalms Group of the SBL during the 1995 Annual Meeting in Philadelphia. Personal copy from P. D. Miller.

_____. "Vocative Lamed in the Psalter: A Reconsideration." *UF* 11 (1979): 617–639.

Miranda, J. P. *Der Vater, der mich gesandt hat: Religionsgeschichtliche Untersuchungen zu den johanneischen Sendungsformeln: Zugleich ein Beitrag zur johanneischen Christologie und Ekklesiologie*. Europäische Hochschulschriften 23/7. Bern: Herbert Lang; Frankfurt/M.: Peter Lang, 1972.

_____. *Die Sendung Jesu im vierten Evangelium: Religions- und theologiegeschichtliche Untersuchungen zu den Sendungsformeln*. SBS 87. Stuttgart: Katholisches Bibelwerk, 1977.

Mitchell, D. C. *The Message of the Psalter: An Eschatological Programme in the Book of Psalms*. JSOTSup 252. Sheffield: Sheffield Academic Press, 1997.

Moessner, D. P. *Lord of the Banquet: The Literary and Theological Significance of the Lukan Travel Narrative*. Minneapolis: Fortress, 1989.

Mollat, D. "Le bon pasteur. Jean 10, 11–18. 26–30." *BVC* 52 (1963): 25–35.

Moloney, F. "The Fourth Gospel's Presentation of Jesus as 'The Christ' and J. A. T. Robinson's *Redating*." *DRev* 95 (1977): 239–253.

Moo, D. J. *The Old Testament in the Gospel Passion Narratives*. Sheffield: Almond, 1983.

Moore, G. F. *Judaism in the First Centuries of the Christian Era: The Age of the Tannaim*. 3 vols. Cambridge: Harvard University Press, 1927–1930. Repr. Peabody, Mass.: Hendrickson, 1997.

Mörchen, R. "Johanneisches 'Jubeln.'" *BZ* 30/2 (1986): 248–250.

Moreton, M. J. "Feast, Sign, and Discourse in John 5." *SE* 4 (1968): 209–213.

Morgan, R. "Fulfillment in the Fourth Gospel: The Old Testament Foundations." *Int* 11 (1957): 155–165.

Morgenstern, J. "The Gates of Righteousness." *HUCA* 6 (1929): 1–37.

Moritz, T. *A Profound Mystery: The Use of the Old Testament in Ephesians*. NovTSup 85. Brill: Leiden, 1996.

Morris, L. *The Gospel According to Matthew*. Grand Rapids: Eerdmans; Leicester: Inter-Varsity, 1992.

_____. *The New Testament and the Jewish Lectionaries*. London: Tyndale, 1964.

Motyer, J. A. "ὡσαννά." *NIDNTT* 1.100.

Moule, C. F. D. *The Gospel according to Mark*. Cambridge: Cambridge University Press, 1965.

Moulton, J. H., W. F. Francis, and N. Turner. *A Grammar of New Testament Greek*. 4 vols. Edinburgh: T&T Clark, 1908–1976.

Mowinckel, S. *He That Cometh*. ET G. W. Anderson. New York: Abingdon Press, 1955.

_____. *Psalmenstudien*. 6 vols. Oslo: Kristiana, 1921–1924.

_____. "Psalms and Wisdom." Pages 205–224 in *Wisdom in Israel and in the Ancient Near East*. Edited by M. Noth and D. W. Thomas. VTSup 3. Leiden: Brill, 1955.

_____. *The Psalms in Israel's Worship*. ET D. R. Ap-Thomas. 2 vols. Oxford: Blackwell, 1962.

Moyise, S. *The Old Testament in the Book of Revelation*. JSNTSup 115. Sheffield: Sheffield Academic Press, 1995.

_____. "Intertextuality and the Book of Revelation." *ExpTim* 104 (1993): 295–298.

Mulder, M. J., ed. *Mikra: Text, Translation, Reading and Interpretation of the Hebrew Bible in Ancient Judaism and Early Christianity*. CRINT. Assen/Maastricht: Van Gorcum, 1990.

Murray, D. G. "Jesus and the Feasts of the Jews." *DRev* 109 (1991): 217–225.

Neusner, J. "Mishnah and Messiah." Pages 265–282 in *Judaisms and their Messiahs at the Turn of the Christian Era*. Edited by J. Neusner et al. Cambridge: Cambridge University Press, 1987.

_____, W. S. Green, and E. S. Frerichs, eds. *Judaisms and their Messiahs at the Turn of the Christian Era*. Cambridge: Cambridge University Press, 1987.

Newman, C. C. "From (Wright's) Jesus to (the Church's) Christ: *Can We Get There from Here?*" Pages 281–287 in *Jesus and the Restoration of Israel: A Critical Assessment of N. T. Wright's Jesus and the Victory of God*. Edited by C. C. Newman. Downer's Grove, Ill.: InterVarsity; Carlisle: Paternoster, 1999.

_____, ed. *Jesus & the Restoration of Israel: A Critical Assessment of N. T. Wright's Jesus and the Victory of God*. Downer's Grove, Ill.: InterVarsity; Carlisle: Paternoster, 1999.

Nicholson, G. C. *Death as Departure: The Johannine Descent-Ascent Schema*. SBLDS 63. Chico, Calif.: Scholars Press, 1983.

Nickelsburg, G. W. E. *Jewish Literature Between the Bible and the Mishnah: A Historical and Literary Introduction.* London: SCM Press, 1981.

Nicol, W. *The Semeia in the Fourth Gospel: Tradition and Redaction.* NovTSup 32. Leiden: Brill, 1972.

Nieuviarts, J. *L'Entrée de Jésus à Jérusalem (Mt 21, 1–17): Messianisme et accomplissement des Écritures en Matthieu.* Lectio Divina 176. Paris: Cerf, 1999.

Nineham, D. E. *Saint Mark.* Westminster Pelican Commentaries. Philadelphia: Westminster, 1963.

Nolland, J. *Luke.* 3 vols. WBC 35A–C. Dallas: Word, 1989–1993.

North, C. R. "The Religious Aspects of Hebrew Kingship." *ZAW* 1 (1932).

Oesterley, W. O. E. *The Psalms.* 2 vols. London: SPCK, 1939.

Obermann, A. *Die christologische Erfüllung der Schrift im Johannesevangelium: Eine Untersuchung zur johanneischen Hermeneutik anhand der Schriftzitate.* WUNT 2/83. Tübingen: Mohr Siebeck, 1996.

Ogg, G. "The Age of Jesus When He Taught." *NTS* 5 (1958–1959): 291–298.

O'Rourke, J. J. "Jo 10.1–18: Series Parabolarum." *VD* 42 (1964): 22–25.

Painter, J. *The Quest for the Messiah: The History, Literature and Theology of the Johannine Community.* Edinburgh: T&T Clark, 1991.

_____. "The Quotation of Scripture and Unbelief in John 12.36B–43." Pages 429–445 in *The Gospels and the Scriptures of Israel.* Edited by C. A. Evans and W. R. Stegner. JSNTSup 104. SSEJC 3. Sheffield: Sheffield Academic Press, 1994.

_____. "Tradition, history and interpretation in John 10." Pages 53–74 in *The Shepherd Discourse of John 10 and its Context: Studies by Members of the Johannine Writings Seminar.* Edited by J. Beutler and R. T. Fortna. SNTSMS 67. Cambridge: Cambridge University Press, 1991.

Pao, D. W. *Acts and the Isaianic New Exodus.* WUNT 2/130. Tübingen: Mohr Siebeck, 2000.

Pap, L. I. *Das israelitische Neujahrsfest.* Kampen: J. H. Kok, 1933.

Patai, R. "The 'Control of Rain' in Ancient Palestine." *HUCA* 14 (1939): 251–286.

_____. *Man and Temple in Ancient Jewish Myth and Ritual.* London, 1947.

Patsch, H. "Der Einzug Jesu in Jerusalem: Ein historischer Versuch." *ZTK* 68 (1971): 1–26.

Paulien, J. "Elusive Allusions: The Problematic Use of the Old Testament in Revelation." *BR* 33 (1988): 37–53.

Pender, W. C. "The Christological Interpretation of Old Testament Stone and Rock Texts in the New Testament." Ph.D. diss., Duke University, 1984.

Perowne, J. J. S. *The Book of Psalms.* 2 vols. London: Bell and Daldy, 1868.

Peters, J. P. *The Psalms as Liturgies.* London: Hodder and Stoughton, 1922.

Petuchowski, J. J. "'Hoshi'ah na' in Psalm 118.25: A Prayer for Rain." *VT* 5 (1955): 266–271.

Pietrantonio, R. "El Mesías permanece para siempre: Juan 12:12–36." *RevistB* 47/3 (1985): 121–142.

_____. "Los 'ioudaioi' en el Evangelio de Juan." *RevistB* 47/1–2 (1985): 27–41.

Piper, O. A. "Unchanging Promises: Exodus in the New Testament." *Int* 11 (1957): 3–22.

Plummer, A. *A Critical and Exegetical Commentary on the Gospel According to Luke.* 5th ed. ICC. Edinburgh: T & T Clark, 1922.

Pollard, T. E. "The Exegesis of John X. 30 in the Early Trinitarian Controversies." *NTS* 3 (1956–1957): 334–349.

Pomykale, K. E. *The Davidic Dynasty Tradition in Early Judaism: Its History and Significance for Messianism.* SBLEJL 7. Atlanta: Scholars Press, 1995.

Pope, M. H. "Hosanna." 3.290–291 in *Anchor Bible Dictionary*. Edited by D. N. Freedman. 6 vols. New York: Doubleday, 1992.

———. "Hosanna—What It *Really* Means." *BR* 4/1 (1988): 16–25.

———. "Vestiges of Vocative Lamedh in the Bible." *UF* 20 (1988): 201–207.

Porter, S. E. "Can Traditional Exegesis Enlighten Literary Analysis of the Fourth Gospel? An Examination of the Old Testament Fulfilment Motif and the Passover Theme." Pages 398–428 in *The Gospels and the Scriptures of Israel*. Edited by C. A. Evans and W. R. Stegner. JSNTSup 104. SSEJC 3. Sheffield: Sheffield Academic Press, 1994.

———. "The Use of the Old Testament in the New Testament: A Brief Comment on Method and Terminology." Pages 79–96 in *Early Christian Interpretation of the Scriptures of Israel: Investigations and Proposals*. Edited by C. A. Evans and J. A. Sanders. JSNTSup 148. SSEJC 5. Sheffield: Sheffield Academic Press, 1997.

Potterie, I. de la. "Le Bon Pasteur." Pages 927–968 in *Populus Dei II: Studi in onore del Card. A. Ottaviani*. Rome: Comunio, 1970.

Price, S. R. F. *Rituals and Power: The Roman Imperial Cult in Asia Minor*. Cambridge: Cambridge University Press, 1984.

Probst, A. "Jésus et Yahvé." *RRef* 41 (1990): 44–45.

Pryor, J. W. "The Johannine Son of Man and the Descent-Ascent Motif." *JETS* 34/3 (1991): 341–351.

Quasten, J. "The Parable of the Good Shepherd: Jn 10:1–21." *CBQ* 10 (1948): 1–12, 151–169.

Rabinowitz, L. I. "The Book of Psalms: In the Talmud and Midrash and in the Liturgy." 13.1322–1325 in *Encyclopaedia Judaica*. Edited by C. Roth. 16 vols. Jerusalem, 1972.

Rabinowitz, P. J. "Truth in Fiction: A Reexamination of Audiences." *Critical Inquiry* 4 (1977): 121–141.

Rad, G. von. "ἡμέρα." *TDNT* 2.943–947.

———. "מלך and מלכות in the OT." 1.565–571 in "βασιλεύς κτλ." *TDNT* 1.564–593.

———. *The Problem of the Hexateuch and Other Essays*. ET E. W. Trueman. Edinburgh and London: Dicken, Oliver & Boyd, 1966.

Rankin, O. S. *The Origins of the Festival of Hanukkah: The Jewish New-Age Festival*. Edinburgh: T&T Clark, 1930.

Rapinchuk, M. E. "The End of the Exile: A Neglected Aspect of Matthean Christological Typology." Ph.D. diss., Trinity Evangelical Divinity School, 1996.

Reif, S. C. Review of D. I. Brewer, *Techniques and Assumptions in Jewish Exegesis Before 70 CE*. *VT* 44 (1994): 422.

Reim, G. "Nordreich–Südreich. Der vierte Evangelist als Vertreter christlicher Nordreichs-theologie." *BZ* 36 (1992): 235–240.

———. *Studien zum alttestamentlichen Hintergrund des Johannesevangeliums*. SNTSMS 22. Cambridge: Cambridge University Press, 1974.

Reinhartz, A. *The Word in the World: The Cosmological Tale in the Fourth Gospel*. SBLMS 45. Atlanta: Scholars Press, 1992.

Rensberger, D. *Overcoming the World: Politics and Community in the Gospel of John*. Cambridge: Cambridge University Press, 1989.

Ringren, H. *Israelitische Religion*. Stuttgart: W. Kohlhammer, 1963.

Robert, R. "Étude littéraire de Jean VIII, 21–59." *RThom* 89 (1989): 71–84.

———. "Le malentendu sur le Nom divin au chapitre VIII du quatrième évangile." *RThom* 88 (1988): 278–287.

Robertson, R. G. "Introduction to Ezekiel the Tragedian." 2.803–807 in *The Old Testament Pseudepigrapha*. Edited by J. H. Charlesworth. 2 vols. Garden City, N.Y.: Doubleday, 1985.

Robinson, J. A. T. "Elijah, John, and Jesus: an Essay in Detection." *NTS* 4 (1957–1958): 263–281.

———. "The Parable of John 10.1–5." *ZNW* 46 (1955): 233–240.

Robinson, J. M. "Die Hodajot-Formel in Gebet und Hymnus des Früh-Christentums." Pages 194–235 in *Apophoreta*. FS Ernest Haenchen. BZNW 30. Leiden: Brill, 1964.

Robinson, W. "Psalm 118: A Liturgy for the Admission of a Proselyte." *CQR* 144 (1947): 179–183.

Rodgerson, J. W., and J. W. McKay. *Psalms 101–150*. The Cambridge Commentary on the New English Bible. Cambridge: Cambridge University Press, 1977.

Rodríguez Ruiz, M. "El discurso del Buen Pastor (Jn 10,1–18). Coherencia teologico-literaria e interpretacion." *EstBib* 48 (1990): 5–45

Roland, C. C. "Apocalyptic Literature." Pages 170–189 in *It is Written: Scripture Citing Scripture: Essays in Honour of Barnabas Lindars*. Edited by D. A. Carson and H. G. M. Williamson. Cambridge: Cambridge University Press, 1986.

Rosner, B. S. *Paul, Scripture and Ethics: A Study of 1 Corinthians 5–7*. AGJU 22. Brill: Leiden, 1994.

Roth, C. "Messianic Symbols in Palestinian Archaeology." *PEQ* 87 (1955): 151–164.

Roth, W. "Scriptural Coding in the Fourth Gospel." *BR* 32 (1987): 6–29.

Rousseau, J. J., and R. Arav. *Jesus and His World: An Archaeological and Cultural Dictionary*. Minneapolis: Fortress, 1995.

Rowley, H. H. *Worship in Ancient Israel: Its Forms and Meaning*. London: SPCK, 1967.

Rubenstein, J. L. *The History of Sukkot in the Second Temple and Rabbinic Periods*. BJS 302. Atlanta: Scholars Press, 1995.

Rusche, H. "Das letzte gemeinsame Gebet Jesu mit seinen Jüngern. Der Psalm 136." *Wissenschaft und Weisheit* 51 (1988): 210–212.

Sabbe, M. "John 10 and its relationship to the Synoptic Gospels." Pages 75–93 in *The Shepherd Discourse of John 10 and its Context: Studies by Members of the Johannine Writings Seminar*. Edited by J. Beutler and R. T. Fortna. SNTSMS 67. Cambridge: Cambridge University Press, 1991.

Safrai, S. "Pilgrimage to Jerusalem at the end of the Second Temple Period." Pages 12–21 in *Studies on the Jewish Background of the New Testament*. Edited by O. Michel. Assen: Van Gordum, 1969.

Sahlin, H. *Zur Typologie des Johannesevangeliums*. UUA 1950/4. Uppsala: Lundequistska 1950.

Saldarini, A. J. Review of D. I. Brewer, *Techniques and Assumptions in Jewish Exegesis Before 70 CE*. *JBL* 113 (1994): 719–720.

Sanders, E. P. *Jesus and Judaism*. Philadelphia: Fortress Press, 1985.

———. *Judaism: Practice and Belief, 63 BCE–66 CE*. London: SCM Press; Philadelphia: Trinity Press International, 1994.

Sanders, J. A. "A New Testament Hermeneutic Fabric: Psalm 118 in the Entrance Narrative." Pages 177–190 in *Early Jewish and Christian Exegesis: Studies in Memory of W. H. Brownlee*. Edited by C. A. Evans and W. F. Stinespring. Homage Series 10. Atlanta: Scholars Press, 1987.

———. "Paul and Theological History." Pages 52–57 in *Paul and the Scriptures of Israel*. Edited by C. A. Evans and J. A. Sanders. JSNTSup 83. SSEJC 1. Sheffield: JSOT Press, 1992.

Sandmell, S. "Parallelomania." *JBL* 81 (1962): 1–13.

Sandvik, B. *Das Kommen des Herrn beim Abendmahl im Neuen Testament.* ATANT 58. Zürich: Zwigli, 1970.

Schaper, J. *Eschatology in the Greek Psalter.* WUNT 2/76. Tübingen: J.C.B. Mohr (Paul Siebeck), 1995.

Schenke, L. "Das Rätsel von Tür und Hirt. Wer es löst, hat gewonnen!" *TTZ* 105 (1996): 81–100.

Schmidt, H. *Die Thronfahrt Jahwes am Fest der Jahreswende im alten Israel.* Tübingen: J.C.B. Mohr (Paul Siebeck), 1927.

Schnackenburg, R. "'Der Vater, der mich gesandt hat': Zur johanneischen Christologie": Pages 274–291 in *Anfänge der Christologie: Festschrift für Ferdinand Hahn zum 65. Geburtstag.* Edited by C. Breytenbach and H. Paulsen. Göttingen: Vandenhoeck & Ruprecht, 1991.

_____. *The Gospel According to John.* ET K. Smyth, C. Hastings et al. 3 vols. HTCNT. London: Burns & Oates, 1968–1982.

Schneider, J. "ἔρχομαι." *TDNT* 2.666–675.

_____. "Zur Komposition von Joh. 10." ConBNT 11. FS A. Fridrichsen. Lund: Gleerup, 1947: 220–225.

Schrenk, G. "πατήρ." *TDNT* 5.974–1014.

Schuchard, B. G. *Scripture within Scripture: The Interrelationship of Form and Function in the Explicit Old Testament Citations in the Gospel of John.* SBLDS 133. Atlanta: Scholars Press, 1992.

Schürer, E. *The History of the Jewish People in the Age of Jesus Christ (175 B.C.–A.D. 135).* Rev. and ed. by G. Vermes, F. Millar, and M. Black. 3 vols. Edinburgh: T&T Clark, 1973–1987,

Schweizer, E. *Ego Eimi: Die religionsgeschichtliche Herkunft und theologische Bedeutung der johanneischen Bildreden, zugleich ein Beitrag zur Quellenfrage des vierten Evangeliums.* FRLANT 56. Göttingen: Vandenhoeck & Ruprecht, 1939.

_____. *The Good News According to Mark.* ET D. H. Madvig. Atlanta: John Knox Press, 1970.

_____. *The Good News According to Matthew.* ET D. E. Green. Atlanta: John Knox Press, 1975.

Scott, J. A. "'For as many as are of works of the law are under a curse' (Galatians 3.10)." Pages 187–221 in *Paul and the Scriptures of Israel.* Edited by C. A. Evans and J. A. Sanders. JSNTSup 83. SSEJC 1. Sheffield: JSOT Press, 1992.

Scott, J. J. Jr. *Customs and Controversies: Intertestamental Jewish Backgrounds of the New Testament.* Grand Rapids: Baker, 1995.

Scott, J. M., ed. *Exile: Old Testament, Jewish and Christian Conceptions.* Leiden: Brill, 1997.

Segal, J. B. *The Hebrew Passover: From the Earliest Times to A.D. 70.* London Oriental Series 12. London: Oxford University Press, 1963.

Segovia, F. F. "The Journey(s) of Jesus to Jerusalem: Plotting and Gospel Intertextuality." Pages 535–541in *John and the Synoptics.* Edited by A. Denaux. Bibliotheca Ephemeridum Theologicarum Lovaniensium CI. Leuven: Leuven University Press, 1992.

Seybold, K. *Die Wallfahrtspsalmen: Studien zur Enstehungsgeschichte von Psalm 120–134.* Biblische-Theologische Studien 3. Neukirchen-Vluyn: Neukirchener Verlag, 1978.

Shirbroun, G. F. "The Giving of the Name of God to Jesus in John 17:11, 12." Ph.D. diss., Princeton Theological Seminary, 1985.

Simonis, A. J. *Die Hirtenrede im Johannes-Evangelium: Versuch einer Analyse von Johannes 10,1–18 nach Entstehung, Hintergrund und Inhalt.* AnBib 29. Rome: Pontifical Bible Institute, 1967.

Skehan, P. W. "A Liturgical Complex in 11QPs[a]." *CBQ* 34 (1973): 195–205.

_____. "A Psalm Manuscript From Qumran (4Q Ps[b])." *CBQ* 26 (1964): 313–322.

Smith, C. W. F. "No Time for Figs." *JBL* 79 (1960): 315–327.

_____. "Tabernacles in the Fourth Gospel and Mark." *NTS* 9 (1962–1963): 130–146.

Smith, D. M. *John Among the Gospels: The Relationship in Twentieth-Century Research.* Minneapolis: Fortress, 1992.

_____. "John and the Synoptics: Some Dimensions of the Problem." Pages 145–172 in *Johannine Christianity: Essays on its Setting, Sources, and Theology.* Columbia, S.C.: University of South Carolina Press, 1984.

_____. "John, the Synoptics, and the Canonical Approach to Exegesis." Pages 166–180 in *Tradition and Interpretation in the New Testament.* Edited by G. F. Hawthorne and O. Betz. Grand Rapids: Eerdmans; Tübingen: J.C.B. Mohr (Paul Siebeck), 1987.

_____. "John 12:12ff. and the Question of John's use of the Synoptics." Pages 97–105 in *Johannine Christianity: Essays on its Setting, Sources, and Theology.* Columbia, S.C.: University of South Carolina Press, 1984. Repr. from *JBL* 82 (1963): 58–64.

_____. "The Setting and Shape of a Johannine Narrative Source." Pages 80–93 in *Johannine Christianity: Essays on its Setting, Sources, and Theology.* Columbia, S.C.: University of South Carolina Press, 1984. Repr. from *JBL* 95 (1976): 231–241.

Smith, M. "Goodenough's Jewish Symbols in Retrospect." *JBL* 86 (1967): 53–68.

Smith, R. H. "Exodus Typology in the Fourth Gospel." *JBL* 81 (1962): 329–342.

Snaith, N. H. *The Jewish New Year Festival: Its Origins and Development.* London, 1948.

Snodgrass, K. "The Christological Stone Testimonia in the New Testament." Ph.D. diss., University of St. Andrews, 1973.

_____. *The Parable of the Wicked Tenants: An Inquiry into Parable Interpretation.* WUNT 27. Tübingen: J.C.B. Mohr (Paul Siebeck), 1983.

_____. "The Use of the Old Testament in the New." Pages 29–51 in *The Right Doctrine from the Wrong Texts?* Edited by G. K. Beale. Grand Rapids: Baker, 1994.

Stanley, C. D. *Paul and the Language of Scripture: Citation Technique in the Pauline Epistles and Contemporary Literature.* SNTSMS 72. Cambridge: Cambridge University Press, 1992.

_____. "The Social Environment of 'Free' Biblical Quotations in the New Testament." Pages 18–27 in *Early Christian Interpretation of the Scriptures of Israel: Investigations and Proposals.* Edited by C. A. Evans and J. A. Sanders. JSNTSup 148. SSEJC 5. Sheffield: Sheffield Academic Press, 1997.

Stather Hunt, B. P. W. *Some Johannine Problems.* London: Skeffington, 1958.

Stauffer, E. *Jesus and His Story.* ET R. and C. Winston. New York: Knopf, 1960.

_____. "Probleme der Priestertradition." *TLZ* 81 (1956): 135–150.

Stein, S. "The Liturgy of Hanukkah and the First Two Books of Maccabees." *JJS* 5 (1954): 100–106; 148–155.

Strack, H. L. and P. Billerbeck. *Kommentar zum Neuen Testament aus Talmud und Midrasch.* 4 vols. 3rd ed. Munich: Beck, 1951–1956.

Strauss, M. L. *The Davidic Messiah in Luke-Acts: The Promise and its Fulfillment in Lukan Christology.* JSNTSup 110. Sheffield: Sheffield Academic Press, 1995.

Stuhlmacher, P. *Biblische Theologie des Neuen Testaments.* 2 vols. Göttingen: Vandenhoeck & Ruprecht, 1999.

Sundberg, A. C. "On Testimonies." *NovT* 3 (1959): 268–281. Repr. as "Response Against C. H. Dodd's View: On Testimonies." Pages 182–194 in *The Right Doctrine from* the Wrong Texts? Essays on the Use of the Old Testament in the New.* Edited by G. K. Beale. Grand Rapids: Baker, 1994.

Swancutt, D. M. "Hungers Assuaged by the Bread From Heaven: 'Eating Jesus' as Isaian Call to Belief: The Confluence of Isaiah 55 and Psalm 78(77) in John 6.22–71." Pages 218–251 in *Early Christian Interpretation of the Scriptures of Israel: Investigations and Proposals.* Edited by C. A. Evans and J. A. Sanders. JSNTSup 148. SSEJC 5. Sheffield: Sheffield Academic Press, 1997.

Swartley, W. M. *Israel's Scripture Traditions and the Synoptic Gospels.* Peabody, Mass.: Hendrickson, 1994.

Swete, H. B. *The Gospel according to St. Mark.* London: Macmillan, 1908.

Talmon, S. *"Pisqah be'emsa' pasuq* and 11QPs^a." *Textus* 5 (1966): 11–21.

Taylor, V. *The Gospel According to St. Mark.* 2nd ed. London: Macmillan; New York: St. Martin's, 1966.

Temple, S. *The Core of the Fourth Gospel.* London: Mowbrays, 1975.

Tenney, M. C. "Literary Keys to the Fourth Gospel: The Old Testament and the Fourth Gospel." *BSac* 120 (1963): 300–308.

Thackeray, H. St. J. *The Septuagint and Jewish Worship: A Study in Origins.* London: Oxford University Press, 1921.

Thompson, M. *Clothed with Christ: The Example and Teaching of Jesus in Romans 12.1–15.13.* JSNTSup 59. Sheffield: JSOT Press, 1991.

Thyen, H. "Johannes 10 im Kontext des vierten Evangeliums." Pages 116–134 in *The Shepherd Discourse of John 10 and its Context: Studies by Members of the Johannine Writings Seminar.* Edited by J. Beutler and R. T. Fortna. SNTSMS 67. Cambridge: Cambridge University Press, 1991.

Tilborg, S. van. "Matthew 27.3–10: an Intertextual Reading." Pages 159–174 in *Intertextuality in Biblical Writings.* Edited by S. Draisma. Kampen: J. H. Kok, 1989.

———. *Reading John in Ephesus.* NovTSup 83. Leiden: Brill, 1996.

Torrey, C. C. "The Aramaic Origin of the Gospel of John." *HTR* 16 (1923): 305–344.

———. *The Four Gospels: A New Translation.* 2nd ed. New York and London: Harper, 1933.

———. *Our Translated Gospels.* New York and London: Harper, 1936.

Tragan, P.-R. *La parabole du 'Pasteur' et ses explications: Jean, 10,1–18: La genèse, les milieux littéraires.* SA 67. Rome: Editrice Anselmiana, 1980.

Tsuchido, K. "Tradition and Redaction in John 12.1–42." *NTS* 30 (1984): 609–619.

Tuckett, C. M. "Introduction." Pages xiii–xxiv in *The Scriptures in the Gospels.* Edited by C. M. Tuckett. Leuven: Leuven University Press, 1997.

———, ed. *The Scriptures in the Gospels.* Leuven: Leuven University Press, 1997.

Tuñí, J. O. "Personajes veterotestamentarios en el Evangelio de Juan." *Revista Latinoamericana de Teologia* 10/30 (1993): 279–292.

Turner, J. D. "The history of religions background of John 10." Pages 33–52 in *The Shepherd Discourse of John 10 and its Context: Studies by Members of the Johannine Writings Seminar.* Edited by J. Beutler and R. T. Fortna. SNTSMS 67. Cambridge: Cambridge University Press, 1991.

Ulfgard, H. *Feast and Future: Revelation 7:9–17 and the Feast of Tabernacles.* Stockholm: Almqvist & Wiksell, 1989.

Urban, L. and P. Henry. "'Before Abraham was I am': Does Philo Explain John 8:56–58?" *SPhilo* 6 (1979–1980): 157–195.

Van Wolde, E. "Texts in Dialogue with Texts: Intertextuality in the Ruth and Tamar Narratives." *BibInt* 5 (1997): 1–28.

———. "Trendy Intertextuality?" Pages 43–49 in *Intertextuality in Biblical Writings: Essays in honour of Bas van Iersel.* Edited by S. Draisma. Kampen: J. H. Kok, 1989.

VanderKam, J. C. "Hanukkah: Its Timing and Significance According to 1 and 2 Macca-
bees." *JSP* 1(1987): 23–40.
_____. "John 10 and the Feast of the Dedication." Pages 203–214 in *Of Scribes and
Scrolls: Studies in the Hebrew Bible, Intertestamental Judaism and Christian
Origins.* Edited by H. W. Attridge. Lanham: University Press of America, 1990.
VanGemeren, W. A. *Psalms.* Vol. 5 of The Expositor's Bible Commentary. Grand Rapids:
Zondervan, 1991.
Vargha, T. "'Abraham . . . exultavit, ut videret diem meum': Ioh. 8, 56." *VD* 10 (1930):
43–46.
Vaux, R. de. *Ancient Israel: Its Life and Institutions.* ET J. McHugh. London: Darton,
Longman & Todd, 1962.
Velasco Arenas, J. "'Yo soy la puerta' (Jn 10,7.9). Trasfondo y sentido de la imagen
cristológica de la puerta." *Carmelus* (Rome) 37/1 (1990): 38–80.
Vermes, G. *Jesus the Jew: A Historian's Reading of the Gospels.* London: Collins, 1973.
Verseput, D. J. "Jesus' Pilgrimage to Jerusalem and Encounter in the Temple: A Geogra-
phical Motif in Matthew's Gospel." *NovT* 36 (1994): 105–121.
Visser 't Hooft, W. A. "Triumphalism in the Gospels." *SJT* 38 (1985): 491–504.
Volz, P. *Das Neujahrsfest Yahwes.* 1912.
Vorster, W. S. "Intertextuality and Redaktionsgeschichte." Pages 15–26 in *Intertextuality
in Biblical Writings: Essays in honour of Bas van Iersel.* Edited by S. Draisma.
Kampen: J. H. Kok, 1989.
Wacholder, B. Z. "David's Eschatological Psalter: 11Q Psalms[a]." *HUCA* 59 (1988): 23–72.
Wagner, J. R. "Psalm 118 in Luke-Acts: Tracing a Narrative Thread." Pages 154–178
in *Early Christian Interpretation of the Scriptures of Israel: Investigations and
Proposals.* Edited by C. A. Evans and J. A. Sanders. JSNTSup 148. SSEJC 5.
Sheffield: Sheffield Academic Press, 1997.
Wahlde, U. C. von. "The Johannine 'Jews': A Critical Survey." *NTS* 28 (1982): 33–60.
Watts, R. E. "Consolation or Confrontation? Isaiah 40–55 and the Delay of the New
Exodus." *TynBul* 41/1 (1990): 31–59.
_____. *Isaiah's New Exodus and Mark.* WUNT 2/88. Tübingen: J.C.B. Mohr (Paul Sie-
beck), 1997.
Webb, R. L. *John the Baptizer and Prophet: A Socio-Historical Study.* JSNTSup 62.
Sheffield: Sheffield Academic Press, 1991.
Weigandt, P. "Zum Text von Jon X 7." *NovT* 9 (1967): 43–51.
Weiser, A. *The Psalms.* ET H. Hartwell. London: SCM Press, 1962.
Weren, W. "Jesus' Entry Into Jerusalem: Mt 21,1–17 in the Light of the Hebrew Bible
and the Septuagint." Pages 117–141 in *The Scriptures in the Gospels.* Edited
by C. M. Tuckett. Leuven: Leuven University Press, 1997.
_____. "Psalm 2 in Luke-Acts: an Intertextual Study." Pages 189–203 in *Intertextuality
in Biblical Writings.* Edited by S. Draisma. Kampen: J. H. Kok, 1989.
Werner, E. "'Hosanna' in the Gospels." *JBL* 65 (1946): 97–122.
Westermann, C. *The Gospel of John in Light of the Old Testament.* ET S. Schatzman.
Peabody, Mass.: Hendrickson, 1988.
_____. *Praise and Lament in the Psalms.* ET K. R. Crim and R. N. Soulen. Edinburgh:
T&T Clark, 1981.
_____. *The Psalms: Structure, Content and Message.* ET R. D. Gehrke. Minneapolis:
Augsburg, 1980.
Wilcox, M. "The 'Prayer' of Jesus in John XI.41b–42." *NTS* 24 (1977–1978): 128–132.
Wiles, M. F. *The Spiritual Gospel: The Interpretation of the Fourth Gospel in the Early
Church.* Cambridge: Cambridge University Press, 1960.

Williams, C. H. *I am He: The Interpretation of "Ani Hu" in Jewish and Early Christian Literature.* WUNT 2/113. Tübingen: Mohr Siebeck, 1999.

Williams, H. H. Drake III. *The Wisdom of the Wise: The Presence and Function of Scripture within 1 Cor. 1:18–3:23.* AGJU 49. Leiden: Brill, 2001.

Williford, D. D. "A Study of the Religious Feasts as Background for the Organization and Message of the Gospel of John." Ph.D. diss., Southwestern Baptist Theological Seminary, 1981.

Wilson, G. H. *The Editing of the Hebrew Psalter.* Chico, Calif.: Scholars Press, 1985.

_____. "Shaping the Psalter: A Consideration of Editorial Linkage in the Book of Psalms." Pages 72–82 in *The Shape and Shaping of the Psalter.* Edited by J. C. McCann. JSOTSup 159. Sheffield: JSOT Press, 1993.

_____. "Understanding the Purposeful Arrangement of Psalms in the Psalter: Pitfalls and Promise." Pages 42–51 in *The Shape and Shaping of the Psalter.* Edited by J. C. McCann. JSOTSup 159. Sheffield: JSOT Press, 1993.

Wintermute, O. S. "Jubilees: A New Translation and Introduction." 2.35–51 in *The Old Testament Pseudepigrapha.* Edited by J. H. Charlesworth. 2 vols. ABRL. New York: Doubleday, 1985.

Wright, N. T. "In Grateful Dialogue: *A Response.*" Pages 244–277 in *Jesus and the Restoration of Israel: A Critical Assessment of N. T. Wright's* Jesus and the Victory of God. Edited by C. C. Newman. Downer's Grove, Ill.: InterVarsity; Carlisle: Paternoster, 1999.

_____. *Jesus and the Victory of God.* Vol. 2 of *Christian Origins and the Question of God.* Minneapolis: Fortress, 1996.

_____. *The New Testament and the People of God.* Vol. 1 of *Christian Origins and the Question of God.* Minneapolis: Fortress, 1992.

Wood, H. G. "Interpreting This Time." *NTS* 2 (1956): 262–266.

Wyller, E. A. "In Solomon's Porch: A Henological Analysis of the Architectonic of the Fourth Gospel." *ST* 42 (1988): 151–167.

Yadin, Y. "Another Fragment (E) of the Psalms Scroll from Qumran Cave 11 (11QPs^a)." *Textus* 5 (1966): 1–10.

_____. "More on the Letters of Bar Kochba." *BA* 24 (1961): 89–92.

Yee, G. A. *Jewish Feasts and The Gospel of John.* Wilmington, Del.: Michael Glazier, 1989.

Young, F. W. "A Study of the Relation of Isaiah to the Fourth Gospel." *ZNW* 46 (1955): 215–231.

Zeitlin, S. "The Hallel: A Historical Study of the Canonization of the Hebrew Liturgy." *JQR* 53 (1962): 22–29.

_____. "Hanukkah: Its Origin and its Significance." *JQR* 29 (1938–1939): 1–36.

Zenger, E. "New Approaches to the Study of the Psalms." *Proceedings of the Irish Biblical Association* 17 (1994): 37–54.

Zerr, B. *The Psalms: A New Translation.* New York: Paulist, 1978.

Zerwick, M. *Biblical Greek Illustrated by Examples.* ET J. Smith. Scripta Pontificii Instituti Biblici 114. Rome, 1963.

Zimmerman, H. "Das Absolute Ἐγώ εἰμι als die neutestamentliche Offenbarungsformel." *BZ* 4/1 (1960): 54–69, 266–276.

Index of References

Contents:
1. Old Testament;
2. Old Testament Apocrypha;
3. Pseudepigrapha;
4. New Testament;
5. Qumran;
6. Hellenistic-Jewish Writings;
7. Rabbinic Writings;
8. Early Christian and Patristic Literature;
9. Graeco-Roman Writings.

1. Old Testament

Genesis

2.11	354n
2.13	354n
15	292, 293n
15.12ff	294n
17	295n
17.17	293n, 294
18.1–15	294n
21.1–7	294
22.8	294, 294n
24.1	293
49	42n, 260, 260n, 273n, 276n
49.10	108n, 248n, 276
49.10–11	276
49.10–12	260, 265n
49.11	107n, 276, 276n, 282

Exodus

3.12	160n, 161n
3.14	308
4.8	161n
4.9	161n
4.14	288n
4.17	161n
4.28	161n
4.30	161n
7.3	161n

7.14–24	160n
8.23	161n
9.1–7	160n
9.8–12	160n
9.13–35	160n
10.1	161n
10.1–20	160n
10.2	161n
10.21–29	160n
11.1–12.32	160n
12.2	79n
12.13	161n
12.22	157
12.34	157
12.46	142
13.9	161n
13.16	161n
14–15	78, 82
14.11	78n
14.30–31	78n
15	78n, 128n
15.1–18	77
15.2a	77
15.2b	77
15.6	77, 77n
15.12	77n
15.18	237n
15.23–26	160n
15.24	158
16.2	158
16.4	141n

3. Pseudepigrapha

4. New Testament

6. Hellenistic-Jewish Writings

Josephus

8. Early Christian and Patristic Literature

9. Graeco-Roman Writings

Selective Index of Modern Authors

Index of Subjects

Wissenschaftliche Untersuchungen zum Neuen Testament

Alphabetical Index of the First and Second Series

Wissenschaftliche Untersuchungen zum Neuen Testament

- Studien zur Theologie, Sprache und Umwelt des Neuen Testaments. Ed. von D. Sänger. 1998. *Volume 107.*
Burnett, Richard: Karl Barth's Theological Exegesis. 2001. *Volume II/145.*
Byrskog, Samuel: Story as History – History as Story. 2000. *Volume 123.*
Cancik, Hubert (Ed.): Markus-Philologie. 1984. *Volume 33.*
Capes, David B.: Old Testament Yaweh Texts in Paul's Christology. 1992. *Volume II/47.*
Caragounis, Chrys C.: The Son of Man. 1986. *Volume 38.*
- see Fridrichsen, Anton.
Carleton Paget, James: The Epistle of Barnabas. 1994. *Volume II/64.*
Carson, D.A., O'Brien, Peter T. and Mark Seifrid (Ed.): Justification and Variegated Nomism: A Fresh Appraisal of Paul and Second Temple Judaism. Volume 1: The Complexities of Second Temple Judaism. *Volume II/140.*
Ciampa, Roy E.: The Presence and Function of Scripture in Galatians 1 and 2. 1998. *Volume II/102.*
Classen, Carl Joachim: Rhetorical Criticsm of the New Testament. 2000. *Volume 128.*
Crump, David: Jesus the Intercessor. 1992. *Volume II/49.*
Dahl, Nils Alstrup: Studies in Ephesians. 2000. *Volume 131.*
Deines, Roland: Jüdische Steingefäße und pharisäische Frömmigkeit. 1993. *Volume II/52.*
- Die Pharisäer. 1997. *Volume 101.*
Dettwiler, Andreas and Jean Zumstein (Ed.): Kreuzestheologie im Neuen Testament. 2002. *Volume 151.*
Dietzfelbinger, Christian: Der Abschied des Kommenden. 1997. *Volume 95.*
Dobbeler, Axel von: Glaube als Teilhabe. 1987. *Volume II/22.*
Du Toit, David S.: Theios Anthropos. 1997. *Volume II/91*
Dunn, James D.G. (Ed.): Jews and Christians. 1992. *Volume 66.*
- Paul and the Mosaic Law. 1996. *Volume 89.*
Dunn, James D.G., Hans Klein, Ulrich Luz and Vasile Mihoc (Ed.): Auslegung der Bibel in orthodoxer und westlicher Perspektive. 2000. *Volume 130.*
Ebertz, Michael N.: Das Charisma des Gekreuzigten. 1987. *Volume 45.*
Eckstein, Hans-Joachim: Der Begriff Syneidesis bei Paulus. 1983. *Volume II/10.*
- Verheißung und Gesetz. 1996. *Volume 86.*
Ego, Beate: Im Himmel wie auf Erden. 1989. *Volume II/34*

Ego, Beate and Lange, Armin with Pilhofer, Peter (Ed.): Gemeinde ohne Tempel – Community without Temple. 1999. *Volume 118.*
Eisen, Ute E.: see Paulsen, Henning.
Ellis, E. Earle: Prophecy and Hermeneutic in Early Christianity. 1978. *Volume 18.*
- The Old Testament in Early Christianity. 1991. *Volume 54.*
Endo, Masanobu: Creation and Christology. 2002. *Volume 149.*
Ennulat, Andreas: Die 'Minor Agreements'. 1994. *Volume II/62.*
Ensor, Peter W.: Jesus and His 'Works'. 1996. *Volume II/85.*
Eskola, Timo: Messiah and the Throne. 2001. *Volume II/142.*
- Theodicy and Predestination in Pauline Soteriology. 1998. *Volume II/100.*
Fatehi, Mehrdad: The Spirit's Relation to the Risen Lord in Paul. 2000. *Volume II/128.*
Feldmeier, Reinhard: Die Krisis des Gottessohnes. 1987. *Volume II/21.*
- Die Christen als Fremde. 1992. *Volume 64.*
Feldmeier, Reinhard and Ulrich Heckel (Ed.): Die Heiden. 1994. *Volume 70.*
Fletcher-Louis, Crispin H.T.: Luke-Acts: Angels, Christology and Soteriology. 1997. *Volume II/94.*
Förster, Niclas: Marcus Magus. 1999. *Volume 114.*
Forbes, Christopher Brian: Prophecy and Inspired Speech in Early Christianity and its Hellenistic Environment. 1995. *Volume II/75.*
Fornberg, Tord: see Fridrichsen, Anton.
Fossum, Jarl E.: The Name of God and the Angel of the Lord. 1985. *Volume 36.*
Fotopoulos, John: Food Offered to Idols in Roman Corinth. 2003. *Volume II/151.*
Frenschkowski, Marco: Offenbarung und Epiphanie. Volume 1 1995. *Volume II/79* – Volume 2 1997. *Volume II/80.*
Frey, Jörg: Eugen Drewermann und die biblische Exegese. 1995. *Volume II/71.*
- Die johanneische Eschatologie. Volume I. 1997. *Volume 96.* – Volume II. 1998. *Volume 110.*
- Volume III. 2000. *Volume 117.*
Freyne, Sean: Galilee and Gospel. 2000. *Volume 125.*
Fridrichsen, Anton: Exegetical Writings. Edited by C.C. Caragounis and T. Fornberg. 1994. *Volume 76.*
Garlington, Don B.: 'The Obedience of Faith'. 1991. *Volume II/38.*
- Faith, Obedience, and Perseverance. 1994. *Volume 79.*

Garnet, Paul: Salvation and Atonement in the Qumran Scrolls. 1977. *Volume II/3.*

Gese, Michael: Das Vermächtnis des Apostels. 1997. *Volume II/99.*

Gräbe, Petrus J.: The Power of God in Paul's Letters. 2000. *Volume II/123.*

Gräßer, Erich: Der Alte Bund im Neuen. 1985. *Volume 35.*

– Forschungen zur Apostelgeschichte. 2001. *Volume 137.*

Green, Joel B.: The Death of Jesus. 1988. *Volume II/33.*

Gundry Volf, Judith M.: Paul and Perseverance. 1990. *Volume II/37.*

Hafemann, Scott J.: Suffering and the Spirit. 1986. *Volume II/19.*

– Paul, Moses, and the History of Israel. 1995. *Volume 81.*

Hahn, Johannes (Ed.): Zerstörungen des Jerusalemer Tempels. 2002. *Volume 147.*

Hannah, Darrel D.: Michael and Christ. 1999. *Volume II/109.*

Hamid-Khani, Saeed: Relevation and Concealment of Christ. 2000. *Volume II/120.*

Hartman, Lars: Text-Centered New Testament Studies. Ed. von D. Hellholm. 1997. *Volume 102.*

Hartog, Paul: Polycarp and the New Testament. 2001. *Volume II/134.*

Heckel, Theo K.: Der Innere Mensch. 1993. *Volume II/53.*

– Vom Evangelium des Markus zum viergestaltigen Evangelium. 1999. *Volume 120.*

Heckel, Ulrich: Kraft in Schwachheit. 1993. *Volume II/56.*

– Der Segen im Neuen Testament. 2002. *Volume 150.*

– see *Feldmeier, Reinhard.*

– see *Hengel, Martin.*

Heiligenthal, Roman: Werke als Zeichen. 1983. *Volume II/9.*

Hellholm, D.: see *Hartman, Lars.*

Hemer, Colin J.: The Book of Acts in the Setting of Hellenistic History. 1989. *Volume 49.*

Hengel, Martin: Judentum und Hellenismus. 1969, ³1988. *Volume 10.*

– Die johanneische Frage. 1993. *Volume 67.*

– Judaica et Hellenistica.
Kleine Schriften I. 1996. *Volume 90.*

– Judaica, Hellenistica et Christiana.
Kleine Schriften II. 1999. *Volume 109.*

– Paulus und Jakobus.
Kleine Schriften III. 2002. *Volume 141.*

Hengel, Martin and *Ulrich Heckel* (Ed.): Paulus und das antike Judentum. 1991. *Volume 58.*

Hengel, Martin and *Hermut Löhr* (Ed.): Schriftauslegung im antiken Judentum und im Urchristentum. 1994. *Volume 73.*

Hengel, Martin and *Anna Maria Schwemer:* Paulus zwischen Damaskus und Antiochien. 1998. *Volume 108.*

– Der messianische Anspruch Jesu und die Anfänge der Christologie. 2001. *Volume 138.*

Hengel, Martin and *Anna Maria Schwemer* (Ed.): Königsherrschaft Gottes und himmlischer Kult. 1991. *Volume 55.*

– Die Septuaginta. 1994. *Volume 72.*

Hengel, Martin; Siegfried Mittmann and *Anna Maria Schwemer* (Ed.): La Cité de Dieu / Die Stadt Gottes. 2000. *Volume 129.*

Herrenbrück, Fritz: Jesus und die Zöllner. 1990. *Volume II/41.*

Herzer, Jens: Paulus oder Petrus? 1998. *Volume 103.*

Hoegen-Rohls, Christina: Der nachösterliche Johannes. 1996. *Volume II/84.*

Hofius, Otfried: Katapausis. 1970. *Volume 11.*

– Der Vorhang vor dem Thron Gottes. 1972. *Volume 14.*

– Der Christushymnus Philipper 2,6-11. 1976, ²1991. *Volume 17.*

– Paulusstudien. 1989, ²1994. *Volume 51.*

– Neutestamentliche Studien. 2000. *Volume 132.*

– Paulusstudien II. 2002. *Volume 143.*

Hofius, Otfried and *Hans-Christian Kammler:* Johannesstudien. 1996. *Volume 88.*

Holtz, Traugott: Geschichte und Theologie des Urchristentums. 1991. *Volume 57.*

Hommel, Hildebrecht: Sebasmata. Volume 1 1983. *Volume 31* – Volume 2 1984. *Volume 32.*

Hvalvik, Reidar: The Struggle for Scripture and Covenant. 1996. *Volume II/82.*

Joubert, Stephan: Paul as Benefactor. 2000. *Volume II/124.*

Jungbauer, Harry: „Ehre Vater und Mutter". 2002. *Volume II/146.*

Kähler, Christoph: Jesu Gleichnisse als Poesie und Therapie. 1995. *Volume 78.*

Kamlah, Ehrhard: Die Form der katalogischen Paränese im Neuen Testament. 1964. *Volume 7.*

Kammler, Hans-Christian: Christologie und Eschatologie. 2000. *Volume 126.*

– see *Hofius, Otfried.*

Kelhoffer, James A.: Miracle and Mission. 1999. *Volume II/112.*

Kieffer, René and *Jan Bergman (Ed.):* La Main de Dieu / Die Hand Gottes. 1997. *Volume 94.*

Kim, Seyoon: The Origin of Paul's Gospel. 1981, ²1984. *Volume II/4.*

– "The 'Son of Man'" as the Son of God. 1983. *Volume 30.*

Klauck, Hans-Josef: Religion und Gesellschaft im frühen Christentum. 2003. *Volume 152.*

Klein, Hans: see *Dunn, James D.G..*

Kleinknecht, Karl Th.: Der leidende Gerechtfertigte. 1984, ²1988. *Volume II/13.*

Klinghardt, Matthias: Gesetz und Volk Gottes. 1988. *Volume II/32.*

Köhler, Wolf-Dietrich: Rezeption des Matthäusevangeliums in der Zeit vor Irenäus. 1987. *Volume II/24.*

Korn, Manfred: Die Geschichte Jesu in veränderter Zeit. 1993. *Volume II/51.*

Koskenniemi, Erkki: Apollonios von Tyana in der neutestamentlichen Exegese. 1994. *Volume II/61.*

Kraus, Thomas J.: Sprache, Stil und historischer Ort des zweiten Petrusbriefes. 2001. *Volume II/136.*

Kraus, Wolfgang: Das Volk Gottes. 1996. *Volume 85.*

– see *Walter, Nikolaus.*

Kreplin, Matthias: Das Selbstverständnis Jesu. 2001. *Volume II/141.*

Kuhn, Karl G.: Achtzehngebet und Vaterunser und der Reim. 1950. *Volume 1.*

Kvalbein, Hans: see *Ådna, Jostein.*

Laansma, Jon: I Will Give You Rest. 1997. *Volume II/98.*

Labahn, Michael: Offenbarung in Zeichen und Wort. 2000. *Volume II/117.*

Lange, Armin: see *Ego, Beate.*

Lampe, Peter: Die stadtrömischen Christen in den ersten beiden Jahrhunderten. 1987, ²1989. *Volume II/18.*

Landmesser, Christof: Wahrheit als Grundbegriff neutestamentlicher Wissenschaft. 1999. *Volume 113.*

– Jüngerberufung und Zuwendung zu Gott. 2000. *Volume 133.*

Lau, Andrew: Manifest in Flesh. 1996. *Volume II/86.*

Lee, Pilchan: The New Jerusalem in the Book of Relevation. 2000. *Volume II/129.*

Lichtenberger, Hermann: see *Avemarie, Friedrich.*

Lieu, Samuel N.C.: Manichaeism in the Later Roman Empire and Medieval China. ²1992. *Volume 63.*

Loader, William R.G.: Jesus' Attitude Towards the Law. 1997. *Volume II/97.*

Löhr, Gebhard: Verherrlichung Gottes durch Philosophie. 1997. *Volume 97.*

Löhr, Hermut: see *Hengel, Martin.*

Löhr, Winrich Alfried: Basilides und seine Schule. 1995. *Volume 83.*

Luomanen, Petri: Entering the Kingdom of Heaven. 1998. *Volume II/101.*

Luz, Ulrich: see *Dunn, James D.G.*

Maier, Gerhard: Mensch und freier Wille. 1971. *Volume 12.*

– Die Johannesoffenbarung und die Kirche. 1981. *Volume 25.*

Markschies, Christoph: Valentinus Gnosticus? 1992. *Volume 65.*

Marshall, Peter: Enmity in Corinth: Social Conventions in Paul's Relations with the Corinthians. 1987. *Volume II/23.*

Mayer, Annemarie: Sprache der Einheit im Epheserbrief und in der Ökumene. 2002. *Volume II/150.*

McDonough, Sean M.: YHWH at Patmos: Rev. 1:4 in its Hellenistic and Early Jewish Setting. 1999. *Volume II/107.*

McGlynn, Moyna: Divine Judgement and Divine Benevolence in the Book of Wisdom. 2001. *Volume II/139.*

Meade, David G.: Pseudonymity and Canon. 1986. *Volume 39.*

Meadors, Edward P.: Jesus the Messianic Herald of Salvation. 1995. *Volume II/72.*

Meißner, Stefan: Die Heimholung des Ketzers. 1996. *Volume II/87.*

Mell, Ulrich: Die „anderen" Winzer. 1994. *Volume 77.*

Mengel, Berthold: Studien zum Philipperbrief. 1982. *Volume II/8.*

Merkel, Helmut: Die Widersprüche zwischen den Evangelien. 1971. *Volume 13.*

Merklein, Helmut: Studien zu Jesus und Paulus. Volume 1 1987. *Volume 43.* – Volume 2 1998. *Volume 105.*

Metzler, Karin: Der griechische Begriff des Verzeihens. 1991. *Volume II/44.*

Metzner, Rainer: Die Rezeption des Matthäusevangeliums im 1. Petrusbrief. 1995. *Volume II/74.*

– Das Verständnis der Sünde im Johannesevangelium. 2000. *Volume 122.*

Mihoc, Vasile: see *Dunn, James D.G..*

Mittmann, Siegfried: see *Hengel, Martin.*

Mittmann-Richert, Ulrike: Magnifikat und Benediktus. 1996. *Volume II/90.*

Mußner, Franz: Jesus von Nazareth im Umfeld Israels und der Urkirche. Ed. von M. Theobald. 1998. *Volume 111.*

Niebuhr, Karl-Wilhelm: Gesetz und Paränese. 1987. *Volume II/28.*

– Heidenapostel aus Israel. 1992. *Volume 62.*

Nielsen, Anders E.: "Until it is Fullfilled". 2000. *Volume II/126.*

Nissen, Andreas: Gott und der Nächste im antiken Judentum. 1974. *Volume 15.*

Noack, Christian: Gottesbewußtsein. 2000. *Volume II/116.*

Noormann, Rolf: Irenäus als Paulusinterpret. 1994. *Volume II/66.*

Obermann, Andreas: Die christologische Erfüllung der Schrift im Johannesevangelium. 1996. *Volume II/83.*

Okure, Teresa: The Johannine Approach to Mission. 1988. *Volume II/31.*

Oropeza, B. J.: Paul and Apostasy. 2000. *Volume II/115.*

Ostmeyer, Karl-Heinrich: Taufe und Typos. 2000. *Volume II/118.*

Paulsen, Henning: Studien zur Literatur und Geschichte des frühen Christentums. Ed. von Ute E. Eisen. 1997. *Volume 99.*

Pao, David W.: Acts and the Isaianic New Exodus. 2000. *Volume II/130.*

Park, Eung Chun: The Mission Discourse in Matthew's Interpretation. 1995. *Volume II/81.*

Park, Joseph S.: Conceptions of Afterlife in Jewish Insriptions. 2000. *Volume II/121.*

Pate, C. Marvin: The Reverse of the Curse. 2000. *Volume II/114.*

Philonenko, Marc (Ed.): Le Trône de Dieu. 1993. *Volume 69.*

Pilhofer, Peter: Presbyteron Kreitton. 1990. *Volume II/39.*

– Philippi. Volume 1 1995. *Volume 87.* – Volume 2 2000. *Volume 119.*

– Die frühen Christen und ihre Welt. 2002. *Volume 145.*

– see *Ego, Beate.*

Pöhlmann, Wolfgang: Der Verlorene Sohn und das Haus. 1993. *Volume 68.*

Pokorný, Petr and *Josef B. Souček:* Bibelauslegung als Theologie. 1997. *Volume 100.*

Pokorný, Petr and *Jan Roskovec* (Ed.): Philosophical Hermeneutics and Biblical Exegesis. 2002. *Volume 153.*

Porter, Stanley E.: The Paul of Acts. 1999. *Volume 115.*

Prieur, Alexander: Die Verkündigung der Gottesherrschaft. 1996. *Volume II/89.*

Probst, Hermann: Paulus und der Brief. 1991. *Volume II/45.*

Räisänen, Heikki: Paul and the Law. 1983, [2]1987. *Volume 29.*

Rehkopf, Friedrich: Die lukanische Sonderquelle. 1959. *Volume 5.*

Rein, Matthias: Die Heilung des Blindgeborenen (Joh 9). 1995. *Volume II/73.*

Reinmuth, Eckart: Pseudo-Philo und Lukas. 1994. *Volume 74.*

Reiser, Marius: Syntax und Stil des Markusevangeliums. 1984. *Volume II/11.*

Richards, E. Randolph: The Secretary in the Letters of Paul. 1991. *Volume II/42.*

Riesner, Rainer: Jesus als Lehrer. 1981, [3]1988. *Volume II/7.*

– Die Frühzeit des Apostels Paulus. 1994. *Volume 71.*

Rissi, Mathias: Die Theologie des Hebräerbriefs. 1987. *Volume 41.*

Roskovec, Jan: see *Pokorný, Petr.*

Röhser, Günter: Metaphorik und Personifikation der Sünde. 1987. *Volume II/25.*

Rose, Christian: Die Wolke der Zeugen. 1994. *Volume II/60.*

Rüegger, Hans-Ulrich: Verstehen, was Markus erzählt. 2002. *Volume II/155.*

Rüger, Hans Peter: Die Weisheitsschrift aus der Kairoer Geniza. 1991. *Volume 53.*

Sänger, Dieter: Antikes Judentum und die Mysterien. 1980. *Volume II/5.*

– Die Verkündigung des Gekreuzigten und Israel. 1994. *Volume 75.*

– see *Burchard, Christoph*

Salzmann, Jorg Christian: Lehren und Ermahnen. 1994. *Volume II/59.*

Sandnes, Karl Olav: Paul – One of the Prophets? 1991. *Volume II/43.*

Sato, Migaku: Q und Prophetie. 1988. *Volume II/29.*

Schaper, Joachim: Eschatology in the Greek Psalter. 1995. *Volume II/76.*

Schimanowski, Gottfried: Die himmlische Liturgie in der Apokalypse des Johannes. 2002. *Volume II/154.*

– Weisheit und Messias. 1985. *Volume II/17.*

Schlichting, Günter: Ein jüdisches Leben Jesu. 1982. *Volume 24.*

Schnabel, Eckhard J.: Law and Wisdom from Ben Sira to Paul. 1985. *Volume II/16.*

Schutter, William L.: Hermeneutic and Composition in I Peter. 1989. *Volume II/30.*

Schwartz, Daniel R.: Studies in the Jewish Background of Christianity. 1992. *Volume 60.*

Schwemer, Anna Maria: see *Hengel, Martin*

Scott, James M.: Adoption as Sons of God. 1992. *Volume II/48.*

– Paul and the Nations. 1995. *Volume 84.*

Shum, Shiu-Lun: Paul's Use of Isaiah in Romans. 2002. *Volume II/156.*

Siegert, Folker: Drei hellenistisch-jüdische Predigten. Teil I 1980. *Volume 20* – Teil II 1992. *Volume 61.*

– Nag-Hammadi-Register. 1982. *Volume 26.*

– Argumentation bei Paulus. 1985. *Volume 34.*

– Philon von Alexandrien. 1988. *Volume 46.*

Simon, Marcel: Le christianisme antique et son contexte religieux I/II. 1981. *Volume 23.*

Snodgrass, Klyne: The Parable of the Wicked Tenants. 1983. *Volume 27.*

Söding, Thomas: Das Wort vom Kreuz. 1997. *Volume 93.*
- see *Thüsing, Wilhelm.*
Sommer, Urs: Die Passionsgeschichte des Markusevangeliums. 1993. *Volume II/58.*
Souček, Josef B.: see *Pokorný, Petr.*
Spangenberg, Volker: Herrlichkeit des Neuen Bundes. 1993. *Volume II/55.*
Spanje, T.E. van: Inconsistency in Paul? 1999. *Volume II/110.*
Speyer, Wolfgang: Frühes Christentum im antiken Strahlungsfeld. Volume I: 1989. *Volume 50.*
- Volume II: 1999. *Volume 116.*
Stadelmann, Helge: Ben Sira als Schriftgelehrter. 1980. *Volume II/6.*
Stenschke, Christoph W.: Luke's Portrait of Gentiles Prior to Their Coming to Faith. *Volume II/108.*
Stettler, Christian: Der Kolosserhymnus. 2000. *Volume II/131.*
Stettler, Hanna: Die Christologie der Pastoralbriefe. 1998. *Volume II/105.*
Strobel, August: Die Stunde der Wahrheit. 1980. *Volume 21.*
Stroumsa, Guy G.: Barbarian Philosophy. 1999. *Volume 112.*
Stuckenbruck, Loren T.: Angel Veneration and Christology. 1995. *Volume II/70.*
Stuhlmacher, Peter (Ed.): Das Evangelium und die Evangelien. 1983. *Volume 28.*
- Biblische Theologie und Evangelium. 2002. *Volume 146.*
Sung, Chong-Hyon: Vergebung der Sünden. 1993. *Volume II/57.*
Tajra, Harry W.: The Trial of St. Paul. 1989. *Volume II/35.*
- The Martyrdom of St.Paul. 1994. *Volume II/67.*
Theißen, Gerd: Studien zur Soziologie des Urchristentums. 1979, ³1989. *Volume 19.*
Theobald, Michael: Studien zum Römerbrief. 2001. *Volume 136.*
Theobald, Michael: see *Mußner, Franz.*
Thornton, Claus-Jürgen: Der Zeuge des Zeugen. 1991. *Volume 56.*
Thüsing, Wilhelm: Studien zur neutestamentlichen Theologie. Ed. von Thomas Söding. 1995. *Volume 82.*
Thurén, Lauri: Derhethorizing Paul. 2000. *Volume 124.*

Treloar, Geoffrey R.: Lightfoot the Historian. 1998. *Volume II/103.*
Tsuji, Manabu: Glaube zwischen Vollkommenheit und Verweltlichung. 1997. *Volume II/93*
Twelftree, Graham H.: Jesus the Exorcist. 1993. *Volume II/54.*
Urban, Christina: Das Menschenbild nach dem Johannesevangelium. 2001. *Volume II/137.*
Visotzky, Burton L.: Fathers of the World. 1995. *Volume 80.*
Vollenweider, Samuel: Horizonte neutestamentlicher Christologie. 2002. *Volume 144.*
Vos, Johan S.: Die Kunst der Argumentation bei Paulus. 2002. *Volume 149.*
Wagener, Ulrike: Die Ordnung des „Hauses Gottes". 1994. *Volume II/65.*
Walker, Donald D.: Paul's Offer of Leniency (2 Cor 10:1). 2002. *Volume II/152.*
Walter, Nikolaus: Praeparatio Evangelica. Ed. von Wolfgang Kraus und Florian Wilk. 1997. *Volume 98.*
Wander, Bernd: Gottesfürchtige und Sympathisanten. 1998. *Volume 104.*
Watts, Rikki: Isaiah's New Exodus and Mark. 1997. *Volume II/88.*
Wedderburn, A.J.M.: Baptism and Resurrection. 1987. *Volume 44.*
Wegner, Uwe: Der Hauptmann von Kafarnaum. 1985. *Volume II/14.*
Welck, Christian: Erzählte ‚Zeichen'. 1994. *Volume II/69.*
Wiarda, Timothy: Peter in the Gospels . 2000. *Volume II/127.*
Wilk, Florian: see *Walter, Nikolaus.*
Williams, Catrin H.: I am He. 2000. *Volume II/113.*
Wilson, Walter T.: Love without Pretense. 1991. *Volume II/46.*
Wisdom, Jeffrey: Blessing for the Nations and the Curse of the Law. 2001. *Volume II/133.*
Wucherpfennig, Ansgar: Heracleon Philologus. 2002. *Volume 142.*
Yeung, Maureen: Faith in Jesus and Paul. 2002. *Volume II/147.*
Zimmermann, Alfred E.: Die urchristlichen Lehrer. 1984, ²1988. *Volume II/12.*
Zimmermann, Johannes: Messianische Texte aus Qumran. 1998. *Volume II/104.*
Zimmermann, Ruben: Geschlechtermetaphorik und Gottesverhältnis. 2001. *Volume II/122.*
Zumstein, Jean: see *Dettwiler, Andreas*

For a complete catalogue please write to the publisher
Mohr Siebeck • P.O. Box 2030 • D–72010 Tübingen/Germany
Up-to-date information on the internet at www.mohr.de